European Public Law

ONE WEEK LOAN

Books are to be returned on or before the last date below

Law in Context

Below is a listing of the more recent publications in the Law in Context Series

Editors: William Twining (University College, London) and Christopher McCrudden (Lincoln College, Oxford)

European Public Law

Patrick Birkinshaw LLB

Professor of Public Law, Hull University Law School;
Director, Institute of European Public Law, Hull University;
Barrister

Butterworths
LexisNexis™

Members of the LexisNexis Group worldwide

United Kingdom	LexisNexis Butterworths Tolley, a Division of Reed Elsevier (UK) Ltd, Halsbury House, 35 Chancery Lane, LONDON, WC2A 1EL, and 4 Hill Street, EDINBURGH EH2 3JZ
Argentina	LexisNexis Argentina, BUENOS AIRES
Australia	LexisNexis Butterworths, CHATSWOOD, New South Wales
Austria	LexisNexis Verlag ARD Orac GmbH & Co KG, VIENNA
Canada	LexisNexis Butterworths, MARKHAM, Ontario
Chile	LexisNexis Chile Ltda, SANTIAGO DE CHILE
Czech Republic	Nakladatelství Orac sro, PRAGUE
France	Editions du Juris-Classeur SA, PARIS
Hong Kong	LexisNexis Butterworths, HONG KONG
Hungary	HVG-Orac, BUDAPEST
India	LexisNexis Butterworths, NEW DELHI
Ireland	Butterworths (Ireland) Ltd, DUBLIN
Italy	Giuffrè Editore, MILAN
Malaysia	Malayan Law Journal Sdn Bhd, KUALA LUMPUR
New Zealand	LexisNexis Butterworths, WELLINGTON
Poland	Wydawnictwo Prawnicze LexisNexis, WARSAW
Singapore	LexisNexis Butterworths, SINGAPORE
South Africa	LexisNexis Butterworths, DURBAN
Switzerland	Stämpfli Verlag AG, BERNE
USA	LexisNexis, DAYTON, Ohio

A CIP Catalogue record for this book is available from the British Library.

ISBN 0 406 94288 9

Printed and bound in Great Britain by William Clowes Limited, Beccles and London

Visit Butterworths LexisNexis *direct* at www.butterworths.com

Preface

The European context in which our domestic public law is developing –
and by public law I include constitutional law, administrative and regulatory
law and human rights – has established the conditions for a series of striking
developments in our public law. Legal sovereignty, principles of judicial
review and human rights protection have all been fundamentally and
permanently affected by our membership of the European Union and our
presence in Europe. Many features of our domestic public law are
unrecognisable from ten years ago, let alone thirty when the United
Kingdom acceded to the European Economic Community, as it then was.
A constitution for the European Union, economic and monetary union,
the growing implications of devolution and subsidiarity within the state
and the impact of the Human Rights Act 1998 will effect further
transformations. To fail to appreciate the European context in which our
domestic law is developing is to fail to comprehend our public law.

Context is one thing. Questions are another. Is the influence of European
law and legal thought on domestic law a one-way process? Has our
domestic law influenced European legal thought including the law of the
European Community, the jurisprudence of Member States and the
jurisprudence of the Court of Human Rights at Strasbourg? To what extent
are other national systems influencing Community law and, either directly
or indirectly, each other? This book asks if such reciprocal influences are
taking place; to what extent is a European public law emerging? I can only
speak of the position with respect to English and Welsh public law. Similar
questions are being asked in other Member States. I make reference to
developments in other countries, but I have to concentrate my attention
on the system I know best. Is there something called European public law

emerging? Is there something which is quite distinctive although not a 'system' possessing its own jurisdiction, courts and tribunals? Is European public law a body of thought, practice and principles reflecting an increasingly shared perspective on the relationship between power, its exercise and its control in Europe today?

I am grateful to the many friends and colleagues who assisted me in this present endeavour. Jurgen Schwarze, Roger Errera, Mario Chiti, Jeffrey Jowell and Douglas Lewis have in different ways, and along with countless others, provided instruction. Tony Prosser, Chris Kerse, John Bell, Ian Harden, Stephen Tierney, David Bonner and Gordon Anthony read chapters and/or offered valued and valuable advice. The fact that it may not always have been totally accepted left me weaker. To my colleagues Mike Feintuck, Martina Kunnecke, John Hopkins, Gary Edles and Mike Varney I am grateful in particular for their advice in specific areas. The imperfections in the final product are mine alone.

Chapter 4 had its origins as a chapter in Professor Schwarze (ed) *The Birth of a European Constitutional Order* (2000) and Chapter 8 was originally a co-authored chapter with Professor Jowell in Schwarze (ed) *Administrative Law Under European Influence* (1996). Both chapters have been substantially rewritten and updated.

Patrick Birkinshaw
2 January 2003

Contents

Part one

Some basic issues

Chapter 1

Introductory thoughts on what is European public law   3

Chapter 2

Law and government: a comparative tour   31

Chapter 3

The Community and national systems and their contribution to European public law   93

Chapter 4

The main features of UK constitutional law and European integration 153

Part two

Some key issues

Chapter 5

'A Closer Union ... in which decisions are taken ... as closely as possible to the Citizen' – subsidiarity and devolution   219

Chapter 6

'... as openly as possible ...': openness and access to information   255

Chapter 7

National participation in Community affairs: democracy, the UK Parliament and the EU   289

Chapter 10

Principles of liability   435

Chapter 11

The EU Ombudsman, complaints and internal complaints and grievance procedures   479

Chapter 12

Competition, regulation and the market   517

Part three

Some questions and future issues

Chapter 13

Does European public law exist?   561

Chapter 14

Future considerations 583

Table of statutes

Table of EU legislation

List of cases

V

W

X

Y

Decisions of the European Court of Justice are listed below numerically.
These decisions are also included in the preceding alphabetical list.

Part one

Some basic issues

Chapter 1

Introductory thoughts on what is European public law

This is a book about European public law. It must be immediately emphasised that it is not a comparative treatise of the public law systems of each European state. My linguistic limitations,[1] my ignorance and the demands of publishers would prevent such a task. It is more accurate to suggest that this work is a study of the impact of European legal thought and practice, and on 'being in Europe', on British, and more specifically English public law, its thought and practice. 'Public law' itself is an expression that is contested among English lawyers who either deny there is any system comparable with continental traditions or believe that there is little that needs to be treated as distinctly 'public' in our law. I do examine, for comparative purposes, the constitutional and administrative systems of France, Germany and the European Union (EU) albeit too briefly.

European public law is concerned with the development of the public law of European states and their influence upon, and their influence in turn by, the developing law of the European Community or European Union as it is increasingly called. The subject is not restricted to the public law of Member States but potentially covers the public law of all European states and those further afield who have been influenced by European legal systems usually through forms of imperialism or colonisation. It is also

---

[1] David Edwards has stated that linguistic barriers in the ECJ have prevented the development of an 'oral tradition' similar to some legal systems in Member States in B Markesinis ed *The British Contribution to the Europe of the Twenty-first Century* (2002) ch 3. See also Markesinis ed *Gradual Convergence: Foreign Ideas, Foreign Influence and English Law on the Eve of the Twenty-first Century* (1994).

concerned with the influence of the European Convention on Human Rights (ECHR) upon the substantive and procedural law of nations that are members of the Council of Europe and the influence of the Convention and judgments of the European Court of Human Rights (CHR) on the decisions of the European Court of Justice (ECJ). Judgments of the ECJ have been influenced by doctrines of fundamental human rights contained in the Convention and in the constitutions of Member States. Indeed, the principles of the ECHR constitute a part of the body of general principles of law which informs the Court's development.

There will be no suggestion that legal systems borrow lock, stock and barrel from other systems or that an amorphous homogenised entity is going to do for the legal traditions in Europe what McDonald's has arguably done to its culinary traditions. Flowers that blossom in one soil, wane and wither in another. It was very popular to argue for convergence in laws of the Community, very often advocated by those who had a strong Community agenda in order to assist the process of greater European integration.[2] Community law was after all to be primarily enforced through the courts of Member States. Remedies in domestic courts for breaches of Community law operate in accordance with national procedural and remedial rules but subject to two constraints. They must be no less favourable when applied to Community claims than when applied to similar claims in domestic law and national rules must not make it virtually impossible or excessively difficult to exercise Community rights.[3] These are the doctrines of equivalence and effectiveness.[4] Commercial and legal integration require a legally stable framework in which to operate and vicissitudes brought about by too great a legal disparity would upset or prevent that stability. The doctrines seek to ensure a broad consistency in application. They cannot, and do not guarantee uniformity.

Comparative lawyers wrote of how 'legal transplantation' provides the main source of legal change.[5] An older generation of comparative lawyers

---

2   J Schwarze *European Administrative Law* (1992).

3   Case 33/76 *Rewe* [1976] ECR 1989; Case 222/86 *Heylens* [1987] ECR 4097. A Biondi (1999) 36 CML Rev 1271; R Craufurd Smith in P Craig and G de Burca *The Evolution of EU Law* (1999) ch 8; T Heukels and J Tib in *Convergence and Divergence in European Public Law* (2002) P Beaumont, C Lyons and N Walker, ch 7.

4   See p 450 et seq.

5   Alan Watson *The Evolution of Law* (1985); *Legal Transplants* (1994, 2nd ed); (1996) LQR 79.

warned about the 'misuses' of comparative law, noting how some legal institutions are culturally 'deeply embedded' while others are effectively insulated from 'culture and society'.[6] The latter may be subject to legal transfer but in the case of the former it may be impossible. Laws based upon religious or moral beliefs provide an obvious example of the former.

A reaction to Europeanisation has set in from those who see 'convergence' of legal cultures as impossible and/or bad and/or overstated. Its impossibility lies in the fact that convergence overestimates the capability of converging two or more different legal traditions because of their cultural, linguistic, historical and socio-political differences. Its badness lies in varying assumptions about the distorting effect that lumping or forcing together institutions from different traditions will have so that what emerges will not serve a useful purpose, either practical or theoretical.[7] In so far as a case sometimes may have to be overstated to be made effectively, then one must be cautious not to exaggerate. Teubner for instance has related how the doctrine of 'good faith' in contract[8] was introduced into English law by virtue of a regulation made in accordance with an EC Directive.[9] Relying upon judicial dicta he describes the doctrine as 'inherently repugnant' and 'unworkable in practice'.[10] Ignoring the context in which the statements were made and simply grafting on one doctrine from another system because of some supposed beneficial effect it will have will appear to be at least naïve.

But, it must be emphasised this is not argued for in this present work. What a judge in one system may do is use a doctrine from another to reach a just solution to a case before the court. But in using that doctrine, the judge may modify it and use it for purposes that may not be an exact replica of its use in the 'lending' jurisdiction. But its use in the borrowing jurisdiction

---

[6] O Kahn-Freund 'On Uses and Misuses of Comparative Law' in *Selected Writings* (1978) and (1974) MLR 1. On more recent authors, see: B Markesinis *Foreign Law and Comparative Methodology: A Subject and a Thesis* (1997) and *Always the Same Path* (2001).

[7] See P Legrand (1995) Mod LR 262; P Legrand (1997) Mod LR 44 and in P Beaumont, C Lyons and N Walker (2002); C Harlow in Beaumont et al.

[8] 'Good faith' refers to being open and straight in one's contractual arrangements: 'playing it fair', playing with one's cards laid on the table face-up etc.

[9] Directive 93/13/EEC and SI 1994/3159.

[10] G Teubner in F Snyder ed *The Europeanisation of Law* (2000) citing *Walford v Miles* [1992] 1 All ER 453. The regulation concerns unfair terms in consumer contracts; *Walford* concerned a commercial agreement.

may enhance the capability of that judge to provide a just solution which in the doctrine's absence may not be possible under existing law. Proportionality, a concept which I deal with in Chapter 8 and elsewhere in this book, has different nuances in EC, German and now English law. Its utility and the difference it will make to decisions reviewing executive action has been dramatically illustrated by the House of Lords in *R (Daly) v Secretary of State for the Home Department*.[11] The 'borrowing', after initial reluctance, has been of fundamental importance. So long as we are aware of nuances of meaning and differences in points of detail, we should not deny the benefits of mutual influence. Chaucer wrote in English and had a decisive influence on the course of English language and literature, guaranteeing that we would today speak English, although the English we speak sounds completely different to that of Chaucer. To a modern ear, Chaucer sometimes sounds very French. He would not have written without a knowledge of French and French literature. He borrowed liberally. Did he do wrong?

There is a sense of anti-globalisation and anti-Europeanisation behind such attacks and perhaps a fear of some sense of pending legal imperialism driven by economic and commercial determinism.[12] As between different cultures, legal or otherwise, I join in with an exclamation of *'Vive la difference!'* But we should refuse to deny the obvious benefits that may be gained by influences and developments outside our own or to close our eyes to the degree of mutual influence that *is* taking place.

Other observers have noted the particular difficulties in attempting to incorporate a 'system' of public law into a foreign political structure. The example often referred to is French *Droit Administratif* and its introduction into English law, or more accurately the development of a separate *system* of public law within England and Wales.[13] The 'system' had developed in a very different political and historical environment shaped very strongly by a separation of powers matrix and very different conceptions of the end objectives of subjecting government and public authorities to legal process. It would be unthinkable not because it would introduce 'the very essence of tyranny' as Professor Max Beloff referred to *droit administratif*

---

11   [2001] UKHL 26, [2001] 3 All ER 433.

12   On 'law stuff' and globalisation, see W Twining *Globalisation and Legal Theory: Some Legal Implications* (2000); N D Lewis *Law and Governance* (2001); B de Sousa Santos *Toward a New Legal Common Sense* (2nd ed, 2002); on globalisation: J Stiglitz *Globalisation and its Discontents* (2002); on judicial globalisation A-M Slaughter (2000) 40 *Virginia Journal of International Law* 1102.

13   J W F Allison *A Continental Distinction in the Common Law* (2000 pb).

over a decade ago.[14] It would be unthinkable because as a system it is alien to the English way of relating legal control to governmental purpose. This is obvious to anyone who as I have, has sat and observed proceedings in the Conseil d'Etat in Paris or the Administrative Tribunal (a court!) in that city. The procedures are completely different to English judicial process in judicial review (see Chapter 3). But, might there be benefit in organising our administrative courts on a regular provincial basis as do the French rather than insisting that claimants come to London for hearings before the Administrative Court?[15] Judges have commented that this concentration in London has thwarted expertise in public law in the provinces in England and Wales.

Convergence, cross-fertilisation and 'spill-over'

Professor Bell has argued that while convergence may be too strong an expression for the processes of mutual influence that are taking place, although in some areas that is an accurate expression (see competition law in Chapter 12 for instance), he prefers other terms which more accurately reflect the phenomenon. These are 'cross-fertilisation' and 'spill-over' a term that others have suggested. Citing Professor Schwarze's book on *Administrative Law Under European Influence*[16] Bell described how when national rapporteurs, of which the present author was one, were asked about the European impact on their national administrative law, they identified administrative law in different ways and spoke of different things.[17] For some it meant judicial review. Others were more concerned with ombudsmen techniques and processes aimed at furthering public goals. This is hardly surprising since if one asks an American what administrative law means the answer will be agency procedures and

---

14 HL Debs col 690 (18 April 1989). This crudely exaggerates Dicey's view. Dicey stated that the term 'administrative law' was unknown to English judges and counsel without further explanation. Maitland believed that in 1888, just after the first edition of Dicey's work, over half the cases in the Queen's Bench Division concerned rules of administrative law. Beloff's intervention came under questions on the subject of 'Executive Powers: Complaints Procedure.'

15 CPR 1998, Part 54 allows the Administrative Court to sit in Cardiff and elsewhere. The creation of the Administrative Court coincided with the introduction of the HRA 1998 in October 2000.

16 (1996).

17 J Bell in J Beatson and T Tridimas *New Directions in European Public Law* (1998) ch 11.

powers. Judicial review is a separate heading within administrative law. It is clear from Schwarze's book, and the proceedings which took place in 1994, that there was occurring a significant degree of penetration into national systems of concepts from EC and ECHR law in relation to judicial review while there were also similar developments concerning privatisation and regulation, liability, interim relief and human rights.

Bell suggests that cross-fertilisation, which is more indirect than transplantation and convergence, is 'an external stimulus promot[ing] an evolution within the receiving legal system. The evolution involves an internal adaptation by the receiving legal system in its own way. The new development is a distinctive but organic product of that system rather than a bolt-on.'[18] With respect, I believe this description captures both accurately and subtly the process of mutual influence that is taking place between European legal systems. I would add, that in some senses as I shall soon describe, there may well be signs of common law procedures being influenced by civil law procedures (see below) and there may be areas where 'convergence' willy nilly *is* taking place. I return to these points. What is obvious, however, is the all pervasive and fundamental influence that European legal thought, and the fact of being in Europe, have had on English and UK public law.

When I began my legal studies in 1972, Community law was a component of the introductory English Legal System course. It was widely ignored by most students as irrelevant. We shared with Parliament and the legal community an ignorance of the full effect of Community law on our domestic legal order although in our case this ignorance was more excusable! When in 1981, Lord Diplock stated that the development of a coherent system of administrative law in England was the greatest judicial creation in his lifetime,[19] he was thinking primarily of that law in its domestic setting, although he famously suggested that proportionality may in the future enter the judicial lexicon as an aid to judicial review.[20] It was at about that time that case law began to grapple with the full implications of

---

[18]   J Bell in J Beatson and T Tridimas *New Directions in European Public Law* (1998) p 147.

[19]   *IRC v National Federation of Self-Employed and Small Businesses Ltd* [1981] 2 All ER 93, 104g.

[20]   *Council for Civil Service Unions v Minister for the Civil Service* [1984] 3 All ER 935, 950j: 'I have in mind particularly the possible adoption in the future of the principle of "proportionality" which is recognised in the administrative law of several of our fellow members of the European Economic Community.'

sovereignty and the European Communities Act 1972 (ECA 1972), s 2. But on a personal level, I soon realised that domestic public law was increasingly operating in a European context to such an extent that one could not practise or work in our domestic law without a growing appreciation of that context. In other words, without appreciating the European context in which our domestic law was operating, one was less and less likely to fully understand the progress of domestic public law. The point became crystal clear when in 1989 I was asked to be the UK rapporteur for the 1990 FIDE Congress in Madrid on the subject of public procurement and the impact of the Directives on national systems of law.

The Directives[21] basically addressed the position of contracts placed by public authorities in two basic areas: for goods and services. They have since been extended to cover services and public utilities and remedies.[22] In the 1980s, there was a prevailing feeling in the Commission that the existing Directives which sought to introduce transparency into notoriously closed markets protecting national champions and which attempted to place legal regulation on pre-contract procedures in which bidders are chosen, had been largely ignored. The Commission wished to strengthen the Directives and to add to them. In the area of public contracts in the UK, the subject had been devoid of any effective oversight – legislative or judicial – and it was assumed that the common law of contract would apply equally to government contracts as in contracts between private parties. In fact, public procurement spawned a vast network of subterranean and political processes in which 'the rules' were spelled out and in which judicial decisions would have no impact whatsoever. Grievances simply did not go to the courts: it was not in the interests of government or contractors to have a judicial determination of their dispute. In the case of the former, because judicial decisions might confine discretion exercised through contract in a way that would interfere with government prerogative; in the latter, because contractors would fear prejudice if they complained about aspects of a contract either at pre-allocation or at performance stage. They might be struck off tendering lists or not selected if included. We shall see that not only did the Directives apply to pre-contractual allocation of government contracts, but the area of public contracts has become much more subject to judicial decision (Chapter 12). There are dangers of post hoc/propter hoc reasoning but it is remarkable how for decades the litigation on government contracts, which was both

21   See Ch 12, p 546.
22   See Ch 12, p 546.

minimal and deeply unsatisfactory, suddenly began to attract legal attention.

More generally, some Directives in the UK, especially the Procurement Directives, were not originally implemented by legal devices but by administrative means: by the use of Treasury guidelines and Departmental circulars. Following a series of judgments of the ECJ,[23] that court has stated that a specific legislative act is not necessary to transpose a Directive. However, mere administrative practices which may not be publicised or which may be changed at will could not be regarded as a proper fulfilment of the obligation imposed on the Member States by Article 249 [189] EC. Furthermore, the ECJ has held that where a Directive is intended to create rights for individuals, the implications for the legal position arising from implementing measures for such individuals must be sufficiently clear, precise and transparent and the persons concerned must be fully aware of their rights. Those individuals must, where appropriate, be afforded the possibility of relying upon them before national courts.[24] Ambiguous or non published legislation which does not give sufficient guidance on whether an individual may rely upon EC law would not fulfil the duty to transpose a Directive into national law.[25] The British government has abandoned the attempt at implementation by administrative devices in the case of procurement and elsewhere and has resorted to subordinate legislation – subordinate legislation is legislation approved by Parliament. These regulations spell out in generally clear terms the nature of procedural and substantive rights for individuals and are a tremendous advance on the completely discretionary regime which they replaced and which in many cases were probably not legally enforceable.[26]

It has to be said that regulation by administrative guidance has been a standard practice among administrators in the UK. The practice is covered by the soubriquet 'soft law', meaning a resort to non-legally binding devices around which regulators/overseers may exhort, encourage, negotiate or dictate an outcome. Too often, where the administered were concerned and

---

23   Eg Case 116/86 *Commission v Italy* [1988] ECR 1323; Case 429/85 *Commission v Italy* [1988] ECR 843; Case 168/83 *Commission v Italy* [1986] ECR 2945.

24   Case 29/84 *Commission v Germany* [1985] ECR 1661 and Case 363/85 *Commission v Italy* [1987] ECR 1733.

25   Case 116/86 *Commission v Italy* [1988] ECR 1323, para 212.

26   Birkinshaw, *L'Application Dans Les Etats Membres Des Directives Sur Les Marchés Publics*: 'Grand Britannique' FIDE Vol 1 Madrid (1990) 287.

where they lacked power, all the advantages were in favour of the powerful and manipulative.

The catalogue of examples of influence of European legal thought on domestic law which will be examined in this book, is striking.

The most dramatic has been the full realisation that Parliamentary legislation is no longer sovereign within the UK in a field covered by Community competence. We shall see that this was no more than the jurisprudence of the ECJ demanded in the famous decisions of *van Gend en Loos*[27] and *Costa v ENEL*[28] which are examined in detail in Chapter 2 together with *Simmenthal*[29] which established that directly effective provisions of Community law 'render inapplicable any conflicting provision of national law' even constitutional law and human rights.[30] In *Factortame v Secretary of State (No 2)* the House of Lords realised there was no option but to disapply an Act of Parliament by issuing an injunction. The terms of the Act authorised breaches of the non-discrimination provisions of the Treaty of Rome.[31] The decision was made when a preliminary judgment of the ECJ holding that there should be no barriers to the effective enforcement of Community law was delivered to the Law Lords. The full effectiveness of Community law and the rights it protected had to be maintained:

> The full effectiveness of Community law would be ... impaired if a rule of national law could prevent a court seised of a dispute governed by Community law from granting interim relief in order to ensure the full effectiveness of the judgement to be given on the existence of the rights claimed under Community law. It follows that a court which in those circumstances would grant interim relief, if it were not for a rule of national law, is obliged to set aside that rule.[32]

It was clear that Community law required by way of legal obligation the non-application of an Act of Parliament even if that upset one of the central organising concepts of British constitutionalism. In a subsequent decision involving the challenge by the Equal Opportunities Commission of certain sections of the Employment Protection (Consolidation) Act 1978 which it

---

[27]   Case 26/62 [1963] ECR 1.
[28]   Case 6/64 [1964] ECR 585.
[29]   Case 106/77 [1978] ECR 629.
[30]   Case 11/70 *Internationale Handelsgesellschaft* [1970] ECR 1125.
[31]   [1991] 1 All ER 70 (ECJ and HL).
[32]   Based on Article 10 [5] EC co-operation: see Ch 3, p 100 et seq.

claimed contravened the Article 141 [119] EC and certain Directives,[33] the House of Lords declared that they had the ability to declare whether provisions in primary legislation of the UK Parliament were incompatible with Community law – and so ruled on the authority of *Factortame* and decisions of the ECJ, but not, it should be noted, after a reference this time to the ECJ for a preliminary ruling.[34]

Secondly, since the early 1960s, the ECJ has been active, with varying degrees of urgency, in filling lacunas in the Treaty of Rome and its amendments. This has been particularly emphatic in the areas of legal supremacy and in the doctrine of direct effect – that the Treaty may well create rights for individuals which they may pursue in their own national courts.[35] The Community differed from organisations established by international treaties because it conferred rights on individuals and not simply on nations. The ECJ developed general principles of law under the influence of the legal regimes of Member States and these have been influential in shaping domestic law, particularly, but far from exclusively, the doctrine of proportionality in judicial review. Another area of judicial development has been the establishment of a law of liability where Member States are in breach of Community law and where the conditions for imposing liabilty for such breaches are satisfied. The law was formulated in *Brasserie du Pêcheur* and *Factortame III*[36] and in the decision which preceded them in *Francovich*.[37] This developed from case law of the ECJ which decided upon the conditions of liability of Community institutions for breaches of Community law when individuals were injured and which were decided under Article 288 [215] EC which specifically enjoins the ECJ to take inspiration from the 'general principles common to the laws of the Member States'. It will be seen how these developments have impacted on domestic law.

What is not so widely remarked upon is the decision in the Court of Appeal in *Factortame (No 5)* which concerned a possible remedy for a breach of a superior rule of law by domestic legislation: 'we leave for consideration

---

33   *Equal Opportunities Commission v Secretary of State for Employment* [1994] 1 All ER 910, HL. The challenge concerned the use of a public law remedy of a declaration in a manner which previous authorities had ruled non-permissible: see Lord Keith at pp 919–20.

34   G Anthony *UK Public Law and European Law* (2002) p 92.

35   *Van Gend en Loos* Case 26/62 [1963] ECR 1.

36   Cases C-46/93 and 48/93 [1996] ECR I-1029.

37   Case C-6 and 9/90 [1991] ECR I-5357.

on another occasion the circumstances, if any, in which, quite apart from any requirement of Community law, our law will give a remedy for damage caused by legislation enacted in breach of a superior legal rule.' Traditionally this remedy has not been available in our law. Now that it is undoubtedly available in circumstances which contain a Community law element it may be right on some future occasion to re-examine that tradition.' Are the courts then countenancing a 'rule of law' superior to legislation which does not derive from Community law?[38] As we shall see in Chapter 4 (p 174 et seq) domestic judges are giving recognition to 'constitutional statutes' conferring it would seem a higher status to these measures than to non-constitutional measures – a 'hierarchy of norms' or a hierarchy of statutes.[39]

Thirdly, the requirements of harmonisation and approximation which are contained in Article 95 [100a] EC and other measures introduced by the Single European Act 1987 which relate to the Council's powers in Article 95(1) to 'adopt the measures for the approximation of the provisions laid down by law, regulation or administrative action in Member States which have as their object the establishment and functioning of the internal market'[40] are relevant to the discussion of growing convergence and European public law. Harmonisation was referred to as the method or policy through which internal barriers within the Community to Community trade were dismantled and in their place would emerge a truly common and unified Community system – the internal market.

Laws of direct relevance to the internal market and which cover basic freedoms of the Community (though not in relation to fiscal policy or free movement of persons or rights or interests of employees) were to be approximised to help realise the internal market.[41] Under Article 95(1), which is a residuary provision and one of several relevant provisions, legislation intended to complete the internal market could be passed through the Council by Qualified Majority Voting under the co-decision procedure in Article 251[189b] EC (see Chapter 2, p 41). Article 95(4) refers to 'harmonisation'. The expression 'approximation' although used

---

[38]   [1998] 3 CMLR 193, [1998] Eu LR 456.
[39]   *Thoburn v Sunderland City Council* [2002] EWHC 195 (Admin), [2002] 4 All ER 156.
[40]   The internal market was the first of three stages to bring about EU. The other two were monetary and political union.
[41]   See however, Article 95(2) EC. Article 95 EC is a residual measure and must not be used where other provisions apply under the Treaty.

interchangeably is now preferred because it has less of a centripetalist connotation. The subject areas in which laws have been or are being are approximated under relevant provisions include: company law, VAT, environmental regulation, health and safety at work, consumer protection, public procurement, data protection, competition law and financial services. Because it is ordained that approximation shall take place, that does not entail a neat and tidy practice. Doubtless, there are fifteen (and soon more) ways to skin a cat. The detail and procedure adopted will differ, but the substantive provisions will have to be consistent with European requirements. Member States may be allowed to maintain national provisions covered by the harmonisation measures only on grounds identified in Article 95(4) and (5).

The last sphere of European influence concerns the European Convention on Human Rights and the role of the Court of Human Rights – and that court has described the ECHR as 'a constitutional instrument of European public order.'[42] The court was reformed with effect from 1 January 1999.[43] Long before the UK incorporated the Convention into domestic law by virtue of the Human Rights Act 1998 (HRA 1998), it was clear that the Convention was going to have a profound impact on our governmental and administrative and legal practice. 'The [domestic] court should take the convention into account' said Lord Denning. 'They should take it into account whenever interpreting a statute which affects the rights and liberties of the individual.'[44] To single out one area where the impact was felt, one could turn to prison administration where decisions such as *Golder v UK*[45] and *Silver v UK*[46] showed emphatically that prisons were not to be allowed to continue as completely closed societies, so that in order to satisfy the requirements of Articles 6 and 8 ECHR when prisoners were subject to prison disciplinary proceedings or sought legal advice, they would have to be allowed access to a lawyer and ultimately the courts. The age-old reference to prerogative powers and the fact that government could do what anyone else might lawfully do to intercept communications were seen for what they were – a legacy of a feudal tradition. Such practices now had to be based on legislation. The attitude of national courts and

---

42   *Loizidou v Turkey* (1995) Series A Volume 310, 27, para 75.
43   Protocol No 11 ECHR: www.coe.int.
44   *R v Secretary of State for the Home Department, ex p Bhajan Singh* [1975] 2 All ER 1081 at 1083.
45   (1975) 1 EHRR 524.
46   (1983) 5 EHRR 347.

the government to the CHR was not always constructive; it was sometimes churlish. The decision by the Law Lords in *Brind*[47] where the Law Lords ruled that the Convention, specifically Article 10 providing for freedom of speech, could have no role to play when the powers of the statute and regulations made thereunder were clear. The Convention had no role to play in interpreting and limiting the exercise of a discretion by the executive – in this case banning voice broadcasts of members of proscribed organisations in Northern Ireland. Furthermore, proportionality was not a principle of English common law but a continental ground of judicial review.[48] The decision is indicative of a rigid division between the realms of European legal thought and the domestic legal order. I say more about this further on in this chapter. But even while the judgment in *Brind* was being given, the growing confluence of European and domestic legal orders was well under way.

I should pause to make the point that while I have spoken so far about the influence of European legal thought on domestic systems, the European systems which existed in the Community and even many of those that were members of the Council of Europe bore more proximity to a Roman model of public law than did the English or the broader UK model. Bell has been vigilant to point out that Roman law has been more influential in helping to shape private law continental systems than in shaping public law systems.[49] That point is taken, but until 1973, the dominant tradition in Member States was still one influenced by Roman law – the common law and Scandinavian systems were yet to sign up. Dominant in that tradition was a separation of public and private realms. In Justinian's *Institutes* (Book 1 Title I) law is divided into two branches, public law and private law. The former concerns the constitutional law of the Roman state, administrative law,[50] criminal law and *ius sacram* or religious law. Private law is concerned with relationships between individuals. The *Institutes* concentrate on private law. Definitions of public law are politically driven – they are forged by, and emerge from, the cauldron of political upheaval and conflict which has meant that apart from the division of public and private, the actual content of public law has not been subjected to the influence of Roman law as has private law. On the continent, Roman law was 'received' by

---

47 [1991] 1 All ER 720, HL.
48 Although there was some divergence of opinion on the proportionality point. See Ch 8, p 333 et seq.
49 J Beatson and T Tridimas *New Directions in European Public Law* (1998).
50 R W Lee *Elements of Roman Law* (1956, 4th ed) p 35.

universities especially in Germany and France while Italy carried on a tradition that never quite disappeared. In England, by contrast, when the flirtation with Roman law ended with Cardinal Wolsey's death in 1529 and when a separate system of public law administered through the Prerogative courts was abolished in 1642, English public law operated within the common law, not as public common law,[51] but simply as common law. Public law, as Maitland famously observed, was ubiquitous; it was not systematic. Formal division meant very little although there was no judicial review of private power;[52] what was important was how bodies were created and what powers and duties they exercised, and how they were exercised, for the purpose of judicial review. As we know, the inherent flexibility and malleability of this approach, although subject to long periods of ossification, also allowed the law to be applied and extended to ever changing patterns of government organisation and activity when the judiciary felt impelled to act. It was subject to fits and starts and not stable progression.

Nevertheless, despite these cultural eccentricities of the common law, the influence of European law and legal thought are being emphasised regularly and with growing authority.

In a publication of lectures delivered at the British Academy in 2002,[53] Lord Woolf quoted Lord Denning's famous quotation from *Bulmer and Bollinger*[54] of how the tidal waves of Community law were flowing into our estuaries. Lord Woolf carried on the quotation where Denning indicated the limited effect Community law has on those parts of English law which are untouched by Community law and 'which does not touch any of the matters which concern solely England and the people in it.' 'These are still governed by English law.'[55] While of course there are areas that are untouched by Community law, succession and real property law, many areas hitherto untouched such as criminal law, contract, commercial law

51   See C Hilson (2003) 9 European Public Law 125.
52   Coke CJ in *Bagg's* case (1615) Co Inst iv 71 spoke of the Court of King's Bench rectifying all private as well as public wrongs. Abuse of private power could be addressed through the law on common callings, restraint of trade and abuse of market power. It was interstitial.
53   B Markesinis ed *The British Contribution to the Europe of the Twenty-first Century: The British Academy Lectures* (2002) Hart.
54   *HP Bulmer v J Bollinger SA* [1974] Ch 401.
55   Lord Woolf in B Markesinis ed *The British Contribution to the Europe of the Twenty-first Century* (2002) ch 1, 'The Tides of Change.'

let alone our public law, labour law, company law and so on are directly affected by Community law. Even family law is now heavily influenced by the ECHR and the HRA 1998. Woolf begins by showing why he believes that there has been a process of cross-fertilisation of mutual influences[56] and he illustrates the influence of the common law on Community law. The ECJ has become more influenced by common law style of judgments, by the use of precedent and the manner in which previous case law is distinguished and departed from, by the invocation of general principles of substantive law. The 'role of case law and the handling of precedent are not as fundamentally and irreconcilably dissimilar as some may contend.'[57] The ECJ's work is a fusion of different legal traditions in the EU. Although one should not over-exaggerate the differences between the civil and common law traditions, on the whole the Court followed previous judgments although it did not consider itself strictly bound by them. There was a natural reluctance to depart from them. Although case law was resorted to, the Court preferred vaguer references to 'the settled case law of the Court.'[58] The use of case law has certainly become more systematic and in *HAG II* for the first time in 35 years, the ECJ effectively overruled an earlier judgment.[59] The consequence believes Woolf, is a breaking away from the 'syllogistic style' of judgments in the ECJ which were influenced by the French superior courts.

That Court, argues Woolf, has been far more concerned with fleshing out the Treaty to give it specific shape, judges have been more prepared to intervene in the style of common law judges to resolve points of ambiguity

---

[56] B Markesinis ed *The British Contribution to the Europe of the Twenty-first Century* (2002); Bell in J Beatson and T Tridimas *New Directions in European Public Law* (1998).

[57] Page 4. See Case C-10/89 *Hag II* [1990] ECR I-3711 and the reconsideration of an earlier case Case –192/73 *Hag I* [1974] ECR 731 which the ECJ ruled was wrongly decided.

[58] Lord Woolf in B Markesinis ed *The British Contribution to the Europe of the Twenty-first Century* (2002). See A Arnull in M Andenas ed *English Public Law and the Common Law of Europe* (1998) p 93.

[59] Case C-10/89 [1990] ECR I-3711 declaring *Van Zuylen v HAG (HAG I)* Case 192/73 [1974] ECR 731 had been wrongly decided. See also *Parliament v Council* Case 70/88 [1990] ECR I-2041 (Chernobyl) and *Parliament v Council* Case 302/87 [1988] ECR 5615 (Comitology) and Parliament's capacity to bring proceedings under Article 230 EC; the earlier decision was effectively overruled although this was not stated. On the position of the CFI, see Case T-162/94 *NMB France v Commission* [1997] ECR II-427 and A Arnull in M Andenas (ed) *English Public Law and the Common Law of Europe* (1998) pp124-27.

in proceedings before them[60] and there has been a notable interest in providing effective remedies for breaches of Community law in national courts which, believes Woolf, owes much to the common law's preoccupation with effective remedies rather than abstract rights.

As I shall point out later, there may be reasons why judges have become more receptive to outside influences. It may fit in with a realisation that domestic remedies required re-invigoration and that inspiration from elsewhere was needed. As Anthony has suggested,[61] it may well be that the domestic situation was ripe for influence. One of the most interesting areas where European influence has spilled over into a purely domestic situation concerned the case of the asylum seeker from Zaire who faced deportation, and a possibly hostile reaction in Zaire, and who by court order was to be kept within the UK pending consideration of his case. In breach of this order, the Home Office ordered his removal to Paris and thence to Zaire. This was a clear breach of a judicial injunction. But, the House of Lords had confirmed in the first *Factortame* case that injunctions could not issue against the Crown. Eventually, as we have seen, injunctions did issue against the Secretary of State (acting on behalf of, and for all intents and purposes as, the Crown[62]) but this was as a direct consequence of the application of Community law in previous litigation. As Lord Woolf expressed the point in *M v Home Office*[63] 'so that the unhappy situation now exists that while a citizen is entitled to obtain injunctive relief (including interim relief) against the Crown or an officer of the Crown to protect his interests under Community law he cannot do so in respect of his other interests (ie, purely domestic) which may be just as important.' The law decided in the original *Factortame* judgment that injunctions could not issue against the Crown or its officers was shown by Woolf to have been decided on inadequate examination of the authorities and precedents. They had got the law wrong not only in its Community setting, and on which the ECJ had to advise, but also in its domestic setting. Injunctions may issue against a Minister of the Crown, or a Crown servant, 'on the public law side' regardless of whether a question of Community or domestic law was involved.

---

[60]   Though cf David Edwards' point on advocacy in note 1 above.

[61]   G Anthony *UK Public Law and European Law* (2002) p 92.

[62]   Sir S Sedley 'The Crown in its Own Courts' in C Forsyth and I Hare eds *The Golden Metwand and the Crooked Cord* (1998) p 253.

[63]   [1993] 3 All ER 537 at 551a. On the position on enforcement orders in Scotland and the Crown, see Ch 3, note 67.

But there are still many signs that there are judicial pockets of resistance to allowing European influence to overspill where it is not strictly necessary to resolve an issue before the court. We have been reminded that the general principles of Community law are not legally binding where a case has no Community dimension whereas domestic measures even if ostensibly outside the area of EC competence *must not* contravene the EC Treaty and EC secondary legislation.[64]

Lord Woolf has not asserted that this is simply a one-way process of influence. The traditions of codification on the continent have made their impact in our domestic law in one of the preserves of the common law – civil procedure. He cites the Civil Procedure Rules as an example of a 'new trend' to codification in common law:

> I think it fair to say that the result has been the creation of a system that is generally accepted as being far better organised, more proportionate and cost effective, and fair, not only for lawyers, but for unrepresented and represented litigants as well.

He continues that while the Civil Procedure Rules were designed to provide a comprehensive code of procedure for the English and Welsh courts, they were heavily influenced by the practices in continental jurisdictions. 'They have been described as being positioned mid channel.'[65] Jacob has described how English case law is itself relying less on precedent which is being modified becoming more like guidance in the civil tradition.[66] It is not only in civil procedure where Woolf believes the influence of the civil system's codification is being felt, but also in criminal law where Sir Robin Auld has recommended codification in the 'criminal justice system' covering the substantive law, evidence, procedure and sentencing under a new Criminal Justice Council supported by, or working with, the Law Commission.

One example of how procedure was influenced by the impact of Community law concerns statutory interpretation and the removal of the exclusionary rule which prohibited (with limited success) judges from citing Hansard and the record of Parliamentary proceedings in their judgments. This would

---

64   *R v MAFF, ex p First City Trading Ltd* [1997] 1 CMLR 250, Laws J.
65   Lord Woolf in B Markesinis ed *The British Contribution to the Europe of the Twenty-first Century* (2002), pp 10–11.
66   J Jacob *Civil Litigation: Practice and Tradition in a Shifting Culture* (2001) pp 10 et seq; also D N MacCormick and R S Summers *Interpreting Precedent* (1995).

add to delay, uncertainty and usurped the constitutional position of the courts as interpreters of the law.[67] But the door had already been opened when five years previously the House of Lords had consulted Hansard and statements made by a Minister when introducing a draft instrument into Parliament which implemented Community provisions. The instrument was not subject to revision in Parliamentary Committee and 'it was entirely legitimate, for the purpose of ascertaining the intention of Parliament, for the court to refer to Hansard in order to take into account the terms in which the draft was presented by the responsible Minister' so as to interpret norms which had been incorporated into English law to fulfil UK obligations.[68] So in *Pepper v Hart*, where a question solely of domestic law was concerned, in order to give effect to the 'purposive approach' adopted by the courts to interpret legislation, it would be proper to refer to Parliamentary material to aid statutory construction where a provision was ambiguous, obscure or the literal interpretation would lead to an absurdity and the statements were clear. The range of statements covered was also circumscribed and covered ministerial statements or those of other promoters of Bills leading to enactment of the Bill.[69]

The HRA 1998 will give British and Northern Ireland judges the opportunity to apply provisions of the European Convention of Human Rights as incorporated into domestic law in a manner which has to have regard to the judgments and decisions of the CHR and other matters[70] but which does not slavishly adhere to them. As we shall see elsewhere (Chapter 9), several judges have seen the incorporation as an opportunity to apply a domestic gloss to Convention jurisprudence; to give it a distinctly British tone. The words of Lord Hope are illustrative:

> Nevertheless, there is good reason to think that, now that they [domestic judges] are able to engage themselves directly in issues about the application of Convention rights to our laws and practices, our judges will have an increasing influence on the development of the jurisprudence

---

[67] *Pepper v Hart* [1993] 1 All ER 42, 59–60.

[68] *Pickstone v Freemans plc* [1988] 2 All ER 803, HL.

[69] A broader test applies to EU provisions than domestic ie to ascertain the object of a measure as a whole and not simply where the provision to be interpreted was unclear: in *Thoburn* note 39, Laws LJ did not believe the rule in *Pepper* applied to construe 'constitutional measures' and in *Robinson v Secretary of State for Northern Ireland* [2002] UKHL 32, para 40, [2002] All ER (D) 364 (Jul) Lord Hoffman believed invocation of *Pepper* was a 'last resort'.

[70] The Commission on Human Rights and the Committee of Ministers.

of the courts [EU and CHR]. In particular, the opportunity now exists for our judges to demonstrate, by means of reasoned judgments based upon established Convention law principles, how the basic human rights which are enshrined in the Convention can be respected without risk to the rule of law or to the established values of our democracy.[71]

So the influence of European thought on our law is apparent. This is not best described as a 'transplant' and nor is it a convergence by design. It is simply that different systems have to work in ever increasing proximity and borrowing or influencing are standard and universal human characteristics. Some may fear that all this amounts to is the exploitation by a sophisticated legal profession in the UK of opportunities to advance the interests of powerful commercial clients. Lord Woolf felt that commercial law was an area where English law could have a wide influence in Europe.[72] Some may see this as naked instrumentalism. There are old arguments here about law as a tool of oppression to be exploited by dominant classes. Law will always be used by the powerful, public or private, more than by the economically weak. Or law will be used for different purposes by the powerful: trouble avoidance rather than damage repair. The question is whether the content of law reflects values which protect us all and which foster democratic protection and advancement of human rights. My own belief is that the developments in the UK under European influence have advanced those values. This is not to say that other processes cannot advance them also. Courts are not alone in providing protection to those subject to improper domination and worse. But what we have seen courts do has been an advance for the good where the philosophy of the common law has been invigorated by European influence.

A multi-dimensional process

I spoke earlier about a two-way process that is taking place. Much of what has been spoken of above concerns European influence on our domestic order. There have been hints of domestic influence on the European orders – the common law practice of precedent and the adoption of something which, if not an exact replica, has certainly absorbed some of the features

---

[71] (2000) 5 EHRL Rev 439.
[72] Page 12; and see R Goode 'Europe and English Commercial Law' in B Markesinis ed *The British Contribution to the Europe of the Twenty-first Century* (2002).

of the precedential approach have been identified. In Chapter 3 I will point out how the influence has gone from the Member States to the Community and elsewhere I will address domestic influence on the CHR (see Chapter 9). Reference has already been made to the ECJ's use of Member State systems to help fashion a law of liability for Community institutions which was then used to establish the basis of liability for Member State breaches of Community law. In *A M & S v Commission*, the ECJ observed in establishing a form of legal professional privilege whereby communications between a lawyer and their clients are privileged, that 'Community Law derives not only from the economic but also the legal interpenetration of the Member States.'[73] Advocate General Fennelly has observed that '*Audi alteram partem* (or the principles of natural justice/fair procedure) was introduced in 1974 in *Transocean Marine Paint v Commission* and droits de la defense were soon elevated to the status of a 'fundamental principle of Community law' in *Hoffman la Roche v Commission*.'[74] In this latter category it is worth mentioning the decision in *British Aerospace and Rover Group Holdings v Commission*[75] where it was held if the Commission attempts to recover aid from a recipient without complying with the Article 88(2) [93(2)] EC procedure, the decision of the Commission that any aid given by the state must be repaid may be struck down by the Court where the concerned parties, including the beneficiary of the aid, were not notified and thereby denied the right to be heard before the decision on repayment was made.

I have already pointed out how general principles were borrowed from domestic legal orders and how in the case of proportionality it was used by the ECJ and then found its way into English law. There was criticism by German commentators about the manner in which the ECJ used, or failed properly to use the concept in the famous 'bananas' judgment in 1994 when a former judge of the ECJ and a leading legal commentator in Germany argued that that court's treatment of proportionality had brought 'judicial control to a minimum'.[76] As will be seen in Chapter 2, where the ECJ borrows

---

73   Case 155/79 [1982] ECR 1575; legal professional privilege is a common law doctrine and there are modifications for 'in-house' lawyers under EC law.
74   Case 85/76 [1979] ECR 461: Fennelly in Andenas ed *English Public Law and the Common Law of Europe* (1998). See Case C-315/99 P *Ismeri Europa Srl v Court of Auditors* [2001] ECR I-5281 on fair procedure.
75   Case 294/90 [1992] 1 CMLR 853.
76   *Germany v Council* Case C-280/93 [1994] ECR I-4973 and U Everling [1996] CML Rev 401 and Fennelly in Andenas ed *English Public Law and the Common Law of Europe* (1998), pp 16–17. See Chs 2 and 8.

from a Member State it cannot apply a doctrine in necessarily the same way as would the Member State. The ECJ and Court of First Instance (CFI) have to apply legal principles in a Community context and it cannot be bound by the interpretation or application that a court in a Member State, applying domestic law, might give. This has been seen particularly in the field of human rights (Chapter 2, p 55 et seq). We should not forget, as the rest of this chapter suggests, that there is likely to be increasing influence of domestic systems on each other through their influence on Community law. There has been a pooling of sovereignties and a pooling of ideas from which we have all benefited.

At a time when the Convention under Valerie Giscard D'Estaing has been mandated by the European Council to come forth with ideas for a constitution for Europe, a great deal of work has gone into examining whether European integration is having an impact on national constitutions so that it is possible to identify very similar influences having similar effects, indeed if not bringing them in any way closer together in points of detail.

> The mutual influences of national and European law unmistakenly cause an approximation of the respective national legal systems – even though national particularities continue to persist which determine the character of any national constitutional order to a considerable extent. Thus, it can be shown that a growing concordance has evolved in the process of European integration not only between European and national constitutional law but also between the respective constitutional orders of the Member States. In keeping with Konrad Hesse's recent conclusions, certain elements of this development could indeed be viewed as the framework of a 'common European constitutional order.'[77]

To recapitulate: European public law is concerned with the influence of Community law and Convention law on European states. It is concerned with the influence of the laws of those states on the Community and CHR. It is concerned whether the influence operates directly by one Member State upon another, but more realistically through the mediation of the EU courts and the CHR. As well as this evolving constitutional and administrative law of the EC and of its Member States and of its non-Member States, and the refinement of the law relating to human rights in modern Europe, there is a wide area – a sort of hybrid – which has grown from relationships

---

[77] H Schafer in J Schwarze *The Birth of a European Constitutional Order* (2000) at p 464.

dominated by private law but where a growing public interest has ensured more regulatory involvement by national and EC government. Here we include environmental law, labour relations, equality, competition and regulation of mergers, state support for industry and public procurement, regulation of utilities and social welfare.

No one can honestly say that the division between public and private law in any jurisdiction represents the outcome of rational conceptualisation – or at least not completely so. Some will doubtless want to refine the nature of the distinction; others to argue that increasingly it is of little consequence. And in a sense I am sympathetic with Emile Durkheim who over a century ago expressed the view that 'All law is public law'[78]. All law is social, he continued, and all the functions of society are social. 'There are [no functions] ... which are not, in greater or lesser degree, under the supervision of action by governmental bodies.'

It is a statement of fact and not wishful thinking to say that public law suffuses our existence in Europe and in each European State whether it be in our relationships with officialdom or some aspect of the State or in our relationships with each other. We are more administered and more ruled than we were thirty years ago. We are more spied upon and more regulated. More and more lawyers and more and more legal discourse throughout Europe and throughout the world embrace complex social and state developments in terms of powers and jurisdiction, procedural regularity and human rights, discretion and natural justice or fairness in action. This is as true in the United Kingdom as elsewhere.

How are we, if at all, influencing each other in the development of our public law systems? How are national systems of law being influenced by EC law and is there a clear vision of European public law emerging? National systems will retain their distinction and they will remain distinct from supra national entities. But they will be subject to more international influence in the way their systems develop. In Trieste, at a seminar organised by the Council of Europe for states from south east Europe, I was asked pointedly: 'What system should Bulgaria adopt?' Where was my suggestion of a legal panacea? I suspect there was a recollection in the questioner's mind and a hint of the free marketeers who invaded the Soviet Union and Eastern Europe to advise on wholesale importation of Anglo Saxon capitalism

---

[78]   Emile Durkheim *The Division of Labour in Society* (1933) The Free Press, p 127.

without delay – invariably with disastrous consequences for social solidarity and cohesion. Bulgaria should adopt no *system*: but any country should learn what others are doing about common problems and what approaches are being shared and how, if at all, legal doctrine and practice are coming together. What have we to learn from each other?

The pragmatism of the English may have been resistant to refined, abstract or rational models of law, so common in the continental tradition and which have had more of an impact on the shaping of EC law than has the English system – if 'system' is the correct phrase. And this is no place to rehearse why a relatively stable political framework has not until comparatively recently felt the need for a developed system of public law. The need is becoming increasingly felt and our presence in Europe is making us all ever more keenly aware of that need. However, we have, along with all other jurisdictions in Europe, rich traditions and wide experience in a variety of practices including the use of tribunals and inquiries which have helped to judicialise the administrative process and also in our experience with Ombudsmen, a concept borrowed in the UK from Scandinavia by way of New Zealand.

As the world moves ever closer together temporally and in terms of communication and as ancient barriers and not so ancient evaporate or are dismantled, and new ones emerge, we must increasingly seek enlightenment from each other to see how political power may be tempered with legal discipline. What have different jurisdictions learned about the relationship between law and politics and what are comparatively recent ones, by which I include the EC, doing and learning about the balance between might and right? The problems are increasingly of an international dimension and posed by bodies which are not governmental in nature or, more precisely, in form. And they occur whether we like it or not when we are being pulled towards ever closer union and co-operation. I have already quoted from Durkheim and I conclude this section with a prescient passage of the same author from his classic work on *The Division of Labour in Society* where he wrote of the nature of an international society:

> Truly ... we must recognise that this ideal [international society] is not on the verge of being integrally realised, for there are too many intellectual and moral diversities between different social types existing together on the earth to admit of fraternalization in the same society. But what is possible is that societies of the same type may come together, and it is, indeed, in this direction that evolution appears to move. We have

already seen that among European peoples there is a tendency to form, by spontaneous movement, a European Society which has, at present, some idea of itself and the beginning of organisation. If the formation of a single human society is forever impossible ... at least the formation of continually larger societies brings us vaguely nearer that goal.[79]

Chapter outlines

It will help if I set out the outline of the contents of chapters at this early stage.

In this chapter, the primary concern was the question: what is European public law? It is not simply an examination of the national context of Community law. The inquiry focused on some introductory questions concerning: what has happened to English public law under *European* influence and what influence in return is English public law having on Community law? Is something new and different emerging? In later chapters, these questions will also be asked about French and German law. Are there signs of national systems borrowing from each other as well as from Community law and also from the ECHR? Are claims for European public law exaggerated? Chapter 13 attempts to deal in more detail with this latter question. By that time, readers will have the evidence before them.

In the following chapter it will be necessary to say something about the relationship between law and government in the EC, France, Germany and the UK. The traditions and constitutional cultures and institutional frameworks are very different and have to be explained in order to appreciate any limitations to possibilities in European public law's development. The United Kingdom's sovereign Parliament will dictate the terms of constitutional and even administrative law development in the UK and Germany's strict observance of constitutional guarantees of fundamental rights and democratic government will affect developments in that country. In the French tradition the strong executive and a weak Parliament partly explain the emergence of a strong system of *droit administratif* and a limited *conseil constitutionnel*. The different traditions will have to be explained to inform what follows.

---

[79]   Emile Durkheim *The Division of Labour in Society* (1933) The Free Press, p 405.

Chapter 3 will examine the contribution of the French, German and English (sic) legal cultures to the development of European public law. Specific themes will be looked at in chapters in Part Two eg, Principles of Review and Principles of Liability.

Chapter 4 will assess in detail the impact of European integration on UK constitutional law, now of course subject to devolution. It is a very rich story.

In Part two, I wish to tease out the major themes confronted in Part One by looking at specific areas. I hope these will be self explanatory. Chapter 5 will concentrate on devolution within the UK and subsidiary within Europe.

Chapter 6 examines the familiar themes of openness and access to information within Europe. Increasing conflict is seen between the more liberal tendencies of some Member States and the less liberal tendencies of the EU, especially the Council and Commission. Specifically, and very briefly, how will the UK's regimes – for there are to be four as a consequence of devolution – react to the EU system? How might the Scottish regime influence the English and so on? The chapter will concentrate on the position within the Union.

Chapter 7 examines our national Parliament and review of legislation and EU policy and its role alongside the European Parliament (although the latter is a partner in EU legislation). It concentrates on the role of national parliaments in the Community architecture. What needs to be introduced into such oversight – more national or more European oriented bodies or a combination?

In Chapter 8 there is an examination of the principles of review now being employed by English courts and the extent to which these principles have been influenced by European doctrines. Chapter 9 examines the contribution of human rights protection and the European influence in that subject. Within two years of coming into effect, the Human Rights Act 1998 was already making a deep impact on judicial control of governmental decisions affecting individuals. How adequate is the coverage of the concept of human rights that the HRA addresses? What, for instance, of third generation rights such as information and participation in decision-making, environmental regulation let alone second generation rights such as social and economic rights? What concept of citizenship is conveyed by the HRA and the ECHR?

Chapter 10 covers an area of substantive principles of law, on the liability of public authorities in which the jurisprudence of EC law and the CHR has been influential in developing the liability of public authorities for tortious wrong-doing.

In Chapter 11, I examine the EU Ombudsman and other devices for dealing with grievances/complaints of citizens both in a European and in a domestic context. In the subject of grievance redress, too much attention is perhaps paid to courts. Growing interdependence is likely to be an emerging feature of Ombudsman activity as the EU expands. And what of redress within EU institutions themselves before the Ombudsman intervenes?

The subject matter of Chapter 12 is broad and deals with competition, regulation and markets with reference to provision of essential services, problems associated with regulation in a European context and in competition law the fact that UK law has virtually incorporated the EC provisions for its domestic use. While the chapter offers some examples of glaring EC influence in shaping domestic law, it also reveals some of the greatest divergences between some continental traditions and Anglo Saxon approaches to the provision of essential services.

While the coverage in Part two is broad, there are some obvious omissions. One such could be discrimination. Although this will not feature as a chapter in its own right, it will de discussed in the chapter on human rights (where the ECHR is seriously deficient, although in the process of development). Another omission might be economic law or law and monetary policy as part of public law. I address the impact of the Economic and Monetary Union in the concluding chapter on Future Questions. I am open to criticism about what might be omitted, including social and employment policy and environmental regulation but I cannot cover every area in a comprehensive or even fleeting fashion. Nor has it been my intention to give textbook treatment to topics. Pursuing themes has been my objective.

Part three will look forward to the future but will also cover present work so that in Chapter 13 it will be asked whether European public law exists? I accept that it might be objected that such a chapter should be at the beginning of the book to inform the book's unfolding discussion. I have placed it near the end to offer a reflection on what has come before. It may, alternatively, be read after this present chapter by those who wish to address broad arguments about the existence of European public law.

The final chapter will include discussion of present and future questions such as EMU, codifying European administrative law and possible influence of codes of good administrative practice produced by the EU Ombudsman, which is discussed in Chapter 7 and the impact of the new EU Charter of Fundamental Rights discussed in Chapter 9. Is codification desirable or possible? Will the inevitable result be a written constitution for Europe – currently very much on the agenda with the Convention under former French President Giscard D'Estaing discussing Europe's future? The Convention will produce a report, probably by June 2003, which will be the basis of intergovernmental discussions at the European Council – the meeting of the heads of state of Member States. The report will not be binding (see Chapter 14, p 600 et seq and <http://european-convention.eu.int>). On 28 October 2002, a preliminary draft constitution was produced after various papers from working groups. What will the impact of these developments be, if they come to pass, on a country like the UK which does not even *possess* a written constitution?

The last chapter will seek to mesh these developments in the field of European public law with wider, international or global developments. Principles of national European systems are pervasive throughout the world; in the Commonwealth and common law world as well as in the French speaking world and so on. European law's influence is also spreading ever eastwards. What consequences are we likely to witness? What contribution can, or should, European public law make to global order and governance? These questions are posed rather than answered.

Chapter 2

Law and government: a comparative tour[1]

This chapter offers a comparative analysis of the relationship between law and government. Government is organised through politics – or more precisely through the power resulting from political success. Politics concerns the battleground in which differing views of the good life centring around political groups or parties compete for ascendancy, usually by appeal to mass support and electoral victory. Law is a body of precepts, principles, rules and norms emerging through the political process in the form of legislation or regulations or orders, or it is something which emerges from judicial decisions, 'jurisprudence' as it is known on the continent; case law in the common law tradition.

Legislative rules are very often not self explanatory but have to be interpreted by courts as well as by others. Doctrines on interpretation set guidelines on how the interpretation of law should be conducted. The common law has developed various canons of construction built upon the plain meaning of the words, what problem was a statute or a section attempting to address or rectify, or what interpretation makes best sense? In the US, legislative intent, or what legislators intended in drafting legislation, has been a central method in interpreting legislation and forms of this approach are being adopted in England. These are not so much rules, but guidelines. In the common law, the judge is described as an oracle of the law and helps develop the law around the doctrine of precedent and

1   The 1996 FIDE conference was devoted in one of its sessions to *National Constitutional Law and European Integration* FIDE Kongress Vol I Berlin (1996). The 2002 Congress has a session on *EU Law and National Constitutions* www.FIDE2002.ORG/reportseulaw.htm.

stare decisis – in simple terms, a lower court is bound by the *ratio decidendi* of a superior court – and filling in the gaps left by the legislature. In the civil law tradition which has been highly influential on the development of Community law, the judge is not a law maker; the judge makes a decision under the law applying general legal principle contained in a code to a set of facts. There is, in this approach, little room for precedent. To be bound by previous decisions is to give the force of legislation to those decisions instead of treating them as a legally authoritative answer to the question before the previous court.

Law sets limits to the process of government and governance. If no legal limits are set on what government may do, there is a likelihood of tyranny. The rules of government are set out in constitutions. Written constitutions are given a special or primary status in a nation's legal order. These invariably separate the basic powers of government functionally and institutionally in order to minimise opportunities for power to become corrupted through being confused. Three specific functions are identified: governing or executive power; legislating or legislative power; and adjudicating or applying the law. These powers are entrusted to three separate institutions: the government, the legislature and the judiciary.[2] The EU does not possess a separation of powers in the classic sense. The legislature involves three institutions. The Council and Commission both act in executive capacities. The courts applying Community law comprise national courts as well as domestic courts of Member States. The EU is built on the basis of interest representation.

As well as separating power horizontally, constitutions may devolve power vertically to establish federal or other forms of devolved government. Constitutions define the terms of the relationship and the powers allocated between the institutions of government and between layers of government and between these institutions and the people they govern. They invariably define the relationship between the nation state and international organisations and the domestic legal implications of Treaties that are ratified. Since the French drafted their first constitution in 1791, to which the 1789 Declaration of the Rights of Man was a preamble, that document has had a profound influence both within Europe and beyond in setting the terms of the relationship between government and law. It was itself inspired by American constitutionalism.

---

[2]   M J C Vile *Constitutionalism* (1967); K C Wheare *Modern Constitutions* (1966, 2nd ed).

Today, however, the constitutions of nation states display multifarious variations in how they tackle the task of setting limits to the political power of government. In Germany for instance, there is a constitutional court with powers to review federal and state legislation and their conformity with the federal constitution (the Basic Law) and numerous other powers conferred specifically in the federal constitution. These powers include 'public international law actions' which confer on the Constitutional Court alone power to determine whether rules of public international law are an integral part of federal law creating rights and duties for persons resident in Germany.[3] In Germany, as in many European states, review of legislation may be abstract – there is no actual case or controversy in existence which needs to be resolved – and which applies to legislation at various stages of its development. Review of legislation may also, or as in the case of the US *only*, apply to legislation when enacted. In this situation, a concrete dispute or case has to be in existence. This was all alien to the UK until the decision in *Factortame*[4] forced UK courts to disapply UK statutes which contravened the EC Treaty and until the devolution Acts allowed Scottish and Northern Irish devolved legislation to be judicially challenged both before and after enactment (see p 194 et seq and p 232 et seq).[5]

European public law has emerged from a variety of traditions found in Member States of the EU, from the Union itself and from the ECHR. We need to have some idea of the relationship between law and government in differing systems in order to gain an understanding of the matrices in which European public law emerged. Public law is very much defined by a wider political context; a context within which government and ways of governing must operate as well as delivering the benefits to be gained from government. There is no state in the world today in which a constitution of some sort does not set the framework for government. Although their existence is commonplace, constitutions are very much a framework for government – the detailed practice is to be found elsewhere. Behind every formal constitution is a living constitution just as behind formal legal provisions lies the 'living law' in Ehrlich's vivid phrase.[6] They are 'highly

---

3   D P Kommers *The Constitutional Jurisprudence of the Federal Republic of Germany* (1997, 2nd ed) p 10.

4   *R v Secretary of State for Transport, ex p Factortame* Case C-213/89 [1991] 1 All ER 70 (ECJ and HL).

5   Northern Ireland legislation was subject to judicial review in the Privy Council under the Government of Ireland Act 1920.

6   E Ehrlich (1922) 36 Harvard Law Rev 130.

incomplete, if not misleading, guides to actual practice to what is often called the "working constitution" or the "governance" of a country.'[7]

New Zealand and Israel have both succumbed to some form of written basic law, which is what a constitution is. The UK alone does not possess a single constitutional document which is given the form of superior law. Its constitution is contained in a variety of statutes, legal presumptions and working assumptions of constitutional practice known as conventions. This is developed in Chapter 4.

Constitutions invariably follow political upheaval or change, whether traumatic or otherwise, and embrace a new set of values and a definition of how power should be organised within a state. They often constitute a break with the past and a deliberate attempt to introduce a new way of doing things. They might make provision for basic human rights. The only, and long defunct, written English constitution of 1653, the 'Instrument of Government' certainly introduced a novel mode for the conduct of government in England which had now despatched with its Crown. It said nothing about human rights apart from a very limited form of Christian toleratism. It lasted six years before the old order under the Crown was restored. The 'old order' was constitutionalised in 1689 by an Act of Parliament, the Bill of Rights. It reinforced what in England many had believed to be the fundamental principles of good government. The American constitution adopted in 1789 was a deliberate attempt to guarantee by law a balance of governmental powers in order to expel from government the abuse of executive or Crown prerogative that had imposed taxes without consent and which had thwarted freedom of speech. Protection of some human rights followed shortly after. The first constitution of France usurped the position of the *ancien regime* and famously heralded the rights of man. Successive constitutions altered the balance of power between the executive and the legislature until in the fifth republic of 1958 the balance swung back to the executive when the fifth constitution was duly approved by a popular referendum in September of that year.

Germany's constitution was rebuilt in 1949 after the nazi regime and had to accommodate a divided Germany and attempted to guarantee that the

---

[7]   S Finer, V Bogdanor and B Rudden *Comparing Constitutions* (1994) p 1. There are degrees of divergence between written constitutions and political practice; some nations eg the US, are comfortable with constitutional flexibility. Others, eg Germany, require a more rigid fidelity of political practice to the Basic Law: D P Kommers *The Constitutional Jurisprudence of the Federal Republic of Germany* (1997, 2nd ed) p 39.

Federal German state would not descend into the depravations from which it had recently emerged. It set a high premium on fundamental human rights, democratic government and protection for the regions in Germany, the Lander. In fact several provisions are unamendable: those concerning the Lander and democracy. The German constitution set its premium on a state in which law and the protection of rights was supreme under values contained in the Basic Law – a *Rechtsstaat* – and this is evidenced by the extent to which financial law concerning financial relations between the federal state and the Lander are set out in constitutional law.[8]

There is no point in introducing the quirks and foibles of several other states in Europe other then to mention the point that several bear testimony to the fact that they were heavily influenced by the French model, that those of Italy, Portugal and Spain emerged after periods of totalitarian rule in 1946, 1976 and 1978 respectively, that some give special pre-eminence to religious belief and doctrine, and that some do not follow the French or German inspired models – the Scandinavian examples are relevant here. Finally, as we shall see in Chapter 4, the UK is an exception in that it has decided that while lip-service is paid to the supremacy of law in the form of the rule of law, this supremacy is not encased or guaranteed in any higher entrenched law applied by a constitutional or supreme court.

As the past history of written constitutions was driven by the desire to give definition to a new moment of government under a new concordat, the present is dominated by the desire to give expression to arrangements forged by international alliances which transcend the traditional form of Treaty. The most developed is the Treaty of Rome and its successors which does not simply establish a relationship between Member States which is bound by international law but which also establishes, the ECJ has made clear, a 'new legal order of international law for the benefit of which states have limited their sovereign rights......... [and which] .....is also intended to confer upon them rights which become part of their legal heritage.'[9] Less developed forms of such organisations exist elsewhere in the world including the North American Free Trade Association (see Chapter 14, p 613 et seq). Unlike the United Nations, the Community created

---

8   D P Kommers *The Constitutional Jurisprudence of the Federal Republic of Germany* (1997, 2nd ed) pp 90–96; Arts 104a–115 Basic Law. On the German Constitutional Court's decision on the compatibility of the Finance Equalisation Act with the Basic Law, see: M Aziz (2000) European Public Law 217.

9   *NV Algemene Transporten Expedite Onderneming van Gend en Loos v Nederlandse Administratie der Belastingen* 'Van Gend en Loos' Case 26/62 [1963] ECR 1.

by the Treaty of Rome has given rights to Member States *and* to citizens and has established a legal order superior to that of Member States' legal orders: 'the Member States have limited their sovereign rights, albeit within limited fields,[10] and have thus created a body of law which binds both their nationals and themselves.'[11] Some of the features of the Treaty on the European Union (TEU) introduced in Amsterdam retain a purely traditional intergovernmental compact although they draw on the organs of the Community and have given the ECJ an enhanced albeit confined role in, for instance, police and judicial co-operation in criminal affairs.

What is the nature and form of this new legal order?

The European Union's Legal Order[12]

The European Council at Laeken in December 2001 established a convention to investigate the future of the EU and in particular a Constitution for the Union and a simplification and revision of existing treaties. This investigation is in preparation for the European Council which will take place in 2004 (see p 600 et seq for a preliminary draft constitution).[13] The Convention is guided by a Praesidium which sits in private and various working groups have been established (p ... below) to report on specific subjects. There is also a 'Youth Convention'. The Convention will be examined in Chapter 14 but one point among many being discussed – there are 11 working groups reporting to the Convention – is the question of a legal personality for the EU which would be likely to have very important repercussions for the existing Union framework. Under Article 281 [210] EC, the Community is given legal personality (as are Euratom and the European Coal and Steel Community (ECSC) under their Treaties) and enjoys the 'most extensive legal capacity accorded to legal persons' under the laws of the Member States within those states.

---

10   The ECJ has expressed the point that such limitations have taken place in ever wider fields: *First EEA case Op 1/91* [1991] ECR I-6079 para 21.
11   Case 6/64 *Flaminio Costa v ENEL* [1964] ECR 585.
12   See Sir G Slynn *Introducing a European Legal Order* (1992); J Weiler *The Constitution of Europe* (1999); Z Bankowski and A.Scott eds. *The European Union and its Order: The Legal Theory of European Integration* (2000): I Harden (1994) Public Law 609.
13   On the *Future of the EU and a Constitution* see: www.european-convention.eu.int and www.europa.eu.int/futurum/index_en. See also HL 163 (2001–02) for the select committee of the House of Lords on European Union on the Convention and FIDE 2002, note 1 above *Commission Report* by P Oliver.

The TEU presently constitutes the Community's legal order – the Community is a component of the EU. The TEU is the constitution of the Community and Union creating the institutions of the Community, together with the objectives, powers and tasks of the EU and Community.[14] What is meant by 'Union' and 'Community' are discussed below. The ECJ has described the Community as one based on the rule of law.[15] A prevailing call for a European Constitution which refuses to accept the TEU as a coherent constitutional document comes from the left, the right, perfectionists and pragmatists. The left wishes to see a constitution allowing for full and unqualified federalism, integration and a much richer form of citizenship than is currently provided in Articles 17–22 [8–8e] EC.[16] In this latter feature, the distinction between those who belong to the Union and those who do not causes the left great difficulty. Central to its aims is a constitution which enshrines these points as matters of legal detail to be argued in judicial fora. For the right, a constitution needs to set out clearly the limitations of the institutions of the Community, especially the court so that it cannot make decisions which 'bend the rules'. The perfectionists seek a legally perfect document which adds protection of human rights to the legal norms of the Treaty and which establishes a new model of legislative chambers to replace the existing Council and European Parliament and which sets out more clearly the division of powers between the tiers of government: union, national, regional and possibly local. It shares with the left the desire to reduce opt outs, as well as a reduction of those powers for Member States to proceed at different levels and at different speed. While its ambitions may be regarded by some as utopian, their view is that the present arrangements which political leaders regard as a result of pragmatic compromise and fudging, are distinctly dystopian. Pragmatists may take many forms, and may share in some of the above ideals but their concern is to enhance the effectiveness and workability of the EU and Community. A constitution would provide much needed direction and clarity in the relationship between the Community, the EU and Member States. That relationship is one that has forged a multi-level system of governance where many essential tasks can only be effected through cooperation, shared arrangements, flexibility and complementary competencies.

[14] 'A constitutional charter of the Community': see *EEA* case note 10 and *Les Verts v European Parliament* [1986] ECR 1339.

[15] *European Parliament v Council* Case C-70/88 [1990] ECR I-2041.

[16] Which basically provide European citizens in other Member States with rights on voting and standing as candidates in municipal and European Parliament elections; petitioning the European Parliament; communicating to the institutions of the EC in their own language; and complaining to the EU Ombudsman. These are added to rights of free movement and residence.

The story of the origins of the three original communities: European Economic Community (EEC), ECSC and the European Atomic Energy Community (EAEC) has been exhaustively rehearsed.[17] Today the European Community (EC)[18] refers to Title II TEU, ie that part of the Treaty which is incorporated into UK law by virtue of the European Communities Act 1972 and which was formerly called the EEC. It is known as the First Pillar of the European Union – the EC. There are two other pillars to the EU which are described below. Legally and constitutionally the First Pillar is the most significant part of the TEU because of its incorporation into our domestic legal order by virtue of the 1972 Act and subsequent amendments. A little needs to be said about the scope of the Common Provisions of the EU contained in Title I TEU which embrace and set a wider context to Community aspirations.

Title I TEU concerns the Common Provisions of the European Union. Article 1 TEU states that the Treaty marks a new stage in the process of creating 'an ever closer union among the peoples of Europe, in which decisions are taken as openly as possible and as closely as possible to the citizen.' These points I develop in Chapters 5 and 6. It continues that the EU shall be founded on the European Communities 'supplemented by the policies and forms of co-operation established by this Treaty', ie the second and third pillars. Its task is defined as the organisation of relations between the Member States and between their peoples 'in a manner demonstrating consistency and solidarity.'

Article 2 TEU spells out the objectives of the EU much of which is directly relevant to the EC – eg strengthening the protection of the rights and interests of nationals of Member States through the introduction of citizenship of the EU – but in other respects is not a part of Community competence such as asserting its identity on the international scene through the Common Foreign and Security Policy (the Second Pillar) including a common defence policy. The fourth indent refers to matters which cover both the TEU and EC, ie freedom of movement, external border controls, asylum and immigration and the prevention and combating of crime. The

---

[17]   See K Lenaerts and P Van Nuffel, ed R Bray *Constitutional Law of the European Union* (1999) ch 1.

[18]   ECSC and EAEC are effectively absorbed within the European Community and are a part of UK law by virtue of the European Communities Act 1972, s 2(1). Titles III and IV TEU deal with the ECSC and EAEC respectively.

fifth indent refers to the maintenance and strengthening of the *acquis communautaire* (see p 95 below) and revision of policies and forms of cooperation introduced in the TEU 'with the aim of ensuring the effectiveness of the mechanisms and the institutions of the Community.'

Article 3 TEU states that the EU shall be served by a single institutional framework ie those institutions created for the EC, and Article 4 TEU makes special reference to the position of the European Council – the meetings or 'summits' of the heads of state or government of Member States and the President of the European Commission. The European Parliament, the Council and the Commission, the ECJ and Court of Auditors, bodies created by the Community, shall exercise their powers under the conditions and for the purposes of the Community Treaties and the TEU. Articles 6 and 7 TEU are dealt with below.

This is not an easy or accessible structure. It has not been assisted by a re-numbering of Treaty Articles when the TEU was revised at Amsterdam (ToA) in 1997. The EU is attempting a complex exercise – a framework for collective action among sovereign states building on collective, representative and electoral models. Its very complexity has produced countless accusations of a lack of transparency, exacerbated by secretive practices of the Council and Commission in particular and satellite bodies created by those institutions. The Convention under former French President Valerie Giscard D'Estaing has been charged by the European Council with the task of producing a draft straightforward constitution for a Community which is facing eastward and southern expansion and which since January 2002 has a shared Euro currency in all but three Member States. One working group under the Convention has suggested a single legal personality for the EU including the EC to help to simplify its structure (see below p 68).

The First Pillar of the European Union

The EC is the First Pillar of the EU, although it has also absorbed the two other Communities ECSC and EAEC.[19] Article 2 EC sets out objectives and

---

[19]   The three Treaties governing the Communities prescribe the tasks of the Communities in order to attain clearly circumscribed objectives (See ECSC, Art 2, first para; EAEC, Art 1). The ECSC no longer exists.

tasks of the EC and these are further developed in Articles 3 and 4 EC. The Community's task is to promote a 'harmonious, balanced and sustainable development of economic activities, a high level of employment and of social protection, equality between men and women, sustainable and non-inflationary growth, a high degree of competitiveness and convergence of economic performance, a high level of protection and improvement of the quality of the environment, the raising of the standard of living and quality of life, and economic and social cohesion and solidarity among Member States.' This will be by virtue of establishing a common market and an economic and monetary union together with the activities set out in Article 3 EC concerning the common market and other items going beyond a common market, eg an environmental policy, education and training of quality and 'the flowering of the cultures of the Member States', health protection, energy, civil protection and tourism. All these activities will seek to promote equality between men and women.

Article 4 EC makes provision for the adoption of an economic policy based on close co-ordination of Member States economic interests and on the internal market. Specifically, Article 4(2) states that the activities shall include the introduction of a European Monetary System which reached its fulfilment with the introduction of the Euro in January 2002 although not for the three Member States which opted out – the UK, Denmark and Sweden.[20]

In the Common Provisions of the TEU it is proclaimed that the EU is built on the Rule of Law.[21] Article 5 [3b] EC states that the Community shall act within the powers conferred upon it by the Treaty and its objectives – it will operate intra vires. It possesses no Kompetenz-Kompetenz or power to *extend* its own powers. The absence of clearly defined boundaries in many competencies makes this sound easier than it is in practice where so much is subject to interpretation.

Article 7 [4] EC establishes the major institutions of the Community. As well as the following bodies, Article 7 established the Court of Auditors, an Economic and Social Committee and a Committee of the Regions, a

---

20   See Ch 14, p 584 et seq.
21   See the ECJ in *Les Verts* above note 14.

European System of Central Banks and the European Central Bank, and the European Investment Bank.

The pre-eminent executive body which has to act in accordance with powers conferred by the Treaty, and therefore by Member States, is the Council of Ministers (now Council of the EU) (Articles 202–210 [145–154] EC) which is not to be confused with the European Council. The latter has no formal role in the EC Treaty.[22] The Council of Ministers consists of Ministers of Member States chosen for the subject speciality with which the Council is dealing.[23] It has a Committee of Permanent Representatives (Article 207 EC) which carries out tasks assigned to it including preparation of the agenda for Council meetings. It comprises national officials working at two levels.[24] Numerous working parties and committees set up under the TEU assist in the legislative process.

The Council of the EU is a joint partner in legislation with the European Parliament which since 1979 has been directly elected with representatives elected in national constituencies according to allocations under the EC Treaty. These figures were amended at Nice. Under the Treaty of Nice the total number of MEPs is limited to 732. The authority and standing of the European Parliament have grown since its early years when a non-directly elected 'Assembly' only had to be consulted by the Council in the legislative process and had limited powers in the budgetary process. Progressively, the European Parliament became involved with the co-operation procedure in legislation and this was followed by the co-decision procedure in 1993 which applies to all internal market provisions.[25] The co-decision procedure established in Article 251 [189b] EC allows for a Conciliation Committee to be established where the Council and European Parliament cannot agree legislative proposals. Basically, under Article 251, legislation cannot be made without the European Parliament's approval. The European Parliament's role in the budget has been enhanced. It also

---

[22] See Article 4 TEU and above for membership.
[23] Its Presidency is chosen on a six monthly basis.
[24] COREPER I and II. The latter is more important and has an important liaison role with national governments.
[25] The internal market was the first stage of three stages towards European Union. It was introduced by the Single European Act 1987 and sought to bring about a single economic area among Member States without internal borders.

engages in a supervisory role over the other institutions, especially the Commission.[26]

The European Commission (Articles 211–219 [155–163] EC) is the law enforcer, law preparer, policy initiator, adviser, a law maker and general guardian and overseer of the Community's interests. The Commissioners must be 'completely independent in the performance of their duties' (Article 213) seeking instructions from no government or 'any other body.' It comprises twenty members headed by a President. It is a collegial body which may decide on a majority vote. There are about 18,000 administrators and translators, interpreters and researchers. It is accompanied by a satellite of committees known as 'Comitology committees' and other committees, agencies and other advisory bodies which have caused increasing concern because of the closed and confidential manner in which such bodies advise on the detailed and technical contents of law initiatives and policy development and implementation. These committees comprise national civil servants and members of special interest groups and scientific/specialist advisers. The committees spent about 19.5m Euros in 1998 and numbered 477 committees.[27] A Council Decision of 1999 has sought to introduce greater safeguards into the operation of committees (see Chapter 6, p 262) Some commentators see the potential in Comitology committees to offer a means of legitimising transnational governance and 'deliberative supra-nationalism' – that framework of compromise, negotiation and shared competencies in which the Community has to operate.[28] Also causing concern has been the development of agencies by the Council and Commission which, like committees, are not subject to the supervision of the ECJ or Court of First Instance.

An important amendment to the EC Treaty at Nice now allows the President of the Commission to demand the resignation of an individual member of the Commission after obtaining the approval of the College of

---

[26]   The institutions are described in basic texts: see P Craig and G de Burca *EU Law: Text and Materials* ch 2 (2002, 3rd ed).

[27]   C Joerges and E Vos eds. *EU Committees: Social Regulation, Law and Politics* (1999) ch 2, p 20. Also R Pedler and G Schafer *Shaping European Law and Policy: The Role of Committees and Comitology in the Political Process* (1996). Some have put their number as high as 1,000: de Burca in P Craig and G de Burca *The Evolution of EU Law* (1998) ch 2. The Council also has its advisory committees.

[28]   C Joerges (2002) ELJ 133. See N Bernard *Multilevel Governance in the European Union* (2002).

Commissioners. This reform was introduced to end the log-jam which previously existed whereby only the Commission as a whole could be asked to resign by the European Parliament. The Cresson episode, which included favouritism in appointments, brought home the desirability of placing a power to insist on resignation of one Commissioner in the hands of the President.[29] In June 2002, it was reported that the then President of the Commission wished to reform the Commission so that his power would be enhanced allowing him to preside over a Cabinet of Vice Presidents.[30]

The European Court of Justice (ECJ) and the Court of First Instance (CFI) (Articles 220–245 [164–188] EC) are charged with ensuring that in the interpretation and application of this Treaty the law is observed (Article 220). The judges of the ECJ,[31] its Advocates General and those of the CFI shall be chosen from persons whose independence is beyond doubt and who possess the requisite ability.[32] The Treaty of Nice made considerable amendments to the jurisdiction of the two courts giving the CFI a general jurisdiction for all actions of annulment and other items not reserved for the ECJ and which also allowed for preliminary references (below) to be made to the CFI in specific areas laid down in statute. There are in addition judicial panels of the CFI over which the CFI will act as a court of appeal, with further review in the ECJ. The appellate work of the ECJ is likely to grow significantly.[33]

The ECJ, and now the CFI, are given powers of judicial review of Community institutions under the terms of Article 230. This aspect may be dealt with in the next chapter when we examine the EC as a system of administrative law. Of significant importance to its constitutional structure, however, is

---

[29] See Ch 6 p 261 on the fall-out to the Cresson episode. See the Commissioner N Kinnock (2002) 73 Political Qu 21. But after various reforms in the Commission, a former chief accountant of the Commission criticised its inability to control fraud and accused Neil Kinnock and the Commission of a 'cover-up' and was suspended: *Financial Times* (2002) 1 and 3 August.

[30] *Financial Times* (2002) 19 June.

[31] Comprising one judge per Member State for the ECJ and CFI.

[32] In relation to the ECJ, this includes juriconsultants of recognised competence, Article 223 EC. See generally: N Brown and T Kennedy *The Court of Justice of the European Communities* (2000, 5th ed); A Dashwood and A Johnston eds *The Future of the Judicial System of the European Union* (2001) D O'Keeffe ed *Judicial Review in European Union Law* (2000); K Alter *Establishing the Supremacy of European Law* (2001).

[33] K St C Bradley in *20 Yearbook of European Law 2001* (2002) OUP.

the role of the ECJ in hearing preliminary references on points of Community law from Member State courts. Article 234 [177] EC is as follows:

> The Court of Justice [now also the CFI] shall have jurisdiction to give preliminary rulings concerning:
> (a) the interpretation of this Treaty;
> (b) the validity and interpretation of acts of the institutions of the Community and of the European Central Bank;
> (c) the interpretation of the statutes of bodies established by an act of the Council, where those statutes so provide

A court or tribunal in a Member State may refer such a matter to the appropriate court for a ruling where it considers that a decision of the court is necessary to enable it to give judgment. Where the national court or tribunal is a court of final instance, any such question must be referred to the ECJ or CFI. In addition to the reference under Article 234, references may also be made under Title IV Article 68 EC (concerning visas, asylum and immigration) and under the Third Pillar, Article 35 TEU (see below).

Article 234 EC is a subject of undoubted constitutional importance for the role of the ECJ, and now the CFI. It is the principal means by which the details of Community law have been developed. It is the process by which the ECJ has provided for a uniform interpretation of Community law within Member States. The law is applied by the ECJ and the matter is sent back to the national court or tribunal for it to apply to the facts before the national court. Findings of fact are for national courts and these powers may be jealously protected.[34] The doctrine of *acte clair* has been developed to allow Member State courts not to refer such a question where 'it [national court] has established that the question raised is irrelevant or that the Community provision in question is so obvious as to leave no scope for any reasonable doubt.'[35] This would be considered in the light of the 'specific characteristics of Community law, the particular difficulties to which its interpretation gives rise [including the fact that Community legislation is drafted in several languages] and the risk of divergences in judicial decisions within the Community.'[36] Some saw this as a process of

---

34 The ECJ and CFI have no jurisdiction in relation to findings of fact under Art 234: *Arsenal Football Club plc v Reed* [2002] EWHC 2695 (Ch) [2003] 1 All ER 137; Case 51/75 *EMI Records Ltd v CBS UK Ltd* [1976] ECR 811.

35 *CILFIT* Case 283/81 [1982] ECR 3415, para 17.

36 *CILFIT* Case 283/81 [1982] ECR 3415, para 17.

give and take so that there should be a spirit of compromise by the ECJ and national courts in the development of Community law – it also encouraged the development of precedent by national courts interpreting Community law cases but in a manner which may be partial to national predilections or sympathies.[37] Arnull, on the other hand, sees the *CILFIT* decision in which the above quote appears as one which may 'only jeopardise the uniform application of the Treaty.'[38] Craig and de Burca believe the original relationship between the European and national courts no longer represents reality. Originally conceived as a horizontal and bilateral relationship, it is one which is becoming more vertical and multilateral. This has been brought about by a variety of factors including:

> the assertion of the supremacy of Community law over national law; the development of a system of de facto precedent; the qualified support for the *acte clair* doctrine; the sectoral devolution of responsibility to national courts; the desire of the ECJ to exercise control over the type of case which it will hear; and the blurring of the line between interpretation and application.[39]

The end result many believe has been the establishment of the ECJ as a constitutional court of the Community in which national courts will also interpret and apply Community law.[40] From the early 1960s, the ECJ had shown propensity for the assumption of a constitutional role in its work, as profound in its own way as the decision in *Marbury v Madison*[41] where the US Supreme Court in the decision of Marshall CJ inferred a power of judicial review in that court to assess the consistency of federal and state legislation with the constitution.

---

[37] G Mancini and D Keeling (1991) 11 Yearbook of European Law 1. See P Craig and G de Burca *EU Law: Text Cases and Materials* (3rd ed) pp 439 et seq.

[38] (1989) Mod LR 622. An empirical study quoted by Arnull showed that non-reference was a significant feature of UK courts. For the details relating to the application of Art 234 and the English approach to references see Craig and de Burca *EU Law: Text and Materials* ch 2 (2002, 3rd ed).

[39] Craig and de Burca *EU Law: Text and Materials* ch 2 (2002, 3rd ed) p 479. See also, T de la Mare in Craig and de Burca *The Evolution of EU Law* (1998), ch 6.

[40] Craig and de Burca *EU Law: Text and Materials* ch 2 (2002, 3rd ed). See more generally, A-M Slaughter, A Stone Sweet and J Weiler eds *The European Courts and National Courts: Doctrine and Jurisprudence* (1998). The ECJ has been heavily criticised for being a court with a 'mission' which has abused its position: see Ch 4, p 201 et seq.

[41] 1 Cranch 137 (1803).

The ECJ, direct effect and legal sovereignty

The doctrine of direct effect was introduced by the ECJ in the famous *Van Gend en Loos* decision in 1963. It was referred to above and in Chapter 1 and its importance will reverberate throughout this book. It is a development of striking constitutional significance establishing that where relevant criteria are satisfied, provisions of Treaties, and subsequently Directives although additional qualifications would apply, may be directly effective in Member States' legal systems and may therefore be invoked by individual litigants in national courts and not simply by state representatives in a supra national court. Directly effective provisions in treaties may be invoked against Member States or, if appropriate, against individuals. Provisions in Directives are only effective against the state or 'emanations of the state' (see p 97 et seq).[42] The provisions must be clear, precise and unconditional, where in other words, it is legally complete and self executing. The rights derive solely from Community law and are not dependent upon implementation by national law into the domestic arena although they are enforced through national courts. It was a truly revolutionary position. In the judgment the ECJ referred to the new international order created by the Treaty [of Rome] as follows:

> this Treaty is more than an agreement which merely creates mutual obligations between the contracting states ..... It is also confirmed more specifically by the establishment of institutions endowed with sovereign rights ....

> The conclusion to be drawn from this is that the Community constitutes a new legal order of international law for the benefit of which the states have limited their sovereign rights, albeit within limited fields, and the subjects of which comprise not only Member States but also their nationals.[43]

Just after the decision in *Van Gend en Loos*, the ECJ gave judgment in another case of enormous constitutional consequence. This was *Costa v*

---

42 Vertically directly effective. Provisions in Directives may only be so effective after the time for their implementation has expired but a Member State may not do acts which undermine the impact of the Directive in the period prior to implementation: Case C-129/96 *I-E Wallonie ASBL v Région Wallonie* [1997] ECR I-7411. On the direct horizontal effect of Treaty provisions on an individual, see: Case C-453/99 *Courage Ltd v B Creham* [2001] ECR I-6297 (Ch 12, p 523).

43 Case 26/62 [1963] ECR 1.

ENEL[44] where the ECJ described the Community as one of 'unlimited duration' having its own institutions, its own personality, its own legal capacity and power of legal representation on the international plane and, more particularly, real powers stemming from a limitation of sovereignty or a transfer of powers from the Member States to the Community the latter of which have created a body of law which is binding over both their nationals and themselves in rights and obligations arising under the Treaty. Such a transfer, the ECJ held, 'carries with it a permanent limitation of sovereign rights'.

Community law made it impossible therefore for Member States to adopt a contradictory measure taking precedence over a legal system 'accepted by them on a basis of reciprocity'. To allow such would be to subvert the 'executive force' of Community law which cannot vary from one Member State to another. Treaty conditions would be contingent and not unconditional if a subsequent legal measure of a Member State could challenge their authority.

The law stemming from the treaty, an independent source of law, could not, because of its special and original nature, be overridden by domestic legal provisions, however framed, without being deprived of its character as Community law and without the legal basis of the Community being called into question.

The Court followed *Van Gend en Loos* in holding that under specified conditions, articles of the Treaty could be directly effective in national legal systems and their courts.

In *Internationale Handelsgesellschaft*[45] the ECJ emphasised that Community law by virtue of its independent nature cannot be overridden by national law adding that not even an appeal to 'fundamental rights' could override Community law which itself respects such rights and which form an 'integral part of the general principles of law' and whose protection 'must be ensured within the structure and objectives of the Community' (see below). From this it follows that national courts must enforce Community law in its entirety and give full effect to it and to rights conferred on individuals and they should not wait for annulment or repeal of inconsistent legal measures by domestic legislatures or constitutional

[44]   Case 6/64 [1964] ECR 585.
[45]   Case 11/70 [1970] ECR 1125.

organs. National courts must accordingly 'set aside any provision of national law which may conflict with it, whether prior or subsequent to the Community rule.[46] The full impact of these decisions was to be felt in the UK in the *Factortame* saga as we shall see (p 194 et seq).

From the perspective of the ECJ, the relation of Member States and their laws to the Community is determined by Community law and not by national constitutional laws. If the latter were the case, there could be 15, and soon more, different versions of what that relationship was. What has to be established now is how constitutions in Member States accommodated both a transfer of sovereignty to the Community, in limited but ever expanding fields, as well as the principles on legal sovereignty and direct effect spelt out in the above decisions of the ECJ. In doing this, and after discussing Member State approaches in general, I will look in particular at three very different constitutions: France, Germany and the UK. These will give some idea of the variety of responses to the assertion that Community law is sovereign and how those constitutions have accommodated and responded to such claims. This should provide an insight into how constitutions operate in those countries. It will help illustrate the relationship between politics and law that we set out to explore. It will also bring home how in spite of considerable differences, the practical (if not theoretical) difficulties in accommodating enormous constitutional change have been completely overcome. Constitutions, that most idiosyncratic of national identities, have prepared the way for their own integration without, it might seem, realising it.

Accommodating the 'New Legal Order'

The ECJ's decision confirming the primacy of EC law was not applied automatically in each Member State within its own legal system. For those states that were 'monist', that is where it was accepted that domestic and international legal orders were a part of a continuing legal or normative order and in which international law is superior, an automatic incorporation of international norms may be possible. In such states, eg Austria and Luxembourg, the supremacy of Community law was readily accepted. Where a state is dualist in its approach to international law it does not accept that international law and domestic law are part of one normative legal order.

---

[46]   *Simmenthal II* [Case 106/77 [1978] ECR 629, para 21.

Rather, there are two distinct legal orders and international norms can only be introduced into the domestic legal order by appropriate domestic legal measures. If this latter is the case, and if the domestic order stipulates the sovereignty of domestic law, as in the case of the UK and parliamentary legislation, from a domestic perspective, it is the sovereignty of domestic law that will be in the ascendant. As Lenaerts expresses the point: 'If the principle of the primacy of Community law is given no legal force superior to the provision incorporating it, the process of incorporation does not secure primacy for Community law.'[47]

In some states, the primacy of Community law is recognised not because of the specific nature of Community law 'but on the provision of the constitution which recognises the primacy of international law or which authorises the transfer of powers to a supranational authority.'[48] For the Community, its legal order is sovereign in the Community field regardless of what Member States believe and regardless of what their own constitutional courts may say in relation to the constitutionality of Community measures. *Simmenthal II* made clear that the 'principle of precedence of Community law' ensured that directly applicable (and effective) provisions of Community law render automatically inapplicable any conflicting provisions of national law and also preclude the valid adoption of new national measures insofar as they would be incompatible with Community law.[49] This has been particularly important in Germany as we shall soon see.

While Member States accept the sovereignty of Community law by virtue of provisions in constitutions recognising the superiority of international law over national law or by laws transferring sovereignty to international bodies, many reserve a right to review the constitutionality of Community measures infringing basic constitutional rights or fundamental human rights. No such successful review of a Community measure has been made, although they have been threatened. The case law of the German Constitutional Court has reserved a power to that Court to review the constitutionality of transfers of sovereignty to the Community (below) and

---

[47] K Lenaerts and P Van Nuffel, ed R Bray *Constitutional Law of the European Union* (1999), p 514. See FIDE 2002, note 1 above, *General Report* J Duthiel de la Rochère and I Pernice.

[48] K Lenaerts and P Van Nuffel, ed R Bray *Constitutional Law of the European Union* (1999) p 514.

[49] *Simmenthal II* Case 106/77 [1978] ECR 629, para 17.

the Irish Supreme Court has stated that it would not permit a constitutional right to life of an unborn child to be overbourne by some 'possible or putative right which might exist in European Law.'[50] The Danish Supreme Court has ruled that Danish courts must comply with judgments of the ECJ unless they have good cause to believe that a Community measure is ultra vires the Danish constitution. In such a case, the Danish Court must refer the question to the ECJ for clarification. Only after such a clarification, 'and in exceptional circumstances' may a Danish court declare a Community measure ultra vires. The domestic court may rule on the ultra vires nature of a Community measure which though upheld by the ECJ, nevertheless 'is based on an application of the Treaty which lies beyond the surrender of sovereignty according to the [Danish] Act of Accession.'[51] On such a question, *under Danish law,* the Danish court has the final say.

While the constitution may confer supremacy of Community law over domestic law, it may be silent on the question of superiority over the constitution. In those constitutions which have given precedence to Community law over domestic law, a further question arises as to whether the Community order is superior to the constitution or whether Community law stands to be appraised subject to the constitution. In some Member States, the position is not clear: Spain is an example where 'the status of Community law vis à vis the constitution is unclear, since the constitution places limits on the transfer of powers to the Community'[52] under Article 93 of the Constitution. As elsewhere, there is a marked reluctance to attack the primacy of Community law either in ordinary courts or in the constitutional court. In other constitutions, it is often left unspecified but

---

[50] *Society for the Protection of the Unborn Child (Ireland) Ltd v Grogan* [1990] 1 CMLR 689 *per* Finlay CJ at 699. The right to life was guaranteed by Art 40.3.3 of the Irish Constitution. Irish students were issuing leaflets for pregnant women advising them of the addresses of abortion facilities in the Britain. An injunction was issued preventing the leaflets being disseminated and it was argued that this breached Art 50 [60] EC which provides for the freedom to provide and receive services. See *Crotty v An Taoiseach* [1987] IR 713 *per* Walsh J at 783 on possible constitutional limits to transfers of sovereignty and on the initial negative Irish reaction to Nice, G Hogan (2001) European Public Law 565 and Irish report, FIDE 2002 at www.FIDE2002.ORG/reportseulaw.

[51] Danish Supreme Court, Case No 1 361/1997. Judgment of 6 April 1998 *Hanne Norup Carlsen v Prime Minister P N Rasmussen* [1999] 3 CMLR 854 and quotes from J Schwarze (1999) *European Public Law* 227, 237. See the 2002 FIDE Convention at www.FIDE2002.ORG/reportseulaw.

[52] K Lenaerts and P Van Nuffel in R Bray ed *Constitutional Law of the European Union* (1999) p 525.

is a matter of logical deduction. Belgium accepts the primacy of Community law but also holds that it has power to review the constitutionality of treaties. In France, the constitution must be amended if measures contrary to the constitution are to be ratified (below). The Italian Constitution of 1948, Article 11 authorised a transfer of competence to the Community but until 1984 questions of conflict between a Community measure having direct effect and a national law had to be referred to the Constitutional Court (CC). That position changed in that year[53] where it was decided that Italian courts must disapply conflicting national measures and apply rules of Community law. The Constitutional Court reserved to itself the power to review the constitutionality of domestic measures which are alleged expressly to attempt to prevent performance of Community measures. In 1994, the Constitutional Court refused to take such a review when the ordinary court had not ruled on whether the two measures, ie the national and Community, were in fact compatible. The Constitutional court also reserves the right to rule on a Community provision which allegedly breaches human rights or basic principles of the Italian legal order[54] as does the Greek Constitutional Court. Denmark was referred to above.

Either expressly, or by implication, no Member State has ceded ultimate sovereignty, but that is not to say that the nature of such sovereignty is not vitally affected by Community membership. A sovereignty that is pluralistic, says MacCormick, rather than monistic and one which is interactive not hierarchical.[55]

The Community and the individual

It is worth pointing out that in 1967, the UK Lord Chancellor observed:

> Community law has little direct effect on the ordinary life of private citizens. In so far as it imposes obligations, it does so mostly in relation to industrial and commercial activities and does not touch citizens in their private capacities. [56]

---

[53] *Granital* Judgment No 170/84 of 8 June 1984. See the Italian Constitution Act n 3 18 October 2001 which includes European Integration as an objective of national constitutional order and provides for the supremacy of Community law over ordinary Italian legislation.

[54] *Frontini* [1974] 2 CMLR 372.

[55] N MacCormick *Questioning Sovereignty* (1999).

[56] HL Debs col 1197 at col 1203 (8 May 1967).

Although totally wrong, that statement must be judged on the situation as it existed in 1967, not with the benefit of hindsight or recent developments such as the creation of EU Citizenship introduced under the TEU at Maastricht. The right of citizenship confers various voting rights, rights of access to the EU Ombudsman, rights to petition the European Parliament and the right to write to Community institutions as set out in Article 7 (EC) and the Ombudsman in their own language with a similar right of reply in addition to rights of free movement and residence. The implications of this citizenship are now working their way through the courts.[57]

However, even in the days of the 1960s, the Lord Chancellor seemed to overlook what is without doubt the most revolutionary aspect of the judgments of the European Court of Justice, viz the doctrine of direct effect whereby citizens *could* invoke rights under the Community Treaties in their own domestic courts even where they had not been implemented by a Member State's legislature.[58] Indeed increasing non-implementation was the reason why the ECJ developed the doctrine of direct effect. This was nothing less than revolutionary in the context of international organisations. The Community is 'a new legal order of international law.' The ECJ and the EC have not only been seeking to create rights for individuals in numerous areas, but they have been anxious to provide effective remedies when things go wrong. These remedies exist not only through the courts, both in Luxembourg and in each Member State[59] but also with the creation of the EU Ombudsman and the right of petition as described above. The EC now primarily concerns the individual. The Treaty of the EC constitutes 'the constitutional charter of a Community based on the rule of law' which has direct relevance to individuals and is according to the ECJ 'a new legal order'.[60]

The Community is a creature of international law by which Member States agreed to impose limitations upon their sovereignty in defined but ever growing areas (the four freedoms to establish a common market[61] plus

---

57   Especially in relation to free movement and residence rights although the position is not clear (see Ch 9 p 372 et seq). On the EU Ombudsman and petitioning Parliament see Ch 11.

58   Case 26/62 *Van Gend en Loos* [1963] ECR 1.

59   As a consequence of their direct effectiveness, or direct applicability in the case of EC regulations.

60   *Opinion 1/91 (First EEA Opinion)* [1991] ECR I-6079.

61   Free movement of persons, goods, capital and services.

economic and monetary union, social policies and equality between men and women, a new power to take appropriate action against discrimination and so on) and to impose upon themselves legal obligations within their own legal systems without further enactment. This latter was to be achieved by Community Regulations and was known as 'direct applicability' and is provided for within the Treaty: Article 249 [189] EC. It is not the same as direct effect (above) which was judicially created. This Community was to be for 'an unlimited period' (Article 312 [240] EC).[62]

In the reception of Community law, the reservation felt by many states concerned the question of the relationship of Community norms with human rights provisions within their own constitutions.

Human rights and the European Union

An increasing concern of the Community and EU, and one which again concerns individuals, has been with the protection of human rights. This concern has been witnessed in the ECJ's case law, although the sometimes diffident nature of its protection has caused a good deal of critical comment.[63] I return to the role of the court in the next section. In December 2000, the Presidents of the Council, Commission and European Parliament agreed to a Charter of Fundamental Rights for the EU and the Charter was 'solemnly proclaimed' at the European Council at Nice in December 2000. I will look at this, the most important development in human rights protection in the EU, below and in Chapter 9.

Until Maastricht in 1992, the treaties were silent on fundamental human rights unless they coincided with economic rights such as equal pay. With reference to the EU and under Title I Article 6(1) TEU[64] 'The Common Provisions' (which has been amended most recently by the Treaty of Amsterdam (ToA)) in 1997 it declares that: 'The Union [which includes the Community] is founded on the principles of liberty, democracy, respect

---

62   Although Greenland left the Community in 1985. Departure would necessitate amendment to the Treaty.

63   See eg, Case 60, 61/84 *Cinéthèque* [1985] ECR 2605; Case C-159/90 *Grogan* [1991] ECR I-4685; Case C-299/95 *Kremzow* [1997] ECR I-2629; Case C-249/96 *Grant v South-West Trains* [1998] ECR I-621. P Alston, M Bustelo and J Heenan eds *The EU and Human Rights* (1999, OUP).

64   There are eight Titles in the TEU, Title II of which concerns the EC, see above. Title VI concerns Police and Judicial Cooperation in Criminal Affairs.

for human rights and fundamental freedoms, and the rule of law, principles which are common to the Member States.' [65] By virtue of Article 7 TEU the Council may unanimously determine the existence of a persistent breach by a Member State of the above provisions who may then have certain of its rights under the Treaty suspended by qualified majority while its Treaty obligations continue. Article 309 EC applies these provisions to the EC Treaty and to the Communities. After the Treaty of Amsterdam, this 'judicial' decision is taken by the Council, it should be noted, and not the ECJ although it was expected that such action would only follow a judgment of the CHR which had not been complied with. Following the Treaty of Nice in 2000, the ECJ now has jurisdiction over the 'purely procedural stipulations' in Article 7 TEU. A request may be made by the Member State concerned to the Court within one month of the determination of the Council. The Article 7 procedures were revised at Nice so that a Member State must be heard by the Council before it makes a determination. The Council may also call upon 'independent persons' to submit within a reasonable time limit a report on the situation in the Member State concerned.

Title I Article 6(2) TEU states that the EU, including the Community, shall respect fundamental rights as guaranteed by the ECHR and as they result from the constitutional traditions common to the Member States as general principles of Community law. By virtue of Article 46(d) TEU, the ECJ may apply this provision to 'action of the institutions of the Community' [does not refer to Member States] insofar as the court has jurisdiction over such actions by virtue of the EC Treaty and the TEU. This clearly covers the Council, Commission and European Parliament and it affords the ECJ jurisdiction over Community organs to protect human rights where those organs interface with individuals.[66] The ECJ may apply this provision to the Third Pillar under the conditions set out in Article 35 TEU and to the provisions brought from that Pillar into the Community (ie First) Pillar at Amsterdam. Human rights protection is also a feature of accession procedures for new Member States.[67]

---

[65]   As amended by the Treaty of Amsterdam (ToA).

[66]   This spells out what was existing practice. For the application by ECJ of the ECHR where Member States are implementing or derogating from Community law: Case 201, 202/85 *Klensch* [1986] ECR 3477: Case 5/88 *Wachauf* [1989] ECR 2609; Case 60, 61/84 *Federation Nationale des Cinemas Francais* [1985] ECR 2605; Case 260/89 *Elliniki Radiophonia Tileorasi* [1991] ECR-I 2925. Cf *Sodemare* Case C-70/95 [1997] ECR I-3395 and giving reasons under Article 253 [190] EC.

[67]   It is a complaint from such states that the *acquis communautaire* does not include their own acquired principles of legality and constitutionality.

Freedom of movement of persons is a central feature of the EU and Community and by Title I Article 2(iv) TEU, it is expressly stated that one of the EU's objectives is: 'to maintain and develop the EU as an area of freedom, security and justice, in which the free movement of persons is assured in conjunction with appropriate measures with respect to external border controls, asylum, immigration and the prevention and combating of crime.' It is accepted within the Community that there are grounds of security or public order which necessitate restrictions on free movement of persons and also goods on grounds of public policy, health and security and in the case of goods alone, public morality. Both the UK and Ireland derogated from that part of the EC Treaty which was introduced from the Third Pillar and which, *inter alia*, concerned facilitation of the free movement of persons.

The ECJ and human rights

The above passages reflect a grand endorsement of human rights protection. But it was not always so. The Treaty of Rome did not contain a Bill of Rights – rather like the constitution of the fifth republic of France. The building of a fundamental rights tradition until Maastricht and Amsterdam was left to the ECJ, as was the doctrine of direct effect and supremacy, although the Treaty does contain some fundamental rights in its provisions scattered throughout the Treaty.[68] Gradually, and somewhat reluctantly, and here it was prompted by the German Constitutional Court (see below), the ECJ embraced the doctrine of fundamental human rights having originally rejected the idea that the Community legal order was bound by the fundamental rights guaranteed by Member States' constitutions.[69] In *Internationale Handelsgesellschaft*[70] fundamental rights were recognised as a part of the general principles of Community law. But they are not free-standing agents. Such rights 'must be ensured *within the framework of the structure and objectives of the Community.*'[71] There

---

[68] Eg, Art 13 introduced at Amsterdam as a legal basis for wide ranging Directives on anti discrimination covering a broad spectrum of discriminatory activities; Rights fundamental to the Treaty include: Art 12 on non-discrimination; Art 141 on equal pay; Art 34(2), Art 39(2) both dealing with specific cases of non discrimination: see Case C-281/98 *Angonese* [2000] ECR I-4139; Union Citizenship under Part II of Title I and naturally the four basic freedoms. See also: Arts 3(2) and 177 EC.

[69] *Stauder v City of Ulm* 26/69 [1969] ECR 419.

[70] Case 11/70 [1970] ECR 1125.

[71] Emphasis added.

followed case law[72] in which international treaties of which Member States are signatories and in which they have collaborated may provide guidelines for the development of human rights protection. In *Rutili*,[73] first reference to the ECHR was made by the ECJ. The approach of the ECJ was to seek Member State constitutional inspiration, including the international norms that they had agreed, but not domination. The Community had its own agenda and human rights protection, while fundamental, might not give the same results under Community law as under national interpretations. Nevertheless, the fears expressed by the German Constitutional Court on human rights protection were to a considerable extent resolved. But a blank cheque was not signed by that Court (below). As Alston and Weiler have expressed the point:

> In its jurisprudence, the [ECJ] has articulated three critical constitutional principles which inform this field. The first affirms that 'respect for human rights' is a condition for the lawfulness of Community acts. The second affirms that it is the positive duty of the institutions 'to ensure the observance of fundamental rights'. In other words, they are obligated not simply to refrain from violating them, but to ensure they are observed within the respective constitutional roles played by each institution. Finally, the human rights jurisdiction of the Community extends only 'in the fields of Community law.[74]

The attitude of the ECJ to human rights protection under Community law is neatly summed up in *Kremzow*[75] where it declared: 'fundamental rights form an integral part of the general principles of Community law.' The ECJ draws inspiration from the constitutional traditions common to the Member States and from international treaties on which Member States have collaborated or to which they are signatories. In this range the ECHR has 'special significance'. Measures are not acceptable in a Community which are incompatible with human rights.

The ECJ has recognised the following as fundamental human rights (FHR) within the general principles of law under the Community legal order; it may be objected that those towards the end are general principles of law

72   *Nold* Case 4/73 [1974] ECR 491.
73   Case 36/75 [1975] ECR 1219 – followed by *Hauer* Case 44/79 [1979] ECR 3727.
74   Alston and Weiler, in P Alston, M Bustelo and J Heenan eds *The EU and Human Rights* (1999) OUP p 25. See J Coppell and A O'Neill (1992) 29 CML Rev 669 and J Weiler and N Lockhart (1995) CML Rev 51, 579.
75   Case C-299/95 [1997] ECR I-2629 at 2645.

rather than FHRs.[76] Many new FHRs contained in the EU Charter of Fundamental Rights are traditionally more like general principles it could be argued (see below) or social rights.

Those recognised by the ECJ (and CFI) include: freedom of expression;[77] freedom of religion;[78] freedom of association;[79] right to privacy, family life and protection of the home[80] and the ECJ has referred to a Community provision (Data Protection Directive 95/46/EC) as a source of inspiration for a FHR;[81] to medical confidentiality;[82] right to property;[83] freedom to pursue one's trade or business [ditto]; non-retroactivity of penal measures;[84] right to judicial remedy for protection of one's rights;[85] rights to a fair procedure;[86] there must be a legal basis for interfering in private affairs;[87] equality[88] going beyond that provided in Treaty Articles and regulations and Directives; non-discrimination on grounds of sex;[89] rights to paid annual leave,[90] and in short all fundamental rights recognised by the ECHR, relevant treaties and the constitutional traditions of Member States.

The most recent addition has been a right to access to documents and information exemplified by the ECJ's decision in *Hautala* in December

---

76   On general principles see T Tridimas *The General Principles of EC Law* (1999, OUP).

77   *Elliniki Radiophonia* Case C-260/89 [1991] ECR I-2925; *Bauer Verlag* Case C-368/95 [1997] ECR I-3689; Case C-150/98P *Economic and Social Committee v E* [1999] ECR I-8877.

78   Case 130/75 *Vivien Prais v Council* [1976] ECR 1589 at 1599.

79   Case C-415/93 *Bosman* [1995] ECR I-4921 at 5065.

80   Case 136/79 *National Panasonic v Commission* [1980] ECR 2033 at 2056; Case 249/86 *Commission v Germany* [1989] ECR 1263 at 1290; Case C-404/92P *X v Commission* [1994] ECR I-4737 at 4789.

81   Case C-369/98 *ex p Fisher* [2000] ECR I-6751.

82   Case C-404/92P *X v EC Commission* [1994] ECR I-4737;

83   *Nold* Case 4/73 [1974] ECR 491 and *Hauer* Case 44/73 [1979] ECR 3727. Compare Case C-84/95 *Bosphorus* [1996] ECR I-3935 and *Bosphorus v Ireland* on admissibility CHR 13/9/01.

84   Case 63/83 *R v Kirk* [1984] ECR 2689 at 2718.

85   Case 222/84 *Johnston v Chief Constable RUC* [1986] ECR 1651.

86   Case 374/87 *Orkem v Commission* [1989] ECR 3283 – see K Lenaerts and J Vanhamme (1997) 34 CML Rev 531; and to defence: Case C-7/98 *Krombach v Bamberski* [2000] ECR I-1935.

87   Case 46/87 *Hoechst v Commission* [1989] ECR 2859.

88   Case 8/78 *Milac* [1978] ECR 1721.

89   Case C-50/96, *Deutsche Telekom v Schröder* [2000] ECR I-743.

90   Case C-173/99 *BECTU* [2001] ECR I-4881.

2001[91] and under Article 255 EC, Regulation 1049/2002/EC and Decisions of the European Parliament, Council and Commission. The case, as will be seen in Chapter 6 (p 269 et seq), is a remarkable example of the interplay and influence of Member State laws on the jurisprudence of the Community's courts. 'The Court has seldom refused to include an alleged right into its capacious bag of general principles; but it has been more cautious in finding an actual violation of those rights.'[92]

This has been evidenced in well known cases where the ECJ has found that either a point of Community law was not involved, or not transgressed[93] – this latter decision in *Cinéthèque* which involved a derogation from Community provisions must be doubted since the *ERT* and *Bauer Verlag* decisions below. However, a very difficult point is raised in derogations (not following an Article) as to whether where a derogation is justified on public policy grounds there is any room left for an application of human rights. In other words, does a derogation remove the application of human rights norms because the question is no longer a matter of Community law, but one of domestic law on which Community law cannot speak.[94] The derogations will have to satisfy the tests of necessity, proportionality and discrimination but once through those hurdles, there is no further human rights obstacle to overcome, it has been argued. Although the CHR has found a breach of the Article 10 ECHR protecting freedom of speech and freedom to pass on information in a case with the same facts as *SPUC v Grogan* which was referred to above and which concerned an Irish ban on advertising abortion facilities in Britain,[95] the ECJ ruled that no point of Community law was involved because there was no breach of Article 50 [60] EC relating to freedom to seek services. The students who were prevented from distributing leaflets about abortion facilities in Great Britain were not employed by the abortion clinics. The ECJ and CHR have taken different approaches to cases raising similar points and have come to opposing conclusions. In *Hoechst* (supra) the ECJ found that Article 8 ECHR which protects privacy did not protect companies and business

91   Case C-353/99 P *Council v Hautala* [2002] 1 WLR 1930.
92   de Witte in P Alston, M Bustelo and J Heenan eds *The EU and Human Rights* (1999, OUP) p 869.
93   Case C-159/90 *SPUC v Grogan* [1991] ECR I-4685; Case 60, 61/84 *Cinéthèque* [1985] ECR 2605; Case C-299/95 *Kremzov* [1997] ECR I-2629.
94   F Jacobs (2001) European LR 331.
95   *Open Door Counselling Ltd v Ireland* (1992) 15 EHRR 244.

premises; in *Chappell*,[96] the CHR found that Article 8 did protect an individual on his business premises and more generally the ECHR may well protect the 'human rights' of companies.[97] Different decisions have been made on the right to silence and Article 6 ECHR in a manner which appears inconsistent.[98] Limited use has been made of CHR and Commission jurisprudence relating to rights to marry and privacy and family life in rights of same sex marriages and some case law under Articles 12 and 8 ECHR was not referred to by the ECJ.[99] The ECJ has emphasised that the Convention is a source of jurisprudence for the ECJ. But there have been divergent decisions. The ECJ is applying a Treaty which seeks to integrate and develop a common market; the CHR is applying a basic threshold of human rights protection to European states. Their approach is different. Furthermore, the CHR is getting closer to ruling that provisions of the EU are themselves in breach of the ECHR and that action of the EU's institutions may be in breach of the ECHR.[100]

MSs legislation within the scope of Community law will be assessed in the light of compatibility with fundamental rights and guidance will be given by the ECJ in its interpretation.[101] This has particular relevance to the ECHR. This does not apply, however, to legislation outside Community competence.[102]

---

96 1989 Series A Vol 152 CHR, (1989) 12 EHRR 1.

97 *Niemietz* CHR (1992) Series A Vol 251, (1992) 16 EHRR 97 – but a company must show it is a victim; see Ch 9, pp 406-07.

98 Case 374/87 *Orkem* [1989] ECR 3283 and cf the CHR in: *Funke* [1993] Series A Vol 256-A (1993) 16 EHRR 297. See *Mannesmannröhren-Werke AG v Commission* Case T-112/98 [2001] ECR II-729 – a right to silence could not frustrate the legitimate objectives of Community competition law.

99 Case C-249/96 *Grant v South-West Trains* [1998] ECR I–621: see and compare on transgender rights Case C–13/94 *P v S and Cornwall County Council* [1996] ECR I-2143; *X, Y and Z v UK* (1997) 24 EHRR 143 and more recently *Goodwin v UK* [2002] 2 FCR 577 and *I v UK* [2002] 2 FCR 613.

100 The CHR has ruled that the UK was in breach of the ECHR even though the provision in question denying voting rights in Gibraltar for elections to the European Assembly had been adopted by the EU: *Matthews v UK* CHR (1999) Times, 3 March; see also Case C-364/99 PR *DSR Senator Lines v Commission* [1999] ECR I-8733.

101 Cf Case 314/85 *Foto-Frost* [1987] ECR 4199: the ECJ cannot rule on questions of domestic law outside Community competence.

102 *R v MAFF, ex p First City Trading Ltd* [1997] 1 CMLR 250: Community law principle 'equality' only applies to national measures within Community competence on a strict interpretation.

According to the *Wacchauf* principle, fundamental rights apply when Community measures are executed and made effective in Member States[103] and when Member States derogate from Community measures[104] and whenever national measures fall within the competence of Community law.[105] The points made by Advocate General Jacobs above must be kept in mind and his belief that a proper derogation leaves no scope for human rights protection beyond making out a public policy ground for applying a derogation. By this he means that any human rights consideration is taken on board in deciding whether a public policy interest is successful. It is not a free-standing principle to be applied in its own right after public policy factors have been considered. But the obligation to give reasons for legislative measures and decisions under Article 253 [190] does not apply to a national law implementing a Community measure.[106] The obligation will apply to decisions by national authorities made under Community competence; 'In addition, it should be remembered that the requirements flowing from the protection of Community rights in the Community legal order are also binding on Member States when they implement Community rules.'[107]

The query has been raised whether when implementing a Directive, as opposed to executing a Directive, the *Wachauf* principle applies. It would be incumbent on Member State courts to uphold the fundamental human rights in litigation before them where a matter was within Community competence; the ECJ would give guidance including the application of these principles on a reference under Article 234 and a failure to comply with the provisions could be an issue of enforcement by the Commission. The ECJ could not strike down a national measure but the problem, if problem there is, appears academic. An Opinion of Advocate General Mischo[108] gives very strong support for the view that in transposing and

---

103   Case 5/88 *Wachauf* [1989] ECR 2609.
104   *Elliniki Radiophonia Tileorassi etc* Case C-260/89 [1991] ECR I-2925; see F.Jacobs at note 94.
105   *Vereinigte Familia press Zeitungsverlags etc v H Bauer Verlag*: Case C-368/95 [1997] ECR I-3689.
106   Case C-70/95 *Sodemare* [1997] ECR I-3395.
107   Case C-292/97 *Karlsson* [2000] ECR I-2737.
108   Joined Cases C-20/00 and C-64/00 *Booker Aquaculture Ltd etc v The Scottish Ministers* 20 September 2001, paras 51–59; and see paras 104–132 on a discussion of rights to property in the ECHR and national constitutions *and* the EU Charter of Fundamental Rights.

implementing a Directive, a Member State must conform with the fundamental human rights principles of Community law.

Opinion 2/94 of the ECJ, the ECHR and national traditions

In spite of the undoubted importance of the ECHR in shaping the fundamental human rights of the Community and indeed in now being referred to in the Treaty, the ECJ has ruled that the Community has no power under Article 308 [235] EC or elsewhere, to accede to the ECHR. The Treaty would have to be amended for such an accession.[109] The European Parliament has made various declarations and resolutions on human rights and there was a joint declaration on human rights from the EC institutions in 1977. The case law on human rights would not have been built without the ECHR; in a way that is just as well because there is no reference by the ECJ says Alston (writing in 1999) to a specific constitutional case of a Member State; references to specific legal regimes of a Member State 'are perfunctory and haphazard' says de Witte.[110] The latter author claims that it is only since 1996 that the CHR has been specifically referred to by the ECJ and not simply the ECHR.[111]

We should remember that while the ECJ has been criticised by numerous commentators for its lack of urgency in the protection of human rights, it must be emphasised that it is not a national court but a supranational court striving for the achievement of supranational standards bound by a limited jurisdiction. From the early case law where it invoked the human rights traditions of Member States, the ECJ made clear that it applied those principles in the structure of Community law and its conclusions may differ from those reached by a national constitutional court. It has to deal with states with very different – although converging – standards of human rights protection. This problem is likely to increase as the EU expands. At the heart of most of its disputes are economic conflicts between economic actors or agents where the ground rules of behaviour and rights and duties are fairly clearly set but where fundamental rights arguments add a novel

---

[109]   *Opinion 2/94* [1996] ECR I-1759: Gaja (1996) 33 CML Rev 973.

[110]   P Alston, M Bustelo and J Heenan eds *The EU and Human Rights* (1999) OUP p 878.

[111]   Case C-13/94 *P v S and Cornwall County Council* [1996] ECR I-2143; Case C-74, 129/95 *Criminal Proceedings Against X* [1996] ECR I-6609; *Bauer Verlag* Case C-368/95 [1997] ECR I-3689; and Case C-249/96 *Grant v South-West Trains* [1998] ECR I-621.

and sensitive national dimension. It is not starting with a *tabula rasa* from first premises. It has had to borrow. In one case concerning a ban by Austria on the sale of German journals containing prize competitions which were produced perfectly lawfully in Germany, the case was referred to the ECJ by the Austrian court. There seemed to be a contravention of Article 28 [30] on free movement of goods but the ECJ raised the question of Article 10 ECHR and whether the means adopted were proportionate. One justification for the ban as a 'mandatory requirement' of a national interest[112] might involve the need for press diversity which could be threatened by dominant external media. Press diversity is an aspect of Article 10 freedom of speech, the ECJ believed.[113] The case was remitted to Austria with the guidance that the Austrian court would have to decide whether the ban was proportionate and necessary. Freedom of speech did not simply mean freedom to publish; it also carried with it a consideration of diversity of publication requirements.[114]

Different states may take very different approaches to questions of lawyer-client privilege; privacy; the right to life and abortion; or the procedures that should be adopted to deal with state/citizen disputes and how far they should be formalised or legalised in accordance with Article 6 ECHR. They may, and invariably do, take diametrically opposing approaches on the interpretation of the same fundamental right when their national or nationals' interests are involved. The 'margin of appreciation' for legitimate state discretion will have to be respected. The ECJ has to steer a careful course. De Witte argues that 'this strand of the ECJ's fundamental rights doctrine may raise delicate questions in the relationship between the national and Community legal orders. It requires any national court to act as a "constitutional court" ensuring respect by the national authorities for the fundamental rights of EC law, which may even require them to disregard national constitutional rights as they are normally understood.'[115]

A working group on human rights under the d'Estaing Convention has suggested that the EU Treaty be amended to allow a power of accession

---

112   The famous *Cassis de Dijon* case law: Case 120/78 [1979] ECR 649.
113   Case C-368/95, *Bauer Verlag* [1997] ECR I-3689.
114   In *Informationsverein Lentia v Austria* Series A No 276, (1993) 17 EHRR 93 the CHR allowed interference with freedom of speech for press diversity reasons provided interference is prescribed by law and necessary in a democratic society, para 26. See Case C-353/89 *EC Commission v Netherlands* [1991] ECR I-4069.
115   P Alston, M Bustelo and J Heenan eds *The EU and Human Rights* (1999) OUP p 873.

to the ECHR. This will help bring 'coherence to a greater Europe.' The group was at pains to emphasise the spirit of co-operation between national human rights traditions, the ECHR and the EU. The group reported that the relationship between the CHR and ECJ shall be like that of the CHR to existing constitutional courts. It will be able to give decisions which are binding in international law. It is not clear how conflict between the jurisprudence of the two courts will be avoided or how the CHR's decisions will be other than de facto binding on the domestic courts of Member States on matters within Community competence. (See ch 14 p 600 et seq). Accession would, the group believed, bring the advantage of a judge on the CHR with expertise in Community law.

The EU Charter of Fundamental Human Rights

We should note that the Charter builds substantially on the ECHR including the twelfth protocol on discrimination, the convention on human rights and bio-medicine, the Council of Europe's Social Charter and various other conventions on social and economic rights. It includes a chapter entitled 'Citizens' rights' on good administration including access to information and access to an ombudsman (see Chapters 6 and 11) as well as chapters on 'Dignity', 'Freedoms', 'Equality', 'Solidarity', and 'Justice'. The Charter was 'solemnly proclaimed' at Nice in 2000 by the European Council although it is not a part of the EU or Community Treaty in any formal sense, it reflects provisions which are a part of the *acquis communautaire* and may well act as an inspiration for the development of human rights protection in the Union in the hands of the ECJ and CFI.[116] The provisions of the Charter are addressed to the Institutions of the Community (Article 7 EC) and to Member States 'only when they are implementing Union law' (see above).

The Commission will monitor and audit Community laws to assess consistency with the Charter.[117] It was noted above that the European Council in December 2001 established a convention whose task was to

---

[116] See Advocate General Mischo in *Booker Acquaculture* (above) at para 126; Advocates General Tizzano in *BECTU* Case C-173/99 and Jacobs in *Z v European Parliament* Case C-270/99P (22 March 2001, unreported).

[117] Sec (2000) 380/3 cited in McCrudden Jean Monnet Working Paper, Jean Monnet Program, Harvard Law School 10/2001 www.jeanmonnetprogram.org/papers/01/013001. See the Commission COM (2000) 644 final on the Charter.

consider the future of the EU prior to the European Council in 2004. Among the matters remitted to the convention is the question of whether the Charter should be incorporated within the basic Treaty (below) and whether the EC should accede to the ECHR (above).

There was considerable criticism that in spite of being developed in unprecedented openness, the Charter was still dominated by special interests and the secretariat was supplied by the Council. It has been commented that this is unfortunate for a charter which seeks to place the individual at the heart of the EU. The text and motives for the Charter have been stated as 'ambiguous'.[118] Certainly, any attempt to place individuals in such a vaulted position to replace the economic raison d'etre of the Community will have to address a variety of factors. These include the limited access of individuals to the Community courts and the length of proceedings;[119] the suggested need for a constitutional complaints procedure for individuals to the courts possibly along the lines of German and Spanish models;[120] the desirability of including national measures within such a complaints procedure but national procedures would have to be exhausted first of all; relaxing the standing requirement so that a 'sufficient interest' would suffice; the need for a Human Rights Commissioner and a Directorate General of Human Rights.[121] Alston, for instance, has criticised the human rights' activities of the Commission in development co-operation and trade agreements with developing countries. A lack of transparency made the situation 'unsatisfactory'. Access to country strategy papers and to national indicative programmes is highly restricted 'despite their importance in ensuring that human rights are taken adequately into account in policy making.' European Parliament committees lack full information. The Court of Auditors cannot be seized of an individual

---

[118]   C McCrudden, Jean Monnet Working Paper 10/2001.

[119]   Locus standi requirements for individuals under Art 230 are strict, and see Jacobs AG and recent case law p 106 et seq below. Reference procedures can take over eighteen months and constitute only one stage in a procedure – in the famous *Marshall* litigation it took over 13 years for the claimant to receive a judicial ruling on compensation – it was then remitted to the industrial tribunal for assessment.

[120]   In Germany there is no *actio popularis* and legislation is not usually challengeable by individuals – the court dealing with legislation makes a reference to the Constitutional Court and parties may submit written briefs – but judicial and administrative decisions are challengeable.

[121]   All these points are made by de Witte in P Alston, M Bustelo and J Heenan eds *The EU and Human Rights* (1999) OUP ch 27.

matter and the Community courts cannot adjudicate on a contractual question.[122] If human rights clauses in so many external agreements of the EC were activated there could be a possible flood of litigation before the ECJ.

The EU Ombudsman in his annual report for 2001 has observed with irony that those who 'solemnly proclaimed' the Charter are frequent violators of its provisions (see Chapter 11 and www.european-convention.eu.int for the working group on the Charter of Fundamental Human Rights).

Finally, the group on the Charter under the d'Estaing Convention has recommended that the Charter should be incorporated into the proposed EU constitution (Chapter 14, p 600 et seq). The ECJ and CFI would be bound to apply the Charter; the CHR the Convention. If the Union accedes to the Convention, the ECJ and CFI would be bound in international law by the CHR. Although the Charter states that the meaning and scope of Convention rights contained in the Charter are the same as under the Convention, including the case law of the CHR (Article 52(3) of the Charter), it is hard to see how divergences will not occur in case law.

The Second and Third Pillars of the European Union

The Community is a part of our domestic legal order. The EU also comprises two further pillars in addition to the EC – the Second and Third Pillars (Titles V and VI TEU).[123] These cover Common Foreign and Security Policy and Provisions on Police and Judicial Co-operation in Criminal Matters. The former grew from European Political Co-operation (EPC) and working groups under EPC met and discussed problems concerning judicial co-operation in civil and criminal matters, international terrorism and drug addiction. Co-operation in customs controls and combating criminal activity became essential as the programme for the internal market gathered pace and sought to remove internal controls on border checks on persons.[124]

---

[122] P Alston, M Bustelo and J Heenan eds *The EU and Human Rights* (1999) OUP p 38. ECJ has decided a case of alleged human rights violations in EU sanctions in Yugoslavia: Case C-84/95 *Bosphorus* [1996] ECR I-3953 – no violations. Paradoxically, de Burca believes that the EU displayed a greater interest in human rights outside the Union than within: G de Burca in P Beaumont et al eds *Convergence and Divergence in European Public Law* (2002).

[123] E Denza *The Intergovernmental Pillars of the European Union* (2002).

[124] On the internal market, see p 13 above.

These provisions led to the Schengen Agreement to which the UK and Ireland do not belong.

Under the TEU, the European Council, which was recognised for the first time in the Single European Act 1987, is responsible for providing the EU with the necessary impetus for the development of the Second Pillar and defining the general political guidelines. Article 4 TEU defines the composition of the European Council[125] which is not a part of the Community order. It arose as an informal gathering of Heads of State or Government of Member States from 1961 onwards to resolve difficult problems in the Community. Decisions of the Council can only be implemented in the Community order via Community institutions through procedures set out in the EC Treaty. The European Council decides by unanimous consensus. There has, however, been a growing informal inter-penetration of the European Council and the Community. Under Article 4(iii) TEU, the European Council is under a duty to submit to the European Parliament a report after each of its meetings (every six months) and an annual report on progress achieved by the EU. The European Parliament is informed after the event (see Article 27d TEU).

The Third Pillar on 'Provisions on Police and Judicial Co-operation in Criminal Matters' is of particular importance in the fight against international crime and terrorism. It was originally intended that the Third Pillar, like the Second Pillar, would operate primarily at the inter-governmental or international level, although there was a provision to allow Third Pillar items to become part of the Community order. Under ToA, items relating to the free movement of persons were brought within the First Pillar allowing concentration upon Police and Judicial Co-operation. The Treaty of Nice (Article 29 TEU) makes provision for the closer co-operation through Eurojust (European Judicial Co-operation Unit) of judicial and other competent authorities in accordance with the revised Articles 31 and 32 TEU.

Under Article 34 TEU, provision is now made in relation to police and judicial co-operation under the Third Pillar and for Member States to contribute 'to the pursuit of the objectives of the Union' for adopting common positions; the making of framework decisions to approximate Member States' laws and regulations and which will be binding on Member

---

[125] Heads of State of Member States and President of the Commission assisted by Ministers of foreign affairs of Member States and a 'Member of the Commission.'

States *but not directly effective*; further provision is made to adopt decisions 'for any other purpose consistent with the objectives' of the Third Pillar, which also will be binding but not be directly effective, and to establish conventions. These measures will be taken by unanimous agreement in the Council of the EU, ie there is a national veto. Conventions will enter into force in those states which adopt them once adopted by at least a half of Member States. Measures implementing conventions will be taken by a two thirds majority and measures implementing decisions will be taken by a qualified majority, both in the Council.

Under the Third Pillar, Framework Decisions will be implemented by Member States by methods of their choice and form; in the case of the UK this could be by way of legislation or statutory instrument. The ECJ may rule on the validity and interpretation of Framework Decisions and Decisions and interpret conventions and rule on the validity and interpretation of measures implementing them. Member States may agree by declaration to accept this jurisdiction, otherwise it will not be binding on a Member State ie, it cannot be imposed unilaterally. This follows the pattern set by the Europol Convention in 1995.[126] However, under Article 35(7) TEU, the ECJ will have jurisdiction to rule on disputes between Member States in relation to acts adopted under Article 34 where the Council cannot resolve such disputes.

Article 35(5) TEU states that 'The Court of Justice shall have no jurisdiction to review the validity or proportionality of operations carried out by the police or other law enforcement services of a Member State or the exercise of the responsibilities incumbent upon Member States with regard to the maintenance of law and order and the safeguarding of internal security.' One should also note the limits placed on the jurisdiction of the ECJ in relation to Article 62(1) EC by virtue of Article 68(2) EC. These deal with that part of the Third Pillar that was brought within the First Pillar and provide that the Council may adopt measures ensuring an absence on controls on persons when crossing internal borders, but the ECJ will have no jurisdiction to rule on any measure or decision relating to the maintenance of law and order or relating to internal security. The courts of Member States alone will have jurisdiction on such matters subject to the European Convention on Human Rights. The UK and Ireland have opted out of this part of the Treaty (Title IV EC).

---

[126] Cm 3050. The UK declined jurisdiction under the Convention.

It should be noted that under Article 61(e) EC, the Council may, within five years, adopt measures under the Community Pillar (First Pillar) 'in the field of police and judicial co-operation in criminal matters' to prevent and combat crime. This means that such matters within the Third Pillar will come within the First Pillar and will be a part of Community law. The UK and Ireland derogated from this provision which is also within Title IV EC.

The working group of the d'Estaing Convention was strongly of the view that the EU should have legal personality which should be merged with that of the EC and the pillars would then be otiose. The preliminary draft constitution of the EU provides for the EU, or whatever it is to be called, to have legal personality.

The above sets out the constitutional framework of the EU. Between the Union and Member States, principles of constitutionality such as: sovereignty, subsidiarity (see Chapter 5) and proportionality and sincere cooperation have developed through the Treaties and decisions of the ECJ. The latter principle argues de Witte[127] was inspired by the unwritten German constitutional principle of *Bundestreue*. Articles 43-45 TEU provide for enhanced cooperation between Member States. Our attention will now turn specifically to national constitutions.

France[128]

The Constitution can be seen as an attempt to capture a balance. France has swung between Parliamentary and Executive ascendancy in the driving seat of state governance. It is currently in its fifth Republic which began in 1958 and which after a pro-Parliamentarian 1946 constitution (the first to be a truly written constitution in France) veered towards the executive. The first Republic began in 1789 with the famous and resplendent 'Declaration of the Rights of Man and of the Citizen' which is adopted by the 1958 Constitution. The statement of principles on fundamental rights in the 1946 Constitution is also adopted by the 1958 document. The 1946 Constitution also affirmed fundamental principles recognised by the laws of the Republic and as Bell shows, this includes statutes and provisions in some statutes such as the Press law and Associations law. There are furthermore, 'objectives having constitutional value' which may be invoked

---

[127]   B deWitte in F Snyder ed *The Europeanisation of Law* (2000) p 83.
[128]   J Bell *French Constitutional Law* (1994). See French report FIDE 2002, www.FIDE2002.ORG/reportseulaw.

to limit the scope of the legislature. The Conseil Constitutionnel (below) is, however, limited in its ability to review the power of the legislature as we shall see. Certain *lois* or statutes which deal with matters of government and not fundamental rights also assume constitutional significance, especially in the field of finance and budgets.

The Constitution sets out in Title 1 provisions on sovereignty although the Preamble to the 1958 Constitution declares that 'The French people solemnly proclaims its attachment to the rights of man and to the principles of national sovereignty and its institutions are based on 'the common ideal of liberty, equality, and fraternity, and conceived with a view to their democratic development'. Title 2 covers the President who is charged with supervising respect for the constitution and the nation's independence and who is now elected by direct universal suffrage for a term of five years. The President is given emergency powers on terms set out in Article 16 and under stringent safeguards. He appoints the Prime Minister and on his recommendation, members of the government. Title 3 concerns the government, which has to determine and conduct national policy and which has the administration and army at its disposal. Members of the government cannot be members of either chamber of the Parliament – a separation of powers completely alien to the British structure – and government answers to Parliament within the terms set out in Articles 49 and 50 which contain the provisions on a vote of confidence, motion of censure, and resignation. Title 4 concerns Parliament, its composition, structure, meetings and extraordinary sessions. Members of the government shall have access to both chambers and shall be heard on request.

Within its written constitution, the closest France comes to a constitutional court is the Conseil Constitutionnel established by Title 7 of the constitution of 1958. It acts as an election court for parliamentary and presidential elections, monitors the validity of referenda and declares their result. The constitution may be changed by a procedure laid down in the Constitution or by a referendum as occurred after the Maastricht Treaty in 1992 and which the Government very nearly lost. It also reviews Bills to rule on their constitutionality. All organic Bills, ie dealing with the organisation of government and public power, must be referred to the Conseil Constitutionnel along with standing orders of the Parliamentary Chambers. Other Bills may be referred by various parties as set out in article 61: 'by the President of the Republic, the Prime Minister, the President of the National Assembly, the President of the Senate, or sixty deputies (MPs) or sixty senators.'[129] Once promulgated or enacted, an Act cannot be reviewed by the Conseil Constitutionnel . It would be wrong, however, to deduce that the French Parliament is a sovereign legislature. Its legislative powers are set out in Article 34 of the Constitution which is the first Article in Title 5 dealing with relations between Parliament and the Government.

Article 34 spells out what must be provided for by legislation passed by Parliament. 'Loi shall determine the rules concerning: civil rights and fundamental safeguards relating to civil liberties; burdens concerning national defence; nationality and status and capacity and succession; the determination of crimes and torts and penalties; criminal procedure; creation of new types of court and status of judges; taxation and local taxes; issue of currency. It also includes: electoral systems for Parliamentary and local elections; creation of categories of public corporation; privatisation and nationalisation; and 'fundamental guarantees for civil and military servants of the state'. Furthermore, Loi shall lay down the 'fundamental principles' of national defence; local administration and authorities' resources and powers; education; property and commercial rights and obligations; and labour, trade union and social security. However, other Articles also confer legislative power upon Parliament[130] as do constitutional documents such as the Rights of Man 1789 and the Preamble to the 1946 Constitution which are incorporated into the 1958 Constitution together with fundamental or general principles of law long recognised by the Conseil d'Etat, the body which stands at the head of French public law, the *droit administratif* (see Chapter 3). These general principles are not expressly in the Constitution but their inspiration is drawn from the Declaration of 1789 and the Preamble of 1946 and from the 'fundamental principles recognised by the laws of the Constitution.'[131] They may be either of constitutional or legislative significance (the latter is less elevated as they may be overridden by express loi and only bind the executive whereas the former bind both). Included in this category in terms of law-making power not contained in Article 34 are matters relating to civil and court procedures and what we would call natural

---

129 See L Favoreu *Les Cours Constitutionelles* (1986) and ditto *Constitutional Review and Legislation* (1988); A Stone Sweet *The Birth of Judicial Politics in France: The Constitutional Council in Comparartive Perspective* (1992) cited in P Craig 'Constitutional and Non-Constitutional Review' (2001) *Current Legal Problems* ed M Freeman p 147.

130 Bell *French Constitutional Law* (1994) p 88.

131 Bell *French Constitutional Law* (1994).

justice and rights to legal protection and access to justice. There is no doubt, as Bell suggests, this stems from a keenly felt constitutional tradition in France but to the eyes of an English lawyer it might appear as a recipe for instability and uncertainty. This would be unfair because our own courts in Britain increasingly resort to fundamental principles or the common law of human rights to check executive or other excesses, a stance which attracts similar criticism. It will also be seen in Chapter 4 how recent case law in England has sought to introduce a 'hierarchy of norms' including constitutional norms (p 174 et seq). *Les Principes Generaux du Droit* are also likely to be invoked on the most sensitive of occasions from the point of view of the executive thereby attracting allegations of political bias on the part of the Conseil d'Etat where they are invoked by that body in contentious case law. The *Principes* are also invoked as the device by which principles of Community law are introduced into French law.[132]

The Conseil Constitutionnel has ruled that it can review bills to assess their constitutionality from the perspective of fundamental human rights.[133] It may have been influenced by the German Constitutional Court and case law on the binding nature of the preamble to the German constitution.[134] Like the Treaty of Rome, the French constitution contains no entrenched Bill of Rights as such, although the ECHR takes precedence over national legislation by virtue of the French constitution[135] and has been heavily invoked by the French administrative courts. The Conseil Constitutionnel does not, however, rule unconstitutional lois which are in breach of the ECHR because they have been promulgated as loi. Bruno de Witte has argued that the jurisprudence of the Conseil Constitutionnel resembles the human rights case law of the ECJ by its creative 'manipulation of the sources of law' making fundamental rights a part of higher law not intended by the drafters of the 1958 constitution or those of the Treaty of Rome. A second similarity is 'the importance assumed by general principles' derived from a variety of relevant sources – 'pre 1946 legislation and beyond' in

---

[132] See (2002) 19 AJDA November 1219: *Syndicat national de l'industrie pharmaceutique et autres* CE 3/12/01. I am grateful to John Bell for this reference.

[133] *Liberté d'association Conseil Constitutionnel* decision no 7 71-44 DC of 16 July 1971; see Bell pp 270 et seq for translations of leading decisions of the Conseil Constitutionnel . See L Favoreu et al *Droits des Libertés Fondamentales* (2000).

[134] Below and de Witte in P Alston, M Bustelo and J Heenan eds *The EU and Human Rights* (1999) OUP, p 865 citing P Häberle (1992) *Juristen Zeitung* 1037.

[135] Article 55 and the principle of 'reciprocity' below in text.

the case of France and the ECJ's reference to the 'common constitutional traditions of the Member States.'[136]

The constitution allows the supremacy of legislation once enacted but it is legislation from a limited legislature which does not profess the right to rule on any subject or the power to legislate on any matter whatsoever which the UK Parliament in its extreme version of sovereignty, or rather the extreme version of its claimants' theories, espouses. It is a limited legislature. Furthermore, as outlined above, the Conseil Constitutionnel may rule on the constitutionality of Bills referred to it before they have received Presidential assent to ensure they comply with the constitution and constitutional principles – abstract review. Details of leading case law are translated in Professor Bell's book on *French Constitutional Law*.[137]

Article 37 merely states in its first part that 'Matters other than those within the province of a loi have a regulatory character' and are to be made in the form of *règlements* or regulations by the executive. There are also complicated provisions to allow 'texts' in the form of a loi covering such matters to be modified by decree after the Conseil d'Etat has advised on them. Texts passed after the 1958 constitution can only be modified where the Conseil Constitutionnel has declared that they are of a regulatory character in compliance with the first part of Article 37. Government may also ask the Parlement for authority to take measures in the form of *ordonnances* to implement its programme even though such measures would normally be within the province of a loi. They are effective for a limited period after which they may only be amended by a loi operating within the province of loi. They are made in the Council of Ministers, presided over by the President, on the advice of the Conseil d'Etat (C d'E). The Conseil d'Etat not only operates in this advisory a priori role but may also review an ordonnance in respect of its legality but not once it is ratified by Parliament. According to French legal doctrine, it then ceases to be administrative and becomes Parliamentary. Although they come into effect once they are published, they lapse if a bill to ratify them is not laid before Parliament by the date fixed in the enabling law. The enabling laws, for this is a delegation of legislative power to the executive by Parliament and carried wide fears of executive abuse, are reviewable in their Bill form by the Conseil Constitutionnel to ensure proper use of Article 38 and compliance with Article 34.

---

[136]   de Witte, note 134 above.
[137]   Bell in F Snyder ed *The Europeanisation of Law* (2000).

Certainly, ordonnances have been used to carry out reform of competition law and public service retirements and pensions – the latter a matter of burning significance in France. The President has also refused to sign an ordonnance although it appears under the constitution Article 13 that he has little scope for this but this has occurred where the Conseil Constitutionnel had provided interpretations arguably supporting such a course. 'The President is safest when he is following a lead that the Conseil has given as to what the Constitution requires.'[138] President Mitterrand refused to sign a wide ranging ordonnance authorising privatisation and another concerning electoral reform. Bell states how in both cases a loi was subsequently passed and either not referred or objected to by the Conseil Constitutionnel. '

The fifth Republic made no mention of the EEC although just before its inauguration the Gaullists attempted to have the Bill ratifying the Treaty of Rome despatched before a *Comité Constitutionnel* on the grounds that it was not compatible with national sovereignty. The relationship between French law and international law, including Community law was governed by Title 6 of the Constitution (Articles 52–55) entitled 'Treaties and International Agreements' although in 1992 Title 14 was added to the Constitution entitled 'European Communities and European Union' – the first specific reference to the EU in the constitution – in order to amend the constitution to incorporate the Maastricht revisions.[139]

Under Article 52, treaties are ratified by the President unless they fall within the group of treaties requiring Parliamentary ratification or approval by loi under Article 53. These include peace, trade, organisation of the international community, those requiring state expenditure or those which will cause amendments to primary legislation or affect the status of persons. They only come into effect after ratification or approval.[140] By virtue of Article 55, treaties once published and provisions which are duly ratified or approved have a higher authority than lois subject to their implementation by the other party ('reciprocity'). This is the position with the ECHR. Treaties in other words take precedence over lois but are under

---

[138] Bell *French Constitutional Law* (1994) p 107.

[139] On the relationship to International law and Reception of Community law and the problem of *Droit Administratif* see Manin (1991) CMLR 499; Oliver (1994) ICLQ 1; see further Bonnie below and Millns (1999) EPL 6.

[140] In the UK there is no requirement for treaties to be approved by Parliament except under the terms of the European Assembly Elections Act 1978; see p 199.

the constitution in a hierarchy of norms. This formulation has not been without profound difficulties. By virtue of Article 54, the Conseil Constitutionnel may declare a clause in an international agreement, which is referred to it as specified, contrary to the constitution. It cannot therefore be ratified or approved until after a revision of the Constitution. Title 14 of the Constitution (Articles 88(1)–(4)) were introduced as mentioned above to cater for incompatibilities between the Maastricht TEU and constitutional provisions concerning EU citizenship, immigration provisions and monetary union. Article 88(4) increased the scope of consultation of the Parliament by the government on EU proposals including those having legislative effect. Further amendments followed the Amsterdam Treaty. However, as Bonnie believes, the current approach based on piecemeal review of the constitution 'impliedly excludes the insertion of a general clause of transfer of competencies in the French constitution' such as Article 23 of the German constitution, leading in France to the need for amendment not only when new areas of state sovereignty are transferred 'but also each time a further stage of integration is reached within areas of competencies already transferred.'[141] It should be pointed out that reciprocity was satisfied even though there were opt outs from relevant provisions of the Treaty by Member States. Once the constitution is amended, it allows for the sovereignty of Community measures and their direct effect. But these are matters which the Conseil d'Etat, unlike the Cour de Cassation, took a long time to accept. France has three supreme courts and their approach to the question of the relationship between an international order and the domestic legal order has differed.

The Conseil Constitutionnel has refused to rule under Article 61 that a proposed loi is unconstitutional because of incompatibility with a treaty although the constitution sets out the superiority of treaties over lois. Provisions of treaties and international agreements are not a part of the constitution. The Conseil Constitutionnel has therefore felt unable to rule on the question. This was its decision in the Abortion loi case in 1975 where the Conseil Constitutionnel believed that superiority is 'relative' to the subject matter of a particular Treaty and contingent on implementation by all parties to the Treaty. The Treaty in question was the ECHR. 'A statute which is contrary to the Treaty, will not, by virtue of that fact alone, be contrary to the Constitution'.[142] The decision was heavily criticised in

---

[141]   A.Bonnie (1998) EPL 517 at 530.
[142]   Translation by D Pollard: see D Pollard (1992-1995) 30 *Irish Jurist* 79; Conseil Constitutionnel decision no 74-54 DC of 15 January 1975.

France and since that date the Conseil Constitutionnel has considered whether an electoral law conformed to the First Protocol ECHR (below). The matter concerned an election to Parliament over which the Conseil Constitutionnel possessed jurisdiction. The decision was seen as a development by the Conseil Constitutionnel. The Strasbourg CHR has struck down retrospective legislative powers validating contracts between the social security authority and employees.[143] In 1994, the Conseil Constitutionnel ruled the measure in question was constitutional. Lenoir is of the opinion that despite these limitations to the Conseil Constitutionnel's approach, it has contributed to establishing the supremacy of European law. It has also, she maintains, not applied the reciprocity provisions to the enforcement of treaties in Article 55 and 88(2) and (3) in the case of Community law and the ECHR because Community law has its own enforcement mechanisms and 'reciprocity' does not apply to humanitarian principles of international law which preclude the operation of such a clause.[144]

From 1931, it has been accepted that Treaties take precedence over lois but only originally where the Treaty came after the loi. This was the position accepted by the Cour de Cassation, the civil court of appeal. In *Jacques Vabre* in 1975, the Cour de Cassation ruled that an incompatibility between a subsequent French loi and a prior Treaty (the Treaty of Rome) had to be resolved in favour of the Treaty and the incompatible domestic law would have to be disapplied. The Community measure was directly effective. In a way the constitutionality of the statute was not in question; simply whether the treaty obligations prevailed. The Cour de Cassation followed this decision with others which more emphatically recognised the superiority of Community measures without recourse to the constitution.

The Conseil d'Etat (Cd'E) had resisted the implications of Community sovereignty on considerations based on constitutional arguments. That court accepted that where a Treaty came after a loi, the Treaty, where there was an incompatibility, took precedence. However, in 1968, the C d'E

---

143 *Zielinski v France* Joined Applications Nos 24846/94 and 34165/96 to 34173/96 CHR 28 October 1999.

144 N Lenoir in B Markesinis ed *The British Contribution to the Europe of the Twenty First Century* ch 17, p 253 citing: Conseil Constitutionnel Decision No 98-408, 22 January 1999 in *Recueil* p 29. She writes that although France refuses to ratify the Vienna Convention on the Law of Treaties, 'almost all the principles established by this Convention have been introduced through the case law of the Conseil Constitutionnel into domestic constitutional law'.

refused to rule that a loi (actually an ordonnance with force of loi) passed subsequent to a Treaty was superseded by the Treaty provision. The C d'E subsequently refused to enforce a Directive which would have rendered unlawful an administrative decision, and also quashed a decision of a Tribunal Administratif of Paris referring the question to the ECJ under Article 234 [177] EC (*Société International* (1985) and *Cohn-Bendit* (1978)). Subsequent decisions of the C d'E repeated the effect of the 1968 decision. To review a statute in the light of a prior Treaty was the equivalent of reviewing its constitutionality which only the Conseil Constitutionnel could do and then only by abstract review in the case of Bills. The C d'E had shown itself blind to the special position of Community law and the influence which elsewhere international law was having on the domestic legal order. To rule in such a manner would breach the separation of powers which as we shall see in the next chapter was a reason why the ordinary courts in France were forbidden to meddle in administrative affairs and why the C d'E was established as an administrative court.

In 1989 in *Nicolo* (CE 20 October 1989)[145], the C d'E finally accepted the lead of the Conseil Constitutionnel in the decision of 1988 on Parliamentary elections, where the Conseil Constitutionnel ruled that as an electoral court, and not a constitutional court, it could rule that an electoral code did conform with the ECHR and by implication it could rule on whether it did not conform. It could not make a ruling on constitutionality under Article 61. In accepting that the C d'E could rule that a statute promulgated after a Treaty did conform with a Treaty provision, by implication, subsequently realised in following case law, it could rule that a statute did not. The C d'E accepted that its position adopted before this case, which was another electoral case involving elections to the European Parliament, had made it stand out ostentatiously in Europe in resisting the superiority of Community law because of an inconsistent and later statute, a position which diverged diametrically from that adopted in the French civil courts. The days of unqualified supremacy of municipal law over norms of international law, especially Community law, were over. In saying this, it noted that much of its law on employment, economic affairs and human rights laws originated in international treaties. In *Boisdet* in 1990, the C d'E ruled that ministerial decisions in relation to agricultural markets made under enabling powers from a 1980 loi were incompatible with an EEC Regulation 1035/72 ie, prior in time, after a ruling had been given on a reference to the ECJ which ruled the domestic measures were incompatible with the EC

---

145   R Errera (1990) Public Law 134. J-C Bonichot AJDA Special Issue 20 June 1996, 15.

regulation. The statute was incompatible with EC law the C d'E held. In *SA Rothman* (1992) the C d'E held that a Ministerial decree based on a 1976 statute contravened a 1972 Directive as well as Treaty provisions and two judgments of the ECJ which followed enforcement action by the ECJ under Articles 169 and 171.

However, following the *Francovich* ruling[146] (see Chapter 10) concerning Member State liability under Community law for failing to implement a Directive, it was held that if implementation of EC Directives was ineffective, a liability would follow. Where however, there was no implementation by Parliament there would be no liability in French law. This flies in the face of EU law.

Germany[147]

The German constitution, the 'Basic Law', owed a great deal to earlier 'German constitutional tradition'[148] and 'significant traces of liberal German, pan European and North American constitutional traditions are noticeable in the German constitution, the *Grundgesetz*.'[149] The constitution emerged from the post-war allied occupation of Germany which saw Germany split into four zones and a separate command structure for Berlin, and then effectively (*de facto*) further divided into two countries: each zone was controlled by an allied power with the German Democratic Republic under Russian control. In 1948, the three Allied Powers responded to the emergence of the German Democratic Republic by authorising the heads of the eleven Lander (regional) governments in their zones to convene a constituent assembly – a Parliamentary Council – comprising Lander representatives who were requested to draft a constitution 'both democratic and federal'.[150] Its preamble states that it was adopted by the German people 'by virtue of their constituent power' although it was never subjected to a referendum and it was approved in its final form by the Parliamentary Council

---

146 Cases C-6 and 9/90 [1991] ECR I-5357. On implementation, see *Cabinet Revert et Badelon* and *Dangeville* (CE Ass 30 October 1996). Cf *Compagnie Alitalia* (CE 3 February 1987).
147 A detailed text in English on constitutional jurisprudence in Germany is: D P Kommers *The Constitutional Jurisprudence of the Federal Republic of Germany* (1997) 2nd ed.
148 S Finer, V Bogdanor and B Rudden *Comparing Constitutions* (1994) p 10.
149 J Schwarze ed *The Birth of a European Constitutional Order* (2000) p 469.
150 S Finer, V Bogdanor and B Rudden *Comparing Constitutions* (1994) p 11.

and came into effect when duly ratified by the requisite number of Lander in May 1949. In 1990, Germany was re-unified by the unification treaty and the Basic Law covers all 16 Lander.[151]

An overriding preoccupation of the drafters of the Basic Law was the desire to prevent the tyranny of government witnessed in the 1930s and 1940s and the accompanying destruction of human rights and humanity. The system of federal government and the importance of the Lander as expressions of democratic government and popular involvement along with protection of human rights have been particularly central concerns of the constitution. Consequently, although the Basic Law may be amended by two thirds majority in both Houses, the *Bundestag* the Lower House and the *Bundesrat* the Upper House,[152] Article 79(3) states that 'Amendments of this Basic Law affecting the division of the Federation into the Lander, the participation on principle of the Lander in legislation, or the basic principles laid down in articles 1 and 20 shall be inadmissible.' These provisions are unamendable. No part of the US constitution is unamendable (though some provisions are difficult to amend) nor any part of the Russian constitution for that matter. The UK constitution can in theory be amended – any part – by express legislation. The French constitution declares unamendable the Republican form of government in France, but nothing else. Both the central state and the constituent states or Lander are 'qualified as states which co-exist independently with equal rights.'[153]

Article 1 protects human dignity and human rights and states that Articles 2–19 (the basic rights) are directly enforceable law binding the legislature, executive and the courts. It should be noted that basic rights are placed at the beginning of the Basic Law. Article 20 which sets out that the Federal Republic of Germany is a 'democratic and social federal state' that 'all state authority shall emanate from the people' that 'legislation shall be subject to the constitutional order' and 'the executive and the judiciary shall be bound by law and justice.' The third part of Article 20 gives Germans the

---

[151] See *The Unification of Germany in 1990* Press and Information Office of the Federal Government, Bonn (1991).

[152] The *Bundestag* is elected by popular vote for a four year term; the *Bundesrat* comprises 68 members nominated by the 16 Lander and whose number and voting power depend upon the size of the Lander they represent; the office of President is largely symbolic and that of Head of Government, the Chancellor, is given greater legal protection than is that of British Prime Minister.

[153] J Schwarze ed *The Birth of a European Constitutional Order* (2000) p 474. See further Ch 5.

right to resist 'any person seeking to abolish this constitutional order, should no other remedy be possible.' It does not impose a duty.

The provisions on federal structure are 'lengthy and complex'[154] and it has been pointed out that the attempt in Article 72(2) to spell out the conditions under which Federal government may exercise concurrent legislative competence with the Lander 'seems to have inspired the EC's new notion of subsidiarity.' The Maastricht judgment (below) raised the principle to a binding constitutional norm.[155] 'With the Maastricht decision, finally, the court appears ready to reassess the federal state relationship in terms of the principle of subsidiarity.'[156] The powers in Article 23 which include transfer of sovereign power by law with the consent of the *Bundesrat* subject to constitutional safeguards such as subsidiarity and human rights protection comparable with that under the Basic Law, allow the Constitutional Court to review such transfers which are stated to be in breach of subsidiarity.

The Basic Law established the Constitutional Court (*Bundes-verfassungsgericht: BVerfG*) which sits in two senates: one dealing with human rights litigation and the other dealing with disputes between government institutions and political disputes. Kommers emphasises that the Germans wanted as constitutional judges persons who had wider experience and maturity than ordinary judges. The BVerfG's complement of 16 judges is appointed by the Judicial Selection Committee of the *Bundestag* (8 judges) and by the *Bundesrat* (8 judges). A two thirds vote is required in each body. The appointments are made on an equal allocation to 'each side of politics'. Appointments are 'highly politicised',[157] are for a 12-year duration and since 1970, judges may deliver dissenting judgments.

For a court based in a civil law tradition, the BVerfG is unique in Germany in allowing dissenting judgments to be published. This was a reflection of American influence. Its jurisdiction is contained in the Basic Law together with its own statute and as well as referring to the impeachment of the President and dismissal of judges, it may rule on the constitutionality of

---

154 S Finer, V Bogdanor and B Rudden *Comparing Constitutions* (1994) p 19.
155 Article 5 EC and see Chapter 5; and D P Kommers *The Constitutional Jurisprudence of the Federal Republic of Germany* (1997, 2nd ed) p 113.
156 D P Kommers *The Constitutional Jurisprudence of the Federal Republic of Germany* (1997, 2nd ed) p 114.
157 D P Kommers *The Constitutional Jurisprudence of the Federal Republic of Germany* (1997, 2nd ed) p 22.

political parties. It has outlawed both a neo Nazi political party and the Communist party but such a matter may only be referred by the legislature or the executive. Legislation may be referred to the Court by the government or one third of the members of the Bundestag to rule on its constitutional validity (an 'abstract review) and a court must refer to the BVerfG the question of whether a statute is constitutional where the referring court needs to know that answer to decide the case before it. The process has been likened to that in Community law under Article 234 EC and preliminary rulings (see above p 44). Under Articles 25 and 100(2), a court may request the BVerfG's answer on whether a norm of international law creates directly effective rights for individuals in the German legal system.

Until 1969, individuals did not have *locus standi* to bring proceedings before the BVerfG. In that year, however, a constitutional amendment allowed an individual claiming that his constitutional rights have been infringed by the state to file a complaint with the BVerfG after exhausting all other remedies.[158] Very rarely will an individual be allowed to bring a complaint against legislation. Individuals are limited to a challenge in 'concrete disputes' as opposed to abstract reviews of the constitutionality of legislation. Under UK devolution legislation, legislation of the devolved legislatures may be challenged when in Bill form but only by the law officers (see Chapter 5, p 232 et seq). Also notable in constitutional jurisprudence has been the horizontal impact of basic human rights between individuals and not simply as between organs of the state and citizens: *Drittwirkung der Grundrechte* a point I refer to in Chapter 9, pp 432-433.

Transfer of sovereignty

The major constitutional problem to confront the BVerfG, however, has concerned the question of the transfer of sovereign power. Under Article 25 Basic Law, the basic rules of public international law are an integral part of federal law and take priority over statutes and create directly effective rights for inhabitants of the federal territory. The BVerfG has held that Treaty provisions are applicable in German courts and that they take priority over earlier and later national law and secondary EC regulations are directly valid in Germany and supreme over federal law. This has been accepted because of the existence of domestic statutes approving Community

---

[158]   Article 93.1(4a) and (4b).

Treaties; but it is accepted to the extent that Community law remains within the limits established in the Basic Law.

However, this Article, ie 25, was not used to transfer sovereignty in relation to EC law. Resort was made to Article 24. Article 24 does not specify how transfer may be achieved nor whether Article 79(2) has to be complied with (this requires a two thirds majority in both Houses.) The BVerfG has held that any transfer of sovereignty must be authorised by statute and requires the requisite majority of both Houses, ie two thirds. On the face of it, it has been said, Article 24 does not allow the transfer of complete sovereignty.[159] Particular problems which would become apparent included: does Article 24 allow the transfer of Lander powers? – a particularly sensitive question given the desire to protect Lander in the constitution; secondly, what is the position of the protection of human rights in Community law and what if such protection was not as robust as in the Basic Law? How would the perceived democratic deficit in the Community brought about by Qualified Majority Voting in the Council of Ministers affect constitutional protection of democracy – what in other words is the position if legislation is passed without the formal approval of German Ministers? Proponents of this later point would still not be assuaged by the increased powers of the European Parliament in the legislative process; it would also be concerned by the secrecy of the legislative process and so on (see Chapters 6 and 7). What would be the EC law impact on German Federalism – to what extent would it be oblivious to the Lander question – or *Landerblind*?

This latter has emerged as the second of two questions that have concentrated the attention of the BVerfG; the first question chronologically was: what is the role of the BVerfG in protecting human rights in a case which involves EC law?

On the first of these questions, the acceptance of the supremacy of Community law, was not sufficient to prevent a challenge to a Community law when it was alleged that the Community measure contravened the protection of human rights established in the Basic Law. The question was referred to the ECJ on a Article 234 [177] EC reference, but it was also referred by the German national court to the BVerfG. The BVerfG held that any transfer of sovereignty to the Community under Article 24 could not undermine the essential safeguards contained in the Basic Law and it

[159]   Foster (1994) Public Law 392.

reviewed the question of the measure's compatibility with the Basic Law in spite of the fact that the ECJ had ruled that there was no breach of human rights in the measure. This was necessary 'so long as' the Community legal order lacked a democratically elected parliament with legislative powers and powers of scrutiny and as long as there was an absence in that order of codified human rights.[160] The ECJ confirmed, as we saw above,[161] that its jurisprudence recognised and protected human rights within the Community legal order. Subsequently, the BVerfG in *Solange II* stated that it would not conduct a review of Community measures in order to assess their compliance with the Basic Law's human rights protection 'so long as' the jurisprudence of the ECJ provided the necessary degree of protection to human rights.[162] The BVerfG did, however, rule that German courts may no longer refer cases to it under Article 100 in order to test the constitutionality of Community measures in relation to their human rights protection.[163] In the Maastricht decision discussed below, the BVerfG believed that human rights would be better protected after that Treaty for reasons already discussed and a fortiori after Amsterdam and the Charter of Fundamental Rights agreed at Nice, although it has been seen that this does not have legal force within the Community legal order. It may well influence legal developments (see pp 63, 388 et seq).

The second of the major Community issues before the BVerfG concerned transfer of sovereignty. In the famous decision on the Maastricht Treaty,[164] the BVerfG reiterated its authority to determine whether transfers of sovereignty effected under Article 24 were within the BL. The burning issue concerned the question of whether the law making role of the Council of Ministers breached Article 20(2) Basic Law because it would be argued that state authority could only be exercised through the 'direct legitimation' of the people. Qualified Majority Voting would allegedly undermine this. The concurrent and residual exclusive powers over legislation of the Lander would be fatally compromised and democracy diminished.

Both Houses of the German Parliament had ratified the Maastricht Treaty in December 1992. The complainants alleged that there were breaches of

---

160   *Solange I* (1974) 37 BVerfGE 271: See J Kokott (1996) European Public Law 237 and 413.

161   Above p 55 et seq.

162   *Solange II* (1986) BVerfGE 73 at 339.

163   Attempts have been made – see the 'Bananas' episode below.

164   *Brunner v European Union Treaty* [1994] 1 CMLR 57.

Article 20 and the requirement that Germany be a democratic state; further breaches were alleged in relation to Article 38 which guaranteed the right to take part in elections and to choose a government and its policies democratically. Furthermore the amendment of Article 23 which provided for greater safeguards in relation to the Community was also criticised because it should have been approved by referendum. Much of the BVerfG's decision concerns admissibility but the court decided to hear the case in spite of an absence of an individual's rights. The Court believed that only the claims concerning Article 38 contained any possibility of infringement. Transfers of power to the Community had the consequence that the Bundestag would reduce its authority over certain policy areas with a consequential diminution or absence of voters' influence.

The court ruled that the German Accession Act and Maastricht were compatible with the Basic Law for the present proceedings but the court sent out some warning barbs. The provisions of Article 38 would prevent a transfer of powers if the democratic context of the right under Article 38 became so undermined as to be meaningless.[165] The German Accession Act must state with sufficient clarity what the scope of transferred powers is, and that article does not allow a general transfer of powers. As Foster rightly says, this could have serious implications for the future if the EU developed laws that were not compatible with the German Accession Act. The Community legal order is *pro tanto* 'subject to the approval of the BVerfG.' The court would itself review whether Community acts were within the limits of the Treaty provisions approved by the Accession Law. The Community institutions, including the ECJ, had no authority to confer powers upon themselves that were not provided by the treaties and Member States – there was no *Kompetenz-Kompetenz*.[166] German state

---

[165] See Art 6(3) TEU which states that the EU will respect the national identities of Member States.

[166] There were comments about the absence of a national democratic structure preventing the spiritual homogeneity of a people: a sort of *volksgeist*. But potential was seen in the Community for fuller democratic legitimation possibly justifying fuller transfers of power. In 1998, a challenge was made by way of constitutional complaint to the BVerfG against the introduction of the 'Euro'. The challenge was thrown out because it was completely unjustified and there was no need to exercise any form of constitutional review. However, the German constitution had to be amended following the decision of the ECJ in Case C-285/98 *Kreil v Germany* [2000] ECR I-0069 when it decided that the constitutional prohibition on women joining the armed services contravened the equal treatment provisions: J Schwarze 3 *Cambridge Yearbook of European Legal Studies 2000* (2001). See, however, Case C-273/97 *Sirdir v Army Board* [1999] ECR I-7403.

authorities would not be allowed to apply such provisions breaching the Basic Law in Germany for constitutional reasons.

In order to accommodate Germany's participation in the EU and in an attempt to assuage the anxieties released in the constitutional case law, a new Article 23 was inserted by federal statute in December 1992 (the Accession Statute) as stated above. This expresses the belief that the EU is bound by democratic, law governed, social and federative principles as well as subsidiarity and 'guarantees a protection of basic rights essentially comparable to that of the Basic Law.' The Republic may transfer sovereign powers to the Community but only where the Bundesrat has consented to the statute and Article 79(2) and (3) govern the 'foundation of the European Union' and amendments to its treaties. Article 79(3) 'enshrines the principle of human dignity, the rule of law and the principle of democracy as sacrosanct.'[167] Comprehensive and timely information must be given to the Bundestag and Bundesrat by the Federal government about 'the affairs of the EU and the former must be consulted in EU legal measures in which federal government participates. Additional safeguards are contained for the Lander and Bundesrat and on certain items the opinion of the Bundesrat is 'authoritative' and representative rights may be transferred to a nominee of the Bundesrat where a question on legislation concerns the exclusive power of the Lander.[168]

A long-running saga has involved the Community's regime for importing bananas which German importers claimed breached their fundamental property rights to trade and which was also alleged to breach the GATT which was an international obligation with priority to Community law by virtue of Article 307 [234] EC. Ultimately, the BVerfG declared the challenge inadmissible, although the traders did win a partial victory in the ECJ when part of the Regulation in question was annulled. The ECJ refused to rule on whether the GATT (WTO) provision was directly effective.[169] The case is considered to have exemplified a more constructive relationship between the BVerfG and ECJ – evidence of which was in the Maastricht decision. It also raises fundamental difficulties about the nature of European and National constitutionalism.

---

[167]   J Schwarze ed *The Birth of a European Constitutional Order* (2000) p 498.

[168]   See also Art 24(1a) inserted in December 1992.

[169]   See Case 280/93 *Germany v Council* [1994] ECR I-4973 and Case C-122/95 [1998] ECR I-973; Case 364, 365/95 *T Port GmbH* [1998] ECR I-1023. U Everling 33 CMLR 401. A Peters (2000) 43 *German Yearbook of International Law* 276 and F Hoffmeister (2001) CML Rev 791.

The final point to note is that the ECHR in Germany operates as an ordinary statute and decisions of the CHR have gained in influence in Germany.[170] The BVerfG has stated that 'the jurisdiction of the CHR helps to ascertain the content and the reach of human rights and fundamental general principles in connection with the rule of law in the *Grundgesetz*.'[171] However, it is difficult to see cases where the ECHR has made a positive difference to outcome; it has usually been used to reinforce a conclusion already reached and Article 6 ECHR has been particularly notable in this regard. The CHR has objected to the excessive delay involved in proceedings involving the BVerfG.[172] The BVerfG has 'almost neutralised' the *lex posterior* principle – a law subsequent to the ECHR takes precedence – in several cases in saying that the legislator cannot be presumed to have intended to violate international standards of this nature intentionally.[173]

British constitutionalism

To make some kind of preliminary assessment of the impact of European thought on English constitutional law, an inevitable consequence of increasing European integration, it is necessary to say something about the prevailing culture of English (sic) constitutionalism and law.

In a phrase, the English tradition has been insular, if not isolated, legally. Although the influence of our constitutional and legal thought was felt throughout the British Isles and Empire and then Commonwealth and in the US, we were resistant to outside influence in these areas. As early as the reign of Edward I (1272–1307), said Maitland, English lawyers became 'more and more utterly ignorant of any law but their own.' We progressed by the 'crude English method of development' as Marx said of Darwin. What we lost was juristic coherence; what we gained, argued Maitland, was an absence of absolutism which accompanied Roman law influence.[174]

---

[170] J Schwarze ed *The Birth of a European Constitutional Order* (2000) pp 534–5.
[171] BverfG 74, p 358 at 370: cited in J Schwarze ed *The Birth of a European Constitutional Order* (2000) p 535.
[172] *FW Pammel v Germany* EuGRZ (1997) 310 and *M Probsmeier v Germany* EuGRZ (1997) 405: J Schwarze ed *The Birth of a European Constitutional Order* (2000) p 535. Similar problems have occurred with Italian courts.
[173] BVerfG 74 p 358 at 370 cited in E Smith in J Beatson and T Tridimas eds. *New Directions in European Public Law* (1998) at 118.
[174] F W Maitland *The Constitutional History of England* (1955, CUP) p 22.

What the English developed, and what supplanted existing arrangements in Wales, Scotland and Ireland and then Northern Ireland was a *sui generis* or a 'one off' constitution the characteristics of which are unique. To those brought up in other traditions, especially the civil tradition on which the law of the EU is built, our approach appears increasingly idiosyncratic. To compound the absence of a dominant civil jurisdiction in the English tradition, [175] our constitution was not the product of revolution or tectonic political upheaval which begot a new and written constitution setting out the new order. If the English had a revolution, it took place in America and our constitutional revolution occurred in the US! As has been so often explained, the so called revolution of 1688-1689 in England re-established an existing order and clarified what many believed to be the underlying principles of English constitutionalism. The result is that our constitution remains unwritten – the only such constitution now in the western democratic world and we possess no supreme or constitutional court to interpret such a constitution.

The result of our history has been:
1. There is no strict separation of powers through which official power is checked and restrained (note, however, the EC itself, where a strict separation of powers does not exist) but the threat of government excesses was checked through a 'balanced' constitution, an independent judiciary and adherence to the rule of law.
2. An enormous residue of discretion, especially in relation to the prerogative (eg on themes such as national security, public order and so on) as well as under statute – per contra the *Rechtsstaat* ideal in Germany where the citizens' position is built on clearly defined rights which can only be interfered with through clearly defined legal norms.
3. The breadth and ambiguity of the expression 'the Crown' as the executive power in the state. In terms of law and order, for instance, the police are officers of the Crown but not servants of the Crown around which terms a good deal of legal argument and enveloping fog exist.
4. Until recently there was a very small role for the courts in the process of government; our constitution worked through non-legally enforceable conventions and government was answerable politically and primarily in the House of Commons. It was best to keep law and politics separate.

---

[175]   Admiralty and ecclesiastical law were subject to a civil law influence.

5. The linchpin of this structure, and its most important feature, was Parliamentary Sovereignty with all its implications including *dualism in international law*. That means that international law exists on a different level to municipal law and cannot become part of our municipal or domestic law until implemented through Parliament by statute or powers conferred through Parliament under statute. The *Pinochet* judgments of the House of Lords (which are examined at p 165 et seq)[176] constituted a powerful statement about the influence of international law in domestic law, albeit in a manner which did not affront Parliamentary sovereignty, and continue a trend in the interpretation of domestic law according to international norms which has developed significantly since our advent to the EEC, as it then was, in 1973 (see Chapter 4).

Basic doctrines do not, thirty years after incorporation of Community law, have that ring of crystal-clear certainty. In the famous *Factortame* litigation, in the Court of Appeal in 1989 Bingham LJ stated that Community law prevails over inconsistent domestic law. Any inconsistent domestic law preventing the application of directly effective Community law was 'bad'. 'To that extent, a UK statute is no longer inviolable as it once was.' 'Bad' means the *domestic* court would have to disapply it. This position was endorsed by the ECJ and subsequently the House of Lords.[177]

Although the EC does not have the power in the Treaty to accede to the ECHR,[178] the latter is a part of the *acquis communautaire* which was referred to above and on which the Community is built and which forms a part of the general principles of Community law from which the ECJ can draw inspiration. It may also thereby, as Sir Leslie Scarman pointed out in 1974, be indirectly a part of UK law, long before the HRA 1998 (Chapter 9) incorporated the Convention into UK law in October 2000.[179]

In the UK, the general approach has been that the ECHR is a part of our international obligations alone. There has been until recently a noted reluctance to accept the philosophy of the Convention by the British government and also judiciary. And yet a crucial influence on its drafting

---

[176] [1998] 4 All ER 897, HL and *(No 3)* [1999] 2 All ER 97, HL.
[177] [1989] 2 CMLR 353, 403–04, CA.
[178] *Opinion 2/94* [1996] ECR I-1759.
[179] *English Law – The New Dimension* (1974).

came from British lawyers and the increasingly accepted official view is that the Convention rights echo back to those in Magna Carta.[180]

The judges have used the Convention and interpretations of the Convention by the Court and Commission of Human Rights in Strasbourg to aid in the interpretation of British statutes and crucially to develop the common law, this latter after an initial refusal to do so. Where, however, action is authorised by a statute which is not ambiguous or by regulations made under a statute which are in other respects *intra vires,* there has been little role for the ECHR in domestic litigation.[181] The matter may then proceed on a petition by an individual to the CHR in Strasbourg for a ruling under the Convention. That court's rulings have generally been accepted by the UK government, but there have been notable derogations from its rulings.[182]

The influence of the judgments of the CHR has been pivotal in several areas of sensitive national administration. The impact has been felt in the armed services when the CHR held that the Ministry of Defence and relevant authorities had breached the provisions of Articles 8 and 13 ECHR by banning homosexuals from being members of the armed forces. It was their orientation which had caused the ban not their behaviour.[183] Reforms of British laws have followed rulings on the breach of privacy under Article 8 by telephone tapping and by bugging,[184] in the field of prison administration and Article 6 which concerns the right to a fair trial,[185] and in the field of police administration and criminal investigation.[186] The Court

---

180   See *Rights Brought Home* Cm. 3782. T Plucknett *A Concise History of the Common Law* (1956, 5th ed) observes a suggestion that Magna Carta may have possessed a Spanish influence, p 25.

181   *R v Secretary of State for the Home Department, ex p Brind* [1991] 1 All ER 720, HL.

182   *Brogan v UK* (1988) 11 EHRR 117 and detention in Northern Ireland breaching Article 5(3), and (5); cf *Brannigan* (1993) 17 EHRR 539 on the UK use of the derogation from Art 5 (3).

183   The English decision is: *R v Ministry of Defence, ex p Smith* [1996] 1 All ER 257, CA. See *Lustig-Prean and Beckett v UK* (1999) 29 EHRR 548 and *Smith and Grady v UK* [1999] IRLR 734. See the ECJ in *Grant v South-West Trains* Case C-249/96 [1998] ECR I-621.

184   *Malone v UK* (1984) 7 EHRR 14; *Halford v UK* (1997) 24 EHRR 253.

185   *Golder v UK* (1975) 1 EHRR 524; *Silver v UK* (1983) 5 EHRR 347; *Campbell and Fell etc* (1984) 7 EHRR 165.

186   *Murray v UK* (1996) 22 EHRR 29; *Steel v UK* (1998) 5 BHRC 339; *Saunders v UK* (1996) 23 EHRR 313.

has also ruled that the immunity of the police under English law from actions for negligence for their actions in investigating crime was also a breach of Article 6 in so far as it denied a claimant the right to have their civil rights upheld in an independent court. The Court believed that the police had been granted a blanket immunity which was disproportionate and therefore an unjustifiable restriction on the claimant's right of access to the court.[187] This will allow actions to proceed, but it does not mean that they will meet with any greater chance of success.[188] The influence of the Court has also been significant in overruling government pleas of national security and public order to allow access to justice under Article 6 although one of the cases actually concerned a question of EC law.[189] The case law has also been important in freedom of speech and publication under Article 10, seeking to confine unnecessarily wide defamation laws and in giving greater protection to privacy.

Crucially, the CHR prompted English judges to review their role in protecting human rights under domestic law. This was illustrated famously in the *Spycatcher* litigation[190] where the Government sought a world-wide ban on reporting of Peter Wright's book of that name. Early on in that litigation Lord Bridge, a member of no bleeding hearts' club, voiced his concerns, prompted by the Government's actions, about the absence of appropriate protection for fundamental human rights in the UK.[191] By exposing statutory language to ever increasingly detailed scrutiny so that any interference with human rights had to be explicitly justified and by expecting the most rigorous justification for official action or decisions where such rights were interfered with, the courts have fashioned in Laws J's famous phrase 'a common law of human rights'.[192]

---

[187] *Osman v UK* (1998) 5 BHRC 293.

[188] See eg: *Barrett v Enfield London Borough Council* [1999] 3 All ER 193 and in particular the dicta of Lord Browne-Wilkinson at 199.

[189] Case 222/84 *Johnston v Chief Constable RUC* [1986] 3 All ER 135 (see above) the EC case; *Tinnelly and Son v UK* (1998) 27 EHRR 249, ECtHR. See also *Chahal v UK* (1996) 23 EHRR 413 where the court ruled that national security could not override a fair and independent procedure for deportation under Art 5(4) ECHR.

[190] *A-G v Guardian Newspapers (No 2)* [1988] 3 All ER 545.

[191] *A-G v Guardian Newspapers* [1987] 3 All ER 316 at 346.

[192] In *Witham* below. And see: *A-G v Guardian Newspapers (No 2)* above; *Derbyshire County Council v Times Newspapers Ltd* below; *R v Secretary of Sate for the Home Department, ex p Leech* [1993] 4 All ER 539; *R v Secretary of State for the Home Department, ex p McQuillan* below; *R v Secretary of State for Defence,*

In *Derbyshire County Council v The Sunday Times Newspapers Ltd*[193]
freedom of speech was given constitutional protection without reference
in the House of Lords to the Convention and Article 10. Elsewhere the
judges have noted how the Convention and the common law march hand
in hand, seeking to protect the same rights and standards. The most
illustrative statement comes from Sedley J in *McQuillan*[194] and is examined
in Chapter 9 (p 382). From this common law of human rights, a
constitutional jurisprudence is emerging.

Finally, the HRA 1998, as other chapters describe, has incorporated the
Convention into our domestic law and courts will have to have regard to
the jurisprudence of the court and the now disbanded Commission in
Strasbourg. There appeared to be official disparities as to whether the Act
'incorporates' the Convention or not but the Home Secretary in the Second
Reading referred to the Bill as one 'incorporating the Convention'. The
Act's impact will be enormous. One point I would note is that under section
11, the Act does not restrict any human rights or freedoms existing under
other laws effective in any part of the UK. This would include common law
and would allow invocation of the case law adverted to above. This could
be important because on a judicial review application using such authorities
the applicant will not be confined by the circumscribed rules of standing
under the 1998 legislation which only concern a 'victim'.[195]

Conclusion

Constitutions are political as well as legal beasts. The British have politicised
their constitution whereas the Germans have sought to subject
constitutional analysis to the closest of legalistic scrutiny. The approach
of the French falls somewhere between the two. The EU's constitution at
present – the treaties – are also a mixture of political and legal inspiration
and are subject to constant political revision as well as judicial
interpretation. The outcome of Giscard d'Estaing's convention which I
spoke of earlier in this chapter will probably be a fairly straightforward and

---

ex p Smith [1996] 1 All ER 257; *R v Secretary of State for Social Security, ex p
JCWI* [1996] 4 All ER 385; *R v Lord Chancellor, ex p Witham* [1997] 2 All ER
779; *R v Secretary of State for the Home Department, ex p Simms* [1999] 3 All
ER 400.

193   [1993] AC 534.
194   [1995] 4 All ER 400 at 422 h-j.
195   See s 7(1) which refers to a 'victim' bringing proceedings.

simple statement of basic principles with little elaboration or qualification. It is difficult to see consensus on any other and more detailed text acting as a constitution for Europe. From an amazing disparity of constitutions, there is remarkable similarity on priorities and concerns: democracy, human rights, the security of national cultures and traditions within a Community based on the rule of law. It is a testament to an increasing sensitivity to converging themes in European constitutions. In the next chapter, there will be an examination of the influence of public law traditions on European thought and on national thought.

Chapter 3

The Community and national systems and their contribution to European public law

In the previous chapter I examined the existing constitutional framework within the EU and the constitutional traditions of several influential Member States and the matrix in which public law – the relationship between law and politics – emerged. In this chapter there will be an examination of the contribution that the administrative legal systems and the Community legal system have made to European public law. Before I examine the contribution of national systems to the development of European public law, it is necessary to examine some concepts and provisions deriving from the Treaty and the Community which have had a pronounced effect on allowing the ECJ to draw inspiration from the Member States and elsewhere in order to create a jurisprudence of Community law. Community law, it has been said,[1] is a system of administrative law originally concentrating on economic matters and extending its reach into environmental, social, financial and constitutional affairs. Schwarze, in the major study of European administrative law, describes it as a Community built on administrative law. In saying so, he emphasises the point that there is not simply an academic interest in pursuing the emergence of European administrative law, but there are substantial reasons of practical necessity. Community law is in constant need of inspiration and growth to meet its tasks, which include integration. As well as the provisions in the Treaty which provide for judicial review, he describes how 'by far the greatest number of legal principles governing administrative activity recognised today in Community law originate in the creative law-making and decision-making process of the

---

[1]   J Schwarze *European Administrative Law* (1992) p 4.

ECJ.'[2] As in national systems, administrative law has expanded 'primarily through judicial decisions.' This is certainly very true of systems which manifest a complete contrast in their approach to administrative law: the English and the French.

As early as 1954 Lagrange AG in *ASSIDER v High Authority*[3] conducted a comparative analysis of the concept 'misuse of powers' and in the *Algera*[4] decision in 1957, the ECJ stated that it could draw on inspiration from the law of Member States where the Treaty offered no solution to a problem, in this case the revocation of administrative acts. The same Advocate General conducted an examination of national rules on the topic. *Algera*, says Schwarze, 'constitutes the starting point and bench-mark for the judicial practice of the European Court in the area of general administrative law'.[5] In *A M & S v Commission*, the ECJ observed that Community Law derives not only from the economic but also the legal interpenetration of the Member States 'involving a two way traffic of legal principles between Community and national law.'[6] The case drew on the English common law principles of legal professional privilege (though with some important modifications) to incorporate the doctrine within Community law.

The English principle of *audi alteram partem*, that is conducting a fair hearing whenever an individual person's identifiable interests stand to be adversely affected by official decision-making was introduced in 1974 in *Transocean Marine Paint v Commission*[7] and 'droits de la defense' as it is known in French law, were soon elevated to the status of a 'fundamental principle of Community law' in *Hoffman la Roche v Commission*.[8] A raft of other fundamental or general principles has been taken from Member States public law (specifically administrative law) and have been applied to Community institutions or to national institutions applying Community

---

2   Pages 4–5 published in 1992 when ECJ at the height of its creativity. See also: H P Nehl *Principles of Administrative Procedure in EC Law* (1999).

3   Case 3/54 [1954–56] ECR 63.

4   Joined Cases 7/56 & 3-7/57 *Algera v Common Assembly* [1957] ECR 39.

5   Joined Cases 7/56 & 3-7/57 *Algera v Common Assembly* [1957] ECR 39 at p 5. Tridimas *The General Principles of EC Law* (2000) p 16, believes that the two first Advocate Generals of the Court Roemer and Lagrange both had a seminal influence in establishing principles of administrative law for the Community; the former was German and the latter French.

6   Case 155/79 [1982] ECR 1575 and establishment of legal professional privilege.

7   Case 17/74 [1974] ECR 1063.

8   Case 85/76 [1979] ECR 461: Fennelly in M Andenas ed *English Public Law and the Common Law of Europe* (1998) at p 7. Procedural fairness has been a strong point of English public law since the early 1960s. See p 356 et seq below.

measures. The way such principles or legal concepts are applied by the ECJ may not take the precise shape that they would in a national system for reasons we identified when discussing the jurisprudence of human rights and its absorption by the ECJ in the previous chapter (p 55 et seq), but the influence is none the less palpable. For it is an obvious point that the Community not only had to borrow to develop its own jurisprudence, but Community law is unable to be enforced by the institutions created by the Treaties alone, but has to rely to an ever increasing extent on national authorities for enforcement of Community law.

Acquis Communautaire and principles of Community law

When a new Member State accedes to the Community it subscribes to the '*Acquis Communautaire*' – one might ask whether the phrase is now *Acquis de l'Union*? – and the general principles of law that are part of the Community's heritage. Strangely perhaps, the only references to the acquis communautaire in the TEU are not in the part of the Treaty dealing with Community law. The obligation is explicitly stipulated in Accession Agreements. When the UK joined the Community in 1973, for instance, the principles of sovereignty of Community law and direct effect (see chapter 2) were well established and were binding on the UK.[9] The acquis communautaire connotes that 'body of objectives, substantive rules, policies, laws, rights, obligations, remedies and case law which are fundamental to the development of the Community legal order.'[10] This would also include naturally the case law of the ECJ and now the CFI as influenced by Member States. Robinson explains how the legislative acts comprising the acquis communautaire were set out in May 1992 in annexes to the European Economic Area Agreement, each annexe covering a specific sector. In all, 1,600 legislative acts were identified. The acquis communautaire has been described as the sum total of decisions and rules whether legally binding or not upon which the Community is based and upon which its direction is driven.[11] It is understandably described as 'amorphous'.

Among the general principles are included: proportionality in the exercise of public power (see Chapter 8); the supremacy of the rule of law or the

---

9   Lord Bridge makes the point graphically in *Factortame (No 2)* [1991] 1 All ER 70 at 107-08. See p 195 below.
10   Robinson in *Butterworth's Expert Guide to the European Union* (1997) pp 3–4.
11   Mathijsen *A Guide to European Union Law* (1999, 7th ed) p 6, fn 9.

principle of administration and government through law if we unpack Dicey's loaded version which exalted private law over public law; legitimate expectation (both substantive and procedural – see Chapter 8) that authorities will act in accordance with their assurances and fairly; legal certainty; equality and non-discrimination; environmental protection; openness and transparency in the operation of public bodies; fair procedure or natural justice; the principle of effectiveness (which has been a driving force behind many of the most important developments in Community law including liability for breaches of Community law and consistent construction of domestic measures with Community provisions): giving reasons for decisions which arose as a general principle after it was placed in the Treaty specifically in relation to the adoption of regulations, Directives or decisions by the Council and European Parliament, or by the Council of Commission (Article 253 [190] EC); due care in the performance of administrative functions and obtaining all relevant evidence and information; restitution for monies wrongly paid to public authorities (see Chapter 10).

The general principles will be dealt with throughout chapters of this book and their use by the ECJ has been exhaustively covered elsewhere.[12] It is worth indicating that the articulation of a duty to give reasons in Community legislation imposed by Article 253 EC was pivotal in establishing a general principle to give reasons for adverse decisions. A failure so to provide will lead to the annulling of the legislation or decision.[13] In *Germany v Commission*[14] the ECJ ruled why the giving of reasons was crucial:

> In imposing upon the Commission the obligation to state reasons for its decisions, Article 253 is not taking mere formal considerations into account but seeks to give an opportunity to the parties of defending their rights, to the Court of exercising its supervisory functions and to Member states and to all interested nationals of ascertaining the circumstances in which the Commission has applied the Treaty. (p 69)

Failure to comply would appear to be both an infringement of an essential procedural requirement and infringement of the Treaty.

---

[12]   On general principles see T Tridimas *The General Principles of EC Law* (2000) OUP.

[13]   Case 131/86 *UK v Council* [1988] ECR 905.

[14]   Case 24/62 [1963] ECR 63.

Principles of good administration have been formulated by the European Ombudsman in a Code on good administrative behaviour and also by the Commission and these principles themselves lean on standards taken from the judicial decisions of the ECJ.[15] This Code attempts to explain in more detail what the Charter of Fundamental Rights of the European Union, which was adopted in Nice in December 2000, means when it describes the 'right to good administration and the right to complain to the European Ombudsman against maladministration' (Chapter 11).

Since 1970, as was seen in Chapter 2, the ECJ has held that fundamental human rights are a part of the general principles of Community law (p 55 et seq). This followed *Stork v High Authority* where the ECJ refused to subject Community law to an examination of its protection of human rights in the light of such protection provided by Member States constitutions because to do so would qualify Community supremacy. The German reaction to this has been explained above in Chapter 2.

The above corpus of the *Acquis Communautaire* and the principles of law including human rights apply in domestic courts as a matter of law when those courts are enforcing Community law, and in its implementation. They have also spilled over into domestic law where no question of Community law is involved and have been applied to secure consistent development of domestic law and Community law. Domestic courts have, however, refused to apply Community law to purely domestic provisions. This development has been well chronicled.[16] Before examining these principles below and again in Chapter 8 in an English setting, I need to address some points.

Direct effect of Directives

In the previous chapter it was seen how provisions in treaties could be directly effective and how far reaching that doctrine, together with sovereignty, had been. The Treaty provides (Article 249 [189] EC) that

---

[15] *The European Code of Good Administrative Behaviour* European Ombudsman (2002); see Ch 12.

[16] For the views of the author and Professor Jeffrey Jowell QC see: J Jowell and P Birkinshaw 'The United Kingdom' in J Schwarze (ed) *Administrative Law Under European Influence* (1996) at p 273. See G Anthony *UK Public Law and European Law* (2002) for an interesting appraisal.

regulations have general application, are binding in their entirety and are directly applicable in all Member States. They are binding legal instruments requiring no further implementing measures.

After UK accession in 1973, the ECJ decided[17] that Directives could, in appropriate circumstances – in spite of being addressed to the Member State to implement in a form and by methods which it was within their choice (ie discretion) to designate[18] – be directly effective like Treaty obligations *but only in a vertical fashion as against an emanation of the State,* which as well as central government includes local authorities, public corporations and the police forces: *Johnston v Chief Constable RUC*[19] was the decision of the ECJ which held that police forces were 'emanations of the State', a ruling which did not fall easily into our conventional philosophy about the police, ie officers were not agents of the state or state bodies or servants of the Crown but independent of executive authority. *Marshall v Southampton and South-West Hampshire Area Health Authority*[20] held that the doctrine applied to health authorities and, in an English case, privatised industries[21] a direction pointed out by the Advocate General in the case *Foster v British Gas.*[22] The English Court of Appeal has ruled that the Motor Insurers' Bureau, a private company in form, was not an emanation of the state. This is a body which administers the scheme for compensating victims of uninsured drivers and which the UK government has chosen as the means for meeting obligations under an EC Directive (84/5/EEC). In Ireland, the Circuit Court has accepted that the Irish analogue was an emanation of the state.[23]

17   Case 41/74 *Van Duyn v Home Office* [1974] ECR 1337.
18   The ECJ has spelt out the requirements that must be satisfied for proper implementation: Case C-29/84 *Commission v Germany* [1985] ECR 1661; Case C-58/89 *Commission v Germany* [1991] ECR I-4983.
19   Case 222/84 [1986] 3 All ER 135.
20   *Marshall* Case 152/84 [1986] ECR 723 and see the influential Opinion of Advocate General Slynn.
21   *Griffin v South-West Water Services Ltd* [1995] IRLR 15. See also *NUT v Governing Body St Mary's Church of England Junior School* [1997] 3 CMLR 360.
22   Case C-188/89 [1990] ECR I-3313.
23   *White v White and Motor Insurers' Bureau* [1999] 1 CMLR 1251, CA; the point was not ruled on by the House of Lords: [2001] 2 CMLR 1 (HL); see Case C-63/01 *Evans v Secretary of State and Motor Insurers' Buereau* (24 October 2002, unreported) for a reference to the ECJ; in Ireland *Dublin Bus v Motor Insurers' Bureau of Ireland* McMahon J (29 October 1999, unreported): see C Costello and S Drake (2003) 9 European Public Law forthcoming. For liability of bodies for breaches of Community law, irrespective of their public law status, see Ch 10 p 449.

The 'appropriate circumstances' were basically that the relevant obligations in a measure had to be clear, precise, unconditional and incapable of further legal perfection or 'complete'. The time for implementation of the Directive had also to have passed.[24] In *Van Duyn*, the ECJ ruled that the Directive, which concerned freedom of movement of persons, was directly effective although the Member State had acted within Community law in refusing entry to a foreign national who was seeking to enter the UK to take up a position with the Church of Scientology. The refusal of the UK authorities, the ECJ believed, was based on a public policy derogation which clearly gave considerable discretion to the national authority but which nonetheless did not negative the principle of direct effect of a Directive. The ECJ was determined to give full effect to Community law and to make Directives effective at the suit of individuals before national courts where the duty was imposed on the state or its emanations.[25]

There has been resistance by Member States to the full impact of direct effectiveness and the Protocol on the application of the principles of proportionality and subsidiarity may assuage anxieties of Member States. This provides that in law making by the Community, Directives should be preferred to regulations and framework or broad-based Directives to 'detailed measures', ie instruments which are less easily interpreted as directly effective (para 6). The latter are less likely to be construed by the ECJ as creating rights, either directly or indirectly for individuals. It must be said that the ECJ has fashioned a jurisprudence which has created an indirect and incidental liability on third parties because of failures by a Member State to implement a Directive (see below).[26]

Under the Amsterdam Treaty obligations may be introduced by unanimous action under the Third Pillar on Police and Judicial Cooperation where Member States agree by way of 'Framework Decisions' to approximate laws and regulations of the Member States. Article 34 TEU specifically states that such decisions shall not entail direct effect. Curtin and Dekker query whether this allows one to infer direct applicability.[27]

---

24   Case 148/78 *Ratti* [1979] ECR 1629.
25   See *Marshall* Case 152/84 [1986] ECR 723.
26   See P Craig and G de Búrca *EU Law: Text, Cases and Materials* (2002, 3rd ed) pp 216 et seq and see Ch 4 pp 191-192 and 102-103 below.
27   D Curtin and I Dekker in P Beaumont, C Lyons and N Walker eds *Convergence and Divergence in European Public Law* (2002) ch 4.

Where a Directive is not implemented within the required period, a Member State may be liable to those who have clearly defined rights under the Directive and where other legal requirements are met.[28] Member States may also be liable in damages for breaches of Community law – including non-implementation – to injured parties where the relevant criteria are established. Such criteria were shaped by the court under the non-contractual liability provisions of Article 288 [215] EC which was designed to establish criteria of liability for the institutions of the Community (see Chapter 10). This article specifically refers to the ECJ borrowing from the principles common to the laws of the Member States. To extend the provisions to serious breaches of Community law by Member States is another example of the ECJ in its most creative jurisprudential mode and is a point that is dealt with in Chapter 10.[29]

Article 228 EC has recently been repeated as a fundamental right of the Union in the Charter of Fundamental Rights of the EU. Article 47 of that Charter provides that 'Everyone whose rights and freedoms guaranteed by the law of the Union are violated has the right to an effective remedy before a tribunal' under the terms of the article.

Article 10 [5] EC and co-operation

It will be recalled from the previous chapter that 'Co-operation' was a constitutional principle existing between the Community and Member States and was influenced by the German doctrine of '*Bundestreue*'.[30] The theme of co-operation between the institutions of the Member States and the institutions of the Community is contained in Article 10 EC. It states quite simply that:

---

28   Case C-6/9/90 *Francovich* [1991] ECR I-5357.
29   And has seen its detractors as well as supporters. See: *Francovich* above; Case C-48/93 *R v Secretary of State for Transport, ex p Factortame Ltd* [1996] ECR I-1029; Case C-392/93 *R v HM Treasury, ex p BT plc* [1996] ECR I-1631; Case C-5/94 *R v MAFF, ex p Hedley Lomas* [1996] ECR I-2553 etc. In *Bergaderm v Commission* Case C-352/98P [2000] ECR I-5291 the principles of *Brasserie* were applied to Community institutions for breaches of Community law.
30   B de Witte in F Snyder ed *The Europeanisation of Law* (2000) at p 83 and references cited. Cooperation between Member States underpins the doctrine of mutual recognition in the famous *Cassis de Dijon* decision and in Case C-340/89 *Vlassopoulou* [1991] ECR I-2357.

Member States shall take all appropriate measures, whether general or particular, to ensure fulfilment of the obligations arising out of this Treaty or resulting from action taken by the institutions of the Community. They shall facilitate the achievement of the Community's tasks.

They shall abstain from any measure which could jeopardise the attainment of the objectives of this Treaty.

As well as embodying the general principle that national courts must apply Community law as interpreted by the ECJ and CFI, Article 10 EC has also been the inspiration behind, or which has given assistance to, some of the most far reaching of ECJ decisions concerning direct effect and liability. Article 10 has also been pivotal in the development of co-operation between the ECJ and national courts in one further area which it will be useful to address at this stage: the interpretation of domestic law so as to comply with Directives which are not directly effective; which do not, that is, have an effect on a state body or an emanation of the state. We have seen that the ECJ has developed the doctrine of direct effect not only in relation to Treaty provisions (see Chapter 2) but also for unimplemented Directives where the necessary conditions are established. By this process, individuals may enforce rights in the Treaty or Directives through their domestic courts. But direct effect of unimplemented Directives only applies against the state or emanations of the state, ie public authorities and only after the date for implementation has passed.[31] Before that date, a Directive cannot be invoked by an individual directly but a Member State must not do anything to frustrate or seriously compromise the result to be achieved by the Directive, ie by adopting conflicting national measures.[32]

The ECJ has ruled that Directives that are not implemented by a Member State cannot confer rights on individuals against other individuals who are not representing the state or acting in some public capacity. They have no direct horizontal effect.[33] This could cause serious inequality and injustice in the application of Community law – eg, a public employer may have obligations caste upon it which a multi-national private employer can avoid.

---

[31] See above. For privatised industries, see AG W van Gerven in Case C-188/89 *Foster v British Gas* [1990] ECR I-3313 and *Griffin* note 21above.

[32] *Inter-Environment Wallonie ASBL v Région Wallonie* Case C-129/96 [1997] ECR I-7411.

[33] Case C-91/92 *Faccini Dori* [1994] ECR I-3325. Although some AGs have attempted to get the ECJ to move so far: see Walter van Gerven *The Horizontal Effect of Directive Provisions Revisited – the Reality of Catchwords* IEPL, University of Hull (1993).

Directives which are not directly effective because they do not take effect vertically or have not been implemented, must nonetheless be invoked by national courts to interpret domestic measures to achieve consistency and uniform interpretation of domestic law in conformity with Community law. In *Von Colson and Kamann*[34] the ECJ invoked the principle of co-operation in Article 10 [5] EC and the duty on the state, including its courts, to take all appropriate measures, whether general or particular, to ensure the fulfilment of Community obligations. This duty in Article 10 was combined with the Member State's obligation under Article 249 [189] to achieve the result envisaged by a Directive. By this combination, the ECJ established that national courts must as a general principle interpret domestic measures in the light of the wording and purpose of the Directive in order to achieve the obligation in Article 249, viz, the result envisaged by a Directive. In *Von Colson* the domestic measure in question was a provision under the Equal Treatment Directive (Article 6) which attempted to implement a Directive and to that extent was consistent with those national systems which hold that a domestic measure may be interpreted in accordance with international provisions under certain conditions.[35] The applicants had unsuccessfully applied for jobs in prisons; their lack of success related to their sex. The national court only allowed them reimbursement for travel expenses on a 'loss of expectation' basis. The purpose of the Directive, the ECJ held, is to provide real equality of opportunity to male and females in employment markets and this necessitated sanctions giving real and effective protection before judicial bodies. They would also have to act as an appropriate deterrent.[36] However, the decision of the ECJ in *Marleasing* made it clear that the duty of co-operation applies in the interpretation of domestic measures which precede as well as succeed a Directive which is not directly effective.[37] The national court is under a duty to interpret such preceding measures in the light of the wording and purpose of the Directive. The ECJ has seen limits to this doctrine so that a national court does not have to interpret a measure in a manner which is against the domestic provision or *contra legem*. But it is a general duty so all relevant domestic measures should be included within its ambit. (See Chapter 4, p 192).

---

[34]   Case 14/83 [1984] ECR 1891.
[35]   See Ch 4 on the UK, p 186 et seq.
[36]   See Case C-271/91 *Marshall (No 2)* [1993] ECR I-4367 etc Ch 4 p 474.
[37]   Case C-106/89 [1990] ECR I-4135. The case concerned nullification of a company's articles because incorporation was used to defraud creditors. The EC Directive did not allow fraud as a ground of nullity.

Marleasing has been a very controversial decision because of the widespread feeling that if extended too far, it could undermine one of the fundamental principles of the Community legal edifice: legal certainty. Some limits imposed on this doctrine will be discussed in the next chapter but it should be noted that in spite of its path-breaking initial impact, the application of the principle has generally been qualified by the ECJ. There have, however, been strong directions to national courts to interpret domestic measures in accordance with unimplemented Directives with possible legal consequences for private parties.[38] And a failure by the state to comply with Directives has caused other difficulties for private parties. Although Directives cannot be used to perfect an imperfect criminal liability which is contained in a domestic measure[39] their existence may lead to the non-recognition by national courts of domestic laws which has consequential effects on relations between private individuals and which is bound to complicate the giving of legal advice on such questions.[40]

After some uncertainty, English courts have acted consistently with the ruling in *Marleasing* (see p 186 et seq below). The ECJ itself has pointed out that application of the *Marleasing* doctrine may not always be possible. In fact in recent years, the ECJ initially stepped back from its creative phase, reluctant to push judicial remedies too far against prevailing orthodoxy. But as seen above, recent case law has applied the doctrine with renewed vigour. The situation is not free from doubt. In *Faccini Dori* the ECJ also adverted to the possibility of an individual resorting to *Francovich* liability where a Directive remained unimplemented, a point referred to above and developed in Chapter 10. It need only be pointed out at this stage that the creation by the ECJ of a liability of a Member State to pay damages where that Member State through one of its organs of government breaches Community law is another manifestation of co-operation as well as the effectiveness of Community law.

Curtin and Dekker see Article 10 as a significant agent in helping to produce greater degrees of convergence within the Community and domestic legal

---

[38]   Case C-456/98 *Centrosteel v Adipol* [2000] ECR I-6007; Case C-240/244/98 *Océano Grupo Editorial v Rocio Murciano Quintero* [2000] ECR I-4941.
[39]   Case 80/86 *Kolpinghuis Nijmegen BV* [1987] ECR 3969; Case C-168/95 *Luciano Arcaro* [1996] ECR I-4705.
[40]   Case C-194/94 *CIA Security* [1996] ECR I-2201; Case C-443/98 *Unilever Italia SpA* [2000] ECR I-7535; see eg *R v Durham City Council, ex p Huddlestone* [2000] 1 WLR 1484, CA at p 192 below

orders.[41] If appropriate limits are not placed on the doctrines of indirect and incidental horizontal effect, it could prove a cause of resentment and be counter-productive.

Co-operation also characterises the operation of the Community Third Pillar on Police and Judicial Cooperation in Criminal Affairs which is crucially important for policing activity just as co-operation features in the Second Pillar. This will have a pronounced impact on criminal administration and policing. An aspect of co-operation in relation to the Community and a Member State in relation to law enforcement occurred in the case of *Zwartveld*.[42] In this case, officials in the Commission, against their wishes, had to hand over Commission documents relating to the rigging of fish markets in Holland to the Dutch criminal investigating authorities in order to assist the latter in their enquiries. This did not cover a Community item but was enjoined through the instrumentality of Article 10 [5] EC which the ECJ took to mean the duty of 'sincere cooperation' that should exist under Article 10 between national authorities and the Community organs, as well as the duty on the Commission to ensure that the Treaty was applied under Article 211 [155] EC along with the ECJ's own duty to ensure that the law was observed in the interpretation and application of the Treaty (Article 220 [164] EC). The court saw itself attempting to uphold the rule of law. It is another illustration of the ECJ engaging in constructive jurisprudence and one with strong analogical potential in the area of law enforcement.

Is the Community a system of administrative law?

In the previous chapter we examined the constitutional order of the Community and its relationship to national constitutions. It has been claimed, as was seen above, that the system of Community law is in fact a system of administrative law. This might appear a little strange given that much of the corpus of Community law concerns exports and imports,

41 Op cit note 27.
42 Case C-2/88 Imm [1990] ECR I-3365. The Mutual Assistance Regulation 515/ 97/EC (OJ 1997 L82/1) provides for the mutual exchange of information between competent national authorities in Member States and between them and the Commission on customs and agricultural affairs and there is a computer database to facilitate such exchange. See also the Administrative Sanctions Regulation (2988/95/EC) and the European Inspections Regulation 215/96/EC: see Bernard *Multi Level Governance in the European Union* (2002) pp 169 et seq.

movement of persons, capital and businesses, competition, sex equality and employment law. Increasingly the concerns of Community law have embraced environmental and regulatory law. Definitions of administrative law are notoriously tendentious; is it merely the rules of the mighty state and its courts seeking to simplify or make more effective the process of rule and public control? Is it the law relating to public service (see Chapter 12)? Is it the promise to provide opportunities for the ruled to engage with decision-makers in the process of rule and participate in government. Is it the control of government and its agencies by judicial means? Is it the corpus of law dealing with public welfare as an expression of public interest in areas where we cannot avoid collective organisation such as education, environmental welfare, immigration, public safety and so on? In some systems of administrative law, the subject is seen very much as the rules and principles invoked by courts in setting limits on what those wielding public power may do. In other systems, the concentration, while not ignoring such aspects, will focus on how public authorities make decisions and how they are rendered coherent and accountable by internal devices such as public hearings, ombudsman techniques, complaints procedures, independent audit and inspection. Furthermore, the model of administrative law that is used is to a large extent one that assumes an interventionist state whether via the direct provision of services or whether by regulation of activities and where there are clear divisions between the public and private realms. A clear bifurcation has been replaced by a greater degree of ambiguity and obscurity. These tensions reveal themselves in Community law also.

It should be recalled that the Community is an entity bound by the rule of law (Article 5 EC first paragraph). In so far as it can claim to be a system, there are numerous examples of such a phenomenon. There is no need to deal with these points in detail because they are well covered by numerous texts elsewhere.[43] But an outline will help our enquiry.

Judicial Review: There is a power of judicial review modelled on the French *droit administratif.* This is contained in Article 230 [173] EC, with further provisions in Articles 231 [174], 232 [175] – the latter constituting a remedy for failure to act or inactivity by the Council, European Parliament or Commission under the Treaty. Under Article 233 [176] EC, where a

---

[43] Again P Craig and G de Burca *EU Law: Cases and Materials* (2002, 3rd ed). See also: D O'Keeffe ed *Liber Amicorum in Honour of Lord Slynn of Hadley: Judicial Review in European Union Law* (2000).

declaration has been given on voidness or failure to act in breach of the Treaty of Rome as amended, the defaulting institution has to take the necessary measures to comply with the judgment (this does not affect any obligation to make good damage caused as a consequence of a breach of Community law under Article 288 [215] EC, second paragraph). Article 241 [184] EC also provides an opportunity for judicial review. This last Article concerns the power of any party to raise a plea of illegality in proceedings in which a regulation is in issue, ie a collateral challenge as opposed to a direct one under Article 230.

Under Article 230, the ECJ and CFI will have power to review the legality of acts adopted jointly by the European Parliament and Council, acts of the Council, of the Commission and the European Central Bank. Measures which are illegal, on grounds which owe their provenance to French public law (see below), will be annulled save that certain effects of regulations may be preserved to avoid injustice where annulment may cause adverse retrospective consequences (Article 231 EC). 'Acts' includes legislative and administrative measures and in the case of the European Parliament 'acts' intended to produce legal effects vis à vis third parties.[44] The Treaty of Amsterdam added that the acts of various additional bodies may also be reviewed by the ECJ such as the European Investment Bank and European Monetary Institute (a transitional body). Time limits of two months to bring the action are strictly applied. The ECJ will deal with applications by the Institutions of the Community and Member States; the CFI will now deal with applications by individuals.

Individuals, either personal or corporate, are at a distinct disadvantage in challenging regulations in that they have to establish locus standi by establishing that a regulation 'is of direct and individual concern to' that individual. This has proved an enormously obdurate barrier in numerous cases because regulations are collective measures.[45] It constituted nothing less than a 'denial of access to the court for a judicial remedy' a criticism

---

44   Case 294/83 *Les Verts v European Parliament* [1986] ECR 1339.
45   To establish an interest, an individual would have to satisfy the court that a regulation was of direct and individual concern to that applicant, in effect a decision albeit in the form of a regulation. The ECJ in the past has not been generous: but see Case C-309/89 *Codorniu* [1994] ECR I-1853. There are also serious problems where a decision is addressed to another, eg a national government: Case 25/62 *Plaumann v Commission* [1963] ECR 95.

which the ECJ had frequently levelled against decisions of national courts.[46] The ECJ has relied on the availability of a remedy in a national court which would have to make a reference under Article 244 (below) as a reason for not extending locus standi provisions. This was a redundant reason for a variety of reasons, not least being the fact that in the absence of national implementing measures, there may be nothing to refer by the national court to the CFI. Furthermore, the questions of law referred to the CFI by the national court may not represent the actual grievance of the applicant for relief.

In case law in 2002, Advocate General Jacobs described the locus standi requirement under Article 230 as 'one of the least satisfactory aspects of the Community legal system' and after a comprehensive review of academic comment suggested that an individual is individually concerned where 'the measure has, or is liable to have, a substantial adverse effect on his interests.' This might be more demanding than the test of 'sufficient interest' set out for locus standi in English judicial review, but Jacobs saw it removing the anomaly that the more people affected by a measure, the less likely a judicial remedy was.[47] The opinion of the Advocate General was given in a case on appeal from the CFI. The CFI has also produced a judgment which had the effect of considerably liberalising locus standi under Article 230.[48] The CFI established that a reference under Article 234 was not possible on the facts and remedies for damages under Article 288 [215] second paragraph, could not be regarded 'in the light of Articles 6 and 13 ECHR and of Article 47 Charter of Fundamental Rights of the European Union as guaranteeing persons the right to an effective remedy' to challenge measures of general applicability which affects directly their legal situation. The CFI reconsidered the restrictive test for locus standi relating to an individual stating that 'a natural or legal person is to be regarded as individually concerned by a Community measure of general application that concerns him directly if the measure in question affects his legal position, in a manner which is both definite and immediate, by restricting his rights or by imposing obligations on him' (para 51). The number of others similarly affected is of no relevance. This is an undeniably

---

46 Case 294/83 *Les Verts v European Parliament* [1986] ECR 1339, para 23 and Case 222/84 *Johnston v Chief Constable RUC* [1986] ECR 1651, para 18.

47 *Unión de Pequenos Agricultores v Council of the European Union* Case C-50/00 P, para 102(4).

48 Case T -177/01, *Jégo-Quéré et Cie SA v Commission* [2002] All ER (EC) 932.

liberal development in relation to standing bringing the Community position closer to English and other national rules of standing.

However, the case in which Advocate General Jacobs gave his opinion was heard in the ECJ where that court noted that any change in standing had to be made by Member States under Article 48 TEU. The ECJ held that Community courts or national courts could be the place to challenge Community measures of general application by Article 241 or in the latter case Article 234, paragraphs (2) and (3). In the case of a challenge before a national court, an applicant would proceed under the preliminary reference procedure under Article 234 EC (Chapter 2 p 44 and below). The ECJ, however, could not review national procedures to see whether they allowed such a challenge before domestic courts thereby allowing the ECJ to take a direct challenge if they did not.[49] The Treaty had established a 'complete system of legal remedies and procedures' and the ECJ, in spite of widespread criticism, was not inclined to re-orient established principles.

A French influence in judicial review

From the point of view of domestic influence on Community law, the similarity of judicial review powers of the ECJ, and CFI, and those available in French public law must be emphasised. Article 230 EC was outlined above but the specific powers of review within the Article are as follows:

Lack of competence meaning an absence of the necessary power to act. French law has as a ground of review: *incompetence*. This ground is not frequently invoked in Community law because powers are interpreted broadly. It has been used to challenge unlawful delegations. In French law, this ground of attack is used when a measure and factual situation require examination and interpretation; a decision is not, in other words, ex facie void.

The second ground of review is infringement of an essential procedural requirement. French law provides a review for *vice de forme* – procedural errors and the distinction between essential and non-essential requirements was imported from French law.

---

[49]   *Unión de Pequenos Agricultores v Council of the European Union* Case C-50/00 P (25 July 2002, unreported), ECJ.

The third ground is infringement of the Treaty or of any rule of law relating to its application. A rule of law would include the general principles of law as well as all rules of Community law other than those in the Treaty to which specific reference is made (EC, ECSC and Euratom). In French law *violation de la loi* covers similar grounds in so far as it covers errors of law, but French law as we shall see affords a very careful scrutiny over fact-finding processes by the administrative courts. A mistake of fact is reviewable in Community law under this heading but not as extensively as under French law (see below) and in review cases, the ECJ and CFI adopt generally a low intensity of review although in competition cases, the CFI has been accused by the Commission of adopting a form of review which challenges the merits of Commission decisions on mergers (Chapter 12 note 6). Principles such as proportionality do afford an opportunity for the ECJ to exact a more searching scrutiny of measures than obtains under more self-effacing tests for review such as those in the English *Wednesbury* decision (see Chapter 8) but even here, there are significant differences between the scrutiny adopted by the Community courts and domestic courts.

The fourth ground of review is misuse of powers and once again the doctrine was developed by the French ground of review *detournement de pouvoir*. In French law this is very much concerned with motive; likewise in Community law. Motives may be either subjectively irregular; they are used for a private purpose such as profit, spite, bad faith. Or they may not be vitiated in this subjective sense but a power is being exercised for a purpose that does not exist, or disproportionately. In English law, the first subjectively vitiated exercise of power is analogous to misfeasance of public office.[50]

Enforcement: Article 226 [169] EC provides for a system of enforcement where the Commission believes a Member State has failed to fulfil an obligation under the Treaty (see Chapter 11 p 481).[51] Under Article 226 [169] EC, the Commission shall deliver a reasoned opinion on the matter after the State concerned has been given the opportunity to submit its observations. If the State does not comply within the period laid down by the Commission in its opinion, the Commission may bring the matter before the ECJ. Article 228 [171] EC allows for lump sum penalties to be awarded

---

[50] *Three Rivers District Council v Bank of England (No 3)* [2001] UKHL 16, [2000] 3 All ER 1, HL and [2001] 2 All ER 513.

[51] See R Rawlings (2000) 6 ELJ 4 for a critique of the approach of the Commission in these procedures and also A. Bonnie (1998) EL Rev 537.

against a Member State which has been found in breach of its Treaty obligations by the ECJ but which has not taken the 'necessary measures' to comply with the judgment.[52]

Article 226 has spawned a considerable body of guidance on internal procedures and practices in relation to the manner in which the Commission conducts itself and these practices have been investigated by the EU Ombudsman. The practice within the article raises very important questions about the Community/Member State partnership in enforcement proceedings and the role of national bodies in enforcing Community measures. Much of the information on which the Commission relies to activate Article 226 comes from complainants within the Member States who, in turn, very often feel aggrieved about the manner in which the Commission exercises its powers under Article 226. This is a subject which ties in with themes addressed more fully in Chapter 11. The Commission cannot be reviewed in the ECJ under Article 232 for the manner in which it exercise its powers under Article 226 and the ECJ is reluctant to challenge the Commission's discretion on how it proceeds, or not, under the Article. Legal advice for complainants can be obtained under the EURO JUS system of part time lawyers in Commission offices in Member States. The EU Ombudsman has been of the view that effective enforcement is really about decentralising Community law enforcement to Member States (see p 481 et seq).

Preliminary Reference: Article 234 [177] EC provides for the ECJ and after Nice the CFI to give preliminary rulings concerning the interpretation of the Treaty, the validity and interpretation of acts of the Community institutions and the European Central Bank, and the interpretation of statutes of bodies established by an act of the Council, where that is provided for. References, it will be recalled, are made by national courts or tribunals. This provision, which has been crucial for the uniform interpretation and application of Community measures, was examined in Chapter 2 (p 44 et seq).

Paragraphs (2) and (3) of Article 234 make provision for national courts to refer to the ECJ questions concerning the 'validity .... of acts of the institutions of the Community and European Central Bank.' This is a form

---

52   Only one judgment had been given by the ECJ under Art 228(2) between 1 November 1993 and the beginning of 2002: Case C-387/97 *Commission v Greece* [2000] ECR I-5047. Proceedings have been initiated against several states.

of indirect challenge of Community measures because such measures cannot be challenged directly in national courts.[53] Only national measures implementing Community provisions or putting them into effect can be so challenged and interim relief disapplying domestic measures may be given by the national court.[54]

Secondary law making powers: Article 249 [189] EC provides for the making of secondary legislation either jointly by the European Parliament and Council, by the Council and by the Commission and for the taking of legally binding decisions affecting those to whom they are addressed. The legislation is in the form of regulations and Directives. The former are of general application and are directly applicable in all Member States as we have seen. Directives were discussed above. Innominate measures having legal effect may also be reviewed.

Article 308 [235] EC contains powers to take 'appropriate measures' under procedures in the article where it is necessary to attain Community objectives 'in the course of the operation of the common market and the Treaty has not provided the necessary powers.' The Council acts unanimously on a Commission proposal and has to consult the European Parliament.

Audit: There is also a Court of Auditors established under Article 7 [4] EC. A point to be noted at this stage is that Community law followed the continental model in possessing a court to deal with questions of public finance and accounting. France for instance has a Cour des Comptes. However, the EU model does not have the judicial functions that its name suggests and there is not a unified continental system of financial control and accounting.[55] Furthermore, the Court is linked to the European Parliament in a manner approximating to the British model and the National Audit Office, and this differs fundamentally from the French model. Its confused antecedents and the absence of a Finance Ministry have left the Court in an unsatisfactory position, it is argued.[56] The Court is the auditor

---

53   Case 314/85 *Foto-Frost* [1987] ECR 4199; Case C-92/89 *Zuckerfabrik* [1991] ECR I-415 and see Cases C-376/98 C-74/99 *Germany v European Parliament* [2000] All ER (EC) 769.

54   See *R v Secretary of State for Health, ex p Imperial Tobacco* [2001] 1 All ER 850, HL and *Germany v European Parliament* [2000] All ER (EC) 769. National courts have to follow strict procedures established by the ECJ.

55   Harden, White and Donnelly (1995) European Public Law p 599: see www.eca.eu.int.

56   Harden, White and Donnelly (1995) European Public Law pp 629–30.

of the Community and bodies established by the Community insofar as it is not barred from investigating their finances. It operates over the budgetary and financial procedures of the Community and provisions on internal audit. The approaches of Member States to audit within their own systems is very different and Harden and colleagues were of the view that arrangements in the Community – where 80% of Community general budget was spent within Member States – required 'a degree of harmonisation of national systems of financial control and management and of external audit.'[57]

The Court of Auditors' powers are contained in Articles 246–248 [188a-c] EC and it has, after Nice, power to draw up its own rules of procedure approved by the Council on qualified majority. Its powers include a right to documents and information necessary to carry out its tasks and on the spot examinations. Special provisions apply to the European Investment Bank. It should also be noted that as an institution of the Community it is able to bring proceedings before the Court under Article 232 [175] EC (above), failing to act. A European Anti-Fraud Office (Olaf) was established by Commission Decision 99/352 (see Chapter 11 p 481).

The formal trappings of a system of administrative law are in existence. To these can be added an EU Ombudsman, access to information legislation and provision to petition the European Parliament as well as numerous provisions relating to specific areas such as the environment, employment

---

57   Harden, White and Donnelly (1995) European Public Law p 632. In the UK, the use of specialist courts as a means for overseeing accounts and finances is unknown in central government since the *cursus scacarrii* although courts play a role in local government audit: Local Government Act 2000, ss 90–91 amending Audit Commission Act 1998. Questions involving finance do of course come before the courts when an issue of vires is involved: in the early 1980s the Leader of the GLC was embroiled in a dispute over a heavily subsidised transport policy which was attacked for being unlawful. Questions of central-local finance and expenditure have been resolved through the courts when, in this case, central government was accused, unsuccessfully, of acting unlawfully. In the most recent case of significance the government, it was held, had acted unlawfully in allocating funds for overseas aid which were not covered by the governing legislation: *R v Secretary of State for Commonwealth and Foreign Affairs, ex p WDM* [1995] 1 All ER 611. The main body of auditing in central government and in local government and other public bodies is undertaken by the National Audit Office which has the CAG at its head and by the Audit Commission. The CAG reports to the Public Accounts Committee of the House of Commons which publishes reports and accounts.

and so on. One notable omission is a developed system of regulatory law, which is a common feature of common law jurisdictions. To this I shall return (Chapters 6, p 259 and 12, p 534). Earlier in this chapter it was seen how Community law leaned heavily on the administrative law of Member States. It is time to look more closely at national systems of administrative law.

France

In the previous chapter the constitution of France was examined in an overview of legal and governmental relationships. Part of that relationship in France saw a distinct contribution to the jurisprudence of public law in the form of the system of *droit administratif*. We noted above how a right to good administration through law was one of the general principles of the Community law adopted by the ECJ. In France *Droit Administratif* means not only the whole corpus of administrative law but also the principles which should inform good administration. This body of public law has been the most influential form of law in its influence on EC law, especially in the formative years: this is true not only in terms of procedure but also substance. Forms of relief developed in French public law have been invoked directly in the ECJ eg *detournement de pouvoir* or abuse of power.[58] And what would strike an English person as strange is the fact that grievances of those employed by the Community institutions are dealt with by the one of the Community courts, the CFI, in much the same manner in which the administrative law courts in France are occupied, very significantly, with grievances of public servants. This is an aspect of *droit administratif* shared with other continental systems.

The history and influence of *droit administratif* have imparted a great self confidence in public law scholarship and practice in France although there are frequent assaults and rebuttals on the ideological underpinnings of a branch of law that subjects government and administration to the principles of *legalité*.

---

[58] The leading text in English is N Brown and J Bell *French Administrative Law* (1998, 5th ed). See also J Bell *French Legal Cultures* (2001).

Droit Administratif

Droit administratif has a particularly fascinating history.[59] Before the French Revolution of 1789, France had witnessed continuing conflict between the executive power of the King and powerful Ministers exercised through the Conseil du Roi on the one side and the local Parlements, of which there were twelve, on the other. These latter bodies acted as courts and executive authorities in their locality, including Paris, and frequently interfered with decisions of officers sent out by the chief secretary of state, Cardinal Richelieu, by issuing in effect decrees nullifying their decisions. To counter this interference, in 1641, the Edict of Saint Germain forbade Parlements from hearing and judging any cases involving any business concerned with the state, government and administration. These matters were reserved to the King and his officers. As Brown and Bell observe, conflict nonetheless continued.[60] This history had a significant influence after events in 1789 when in 1790, the Law of 16–24 August 1790 prohibited 'ordinary' courts from interfering in any manner in administration, or calling officials to account for their actions. Breach of this provision in Article 13 was a criminal offence. 'Judicial functions are distinct' the article states 'and will always remain separate from administrative functions'. The article, which continued the spirit of judicial and executive separation witnessed by the Edict of St Germain, was confirmed by decree in 1795. Doubtless there is an appreciable element of Montesquieu's influence in this law and its belief in the desirability of the separation of powers. It resulted in the executive being judge of its own cause; the expulsion of ordinary courts meant that *droit administratif* would emerge to fill the void and provide independent adjudication over the executive and administration.

Indeed, the argument has been made that the French tradition of separate systems of public and private law springs from this conceptual distinction which is not present in the English system, the latter of which therefore lacks the basis on which to build a separate system of public law.[61] The English do not have a refined and distinct system of public law such as the

---

[59]   J Massot and J Marimbert *The Conseil d'Etat* (1988); A-S Meschariakoff *Histoire du droit administratif* (Paris, 1985); *Le Conseil d'Etat 1799–1974* (1974) Centre de la Recherche Scientifique, Paris; for a standard text see: *Droit Administratif* J Rivero and J Waline Dalloz (1998, 17th ed).

[60]   N Brown and J Bell *French Administrative Law* (1998, 5th ed) ch 3.

[61]   J W F Allison *A Continental Distinction in the Common Law* (2000 pb); see also Lord Wilberforce in *Davy v Spelthorne Borough Council* [1983] 3 All ER 278.

French. The French system was thought through and conceptualised in order to advance *service public* and protect the citizen. The English approach fastened 'not on principles but on remedies'.[62] Some forms of relief were truly constitutional in their significance for liberty: habeas corpus. But judges moulded other forms of public law remedy to focus on proprietorial or narrowly focused forms of relief. Nevertheless, English judges have developed a sophisticated and powerful body of judicial review which has borrowed liberally from European legal thought, if not noticeably from the French system. While it has grown immeasurably in scope and self confidence in the last thirty years, it would be wrong to describe it as a separate system in the sense of French public law. 'But by an extension of remedies and a flexible procedure it can be said that something resembling a system of public law is being developed.'[63]

THE CONSEIL D'ETAT (http://www.conseil-etat.fr/)

The story of how the *Conseil d'Etat* was created by Napoleon to oversee the administration, to act as a drafter of laws and regulations, to operate as an advisory body and as a body 'to resolve difficulties which might occur in the course of administration' is well recounted by Brown and Bell.[64] The vacuum created by the prohibition on ordinary courts dealing with administrative affairs described above was filled, to some extent, by allowing complaints to be made to Ministers with a further appeal to the *Conseil d'Etat*. They were not, however, acting in any sense as a court of law but merely advised the Head of State.[65] In the Law of 24 May 1872 the *Conseil d'Etat* was given the power to issue judgments in the name of the French people, as with other French courts. Until the development of the doctrine of *astreinte*[66] which in 1995 was extended to the lower administrative courts, it had no means of enforcing its judgment. Before seeking to censure this feature of the court's operation, we should recall that it was only after the decision in *M v Home Office*[67] that English courts could issue an injunction

---

[62]   Lord Wilberforce in *Davy v Spelthorne Borough Council* [1983] 3 All ER 278 at 285.

[63]   Lord Wilberforce in *Davy v Spelthorne Borough Council* [1983] 3 All ER 278 at 285. See S Flogaïtis *Administrative Law et Droit Administratif* (1986) Paris.

[64]   N Brown and J Bell *French Administrative Law* (1998, 5th ed) ch 3.

[65]   The Bill of Rights 1689 allowed petitioning of the Crown without punishment and would invariably in important cases be dealt with by a Minister.

[66]   Which allows fines to be imposed where a judgment is not complied with.

[67]   [1993] 3 All ER 537, HL. Previous case law where injunctions were issued were overruled by *Factortame v Secretary of State for Transport* [1989] 2 All ER 692,

against a Minister in his official capacity and would hold a Minister liable for contempt as a servant of the Crown where he breached a coercive order of the court or an injunction. The courts would not enforce contempt proceedings in England; enforcement would be by Parliament.

By 1889 in *Cadot*, the *Conseil d'Etat* allowed complainants to come to it directly rather than having to go to a Minister first. It is interesting to compare the practice of many public sector ombudsmen in the UK who either have to receive a complaint via an MP and not directly (the Parliamentary Commissioner) or who have to ensure that grievances have been made to the authority complained about before coming to the ombudsman.[68] It started to sit as a *public* court in 1831 giving published judgments with reasons. It is, as far as any court can be, truly relatively independent. Its lack of independence was, however, criticised by Dicey who believed it was the executive standing in judgment of itself, a view which he modified.

The *Conseil d'Etat* today stands at the apex of a court structure involving *tribunaux administratifs* which are courts and not tribunals as we would understand that term[69] and which deal with most cases of first instance, and at appeal level the regional *cours administratives d'appel*. There are 36 *tribunaux administratifs* and 7 appeal courts. The *Conseil d'Etat* has a small first instance and last instance jurisdiction amounting to just over 2000 cases in 1998 and a supervisory jurisdiction. The *tribunaux administratifs* dealt with almost 111,000 cases and appeal courts 11,651.[70] The Conseil still maintains its role as a government adviser on Bills and draft regulations and other matters. [71] In fact its judicial business is dealt with by one section of six sections and is itself split into various sub-sections. The non-judicial sections are mainly involved in advisory work

---

HL which was itself subsequently overruled in effect by *Factortame (No 2)* [1991] 1 All ER 70, HL when the case returned from the ECJ: see p 194 et seq below. The Crown Proceedings Act 1947 took away a right from the Scots to obtain coercive orders against the Crown that the Scots claimed always to have possessed: Prosser and Mullan (1995) *European Public Law* 46 and cf *Davidson v Scottish Ministers* 2002 SLT 420 Inner House.

68   And note the provision in the Employment Act 2002, s 32.
69   With significant lay representation.
70   J Bell *French Administrative Cultures* pp 31–2.
71   The CE has been very critical of measures allowing greater decentralisation within France, even though such measures, as 'organic laws', would have to be approved by the Conseil Constitutionnel (Ch 2, p 69 et seq).

relating to home affairs, government finance, public works, social matters and a *Section du Rapport et des Etudes* which is responsible for research and publications including the annual report. It operates as a 'think-tank' casting an appraising eye on future developments. It also overseas the execution of judgments.

There is also an Ombudsman, the Mediateur, and a variety of in-house and other administrative bodies dealing with grievances. The Mediateur shares the characteristic of the British Parliamentary Ombudsman in that he may only be approached via an elected MP (Deputy).[72] Interest in alternative dispute resolution has grown and efforts to enhance the use of conciliation procedures before going to court have been common-place. An implementing decree of 1991 established a national conciliation committee for conciliation in the subject area of public contracts made by state and public administrative bodies and in 1995 the Prime Minister issued a circular emphasising the need to attempt to settle disputes before going to court.

The recruits to the *Conseil d'Etat* emerge from the Ecole Nationale d'Administration.[73] They are trained as administrators and lawyers but generally only those going to the *Conseil d'Etat*, the best of the graduates, will actively be involved in both administrative and judicial business. Recruits to the *tribunaux administratifs* (which were established in 1953) and the *Cours Administratives d'Appel* (1989) are more focused on judicial business alone although the seven presidents of the *Cours Administratives d'Appels* are conseillers of the Cd'E. Change and leadership are very much driven by the *Conseil d'Etat* in Paris although appeal courts are contributing to important developments in legal doctrine, in for instance, liability. The judges at the top level in the *Conseil d'Etat* are fully trained as high level administrators and more willing therefore, to make evaluations based on appraisal of factual situations or as Bell suggests in 'manifest error in evaluation' than would English judges brought up in a tradition of reluctance to appraise subjective expertise or facts in the absence of a

---

[72] Sri Lanka was the only other country to impose this inhibition. The House of Commons Public Administration Committee has recommended that this practice be terminated and access should be direct. In 1999, the Mediateur received 51,189. He covers local government and other public authorities. The Parliamentary Ombudsman in the UK received 1,721 cases in 2000–2001 but these only cover central government and specified agencies.

[73] J Bell *French Administrative Cultures* pp 30 et seq.

glaring error of law. The HRA 1998 (see Chapter 9) will prompt a more exacting scrutiny by British and Northern Irish judges but they are not necessarily skilled administrators or trained as such.

The method of Droit Administratif

Droit administratif is not codified.[74] *Droit adminisitratif* relies upon a case based methodology and the legal principles are judicially developed, not unlike common law, although the strict doctrine of *stare decisis* or precedent does not apply to the *Conseil d'Etat*. In this it follows a continental tradition. The courts cannot issue generally applicable and binding rules. To allow the judges to do so would contravene the separation of powers by affording them a legislative role. The decisions of the *Conseil d'Etat* in a specific case are binding on the lower courts and the administration as are the decisions of the appeal courts. There is a settled practice, however, of lower courts following judgments of the *Conseil d'Etat* whose judgments may only be reversed by the *Conseil d'Etat*. There will be an overwhelming persuasive force in decisions of the *Conseil d'Etat*.[75] Nonetheless, the decisions of the administrative courts are regarded by authorities as binding law and the authorities that breach them suffer the same consequences as if they had breached written law. Where a decision cannot stand with other inconsistent decisions of the *Conseil d'Etat*, they must be revoked even though the decision has not been challenged in court. It must be said that until comparatively recently the courts have had no means of enforcing their decisions (see below). As we have seen elsewhere (Chapter 1) the argument has been made that in England under the influence of the Woolf reforms to our civil procedure, *stare decisis* is itself subject to transformation so that it no longer operates as a constraint, if that is the right word, on judicial decision making. Something more like a civil system is developing whereby decisions are made on the merits of the case under broad principle.

The reason why case law which is not built on precedent is preferred is because it is felt that the jurisprudence of the administrative courts should

---

74   Although areas of substantive public law as opposed to judicial review and public liability are codified, such as planning and development: *Code de L'Urbanisme: Commenté* Dalloz (2000). The *Code Administratif* Dalloz (2000) is a collection of relevant laws and regulations.

75   J Bell *French Administrative Cultures* p 188 and specifically tax cases.

be as flexible as possible to do justice between what are often very unequal parties: the state in its various guises and individuals whether citizen, alien, corporate or individual person.

Crucial as the case law has been in the development of French administrative law, that law has also been built on constitutional fundamental rights which have been given written expression since the Declaration of the Rights of Man in 1789 and which were also added to and completed by the 1946 Constitution. Legislation also contains provisions on administrative law: as well as the usual areas concerning immigration, the environment, the civil service and the law of public contracts – *contrats administratifs* – has the *Codes des Marchés Publics* which, as in every other Member State, has to take account of the Directives on public procurement (see Chapter 12). Government contracts in England has had remarkably little legislative interference because it was regarded as regulated by the same law as private contracts – common law.[76] This Code is supplemented by standards clause contracts, *Cahiers des Charges*, and by very significant case law principles developed by the *Conseil d'Etat* (below).

The subject matter of administrative law is also contained in regulations of government, *ordonnances,*[77] bye-laws, and decisions affecting an individual or a group. It is usually through regulations that Community law is implemented into French law.

The procedures

To examine a French administrative court's proceedings is a strange experience for an English lawyer. The claimant and their lawyer play a very limited role, sometimes appearing to be little more than observing a discussion involving them. Like the procedure in German administrative courts (below), the case proceeds by an inquisitorial method. A rapporteur is assigned to the case and the rapporteur's role is to enquire into the issues involved in a case, establishing the facts by an investigatory process. This takes place at the end of the written submissions of the parties. There are no barriers such as public interest immunity which apply in litigation in

---

[76] Cf the Local Government (Contracts) Act 1997 for England, Wales and Scotland.
[77] See Ch 2, p 69 et seq on the division of law making powers in France.

England to deny the litigant against a public authority access to documents, increasingly in criminal trials. The rapporteur drafts a report on the facts, a summary of the evidence, the law and a draft judgment. This report will be reviewed by a more senior member of the sub-section to which the rapporteur is assigned (the *reviseur)* before being presented to the *séance d'instruction*. The rapporteur as well as presenting his report of the law and facts will also suggest a solution. The case will be discussed by the whole sous section and the rapport is not shown to the parties to the case and is not made public.[78] The case proceeds to judgment which may involve a variety of possibilities: the sous section alone, joint sections or the presidents of all sous sections involved in litigation or the presidents of all sections of the *Conseil d'Etat*. Procedures at this stage are driven by complexity and the importance of changes in the law: as for instance when in *Nicolo* the *Conseil d'Etat* changed the approach adopted towards EC Directives adopted in *Cohn-Bendit* and decided that the court could examine the conformity of domestic laws with Community law.[79]

The procedure follows various stages and perhaps the most interesting to an English observer, because we have no comparable analogue, is that which involves the *Commissaire du Gouvernement*. The role of the Commissaire is to present an independent assessment of the facts and law as raised by the issue before the *Conseil d'Etat*. He or she is in no sense a government representative. The docket will be handed to the Commissaire when the *séance d'instruction* has completed its role. S/he may conduct further enquiries where s/he believes these to be incomplete. The Commissaire will then produce a report which gives a clear summary of the case to those who may be a member of the court who have not so far participated in the case. Secondly, a Commissaire will seek to align a proposed solution to the development of the case law in a manner which may well presage the future progress of the case law.[80] The Commissaire's conclusions are published and very often become the repository of the law. This is all the more important because the judgments of the court are precise and somewhat clipped documents containing no analysis of the case law or discussion of relevant principles although in more recent years they have tended to be longer. The Commissaire's conclusions are invariably, although not always, followed by the court and his or her conclusions are read to the court in the first part of the judgment known as

---

[78]   J Bell *French Administrative Cultures* p159.
[79]   Chapter 2, p 75 et seq.
[80]   N Brown and J Bell *French Administrative Law* (1998, 5th ed) p 105.

the audience publique. As the name suggests, this is held in public. It is followed by the *délibéré* which sits in private with the Commissaire in attendance and who may be asked for any necessary clarification. Otherwise, s/he does not participate in the *délibéré*. There is no published record of the votes. Brown and Bell describe the secrecy of the *délibéré* as less total than that of a judgment of the ECJ where not even the Advocats General may attend.[81] Interestingly, the *Commissaire du Gouvernement* was the inspiration for the Avocat General in the ECJ who presents an opinion to the ECJ and CFI and which often have a powerful influence on the courts' decisions and the subterranean shifts of the law. They often make wide-ranging reference to academic work as well as judgments.

Nevertheless, despite this influence the *Commissaire du Gouvernement* on the ECJ's procedure, the procedures in the *Conseil d'Etat* were held by the CHR in *Kress*[82] to be a breach of Article 6 of the Convention insofar as the submissions of the *Commissaire du Gouvernement* were not communicated in advance to the applicants; a breach of the fair trial provision also arose from the participation of the *Commissaire du Gouvernement* in the deliberations of the *Conseil d'Etat*.[83] In Emesa Sugar the ECJ ruled that the absence of an opportunity to comment on the Advocate General's opinion is not a breach of Article 6(1) of the ECHR.[84] The CHR had ruled that a breach of Article 6 would occur where a party in a civil or criminal trial was not allowed to have knowledge and comment upon 'an independent member of the national legal service's submissions filed with a view to influencing the court.'[85] The ECJ emphasised that the Advocate General has the same status as judges and is a member of the Court, his Opinion is published and his role is public. There is an 'organic and functional link between the Advocate General and the Court.'[86] The AG does not participate in deliberations. The *Commissaire du Gouvernement* is considered, as Bell expresses it, a part of the 'judicial team.'

---

81 N Brown and J Bell *French Administrative Law* (1998, 5th ed) p 112.
82 *Kress v France* (7 June 2001, unreported), ECtHR.
83 (2001) *Les Petites Affiches* 3 October p 13; (2001) 7-8 *Actualité Juridique du Droit Administratif* 675; 3 *Revue de Droit Public* 895; cited in N Lenoir ch 17 of *The British Contribution of the Twenty-first Century: The British Academy Lectures* ed B Markesinis (Hart, 2002).
84 Case C-17/98 *Emesa Sugar (Free Zone) NV v Aruba* [2000] ECR I-665.
85 *Vermeulen v Belgium* 2 February 1996, Reports 1996-I, 224.
86 Paragraphs 14–16. See Cases C-50/96 and C-270 and 271/97 *Deutsche Telekom AG v Schröder* [2000] ECR I-743.

An important point to reiterate is that the procedure in *droit administratif* does not meet the obstacle of public interest immunity as is the case in England in cases involving judicial review. The rapporteur, as was seen above, is not barred from access to documents or files unless the matter is one which the administrative courts cannot examine such as an act of state or Parliamentary proceedings. One of the great obstacles in English law litigation involving public authorities is the difficulty of obtaining information from public bodies which might assist a litigant.[87] There is a reluctance to allow disclosure of documents or cross examination in judicial review cases in England because this would slow down the process of the court exercising a supervisory jurisdiction.[88]

While English courts have since the decision in *M v The Home Office* improved the position of those seeking interim relief against officers of the Crown, the position of interim relief in France had caused serious problems leading to criticism from the CHR of serious delay in cases where compensation for injury caused by HIV contaminated blood was not paid in the lifetime of the victims.[89] Reforms on this subject have been introduced.[90]

Substance

In the substantive *droit administratif* also there has been a pronounced influence of the French system on EC law, especially when one examines the grounds of judicial review (see below). French *droit administratif* is a system: doubtless with its own foibles but nevertheless a system which the English could not have claimed for their own branch of administrative law until comparatively recently. In English law there is still a division between public law and private law even in cases involving public authorities. Tortious claims, for instance, are common law proceedings on the private law side even for those torts which only public authorities may commit such as misfeasance of public office. Contract is a matter for private

---

[87]   P Birkinshaw *Government and Information: the Law relating to Access, Disclosure and their Regulation* (2001) ch 9.

[88]   *R (G) v Ealing London Borough Council* [2002] 17 LS Gaz R 37: cross examination permissible under new Part 54 CPR 1998.

[89]   J Bell (2001) European Public Law 329.

[90]   J Bell (2001) European Public Law 329.

law – there is no public law for contracts in England although Public Private Partnerships may be getting close to such an entity.[91]

In France, there is a public law of contract and a public law of tort as well as private law liability. It is not always entirely apparent which court has jurisdiction in a matter and there are some arbitrary distinctions drawn. The basic division of public and private liability was drawn up in *Blanco* in 1873 where a road injury arising in the course of performing a public service aimed at satisfying the public need should fall within public law. Today, all road accidents are classified as private law. In matters of dispute as to the governing law, public or private, the *Tribunal des Conflits* will determine the issue. This body comprises four judges from the *Conseil d'Etat* and four from the civil court of appeal, the Cour de Cassation with the Minister of Justice casting the crucial vote in the case of a 'tie'.[92]

All acts of illegality are tortious although the quantum of damages is restricted to actual harm suffered. Where no damage is suffered, there is no liability for damages. Liability is based upon fault, and where a sensitive or difficult task is being performed requiring finely balanced judgments eg policing[93] or tax investigations into fraud or regulatory activities in eg, the financial regulation of a bank, the courts require *faute lourde* or serious fault as opposed to *faute simple*. This requirement of serious fault in cases involving very difficult judgments was confirmed in November 2001 when the *Conseil d'Etat* differed in its approach to a case concerning banking regulation from the Administrative Court of Appeal in Paris. The appeal court had held that *faute simple* was sufficient. The *Conseil d'Etat* required *faute lourde* but found the regulatory body, the *Commission Bancaire,* in breach of their duty to that degree of fault and liable.[94] *Faute lourde* reflects

---

[91] Otherwise known as Private Finance Initiatives: see the Public Accounts Committee HC 460 (2001–02) 'Managing the Relationship to Secure a Successful Partnership in PFI Projects.' M Freedland in C McCrudden ed *Regulation and Deregulation* (1999) ch 8.

[92] Brown and Bell describe an incident in 1997 when a civil judge resigned from the Tribunal when the Minister gave the casting vote, describing this as 'political intervention.' The judge recommended the President of the *Conseil Constitutionnel* should fill this casting role: p 150.

[93] Not all policing is covered by *droit adminisratif.*

[94] Conseil d'Etat 30 November 2001, Kechichian, Ajda (2002) 136; See M Andenas and D Fairgrieve (2002) ICLQ 757. The Commission was not liable for the whole of the damage. The facts are very similar to the *Three Rivers* litigation in England which concerned the aftermath of the collapse of the BCCI bank and allegations

the difficulty involved in the acts of judgment in such activities. There are legions of cases where what is at issue is a question of personal liability or *faute de service* ie, is the public service liable for the wrong that has been done because it was done in the course of delivering a public service or has the public servant gone outside the range of his duty and responsibility.[95]

Liability may also be based on a theory of risk: that in pursuing a dangerous activity, the state or a public undertaker should assume the risk where injury is caused by the activity or in the course of performing it. The risk should not be borne by the individual. Furthermore, pursuit of a legitimate objective by lawful means may cause harm to an individual. In such cases, equality before the law may provide a reason for compensating an innocent victim of such activity.[96]

In England, an illegality is not per se compensable; there must be an interference with a private right for an action to be tortious. This might be constituted by a trespass where an invasion of one's proprietorial rights was based on an illegal instrument or by a false imprisonment following unlawful action. The illegality itself is not actionable although it may be a ground for a remedy under judicial review. In France, an illegality is compensable.

Brown and Bell make the point that French courts, based on their experience of liability and its wide base in France had no difficulty accepting liability for the wrongful implementation of Community law Directives.[97] We saw in Chapter 2 how there was a reluctance to accept liability where a Directive was not implemented at all.

of misfeasance of public office: negligence would have been very difficult to establish based on English authorities. Andenas and Fairgrieve examine further cases on banking regulation in Italy and Germany. In *Three Rivers*, the Law Lords ruled there was no breach of Community law in that the Banking Directive in question did not create rights for individual depositors which the Bank of England had breached by failing to fulfil those obligations to protect depositors: *Three Rivers District Council v Bank of England* [2000] 3 All ER 1, HL. The UK Parliamentary Ombudsman has found maladministration by the Department of Trade and Industry in the famous Barlow Clowes affair: see Ch 10, p 441.

95   See Article 288 [215] EC and Article 12 Protocol on the Privileges and Immunities of the European Communities.

96   N Brown and J Bell *French Administrative Law* (1998, 5th ed) pp 198–200.

97   N Brown and J Bell *French Administrative Law* (1998, 5th ed) p 191 and SA Cabinet Revert et Badelon Dangeville (CE Ass 30 October 1996).

Contrats Administratifs

Not only is there a specific law of delict or tort in France for assessing the liability of public bodies, as we have seen, but there is also a separate law of public contracts or *contrats administratifs* as it is known. There are Community Directives on public purchasing which have regulated the pre-contractual stages of tendering for contracts by public authorities and in some cases private bodies (utilities) which have been given special powers. The French public law has, however, developed separate principles to govern the contractual relations between public bodies and private contractors from those which apply in private contracts. Public bodies may enter either private law contracts or public law contracts whose resolution in the event of dispute will go to the relevant court. Jurisdiction in one particular court may be difficult to establish. Where a contract fulfils a public service need or is characterised by particular terms which are not contained in a normal commercial contract, the tendency would be to classify them as *contrats administratifs*. There are very detailed codes on public contracting in France as well as documents known as *cahiers des charges* setting out detailed provisions on contract allocation procedures and contractual terms.[98]

As the law of public contracts has been shaped in France to give expression to the public interest, the judicial contribution has been to develop principles which allow the courts to adjust and amend contracts to reflect that interest. The doctrine of *fait du prince* allows a contractor to seek relief where the basis of a contract has changed by governmental or public action and the contractor could be faced with a harsh bargain as a consequence. Where a public authority alters the terms of a contract under its powers, the contractor may be entitled to an indemnity for additional duties not originally contained in the agreement. *Imprevision* allows the terms of a contract to be adjusted where unforeseen events which have not resulted from action of the public authority alter the basis of the contract making it uneconomical for the private contractor to perform his part. He may claim an indemnity under this doctrine eg allowing him to demand extra charges for a service.

---

[98] See J Arnould (2001) Pub Proc LR 324 and the 2001 reforms to public contracts' law. This code continued the role of advisory committees to attempt amicable settlement of disputes although they are rarely used.

The French law is far more developed in relation to contracts made by public bodies than English law appears to be. The area of government contracting has seen a great deal of interest in public law challenges by way of judicial review (p 546 et seq below). The Public Private Partnerships which were referred to above have projected the use by UK government and public authorities of contract as a means of carrying on traditional areas of public activity such as public transport, education, hospital provision and road building. These are usually allocated through the most exclusive or secretive procedures allowed under the European Directives, the negotiated procedures. One of the great problems caused by the use by government of contract to achieve its objectives in realisation of policy, service delivery and management is that third parties are not able legally to challenge the contracts. Recent reforms in England concerning privity of contract are not likely to relieve the problem because the object of challenge is usually the terms of the contract and these traditionally are seen in English law as a matter of private law between the contracting parties or persons on whose behalf they contracted or who should benefit from the contract; this is not seen as a question of public law. There are signs that courts in England are approaching this subject with a keener sense that public power is being exercised in such cases and that more than the interests of the contractual parties are involved (see Chapter 12; but see Ch 12 note 126). Traditionally, the public interest aspects in England are catered for by the National Audit Office (or the Audit Commission for local government and NHS bodies) which together with the Public Accounts Committee of the House of Commons, has helped to formulate many of the rules of good government practice in this area; traditionally, the courts have made very little contribution and litigation has been sparse.

In France, as well as the fact that the courts have shown a greater willingness to interpret contracts as falling within the realm of *contrats administratifs*, thereby affording a greater opportunity to attend to the public interest, the courts have also displayed a readiness to allow a judicial review based on *recours pour excès de pouvoirs* (below) by non parties to the contract. In *Wajs et Monnier*[99] the question at stake concerned a motorway concession and applicants for *recours* claimed that the terms of the *cahiers des charges* between the concessionary who would manage the motorway and the public authority meant that they, as users of the motorway, would have to pay for various charges which the consessionary would pass on

[99]   CE Ass 30 October 1996.

to them. He would pass them on because he had to reimburse the public body who had imposed these charges on him – for policing the motorway and for supervising the contract – under the contract.[100]

Judicial review

As noted above, the EC borrowed from the French system directly in relation to judicial review. Underpinning the law of judicial review in France are the *Principes Generaux du Droit*. These are absorbed into Community law via the *acquis communautaire* and also as part of the general corpus of principles of legality underpinning all western legal systems. *Les Principes* are a part of the body of principles which constitute the underlying assumption of administration through law and legality which has informed the development of Community law. *Les Principes* emerged from constitutional doctrines from 1789 and 1946 concerning equality and liberty and the fundamental rights of man. They are essential to the notion of legality although they are not expressly incorporated in any code. They nonetheless inform the content of codes (lois) and must be invoked unless expressly overridden. They have been heavily invoked by the *Conseil d'Etat* since the second world war and are also seen in the operation of the Conseil Constitutionnel and its decisions although the latter tends to base its decisions in legal texts as opposed to judicial creativity. As we saw in the last chapter, such creativity is not unknown in the Constitutional Court. They include such principles as: the presumption of liberty; equality in terms of treatment, sharing of burdens; fair procedures and what the English would call natural justice; judicial protection and the separation of powers; non-retroactivity; and legal certainty (*securité juridique*): in short the doing of justice by proper and fair process. Additional protection has been given for human rights, especially as influenced by the ECHR, family rights, social and economic rights and collective rights such as environmental rights.

Interestingly, although influential in Community law and the shaping of its General Principles of Law (above p 95 et seq) the *Conseil d'Etat* have recently rejected the principle of legitimate expectation as a principle of domestic French law where no question of Community law is involved. It is a doctrine of 'Community law' taken from German law and is present in English and German law. The Administrative Court of Strasbourg had ruled that such a doctrine did exist in domestic law basically in order to protect

[100]   N Brown and J Bell *French Administrative Law* (1998, 5th ed) pp 202 et seq.

individuals against revocation of administrative decisions or rules (*confiance legitime*) but this was rejected by the Conseil d'Etat (CE).[101] It had also been cold-shouldered by the Conseil Constitutionnel. The decision is reminiscent of Laws J in *First City Trading*[102] where a rigid division was drawn between domestic law and Community law. As a leading French commentator has asked: does it make sense to have two different approaches in domestic and in Community law?[103] It is reminiscent of the situation in England where there was a divergence of approach in English courts when they were dealing with questions of interim relief under Community law and domestic law and when they were dealing with unjust enrichment.[104] It needs only to be said that English courts are giving a constitutional status to fundamental principles such as human rights protection and general principles of review have been invoked in English courts though its basis would have to be domestic law where no question of Community law is involved.[105] We saw in Chapter 2 that the ECJ is more circumspect in applying fundamental rights protection than many domestic courts might be. It is perhaps strange that such circumspection should attend the invocation of legitimate expectation.

The relief sought in administrative law courts in France is by way of a claim (a *recours*) for one of four forms of litigation, the first two being the most important. If a court is asked to annul an administrative act as unlawful, the applicant will seek *contentieux de l'annulation* (an action for annulment). Where an administrative jurisdiction is involved, where the administrative body possesses *une juridiction* the relief sought is by way of a *recours en cassation* to the *Conseil d'Etat*. In the *contentieux de pleine juridiction* the applicant is seeking a revision of a decision, not simply its annulment, and damages.

The grounds of review in *droit administratif* find their almost exact analogues in Community law. In Community law it will be recalled that under the Treaty we find the following grounds of judicial review of Community institutions named in Article 230 [173] EC: lack of competence; vice de forme; infringement of the Treaty or of a rule of law; and finally misuse of powers.

---

101   *Societé Mosellane de tractions* CE 9 May 2001.
102   *R v MAFF, ex p First City Trading* [1997] 1 CMLR 250; see p 352 et seq.
103   R Errera (2002) *Public Law* 186 at 187.
104   *Factortame* [1989] 2 All ER 692, HL and *M v Home Office* [1993] 3 All ER 537.
105   *Ex p Pierson* [1997] 3 All ER 577, HL and *Ex p Simms* [1999] 3 All ER 400, HL and *ex p Daly* [2001] UKHL 26, [2001] 3 All ER 433; see p 343 et seq.

Under the *droit administratif* the following grounds for review have been developed by the administrative courts: *L'inexistence:* where a decision obviously lacks an essential component it will be declared void. It is equivalent to 'gross and flagrant' abuse of power: it 'bears illegality upon its forehead' as is said in English case law.[106]

The second ground is *Incompetence* and concerns cases where authority is lacking to make a decision or to regulate in an area. Its analogue in English law is substantive ultra vires. Unlike *l'inexistence*, a factual situation and the relevant and available powers do have to be interpreted to establish the legality of what has been done.

Vicce de forme covers serious procedural defects in a decision as well as breaches of a fair procedure ie not allowing a party to be heard before an adverse decision to his or her interests is taken or by not providing an opportunity to know why a decision is being taken or not being informed of the grounds on which a decision is being made.

Violation de la loi is the fourth ground of review and it is sub-divided into three groups:
1. *erreur de droit* which involves use of a wrong text (law/authorisation) or misinterpretation of applicable laws;
2. *inexactitude materielle des faits* this allows the administrative court to check and assess the facts of a case. It must be tied in with the extensive investigations and role of the rapporteurs which was highlighted above (p 119 et seq);
3. *qualification juridique des faits*: this involves the legal categorisation of facts and errors in judgment in the application of the law to the facts. It has been summed up as the legal categorisation of facts.[107] Measures must be appropriate and justified – proportionality; law must be applied to facts capable of coming within the legal category. Eg do the facts of a case amount to 'misconduct' to merit punishment. Have proper inferences been drawn from the facts. Again, the rapport is essential in establishing the factual basis and circumstances of decisions or actions.

Detournement de pouvoir is the last ground of review and is concerned with such items as deliberate and fraudulent acts or omissions – the 'internal

---

[106] *Guigon* TC 27 June 1966; *Maurice* (CE 15 May 1981).
[107] J.Bell (1986) Public Law 99, 103.

legality' of a decision.[108] 'Abuse of power' is an approximate translation. The procedures adopted in the *droit administratif* allow the court to concentrate upon subjective motivations rather than ostensible justification. Are the motivations directed by an ulterior purpose, or not in the public interest, so that the power conferred is in law abused? We saw above how it had influenced Community law. It should also be recalled that the dossier produced by the rapporteur will allow for a far more exacting examination of subjective factors in a decision than would usually be the case in England, for instance. There has been a tendency in England, still maintained, to ask is the situation 'ex facie' valid and if so to leave it alone. The nature of English judicial review is not going to arm the court with material with which it will be allowed to investigate subjective motives. If evidence of improper motive comes to light, then a court in England may act accordingly. Rarely does such evidence come to light as a direct consequence of the review procedure. Where a question of human rights is concerned, an English court will exercise 'anxious scrutiny' (Chapter 8). *Detournement de pouvoir* has declined in importance in judicial review and courts have tended to concentrate on *violation de la loi* and the absence of essential or probative evidence or facts in a decision rather than examining internal states of mind.

Discretion and merits

One of the points to impress upon the reader is the fact that in *droit administratif*, the merits ('*l'opportunité*') of decisions are not subject to review. This reflects the position in England and in the Community. But, where the merits involve an unacceptable decision, courts will be ready to assert some forms of control. This is a widely shared phenomenon throughout jurisdictions. Where the subject matter of a discretion makes it inappropriate for judicial review, control will not be exercised but such actes de gouvernement are tightly confined and defined. The Conseil d'Etat (CE) has reviewed discretion in some highly sensitive cases where at the time in question, English courts would have been most unlikley to review[109]

---

[108]   N Brown and J Bell *French Administrative Law* (1998, 5th ed) p 245.

[109]   Barel CE 28 May 1954; Imbach (CE 14 May 1948). *Barel* concerned a refusal to allow individuals to sit the entrance examination to the elite Ecole Nationale d'Administration and where the Minister refused to give reasons or hand over relevant files. It was suspected that the refusal was because of suspected Communist affiliations of the candidates. The decision was quashed by the CE and produced

because evidence was not given for decisions or files which were demanded were not disclosed. Their powers of review where a discretion in a loi is given in limited terms is based upon the use of the loi by the authorities and the motives used by the authorities in exercising discretion. The CE has shown some reluctance to review questions concerning aliens and technical questions on, according to Brown and Bell, whether a wine deserves an appellation controlée (but it has reviewed the areas designated for certain *appellations d'origine controlée*).[110] In such matters, like English courts, the French courts will review for manifest unreasonableness or disproportionate exercise of power, even in deportation cases. Where a decision outrages ordinary principles of justice where it reveals a 'manifest error in the assessment of the facts', the courts have been prepared to quash decisions.

However, in the famous *Ville Nouvelle Est* decision,[111] the CE was at pains to emphasise that it was prepared to assess whether a decision on planning matters was justified by the evidence before the planning officials and in the application of a test akin to proportionality to decide whether the decision was justified. It agreed with the Minister's assessment of the evidence and upheld his decision on compulsory purchase to allow a new residential area and a university to be built. It is clear, especially in planning and transport decisions that the CE in particular will draw up *le bilan* – a balance sheet – to assess the pros and cons in a decision to ensure that it is made on a proper basis and analysis of the facts. Quite understandably, there are many politicians and officials who see this as a trespass of the courts into their domain: the assessment of the merits. As in cases of proportionality in England and in Community law, the court will justify its action by saying it is assessing *how* the decision was made, not *why*.

Enforcement

Dicey made much of the fact that in England our rights are common law rights enforced through the ordinary courts. Judgments of courts are enforceable against individuals and institutions in a non-discriminatory

---

a presumption in law that giving no reasons meant acting on bad reasons. In *Imbach* a passport was refused because of alleged Nazi collaboration in the Second World War. The allegation was not supported and the decision was quashed.

110 N Brown and J Bell *French Administrative Law* (1998, 5th ed) p 257.

111 CE 28 May 1971.

manner without fear or favour. In fact the Crown in its personal capacity still enjoys a general immunity from suit in Her Majesty's courts. 'Crown' means two things. First of all, it signifies Her Majesty the Queen. Her immunity is still inviolable. Secondly, 'Crown' represents the organised institutions of government, ie Ministers, civil servants and the departments they preside over or work in, along with other agencies designated by statute as Crown bodies.[112] In case of doubt as to which body should be proceeded against, the Attorney General may be proceeded against. The Crown Proceedings Act 1947 allowed the Crown to be sued in its representative capacity, ie as the executive – the government, where prior to that Act actions could not be maintained against the executive in their official capacity unless the Crown consented. There were limitations but the 1947 legislation allowed government departments to be sued in tort in circumstances where ordinary individuals could be sued. It was always the case that a Minister or a named official could be sued in tort for their personal wrong-doing performed in the line of their duty. A command of the King was no defence to illegality. This personal liability was one of the basic features of the English concept of the rule of law, believed Dicey. *M v Home Office* was crucial in that it established that an injunction could be issued against a Minister, or other Crown servant, under judicial review proceedings when they were proceeded against in their *official capacity* and not simply their *personal capacity*. Enforcement would take place through Parliament even though contempt had been established by failing to comply with a coercive order of the Court.

Decisions of the *Conseil d'Etat* were unenforceable – the *Conseil d'Etat* was historically a purely advisory body even when it was authorised to give decisions in the name of the French people. This had a clear influence on Community law doctrine in that judgments of the ECJ are not enforceable by that court, and neither are judgments of the CFI enforceable by the CFI. Judicial review of Community measures or Decisions will have immediate effect, ie nullity though an exception was seen above (see p 106 above). Judgments in enforcement proceedings brought by the Commission against a Member State are declaratory judgments only, although they are binding and it is assumed they will be obeyed. Articles 228 and 229 EC introduced powers to impose financial penalties where judgments were not complied with (above p 109 et seq).

---

112   *Town Investments Ltd v Department of the Environment* [1977] 1 All ER 813, HL; *M v Home Office* [1993] 3 All ER 537, HL and Lord Templeman's vigorous invocation of the rule of law.

In France, the practice of *astreinte* may be employed to impose daily fines where a judgment debt is not complied with. It may also be imposed as a means of enforcing a successful judicial review of an administrative decision and in this capacity has been invoked to force the Prime Minister to revalue family allowance payments.[113] Judgment debts and fines may be enforced against public bodies. *Astreinte* cannot be applied for until the authority has failed to comply with judgment for six months. It may be requested by either the individual applicant or by the *Section du Rapport* (see above). The invocation of *astreinte* in a judicial review application may not be straightforward. It may be awarded where there is a failure to act under a decision in the applicant's favour or where there is a failure to follow mandatory legal duties, a failure which harms the applicant. *Astreinte* was introduced in 1980 for the CE and for the *tribunaux administratifs* and appeal courts in 1995. It was a procedure that originated in the civil courts. The remedy was applied against central government for the first time in 1997.

Human rights and the ECHR in France

In Professor Schwarze's edited work *Administrative Law under European Influence*[114] many of the national reporters express almost uniform agreement about the growing and considerable influence of the ECHR. The French reporter in fact expresses the view that any 'Europeanisation' of French public law has been through the influence of the ECHR rather than the Community.[115] In the case of the UK, the ECHR has been incorporated now by statute. It was ratified in 1974 by France and individual access to the then HR Commission was only allowed from 1981. The ECHR is a treaty obligation in France, and so it takes priority over loi but is subordinate to the Constitution. Readers will recall the discussion on these points in Chapter 2 (p 74 et seq). The commentator for France in fact spoke of a feeling in France until recently that Community law was seen as something eroding

---

[113] N Brown and J Bell *French Administrative Law* (1998, 5th ed) p 116 and UNDAF, CE 14 March 1997.

[114] It continues *On the Convergence of the Administrative Laws of EU Member States* (1996).

[115] J F Flauss in Schwarze *Administrative Law under European Influence: On the Convergence of the Administrative Laws of EU Member States* (1996) ch 2, p 31; and see Flauss (2000) *Revue francaise de droit constitutionnel* 843.

the specificity of 'our administrative law'.[116] The ECHR has, however, had a greater influence on general procedures and the Conseil d'Etat has referred to the Convention in an increasing number of cases.[117] The Cour de Cassation has been influenced by the ECHR Article 7 (prohibition on retroactive effect of criminal offence) in a judgment concerning the criminal liability of President Chirac prior to his mandate.[118]

Flauss spoke of the EC influencing specific areas such as competition law – and as we shall see in Chapter 12, there is a very close approximation of national laws in this area. A free market based on open competition does not accord with the French doctrine of public service in the national interest. The French have seen the concept of *service public* as a clear influence on Community law's attitude to 'services of general interest' and the Community's softening of approach to monopolies providing a public service, providing they satisfy tests of proportionality.[119] Lenoir believes that regulatory authorities have been encouraged in France by Community law and the *Conseil d'Etat*, but not the Conseil Constitutionnel, has been averse to such bodies (Chapter 12, p 537 et seq). The latter has allowed them to implement a statute with rule-making powers which would usually be reserved to the Prime Minister in France under Article 21 of the Constitution. Such powers may be given to an independent agency 'for measures of limited content and field of application.'[120]

Under the ECHR, Article 6 on procedures and access to justice and Article 8 on protection of family life and privacy are particularly important in cases concerning deportation of aliens. The same articles have been used by the *Conseil d'Etat* (CE) to review disciplinary procedures in prisons, schools and the army, procedures which previously the court refused to review because they were '*mesures d'ordre intérieure.*'[121] French commentators

---

116   Flauss in J Schwarze note 115 at p 101.
117   Twenty four occasions in 1980–81; 851 in 1996: Bell *French Legal Cultures* p 181.
118   Cour de Cassation, Decision No 481, 10 October 2001. Serious crimes by the President in office can only be tried by the High Court of Deputies (MPs): see J Bell *3 Cambridge Yearbook of European Legal Studies* 65 (2002).
119   Case C-320/91 *Procureur du Roi v Corbeau* [1993] ECR I-2533; Case C-393/92 *Municipalité d'Almelo* [1994] ECR I-1477 and see Ch 10 below.
120   N Lenoir in B Markesinis B Markesinis *The German Law of Torts: a Comparative Treatise* (2002, 4th ed) ch 17, p 261.
121   N Lenoir in B Markesinis B Markesinis *The German Law of Torts: a Comparative Treatise* (2002, 4th ed) citing: *Hardouin et Marie* 17 February 1995, *Recueil*

do perceive a tension between the interests of the individual and the supremacy of the public interest[122] – but to be fair, since the events of 11 September 2001, English courts have given a wide margin of discretion to the executive in cases where that balance has to be struck.[123] Curiously, certain features of French law, including its classification of public and private in law are not accepted in EC or ECHR jurisprudence. Conversely, the CE has shown itself willing to accept the implications of the sovereignty of Community law (above p 75 et seq) and has interpreted treaties with the assistance of the ECJ's approach, and that of other foreign courts and not on the advice of the Ministry of Foreign Affairs.[124] It has shown itself ready to look out for influence. More generally, the creation of a duty to give reasons established by law in 1979 was explained as an example of European influence.[125]

The influence of *droit administratif* in Europe and in former French colonies is seen immediately in Italy, where a Council of State exists and where the laws on judicial review are modelled directly on those of France, in Belgium and in Greece and in Community law.

Germany

Germany has seen the development of independent administrative law courts since 1863. There is no equivalent of the *Conseil d'Etat* to act in an advisory capacity to government and public administration; in fact this is a function which is peculiar to the French *Conseil d'Etat* and those models directly derived from the French system and even those latter models do not always possess an advisory capacity.

Whereas in France the development of administrative law followed a central direction under the *Conseil d'Etat*, in Germany the system of administrative

---

p 82; cf in England *R v Board of Visitors of Hull Prison, ex p St Germain* [1979] 1 All ER 701, CA which opened up prison disciplinary hearings to judicial review. On courts martial see ch 5 note 84.

122   Bracconier, cited in J Bell *French Legal Cultures* p 181.
123   *Rehman* [2001] UKHL 47, [2002] 1 All ER 122; *Saadi* [2001] EWCA Civ 1512, [2001] 4 All ER 961; see Ch 8. The Special Immigration Appeal Commission has been more critical (Chs 8 and 9) but has been overruled by the higher courts.
124   Bell note 122 p 181.
125   The presumption of *Barel* did place a duty on authorities to explain and justify adverse decisions.

law emerged from the Lander and not from centralised institutions. The first development took place in Baden-Baden. There followed the Prussian Higher Administrative Court between 1872–75.[126] Schwarze describes how under the Weimar constitution of 1919 and under the Bonn Basic law of 1949 (see Chapter 2), the latter after the Nazi era, the concept of public administration evolved from 'a liberal constitutional system to a State system which integrated social laws and customs.'[127] A familiar pattern emerges of the development of public administration from limited roles of policing and national defence to the full provision of public services from the cradle to the grave. In the UK the provision of public services, ie who provides and quality of service, has been a preoccupation of government under Prime Minister Blair.

Administrative law is influenced by the Basic Law which was examined in Chapter 2. The German Federal Republic is a federally structured democratic state built upon the rule of law and social justice (Articles 20(1) and 28(1)(1) *Grundgesetz* (Basic Law)). The principle of legality of administration places duties on the executive and administration to comply with the law and to be subjected to an authorising statute which circumscribes discretion.

The constitution gives especial prominence to fundamental human rights as we saw in the previous chapter. A statute which contravenes a fundamental right will be subject to judicial review before the BverfG on a reference from the court dealing with the dispute. Schwarze cites German authorities who express the view, often heard elsewhere, that administrative law is constitutional law put into effect.

Federal administrative law has been codified in relation to its procedure since the Federal Administrative Procedure Act of 1976 (VxVfG). In addition, Lander have enacted there own administrative procedure law, which is based considerably on federal law (not unlike the situation in the US). Administrative law has been developed by legislation, academic comment and judicial decision in Germany. Sources of administrative law include statutes, regulations and charters – including charters issued by bodies which in English law would be regarded as private but which in Germany have a status under public law, eg chambers of commerce.

Leading judicial decisions have involved the Federal Administrative Court, the Federal Court of Justice as well as the Federal Constitutional Court

---

[126]   J Schwarze European Administrative Law (1992) pp 114 et seq.

where there are constitutional implications for administrative procedures. The Federal Administrative Court (*Bundesverwaltungsgericht*) is split into eight separate senates comprising a President and five judges. The Federal Administrative Court is in some instances 'explicitly called upon to develop the law further.'[128]

There are general principles of administrative law which have been developed through the cases and a great deal of academic comment has surrounded the question of whether this constitutes 'law'. This is the familiar civil law discussion of the status of case law – judges are not oracles of the law, they merely provide a decision under the law. Certain principles have been implemented into legislation; Schwarze cites 'proportionality' and 'legitimate expectation'.[129] In other cases principles have been developed as 'specific expressions of fundamental constitutional principles'. His view is that the question of whether such principles constitute 'legal resources in their own right' is of no great practical relevance.

The courts have power of review over questions of fact, law and merits and in this latter capacity they are to be distinguished particularly from English courts, French and Community courts. Questions of fact in England are not challengeable per se unless they fall within an error of law – which they can quite easily be made to do if the reviewing court is so inclined by establishing, for instance, that there is no evidence to support a particular conclusion.[130]

The Administrative Act

German administrative law concentrated its object of attack on a prior 'administrative act'. Under the Federal Administrative Procedure Act of 1976, s 35, this essentially involved an individual decision and stands in contradistinction to French law where general and specific measures may be challenged as we saw in the courts. Delegated legislation cannot be annulled, however. There is no doubt that this restriction has had an

---

127 J Schwarze European Administrative Law (1992) pp 115–16.
128 J Schwarze European Administrative Law (1992) p 119 and s 11(4) VwGO (see note 133 above).
129 J Schwarze European Administrative Law (1992) p 120.
130 See de Smith, Woolf and Jowell *Judicial Review of Administrative Action* (1995, 5th ed).

inhibiting effect on the development of administrative law and the German approach to locus standi is also restricted. There may be an 'abstract' constitutional review of legislation in the Constitutional Court as was seen in the previous chapter. The administrative courts are concerned with the infringement of a subjective individual right:

> By contrast with the traditional French approach, under which the role of the courts in securing legal protection has traditionally consisted in the objective supervision of the executive, the German approach towards administrative proceedings is first and foremost the protection of the individual's subjective rights. That much is already expressed in the legal protection guaranteed by Article 19(4)(1) of the Basic law, under which anyone whose rights have been infringed by public authorities has access to legal remedies.[131]

There are signs of change taking place in order to give greater procedural protection to individuals. The field of German administrative law is more concerned with substantive rights and this relates to the fact that administrative rights arise from the constitution. It would be dangerous to consign procedural and substantive rights to fixed and separate categories because they often overlap. However, in 1979, the BVerfG ruled that the state's obligation to protect the health of its citizens (Article 2(2) Basic Law) meant that licensing procedures for nuclear plants had to allow individual citizens to challenge non compliance with safety rules – a development described by Nolte as 'a remarkable one.'[132] Nolte also cites the adoption of a code on data protection in 1983 (ahead of the EC Directive) as an example of procedural sensitivity not usually associated with German Administrative law. But surely rights to data protection are not simply procedural; they are substantive and relate to privacy and integrity? Generally, German administrative law's constitutional mandate to protect individual rights will deny a widespread development of the *actio populari*s.

There are also administrative and legislative forms of relief for citizens' grievances that we can examine elsewhere (Chapter 11) which have to be invoked before an individual may seek relief in the courts. These are internal and formal forms of relief and are more bureaucratic, if not completely unremoved, from internal complaints processes within British public authorities which developed significantly after the Citizen's Charter in 1991.

---

[131]   J Schwarze *European Administrative Law* (1992) p 125.
[132]   (1994) Mod LR 191 at 204.

All public law disputes which are not constitutional in nature are within the jurisdiction of the administrative courts.[133] Claims for breaches of a constitutional fundamental right go to the Constitutional court after exhaustion of all other remedies. Liability under tort is a matter for civil law – a position which differs from France as we saw above.[134] Contract may be a matter of either public or private law and even constitutional law in the case of treaties between federal government and Lander. There is a three-stage procedure involving two levels of appeal and there are in addition special administrative jurisdictions. Relief is for an annulment, a declaration or for a mandatory order.

Administrative procedure

An administrative act must satisfy various requirements set out in the Federal Administrative Procedure Act, eg it has to be in writing, or confirmed in writing if made orally. It must be sufficiently definite and certain, in particular in relation to the addressee, its subject matter and any legal consequences of the act. An act which is written must contain reasons describing the facts and the legal grounds for the decision which were considered in making the decision. The grounds on which a discretion has been exercised must also be given. There are exemptions from the requirement to give reasons where for instance a large number of similar decisions are made or decisions are made by automatic device and reasons are not required for an individual decision. Statute may exempt some decisions from the requirement or decisions may be made publicly by general order. The act must contain a statement setting out a legal remedy against the act, the person to whom application may be made and any time limits – this is under a law of 1960.[135] It has been stated that the 1976 law is not in fact comprehensive as to procedural requirements. Procedure is to be informal unless otherwise required by statute. The administrative authority must act in an inquisitorial capacity to establish relevant facts.[136]

---

[133] Section 40 Order Relating to Administrative Courts VwGO.

[134] See: B Markesinis *The German Law of Torts: a Comparative Treatise* (2002, 4th ed); *Tort Law: Scope of Protection* W van Gerven, Ius Commune Casebooks for the Common Law of Europe (1998); J Bell and A W Bradley eds *Governmental Liability: a Comparative Study* (1991); B Markesinis et al eds *Tortious Liability of Statutory Bodies* (1999).

[135] VwGO; Cf the UK Ombudsman (PCA) has ruled that failure to notify parties of remedies and rights of appeal can constitute maladministration.

[136] M P Singh *German Administraive Law* (1985).

It is essential that the authority ascertains the full facts to make its decision and is given full powers of enquiry to achieve this including the calling of evidence and expert witnesses and power to undertake inspections. The administrative authority is under an obligation to provide information and advice to a citizen to secure the position of the citizen and that the latter is not subject to any prejudice through their ignorance or mistakes.

Generally speaking, an opportunity for a hearing is afforded to parties where their rights are being interfered with in order for them to express themselves on the facts that are material to the decision. A written procedure may suffice. There are a number of exceptions to the hearing right including emergency action, and cases where a decision is made affecting a large number of individuals or the authority wishes the decision to be given automatic effect. It is true to say that English courts would regard this latter with particular jealousy and English law has provided public hearings before many decisions of a collective nature are taken as in the field of planning inquiries and these have featured in recent human rights challenges where an interested person was responsible for making a final decision.[137] Bias must also be absent and it is sufficient to show a 'reasonable apprehension of bias.'[138] In the last few years, there has been a relaxation of procedural requirements in some areas where a defect may be cured in subsequent judicial proceedings. It has been stated this may cause extra and difficult burdens for German courts and may encourage a more relaxed approach by administrators which will not assist the quality of decision-making.[139] It is a form of relaxation which goes beyond those contained in the 1976 law.

A right to inspect the record of a decision exists but not where it would interfere with clearly established principles of personal confidences/privacy or business secrecy or where inspection would cause harm to Federal or Lander government. This is to be distinguished from the Freedom of Information Act 2000 in the UK where there are well in excess of twenty exemptions from access to official information in the UK, many of these

---

137   *R (Alconbury) v Secretary of State* [2001] UKHL 23, [2001] 2 All ER 929: see Ch 9, p 423 et seq.

138   The test of bias in English law has incorporated tests from the CHR and Commonwealth jurisdictions in modifying the test laid down by the House of Lords in *R v Gough* [1993] 2 All ER 724 at 737–38 to 'would the circumstances lead a fair-minded and informed observer to conclude that there was a real possibility that the tribunal was biased': *Porter v Magill* [2002] UKHL 67, [2002] 1 All ER 465.

139   Goller and Schmid (1998) European Public Law 31; M Kunnecke (2002) European Public Law 25.

absolute exemptions as opposed to discretionary ones. There is no federal German access to documents laws outside the realm of data protection.[140] Included in records are statements of parties entitled to participate, expert opinion and any records of evidence.

The authority is liable for the correct application of the law and may be liable for its wrongful application which causes injury. In England there would have to be negligence in the interpretation (very unlikely) or application of the law (again very difficult to establish; see Chapter 9). Furthermore, where the constitutionality of an Act is in question, any decision must be suspended pending determination of relevant questions before the Constitutional Court.

Finally, an administrative act must be notified to all relevant parties including addressees and affected parties and their agents if any. This includes relevant third parties. The Federal Administrative Procedure Act of 1976 details the requirements of how notice may be given.

Failure to comply may lead to annulment but Articles 45 and 46 of the procedural code both allow wide exculpatory provisions where procedures are not followed. It has to be said it is more relaxed than is English law. Two basic reasons for this are that if a body has come to the correct decision in its discretion, it does not matter that it made a procedural error. There are analogues in the common law.[141] Article 44 sets out the grounds for annulling a decision. Secondly, the body is usually enabled to hear a complaint against its decision before the courts are involved and this provides an opportunity for procedural correction.

Grounds for review

There are several grounds for judicial review which are analogous with grounds in other major systems and which it would be obvious would have a significant contribution to make to Community law of judicial review. These include a disregard of form and procedure, and we have seen how procedural requirements are spelt out in the Federal Administrative

---

[140]   The BVerfG emphasised that freedom of opinion is a substantial element in a democratic society: *Lüth* BverfGE 7, 198 et seq. How is freedom of speech assisted by being ill-informed?

[141]   *Cinnamond v British Airport Authority* [1980] 2 All ER 368.

Procedure Act of 1976 and how there are numerous exceptions to these requirements. Other familiar grounds for review include a lack of competence; and an excess of jurisdiction.

There are, however, several grounds of review which appear quite distinct. Together with the general principles of administrative law which have been so influential in Community law and which includes legitimate expectation, equality, and proportionality and which I examine in a moment, there are lack of clarity (English legal analogue: void for uncertainty) legal and factual defects and inconsistency with good morals. This might involve discriminatory action of one kind or another which is not justified and which may well be unconstitutional also. In fact, such principles as equality are seen as constitutional in nature.

There are additional controls for the exercise of discretion by authorities. Traditionally it has been suggested that there was less reliance on control via fair procedure in Germany because the intensity of review of discretion was so high. There are signs that review based on procedure is growing in importance. Review on procedural grounds has been the traditional strong point of English law although it was pretty much comatose until 1964 and the decision in *Ridge v Baldwin*.[142]

Discretion is conventionally strictly controlled in the application of administrative law in Germany. There is a tendency to say in German administrative law that there is only one correct solution to a problem unless the administrative authority is clearly given a choice in its actions. To an English lawyer a phrase such as 'to take action in the public interest' may confer a power that is so broad that effective review is almost impossible where fundamental human rights are not in question. In Germany, however, assuming such a phrase was not unconstitutional, courts will insist that there is one right answer to the manner of the application of the discretion so that courts will control the content of answers to state law exams and come to definite conclusions on whether there should be a restriction on pornographic material to children.[143] As well as strict tests for reasonableness, improper purpose, relevance, failure to exercise discretion, abusing its powers and exceeding its powers (which strictly is a question of ultra vires) there are some home-grown remedies.

---

142   [1964] AC 40.
143   See Nolte (1994) Mod LR 191.

The reviewing courts do not like 'indefinite legal concepts of a normative character' (*unbeststimmte Rechtsbegriffe*). So, resort to 'public interest', 'public need', 'public safety', 'urgency', even the ubiquitous 'unreasonable' and so on, will attract critical attention from the administrative courts. This is because such concepts are inherently value laden and traditionally are seen as subjective and are not therefore entitled to any special dispensation or favour by the administrative courts. There are those who argue that there should be special respect shown for such exercise of discretion. The degree of judicial control is based in the concept of the Rechtsstaat in which one's rights are given the full protection of law. Since the 1970s, however, there is growing evidence of more respect being given to administrative discretion. I shall say more about this in a moment.

Proportionality: we shall come back to this concept on numerous occasions in this book. It was seen earlier in this chapter although its use in the Community has been somewhat confined. The principle has been invoked frequently in cases concerned with the common agricultural policy and in establishing whether derogations from Community measures are justified. In European human rights law it has had a pronounced impact as will be seen in Chapter 9. The principle was developed in Germany as is well known by Prussian courts to provide a means for checking exercise of police powers and incursion into citizens' civil liberties – that they were not excessive. As well as meaning avoidance of excessive use of power and not inflicting unduly harsh or oppressive punishment or burdens, the concept developed a variety of other dimensions. It has come to mean using the least injurious means to achieve an end where several methods to address a problem may be identified. It may also involve assessing whether a particular action or rule is necessary in the circumstances. It involves weighing all the factors that go into a decision to ensure that all factors are given sufficient weight and are properly balanced; it can mean ensuring that there is a proper balancing between the position of the individual and the community and that any loss to an individual is seen in the context of gain to the community whereby the action must be no more than is necessary to achieve legitimate objectives and that action must be suitable. The principle has as its basis the protection of the rights of the individual; the more important the right, the more the courts require by justification to interfere with that right as is graphically shown by English case law.[144]

---

[144] See Lord Steyn in *ex p Daly* Ch 8, p 343 et seq.

In Germany, the courts have shown a readiness to view the individual damage/collective benefit in a context of overall law and order and legal order. So it is not a breach of proportionality to allow the destruction of illegally constructed buildings – in England the common law would insist that a hearing be given now overtaken by detailed statutory procedures. Furthermore, German courts have applied the principle to cases of deportation after commission and conviction of crime. Not every crime deserves to be punished by deportation of a non-national. It was a violation of proportionality where a legal rule required that an unemployed person forfeited their claim to unemployment benefits for a period of two weeks if there was a failure by them to notify the unemployment office of their current status at regular intervals. Nolte believes it might have been different had the requirement only allowed stoppage for one week or if those subject to penalties were from a group which was proved frequently to be guilty of benefit fraud.[145] However, such a suggestion is itself open to question on grounds of discriminatory or unequal treatment.

Equality: the level of judicial scrutiny under equality has increased argues Nolte. At first it was treated in a manner equivalent to arbitrary treatment – fine distinctions in treatment would not attract adverse judicial reaction. It may well be that such fine distinctions are symptomatic of a refined concept of administrative justice providing that such distinctions are explicable within published criteria as is the case in England. The approach of both German and Community courts, argues Nolte, is similar to a more exacting form of review based upon approaches similar to proportionality. The BVerfG has said that the differences must be of such a kind and weight as to justify a differentiation on treatment. An example provided by Nolte is that of different treatment of clerical and manual workers in relation to dismissal periods. The former were entitled to six weeks' notice, the latter to two weeks. One might see some assumptions about status here which bear little relationship to equality!

Legitimate expectation: the origins of this concept in German and Community law are the conferral of protection to prevent an advantage being withdrawn from an individual, in the German case even if the conferral is unlawful. Both Community and German law confer substantive protection. This goes much further than English law as we shall see in Chapter 7. See for instance the Federal Administrative Procedure Act of

---

[145]   Nolte (1994) Mod LR 191.

1976, s 48(2) an unlawful administrative decision granting a pecuniary benefit may not be revoked in so far as the beneficiary has relied upon the decision and his expectation, weighed against the public interest, merits protection. English courts cannot confer benefits which are ultra vires (Chapter 8, p 355). In addition, in England, legitimate expectation confers not only procedural protection but also substantive protection. In the application of Community law, defences available in domestic administrative law such as legitimate expectation afford no defence to the enforceability of Community law.[146] It was seen how the French Conseil d'Etat refused to incorporate legitimate expectation in a purely domestic case (above p 127).

The strict approach adopted to the exercise of discretion was noted above and it should be emphasised that the 'margin of appreciation' or discretion and deference to discretion is more pronounced in ECHR law and even Community law that it is in German law where a margin of appreciation will not protect a decision which is not correct. The 'margin' doctrine is more closely associated with Community and Convention law – and even English law – than German law.

As developed in Community law proportionality is the most commonly invoked principle of review in Community law and although it has a wide area of application it has been particularly important in agricultural law, external trade and cases involving sanctions and penalties including charges. The ECJ has adopted different tests in assessing how appropriate measures are and how necessary they are to achieve legitimate ends according to the subject matter involved; where a Community policy measure is under a review, the court has displayed a marked 'margin of appreciation' towards the measure and the discretion involved in formulating such a measure. Where a national measure affecting one of the four freedoms is involved, the Court has adopted a greater degree of scrutiny. Proportionality also controls the legislative competence of the Community – 'subsidiarity' – under Article 5(3) EC (see Chapter 5).

It is interesting to compare the searching review that takes place in German courts with a more deferential review in the ECJ, particularly where Community measures are concerned. In Community law, a three test approach has been identified: is a measure suitable; is it necessary; and

---

[146] Case C-24/95 *Land Rheinland-Pfalz v Alcan Deutschland GmbH* [1997] ECR I-1591.

even if these are satisfied, does the measure nonetheless still impinge on legitimate interests and rights in a manner which is not justified by the end objectives? It involves a weighing of legitimate and competing factors by the court.

Nolte,[147] from whom the following example is taken, believes that the searching review undertaken by German courts arises from a crisis in German legal and political doctrine after the second world war for reasons which have already been addressed in this book. The adoption of proportionality by the ECJ, however, was not constrained by any crisis but by a desire to ensure a sufficient armoury to establish full protection of Community institutions vis à vis national systems and the sovereignty of Community law. But, such review that took place could not be as invasive as the German level of review. In the *Munich University* case[148], a University wished to import an electronic microscope from Japan. The University wished to be exempted from customs duties in accordance with an EEC regulation. The Commission refused to allow this exemption because microscopes 'of equivalent scientific value' were manufactured in the Community. The argument of the University was that the detailed specifications of the microscope made it distinct and different in quality from any available in the Community. The *Finanzgericht* (Finance Court) in Munich held that the Commission decision was unlawful and granted the exemption. On appeal to the *Bundesfinanzhof* (Federal Finance Court), the appeal court wished to uphold the lower court's rather bold decision but accepted that vis à vis the Commission, the ECJ adopted a less rigorous standard of review than a German court would in the case of a German administrative authority.

In the *Stuttgart University* case[149] the ECJ had set out its standard of review. The court held 'given the technical character of the examination to determine whether apparatus are equivalent, it cannot, save in the event of manifest error of fact and law or misuse of power, find fault with the substance of a decision adopted by the Commission in conformity with its relevant [committee's] opinion.' This compares with the conventional standard of review in English courts where there was generally a marked deference to administrative discretion. As we shall see in Chapters 8 and 9, the position in English law has now developed but not to the extent of

---

147 Nolte (1994) Mod LR 191.
148 Case 269/90 [1991] ECR I-5469.
149 Case 303/87: [1989] ECR 705.

review in Germany in the absence of a human rights' factor deserving 'anxious scrutiny'.

The *Bundesfinanzhof* asked the ECJ under a preliminary reference to review its own approach to judicial review. What concerned the German court was that the approach adopted by the ECJ would deny an 'effective judicial review' under the German constitution (Article 19(4) Grundgesetz). It would, as Nolte suggests, allow an error of law to persist even though not 'manifest'. To an English lawyer, this would raise issues of threshold significance: an error is not an error unless manifest. The court in England will not go hunting for errors. To what extent recent English case law has modified this approach we shall have to see in Chapter 8. The clear implication of the ECJ decision was that the more complicated the decision in terms of subject matter, the less susceptible it would be to review.

German courts are concerned to ensure that the 'right' decision is achieved and that a reasonable complainant can be assured that the eventual decision is the 'right' one. There can be no more dramatic representation of a review on the merits. In England, a decision has to be right, ie correct according to legal requirements, not the right decision ie better than all others. A contentious element in Dworkinian jurisprudence is that hard cases only have one right answer. The Bhof asked the ECJ to reconsider the position. As Nolte points out, the ECJ's response was to find procedural fault with the Commission's decision-making process: the experts who were consulted by the Commission were not possessed of proper formal qualifications; the University had been deprived unfairly of an appropriate hearing. Finally, the Commission had given insufficient reasons for its decision and therefore Article 253 [190] EC had been violated. The ECJ abandoned its approach based on 'manifest error' but did not go for what may be termed a full substantive review.[150] Nolte queries whether the approach of the ECJ, modified from its previous position, might not influence German approaches to confine the exacting nature of their review not only in cases involving Community law but in cases where such law is not involved.[151] The case law concerning the Council regulation on

---

[150] Note the effective compromise reached in the 'Bananas' litigation between German courts and BVerfG and the ECJ: Ch 2, p 84.

[151] Note 147, ibid p 208. It is interesting to compare this approach with that adopted in the USA where reviewing courts are mandated to require that administrative decisions, adjudications and delegated legislation are supported by substantial evidence under the Administrative Procedure Act 1946, but courts give a wide

importation of bananas should be recalled where the ECJ was roundly criticised for not giving fundamental rights protection to German traders that would be given under German law. Eventually the ECJ did rule that the regulation was in breach of the general principle of 'non-discrimination.'[152]

The more fundamental the right to be protected under German law, the more exacting the review of any interference with that right. Similar approaches to this can be seen in English law in cases going back almost twenty years (see Chapters 8 and 9). It also reminds us of the discussion in Chapter 2 concerning the conflict between the BVerfG and the ECJ over the perceived inadequacy of protection of fundamental rights in the Community. The particular legal/political conflict has long been resolved but the underlying problems remain as we saw in Chapter 2.[153] Nolte believed that there are signs of a more relaxed form of review which gives the administration greater leeway.[154]

It must be emphasised that when it comes to collective rights or third generation rights where there is a public interest as opposed to an individual interest, German law is not so accommodating although the decision in the case of nuclear plants was noted above. The primary concern of German administrative courts is with individual rights. In that respect in stands in contradistinction to common law systems. In England, for instance, locus standi is very relaxed and has been used by interest groups to challenge matters of high policy as well as the approval of the Maastricht Treaty (Chapter 4). The attempts to move towards a more liberal approach in locus standi in Community law was also noted as was the ECJ's decision thwarting such a development (p 106 et seq).

---

berth to agency discretion on matters of expertise and substance on subjects within the agencies' remit. However, an exacting form of review may be conducted under the hard-look doctrine where the courts insist agencies take a hard look at all the evidence and material supporting a decision under the 'arbitrary, capricious, and abuse of discretion or otherwise not in accordance with law' provisions of the 1946 Act. Intensity can be variable as can review of agencies' interpretation of legislation affecting their jurisdiction: on the former see *State Farm Mutual* 463 US 29 (1983) and on the latter *Chevron USA Inc v NRDC Inc* 467 US 837 (1984) and *Christensen v Harris County* 529 US 576 (2000) and *US v Mead Corpn* 121 SCt 2164 (2001).

152   Case C-122/95 *Germany v Commission* [1998] ECR I-973 and p 96 above.
153   See J Schwarze in (2002) *European Public Law* 241.
154   Nolte (1994) Mod LR 191: a margin of discretion – *Beurteilungsspielraum.*

Implementation of EC law

In Germany, much of EC law ie Directives, has been implemented by administrative rules or circulars. In most cases they have been 'self-binding' rather than legally normative. In the UK, there are examples where EC provisions were implemented by circulars, and the use of circulars in areas of administration is very common. Problems have been caused in prison administration, social security and immigration in non-EU respects and in public procurement where the Directive was for almost twenty years implemented by a Circular and Treasury guidance. In Germany, when the Clean Air Directive (82/884 EEC) was implemented, Germany supplemented a legal rule with administrative explanatory rules, part of the function of which was to be a component of the implementing measure. This method could achieve flexibility should scientific advances require the use of more developed equipment. This could be achieved by a change in administrative rules without the necessity of formal legislative change. The ECJ ruled that this was unlawful because the rules were ambiguous and because individuals must be able to establish whether a Directive has been properly implemented.[155] This as Nolte explains, would involve a collective right to proper implementation and supervision of the administration, a matter which is not in the German tradition in relation to its citizenry. Schwarze's report in his 1996 publication show the various possibilities on how this may affect the German national system.[156]

ECHR

Although, along with many other European countries, domestic German courts play significant regard in their citations to the ECHR, particularly the BVerfG in Germany, there is a note of apprehension in Schwarze's 1996 book on the topic of the ECHR and its impact on German administrative law. The discussion in Chapter 2 should be recalled (p 85). Furthermore, difficulties have been identified with the Charter of Fundamental Human Rights of the EU from a German position particularly from the perspective of multiplicity of jurisdictions – and a good deal of that Charter specifically addresses the subject of administrative justice.[157]

---

[155] [1991] ECR I-2626.

[156] J Schwarze *Administrative Law Under European Influence* (1996); for a precis, see Schwarze in *Judicial Review in European Union Law* ed D O'Keeffe (2000) ch 29.

[157] J Schwarze in *3 The Cambridge Yearbook of European Legal Studies* ch 17.

English administrative law

The flavour of much of our judicial review will be taken from the contents of following chapters. In European seminars and conferences that I have attended there is always an element of disbelief when the 'mysteries' of the common law are unfolded, particularly in relation to its public law elements. How do they manage with this Khadi system of justice? – as Max Weber saw the common law – seems to be a general impression. The fact that there was no separate system of public law courts and doctrine helped the mystification. It is as much to do with the perception of our law as antiquated; the chains of antique time rattling from the grave. It is also reinforced by discussions concerning the true basis of judicial review in English law and the doctrinal disagreement of whether that basis is the ultra vires doctrine and therefore simply an assertion of Parliamentary Sovereignty; or whether it is common law based and settled on notions of justice and fairness which inform common law of which Parliamentary Sovereignty, and the law of ultra vires, are themselves a part. This in essence is but a variation of the legal positivism/natural law debate. If the common law is the basis of review, then of course the influence of European law on common law will reinforce that law and its scope for review. My own view is that judicial review owes its provenance to both sources and that the spirit of the law and legitimacy which flows from that, can only be reinforced by legislation and not undermined by it. This approach informs, it seems to me, the approach adopted by judges to the HRA 1998 (see Chapter 9). If Parliament passes inhumane or unjust laws, no positivist philosophy will protect that legislation from what it deserves. Matters are never so blunt.[158]

The fact is that administrative law, meaning judicial review, has grown in subtlety and in width and in case-load in the last thirty years. Its heritage goes back centuries, rejuvenated but not reinvented at crucial stages of maturity. In 1977, the number of judicial review case applications amounted to 376. By 2001, it was 4,372.[159] In 1977, judicial review procedure was simplified and in spite of some decisions that reinforced technical divisions the development of the law since then has been directed to make the

---

[158]   Blackstone in the eighteenth century adverted to the possibility of Parliamentary Sovereignty being put to outrageous purposes: 'if ever they unfortunately happen, the prudence of the times must provide new remedies upon new emergencies.' *Commentaries* i 245.

[159]   *Judicial Statistics 2001* Cm 5551 (2002).

procedure more accessible. The most recent reforms have come with a general review of civil procedure and take place under Part 54 of the Civil Procedure Rules 1998. The judges are now attached to the Administrative Court of the QBD and not simply to the Crown Office List. The philosophy of the reforms is set out in 'overriding objectives' in rule 1 of the Rules. These seek basically to enable a court to deal with a case 'justly' and to achieve an equal footing, save expense, in a manner which is proportionate, and expeditiously and fairly. For the first time judicial review may take place outside London, in Cardiff and elsewhere. Scotland and Northern Ireland have their own jurisdictions. The philosophy is to make the Rules as flexible as possible so that it will be possible to move from public law process to private law process without undue obstacles – a practice assisted by judicial decisions.[160] The Rules coincided with the implementation of the ECHR into domestic law.

Almost four hundred years ago, Coke CJ wrote of the inherent powers of the court of King's Bench to correct errors 'so that no wrong or injury publick or private, can be done but that this shall be reformed or punished.'[161] The question has been asked whether we need specific forms of public law redress.[162] As the confusion of public and private becomes more opaque, we should perhaps concentrate on means of challenging the exercise of power for arbitrary, capricious and abusive purposes, whatever the source of power and whatever the instruments of challenge. Make no mistake, there is no significant power that does not somewhere rely upon government support, protection or inaction.

To concentrate on judicial review would be to give a misleading picture of the process of administrative justice which takes place through tribunals, public inquiries and hearings and special commissions and regulatory agencies to name a few. The ombudsman – a Scandinavian import – has spread from the public sector to the private sector where only recently a financial services ombudsman has set up a unified complaints system in money markets, banking and insurance. The doing of justice in the administrative realm was examined in 1957 by the Franks committee[163] and

---

[160]   *Clark v Lincoln and Humberside University* [2000] 3 All ER 752, CA.

[161]   *Bagg's Case* (1615) Co Inst iv 71.

[162]   D Oliver (2002) Public Law 91 and *Common Values and the Public Private Divide* (1999).

[163]   *Report of the Committee on Administrative Tribunals and Enquiries* Cmnd 218 (1957).

its plea for justice, openness and fairness in that realm found a partial response in the Tribunal and Inquiries Act, now of 1992. The English tradition has been a rich if un-coordinated one in terms of the jurisprudence of administrative justice. As I have written elsewhere, courts really are only the tip of the iceburg in this jurisprudence.[164] But they are the tip that has felt the greatest impact from European influence and their jurisprudence has revealed the rich and forceful impression made by principles of public law in Europe.

Conclusion

This chapter began by looking at the proposition that Community law was a system of administrative law: putting public powers into effect and developing means for their operation, regulation and control. In developing that system, the Community had to borrow heavily from the French and the German traditions. These are very different, as has been seen. The influence of human rights protection, a growing intensity of review and a greater sensitivity to openness in decision making are increasingly apparent. They are also features of the recent English contribution to judicial review – a third and very different system. It is time to examine these and other matters more closely in our domestic setting.

---

[164]   P Birkinshaw *Grievances, Remedies and the State* (1994, 2nd ed).

Chapter 4

The main features of UK constitutional law and European integration

The nature of the British constitution

Introduction

One has to explain at the outset a variety of factors concerning Constitutional Law in the UK before one can assess its relationship to European integration and European public law. These factors relate to the peculiar position of the status of constitutional law in the UK, the absence of a written constitution and entrenched Bill of Rights and the fact that in British law the 'state' has no legal identity and is not a legal concept.[1] Our constitution is unwritten and flexible. In the western democratic world we now appear to be alone in not possessing some form of written constitution.

Although there has been an absence of a written constitution since the *Instrument of Government* (1653–60), British political and legal language over the centuries has been rich in its discussion of the principles of the 'Ancient Constitution', built on fealty and feudal bonding, developed

[1]   Although it has been held that the State, without a formal legal identity, can hold property: *Ross v Lord Advocate* [1986] 3 All ER 79, HL. Furthermore, privatised water companies have been held by an English court to be an 'emanation' of the State for the purpose of direct effectiveness of EC Directives: *Griffin v South-West Water Services Ltd* [1995] IRLR 15. 'State' is used in legal expressions such as 'act of state' etc, but with no greater precision than 'government'. On the use of the term state in the UK see Birkinshaw *Grievances, Remedies and the State* (1994, 2nd ed) Sweet and Maxwell, ch 1. One of the sensitive issues concerning the use of the term state relates to the fact that the UK comprises four different countries in a unitary or 'union' structure.

through precedent guiding the custom and practice of the realm, embracing ever wider estates into its body politic.

The absence of revolution cemented an enormous degree of certitude and confidence, so confident that Parliament could put its King 'the *fons et origo*' of all justice, on trial for High Treason for subverting the ancient constitution of the realm. The 'Revolution' and Bill of Rights of 1689 were far from a revolution, rather a reestablishment of ancient order with the Crown at its apex and constitutionalised – though not the executive – and everything thereunder in its rightful place, and it was believed, a place for everyone. That the 'Ancient Constitution' existed was never doubted. What it meant, no-one really knew.[2] What the resolute faith in the Ancient Constitution produced was an unmovable complacency and lack of introspection in our governing classes and a propensity to correlate an existing order with a pre-existing scheme of things. If our system of government was declared 'democratic' it was democratic even though reality belied this epithet in a representative capacity until 1928,[3] much later in the case of Northern Ireland. The Great Reform Bill of 1832 enfranchised 217,000 voters in England and Wales for Parliamentary elections from a population of 16,500,000, adding to 435,000 existing voters.

If our system was built on the Rule of Law and Parliamentary sovereignty, then this was self evidently true even though practice often denied the twin assertions of British constitutionalism. In the latter case, and this may sound strange to a non-British audience, Parliament is dominated by a government – it would not be government if that were not the case – and

---

[2]   Christopher Hill has illustrated this paradox beautifully in *The Intellectual Origins of the English Revolution* (1965, Oxford) p 65 in describing the impeachment of Strafford, the King's Minister:

> In 1641 Strafford was impeached, among other charges, for subverting the fundamental laws of the kingdom. The Commons were just about to vote the charge when the witty and malicious Edmund Waller rose, and with seeming innocence, asked what the fundamental laws of the kingdom were. There was an uneasy silence. No-one dared to attempt a definition which would certainly have divided the heterogeneous majority, agreed only in its view that for Strafford 'stone dead hath no fellow'. The situation was saved by a lawyer who leapt to his feet to say that if Mr Waller did not know what the fundamental laws of the kingdom were, he had no business to be sitting in the House.

[3]   Universal *male* suffrage was virtually achieved in 1884.

what Parliamentary sovereignty effectively produced was *de facto* Executive sovereignty.

A major message in this chapter is that perhaps more than anything this century, the UK accession to Europe has swept away the cobwebs of antique time from our constitution. The New Labour government that came to power in May 1997 carried a commitment to major constitutional change and a 'modern constitution fit for the twenty-first century'.[4] Devolution has changed the face of the country and the ECHR has been incorporated into domestic law. There has been an increasing resort to referenda – including the promise of a referendum before our entry into monetary union and the Euro – and proportional representation. As I write, the final shape of the House of Lords is still unsettled but it is unlikely to be an all elected assembly. Freedom of Information legislation although enacted has been put on hold until 2005 in relation to individual rights of access.

Evolution, historical development and sources of the British constitution

Although the UK possesses no written constitution as such, the UK possesses a variety of constitutional instruments – and many of these have their provenance as English law. These are statutes dating from 1215 which relate to constitutional fundamentals concerning relationships between the Crown – which represents and is symbolic of the 'state' – and individuals and between the Crown and Parliament, between the two Houses of Parliament in the case of dissent between them on legislation, on the duration of Parliament, on the independence of the judiciary and the government of, and union with Scotland and Northern Ireland and various other matters. The devolution statutes and the Human Rights Act have taken their place in this assembly. It is often remarked that the British constitution looks very different from the Scottish side of the border than from the English and this is certainly true of their respective legal systems. It has been made more divergent by devolution statutes (see Chapter 5).

It is not an exaggeration to say that by 1295, we had in England the basic constitutional machinery in place which has survived to this day. The King in Parliament made statutes. The King in his Council made ordinances (now,

---

[4]   *Scotland's Parliament* Cm 3658, para 1.6, HMSO, (1997).

in addition, Her Majesty's ministers and civil servants draft their delegated instruments in departments for Parliamentary approval). The King through his courts administered justice and applied the common law. Parliament as the national assembly comprised three estates of the realm: the Lords Spiritual and Temporal (not all of whom are now hereditary), and the Commons. This was an English constitution which was extended by treaties or acts of union with Scotland in 1707 and Ireland in 1800. Wales has existed as an English principality since 1282 and was united with England in 1536 and the common law of England was applied in Wales from 1543.

By the end of the seventeenth century the English doctrine of Parliamentary sovereignty (see below) was established, reinforced by the Bill of Rights of 1689 which set out the relationship between Crown and Parliament. The doctrine came to mean that there was no subject on which Parliament could not legislate and there was no law above Parliamentary legislation. What was sovereign was the current Parliament, so one Parliament could not bind its successors. There was no judicial review of legislation.

Without a written constitution, the English did not develop a constitutional court. Constitutional questions presented by legislation, prerogative acts or actions of government are dealt with by the ordinary courts in their interpretation of statutes or prerogative instruments or actions. Parliament, the 'highest court in the land' would also regard itself as a constitutional court with unlimited and sovereign powers. When legislating on constitutional matters, the Committee stage of the House of Commons is, for instance, taken as a Committee of the whole House and not by a standing committee.

What in other jurisdictions is catered for by provisions in a written constitution is very often dealt with by conventions or 'custom and practice' of government which are not justiciable *per se* before the courts but which may well be invoked by courts in giving judgments and which may help to shape judicial decisions.[5] These conventions are not subject to explicit or deliberate act of creation. They are evolutionary in character. One such is the 'Ponsonby rule' under which a text of a Treaty is laid before Parliament at least 21 days before ratification which satisfies the requirement that Parliament needs to be informed of Ministers' intentions relating to foreign affairs. However, the uncertain status of conventions is evidenced

---

5   See eg *A-G v Jonathan Cape* [1976] QB 752 and confidentiality of Cabinet proceedings.

by the fact that a Government spokesperson denied that the Ponsonby rule was a convention adding that it was regularly breached.[6] Their enforcement is ultimately a matter of political pressure.

No constitutional provision as such is entrenched or, subject to what is said below, assumes any superior legal status to any other statutory provision. Magna Carta, the Bill of Rights 1689 or the European Communities Act 1972 were ordinary statutes, possessing no greater legal status than the Scotch Whisky Act 1988. But, as stated above, they were regarded as constitutional measures. It is true that Sir John Laws has stated that the 1972 Act, together with other 'constitutional statutes', possess a superior constitutional status.[7] As a matter of law, it is not clear what this means beyond suggesting, as he does, that their constitutional and political significance make them unsuitable candidates for the doctrine of implied repeal by subsequent legislation. The 1972 Act caters for this expressly as we shall see. It is correct to say that judicial decisions have fastened on the concept of 'fundamental human rights' meaning that such rights can only be overridden by the clearest of statutory language. To such rights, Sir John has added 'constitutional statutes' to the lexicon of our legal discourse. These he describes as statutes that condition the state/citizen relationship in a 'general, overarching manner' and which enlarge or *diminish* the scope of fundamental constitutional rights.[8] There has also been strengthening support for a 'hierarchy of norms' meaning that human rights are more important than other rights, and some human rights are

---

[6]   HL Debs cols 1530 et seq (28 February 1996) and Lord Lester's motion for a Treaties (Parliamentary Approval) Bill to provide parliamentary approval of treaties before being ratified, ibid at col 1532.

[7]   *Thoburn v Sunderland City Council* [2002] EWHC 195 (Admin) [2002] 4 All ER 156. The case concerned a prosecution of a market trader for refusing to use metric measures. On the differing status of statutes where they were constitutional documents, ie in Commonwealth countries, see: *Minister of Home Affairs v Fisher* [1980] AC 319, though cf, *Riley v A-G of Jamaica* [1983] 1 AC 719 – both in the Privy Council. Similarly, note *Edwards v A-G* [1930] AC 124 at 136–137 and Sir I. Jennings (1936) 52 LQR 173. In *Robinson v Secretary of State for Northern Ireland* [2002] UKHL 32, [2002] All ER (D) 364 (Jul) the Law Lords by majority held that the Northern Ireland Act 1998 was a 'constitution' and had to be interpreted 'generously and purposively' to allow flexibility in the exercise of political judgment in the face of difficult and unforeseen events. Strict rules of construction would not allow such an approach. The case concerned the election of a First Minister and a Deputy First Minister in Northern Ireland and the holding of an Assembly election within NIA 1998, ss 16(8) and 32(3).

[8]   Emphasis added; p 185b.

more important than other human rights. The more important the right, the more jealously courts will protect them.[9] Laws LJ spoke of a 'hierarchy of statutes', with constitutional measures taking primary position.

There are in addition uncodified principles of common law such as the sovereignty of Parliament, the presumption of the Rule of Law governing governmental activities and other principles such as equality and fairness in action, and now proportionality.[10] These principles are afforded no written constitutional guarantee as such; it is rather presumed that they inhere in the nature of things. They have certainly been used by the courts to shape principles of public law which the English judiciary regard as their most significant achievement since the Second World War.[11] Theoretically there is nothing to prevent these principles being excluded by clear and precise statutory provisions. To do so would run the risk of upsetting the delicate balance of the British constitution where so much is still implicit and dependent upon 'good form' rather than explicit and subject to legal regulation. My own belief is that such a state of affairs will have to move with the times and indeed, there is ample evidence that our constitutional world is changing, particularly in areas of government visited by the HRA 1998 (see Chapter 9). Such a change was at the heart of the Labour government's agenda in 1997–2001. This book attempts to assess that change.

Although the UK is the supposed home of the separation of powers, the UK has no constitutional guarantees of such a separation which are to be found, and which constantly feature as practical problems, in the constitutions of the US, France and Germany for instance.[12] The mish-mash of our constitutional history features in the confusion of roles adopted by the Lord Chancellor, a situation which has come under increasing strain as

---

9   See Sedley J in *R v Secretary of State for the Home Department, ex p McQuillan* [1995] 4 All ER 400; Lord Steyn in *Ex p Daly* [2001] UKHL 26, [2001] 3 All ER 433 and in *McCartan Turkington Breen v Times Newspapers Ltd* [2000] 4 All ER 913 at 928; Lord Hoffman in *R v East Sussex County Council, ex p Reprotech (Pebsham) Ltd* [2002] UKHL 8, [2002] 4 All ER 58. Bieber and Salomé (1996) 33 CML Rev 907.

10   See *Brind v Home Secretary* [1991] 1 All ER 720, HL which held that 'proportionality' was not a discrete head of review in English law although the position is far from unqualified and see below Ch 8.

11   Lord Diplock in *R v IRC, ex p National Federation of Self Employed and Small Businesses* [1982] AC 617, 641. Since 2000, an Administrative Court of the High Court has been established as we saw in Ch 3.

12   M J C Vile *Constitutionalism* (1967).

the Lord Chancellor insists on sitting in appeals to the judicial committee of the House of Lords.[13] An independent judiciary, a sovereign Parliament and the Rule of Law would guarantee the balanced constitution; so it was thought. The fact that our constitution is unwritten and flexible has ensured that the judicial contribution to our constitutional thought and culture has been minimal. The judiciary's most significant contribution has probably been the acceptance of Parliamentary sovereignty in its widest terms. The common law is the repository of the judiciary and the doctrine of Parliamentary sovereignty is ultimately a rule of common law. It is not, and could not be, a statutory creation because any statute is itself subject to the doctrine.

Characteristics of national constitutional law

The powers of government are formally in the hands of the Queen as Head of State, although Ministers govern in the name of the Queen and the Queen only acts through and on the advice of Ministers on whom Parliament confers statutory powers. The Queen's inherent powers are prerogative powers. Although she does exercise certain prerogative powers herself, as appropriately advised, these again are mainly exercised by Ministers. The courts have ruled that the prerogative is subject to judicial review where the subject matter of a prerogative is appropriate for such review.[14] Ministers, by convention, should be members of either House of Parliament although all senior Ministers, apart from the Lord Chancellor, are usually members of the Commons and therefore elected. However, in Mrs Thatcher's government, senior Ministers such as a Trade and Industry Secretary and Foreign Secretary were members of the House of Lords. Central government operates under the identity of the 'Crown' – a notoriously imprecise term in British constitutional law.

The government meets in the Cabinet and is presided over by the Prime Minister. Ministers head Ministries and are answerable to Parliament along

---

[13] See ch 5 and *McGonnell v UK* (2000) 30 EHRR 289; Lord Steyn has attacked this practice which appears to breach Art 6 ECHR (see ch 5, p 247 et seq): The Home Secretary was found to be in breach of Art 5(4) ECHR in overruling the Parole Board: *Stafford v UK* App 46295/99 (2002) 13 BHRC 260, ECtHR.

[14] *Council for Civil Service Unions v Minister for the Civil Service* [1985] AC 374: where the prerogative impacts directly on an individual's rights or legitimate expectations, for instance.

with the Prime Minister for their areas of responsibility. This they fulfil by answering Parliamentary Questions and providing information to Parliament and its Select Committees. Since 1988, the UK has seen the increasing introduction of executive agencies to carry out the operational aspects of government as distinct from the policy making aspects of government which are retained within ministries. The division between these 'Next Steps Agencies' which are under Chief Executives and Ministries under the Minister is far from clear and there are some notorious examples of Ministers interfering with the independence of Chief Executives. Their relationship is not spelt out in laws but in a Framework Document, a form of non-legally binding agreement. About 75% of civil servants work in Next Steps Agencies.

Parliament is the supreme UK legislator and all UK primary legislation is passed by Parliament. By convention more important Bills originate in the Commons, but this is not universally followed. Each Bill has three readings, a committee and a report stage in both Houses. It then receives the Royal Assent and becomes law. Any presumed veto power in the Monarch has not been used since 1707 and, in 1913, George V was advised by the Prime Minister that any attempted veto – on a Bill for home rule for Ireland – would cause a constitutional crisis from which the Crown would not recover.

Most delegated legislation made by statutory instrument has to be approved by Parliament and must conform with the parent Act. Courts may review the legality of delegated legislation but have no review powers over primary legislation. The Human Rights Act 1998 has given the courts a power to issue a declaration of incompatibility where a statute does not conform with the ECHR but this falls short of a power to review statutes (see Chapter 9) Local authorities and other public authorities have powers to make bye-laws which are forms of delegated legislation. The Scottish Parliament has been given power to legislate, but its legislation may be reviewed in the courts where it is ultra vires. The Welsh Assembly may legislate on delegated powers but cannot pass primary legislation.

Form of government

Until devolution (see below) the UK was governed from Whitehall and its legislation was passed in Westminster. England, Wales, Scotland and Northern Ireland are all split into local authorities which have a wide range of statutory powers but which lack any entrenched protection against hostile governments which are able to redesign the whole face of local government by an Act of Parliament passed by a submissive Parliament. This commonly occurred in the Thatcher era and led to many accusations that the former Prime Minister had abused Parliamentary sovereignty. The resulting legislation cannot be challenged in the courts, only interpreted. However, it is widely regarded that the former Prime Minister was forced to resign because of the unpopularity of her reforms of local government taxation.

As well as local authorities, there are numerous non-departmental public bodies, quasi public bodies, regulatory authorities, privatised industries and private bodies carrying out functions under contract for the public sector which make an easy definition of the public sector impossible in a British context. In May 2002, a White Paper outlined plans for elected regional assemblies in England.[15]

A good deal of the relationship between Crown and Parliament, and constitutional niceties concerning their respective powers, may be seen in Parliament's role in implementing treaties and the impact treaties have on domestic law. This discussion will help explain the relationship between Parliament and international affairs.

Parliament and treaties

Because of the doctrine of Parliamentary sovereignty and the consequential acceptance of a dualist theory of international law, treaties cannot *ipso facto* change or amend the law of the land. They are executive acts effected under the royal prerogative and long ago the courts decided that the prerogative cannot alter or amend the law of the land.[16] Ratification by Parliament is not necessary for the UK to be bound internationally. To accept a monist[17] theory of international law, our legal doctrine informs us, would be to subvert Parliamentary sovereignty and to risk a repeat of that abuse of prerogative which led to a civil war in the seventeenth century.

---

[15] Cm 5511 *Your Region, Your Choice.* See Ch 5.
[16] *Case of Proclamations* (1611) 12 Co Rep 74. See the *Parlement Belge* (1878–9) 4 PD 129 at 154.
[17] Legal rights and obligations in treaties become a part of national law without the need for implementing legislation as compared with dualist systems which require such legislation for implementation: see p 48 et seq above.

One may ask: what has this to do with the reality of international relationships today? Be that as it may, the legacy is still keenly felt in our current law and practice. And this is so despite the fact that under EC law, as interpreted by the ECJ, it is EC law that is supreme and is so by virtue of the Treaty and Treaty obligations where states have limited their 'sovereign rights', where EC provisions may have 'direct effect' which is a fluid concept subject to development in the ECJ as we saw in Chapters 2 and 3.[18] Furthermore, the Treaty making power is a prerogative power which the courts will not question constituting as it does an act of state. It is non-justiciable.[19] When the treaty agreeing to our entry into the Common Market was questioned in the courts in 1971 to the effect that the Crown had no power to make the treaty, the courts refused to deal with the matter:

> The general principle applies to this treaty as to any other. The treaty-making power in this country rests not in the courts, but in the Crown, that is Her Majesty acting on the advice of her Ministers. When her Ministers negotiate and sign a Treaty, even a treaty of such paramount importance as this proposed one, they act on behalf of the country as a whole. They exercise the prerogative of the Crown. Their action in so doing cannot be challenged or questioned in these courts.[20]

It is important to realise that British courts take no cognisance of treaties as such – saving what is said below – until they are embodied in laws passed by Parliament 'and then only to the extent that Parliament tells us.'[21]

---

18   Case 26/62 *Van Gend en Loos* [1963] ECR 1; Case 6/64 *Costa v ENEL* [1964] ECR 585; Case 11/70 *Internationale Handelsgesellschaft mbH* [1970] ECR 1125; Case 106/77 *Simmenthal* [1978] ECR 629 etc (Ch 2, p 46 et seq). The ECJ has ruled that provisions of the GATT/WTO are not directly effective within Member States of the Community: *Portugal v Council* Case C-149/96 [1999] ECR I-8395: G de Burca and J Scott eds *The EU and the WTO: Legal and Constitutional Issues* (2002); A Rosas (2000) 37 CML Rev 797.

19   The case law on this point is legion although this must now be read to include *R v Secretary of State for Foreign and Commonwealth Affairs, ex p Rees Mogg* [1994] 1 All ER 457 see below and *Ex p Molyneaux* [1986] 1 WLR 331 where the text of an intergovernmental agreement between the UK and Ireland was examined to see if it contravened any rule of statute, common law or convention. It did not. Treaties may be used by courts as aids to interpretation; see the text below. Treaties do not create individual rights or duties until transposed into domestic law in the UK: see eg *J H Rayner Ltd v Department of Trade and Industry* [1990] 2 AC 418.

20   *Blackburn v A-G* [1971] 2 All ER 1380 at 1382 *per* Lord Denning. See however, note ... supra.

21   *Blackburn v A-G* [1971] 2 All ER 1380 at 1382 *per* Lord Denning.

In the context of the Treaty of Rome Lord Denning expressed the point vividly:

> Even though the Treaty of Rome has been signed, it has no effect, so far as these courts are concerned, until it is made an Act of Parliament. Once it is implemented by an Act of Parliament, these courts must go by the Act of Parliament, and then only to the extent that Parliament tells us.[22]

It is the Act which incorporates the Treaty and makes it effective. It is the Act to which the courts will turn. Ratification by the government does not concern the domestic courts because it does not affect the domestic law; ratification is not incorporation. Ratification is only a question of significance for domestic law where Parliament has provided that any treaty provision must be approved by Act of Parliament before it can be ratified by the government – such is the case with any increase in the powers of the European Parliament under the terms of the European Assembly Elections Act 1978.[23] Ratification is also of significance where revisions to the Treaty of Rome will have to take effect in domestic law. Before revisions in the EC Treaty are brought into force, they have to be ratified by the 'respective constitutional requirements of each Member State' (Title VIII Article 48 TEU). Legislation would therefore be necessary before ratification to implement Treaty obligations into domestic law in the UK.

An attempt was made in the House of Lords in 1996 to introduce a law that would require Parliamentary approval before ratification of treaties by the executive. This attempt to plug the 'democratic deficit' was inspired to some extent by the Second and Third Pillars of the Maastricht Treaty and the absence of supervisory powers by the National Parliament.[24]

However, dualist theories have to bow to certain subtleties of interpretation of our domestic law where the courts have shown an increasing propensity to interpret domestic law, both statutory and common law, according to treaty provisions. Norms of customary international law are accepted as part of domestic law when necessary formalities are complied with. Although treaties are not directly effective in domestic law in the absence

---

[22] *McWhirter v A-G* [1972] CMLR 882 at 886.

[23] Section 6. This is a crucial provision in facilitating litigation which would otherwise be non-justiciable.

[24] Introduced by Lord Lester of Herne Hill QC: HL Debs col 1530, 28 February 1996.

of legislation or in some cases legislative instruments, there is a presumption in our law that statutory provisions will be interpreted in accordance with international obligations when there is ambiguity in the domestic measure.[25] It has even been argued that the requirement of ambiguity has been superseded to the extent that *any* legislation passed subsequent to a treaty will be interpreted in the light of that treaty insofar as the legislation covers the same subject area as the treaty regardless of ambiguity[26] and that such international obligations will assist in the development of the common law, especially in terms of protecting human rights.[27] The pressures for such a development may be growing and were encouraged by the first judgment of the House of Lords in the *Pinochet*

[25]   See *A-G v Guardian Newspapers (No 2)* [1988] 3 All ER 545 (ChD, CA, HL).

[26]   This is an argument that has been expressed forcefully by Murray Hunt in *Using Human Rights Law in English Courts* Ch 1 (1996) who relies on dicta of Lord Diplock in *Garland v British Rail Engineering Ltd* [1983] 2 AC 751 at 771 A-B. The thesis is attractive, but probably overstretched *sic rebus stantibus*. However, in his aid Hunt can now cite the very strong dicta of Lord Browne Wilkinson who in discussing the detention during Her Majesty's pleasure of a young child convicted of murder spoke of the relationship of English statutory provisions to the UN Convention on the Rights of the Child (CRC) (TS 44 (1992) Cm 176) in terms which should be quoted in some detail:

> 'The Convention has not been incorporated into English law. But it is legitimate .... to assume that Parliament has not maintained on the statute book a power capable of being exercised in a manner inconsistent with the Treaty obligations of this country. The Secretary of State contends that he is entitled to fix a tariff which will endure throughout the childhood of the offender [without] any regard to the welfare of the child. Such a policy would infringe the Treaty obligations of this country.'

> It should be noted that the statute *predated* the Convention by almost sixty years: *R v Secretary of State for the Home Department, ex p Venables* [1997] 3 All ER 97 at 123b–d. See Lord Hoffman in *R v Lyons* [2002] UKHL 44, [2002] 4 All ER 1028 (Ch 9, note 93). See further, D Dyzenhaus, M Hunt and M Taggart (2001) Oxford University Commonwealth LJ 5 on Commonwealth case law on the CRC and the status of international human rights law in domestic law.

[27]   See *Ex p Venables* and Lord Browne-Wilkinson above on statutory construction. On the compatibility of the common law with ECHR provisions see: *Derbyshire County Council v Times Newspapers* [1992] 3 All ER 65, CA and [1993] 1 All ER 1011, HL; Sedley J in *R v Secretary of State for the Home Department, ex p McQuillan* [1995] 4 All ER 400 at 422 h–j and *Reynolds v Times Newspapers Ltd* [1999] 4 All ER 609, HL. For a case where the House of Lords refused to allow the right to privacy under ECHR Art 8 to override a question affecting the admissibility of evidence in a criminal trial obtained through a bugging device but for the CHR to rule that such a breach had occurred, see: *R v Khan* [1996] 3 All ER 289, HL and *Khan v UK* (2001) 31 EHRR 45 and the Regulation of Investigatory Powers Act 2000.

case and in the rehearing of that case.[28] As we shall see, these measures were specifically reinforced in the European Communities Act 1972 which authorised UK accession to the Community.

Further comment must be made on an argument that courts will develop domestic law in England under a broader interpretative principle which allows greater opportunity to invoke international standards particularly when seeking to protect human rights; after all the rationale for dualism in English jurisprudence is to prevent Executive excesses not thwart the promotion of human rights.[29] This point can taken up below, but it is interesting to recall the words of A V Dicey who in asserting that judges as 'exponents of morality' could not overrule Acts of Parliament observed:

> Language which might seem to imply this amounts in reality to nothing more than the assertion that the judges, as exponents of morality, when attempting to ascertain what is the meaning to be affixed to an Act of Parliament, will presume that Parliament did not intend to violate the ordinary rules of morality, or the principles of international law, and will therefore, whenever possible, give such an interpretation to a statutory enactment as may be consistent with the doctrines both of private and international morality.[30]

The internationalism of domestic English law may have reached its high water mark in the first *Pinochet* case. In this case the majority of the Law Lords ruled that norms of *international* law outlawing torture, genocide and hostage-taking, showed that such conduct was unacceptable on the part of anyone including a former Head of State and consequently those activities could not be a part of the *official* functions of a *former* Head of State. Because acts of torture and hostage-taking were offences under UK statute law over which the UK had taken extra-territorial jurisdiction, they were therefore not immune from the *domestic* criminal process including extradition in the case of the former President of Chile.[31] A request for extradition had been made by a Spanish magistrate and subsequently by the Spanish government.

---

[28] [1998] 4 All ER 897 and [1999] 2 All ER 97 see below.
[29] Hunt *Using Human Rights Law in English Courts* (1996).
[30] A V Dicey *Law of the Constitution* 10th ed 1961 pp 62–3.
[31] *R v Bow Street Metropolitan Stipendiary Magistrate, ex p Pinochet Ugarte* [1998] 4 All ER 897, HL. D Woodhouse *The Pinochet Case: A Legal and Constitutional Analysis* (2000). On state immunity and torture, see *Al Adsani v UK* App No 35763/97 (21 November 2001, unreported), ECtHR.

However, one of the judges in the case who sided with the majority, Lord Hoffman, was also a Director of Amnesty International Charity Ltd. This body was a subsidiary of Amnesty International, the latter of which had intervened in the *Pinochet* proceedings hoping to secure General Pinochet's eventual trial and conviction for serious crimes against humanity. Lord Hoffman's close relationship to Amnesty International caused a further hearing by a committee of Law Lords into the legal implications of that relationship and its effect on the original judgment. In an unprecedented decision, the Law Lords set aside the first ruling because of Lord Hoffman's close association with one of the parties to the proceedings and because he was a judge in his own cause even though he may not have been personally biased. No investigation into actual bias was made by the Law Lords; it was sufficient that justice must not only be done but must be *seen* to be done.[32] In the retrial of the *Pinochet* case by the Law Lords it was held that while a former head of state could not claim immunity from prosecution or extradition proceedings before a national court for crimes outlawed under international legal order including torture, the offences nonetheless, the majority held, had to be crimes under English law at the time of their commission in order to be subject to the extradition process. The large majority of the 'offences', but not all, were excluded from the extradition process.[33] In this way, perhaps, a balance was achieved between the norms of international law, Parliamentary sovereignty and legal certainty. It is interesting, however, to note how sensitive some of the Law Lords were to the fluid, dynamic and 'living law' quality of international law which is 'a part of the common law' and whose influence on our domestic legal development will continue.

Parliamentary sovereignty and fundamental rights

If we were to sum up in a few words the constitutional heritage of the UK, Parliamentary sovereignty is the linchpin. It has been said that our constitutional history was a commentary on Magna Carta. From the late seventeenth century, it has been a commentary upon Parliamentary sovereignty which we need to examine more closely below. In terms of fundamental human rights, the courts would protect such rights but only

---

[32]   *R v Bow Street etc, ex p Pinochet Ugarte* [1999] 1 All ER 577. On the International Criminal Court, see Ch 14, p 612.

[33]   *R v Bow Street etc, ex p Pinochet Ugarte (No 3)* [1999] 2 All ER 97, HL. Woodhouse *The Pinochet Case: A Legal and Constitutional Analysis* (2000).

to the extent that they were not overridden by legislation, the lawful exercise of police or official discretion or the often oppressive laws of defamation. This afforded them the quality of residual features in the British scheme of things rather than truly fundamental entities (see Chapter 9).[34] I shall comment at some length on the growing sensitivity of judges to fundamental rights' protection and indeed to matters constitutional elsewhere in this book. Their involvement in these matters is of relatively recent provenance and has been promoted to centre-stage by the incorporation of the ECHR into British law (see Chapter 9).

In a British context, the role of law and the courts in terms of government/ citizen relationships was not the advancement of abstract rights but the protection of residual liberties. Our rights were based in property, not abstract entities. Our civil rights were negative: a right *not* to be interfered with in the absence of lawful authority. We could only do what the law did not prohibit. We had no fundamental right *to* anything or to stop the law doing anything. Our right to freedom of speech was only co-extensive with police discretion to allow us to speak. This, many constitutional theorists believe, is the great contribution of the common law technique to our constitution. It is also perceived as a major weakness. In Chapter 9 we shall see how it is subject to fundamental change.

The Rule of Law

Before proceeding to the question of integration, the subject of democracy in the UK and the Rule of Law must be addressed. Dicey's tripartite version of the latter is well known and highly influential: the supremacy of regular law over arbitrary action; the equality of all before the law and the equal applicability of the ordinary common law to everyone except the Crown; and the existence of our constitutional law in the decisions of ordinary courts establishing the rights of ordinary individuals as protected by the common law in concrete and not abstract situations the latter of which are

---

[34]   *Tolstoy Miloslavsky v United Kingdom* (1995) 20 EHRR 442 – damages of £1.5m awarded by an English court for defamation constituted a breach of Art 10 ECHR. On the presence of a *right* to hold a peaceful and non-obstructive assembly on the highway (a reversal of common law doctrine) see: *DPP v Jones* [1999] 2 All ER 257, HL. On the impotence of the courts in the face of wide executive discretion, see *R v Secretary of State, ex p Stafford* [1998] 4 All ER 7, HL reversed by *Stafford v UK* (2002) 13 BHRC 260, ECtHR; cf, *R v Secretary of State ex p Hindley* [2000] 2 All ER 385.

contained in paper constitutions. Our constitution comes from the law; our law does not come from the constitution. Interference with an individual's life, liberty or possessions had to be justified according to clear legislation or common law precedent. Absent such authority then anyone, even the King's Secretary of State, would be acting unlawfully by committing trespass, or worse. But there was nothing to stop the Secretary obtaining the required powers from Parliament in legislation. There was no constitutional control over Parliament and Parliament's sovereignty.[35] There was no guarantee that fundamental rights would not be encroached upon.

Dicey's views have been both criticised and idealised because of their inherent conservatism, their espousal of a formal and not a more substantive form of equality and their need to be remoulded to address the realities of governmental power today.[36] Dicey caught the pragmatic and conservative ethos of the British or rather English constitution. That is how it was seen by politicians and lawyers when he wrote. He did appreciate the basis of moral precepts behind the interpretation of statutes, the common law's protection of moral principle. He was not blind to the problems associated with the impact of Parliamentary sovereignty on the rule of law – viz, the domination of Parliament by an arrogant executive making it a tool of a majority party and destroying its role as the 'grand inquest of the nation'.

What Dicey thought he saw was a system which had stood the test of time and which had, through its genius for balance, prevented abuse or distortion. A Scot, an Irishman or even a Welsh citizen might not have seen it in those terms. But it was how the English elite classes saw it. And their interpretation was the one that counted.

That the Rule of Law needs to be reformulated to suit the pluralism, internationalism and corporatism of the contemporary world, I do not doubt. This book makes a small contribution to the examination of an enhanced

---

[35]   See eg *Brogan v UK* (1988) 11 EHRR 117 and the UK derogation from Art 5(3) ECHR in relation to detention powers concerning Northern Irish suspected terrorists. This derogation was ended in 2001 (SI 2001/3644) but see now the Anti-terrorism, Crime and Security Act 2001, s 23 for a derogation from Art 5(1) ECHR.

[36]   I Harden and N Lewis *The Noble Lie: the Rule of Law and the British Constitution* (1986); J Jowell 'The Rule of Law Today' in J Jowell and D Oliver *The Changing Constitution* (2000, 4th ed).

appreciation of legality and legitimacy as necessary qualities of government, an appreciation which has been stimulated by European influence in our legal consciousness. It would be argued that access to justice, access to information and transparency, proper and full accountability for executive action in all its contemporary forms, participation of the governed in the process of their government beyond elections and optimum opportunity for self fulfilment without *any* form of discrimination are all desiderata of the rule of law today.

The 'Crown'

Central to the legitimation of the British state is the all pervasive 'Crown'. The British have an aversion to sloganising and anthropomorphizing the 'state' and justifying the use of power for the public good through legislative instrument or other devices in the name of the State or the people. Powers are personalised through the entity of the Crown which is presumed to operate in the public interest. Powers of the Crown are operative through the agency of individuals who remain directly and legally accountable for their operation before the ordinary courts of the land, as Dicey expressed the point in his account of the Rule of Law.[37] Britain is not a *Rechtsstaat.* It is not a social state or market state or any other kind of state in a constitutional sense. The notion of the rule of law as outlined above, together with the historical idea of 'freeborn Englishman' might find expression in the term *Justizstaat* but this would be alien to our usage.

The 'Crown' accounts for, or has a central role in, virtually all formal constitutional law.[38] The pervasiveness of the Crown in our constitutional affairs is the primary reason why we did not develop a stricter practice and theory of a separation of powers. There is in the UK a strong presumption that the functions and personnel of government should be split to avoid corruption and tyranny. It is interesting to observe, however, that the only system in the Community which possesses an absence of formal separation of powers in the manner of the UK is the EC. Its executive is its legislature, a role in which it must cooperate and co-decide with the Parliament; its Parliament is not a Parliament as we understand that term although it is adopting more of the techniques of a grand inquisitor. Its judiciary is

---

[37] Dicey, A V *The Law of the Constitution.*
[38] See S Sedley 'The Crown in its Courts' in C Forsyth and I Hare eds *The Golden Metwand and the Crooked Cord* (1998) and (1994) LQR 270.

independent of the other tiers of government but emerge from national courts. Its administration is built on the model of the French fourth republic – elitist and undemocratic.

Democracy

Universal franchise for those over the age of majority did not emerge until, including local government in Northern Ireland 1969; for Parliamentary elections the date was 1928, although the university and business franchises gave about 500,000 electors a double vote until abolished in 1948. Proportional representation has played no role in our elections although the New Labour Government introduced it into European Parliament elections and for elections to the Scottish Parliament, Northern Ireland and Welsh Assemblies. Our system of government operates on a representative democratic model and not a participatory one. Referenda were rare and as recently as 1972 they were regarded as unconstitutional. According to this view, the direct participation of citizens in the legislative process undermined the doctrine of Parliament as the supreme legal, constitutional and political institution in our public law. Such a doctrine was built on *representative* democracy and not *participatory* democracy and was legitimated by electoral processes. How, it was argued, could Ministers be responsible if they had handed over government to the people? In the following 25 years there has been one nationwide referendum, in fact the one and only ever national referendum, where the nation voted to remain in the European Community which achieved a two to one majority in favour (1975) and three regional referenda on Northern Ireland (1973) and Scottish and Welsh devolution (1979). Since May 1997 there have been referenda on Scottish and Welsh devolution and on the peace process in Northern Ireland (which also involved the Republic of Ireland). Other possible topics for example include electoral reform and a promise to hold a referendum before entering into Economic and Monetary Union in the EU.

Polls suggest strong support for referenda on certain issues. Where they are resorted to it has been for major constitutional changes but many fundamental changes have not been preceded by referenda: the Parliament Acts 1911 and 1949 which curtailed the veto power of the unelected House of Lords; the European Communities Act 1972 which authorised our accession to the Community; Mrs Thatcher wanted the Maastricht Treaty to go to a national referendum, a manoeuvre which her Cabinet opponents and Opposition leaders bitterly resisted for fear of losing and seeing the Treaty rejected. Events in France, Denmark and recently Ireland where a referendum initially rejected the Treaty of Nice in May 2001 support their anxiety!

There is no doubt that referenda undermine the pristine notion of Parliamentary sovereignty and representative democracy. Technically, their result is binding on the government not on Parliament. But government by definition controls Parliament. it could be argued that they weaken a government's accountability base by removing responsibility from government to the people; that they could lead to populist, divisive and anti-progressive government and that their use without a written constitution and clear rules for their use will leave them prey to political fixing and expediency.

On the other hand it has been argued:

> a referendum can, theoretically, provide a limited means of entrenchment not otherwise provided for in our constitutional arrangements. This can operate by establishing precedent or convention, which may make it difficult for a government to reverse a measure, without holding a referendum; or by establishing a statutory requirement that a referendum be held before a change may be made.[39]

The Political Parties, Elections and Referendums Act 2000 now makes statutory provision for the conduct of referendums along with an Electoral Commission and donations to political parties.

In the May 1997 Labour Party manifesto, the party promised it would introduce Freedom of Information legislation and a White Paper was promised by July 1997. This gradually slipped back to December 1997 when *Your Right to Know* (Cm 3818) was published and which set out the government's plans for access to information. The complexity of the subject and the different perspective to be gained from government as opposed to so many years in opposition necessitated, the government argued, a Bill that would not be regretted within a short period of enactment.

---

[39] *Report of the Commission on the Conduct of Referendums,* The Constitution Unit, November 1996. The Unit has recommended a statutory Commission to oversee the application of guidelines which the Unit suggested for the conduct of referenda. See *Fifth Report of the Committee on Standards in Public Life* Cm 4057 Vol I (1998) *The Funding of Political Parties in the UK* ch 12.

Their commitment to openness and legislation remained undiminished the responsible government Minister assured us and would go beyond the efforts of the previous government which had only introduced an administrative code giving a right of access to information *not* documents. A full legislative commitment to access to government information, and an appropriately drafted measure, will do much to restore faith in government in the UK, the operation of which has been characterised by 'too much secrecy'. It is a precursor to fuller democratic involvement in the process of rule and will help shift the balance of power from the government to the people; not dramatically, but significantly. The Bill when it was published was disappointing and although subject to considerable amendment and improvement still emerged with significant faults. Furthermore, its full introduction to give rights of access to individuals was deferred until January 2005. (See Chapter 6 p 287 and Cm 4355, May 1999.)

National constitutional law and European integration

From what was said above, domestic law simply took no cognisance of UK membership of international bodies until obligations arose from domestic law. Although treaties may not traditionally be cognisable by the courts except as aids to interpretation, the presence of the Treaty of Rome as amended may well have implications for treaties entered into by British governments where the provisions of the latter are contested as being in breach of obligations under Community law.[40] These treaties may well find themselves being challenged in domestic courts as well as the ECJ for the alleged contravention, the method of challenge depending upon whether the Community provisions were directly effective or not. This might sound a little rarefied, but the *Rees Mogg* litigation which I address below, has illustrated the fact that the question of legality may be put to Treaties by British courts.

Parliamentary sovereignty and transfer of sovereignty

Before the Bill allowing our accession to the Community was passed by Parliament, the Government expressed the view in a White Paper that there was 'no question of any erosion of essential national sovereignty'.[41]

---

[40]   Case C-124/95 *R v HM Treasury, ex p Centro-Com Srl* [1997] All ER (EC) 193.
[41]   *UK and European Communities* Cmnd 4715 para 29 (1971).

Furthermore, the ultimate sovereignty of Parliament was not abridged according to a Government spokesman.[42] Sovereignty may mean several things including the power to limit one's own powers by agreement which, as Lloyd LJ observed in proceedings challenging the provisions concerning Title V of Maastricht (the Common Foreign and Security Policy), constitutes not so much a limitation but an arranging for their exercise.[43] It may mean political sovereignty; here it would be difficult to accept that our political sovereignty has not been affected by membership even if one describes sovereignty as 'pooled' rather than transferred. From a legal perspective the crucial question is whether membership has 'abridged' the sovereignty of the Crown in Parliament as a legislative body – ie, with power to make or unmake any law whatsoever and over whose law no other laws are superior. Nor should it be forgotten that Parliament regards itself as the highest court in the land – the High Court of Parliament – and would probably regard itself as a constitutional court.

The answer to this question of legal sovereignty is still not definitively resolved.[44] This is hardly surprising given the disagreement over the very concept of law in the history and contemporary analysis of jurisprudence and disagreement over how sovereignty is recognised. The usefulness of 'sovereignty' itself is a contested issue in a world increasingly characterised by international co-operation and organisations.[45] Nationalism (a crude form of sovereignty) is still, however, a force to be reckoned with. It is

---

[42]   G Rippon MP HC Debs Vol 831, col 278 (15 February 1972). D Nicol describes how misunderstanding of Community Law was rife among government and opposition spokespersons in the years leading up to the 1972 Act: *European Membership and the Judicialisation of British Politics* (2002). In a White Paper in 1967 on *Legal and Constitutional Implications of UK Membership of the European Communities*, there was no reference to *Van Gend en Loos* or *Costa v ENEL* although their impact was 'sensed'. There were no articles he says in academic legal journals in England, Scotland or Northern Ireland of the two cases at the time of the first two attempts to join the EEC. Mrs Thatcher also opined that there was widespread ignorance of the implications for sovereignty in the lead-in to accession as well as ignorance of the ECJ and its jurisprudence among political leaders: *The Path to Power* (1995) p 497. H W R Wade believed that an annual statute should be passed conferring sovereignty on the Community or that every statute should contain a clause that it was subject to Community law (1972) LQR 1. Cf Lord Bridge in *Factortame* at p 195 below.

[43]   *R v Secretary of State for Foreign and Commonwealth Affairs, ex p Rees Mogg* [1994] 1 All ER 457.

[44]   An opposition attempt to include a declaration of Parliamentary sovereignty in the European Communities Bill failed: D Nicol *European Membership and the Judicialisation of British Politics* (2002).

[45]   MacCormick, N 'Beyond the Sovereign State' (1993) Mod LR 1.

present in the jurisprudence of the *Conseil Constitutionnel* and *BVerfG* as was seen in Chapter 2. The surge to the extreme right in European national politics is a recent manifestation of its vigour. I will address the legal implications of our mode of incorporation in a moment.

The traditional doctrine of Parliamentary sovereignty has not been abridged in a legal sense in that no Parliament can bind a future Parliament to legislate or not legislate on any matter, a point emphasised on several occasions by the New Labour government when promoting its constitutional reforms in its first term of office. It was repeated by the Divisional Court when Laws LJ held that 'the fundamental legal basis of the UK's relationship with the EU rested with the domestic, not the European legal powers.'[46] The 1972 legislation on accession to the Community contains provisions which seek to ensure that the supremacy of Community law cannot be abrogated by the doctrine of *implied repeal*[47] through the operation of a later inconsistent statute. The European Communities Act 1972, s 2(4) does significantly more than that.

In *Thoburn*,[48] Laws LJ took the opportunity to pronounce that the European Communities Act 1972 was a constitutional measure and therefore could not be impliedly repealed. This was not strictly necessary because of the specific provisions in the European Communities Act 1972. In seeking to suggest a common law creation of a 'constitutional statute' Sir John does raise the possibility of an extension of a hierarchy of legal norms which has not hitherto existed *legally* in the UK. His comments (obiter) have far-reaching implications in their claim that ultimately sovereignty is a matter of domestic and not Community law and if a Community measure sought to override a 'constitutional right' guaranteed by the law of England, English courts would have to decide whether the 'general words' of the European Communities Act 1972 could incorporate the measure in domestic law.

---

[46]   *Thoburn v Sunderland City Council* [2002] EWHC 195 (Admin), [2002] 4 All ER 156. If by 'domestic legal powers' he meant powers possessed by Parliament then that statement does not go far enough. If he meant courts possessing the ultimate power, it is revolutionary. He probably meant powers of Parliament interpreted by the courts: it is to the courts that 'the scope and nature of Parliamentary sovereignty are ultimately confided' at p 184a.

[47]   It is more accurate to describe the doctrine as: *implied disapplication.*

[48]   *Thoburn v Sunderland City Council* [2002] EWHC 195 (Admin), [2002] 4 All ER 156.

It is obvious that were Parliament to legislate *expressly* contrary to our EU obligations then a serious *impasse* would operate and could only be satisfactorily resolved at the political level. It is difficult to envisage circumstances in which this would occur unless the will to remain in the Community had ceased to exist in the UK government and Parliament.[49]

Formally, Parliamentary sovereignty still exists in the UK. There have always been limits on the de facto sovereignty of Parliament: there are many matters of government on which it has no say or no control: national security, foreign affairs, declarations of war and monetary policy. In a recess, backbenchers cannot recall Parliament; the initiative remains entirely with the Government. For how much longer the doctrine can exist, or whether it does still exist in its pristine legislative capacity in an unadulterated form, is a matter of considerable conjecture. The sweeping inlets of the EC and the supremacy of EC law – more like a Tsunami than tidal floods[50] – are all too obvious in their impact on the doctrine.

Parliament and accession to Europe

There was a good deal of debate as to whether an Act of Parliament was legally necessary, on the international level or the national level, before ratification in the UK of the Treaty of Accession. The prestigious committee which advised the government felt there were no reasons from the perspective of constitutional law that required Parliamentary approval before ratification, but advised against a general implementing bill before government ratification. Any Bill authorising accession should be restricted to those obligations requiring an 'immediate change in the law of the land':

> So far as the Treaties merely require or envisage some future change in United Kingdom law, we think that constitutional principles at most require that Parliament should formally express its approval of the Treaties generally, before they are ratified. It seems to us, indeed, that in respect of such future changes of the law the interests of Parliament would be

---

[49] It has been judicially claimed that Parliament has enacted legislation which is stated to apply regardless of the European Communities Act 1972: P Craig and G de Burca *EU Law: Cases and Materials* (2002, 3rd ed) p 304. The measure in question is the Fisheries Limits Act 1976 – such words were not in the original statute.

[50] *Bulmer v Bollinger* [1974] 2 All ER 1226, 1231h–j, CA and Lord Denning's famous words.

better served by asking it to pass specific implementing bills from time to time than by seeking its approval to legislation in advance.[51]

In retrospect it is fortuitous that this suggestion was not accepted and that the legislation authorising accession provided for implementation of EC obligations on a continuing basis because Bills implementing Treaty amendments have invariably been contentious and have caused narrow and bitter divisions, especially in the Commons. This is because Bills provide the opportunity for anti-European hostility as well as the usual forces of government opposition seeking to frustrate Government. The enormous majority of the New Labour government has assured an easy passage for the Bill implementing the changes introduced in the Amsterdam and Nice Treaties. Secondary legislation, which is the device invariably employed to implement Community legal duties, has a far less contentious history in terms of implementing Community obligations – though whether they are subject to adequate Parliamentary review procedures is another question. Guidelines are available on whether primary legislation or delegated statutory regulations are the appropriate mode of implementation and problems may emerge before relevant committees of both Houses if it is felt that an inappropriate mode is being employed. There may also be difficulties before the domestic courts on grounds of ultra vires.[52] Specific approval was required under the European Assembly Election Act 1978, s 6 as we saw above whenever the powers of the European Parliament are increased, provisions which operated in the amendments in the UK legislation approving Maastricht. The government only won assent from the Commons for the legislation on a vote of confidence threatening its own future as was also true of the Bill in 1994 which sought to give effect to Treaty obligations to increase the Community budget.[53] If approval by primary legislation were required before the implementation of every Community measure, the relationship between the EC and UK would have been unworkable and not simply outrageously time consuming.

---

[51]   Committee Report, Public Records Office 4 July 1962, advising the Lord Chancellor chaired by Sir Reginald Manningham-Buller A-G comprising inter alios Lord Guest, Diplock LJ, Wilberforce J: PRO LCO 29/108 5280.

[52]   If, for instance, it were felt that the regulations were going beyond the requirements of EC law and they were also beyond the provisions of the enabling domestic legislation. See St J Bates (1996) *Austrian Journal of Public and International Law* 193 and *London Boroughs Transport Committee v Freight Transport Association Ltd* [1991] 1 WLR 828, HL.

[53]   European Communities (Finance) Act 1995.

Parliamentary approval of Maastricht Treaty and European Union

Be that as it may, the approval of the Maastricht Treaty by Parliament – in accordance with the provisions of the European Assembly Election Act 1978, s 6 (p 199 below) – led to some of the most prolonged disputes in Parliament since the end of the Second World War. In fact the government faced defeat both because of its small majority and bitter divisions within its own party on the European question.[54] Defeat would have meant a general election, a scenario only avoided by a resort by the Prime Minister, John Major, to a vote of confidence which was linked to the government's proposal to approve Maastricht although the point has been made that the approval given by Parliament which was necessary for the European Communities (Amendment) Act 1993 to come into effect[55] was never actually given and that a court could have ruled on its legality.[56]

More importantly from a constitutional jurisprudential perspective was the challenge mounted in the courts to the government's attempts to ratify the Treaty and in the alleged failure to obtain appropriate legislation.

The Rees Mogg litigation

The case – described by its protagonist Lord Rees Mogg as 'the most important constitutional case since the seventeenth century' though this was regarded by the judge as hyperbole – was commenced by ordinary process of judicial review for which the applicant was considered to have sufficient interest or locus standi to proceed. Furthermore, the case raised matters of internal Parliamentary proceedings to which great exception was taken in many quarters; the Speaker of the House of Commons ruled that no breach of Parliamentary privilege had occurred. The judge, although he had doubts about whether the matter was justiciable in so far as it related to the competence of the Crown to enter into Treaties, nonetheless gave a ruling on the merits of the case, an approach which is to be welcomed because the case raised a question of legality.

---

[54] The bitterness over Europe still lives on: see Mrs Thatcher *Statecraft: Strategies for a Changing World* (2002), chs 9 and 10.

[55] In accordance with s 7 of the 1993 legislation.

[56] See Marshall (1993) Public Law 402. Cf E Denza *'La Ratification du Traité de Maastricht par le Royame-Uni' Revue du Marché commun et de l'union européenne*, 376 mars 1994 p 172.

In this litigation, the editor of the *Times* newspaper sought a declaration from the court that the Foreign Secretary could not lawfully ratify the TEU because he lacked crucial powers in vital aspects. The challenge was three-pronged. First of all, that in ratifying the Protocol on Social Policy the Government would breach the European Assembly Election Act 1978, s 6 because under paragraph 3 the protocol was annexed to the EC Treaty not the Union Treaty and the approval of the latter under the European Communities (Amendment) Act 1993, s 1(2) did not include approval of the Protocol. This was rejected on the grounds that the protocols were incidental or supplementary to the Union Treaty and were therefore approved and 'the Treaty on European Union' referred to in the 1993 Act, s 1(2) meant the whole of the Union Treaty including the protocols.

Secondly, it was claimed that the government had ratified the Protocol by prerogative and had thereby altered the content of domestic law without explicit statutory authorisation. This was allegedly unlawful because the power of the government to alter or add to Community law under the EC Treaty was limited by statute so that such law could only be amended by statute as provided by the European Communities Act 1972, s 2(1). Once Parliament limits the power of the prerogative by statutory provision it is the statute which takes precedence.[57] This was a subtle argument which rested on the ground that by excluding the operation of the protocol in domestic law, the government had nonetheless altered Community law – 'the fundamental law of the UK' – which would in turn affect our internal law by process of decisions of the ECJ and case law developments influenced by the protocol. The whole of the Treaty had been *approved* by Parliament but any amendment to Community law must be *effected* by specific legislative incorporation. Once again this argument was rejected by Lloyd LJ who held that there was no such limitation to the Treaty making capacity of the Crown.[58] The crucial factor was whether the government wished to alter domestic law and the Protocol was explicitly excluded from those provisions within section 1(1) of the 1993 Act which incorporate Treaty provisions within domestic law.[59] No such alteration was intended by the government.

---

[57]   *A-G* v *De Keyser's Royal Hotel* [1920] AC 508. And note *R* v *Secretary of State for Home Affairs, ex p Fire Brigades' Union* [1995] 2 All ER 244, HL.

[58]   He felt that were this the case then there would have been no need to pass EAEA 1978, s 6 for instance.

[59]   Excluded by the 1993 Act, s 1(1) from Treaties within the 1972 Act, s 1(2) taking effect within domestic law.

The third ground of attack concerned the argument that the prerogative of foreign and security policy had been abandoned without legislative authority. The UK government's agreement to be bound under the Second Pillar was therefore unlawful, it was argued. Title V of the TEU was an exercise of the prerogative and not an abandonment, the court ruled.

Constitutional limitations: international affairs

The traditional doctrine of Parliamentary sovereignty would not countenance the transfer of sovereignty in perpetuity, unless Parliament abolished itself. The fact that the rule of Parliamentary sovereignty pre-exists any claim to such sovereignty and owes its existence to the common law may well mean that the judiciary would not readily accept such an institutional suicide. The doctrine might at best accept some forms of self embracing limitation of which, in traditional terms at least, the European Communities Act 1972 is an example. Government could not abandon its prerogative of foreign affairs without legislative support, which it would be unlikely to obtain, although it may arrange for its exercise as a joint initiative.[60]

In terms of international affairs the membership of the Community has clearly changed emphasis and direction in our foreign policy and international relationships. The movement from Empire to Commonwealth of which the Queen is still Head brought a grouping that was less easily malleable to British wishes and in the 'special relationship' between the UK and US the rapport was less evident from the post Suez era – although it is occasionally rekindled as events post 11 September 2001 revealed. What is interesting is that the Minister with responsibility for our relations with the Community and Treaties is the Secretary of State for *Foreign and Commonwealth Affairs*. The most important development affecting our foreign affairs has come with the Intergovernmental Pillars – the Common Foreign and Security Policy including defence, and Justice and Home Affairs, now police and judicial co-operation in criminal affairs, with our European partners. After 11 September, Parliament legislated to incorporate various Third Pillar matters into domestic law in the Anti-terrorism, Crime and Security Act 2001, s 111 but only until 1 July 2002. This was to provide a common definition for offences and other items. The point was made that by introducing such measures under the section by delegated

---

[60]   *R v Secretary of State for Foreign Affairs, ex p Rees Mogg* [1994] 1 All ER 457 citing *The Case of King's Prerogative in Saltpetre* (1606) 12 Co Rep 12. See on international air traffic agreeements: Case C-466/98 *Commission v UK* (5 November 2002, unreported), ECJ.

instrument, the method bore a relationship to EC law and its implementation. But there was no effective oversight of Third Pillar items and the measures potentially could carry very heavy penalties.

An interesting factor to emerge from the peace settlement in Northern Ireland in the Easter of 1998 was the preparedness of the British government to establish an intergovernmental arrangement to oversee Irish affairs in justice and other items although this could be seen as a development of an initiative begun in 1985 (see Chapter 5 below). The UK has not exercised itself over the effect of GATT on domestic law and EC law in the manner of other Member States.[61]

Intergovernmental Pillars

It is a historical fact that the British do not generally desire to judicialise their politics. The areas covered by the Intergovernmental Pillars are seen in some quarters as areas of high political content which are taking away prerogative from government and oversight from Parliament and which deal in any event with matters which are not covered by the aims of the original Treaty. At the level of xenophobia, this is an outrage to the 'Little Englander' who despises any trend towards internationalism – EU or otherwise. A calmer and still sceptical approach has doubt about the practicality of this Intergovernmental relationship. The view of those who see this as a natural progression from the implications of the Community and EU will none the less approach with apprehension the absence of provisions for Parliamentary review of the two pillars. The House of Commons European Legislation Committee had no scrutiny role whatsoever in terms of the Second and Third Pillars and other committees are fed with a paucity of, or no information, on these matters. Reforms introduced from 1999 have improved the situation (see Chapter 7).

The legality of the Second Pillar and the British government's agreement to that part of the Treaty of European Union was alleged to be unlawful in the *Rees Mogg* litigation in so far as it attempted to abandon the prerogative power without statutory authorisation 'the most interesting of the [challenger's] arguments jurisprudentially; but ... the weakest'.[62] The court was prepared to examine the question on its merits (contra *Blackburn* at note 21 above) although it felt that the matter was non-justiciable and held

---

61   See note 18 above.
62   *R v Secretary of State for Foreign Affairs, ex p Rees Mogg* [1994] 1 All ER 457 at p 468 per Lloyd LJ.

that it constituted an *exercise* of prerogative powers, not their abandonment. 'In the last resort it would be open to the government to denounce the Union Treaty, or at least to fail to comply with its international obligations under Title V.'[63] The claim was rejected on the ground that it was not justiciable or if it were, it failed on the merits. Parliamentary review of Third Pillar proposals is covered in Chapter 7.

The mode of incorporation of Community law

In the process of giving judgment in *Rees Mogg*, Lloyd LJ in a throwaway remark reaffirmed the traditional approach to Parliamentary sovereignty when he said: 'It follows that the protocol is not one of the Treaties covered under the European Communities Act 1972, s 2(1) by which alone Community Treaties have force in domestic law.'[64] We have already spoken of the doctrine of Parliamentary sovereignty and how the doctrine holds that no one Parliament can bind a future Parliament. We need to say something – which will also be relevant for points raised below – about the mode of incorporation of Community law into domestic law because the mode of incorporation will help British and non-British observers appreciate why there has not been that difficulty in the acceptance of EC law as supreme which has been witnessed until recently with the Conseil d'Etat in France[65] and the German Constitutional Court and elsewhere (see Chapter 2, pp 75 and 80).[66]

The courts will look to the words of the statute and they will in cases of doubt refer to the Treaty as an aid to construction: 'and not only as an aid but as an overriding force'.[67] The crucial provision is the European Communities Act 1972, s 2(1). This states:

---

[63]   *R v Secretary of State for Foreign Affairs, ex p Rees Mogg* [1994] 1 All ER 457.

[64]   *R v Secretary of State for Foreign and Commonwealth Affairs, ex p Rees Mogg* [1994] 1 All ER 457 at p 467g. See Laws LJ in *Thoburn v Sunderland City Council* [2002] EWHC 195 (Admin), [2002] 4 All ER 156.

[65]   Until the judgments in *Nicolo* [1990] 1 CMLR 173 and *SA Rothmans International France etc* [1993] 1 CMLR 253; see also P Oliver 'The French Constitution and the Treaty of Maastricht' (1994) 43 ICLQ 1. See Ch 2, p 75 et seq.

[66]   J Kokott (1996) European Public Law 237 and 413; N Foster 'The German Constitution and EC Membership' (1994) Public Law 392 and the Maastricht judgment of the Constitutional Court: (1994) 1 CMLR 57.

[67]   Per Lord Denning in Case 129/79 *Macarthys v Smith* [1979] ICR 785 at 789. NB *Pepper v Hart* [1993] 1 All ER 42, HL.

> All such rights, powers, liabilities, obligations and restrictions from time
> to time created or arising by or under the Treaties, and all such remedies
> and procedures from time to time provided for by or under the Treaties,
> as in accordance with the Treaties are without further enactment to be
> given legal effect or used in the United Kingdom shall be recognised and
> available in law, and be enforced, allowed and followed accordingly; and
> the expression 'enforceable Community right' and similar expressions
> shall be read as referring to one to which this subsection applies.

Section 1(2) defines the 'Treaties' or 'Community Treaties' for the purposes
of s 2(1); the definition may be extended by Order in Council. They include
protocols and annexes. An 'enforceable Community right' is one created
under the Treaties in accordance with the Treaties and their interpretation
by the ECJ. The ECJ created the doctrine of direct effect, ie the creation of
rights for individuals from the Treaty provisions and from Directives (pp
46 and 97). Section 2(1) covers all existing 'rights, powers etc..'. By s 2(2)
provision is made to implement future legal obligations by Order in Council
or regulations—limits are set out in Sch 2 to the Act on what may be the
subject of such subordinate instruments.

Section 2(4) establishes a rule of construction that 'any enactment passed
or to be passed ... shall be construed and have effect subject to the
foregoing provisions of this section'. This provision seeks to ensure that
subsequent legislation is interpreted in a manner which is consistent with
s 2(1) and regulations made under s 2(1). The doctrine of implied repeal
could not override the obligations in s 2(1) and (4). The effect of s 2(4) was
put to the test in a case where market traders were refusing to use metric
measurements as required by statutory orders. When prosecuted under
the orders, one of which was made under the European Communities Act
1972, s 2(2), the respondents argued that s 2(2) was impliedly repealed by
the Weights and Measures Act 1985 which in section 1 set out imperial
and metric measurements as standards of measurement (subject to
amendment). The plain terms of the European Communities Act 1972 would
defeat such a construction. The court chose to address points of wider
constitutional significance (below).

Section 3 makes the decisions of the ECJ on the meaning and effect of EC
law authoritative as precedent for UK courts, that the latter will interpret
Community law obligations in accordance with the provisions of the ECJ.
UK courts treat EC law as a question of law and not fact, the latter of which
is how the question of 'foreign' law is usually treated in English courts.

Section 2(3) authorised public expenditure from the Consolidated Fund or National Loans Fund for community obligations deriving from the Treaties.[68]

The thrust of s 2(1) is that any provisions which are directly effective or directly applicable in Community law are to be treated as directly effective or applicable respectively in domestic courts and those courts must act accordingly. In this way the conventions of standard British legal practice are maintained: judges do what Parliament tells them to do and Parliament has told them that Community law must be accepted on the terms under which it is made or interpreted according to the appropriate Community institutions. The ECJ has told domestic courts that Community law is sovereign in matters of Community competence (p 46 et seq). The limited understanding of leading politicians' and Parliament's comprehension on what these provisions meant before the Bill was enacted was described above.

The supremacy of Community law is recognised by a domestic legal provision because in terms of legal validity it is to the statute that a judge will look, not to the Treaty. The mechanism is crucial because it means that the supremacy of Community law is achieved by an ordinary Act of Parliament and not by any basic constitutional provisions. We have seen Laws LJ's description in the *Thoburn* case of the European Communities Act 1972 as a 'constitutional statute'. Besides limiting the doctrine of implied repeal (disapplication[69]) where matters of constitutional gravity are contained in such a statute, the courts would expect the clearest and most express of formulations to repeal such measures. But this has probably always been the case. No additional *legal* significance is afforded to such statutes by way of entrenchment if Parliament should wish to diminish our rights – Sir John admits as much. That being the case, and in the absence of a written constitution, there are no other basic constitutional provisions which may clash with the recognition of Community law such as inability to rule on the legality of legislation (*Conseil d'Etat*), incompatibility between the constitution and a Union Treaty on eg, protection for tiers of government or democratic representation (Germany) or on special provisions relating to right to life (Ireland).[70] By Act of Parliament, Community law has become a part of 'our law' said Lord Denning and

---

[68]   See below.
[69]   Because the statute can still possibly be applied in non-Community areas.
[70]   See Case C-159/90 *Grogan* [1991] ECR I-4685.

although not 'supplanting 'English law' (sic) it overrides any part that is inconsistent with it.[71]

Bills giving effect in domestic law to those provisions of the Single European Act 1987 which were to be incorporated into law were very short, as indeed were the Bills implementing TEU and Amsterdam and Nice. This was so because the framework had been set by the 1972 legislation which as we have seen allows those parts of the Treaty which are to be incorporated to be named in one sub clause, the Treaty and protocols to be approved for the purposes of section 6 of the European Assembly Elections Act 1978 in another clause and various incidental items.

Judicial acceptance of Community law's supremacy

The comments of Lord Denning above from *Macarthy's v Smith* invite discussion of what it is that EC law actually constitutes. In that case, Lord Denning observed that although EC law does not supplant English law, it 'overrides' any domestic law inconsistent with it. In interpreting domestic provisions covered by a Community competence, the courts will use the Treaty not simply as an aid to construction but as an overriding force in cases of 'doubt': this must include any case where there appears to be an inconsistency between Community law and a domestic provision. I shall say more about this below.

It has been argued that s 2(1) is *sui generis* as it allows for the recognition of the sovereignty of EC law in the UK without resort to doctrines of 'incorporation' of international norms or 'delegation' by Parliament of law-making powers.[72] Incorporation could not account for Community law's continuing development as a body of living law within the body of law enforced through domestic courts. Delegation of sovereignty cannot be made. It allows for the application of directly effective Community law as law in the UK but not as 'part of the law of the UK' as the Solicitor General phrased the point in 1972 when helping to steer the Bill through Parliament.[73] However correct at the time this description was, we would now question its accuracy. The law has evolved.

---

[71]   Case 129/79 *Macarthys v Smith* [1981] 1 All ER 111 at 120.
[72]   Hunt *Using Human Rights Law in English Courts* (1996) pp 56-8.
[73]   G Howe cited in Hunt *Using Human Rights Law in English Courts* (1996) p 56. See also: G Winterton (1977) LQR 591.

Numerous judgments describe EC law as part of English law: 'the law of the EU is itself part of our domestic law.[74] The undesirable nature of 'twin-tracking' has been observed on various occasions whereby the law will give a result or utilise an approach in a case before a domestic court involving EC law, but in a purely domestic case the EC principles will not be invoked eg proportionality[75] or a different result would be achieved under EC law and domestic law, eg issuing an injunction against Ministers of the Crown in their official capacity.[76] There are occasions where the courts will hold that although domestic law must not be inconsistent with Community Treaty provisions, this does not apply where the domestic provision does not affect Community competence. In *R v MAFF, ex p First City Trading*[77] Laws J held that no general principle of Community law, in this case equality, applied to allow the court to rule on a contravention of Community law where the domestic provision in question did not affect Community law competence. Because that competence was unaffected, the domestic provision could not be ruled unlawful on the ground that it breached basic principles of Community law fashioned by the ECJ. Technically the judgment may be correct; if Community law is not affected, Community law cannot apply. But the judgment cannot prevent what we have seen all too readily elsewhere: the influence of Community law may spill over into the development of our domestic law and help shape its contours.

I would argue that the time has arrived when words that were applied to the co-existence of common law and equity which were originally separate jurisdictions in England concerning separate courts but whose powers and principles could both, by virtue of legislation, be exercised by different courts concurrently will increasingly have relevance for EC and domestic law:

> Your Lordships have been referred to the vivid phrase traceable to the first edition of Ashburner, *Principles of Equity* where, in speaking in 1902 of

---

[74] Laws LJ in *Thoburn v Sunderland City Council* [2002] EWHC 195 (Admin) [2002] 4 All ER 156 at p 162g; Lord Woolf MR in *R v HFEC, ex p Blood* [1997] 2 All ER 687 at 691j; in spite of his inconsistency see Denning's comments in *Macarthy's v Smith* above.

[75] See J Jowell (1996) European Public Law 401 and G de Burca (1997) European Public Law 561

[76] *M v Home Office* [1993] 3 All ER 537, HL and Case C-213/89 *R v Secretary of State, ex p Factortame (No 2)* [1991] 1 All ER 70 (ECJ and HL).

[77] [1997] 1 CMLR 250.

the effect of the Supreme Court of Judicature Act he says 'the two streams of jurisdiction' (sc law and equity) – 'though they run in the same channel, run side by side and do not mingle their waters.' My Lords, by 1977 this metaphor has in my view become both mischievous and deceptive. The innate conservatism of English lawyers may have made them slow to recognise that by the Supreme Court of Judicature Act 1873 the two systems of substantive and adjectival law formerly administered by courts of law and Courts of Chancery .... were fused. As at the confluence of the Rhône and Saône, it may be possible for a short distance to discern the source from which each part of the combined stream came, but there comes a point at which this ceases to be possible. If Professor Ashburner's fluvial metaphor is to be retained at all, the waters of the confluent streams of law and equity have surely mingled now.[78]

What I am suggesting is not that Community Law can in any way be overridden by mingling with our domestic law. It is rather suggested that in British courts the two systems are intermingling to such an extent that their application through such courts will cause both to have a profound impact and influence on each other and not simply within areas covered by Community competence within the domestic jurisdiction. This can be seen in other Member States where the Community courts have drawn on national law for inspiration, and have then influenced domestic legal development. The case of *Hautala* in Chapter 6 concerning access to documents is a clear example (p 269 et seq).

Interpretation of domestic measures within the Community competence

The courts have held that where a provision of national law conflicts with a directly effective provision of Community law the latter is supreme. This arises whenever:

[t]here is a conflict or inconsistency between the law contained in an article of the EEC Treaty and the law contained in the internal law of one of the member states, whether passed before or after joining the Community. It says that in any such event the law of the European Community shall prevail over that of the internal law of the member state.[79]

---

[78]   *United Scientific Holdings Ltd v Burnley Borough Council* [1978] AC 904 at 924 *per* Lord Diplock.

[79]   *Shields v Coomes* [1979] 1 All ER 456 at 461 per Lord Denning and *Felixstowe Dock and Railway Co v British Docks Board* [1976] 2 CMLR 655, CA.

Any ambiguity in the domestic statutes or inconsistencies with Community law should be resolved by giving primacy to Community law. Where there is a genuine conflict between domestic law and Community law of the European Communities Act 1972, s 2(4) says that it should be interpreted according to Community law:

> If on close investigation it should appear that our legislation is deficient or inconsistent with Community law by some oversight of our draftsmen then it is our bounden duty to give priority to Community law. Such is the result of section 2(1) and 2(4) of the ... 1972 Act.

> ...I have assumed that our Parliament, whenever it passes legislation, intends to fulfil its obligations under the Treaty. If the time should come when our Parliament deliberately passes an Act with the intention of repudiating the Treaty or any provision in it or intentionally of acting inconsistently with it and says so in express terms then I should have thought that it would be the duty of our courts to follow the statute of our Parliament.[80]

Lord Denning's approach was to start with the EU provisions, establish what they require and then interpret domestic provisions in accordance with such requirements so far as that is not impossible. It inverts the traditional approach which starts with the statute, establishes its plain meaning and then asks to what extent other provisions can fit in with that meaning.

The thrust of the first paragraph of the quotation above was supported in subsequent case law by Lord Diplock in *Garland v British Rail Engineering Ltd*.[81] In *Garland* a female employee complained that her employer was discriminating against her because of her sex in that on retirement, male employees continued to receive travel concessions for their families, whereas female employees did not. A division in opinion had occurred between the Employment Appeal Tribunal and the Court of Appeal (which included Lord Denning) on how the words 'a provision in relation to ... retirement' should be interpreted. If the concession were such

---

80   Case 129/79 *Macarthys v Smith* [1979] 3 All ER 325 at 329 *per* Lord Denning. See, however, Cumming Bruce LJ in the same case and in [1981] 1 All ER 111 at 121. See also *R v Secretary of State for Transport, ex p Factortame* [1989] 2 All ER 692, HL at 700 where it was stated that s 2(4) has the same effect as if a section were included in every subsequent Act of Parliament expressly stipulating that the contents of later statutes were to be without prejudice to directly effective rights under Community Law.

81   Case 12/81 *Garland v British Rail Engineering Ltd* [1983] 2 AC 751.

a provision, it was excluded from the discrimination legislation.[82] Lord Diplock's approach was that if a domestic provision 'without undue straining' could be given two interpretations, one consistent with EC provisions, the other not, then the consistent interpretation should be adopted.

Indeed, in *Garland,* an argument has been advanced that Lord Diplock supported a *general presumption* (emphasis added) of conformity of domestic law with earlier international Treaty norms, *a fortiori* those under the EC Treaty. Such a presumption was not confined to domestic provisions implementing a Treaty which were unclear as traditional doctrine suggests.[83] The end result of that latter case has been that the courts are giving primary emphasis to the interpretation of national law in conformity with Community law. This is achieved not by the process of immediate and direct application of EC law which is the approach of the ECJ whether the national law is prior to or comes after the rule of Community law.[84] It is achieved by reference to the statute. This interpretation is not universally accepted.[85] Hunt, for instance, argues that such an interpretation does not do justice to Lord Diplock's emphasis on consistency with international treaties.[86]

The effect of *Macarthy's v Smith* and *Garland* is that where obligations are in the Treaty or secondary laws, the court must make national measures comply where a meaning consistent with treaty obligations can be produced from the measure in question. Where a domestic provision can be interpreted in different ways, that construction which is consistent with Community law should be chosen. A certain ambivalence has continued especially in relation to implementation of Directives which are not directly effective but where there are certain domestic legislative provisions which are inconsistent with the Directives. Most of the cases have concerned equal treatment. Again the ECJ has made it clear that the legislation whether passed before or after the Directive must be interpreted so as to be consistent with the Directive, a ruling that has attracted criticism from sources which are far from being unsympathetic to the Community and

82   Sex Discrimination Act 1975, s 6(4).
83   *Saloman v Customs and Excise Comrs* [1966] 3 All ER 871.
84   Case 106/77 *Simmenthal* [1978] 3 CMLR 263.
85   G Anthony *UK Public Law and European Law* (2002) pp 78 et seq.
86   M Hunt *Using Human Rights Law in English Courts* (1997).
87   Slynn, Sir G *Introducing a European Legal Order* (1992) at 124.

Community law.[87] British courts had displayed a reluctance to interpret national provisions in such a manner and ECJ decisions themselves,[88] the House of Lords argued, did not require that 'a court of a member state must distort the meaning of a domestic statute so as to conform with Community law which is not directly applicable.'[89] The opinion in *Duke v GEC Reliance* was that s 2(4) had no, or at best limited application, where a provision of EC law was not directly effective and was *preceded* by the relevant national law.

The question in point was whether different retirement ages for men and women, 65 and 60 respectively, were protected from attack for illegality through discrimination on the ground that in the Sex Discrimination Act 1975, s 6(4), it was stated that a statutory prohibition on the grounds of sex did not apply to 'provisions in relation to death or retirement.' In the case, the female worker was required to retire following her 60th birthday. *Marshall I*[90] had ruled that such a difference in the requirement of retirement age was a contravention of Directive 76/207/EEC, and the UK government took on board this ruling by piloting through Parliament the Sex Discrimination Act 1986. But the Act was not retrospective so the appellant in *Duke*, whose claim predated the 1986 Act, could not claim the benefit of that statute. Nor was the Directive in question directly effective, because its enforcement was being sought against an employer who was a private body and not a public authority. Where an Act is passed to give effect to a Directive or other Community obligation 'a British court will seldom encounter difficulty in concluding that the language of the Act is effective for the intended purpose.' But that was not the case here and furthermore the 1974 White Paper *Equality for Women*, (Cmnd 5724, paras 41 and 42) decisions of the EAT and Court of Appeal and 'political' and 'sociological' reality had all helped to determine the parameters of employment conditions at the time in the UK:

> But the construction of a British Act of Parliament is a matter of judgment
> to be determined by British courts and to be derived from the language of

---

[88] Case 14/83 *Von Colson* [1986] 2 CMLR 430. At para 28, the ECJ stated that the national court must interpret the provision 'in so far as it is given discretion to do so under national law.'

[89] *Duke v GEC Reliance Ltd* [1988] 1 All ER 626 at 636, HL: cf, *Finnegan v Clowney Youth Training Programme Ltd* [1990] 2 All ER 546, HL.

[90] Case 152/84 [1986] ECR 723. Denning attacked the *Marshall* decision in the House of Lords but made no reference to his decision in *Macarthy's* or in *Blackburn* [1971] 2 All ER 1380; HL Vol 479 cols 1057–59; D Nicol note 42 above at pp 175–76.

the legislation considered in the light of the circumstances prevailing at the date of enactment. The Act was not passed to give effect to the Equal Treatment Directive.[91]

Lord Templeman gave the unanimous decision of the House of Lords. There had been no breach of Community law in the interpretation favouring discrimination. Furthermore, s 2(4) of the 1972 Act only applied 'where Community provisions are directly applicable' (sic).

Where the legislation followed the Directives, subsequent decisions of the House of Lords have shown a willingness to construe statutes in accordance with Directives even where such a construction was not in accordance with the literal meaning of the statutes but where it corresponded with the intentions of the government in introducing amending regulations.[92] In *Pickstone v Freemans plc,* the decision concerned equal pay for work of equal value where the women in question claimed they were paid less in unjustifiable circumstances than a male doing different work of which their work was of equal value although they were paid the same rate as a male doing work which was the same as theirs. The House of Lords dismissed the employers' appeal who argued that under the Equal Pay Act 1970 as amended, the women's claim was barred under s 1(2)(c) because they were paid the same rate as a male performing the same work. Such a construction, which could legitimately have been made, would mean that Parliament had failed yet again to comply with its obligations under Article 119 of the Treaty.[93] The Minister in presenting the draft regulations to Parliament, made no reference to such an exclusion and the words must be construed 'purposively' to give effect to the 'manifest broad intention' of the Minister and Parliament.[94] If the employers are right 'Parliament simply failed in its purpose and that is a conclusion the court must strive to avoid ... unless it is compulsively driven to it.... Either way, a construction which permits the section to operate as a fulfilment of the UK's obligation under the Treaty involves not so much doing violence to the language of the section as filling a gap by an implication which arises, not from the words used, but from the manifest

91   Note 89, Lord Templeman at 635.
92   *Litster v Forth Dry Dock Co Ltd* [1989] 1 All ER 1134 and *Pickstone v Freemans plc* [1988] 2 All ER 803.
93   This was a reference to a requirement for a job evaluation study to be conducted before a comparison with different kinds of work could be made but no obligation was placed on employers to conduct such a study at an employee's request: *EC Commission v UK* Case 61/81 [1982] ECR 2601.
94   Lord Keith at 807d.

purpose of the Act and the mischief it was intended to remedy.'[95] Following Lord Diplock's observation in *Garland*, it was possible to construe the provision in a manner which was consistent with the UK's express and manifest obligations in a Treaty and a Directive which the regulations were seeking to implement, even though this meant adding necessary words to the domestic provision as spelt out in Lord Templeman's judgment.

The decision 'established that the greater flexibility available to the court in applying a purposive construction to legislation designed to give effect to the UK's treaty obligations to the Community enables the court, where necessary, to supply by implication words appropriate to comply with those obligations.'[96] *Litster v Forth Dry Dock and Engineering Co Ltd* concerned construction of Transfer of Undertakings (Protection of Employment) Regulations 1981 (TUPE) and Council Directive 77/187/EEC.

Lord Oliver said that:

> If the [UK] legislation can reasonably be construed so as to conform with [EC] obligations, obligations which are to be ascertained not only from the wording of the relevant Directive but from the interpretation placed on it by the [ECJ], such a purposive construction will be applied even though, perhaps, it may involve some departure from the strict and literal application of the words which the [UK] legislature has elected to use. (p 140d)

The famous decision of the ECJ in *von Colson*[97] (see Chapter 3, p 102) emphasised the duty of national courts under Article 10 [5] EC to interpret implementing measures in a manner consistent with Directives. This decision did not assist the claimant in *Duke* Lord Templeman believed. *Von Colson* did assist the claimant in *Pickstone v Freemans plc* he believed. There followed a decision of the ECJ[98] which did not restrict the duty to

---

[95]   Lord Oliver at 816g and 817c.
[96]   Lord Oliver in *Litster* [1989] 1 All ER 1134, HL.
[97]   [1984] ECR 1891.
[98]   Case C-106/89 *Marleasing* [1990] ECR I-4135 although the ECJ stated (para 8) 'in so far as possible' and see *Von Colson* [1986] 2 CMLR 430; for limits on this doctrine of interpretation where compatibility is impossible see Case C-334/92 *Wagner Miret v Fondo de Garantía Salarial* [1995] 2 CMLR 49 and the doctrine will not apply to perfect an imperfect national criminal provision: *Kolpinghuis Nijmegen BV* [1987] ECR 3969, and see *R (on the application of the Department of the Environment, Food and Rural Affairs) v ASDA Stores Ltd* [2002] EWHC 1335 (QB) [2002] 2 CMLR 66 – prosecution under EC regulations could only be

the interpretation of implementing measures: it was made clear that national provisions whether implementing EC law or not must be interpreted in the light of relevant Directives – so much is required by Article 10 [5] EC. In subsequent litigation on this point the House of Lords interpreted a statute passed prior to a Directive in accordance with the Directive reversing the ruling of the Court of Appeal though not without indicating certain possible limitations to this approach on the factual circumstances of a future case.[99] The decision in *Marleasing* and the difficulties it has caused, was discussed in Chapter 3, p 102 'Consistent construction' of domestic provisions with those in Directives is a strong feature of the approach in English courts. A further case on the TUPE Regulations featured in *British Fuels Ltd v Baxendale*[100] where the House of Lords produced a decision which left the details of a transferred contract of employment to be determined by domestic law but in a manner which did not continue all the terms and conditions of the former employment but which was consistent with decisions of the ECJ, bar one. In holding that the employee had no contract with the transferee immediately before a take-over and once the contract was terminated by the former employer, the House of Lords disagreed with the ECJ's decision in *Dethier*.[101]

In *R v Durham County Council, ex p Huddleston*[101A] an English court came very close to imposing a direct horizontal duty on an individual arising from a Directive. Such duties may only be imposed against an 'emanation of the state' as we have seen. In *Huddleston* a developer of land was

---

brought where domestic statutes/regulations were in force at the time the EC regulation took effect unless a prior statute expressly included the possibility of future amendment by EC regulations: and note Case C-168/95 *Luciano Arcaro* [1996] ECR I-4705 and see the cases in Ch 2, pp 102-103.

99   *Webb v EMO Air Cargo (UK) Ltd (No2)* [1995] 4 All ER 577 following an Article 177 EC ruling from the ECJ after a preliminary reference by the English court. See Case C-109/00 *Tele Danmark A/S* [2001] ECR I-6993. On the interpretation of a contract in a manner consistent with a Directive (but not on *Marleasing* criteria) and different approaches by the Court of Appeal and Law Lords, see: *White v White and Motor Insurers' Bureau* [1999] 1 CMLR 1251, CA and [2001] UKHL 9, [2001] 2 CMLR 1.

100   [1998] 4 All ER 609.

101   *Dethier* [1998] ECR I-1061. Lord Slynn said the position was *acte clair*. There has been considerable divergence between the ECJ and English courts on the interpretation of TUPE provisions: Case C-13/95 *Süzen* [1997] ECR I-1259; *ECM Ltd v Cox* [1999] 4 All ER 669 and *ADI (UK) Ltd v Willer* [2001] All ER (D) 237.

101A   [2000] 1 WLR 1484, CA.

awarded deemed planning permission under the Planning and Compensation Act 1991 where in fact there had been a procedural irregularity in that no Environmental Impact Assessment had been made in breach of Community law. A relevant Directive had not been implemented properly by the UK. The Court of Appeal, overruling the High Court, ruled that the unimplemented Directive was directly binding upon the public authority and thereby imposed duties on the authority which they could not ignore, or do so only at their peril. The claimant was not claiming a direct entitlement under the Directive which imposed burdens on other individuals; the Court was ensuring that conditions placed upon the securing by an individual of a benefit from the state were enforced and that the benefit was 'within the permitted transposition of Community law.' It is clear that an unimplemented Directive cannot be used to perfect an imperfect criminal indictment. But the development of 'triangular situations' in which individuals gain the benefit of unimplemented Directives because of public law consequences on an official decision has been seen in the ECJ's jurisprudence.[102] What, however, if the effect of the decision in *Huddleston* had been to stop the developer after he had begun to excavate minerals rather than simply to prevent a valid consent being conferred?

It would appear, subject to the limitations seen by the ECJ itself, that the stage has been reached where British courts have accepted that indirectly effective provisions of EC law must be invoked in the construction of domestic measures. To such an extent they take precedence over the literal provisions of national law. Where the inconsistency is deliberate, where in effect Parliament has legislated intentionally against provisions of EC law and these national provisions cannot be interpreted so as to be consistent with Community obligations directly or indirectly effective, the national provisions prevail. At least theoretically. At this stage the conflict will be one of political conflict not legal conflict and has not arisen for decision. If it did, it is unlikely to be resolvable through the domestic courts subject to what is said below. The courts in England have had to rule on domestic provisions in a statute that *clearly* contravened Community measures. The outcome was described as 'revolutionary'.[103] If so, it was a revolution that should have been foreseen.

---

102 See Case 80/86 *Kolpenghuis Nijmegen* [1987] ECR 3969; Case C-168/95 *Arcaro* [1996] ECR I-4705 and the limits of the doctrine in establishing criminal liability; cf Case C-456/98 *Centrosteel v Adipol* [2000] ECR I-6007.
103 W Wade (1996) 112 LQR 568; T Allan (1997) 113 LQR 443.

Parliamentary sovereignty, Factortame and legislating against Europe

No convention was thought to exist at the time of accession or after that the UK Parliament would not legislate against Community law and even if such a convention were thought to have emerged subsequently, it may be overborne by subsequent legislation. Some suggested to the contrary.[104] Inconsistent legislation may well have to state that 'Notwithstanding the provisions of ss 2 (1), 2(4) and 3 of the 1972 Act ....' and then proceed that the present Act's provisions take precedence over inconsistent norms of Community law.[105] Even imagining it brings home how inconceivable such an eventuality would be.

If legislation were passed terminating our membership of the EU, that would face the courts with no alternative but to accept Parliament's will. Laws LJ is probably correct that such an issue of supremacy falls to be determined by domestic law. But the ultimate rule of recognition of that law may be altered with a consistent and long term change in our legal practice. The more interesting practical question is: if Parliament were to legislate inconsistently with directly effective rights of Community law, and deliberately so, in a specific area would the courts *now* come to the view that our membership of the Community is a 'job lot' and that in that instance EC law prevails; the government in other words cannot pick and choose.[106]

---

104   Mitchell, J D B (1966) 15 ICLQ 133 for an expression of a contrary view. See also HL Debs, at cols 1201-02 (8 May 1967) and the views of the former Lord Chancellor that Parliament would not legislate inconsistently with Community law. See T R S Allan (1983) 3 OJLS 22 at 25 who believes that s 2(4) has entrenched s 2(1) to the extent that particular wording will be required to override Community Law. See text above after footnote 104.

105   In *Garland* above Lord Diplock said: 'The instant appeal does not present an appropriate occasion to consider whether, having regard to the express direction as to the construction of enactments 'to be passed' which is contained in s 2(4) [European Communities Act 1972], anything short of an express positive statement in an Act of Parliament passed after 1 January 1973 that a particular provision is intended to be made in breach of an obligation assumed by the UK under a Community Treaty would justify an English court in construing that provision in a manner inconsistent with a Community Treaty obligation of the UK however wide a departure from the prima facie meaning of the language of the provision might be needed in order to achieve consistency' (at p 415d–e).

106   Although there are means to construe the national law in the light of EC law if deliberately contrary to the latter the question is whether the national court will enforce such national law. The dilemma then will switch to the ECJ either because of a reference under Art 234 – if the Community provision is not directly effective

Some of these questions, but not all, were put to the test in the *Factortame* decision where the supremacy of Community law over domestic legislation within the Community competence was dramatically vindicated (see Chapters 2 and 8, pp 87 and 367).[107] In that case a challenge was made by Spanish owners of fishing vessels which because of the terms of the Merchant Shipping Act 1988, could not be registered as British and could not count against the British quota under the Common Fisheries Policy. This the English courts had to accept was a breach of 'fundamental' provisions of the EC Treaty and the UK statute had to be disapplied.

Parliament's acquiescence in Community legal sovereignty was explained by Lord Bridge in *Factortame* where he addresses the view in 'some public comments' that the award of an interim injunction to override domestic legislation in conflict with Community law was 'novel and dangerous':

> If the supremacy within the EC of Community law over the national law of member states was not always inherent in the EEC Treaty, it was certainly well established in the jurisprudence of the Court of Justice long before the UK joined the Community ... whatever limitation of its sovereignty Parliament accepted when it enacted the European Communities Act 1972 was entirely *voluntary*. Under the terms of the 1972 Act it has always been clear that it was the duty of a UK court, when delivering final judgment, to override any rule of national law found to be in conflict with any directly enforceable rule of Community law. Similarly, when decisions of the ECJ have exposed areas of UK statute law which failed to implement Council Directives, Parliament has always loyally accepted the obligation to make appropriate and prompt amendments. [108]

The implications of *Factortame* are still being felt and remain to be fully realised. It may have provided the basis for a fundamental change in what is recognised as our ultimate rule of recognition, how officials – especially judges – recognise ultimate legality. The point was expressed with admirable lucidity by Paul Craig who postulated three conceptual bases on which supremacy may be established after *Factortame*. The third, and most interesting, is as follows:

> there are no rights for the national court to enforce and an interpretation consistent with Community law is not possible – or because of a breach of EC provisions and Arts 226 and 228.

[107] *Factortame v Secretary of State for Transport (No 2)* [1991] 1 All ER 70 (ECJ and HL). The provisions were not *expressly* stipulated in the Merchant Shipping Act 1988 as contrary to Community law.

[108] [1991] 1 All ER at 107–8, emphasis added.

> This is to regard decisions about supremacy as being based on *normative arguments of legal principle the content of which can and will vary across time....*On this view there is no a priori inexorable reason why Parliament, merely because of its very existence, must be regarded as legally omnipotent. The existence of such power, like all power, must be justified by arguments of principle which are normatively convincing. Possible constraints on Parliamentary omnipotence must similarly be reasoned through and defended on normative grounds.[109]

Craig believes that the quotation of Lord Bridge from *Factortame* 'fits well' with his analysis. With echoes of Dworkin, Craig argues that any change in the rule of recognition is achieved through normative and legal argument, not political adaptation by the judiciary. Lord Bridge gave his opinion before the rulings of the German BVerfG in particular raised possible limitations to Community sovereignty, a theme which Laws LJ seems to support in *Thoburn*. It could be argued that Bridge was addressing the situation which so far has faced the UK where there is a clash between Community norms and domestic norms: not a situation which raises questions of constitutional and fundamental right in domestic law. Bridge's concentration is still, understandably enough, on the European Communities Act 1972. The argument he does not address is what meaning can be placed on the statute's words when it is argued that a situation never envisaged by Parliament occurs?

Laws LJ in *Thoburn* made the point clearly that Lord Bridge was referring to the supremacy of the *substantive* provisions of Community law. The sovereignty of Parliament was part of the *legal foundation* which gave Community law its supremacy. The supremacy of Community law had no role to play in establishing the nature of the legal foundation giving it supremacy, because that was reserved to English law, he argued. 'There is nothing in the 1972 Act which allows the [ECJ], or any other institutions of the EU, to touch or qualify the conditions of Parliament's legislative supremacy in the United Kingdom.' (p 183ff)

Where provisions which are allegedly breached are directly effective, the House of Lords in *Factortame* has been prepared to allow the award of interim injunctions against the government effectively disapplying an Act

---

[109]   P Craig in J Jowell and D Oliver *The Changing Constitution* (1999, 4th ed), ch 3, p 79 emph. in original. See T Allan (1997) 113 LQR 443. The first and second possible bases are statutory construction and a technical legal revolution.

of Parliament which was in breach of the EC provisions – a revolutionary event in UK law.[110] The same court has also awarded a declaration in judicial review proceedings that Parliamentary legislation is in breach of Community law.[111] Again, this is evidence that at the highest level the domestic courts are prepared to accept the supremacy of EC law. But that is within a framework in which Community law claims that Community law is supreme and under the rules of the game that is respected.

Organisation of the state: executive power and Parliament

Internal organisation of the state

Since 1979, the British state has seen more internal restructuring than any other comparable democratic western state excluding the consequences of German unification. A great deal of this change has been brought about by non-legal devices to an extent which non-British nationals find remarkable. The general British approach is: 'If it can be done without legislation, why legislate?' Devolution could only be effected through legislation and this subject is addressed in the following chapter.

In retrospect probably the biggest impact on internal organisation following our accession has been the growth of the power of the executive apropos of Parliament.[112] This is particularly acute in the question of democratic review by national parliaments of legislative and policy decisions by European institutions. While national executives and their civil servants are acquiring detailed knowledge and experience of EC decision-making,

---

[110] *Factortame v Secretary of State for Transport (No2)* [1991] 1 All ER 70 (ECJ and HL). In the first *Factortame* decision, when a reference was made to the ECJ, the House of Lords held that an injunction could not issue against the Crown disapplying the statute pending the decision of the ECJ – the judgment was written by Lord Bridge who confessed to some difficulty with the position under Community law. See below on the influence of this case on purely domestic law and award of injunctions against officers of the Crown. See G Anthony Ch 6, note 85 above.

[111] *R v Secretary of State for Employment, ex p Equal Opportunities Commission* [1994] 2 WLR 409. Following this case lower courts disapplied domestic provisions frequently where they did not comply with Community law.

[112] See Birkinshaw, P and Ashiagbor, D 'National Participation in Community Affairs: Democracy, the UK Parliament and the EU' (1996) 33 CMLR 499. And see ch 7 below.

this is not true of opposition leaders and back-benchers. The Treaty of Rome made no provision for the role of national parliaments in legislative oversight except to the extent that they were involved in approving Treaty revisions under domestic constitutional arrangements. The development of Qualified Majority Voting has potentially limited the oversight powers of national parliaments. The advent of joint and codecision making procedures has further promoted the role of the European Parliament.

There have been many developments at the administrative level to facilitate national/EU administrative activity including the creation of new bodies to deal with agricultural intervention and major changes in the Ministry of Agriculture, Fisheries and Food (now a part of the Department for Environment, Food and Rural Affairs) the Department of Trade and Industry and Customs and Excise. The European Secretariat in the Cabinet Office in the UK participates in the making and implementation of EC legislative measures and selects the subjects requiring interdepartmental discussion; it organises the meetings and necessary back-up. The Foreign Office keeps a watching brief on overall developments. Some Community programmes are shared between the Commission and national bodies with each performing distinct tasks that are closely linked. These are distinguished from programmes administered by the Commission itself. Whitehall officials are on the whole comfortable with the process of Europeanisation believes Dyson although tension is revealed in the Treasury.[113] The Office of Fair Trading has ever closer links with Director General IV of the Commission which will be examined in the light of the Competition Act 1998 in Chapter 12. The government established an independent Food Agency to address many of the problems witnessed by the BSE crisis.

One interesting side effect has been a tendency for law in England, Scotland and Northern Ireland to be approximated in ever growing degrees of unity because the Community places obligations on the UK and its laws not those of the separate countries making up the UK. The phenomenon is not novel; the extent of the practice is. Devolution is discussed in the following chapter.

---

[113]   K Dyson in B Markesinis ed *The British Contribution to the Europe of the Twenty-first Century* (2002), ch 11. See also T Daintith (1995) *ELJ* 134.

European Assembly Elections Act 1978, s 6

Before the British accession to the Community in 1973, the preoccupation in Westminster was with loss or otherwise of sovereignty as we have seen. Since that initial period of what was referred to as 'legislative schizophrenia' where it was somehow imagined that the UK might retain its own Parliamentary sovereignty and all that entails while complying with EC sovereignty which we have described, other preoccupations have emerged, all of which emanate from loss of sovereignty. In 1978, the introduction of direct elections to the Assembly was the occasion for the legislation which provided that before the UK ratified any Treaty increasing the powers of the European Parliament, statutory approval had to be given by the Westminster Parliament, the latter no doubt prompted by apprehensions that the European Parliament's newly acquired directly elected basis would encourage it to seek augmentation of its powers at the expense of Westminster. This was a constitutional novelty although approval or 'ratification' as it is sometimes misleadingly called – especially by the British press – had to be given by national parliaments before the coming into force of the Single European Act 1987 and the TEU and subsequent amendments by virtue of Article 236 EC.[114]

Voting rights and unelected representation

Reference has been made to possible movement towards proportional representation in British elections. In October 1998, the Electoral Reform Commission under Europhile Lord Jenkins published its report on Electoral Reform. This recommended an end to 'First past the post' systems for elections and the introduction of a two-vote top-up system to achieve greater and fairer proportionality in representation and to increase voter choice. Such a development will upset many vested interests in both major parties and was hotly contested.[115] Certainly, Jenkins researched extensively into European voting models for ideas. Legislation, however, to remove most of the hereditary peers was predicted to cause major disruption which simply failed to materialise. In the case of the House of Lords, possibilities for long-term replacements and systems of appointment or election are still not free from difficulties, however. Hierarchy based on

---

[114] Repealed at Maastricht and replaced by Art N of the TEU and Title VIII Art 48 Treaty of Amsterdam (ToA).

[115] House of Lords Act 1999.

birth may well be supplanted by hierarchy based on patronage with a minority of elected representatives in the House of Lords.

'Opt outs'

The UK government, together with the Swedish and Danish governments, opted out of European Monetary Union (Chapter 14) although the UK's original opt out of the Social chapter was reversed in 1997.

Under the Amsterdam Treaty, the UK secured opt outs or exemptions from Title IV to maintain its border controls for third country nationals travelling from other Member States and to address the incompatibility between that control and the immediate implementation of Article 14 [7a] EC.[116] The Treaty also provides opportunities for closer cooperation on a voluntary basis: progress towards integration at varying and flexible speeds, or as some might choose to see it something like Joseph's amazing technicolour dream-coat. With the likely expansion of the Community, greater flexibility and different acceleration rates for Member States are inevitable.

Role and function of constitutional adjudication

The ECJ

A problem which has been perceived in many quarters concerns the alleged arrogation to itself by the ECJ of powers approximating to a constitutional court in a federal system – an unwelcome manifestation of judicial self aggrandisement redolent of *Marbury v Madison*[117] where the US Supreme Court inferred a right to judicial review of legislation in the constitution. The argument is that the ECJ has gone beyond its Treaty objectives of ensuring that 'in the interpretation and application of [the] Treaty the law is observed'.[118] In Britain in particular, the exercise or what others would see as an extension of the law on sovereignty of EC law,[119] direct

---

[116]   The internal market shall be without 'internal frontiers'.
[117]   1 Cranch 103 (1803).
[118]   Article 220 [164] EC. See generally T Schilling 'The Autonomy of the Community Legal Order – An Analysis of Possible Foundations' (1996) 37 Harv Int LJ 389.
[119]   See notes 123 and 124 below.

effectiveness and individual rights,[120] the interpretation of domestic laws to comply with non-directly effective Directives whether the former were passed before or after the Directive[121] and the burgeoning area of liability of member states for breaches of EC law[122] are all seen as examples of a court which is overreaching itself in certain quarters.[123] Indeed, it is not uncommon to hear the term 'ultra vires' used in relation to ECJ judgments. This does appear to be inappropriate language to use in relation to the Court, unless it has engaged in the most egregious abuses in its interpretation of the Treaty. The UK government presented a series of suggestions for the Intergovernmental Committee before Amsterdam to rectify 'anomalies' emerging from ECJ judgments. More recent decisions of the ECJ, especially in relation to *locus standi* under Article 230 [173] EC have witnessed the Court adopting a more conventional role (Chapter 3, p 106 et seq). These covered: retrospective effect of judgments; limiting damages on State liability; giving greater emphasis to national time limits; introducing a right of appeal to a full court where chambers would effectively operate as first instance courts; expedited Article 177 references; and providing a streamlined means for amending legislation where the ECJ judgment interprets the law 'contrary to the policy of the Council'. Finally, a request was made for the clarification of the application of subsidiarity in the interpretation of Community law.[124]

---

120 Case 41/74 *van Duyn v Home Office* [1974] ECR 1337; Case 152/84 *Marshall v Southampton and South West Area Health Authority* [1986] ECR 723; Case C-188/89 *Foster v British Gas* [1990] ECR I-3313; etc.

121 Case C-106/89 *Marleasing* [1990] ECR I-4135.

122 Case C-6, 9/90 *Francovich* [1991] ECR I-5357 and the usual suspects: see ch 10.

123 Patrick Neill QC *The European Court of Justice: a Case Study in Judicial Activism* European Policy Forum (1995). See also *The Developing Role of the European Court of Justice* EPF (1995). Neill was critical of just about every major decision taken by the ECJ before 1995 and in its *Opinion 1/91* [1991] ECR I-6079 on the EEA draft treaty he felt that the Court had reasoned that the Treaty of Rome could not be amended to diminish its competence under Art 220 [164] EC ensuring that the law is observed in its application and interpretation of the Treaty: see T Hartley (1992) ICLQ 841. See further: J Weiler and U Haltern in *The European Court and National Courts – Doctrine and Jurisprudence* eds A-M Slaughter, A Sweet and J Weiler (1998) and D O'Keeffe ed *Judicial Review in the European Union* (2000).

124 *The IGC Conference: Memorandum by the UK on the ECJ* July 1996. The point concerning 'contrary to the policy ...' refers to the judgment of the ECJ in Case C-392/92 *Schmidt* [1994] ECR I-1311.

Solutions to conflict

The judges look to the accession statute of 1972, and amendments to that legislation, which provides that supremacy of Community law is accepted by Parliament. The inability of Parliament to entrench its legislation has been noted and nothing could prevent a deliberate and express act of repudiation of the Treaties by Parliament which the courts would have to recognise although it was 'implicit in the acceptance of the Treaties that the UK would not only accept existing Community law but would also refrain from enacting future legislation inconsistent with Community law'.[125] Complete rejection is unlikely. A dilemma caused by a deliberate breach by Parliament of a *provision* of Community law is not, perhaps, so clear cut. I have dealt with this point above. The practical problem has centred around the fact that supremacy is achieved from the British perspective through the mediation of Parliament and from an EC perspective by the terms of the Treaties and their interpretation, and that of the laws arising thereunder operating directly in Member States.

It was seen that the only real problem to have arisen in the British courts concerned the interpretation of statutory provisions which covered the same ground as non-directly effective Directives and which had been made before the Directives. The most recent illustration of this difficulty saw the House of Lords applying the ruling of the ECJ and giving a meaning to the statute which accorded with the Directive; this covered the case of legislation which pre-dated the Directive and was not, therefore, an implementing measure.[126] The position relating to an inconsistent previous statute or regulation and a subsequent Directive has not been finally resolved although the ECJ has itself appreciated that consistent interpretation may not be possible. Other remedies may be available in domestic courts involving state liability for failure to implement within the appropriate time where the necessary conditions are established. The Commission may take action before the ECJ under Articles 226 [169] EC and 228 [171] EC where there is a breach of Community law (see Chapters 3 and 12, pp 109 and 481 et seq).

---

[125]   The Lord Chancellor HL Debs col 1197 (8 May 1967).
[126]   *Webb v EMO (No 2)* [1995] 4 All ER 577, HL. See *British Fuels Ltd v Baxendale* note 100 above and 'consistent construction' of implementing measures.

Solutions provided by national courts

The legality of various payments to the Community in fulfilment of our obligations has been questioned in the courts without success – not surprising given the terms of s 2(3) of the 1972 Act.[127]

The *Rees Mogg* case which has already been treated in some detail provided little in the way of difficulty for judicial determination when the Act implementing the TEU was passed although academic comment has suggested that the judge did oversimplify the issues.[128] An Act of Parliament is only interpretable by the courts in the UK, not reviewable unless the Act contravenes directly enforceable provisions of Community law as occurred in the *Factortame* and *Equal Opportunities* cases. In the latter case the Law Lords were vigilant in their observation that they did not rule on the international Treaty obligations of the British government but on the incompatibility between EC law and domestic law in a statute. The same case also illustrates an important procedural point in that it was incumbent upon the Secretary of State to 'objectively satisfy' or justify why on the facts there were disparities between qualifying threshold periods of employment for part time and full time employees in order to defer the security of employment provisions for the former category and to produce evidence that alleged benefits from the difference, ie increased employment, actually accrued.[129] As a general rule of English law, where a person is challenging the legality of government action the onus of proof is on that person and this is usually faced without the benefit of documents and information from the public body. In such a position, where statistical analysis is concerned the case is a 'non-starter' if one is relying upon the government for the evidence.[130]

One interesting situation has arisen where detailed statistical evidence suggested that the UK government was in breach of the Equal Treatment Directive insofar as the number of women qualifying for the two year

---

[127]   *R v HM Treasury, ex p Smedley* [1985] 1 All ER 589, CA; *Monckton v Lord Advocate* 1995 SLT 1201, OH. In *Rees Mogg* a line of attack which alleged that the dropping of the Social Policy Protocol from the list of the provisions covered by the authorised expenditure within the European Communities Act 1972, s 2(3) was jettisoned when the Treasury claimed that it was covered by the annual Appropriation Act.

[128]   Rawlings, R (1994) Public Law 254 and 367.

[129]   *Equal Opportunities Commission v Secretary of State for Employment* [1994] 1 All ER 910, HL.

[130]   *Enderby v Frenchay Health Authority* Case C-127/92 [1994] 1 All ER 495.

threshold period to be entitled to statutory unfair dismissal protection was significantly lower than men who qualified. The effect of the Order was, therefore, indirectly discriminatory. The order introducing the qualifying period was *pro tanto* declared discriminatory and contrary to the Directive. But the Court of Appeal refused to quash the Order because to do so might cause huge back-claims for compensation and lead to administrative chaos and additionally 'the statistics which can be relied upon to prove indirect discrimination do not remain constant. Thus it may be that at a different time the statistics would point to a different result.'[131] The Court also accepted that it would be extremely reluctant to quash an offending order on the grounds of incompatibility because if the order were in primary legislation the Court would have no power to quash the statute, only to declare its incompatibility with Community law.

On appeal to the House of Lords, the declaration was discharged because the Law Lords believed it would be of no practical effect. But the Law Lords took the opportunity to make some wider points. Lord Hoffman stated that a Directive only affected legal rights as between parties where one of those parties was an emanation of the State and the Directive consequentially was directly effective and except in that case 'Directives do not give rise to rights or restrictions which without further enactment are required to be given legal effect'.[132] The European Communities Act 1972, s 2(4) did not, Lord Hoffman believed, affect the construction of the 1985 Order (or its *validity*) because this would allow a Directive to be used not as a source of rights but as a means of disapplying a restriction on domestic rights where those rights would otherwise be available in domestic law. This he believed was 'unworkable'. Why? Is this not what a purposive approach to statutory interpretation would require – that English law must be read subject to the requirements of EC law?

The inconsistency in question was an indirect act of discrimination; it was disappearing as time passed ie, the number of women caught by the offending provision was declining. Although reference was made to *Faccini Dori*[133] which agreed with the doctrine of interpretation of domestic provisions in a manner consistent with indirect provisions of Community law, any amendment by construction to the Order may have produced an

---

[131]   *R v Secretary of State for Employment, ex p Seymour-Smith* [1996] All ER (EC) 1, CA.

[132]   *R v Secretary of State for Employment, ex p Seymour-Smith* [1997] 2 All ER 273, HL per Lord Hoffman at p 279.

[133]   Case C-91/92 [1994] ECR I-3325.

effect which was directly discriminatory against men. It is probably true to say that the Order could not have been interpreted in any other way. When the case was remitted to the House of Lords from the ECJ, the Law Lords by majority had to decide whether indirect discrimination had taken place and if so whether it was objectively justified by factors unrelated to sex. By majority, it was established that there had been indirect discrimination but that discrimination was justified by objective factors.[134]

One further point should be alluded to. English judges have historically generally viewed legislation as an undesirable encroachment on the unending tapestry and wonder of the common law. They have, consequentially, usually interpreted legislative provisions very strictly and according to self denying ordinances which prohibited courts examining official records of legislative proceedings in either House of Parliament. This was relaxed for the first time officially in 1992.[135] A further and more extensive relaxation had, however, been introduced by the judiciary to deal specifically with statutes and regulations which implemented EC provisions and which pre-dates the 1992 ruling in *Pepper v Hart*.[136] Interpretation of these provisions was to be, one might say, far more 'context sympathetic' an interpretation than would normally be the case and Ministerial statements and explanatory notes were to be referred to for 'purposive' interpretation of domestic measures.

Substantive constitutional law and constitutional adjudication

Recent decisions by British courts bring out a growing awareness of the human rights dimension to executive decision-making and a readiness to acknowledge the increasing constitutional nature of adjudication. These points are dealt with in greater detail in Chapters 8 and 9. The impact of US and other common law courts on constitutional adjudication in the UK has, until recently, been minimal, although it is showing signs of influence

---

[134]   [2000] 1 All ER 857.

[135]   *Pepper v Hart* [1993] 1 All ER 42, HL. On the application of *Pepper to* 'constitutional provisions' see Lord Hoffman in *Robinson v Secretary of State for Northern Ireland* [2002] UKHL 32, [2002] All ER (D) 364 (Jul) note 7 above.

[136]   *Three Rivers District Council v Bank of England (No 2)* [1996] 2 All ER 363 (QBD) following Lord Keith in *Pickstone v Freemans plc* [1988] 2 All ER 803, HL and Lord Diplock in Case 12/81 *Garland v British Rail Engineering Ltd* [1983] 2 AC 751. Note also Lord Templeman's resort to a wide range of materials in *Pickstone v Freemans plc* above note 92.

in freedom of speech case law.[137] The record of the ECJ in constitutional adjudication has been evident since *Van Gend en Loos* and *Costa v ENEL* and in Britain the Directives on equal treatment and protection have been used by courts to disapply offending domestic statutes and for courts to declare them incompatible with EC law.

The evidence is that British courts are much happier protecting individual rights than in adjudicating in institutional conflict. We have not yet reinvented the likes of *Prohibitions del Roy, Bonham's case* or that on *Proclamations*[138] which punctuated constitutional developments in the early seventeenth century. But the progress has nonetheless been remarkable. In *Spycatcher* the courts eventually refused to suppress the publication of the press reports on the book written by a former MI5 operative simply on the say-so of the government that publication would damage the public interest.[139] The case was a water shed in indicating a change in judicial attitudes.

Such intervention in the executive process only several years ago would have been unthinkable. The ruling in May 2002 from the CHR in *Stafford v UK* was that the Home Secretary acted in breach of Article 5 ECHR when he overruled a recommendation from the Parole Board to release a mandatory life prisoner is likely to presage a major change in the role of the Home Secretary in setting tariffs for mandatory life prisoners.[140] In *R v Secretary of State for the Home Department, ex p Anderson* [2002] UKHL

---

137 Clearly their constitutions are not our constitutions despite the fact that there were many features of common law inspiration in them. More recently, adjudication concerned with freedom of speech has made its presence felt. See: *Incorporating the First Amendment* I Loveland (ed) (1998). On the ECJ as a constitutional court, see F Jacobs in D Curtin and D O'Keeffe *Constitutional Adjudication in European Community and National Law* (1992).

138 (1607) 12 Co Rep 63; (1610) 8 Co Rep 113b; (1611) 12 Co Rep 74 – on the King's personal administration of justice; subjecting statutes to judicial review; and denying the Crown the right to change the law by prerogative respectively. On Coke's support for plenary powers of judicial review see *Bagg's* case (1615) 11 Co Rep 93b and Co Inst iv 71, and S A de Smith *Judicial Review of Administrative Action* (1973, 3rd ed) pp 507 et seq.

139 *A-G v Guardian Newspapers Ltd (No 2)* [1988] 3 All ER 545 (ChD, CA and HL).

140 (2002) 13 BHRC 260. The Judicial Committee of the Privy Council has, however, refused to review the failure by a Governor to commute the death penalty for murder to a life sentence: *Reckley v Minister of Public Safety and Immigration (No 2)* [1996] AC 527. See *Pinder v R* [2002] UKPC 46, [2002] 3 WLR 1443 on flogging. D O'Brien (2002) PL 678.

46, [2002] 4 All ER 1089 the Law Lords ruled that the practice of setting such tariffs authorised by statute was in breach of Article 6 ECHR and issued a declaration of incompatibility under the Human Rights Act.

The European constitutional development from a national point of view

Tasks and importance of national constitutional law in the process of integration

The remaining major problem remains from a British perspective that of ultimate 'sovereignty'. The approach was one of let sleeping dogs lie. The Laws judgment in *Thoburn* has kicked the dogs. In theory the approach from the courts is hierarchical; that is what Parliamentary sovereignty means: the judges are lions under the Parliamentary Mace. However, at a more practical level the transfer of sovereignty, in limited if widening areas, to the Community cannot help but influence the judicial psyche. *Factortame* was only decided after a great deal of reluctance by the British courts but its eventual result and the issue of an interim injunction against the Crown to disapply an Act of Parliament pending determination by the ECJ *was* the most dramatic event in constitutional adjudication since the seventeenth century *pace* Lord Rees Mogg.

In many situations the ECJ is effectively delegating important questions of Community law to national courts to decide and this is especially true in the area of liability for breaches of Community law where domestic courts have already shown ways of confining the dramatic impact of ECJ rulings.[141] The ruling in the *Atlanta Bananas* case whereby a national court may issue an interim injunction or relief against a measure based upon a prima facie unlawful EC regulation or directive is further evidence of the co-operative spirit in the relationship between the ECJ and national courts.[142] The case law concerning the banning of tobacco advertising by the making of regulations in England under Directive 98/43/EC revealed

---

[141] See *R v Secretary of State for the Home Department, ex p Gallagher* [1996] 2 CMLR 951, CA and Ch 10, p 460 et seq; *Factortame (No 5)* [1999] 4 All ER 906, HL and compare the reaction of German courts in Ch 10, p 460 et seq.

[142] Case C-465/93 *Atlanta Bananas* [1996] All ER (EC) 31, ECJ developing Case C-143/88 *Zuckerfabrik* [1991] ECR I-415. See the Tobacco cases in note 143.

some divisions of approach in the way the matter should be dealt with.[143] In this case the tobacco company wished to restrain the Secretary of State from making regulations banning such advertising because it was alleged the regulations were attempting to implement a Directive which was ultra vires Community law. There were necessary safeguards which had to be pursued before a Member State court could award such an injunction – including the fact that the legality of the Directive had to be, and had been, referred for a ruling to the ECJ – and the principles of application in relation to such injunctions being awarded by Member State courts had been set out in the ECJ's *Atlanta Bananas* and *Zuckerfabrik* decisions. The Court of Appeal by majority ruled that the relevant test to apply in awarding interim relief was that set out in Community law which, as it happened, was more favourable to the government's case and would have allowed the domestic regulations to be introduced. The Court of Appeal was reluctant to interfere with the legislative activity of the government. Laws LJ believed that the 'Directive is plainly unlawful' but case law of the ECJ prevented a domestic court from ruling on that invalidity.[144] He further felt that the test to apply in awarding interim relief was that formulated under domestic law not Community law because an injunction would not deny or frustrate the effectiveness of Community law since the date of implementation had not arrived. Laws LJ did not believe the plaintiffs had to show 'serious and irreparable harm' as the majority suggested before issuing an injunction. The Court of Appeal was not ruling on the validity of an EU measure; it was ruling on the prospective legality of a domestic measure which was based on a Directive which he felt, but did not rule, was unlawful. If the rules as to vires are not maintained, the rule of law is offended, he believed. He was in favour of awarding an interim injunction.

By the time the House of Lords was seised of the case the ECJ had ruled that the Directive was indeed ultra vires. The majority in the Lords held that the question of which law applied when seeking interim relief to prevent an allegedly unlawful Directive from being implemented by domestic measures was a question of Community law and, but for the decision in *Germany v EP*,[145] a reference on a preliminary point of Community law to

---

[143] *R v Secretary of State for Health, ex p Imperial Tobacco Ltd* [2000] 1 All ER 572, CA; [2001] 1 All ER 850, HL and Case C-376/98 *Germany v European Parliament* [2000] All ER (EC) 769.

[144] Case 314/85 *Foto-Frost* [1987] ECR 4199.

[145] Cases C-376/98 and 74/99 [2000] All ER (EC) 769.

the ECJ would have been obligatory. Lord Hoffman and Lord Millett dissented.

Lord Hoffman stated: 'The argument of the Secretary of State comes to saying that Community law requires the judiciary of a Member State to defer to the executive on the question of when the Directive should be implemented. Once the executive had decided that the Directive should be implemented, the judiciary comes under a Community law obligation to co-operate and should behave as if the Directive were already enforceable.' Enforcement could only be suspended if Community criteria (*Zuckerfabrik*) were established. But this argument interfered, Hoffman argued, with the division of powers between the branches of government in a Member State. Obligations in Community law are placed on all organs of the state regardless of their internal divisions (citing *Marleasing* with approval). The arguments at the interim stage in assessing the balance of public interest in assessing whether an interim injunction should be awarded are not matters of Community law, he believed (p 861). The power in question derived from s 2(2) of the European Communities Act 1972 and Community law only applied on a 'renvoi' from s 2(2) not in its own right. 'The powers of the executive branch of government of the UK are entirely a matter of domestic law' (p 862f–g). This cannot be true; consider the position of directly effective provisions of the EC Treaty and Directives. Consider also, those cases where domestic law has been influenced by Community or Convention law.

The picture of this particular interrelationship is ambivalent with widely different solutions in existence. National courts are, however, providing a crucial role in *developing* Community law.

There are hierarchy and normative tiers but there is also confluence. After thirty years of operating within and adapting to EC law and addressing new and unforeseen vistas, British law is different and lawyers and judges think differently. Lord Woolf above for instance has, in his extra judicial capacity, argued that a power of judicial review of statutes may exist *in extremis*.[146] The comments of that Law Lord would have been unthinkable from a senior judge twenty years ago. Community law suffuses more and more the substance and development of our domestic law.

---

[146]   (1995) *Public Law* 57, 69 and HL Debs Vol 560 cols 1143 et seq (21 January 1995).

Sometimes, as in the case of the prohibition in the British legislation of Sunday trading, the leeway afforded by interpretations of EC law by the ECJ which allowed domestic courts to apply tests of proportionality to the effect of the domestic legislation on Community trade has led to serious discrepancies in the domestic application of the law by different national courts.[147] Relief from a farcical situation only came when the ECJ effectively ruled how the law should be applied domestically (see Chapter 14, p 616 et seq).[148]

Our domestic public law has changed/developed enormously since 1972. Much of this is related to European influence and goes beyond twin tracking or the application of Community law principles in domestic courts when an issue of Community law arises

Emerging problems from integration

The life of constitutional law has been easier in the UK than for our neighbours because of an absence of a written constitution (see Chapter 2). The internal organisation of government in the UK is a matter for the UK and one that has changed dramatically through successful pressure for devolved and regional government – subsidiarity within the state. Such a devolution will necessitate satisfactory machinery to address and resolve conflicts of a kind unseen in the UK since the partition of Ireland in 1922. Now of course there is a Community dimension that was not present in those early years – can Scotland or another region, for instance, be preferred applicants to bring an application to the ECJ under Article 230 [173] EC to annul an EC measure?[149]

I have spoken and will discuss elsewhere in this book the growing awareness and perceived importance of judicial review and how it has been inspired by EC and wider European factors. We simply have no written

---

147   *Wellingborough Borough Council v Payless DIY* [1990] 1 CMLR 773; *Stoke-on-Trent City Council v B & Q* [1990] 2 CMLR 377; *Shrewsbury Borough Council* [1990] 3 CMLR 535; *WH Smith DIY v Peterborough City Council* [1991] 4 All ER 193; *Stoke-on-Trent City Council v B & Q plc* [1991] 4 All ER 221; and *Torfaen v B & Q plc* C - 145/88 [1989] ECR 3851, ECJ. See *Kirklees Metropolitan Borough Council v Wickes Building Supplies Ltd* [1993] AC 227 and a judgment which waived the usual safeguards for the award of interim injunctions where a public authority was seeking that relief.

148   *Stoke-on-Trent City Council v B & Q plc* Case C-169/91 [1993] 1 All ER 481, ECJ.

149   N Burrows (2002) European Public Law 45.

constitution to amend in order to allow compatibility between the constitution and Treaty amendments and nothing to stand in the way of implementation provided proper Parliamentary processes ordained in legislation are followed. The growing constitutional sensitivity of our courts is very much directed to individual human rights. It is also evident in the interpretation by the Privy Council of written constitutions of former colonies and dominions and treaties affecting Commonwealth affairs.[150] With Scottish devolution, and the return of an executive and legislative Assembly to Northern Ireland (Wales will only have delegated secondary legislative powers and not devolved primary powers) that court will have to address questions of conflict between Edinburgh, Belfast and Westminster over domestic and EC affairs. It is unclear whether the judicial committee of the Privy Council will be able to rise to the occasion (see Chapter 5).

In the Report stage of the Scotland Bill in the House of Lords, the government rejected amendments for a Constitutional Court to determine post devolution constitutional disputes. Critics alleged that the Privy Council was too open to political influence by the Lord Chancellor. This interfered with the separation of powers and would produce an English dominated court. The Lord Chancellor, while rejecting the amendments, did appear to leave the door ajar for the possible future establishment of such a court. 'It may be .... longer term thought should be given to the appropriateness of a specialist constitutional court, so I can be encouraging to a limited extent' he stated. This theme is picked up in the next chapter.

Subsidiarity

Subsidiarity is a clear example of a – I am not sure that 'concession' is the right word – solution offered to anxieties raised by the British and German governments in the TEU and the format of which was particularly pressed in the existing wording by the British in the negotiations leading to Maastricht. It is enshrined in Article 5 [3b] EC and a Protocol and is implicit in art 1 TEU. It was an attempt to renationalise and reclaim competences claimed or arrogated by the Community or as Lord Mackenzie Stuart

---

[150] See eg, *New Zealand Maori Council v A-G of New Zealand* [1994] 1 All ER 623, PC; *Pratt v A-G Jamaica* [1993] 4 All ER 769, PC. On the Privy Council and disputes over devolved powers, see: Lord Steyn (1998) EHRLR 153. See also Craig and Walters (1999) Public Law 274.

expressed it: a 'prophylactic against the contagion of Brussels'.[151] That the principle of subsidiarity applies where there are shared competences between Member States and matters are not within the exclusive competence is well known although a list of what are considered Community competences has been drawn up by the Commission.[152] Subsidiarity is one of the subjects committed by the Nice Declaration to examination by Giscard D'Estaing's Convention on the Future of Europe (Chapters 5 and 7).

Devolution has brought increased pressure to bear on subsidiarity within the British and Northern Irish state and on legislative competences, taxation in the case of Scotland and the detailed extent of devolved responsibilities. As we shall see in Chapter 5, the Privy Council has been appointed as the body to hear disputes about such divisions of power, a proposal which was contained in the 1978 Bill and legislation on Scottish devolution. Local authorities in England still would wish for more subsidiarity in their relationship with central government. The implications for devolution for Community membership will be discussed in the following chapter.

In Chapter 5, I examine the measures taken to ensure proper observance of subsidiarity by the institutions of the Community. The *Carvel* litigation informed us that secret concessions and deals – very often against a Member State's national legislature's instructions – were common in the Council.[153]

Conclusion

The impact of doctrines gleaned from domestic systems and their imprint upon British public law – sometimes dramatically so, on other occasions by a process akin to osmosis – have been referred to above (and see Chapters 7, 8 and 9). Lawyers have adapted themselves to EC law. Knowledge of its possibilities is increasing. European Law is a compulsory core subject on the undergraduate law degree and postgraduate courses are developing continually. European public law is finding its way onto the curriculum. The new and newer generations of lawyers are more and

---

151   In *Constitutional Adjudication in EC Law and National Law*, eds Curtin and O'Keefe p 21. See *A Partnership of Nations* FCO Cm 3181 (1996) p 11, a statement of self congratulation by the former UK Government.

152   SEC (92) 1990 final, COM DOC 9649/92.

153   *Carvel v EU Council* [1996] All ER (EC) 53 Case T-194/94 (Ch 6, p 266 et seq).

more familiar with EC law. A new generation of judges is very much at home with EC law and on the whole their attitude is constructive. EC law has added new resources to litigation lawyers particularly in public law.

In terms of institutional links, reference has been made to the links between specialist agencies like the OFT and the EU Competition Commission (Director General IV) and the impact on key departments of EC affairs and their administration and organisation. *The Civil Service Training Directory* prospectus in the UK has more items under 'Europe' in its index than any other subject except 'Management'. Special administrative bodies have been established to address EC matters and special sections within government departments have been created. These include the Intervention Board for Agricultural Produce and major changes have taken place in the former Ministry of Agriculture, Fisheries and Food, whose responsibilities were largely split between a government department and an independent agency because of perceived conflict on interest in food production and effective oversight and consumer protection.[154] The Department of Trade and Industry and Customs and Excise have faced considerable reorganisation because of EC responsibilities. The European Secretariat of the Cabinet Office in the UK participates in the making and implementation of EC law and in the Office of Fair Trading – which polices competition law as well as consumer protection – has ever increasing liaison with Director General IV and provides practical assistance to the latter in its investigations.[155] These links have been strengthened by the Competition Act 1998 (Chapter 12).

There are international organisational networks of lawyers which seek to comprehend the potential and the limits of integration.

From the critical wings there are attacks on the ECJ – not as strident as once they were – and on the developing role and use of the Directive in particular and suggestions have been made to the effect that the Directive should revert to its original design and the Amsterdam Treaty's provision of 'Framework Decisions' under Title VI which are to be implemented in Member States but which are not to be directly effective was noted; that is as a device aimed at achieving increasing harmonisation/approximation of standards under that Title while leaving the details to member states.

---

[154] DEFRA and the Food Standards Agency.
[155] R Whish *Competition Law* (2001, 4th ed); Bender (1991) 6 Pub. Policy & Admin 13.

Nevertheless, the development of direct effect and its extension did more to make the Community an object of significance and meaning to individual citizens than did any comparable development; it did more to rid the EC of its conception as a modern day equivalent of Caesar sending messages to his legates and governors but of no relevance to the citizen:

> Community law has little direct effect on the ordinary life of private citizens. In so far as it imposes obligations, it does so mostly in relation to industrial and commercial activities and does not touch citizens in their private capacities ... By far the greater part of our domestic law would remain unchanged.

said the Lord Chancellor in 1967. [156] The European Monetary System (see Chapter 14, p 584 et seq) and fiscal harmonisation have become more recent ogres for Eurosceptics.

From a constitutional point of view there is no conflict between the sovereignty of EC law and national law. The only problem would come if an unending and unequivocal declaration of sovereignty were demanded from the UK government. We would not be alone in our difficulty. Such a prospect is now unlikely. Rather, the courts have shown themselves generally constructive in the interpretation of EC law and in their use of EC law. Some had to endure extra lessons after hours! But they learned. The opportunities have been seen to use EC law as an aid in what is law's ultimate objective: the protection and the strengthening of the conditions that make democracy possible. In this respect the community and national systems have much to learn. What kind of democracy for instance – more open, more participatory? And if so, through what specific devices?

I personally remain convinced that far more still needs to be achieved to make both the institutions of the EC and EU more open and accessible to its citizens, and far more must be provided to national parliaments to assist them hold their own executives to account for European legislation and policy (see Chapters 5 and 6). The Amsterdam Treaty's provisions on a right of access to information by citizens of the Union and natural or legal persons residing or having their registered office in a Member State (new Article 255) are welcome and the battle over the eventual regulation and implementing decisions can be taken up in Chapter 6.[157] The question of

---

[156]   The Lord Chancellor (Lord Gardiner) see ch 2 note 56 above at cols 1203-04.
[157]   And see Birkinshaw *Freedom of Information: the Law, the Practice and the Ideal* (3rd ed 2001) Ch 8.

the future constitution of Europe is a question currently under the examination of Valerie Giscard d'Estaing's convention to report back to the Intergovernmental Committee in 2004. Central to that question are themes of national/Community relationships involving subsidiarity and shared competencies; the role of national parliaments, transparency in the Community and protection of human rights ie the status of the EU Charter of Fundamental Rights. I address these points in the concluding chapter and elsewhere.

In terms of the UK constitution, it has changed, 'changed utterly' under European influence. Without a written constitution, our judges are thinking constitutionally. The way the constitution operates, and the way courts operate within the constitution, are almost unrecognisable from thirty years ago. But, paradoxically, these changes have not removed the enduring supremacy of common law thought in the practice of our constitution – and in spite of the HRA 1998 and new approaches to sovereignty, the residual role that judicial law should play in our constitution. The implications of the Laws judgment in the *Thoburn* decision are that while his recognition of a 'constitutional statute' by the common law may give us most of the benefits of a written constitution in which fundamental rights are accorded special respect, 'it preserves the sovereignty of the legislature and the flexibility of our uncodified constitution.'

Part two

Some key issues

Part Two

Some key issues

Chapter 5

'A Closer Union ... in which decisions are taken ... as closely as possible to the Citizen' – subsidiarity and devolution

We were reminded recently by an eminent Law Lord[1] that Dicey railed against federalism for producing 'weak government', 'conservatism' and 'legalism'. The latter referred to the predominance of the judiciary over democratically elected government and the fomentation of a spirit of 'legality' among the people. Weak government and conservatism would emerge from a written constitution that would necessarily introduce rigidity into the realm of government. One of the notable features of the British constitution is a flexibility for development which is not repeated in other constitutions. One of the great dangers is that this can lead to elective dictatorship through Parliament controlled by a government with a vast majority. In 2001, the Labour government was elected to office with a majority of 146 seats resting upon 41.7% of the vote or, more dramatically, 25% of the electorate. Dicey's own fears were instilled by his opposition to Home Rule for Ireland which he saw as more destructive of Parliamentary sovereignty than Irish independence. Since Dicey wrote, that independence was achieved for a majority of the counties of Ireland. Although the Northern Ireland question is far from settled, the UK now occupies a place in a Europe where a multi-national federalism has been inexorably developing, and where law has occupied a centre stage in promoting union, integration and human rights. Our national preoccupations on these matters are contained in the HRA 1998, to which I turn in Chapter 9, and in devolution.

---

[1]   Lord Bingham (2002) Public Law 39.

Where devolution has sought to pass power down to Scotland, Wales and Northern Ireland and we await the English regions,[2] that power has been heavily qualified. Furthermore, devolution within the state has occurred following the emergence of more devolved or regional government elsewhere in Europe and perhaps most dramatically of all, the emergence of subsidiarity.[3] Subsidiarity in the EU means in its simplest form, that except in those areas where the Community has exclusive competence to act, then action should be taken at state (or regional) level unless, for stated reasons, this is not the best way forward. The concept of division of powers is the common feature of all federal structures. The German and Austrian constitutions have a form of subsidiarity written into their constitutions. The problems lie in the political decisions relating to the division: that foreign and European affairs, and defence for instance in the UK, are subject to the Westminster regime and not the devolved regimes. The difficulty legally comes in identifying what precisely is involved in verbal formulations calling for an exercise of judgment or balance in what is included within the responsibility of one level rather than another. There is no clearer example of this than Article 5 [3b] EC.

Subsidiarity and proportionality: Article 5 [3b] EC and ToA Protocol

Article 5 EC sets out the operation of subsidiarity in the following terms:

> In areas which do not fall within its exclusive competence, the Community shall take action, in accordance with the principle of subsidiarity, only if and insofar as the objectives of the proposed action cannot be sufficiently achieved by the Member States, and can therefore, by reason of the scale or effects of the proposed action, be better achieved by the Community.

Article 5 was included in the Maastricht Treaty to counterbalance what were widely perceived as centralising federalising tendencies encouraged by dominant forces within the EU.[4] This hotly contested word, which was not strictly necessary for the message which it sought to convey, means that power should be exercised at the lowest appropriate level of government

---

2   Cm 5511, *Your Region, Your Choice: Revitalising the English Regions* (2002).
3   A Toth and J Steiner in D O'Keeffe and P Twomey *Legal Issues of the Maastricht Treaty* (1994); A Estella *The EU Principle of Subsidiarity and its Critique* (2002).
4   Its first appearance in the Single European Act 1987 is in relation to the environment.

unless this is not possible or not efficacious. The Community should only act where it has exclusive power – and exclusive power is a hotly contested aphorism.[5] Or the Community should only act where the 'objectives of the proposed action cannot be sufficiently achieved by the Member States and can therefore, by reason of the scale or effects of the proposed action, be better achieved by the Community.' The Article adds that any action shall not go beyond what is necessary to achieve the objectives of the Treaty ie, it should be proportionate to legitimate objectives. The Community also has to act within the powers conferred by the Treaty and the Treaty's objectives. It is subject to legal control. The doctrine is also justiciable, although the ECJ has been very restrained in the cases where it might have relevance under the doctrine.[6] The strength of feeling on subsidiarity being a justiciable principle is brought out by the House of Commons Committee on European Scrutiny which feels that enforcement of subsidiarity should be a political and not a legal matter.[7] The Committee also felt that an 'ever closer union' is a far from value free aspiration and should be scrapped from the Treaty.[8]

A Protocol added by the Treaty of Amsterdam in 1997 provides greater detail on these matters and refers to subsidiarity as a 'dynamic concept' subject to modification in its application under different circumstances but in a manner consistent with Treaty objectives and powers. It may require action to be expanded within such limits, or to be restricted or discontinued. The principle does not call into question any powers conferred on the Community by the Treaty as interpreted by the ECJ. Each institution shall comply with subsidiarity and proportionality. This means maintaining in full the *acquis communautaire* (see Chapter 3) and institutional balance. It shall not affect principles developed by the ECJ regarding the relationship between Community and national law which are important features of this present book. Furthermore, application of the principle should take into

---

[5]   A Toth and J Steiner in D O'Keeffe and P Twomey eds *Legal Issues in the Maastricht Treaty* (1994) chs 3 and 4.

[6]   Case C-233/94 *Germany v European Parliament and Council* [1997] ECR I-2405; the *Working Time Directive* litigation Case C-84/94 *UK v EU Council* [1996] ECR I-5755 and the *Tobacco Advertising Directive* Case C-376/98 *Germany v EU Parliament and Council* [2000] ECR I-8419.

[7]   HC 152 (2001–02) paras 105–112. COSAC has been recommended as a body to undertake such review: see Ch 7, p 312 et seq and N Bernard *Multilevel Governance in the European Union* (2002).

[8]   But nor is an ever more far removed union value free!

account Article 6(4) TEU: 'the Union shall provide itself with the means necessary to attain its objectives and carry through its policies.'

Community legislation must provide a reasoned justification of compliance with the tests of subsidiarity and proportionality and the Protocol gives guidance on how to meet the requirement that action can be better met by Community action because the Member States are unable sufficiently to achieve the proposed objectives. Detailed guidance is provided on a range of items from transnational aspects, correcting distortion of competition within the Community and the scale of effects. Paragraph (6) states that Community action should be as simple as possible setting out a preference for Directives over regulations and Framework Directives over detailed Directives (the latter of which are more likely to produce direct effect). Community measures should leave as much scope as possible for national decisions consistent with the achievement of objectives. While respecting Community law, 'care should be taken to respect well established national arrangements and the organisation and working of Member States' legal systems.' This should leave available the opportunity for alternative modes of achieving objectives by Member States subject to proper enforcement and where this was appropriate.

The Convention on the Future of Europe established a Working Group to discuss subsidiarity. This Group examined how verification of compliance could be ensured. Specifically, was a mechanism required and if so should it be political or judicial? The European Parliament has favoured a judicial body; the UK prefers a political body. The Group felt that ex ante control was political involving enhanced scrutiny by the national parliaments of draft Community measures. National parliaments should have a right to refer measures to the ECJ for ex post facto review (see Chapter 7, p 317).[9] A further White Paper examined the area of complementary competencies, ie where action is taken by the Community and is limited to supplementing, supporting, or co-ordinating the action of Member States. Where are the points of conflict?

If subsidiarity leads to no action on the part of the Community, the Protocol continues, then in accordance with Article 10 [5] EC on co-operation (see Chapter 3, p 100 et seq) Member States should take all appropriate measures

---

[9]   For the report, and that on national parliaments, see the EU Convention Working Group's report on national parliament's and subsidiary: CONV 286/02 WG I 17 and CONV 353/02 WG IV 17 at http://european-convention.eu.int.

to secure Treaty obligations avoiding any action which could jeopardise such objectives. Given the history of the ECJ's liberal and wide-ranging use of Article 10 in the past, then this provision may not have been strictly necessary.

The Commission shall consult widely in making legislation, publishing consultation documents where appropriate. This is subject to urgency or confidentiality. It also has to justify its legislative proposals with regard to the principle of subsidiarity 'whenever necessary'. A memorandum will provide details.[10] It will explain wherever Community action is financed by the Community budget and the Commission shall seek to minimise burdens and ensure they are proportionate to objectives. It has to submit an annual report to the European Council, European Parliament and Council on the application of the principle. The European Parliament and Council shall also consider Commission proposals and their consistency with Article 5 and further duties apply in relation to the Council and the legislative process.

Article 5 is of course justiciable and as an integral part of the Treaty, the Protocol is also justiciable and could form part of the basis of an Article 230 [173] EC judicial review of Community institutions. A Member State could also be the object of an Article 226 [169] EC enforcement procedure, although such an issue would also be likely to fall under a question of legislating where the Member State has no competence. The ECJ would have to be careful not to rule on the specific measure and its legality, but on the position of the Member State in relation to Community law. The ECJ has had some experience of these provisions. They are not directly effective on individuals. They would necessarily involve such delicate questions and fine balancing of statistical and other analysis to render a very low intensity of review.[11]

The political importance of Article 5 was, however, as a sop to the anti federalists, particularly, but far from exclusively, in the then government party in the Westminster Parliament, and also Germany whose own federal relations influenced the Community model. Its intent was to hedge in the federal tendencies of the European super state.

---

[10]   *Better Lawmaking 1999* COM (1999) 562 final, 2 and *(2000)* COM (2000) 772 final. See further on reinforcing consultation and dialogue and proposals for general principles for consultation: COM(2002)277.

[11]   See note 6.

Making laws at the appropriate level is one issue. One further point that is worth mentioning is the relationship of national legislatures to the law making that takes place in the Community and the taking of measures under the Third Pillar. Certainly in the UK, the treatment of Parliament by the government in the making of European law has been high-handed and arrogant. This has left a serious deficit in the oversight of Community and EU initiatives by the national Parliament. Amendments were made under the ToA to seek to ensure greater provision to national parliaments of consultation documents, information about prospective legislation and Third Pillar proposals[12] and delays were incorporated before formal adoption to give time for scrutiny. The UK President of the Council produced his own proposal for reforms to give Parliament a greater role in scrutiny of European measures in November 1998 and the EU Convention Working Group has made recommendations.[13] We can examine these in Chapter 7.

The forces that supported national supremacy and saw a threat to this supremacy in the ever expanding Community were very often likely to be opposed to devolution within the UK. As the Community attacked a pristine notion of supremacy or sovereignty residing in Parliament from without, devolution arguably undermined that sovereignty from within. That of course depended upon the terms of devolution and whether Parliament had the final say either on reserved matters or ultimately on all matters. The case for devolution had become irresistible by the advent of Blair's first government. We were not alone in Europe in seeing unremitting pressure for devolved power within a national context.[14] In the debate on the future of the EU by the European Convention in early 2002 (see

---

12   *Protocol on the Role of National Parliaments in the European Union.* There were also proposals to facilitate the role of COSAC (The Conference of European Affairs Committees with members from each national Parliament and the European Parliament (Ch 7, p 312)) to allow it to examine 'any legislative proposal or initiative in relation to the establishment of an area of freedom, security and justice which might have a direct bearing on the rights and freedoms of individuals.' The European Parliament, Council and Commission shall be informed and COSAC may address those bodies notably in relation to 'subsidiarity, the area of freedom, security and justice as well as questions regarding fundamental rights'. COSAC's views are not binding on National Parliaments.

13   For the UK Presidency, see Cm 4095 (1998). Reforms in scrutiny in both the Commons and Lords followed in 1999. See note 9 above on the Convention.

14   See J Hopkins *Devolution in Context: Regional, Federal and Devolved Government in the European Union* (2002).

Chapter 2 p 36), discussion of Europe's future on the themes identified by the Final Act of the Nice Intergovernmental Committee included the following subjects: the Charter of Fundamental Rights of the EU[15] and the role of regional government in the working of the EU. This was encouraged by the Liège declaration on regions in November 2001, and was especially relevant to those regions with legislative powers.[16]

The regions then are increasingly making their presence felt in Europe. In terms of overall structure, some of the functions of the Community are state oriented: the state is responsible for breaches of Community law under Article 226 [169] EC even though a sub-state unit was responsible for the breach; the state is a privileged actor in Article 230 [173] EC applications for judicial review; the state can alone veto Treaty revisions ('national'). But as Scott points out, there are numerous Community legal provisions which take note of, or account for the presence of, regional and local government. Direct effect was famously extended to sub-state actors (pp 46 and 97); liability for breach of Community law may involve sub-state actors; flexibility in the implementation of Community law may leave space for regional implementation; Article 203 EC on the Council leaves open the possibility for sub-state ministerial representation in the Council and so on.[17] Some policies give 'voice' to the regions: the Committee of the Regions, Community/state/regional partnerships in funding policies such as structural funding.[18] The fact that the Community was built on relationships with Member States and is to that extent state-directed has, Scott maintains, paradoxically generated pressure for federal relations and for effective regional presence in national policy-making involving Europe to ensure effective national implementation via the regions. In the UK, for instance, Scottish and Northern Irish Ministers have power to make regulations to implement EC law, as do UK Ministers for those regions and a Concordat on Co-ordination of European Union Policy Issues exists between the Scottish Executive and the Westminster government (see below).

15   (2000) OJ 364/01.
16   Made at a meeting of heads of regional government in November 2001.
17   J Scott 'Member States and Regions in Community Law' in P Beaumont et al *Convergence and Divergence in European Public Law* (2002) ch 2, pp 20–21. See also N Bernard *Multilevel Governance in the European Union* (2002).
18   J Scott 'Member States and Regions in Community Law' in P Beaumont et al *Convergence and Divergence in European Public Law* (2002) ch 2, pp 20–21. See also N Bernard *Multilevel Governance in the European Union* (2002).

The Commission White Paper on European Governance (COM (2001) 428 final, 17)

The White Paper is further examined in the section in the following chapter concerning access to information and open government. The White Paper addresses the theme of improving EU policies, regulation and delivery in a partnership with national authorities and deciding whether action is needed at EU level. A feeling remains, however, that the real concern of the White Paper is promotion of the Commission both vis à vis the Council and European Parliament and other Member States. On the role of national parliaments the White Paper has very little to say beyond a single sentence. It refers to the fact that from 2002 onwards, the annual report on the implementation of the Protocol on Subsidiarity and Proportionality will be oriented towards the main objectives of the EU policies. 'It will investigate the extent to which the Union has applied the proportionality and subsidiarity principles in pursuing its main goals' (p 29). After five years one might add!

The Commission thought that best use was not made of the Committee of the Regions established under the Maastricht Treaty – their opinion on legislation and policy proposals goes to the legislature after those proposals have been sent to the latter not before thereby minimising its impact. (p 12). The Committee's membership is organised by Member States and varies considerably according to the federal/regional/devolved structures within those Member States.[19] The Commission was also critical of the use of regional and local democracy by the EU:

> yet the way in which the Union currently works does not allow for adequate interaction in a multi-level partnership; a partnership in which national governments involve their regions and cities fully in European policy-making. Regions and cities often feel that, in spite of their increased responsibility for implementing EU policies, their role as an elected and representative channel interacting with the public on EU policy is not exploited.
>
> There is also criticism that the legislation adopted by the Council and the European Parliament is either too detailed, or insufficiently adapted to local conditions and experience ...
>
> Criticism is not just focused on the Union. The principal responsibility for involving the regional and local level in EU policy remains and should

---

[19]   J Hopkins *Devolution in Context: Regional, Federal and Devolved Government in the European Union* (2002) at pp 202 et seq on the Committee of the Regions.

remain with national administrations. But national governments are often perceived as not adequately involving regional and local actors in preparing their positions on EU policies. Each Member State should foresee adequate mechanisms for wide consultation when discussing EU decisions and implementing EU policies with a territorial dimension. The process of EU policy-making, in particular its timing, should allow Member States to listen to and learn from regional and local experiences. [p 12]

The working group described above suggested that legislative regional assemblies should not be allowed to refer draft Community legislation to the ECJ to assess compliance with subsidiarity as was the case in their suggestion for national parliaments. The Committee of the Regions should have such a right for texts on which it had been consulted.

In calling for a greater sharing of competencies between EU and Member States (including regional and local bodies) the Commission noted that it had been prepared to withdraw proposals for legislation where institutional bargaining between the Council and European Parliament threatened to subvert principles of subsidiarity and proportionality. It also called for a greater degree of separation of the executive and legislature (as in Member States) so that the Commission should carry out executive functions and the Council and European Parliament would be equal partners in legislation. Such a development would allow a reduction of Comitology committees, though quite how is difficult to fathom.

But what of subsidiarity within the state? The EU is a union involving a Community, nations, regions, municipalities and localities. It is multi-level government and multi-level democracy. Ten new Member States will take the union far into the territory of the former Soviet Union and empire and almost to Asia Minor. The EU will seek further integration through further fragmentation. Without being centralist, it will wish to avoid the crisis where 'the centre cannot hold.' While the EU takes stock of its increasing significance in globalisation, and its role in that development, growing perception of regions and localities helps to emphasise identity and local belonging in a bigger scheme of things.

UK devolution

In *Scotland's Parliament* (Cm 3658, 1997), the government set out its plans for devolution in Scotland, to make 'government more accessible, open and accountable' and the government also set out plans for a more limited devolution to Wales. Northern Ireland's programme of devolution was a part of the Good Friday settlement in 1998 seeking peace for the province. In Scotland's case, Home Rule for Scotland had been on the political agenda since adopted by Gladstone's Liberal Party in the 1880s.[20] An attempt in the late 1970s to provide devolved powers failed after referenda in both countries did not achieve the necessary level of votes although detailed legislation had set out the systems of devolved government.[21] Precisely what influence Europe had in promoting subsidiarity within the state is difficult to quantify; eighteen years of Conservative centralisation had caused bitter resentment and not only in Scotland and Wales but in the English regions. But events in Europe certainly informed the background. In 1996, the Conservative government signed the European Charter of Local Self Government (Council of Europe) which states:

> Local authorities shall, within the limits of the law, have full discretion to exercise their initiative with regard to any matter which is not excluded from their competence nor assigned to any other authority.

> Public responsibilities shall generally be exercised, in preference, by those authorities which are closest to the citizen. Allocation of responsibility by another authority should weigh up the extent and nature of the task and requirements of efficiency and economy.

This is an espousal of subsidiarity within the state, and subsidiarity had fastened attention on sharing power and allocating law making power within the Community, and a connection was made with power sharing within the British state. Power sharing is not as broad as devolution which carries varying degrees of legislative, administrative and fiscal implications and self determination in allotted specific areas. But it is a continuation of a theme. The draft legislation which produced devolution within the UK was 'asymmetrical', however, in that the forms of devolution within the UK were not identical. In September 1998, referenda in Scotland and Wales achieved the necessary approval for the go-ahead to regional government and the introduction of the necessary Bills into Parliament at Westminster. For the first time since 1707, Scotland was to possess its own legislature.

---

[20]   See V Bogdanor and also A Bradley in *Constitutional Reform in the United Kingdom: Principles and Precedent* ed J Beatson (1998). Scottish independence is still the paramount objective of the Scottish National Party: see J Murkens, P Jones and M Keating *Scottish Independence: a Practical Guide* (2002).

[21]   The Scotland Act 1978 and the Wales Act 1978.

Following the peace settlement or Belfast agreement in Northern Ireland on Good Friday 1998,[22] referenda in the Republic and in the North of Ireland accepted proposals for a devolved executive and legislative Assembly to Northern Ireland, an Irish North/South Ministerial Council and a British/ Irish Council in which legislative representatives of the Irish Parliament will meet 'regularly' with those from Westminster, Belfast, Edinburgh, Cardiff, the Isle of Man and the Channel Islands; in June 2002, it met for the first time in twenty months. The Northern Ireland Assembly was elected by means of a single transferable vote[23] in June 1998 and has 109 members. The Good Friday Act 1998 makes provision for the appointment of a First Minister and a Deputy Minister by the Assembly on a basis reflecting the spirit of compromise of the Good Friday Agreement so that the First Minister inevitably will be a unionist and the deputy a nationalist. Ministers and junior Ministers are appointed on a complicated basis of proportional representation based upon elections to the Assembly.[24] The Northern Ireland Act 1998 established the legislative framework for devolution to Northern Ireland. Power had been devolved to Northern Ireland between 1922 and 1972 and in spite of elections to an Assembly in 1973 and 1982, direct rule had continued from Westminster. Devolution was not in itself a prized objective for the Northern Irish: it was seen by the Unionists as a means of remaining a part of the UK. The fragile nature of the arrangements was witnessed when in mid October 2002, direct rule was imposed from Westminster for the fourth time since the introduction of devolved government when devolved government broke down. The success of power sharing devolution is central to the long-term success of peaceful co-existence in Northern Ireland.

Welsh devolution (*A Voice for Wales* Cm July 1998) included the creation of a National Assembly for Wales whose functions are performed on behalf of the Crown. Its members (60) are elected to the Assembly based on Parliamentary and regional electoral regions. The Assembly elects one of its members as First secretary who appoints the other secretaries to form

---

[22] Cm 3383 (1998); B Hadfield (1999) Public Law 599.

[23] See Northern Ireland (Elections) Act 1998, s 2(4).

[24] Known as the d'Hondt method: see J Hopkins *Devolution in Context: Regional, Federal and Devolved Government in the European Union* (2002) at p 173. The First Minister's post and that of Deputy are linked by the Northern Ireland Act 1998, s 16 and so resignation of one will necessitate resignation of the other. See *Robinson v Secretary of State for Northern Ireland* [2002] UKHL 32, [2002] All ER (D) 364 (Jul) and the constitutional status of the NI Act 1998 and its interpretation, in particular ss 16(8) and 32(3) and Ch 4 note 7.

the executive. Secretaries work in subject area Assembly committees. Powers are delegated by the Assembly to the secretaries and may be revoked either en masse or in relation to one secretary.

Although the devolution to Wales, which did not devolve primary legislative powers, and to Northern Ireland, which saw the creation of specific bodies relevant to the difficulties of co-existence in the province such as the Northern Ireland Human Rights Commission (see Chapter 9) as well as an Equality Commission which are under duties to promote human rights and eliminate discrimination,[25] differ in fundamental detail from the Scotland Act 1998, there are some striking similarities in the legislation in terms of the mechanics of devolution and judicial review of devolved powers. Specific local features have to be attended to. As equality has a particular resonance in Northern Ireland[26] so, in Wales, has equal protection of the Welsh languages with English.

In relation to Scotland, a legislative Parliament with tax raising powers was introduced by the Scotland Act 1998. It was elected in May 1999. As with the Welsh Assembly, dual mandate is not prohibited so that one may be a member of the devolved body and an MP at Westminster. Its duration is for four years although there is a power for an 'extraordinary general election'. Members (129) are elected either as single constituency representatives or as regional representatives – the latter on a list system seeking to introduce some sense of proportional representation. The statutes of the Parliament, which receive the Royal Assent, are judicially reviewable, including on those occasions where they are incompatible with Convention rights as set out in the Human Rights Act 1998.[27] They will also have to comply with Community law. A Scottish Executive answerable to the Scottish Parliament is appointed from Members by the First Minister approved by Parliament and the Crown. The First Minister will be nominated from the party in Edinburgh able to command a majority and will be appointed by the Crown. In 1999, the Labour government's candidate for this post was the then Secretary of State for Scotland.[28] The Queen will

---

25   See the Northern Ireland Act 1998, ss 90–92 and certificates by the Secretary of State that allegedly discriminatory acts are covered by national security certificates and appeals against such certificates.

26   See the Northern Ireland Act 1998, s 24(1(c).

27   On Scottish legislation see T Mullen (2003) European Public Law Issue 2, forthcoming.

28   The offices of Secretaries of State for Scotland, Northern Ireland and Wales will continue to function as regional representatives within the UK government at Cabinet level. They are responsible for intergovernmental relationships.

remain the Head of State for Scotland. The Scottish civil service will remain a part of the Home civil service although the civil service codes are amended to accommodate the devolved nature of their service. The formal constitutional position of the Scottish executive is the 'Queen in right of the Scottish Administration' conferring a different legal capacity from the 'Queen in right of Her Majesty's Government in the UK'. This is not an example of the famous concept of the two Crowns[29] but is a recognition of the fact that in law the Crown may be divided into different legal personages which may enter into legal relations and be subject to judicial orders, one by the other.

The Edinburgh Parliament will be subject to the overall legislative competence of the Westminster Parliament – which along with the Human Rights Act evidences the New Labour government's unwillingness to compromise Parliamentary sovereignty. The UK Parliament may legislate for devolved Scottish matters[30] – but only after a 'Sewell resolution' (below p 236) and both UK and Scottish Ministers may implement EC law by regulations as was seen above. Under the HRA 1998, judges may declare Acts of the Westminster Parliament incompatible with Convention rights; they cannot declare them ultra vires. Acts of the Scottish Parliament may be declared ultra vires if in breach of the Convention rights or Community law or outwith the powers of the Scottish Parliament. The Executive must also operate within the bounds of Convention rights as defined, Community law and within their devolved competence.

The powers of the Scottish Parliament in terms of its devolved subject matter are deduced from an examination of those items which are the reserve matters of Westminster and which are listed in the Act. A list of devolved matters was set out in the Scottish White Paper.[31] The Scotland Act 1998 followed the pattern of the Northern Ireland Constitution Act 1973 and listed only reserved matters.[32] Although it has been stated that the powers devolved to Northern Ireland are broadly comparable with those devolved

---

[29] The Crown personal and the Crown political: F W Maitland 'The Crown as Corporation' (1901) 18 LQR 131. In Northern Ireland, executive power 'shall continue to be vested in Her Majesty'. There is no similar provision for Scotland.

[30] A Page and A Batey (2002) Public Law 501 'Scotland's Other Parliament ..'; T Mullen (2003) European Public Law Issue 2, forthcoming.

[31] Cm 3658, pp 3–7.

[32] Under the 10th Amendment of the US Constitution, powers are delegated to the US or prohibited to the States. All other powers are reserved to the States or to the people.

to Scotland,[33] the terminology used is different and there is an intermediate category which is 'reserved' but which can be legislated upon by the Assembly but only with the Secretary of State's consent. Any disputes over competence relating to a Bill or its provisions may be referred to the Judicial Committee of the Privy Council by one of the senior law officers.[34] Hopkins has remarked that Scotland and Northern Ireland possess some of the most extensive legislative powers in any regional assemblies in Europe. But the express reservation within the devolution acts for the power of the Westminster Parliament to legislate, effectively on any subject, for the two countries is 'without parallel' among legislative regions in Europe.[35] In Welsh devolution, devolved powers are set out in Orders in Council which are delegated legislation. Some powers are conferred by the Government of Wales Act 1998.

In July 1997, a Green Paper on the future of London government was produced which outlined plans for an elected mayor and an elected assembly for the capital. This was brought into existence by the Greater London Authority Act 1999. Government plans for devolution to the English regions was published in May 2002 on devolution within England (Cm 5511 and see p 251 et seq below).

Legislative competence

The competence of the Scottish Parliament is set out in ss 29 and 30 of the Scotland Act 1998, the latter allowing for modification of powers and designation by Order in Council approved by both Westminster and Edinburgh. Section 29(1) asserts that 'An Act of the Scottish Parliament is not law so far as any provision of the Act is outside the legislative competence of the Parliament.' These sections only make full sense when seen in conjunction with Sch 4 which entrenches certain provisions vis à vis the Scottish Parliament (including the Human Rights Act 1998) and Sch 5 which lists 'reserved' matters, ie for the Westminster Parliament or UK government. The latter is a long schedule covering general reservations

33   R Masterman and R Hazell in A Trench ed *The State of the Nations* (2001) p 206.
34   When home rule extended to Northern Ireland, any question of the constitutionality of Northern Ireland Bills was dealt with by the Privy Council.
35   J Hopkins *Devolution in Context: Regional, Federal and Devolved Government in the European Union* (2002) p 331.

including: the Constitution, political parties and registration and funding, foreign affairs including the EC, public service 'of the State', defence and treason. Part II of Sch 5 lists 'specific reservations' with exceptions. The headings, which contain reserved matters are: financial and economic matters; home affairs; trade and industry; energy; transport; social security; regulation of the professions (the legal professions are not listed); employment; health and medicines; media and culture; and under miscellaneous: judicial remuneration; equal opportunities (with exceptions); control of weapons; ordnance survey; time; and outer space bringing the Part II of Sch 5 provisions to a galactic conclusion. Part III states that bodies with mixed functions are not reserved unless cross-border bodies.

The modification of Scottish private[36] or criminal law is a devolved matter but s 29(4) deals with circumstances where such a modification, which would not otherwise apply to a reserved matter, makes such a modification as it applies to reserved matters. It is to be treated as a reserved matter 'unless the purpose of the provision is to make the law in question apply consistently to reserved matters and otherwise.' The commentators of the Act in *Current Law Statutes* observe of this unclear provision that 'Presumably, those promoting a Bill in the Scottish Parliament will go to some trouble to state their purpose in terms of such consistency.'[37]

Section 29(3) contains an interpretation clause. It states that for the purposes of s 29, the question whether a provision of an Act of the Scottish Parliament relates to a reserved matter is to be determined, subject to s 29(4) (above) by reference to the purpose of the provision, having regard (among other things) to its effect in all the circumstances.' The section seeks to ensure that where a matter is within competence it does not stray outside its vires by incidentally crossing into a reserved matter.[38] Such a cross-over was inevitable given that many areas are not neatly cocooned. 'The interpretation of legislation bridging the reserved and devolved areas will certainly be problematic.'[39]

---

[36] Under s 126(4), references to Scots private law include references to judicial review of administrative action.

[37] C Himsworth and C Munro *Current Law Statutes* (1998) Ch 46, p 46/42.

[38] *Gallagher v Lynn* [1937] AC 863.

[39] Himsworth and Munro *Current Law Statutes* (1998) pp 46–41/42. See also ss 54 and 101.

Section 31(1) imposes a duty on a Minister proposing a Bill to state on or before introduction that in his view the provisions of the Bill are within the legislative competence of the Scottish Parliament. Furthermore, the Presiding Officer of the Scottish Parliament shall issue a decision on or before introduction of a Bill on whether or not it is within competence. This acts simply as a warning. Any question of competence arising from pre-legislative scrutiny may be referred to the Judicial Committee of the Privy Council by a Law Officer including the Advocate General for Scotland appointed under section 87. That officer is the UK government's adviser on Scottish law.[40] The Judicial Committee of the Privy Council has a power to sit in Edinburgh, and also now in Belfast. The Secretary of State may intervene to prevent submission of a Bill for Royal Assent on specified grounds such as incompatibility with international obligations or national security.[41]

Section 34 makes provision for ECJ references for a preliminary ruling under Article 234 EC to test conformity of a Bill with Community law (see Chapter 3, p 44). To avoid interminable delay in judicial proceedings, the Scottish Parliament may resolve to reconsider the Bill. The position of the Scottish Executive applying to the ECJ under Article 230 EC to quash a measure of EC institutions is unchanged. Regions are non-privileged applicants unlike the Member State.[42] This is a matter on which the Committee of the Regions has pressed for reform to allow regional access.

Questions of vires and competence of Scottish Acts and other 'devolution issues' defined in Sch 6 occurring in litigation, and including questions of whether acts or failures to act are compatible with Community or Convention

---

40 See *Davidson v Scottish Ministers* 2002 SLT 420, Inner House on criticism of the Advocate General's failure to make an appearance in litigation involving the Crown.

41 And see the Scotland Act 1998, s 58 and grounds for Secretary of State to intervene by way of order where action of Scottish Executive incompatible with international obligations or national security.

42 For criticism, see N Burrows: (2002) European Public Law 45. Although the UK government defends infraction proceedings against the Community, the Scottish Executive will under the UK/Scottish Executive Concordat be expected to draft a reply and help prepare the case and participate. The Scottish Executive is not in a privileged position in relation to defending its position where a regulation acts contrary (and allegedly unlawfully) against its interests. It is up to the UK to take any action and the Concordat places no obligations upon it to do so. Quaere, the position if a more liberal approach had developed in relation to locus standi under Article 230 EC (p 106 et seq above).

law, may be referred to higher courts[43] and from the higher courts to the Judicial Committee of the Privy Council . In some instances references are mandatory. Appeals from superior courts go to the Judicial Committee of the Privy Council. A devolution issue which arises in proceedings before the House of Lords shall be referred to the Judicial Committee of the Privy Council unless the law lords consider it 'more appropriate, having regard to all the circumstances, that it should determine the issue.' Provision is made for references where the 'issue' arises in Scottish, English and Welsh or Northern Ireland courts. The decision of the Judicial Committee of the Privy Council is binding on all other courts except itself (s 103(1)). Provision is made for institution of proceedings on such issues by the Attorney General, Attorney General (Northern Ireland), Lord Advocate or Advocate General for Scotland and for notice of such proceedings to be given to those officers.[44] No provision is made under human rights litigation in Scotland under the HRA 1998 for the Advocate General to be notified where it affects a devolution point and this has caused difficulties.[45] Courts and tribunals may remove, limit or suspend the retrospective effect of a decision holding a primary or secondary provision in legislation to be outside its competence.[46]

No power exists, the White Paper (p 12) acknowledges, to entrench the existence of the Scottish Parliament but 'popular support for the Scottish Parliament, once established, will make sure that its future in the UK constitution will be secure.' Those who feared that although repeal was unlikely, an erosion of devolved power by implied repeal could take place will take comfort from Sir John Laws' views that constitutional measures,

---

43 See Sch 6, Part II and Part III and Part IV – the latter two deal with proceedings in England and Wales and Northern Ireland where a Scottish devolution issue is raised. Acts of the Scottish Executive were covered by the Convention before the HRA 1998 came into effect because the Scotland Act 1998 was the governing provision: *Starrs v Ruxton* 2000 JC 208.

44 Depending upon the jurisdiction.

45 *Mills v HM Advocate (No 2)* 2001 SLT 1359, where the court dealt with the fact that human rights points can often be raised by a 'victim' either by way of the HRA 1998, s 6 or by the 'devolution issue' procedure through the Scotland Act 1998. Where the former route is chosen there is no requirement to intimate the action to the Advocate General. The High Court of Justiciary on Appeal held that the HRA 1998, s 6 did not affect the operation of the Scotland Act 1998, Sch 6, para 5, and if an issue was raised which fell within the definition of 'devolution issue' in para 1 of Sch 6 to the Scotland Act 1998, there had to be intimation to the Advocate General in accordance with that Schedule.

46 See s 107.

and the devolution Acts are certainly such, cannot be subject to implied repeal (p 174 et seq). We shall see. For the avoidance of doubt, it is expressly stated in s 37 that the Acts of Union of 1706 and 1707 have effect subject to the 1998 Act. Strangely, this seems both to deny and confirm the special status of the 1707 Act in particular.[47]

Freedom of Information legislation in line with proposals for England and Wales, but with some significant modifications, has been introduced for Scotland (Chapter 6, p 287) and a Parliamentary Ombudsman has been established to deal with complaints on devolved items. The UK Parliamentary Commissioner for Administration dealt with complaints from Scotland on matters controlled by Westminster and acted as the Ombudsman for the Assembly. The position is now covered by the Scottish Public Services Ombudsman Act 2002 which has introduced important reforms into the ombudsman system ahead of proposals for models in the UK and England.[48]

Sewell Resolution

Where legislation in Westminster affects a devolved Scottish subject, a Sewell resolution is passed whereby Westminster will legislate for Scotland after seeking consent from the Scottish Parliament. By March 2002, thirty Westminster bills receiving Royal Assent were endorsed by a Sewell resolution at Holyrood.[49] It is a fact that a far greater number of these Bills has been passed than was anticipated. Trench cites the example of the (Westminster) International Criminal Court Act 2001 which although dealing with reserved matters, also touched on criminal law and extradition

---

[47] It was argued that certain articles of the 1707 Act were 'fundamental' and possessed a special status in Scots law which entrenched them against repeal by UK legislation: *MacCormick v Lord Advocate* 1953 SC 396; *Gibson v Lord Advocate* 1975 SLT 134.

[48] Including removal of the MP filter and the combination of a variety of ombudsmen within the new office – a 'one-stop-shop' for complainants.

[49] The Constitution Unit *Monitor* March 2002; did not include the Health Service Commissioners (Amendment) Act 2000 which 'trespassed' onto Scottish matters. See Page and Batey (2002) Public Law 501 'Scotland's Other Parliament'. 'Devolved purposes' does not include 'incidental or consequential changes' to law on non reserved matters made by Westminster bills. It includes those occasions where the Scottish Parliament or Scottish Executive competence is altered. Both Parliaments have legislated to incorporate international obligations.

law which are devolved. The Scots therefore passed their own Act, but a resolution was required because it was impossible not to touch on devolved matters in the Westminster legislation. In the case of Wales, negotiation on primary legislation affecting Wales and how that legislation is implemented is a preoccupation of intergovernmental activity. Each Act affecting Wales creates new and varying problems for administration to such an extent that the settlement in the 1998 Act and the transfer of functions orders is being 'rewritten in small increments by each new Westminster Act.'[50] This has the opposite effect of a Sewell resolution where the Scottish Administration will use provisions of a Westminster Act directly.

Scottish administration and finance

Part II of the Scotland Act 1998 deals with the Scottish Administration, some details of which were referred to above. This part contains the provisions on transfer of powers and devolved competence and shared functions as well as transfer of additional functions under s 63. Section 57 retains the power of Crown (Westminster) Ministers to exercise powers under s 2(2) EC Act in relation to Scotland which they may exercise together with Scottish Ministers. The section also spells out the obvious that Scottish subordinate legislation or acts of Ministers may not be incompatible with Community obligations or Convention rights.[51] Breach of directly enforceable Community rights will be remediable through Scottish courts.

The White Paper identifies roles for Scottish Ministers in Europe eg, in relevant Council meetings, but the Scottish are expected to respect the UK line on policies and will not be possessed of an independent mandate from Westminster on Europe and the Westminster Parliament will have the power to legislate on EU obligations for Scotland. The Edinburgh Parliament has a role to play in the scrutiny of EU legislative proposals and as we observe elsewhere, there is much debate on this issue in the wider context of national Parliaments and their absence from effective scrutiny (Chapter 7). Scotland would have its own representative offices in Brussels.

---

50 See D Bell and A Christie in *The State of the Nations 2001* ed A Trench 2001, p 165.

51 The HRA 1998 defines legislation of the Scottish Parliament as 'subordinate legislation': s 21(1).

Finance is contained in Part III of the Scotland Act 1998. A consolidated fund is established for Scotland and an Auditor General for Scotland (as in Wales). Powers to borrow from the Secretary of State are given, subject to an overall cap. Part IV confers the tax varying power to raise or lower income taxes within a 3p band. As the White Paper states, the UK government will seek to ensure for Scotland an appropriate share of UK public expenditure, in a manner which is objective and transparent and widely accepted. The Scottish Parliament will have maximum freedom to establish its own spending priorities and power to vary central government expenditure in Scotland within defined limits. The UK government will exercise control over public expenditure and borrowing. Problems loom.

Some problems

First, budgetary allocations have favoured Scotland and Wales to England's cost under the so-called Barnett formula which has operated since the days of the previous Labour government. In 2001, Northern Ireland in fact did not fare so well under the formula. Both Scotland and Wales were alleged to have received too much by allocation at the expense of the English regions. Politicians have grown increasingly disenchanted with the formula. To add to its complication is the fact that EU structural funds are allocated according to priorities and Wales is eligible for the highest level of assistance because of the high percentage of its population living in areas possessing 'Objective 1 status'. The Barnet formula, however, drives the allocation of funds received by the UK government – the funds are treated as UK income by HM Treasury because they are paid for by UK tax payers – to UK departments and to the regions because payments to the latter are assessed under the Barnet formula. This could mean England losing out even though it was meant to benefit from the Structural Funds.[52] However, it can cut the other way as the Welsh Assembly found in the 2000–2006 Structural Funds awards when Wales did not receive the priority the EU wished and faced the prospect of cutting back on its programmes. The Treasury had to adjust the Comprehensive Spending Review to compensate Wales. But as Bell and Christie suggest, this might have caused real problems had the UK administration not been so sympathetic to the region. 'So long as the devolved administrations have no legal right to challenge Treasury decisions, they will always be subject to UK macroeconomic priorities. Unlike many other advanced countries,

---

[52]   See D Bell and A Christie in *The State of the Nations 2001* ed A Trench 2001.

there is no arbitration mechanism, such as a constitutional court to resolve such differences.'[53] Nor are there doctrines of federal comity which are reciprocal obligations of cooperation between the nation and the region as developed by the BVerfG in the doctrine of *Bundestreue* – a good faith cooperation undertaking which as was seen in Chapter 2 inspired the provisions of Article 10 [5] EC (p 68).[54] The devolved administrations are in a weak position in relation to settlements made at the centre which may not become critical until there is a political difference between Westminster and the administrations. Such tensions have fuelled arguments for greater fiscal independence for the regions on familiar grounds:[55] that devolved administrations know local needs better than the centre; it will breed pluralism in policy initiatives; they are more flexible in adjustment; they offer protection for local taxpayers and enhance accountability of devolved regimes. On the other hand disparities in policy brought about by fiscal independence may encourage migration, reduce the benefits of economies of scale and reduce the size of the safety net for poorer areas which can only be effectively operated from the centre.[56] If this power imbalance is not addressed, it will only serve to undermine the value of devolution. HM Treasury has power to require Scottish Ministers to provide it with such information as it may reasonably specify (Scotland Act 1998, s 96). In fact, in the alleged absence on leadership on devolution by Whitehall departments, the role and influence of the Treasury in devolution policy has grown.[57]

Secondly, the question of the mid-Lothian issue has not been resolved. This refers to the fact that Scottish MPs in the Westminster Parliament may vote on English matters without a reciprocal right for English MPs to vote on purely Scottish affairs. Furthermore, Scotland is over represented in Westminster on a strictly pro rata basis of constituents to MPs.[58]

---

53   See D Bell and A Christie in *The State of the Nations 2001* ed A Trench 2001, p 148.

54   J Hopkins *Devolution in Context: Regional, Federal and Devolved Government in the European Union* (2002) pp 187 et seq. See p 100 et seq above.

55   See the Layfield report on local government finance in England and Wales: Cmnd 6453 (1976).

56   See D Bell and A Christie in *The State of the Nations 2001* ed A Trench 2001.

57   Institute for Public Policy Research and ESRC 22 July 2002, in *Financial Times* 20 July 2002.

58   See note to s 86 in Himsworth and Munroe *Current Law Statutes* (1998).

A third problem in Wales has been the vagueness of the powers of the National Assembly as well as the fact that the Assembly has no primary legislative capacity:

> It is becoming increasingly difficult for lawyers, voluntary agencies and campaigning organisations advising the public, to gain a clear picture of the National Assembly's powers. As well as the body of powers contained in the Transfer of Functions Order, there are now the effects of two legislative sessions at Westminster, in which a number of different approaches have been taken to drafting Bills that confer powers on the National Assembly. The result is a rapidly expanding and incoherent mass of statutory powers with no overarching logic to the basis of their devolution to the National Assembly.[59]

In Scotland there is a growing realisation that power has not shifted so dramatically northwards.[60] In Scotland, an early concentration on EU and foreign affairs was noted which although a reserved subject 'there was much that the Scottish Parliament had responsibility for that had a significant EU dimension.'[61] The 'top priority' status of this area was witnessed by appointing a Minister for Europe and External Affairs (shared unusually with Education). The Minister was quick to proclaim that 'engagement with Europe cannot be avoided because it permeates so many areas of policy.'[62] Three priorities were established:

1. to monitor and, where necessary, influence the UK line on the forthcoming EU enlargement;
2. to raise Scotland's profile within the EU in relation to the smaller member states, other territorial governments and the EU's institutions;
3. to exchange ideas with other territorial governments on policy.

Mitchell refers to these priorities being adopted by the Scottish Office some years before 'and indeed by many large local authorities'.[63] The Scottish Office had also supported greater Scottish presence overseas (the Scottish Europa Office) a decade earlier or so calls for Scottish trade presence in overseas cities reflected an initiative which had already been supported.

---

[59]   Law Society of England and Wales Submission to the Review of Procedure of the National Assembly for Wales, May 2001, cited in J Osmond in A Trench ed *The State of the Nations 2001*, p 29.

[60]   Trench ed *The State of the Nations 2001*, p 48.

[61]   Trench ed *The State of the Nations 2001*, p 55.

[62]   Trench ed *The State of the Nations 2001*, p 55.

[63]   Trench ed *The State of the Nations 2001*, p 69.

Both Scotland and Wales have 'active representations' in Brussels representing devolved interests, not UK ones. They are a sort of half-way house between unofficial local and regional lobbying interests and diplomatic missions of Member States.[64] In May 2001, the First Minister signed the 'Flanders Declaration' together with other constitutional regions in Europe calling for the involvement of EU devolved governments in preparation for the next Intergovernmental Committee. A report published in December 2001 by the European Committee of the Scottish Parliament followed a seven month inquiry on how the EU should be governed and what Scotland's role in Europe should be. One recommendation was for more involvement by Scottish Ministers and officials in meetings of the Council of the EU and its preparatory working groups.[65]

Under Robin Cook's stewardship as Foreign Secretary, relationships between the Scottish First Minister, who unlike his predecessor had pressed for greater prominence to be given to EU affairs, and Robin Cook had been 'fairly relaxed.' Under Jack Straw however, the Scottish National Party believed that the First Minister had been forced to back down over the Intergovernmental Committee initiative. Certainly, the attention on European connections was small beer compared with the newsworthiness of the Scottish Qualifications Agency fiasco and the mistakes in publicising examination results in 2000 – only bettered by the English 'A level' fiasco in 2002. Nonetheless, ministers from devolved administrations have attended Council meetings containing a devolved interest and have even taken the UK lead.[66] They are there as UK representatives, however, and must maintain the UK line as well as complete confidentiality of the discussions. But, devolved Ministers are not accountable to the UK Parliament; UK Ministers are and they are not responsible for the actions of devolved Ministers. Conversely, the Scottish Parliament has sought information about these meetings from their Ministers for which, being a reserved matter, they have no accountability. 'To create a situation where one Minister attends a meeting, for which they are responsible to a Parliament of which they are not a member but not to the one of which they

[64] Trench ed *The State of the Nations 2001*, pp 168–69.

[65] www.scottish.parliament.uk/official_report/cttee/europe-02/eur02-01-01.

[66] *The State of the Nations 2001* A Trench ed, p 169 and J Hopkins *Devolution in Context: Regional, Federal and Devolved Government in the European Union* (2002) ch 8 who describes regional influence on Brussels. The strongest influence is by German and Belgian regional bodies because of the domestic constitutional guarantees given to those bodies.

are a member, is strange indeed.'[67] The EU was the subject of a Joint Ministerial Committee comprising key players in Cabinet committees and the first and deputy Ministers. Opportunity for influence – in this case on a pending EU summit – are significant but are not guaranteed as in the case of Germany and Belgium whose respective domestic constitutions gives them guaranteed rights to participate.

In Northern Ireland, the preoccupation has been on saving the Belfast Agreement, decommissioning of IRA arms, and keeping devolved government alive. In August 2001, the Northern Ireland Secretary suspended devolution for one day in order to save the institutions of devolution in the face of Loyalist hostility. This was driven by disenchantment with the failure to make progress on arms decommissioning and the enactment of the Police (Northern Ireland) Act 2000 which renamed the RUC the Northern Ireland Police Force. This also introduced an independent Ombudsman for the force breaking away from an English Police Complaints Authority style of complaint resolution although an independent complaints structure for the police is now to be introduced into England under the Police Reform Act 2002. An interesting feature of devolution in Northern Ireland has been an increasing use of litigation in the light of the Belfast Agreement by political parties.[68]

One sensitive feature in Northern Ireland has concerned the working of the Assembly Committees and their right to draft policy papers. Under the UK Freedom of Information Act 2000 – which applies in Northern Ireland – there is an exemption for policy advice. Civil servants were uneasy in Northern Ireland that conventions developed in Westminster on the relationship between select committees and civil servants were not being employed in Northern Ireland. Select Committees may ask for what they want but draft policy papers would not be sent formally to a committee and certainly not for any public hearing. Select committees in Westminster cannot enforce production of papers; this would have to be achieved by a resolution of the House which would of course divide on party lines. The Head of the Northern Ireland Civil Service met Northern Ireland committee chairs on two occasions stating that there were 15 categories of papers that might be difficult to disclose. He nevertheless hoped for the development of conventions on this subject.[69] Possession of security

---

67   *The State of the Nations 2001* A Trench ed, p 169.
68   G Anthony (2002) European Public Law 401.
69   R Wilson and R Wilford in *The State of the Nations 2001* A Trench ed, p 99.

sensitive information by alleged terrorist sympathisers among *Sinn Fein* party workers who had used their position to gain access brought an end to devolved government in Northern Ireland in October 2002 when the Unionist members of the executive resigned. It was expected that direct rule would only be short term.

How does Westminster govern?

By Intergovernmental agreements and concordats and Devolution Guidance Notes establishing the Intergovernmental Relationships. The Memorandum of Understanding on Intergovernmental relations lists five principles governing such relations post devolution: principles of good administration; of cooperation; exchange of scientific, technical and policy information; confidentiality; and accountability. In 2000, Hazell noted the informal and low-key nature of such agreements. Those characteristics have become even more apparent. Resort to formal machinery under the Memorandum of Understanding has not been made.[70] Rawlings showed how from the early days Intergovernmental operations were clothed in confidentiality and that much information from Westminster was given only on that basis. The formal machinery for such Intergovernmental arrangements, the Joint Ministerial Committee, has been little used. Relationships are effected through informal minister/official meetings and relationships are described as 'smooth'.[71] These could in fact be unofficial Joint Ministerial Committees but are simply not referred to as such. Trench described the British/Irish Council and plenary sessions of the North South Ministerial Council as 'off the radar'[72] and Sinn Fein members were barred from the latter which led to a judicial review.[73] Concordats, although subject to annual review, have seen little change to their contents. Newer concordats fulfil different functions to earlier ones and in the case of the Welsh National Assembly and MAFF (DEFRA) it included not only the usual provisions about sharing information and consultation, but also a preoccupation with EU matters including proper implementation of EU

---

[70] Cm 4806 (2000).
[71] *The State of the Nations 2001* A Trench ed, p 155. See *Memorandum of Understanding and Supplementary Agreements* Cm 5240 (Dec 2001); see: www.scotland.gov.uk/concordats/dcms.pdf .
[72] Tench, p 166.
[73] G Anthony (2002) European Public Law 401.

obligations into domestic law. It effectively accentuates what is already contained in the lead Concordat on Co-ordination of EU Policy Issues.[74]

As one might imagine, much of the business is dealt with through Ministerial, and on less sensitive issues, official correspondence. Whitehall main departments established 'devolution units'. There was also a remodelling of some UK departments so that the Lord Chancellor's Department gained human rights, freedom of information and data protection making it more like a Ministry of Justice for England and Wales with additional UK responsibilities. The Cabinet Office and the LCD are jointly responsible for constitutional affairs and the Treasury retains its momentum in controlling financial policy within government although it lost its powers over bank rates under the Bank of England Act 1998 – a necessary pre-cursor to monetary union (Chapter 14, p 584 et seq).

Although contact between departments and devolved administrations was regular and constructive, a feeling persisted among the latter that the centre was less forthcoming with information than was desirable. The special interests of devolved administrations often stood in the way of closer contact between those administrations.

While relations between the devolved administrations and Westminster have worked smoothly and effectively by and large, they have operated in a relationship of informality and a lack of openness and confidentiality. Pluralism in policy development has been seen, so that in freedom of information legislation, although the Scottish model was heavily influenced by the UK Act, some important differences were incorporated.[75] The Scottish Parliament took a different approach to the UK Parliament on the repeal of 'section 28' which placed limits on information about homosexuality in schools. Hunting with dogs was banned in Scotland, but the UK government retreated from what was a manifesto commitment in 1997 in the face of widespread opposition. Student fees were abolished in Scotland, but not in England and Wales. There have also been innovations on public participation in the legislative process in Scotland.[76]

---

[74]   Part II Annex B to Lord Chancellor 2000: *The State of the Nations 2001* A Trench ed, p 158.

[75]   The Scots did not adopt a tribunal to hear appeals from the Scottish Information Commissioner and there are only five absolute exemptions not eight under the Freedom of Information (Scotland) Act 2002 and the test for retaining information is 'prejudice' not 'serious prejudice' (Ch 6, p 287).

[76]   T Mullen (2003) European Public Law Issue 2, forthcoming.

The Leader of the Welsh Assembly has vowed not to use the private sector to improve education as has occurred in England and there are significant divergences from England on health and school administration. Major planning decisions it is vowed will take place in Cardiff not London.

But crucially, in a Europe that has seen pronounced movements towards regional government, the position in the UK gives some of the fewest constitutional and legal guarantees to regional government. The transition may have worked smoothly for the time-being, but in the absence of such guarantees there is less chance to prevent serious disruption to the operation of inter-governmental relationships within the UK should political divergence come to the fore or if a deteriorating economic climate allows the Treasury to dictate financial arrangements that are unacceptable.

The Judicial Committee of the Privy Council – a constitutional court?

The detailed provisions contained in all devolution statutes to deal with devolution disputes or 'issues', ie whether statutes or regulations were within devolved powers or within the ECHR were outlined above. These issues are referred to the Judicial Committee of the Privy Council. The Scottish White Paper spoke of this sitting in Edinburgh, but sittings to 31 July 2001 have only been in London. There have been seven cases to that date, all from Scotland and six involving points of criminal prosecutions and alleged contraventions of the HRA 1998 and the Scotland Act 1998, s 57(2) which prevents a Scottish Minister doing anything in breach of Community or Convention law. In *Anderson, Reid and Doherty v Scottish Ministers and A-G for Scotland* there was a challenge to a Scottish statute which provided for the continuing incarceration of persons suffering in particular from untreatable or psychopathic disorders. The challenge was made under Article 5 ECHR and was dismissed by the Court of Session and went to the Judicial Committee of the Privy Council in July 2001.[77] The Judicial Committee of the Privy Council dismissed the appeal in October 2001.[78]

It should be noted that the preservation of the Scottish High Court of Justiciary after 1707 as the final court of appeal on Scottish criminal matters

---

[77]   2001 SC 1, 16 June 2001 and 2002 SC (PC) 63.
[78]   See Convention Rights (Compliance) (Scotland) Act 2001.

has been disturbed by the role of the Judicial Committee of the Privy Council under these provisions. It is ironic that devolution should transfer this matter to a UK court sitting in England and one which has been accused of displaying an 'apparent ignorance of Scottish law and procedure exhibited in those judgments.'[79] By July 2001, the only Devolution Guidance Note not to be published concerned court proceedings on devolution issues covering Scotland and Wales.

The question of handing this competence to the Judicial Committee of the Privy Council does raise the most pressing of questions about a UK constitutional Court. The UK now has two courts at the apex of the legal system: the House of Lords which hears appeals from England and Wales, Northern Ireland and Scotland (but only in the latter case on civil (including public law) matters); and the Judicial Committee of the Privy Council which deals with appeals from those commonwealth countries which have retained final appeal to that committee – and which has included high profile appeals against death sentences – as well as a variety of 'domestic appeals' on eg professional disciplinary matters from the General Medical Council. Although the work of the two institutions 'overlaps and is carefully coordinated'[80] they are separate institutions with distinct jurisdictions. While membership overlaps, it is not identical. Under devolution this has produced considerable complexity. As we have seen, Bills which raise a devolution issue may be referred by the various Law Officers to the Judicial Committee of the Privy Council to decide whether a provision in a Bill is within the legislative competence of the devolved Parliament/Assembly;[81] devolution issues arising in litigation are dealt with ultimately by the Judicial Committee of the Privy Council. However, it should be recalled that in the Scotland Act 1998, s 32 as (with similar provisions in the Northern Ireland Act): 'Any devolution issue which arises in judicial proceedings in the House of Lords shall be referred to the Judicial Committee of the Privy Council unless the House considers it more appropriate, having regard to all the circumstances, that it should determine the issue.'

So there could be a bifurcation in decision-making. Appeals could come to the House of Lords as the final court of appeal on civil matters from Scotland

---

[79]   R Masterman and J Mitchell in *The State of the Nations 2001* A Trench ed, p 179. See also S Tierney (2001) Public Law 38 and in Boyle et al (eds) *Human Rights and Scots Law* ch 5.

[80]   Le Sueur and Cornes *The Future of the United Kingdom's Highest Courts* (Constitution Unit, 2001) p 25.

[81]   Scotland Act 1998, s 33; Northern Ireland Act 1998, s 11.

(both civil and also criminal from Northern Ireland) even where a point of human rights law was raised, but under the HRA 1998, s 11 which preserves existing human rights law, or by virtue of s 2, but not as a devolution issue. The House could retain it possibly coming to a different conclusion to a similar point decided in the Judicial Committee of the Privy Council. Although the House of Lords does not hear criminal appeals from Scotland, the Judicial Committee of the Privy Council may hear a convention case arising from a criminal prosecution which is not a matter arising from a defect in the court itself (which is not a part of the Scottish executive). Appeals may come from devolved administrations which do not raise 'devolution questions' and so will go to the House of Lords. An appeal on the same point of law may go to the House of Lords from England and Wales but it may raise a devolution question in Scotland or Northern Ireland which takes it to the Judicial Committee of the Privy Council.[82] Furthermore, the Scotland Act 1998, s 103(1)[83] states that 'Any decision of the Judicial Committee of the Privy Council in proceedings under this Act ... shall be binding in all legal proceedings (other than proceedings before the [Judicial] Committee.' On devolution questions therefore, the Judicial Committee's decisions are binding on *all* UK courts except itself. In all other areas, its decisions are of persuasive authority for UK courts and not binding. The House of Lords appellate committee sets binding precedent for all other UK courts in those areas where it hears appeals, with power to depart from its own precedents from a Practice Direction of 1966. There are problems about the relationship between the two courts.

In a lecture given in May 2002, the senior Law Lord, Lord Bingham believed that three factors were responsible for the re-assessment of the present arrangements for dealing with final appeals in the UK. The first concerned the change and projected change in the composition of the House Lords. A smaller House will be less inclined to be agreeable to contain members who, because of professional and ethical inhibitions, cannot play a full role in the affairs of the House. The second reason is the incorporation of the ECHR and the 'unwonted' attraction this has caused to the confusion of roles of the judiciary in the House of Lords and in particular that of the

---

82   *County Properties Ltd v Scottish Ministers* 2000 SLT 965; *R (Holding and Barnes plc v Secretary of State for the Environment* [2001] UKHL 23, [2001] 2 All ER 929. *HM Advocate v R* (2002) Times, 6 December, indicates the problem under SA s 57(2).

83   NIA 1998, s 82(1); GOWA 1998, Sch 8, para 32(b).

Lord Chancellor and whether this confusion breaches Article 6 ECHR. The Convention is concerned with appearances and risks as well as 'actualities' said Bingham. He identified various difficulties that the UK had experienced concerning a lack of independence with judicial tribunals.[84] As with independence, so secondly with impartiality, judges must be more inhibited in the views they express lest they are challenged for a lack of impartiality.[85] 'The result has been to fortify the tradition, already strong, of judicial reticence and to strengthen the steadily growing reluctance of the Law Lords to participate in the legislative business of the House.[86] Reticence may make good judges, argued Bingham, but it makes for poor debaters and legislators 'and serves to weaken the justification for including the Law Lords among the members of the House.'

The third factor concerned the role of the Judicial Committee of the Privy Council and the difficulties I outlined above in its devolution capacity and its relationship to the Appellate Committee.

The way the British have dealt with their final appeal may be symptomatic of the British genius to produce a semblance of order out of chaos. But 'inertia', Lord Bingham believed, 'was not an option'. The 'Law Lords are judges not legislators and do not belong in a House to whose business they can make no more than a slight contribution.'[87]

---

84 For instance in *Findlay v United Kingdom* (1997) 24 EHRR 221, a soldier successfully challenged the manner in which a court martial was organised – even though he had pleaded guilty. See *Morris v UK* [Application No 00038784/97; (26 February 2002, unreported) and note *R v Spear* [2002] UKHL 31, [2002] 3 All ER 1074. In *Starrs v Ruxton* 2000 JC 208 a temporary sheriff's role in the judicial process was successfully challenged under Article 6 ECHR the Scottish trial judge observing that such details could no longer be vouchsafed by convention (custom and practice) and not law. In *Millar v Dickson* [2001] UKPC D4, [2002] 3 All ER 1041 the conduct of temporary sheriffs was considered exemplary and no reason to suspect 'any of the accused suffered substantial injustice (sic)' but Art 6 challenge succeeded. *McGonnell v United Kingdom* (2000) 30 EHRR 289 – plaintiff had legitimate grounds for fearing Bailiff in Guernsey Parliament was influenced by participation in adoption of a planning policy. See also *Davidson v Scottish Ministers (No 2)* 2002 SLT 1231.

85 *Locabail (UK) Ltd v Bayfield Properties Ltd* [2000] QB 451; *Hoekstra v HM Advocate (No 2)* 2000 SLT 602.

86 Cf *Taylor v Lawrence* [2002] EWCA Civ 90, [2002] 2 All ER 353 and non-senior judges.

87 Lord Wilberforce favours membership of legislature of Law Lords to give them that breadth of experience required for judges adopting a broader policy approach to judgments Submission to Royal Commission on Reform of the HLs, Part 16 cited in Le Sueur and Cornes *The Future of the United Kingdom's Highest Courts*

His proposal for change involved four possible models:[88]

1. An amalgamated Appellate Committee and Judicial Committee sitting as the Supreme Court of the UK. This is the simplest solution but is unlikely to be achieved. Devolution disputes were deliberately given to the Judicial Committee and those overseas jurisdictions including the Isle of Mann and Channel Islands would not wish to appeal to a domestic supreme court, he believed. There is also the problem identified with Scottish criminal appeals and there would be no good case to hand these to the new court.

2. A new constitutional court for the UK 'operating alongside the existing courts in the three jurisdictions'. Without a written constitution, it might be difficult to distinguish between those matters that were and were not constitutional reviving 'the public/private formalism which has disfigured the administration of judicial review.' Establishing a constitutional court would downgrade the other supreme court that would decide all non-constitutional appeals. To staff a constitutional court with constitutional experts would run the risk of having judges who would be more in thrall to 'received opinion and current orthodoxy.' Sceptical generalists are less susceptible to such a danger, he believed. Lord Hailsham, it might be added, believed that a written constitution and a constitutional court would require British judges to know something about constitutional law 'about which they were mercifully ignorant'; Bingham believes there is constitutional expertise among the senior judges.

3. A court built on the lines of the ECJ which would hear references from lower courts on points of law. Such a court works well in the EU, he believed, 'uniformity of interpretation is ensured between one Member State and another – an essential condition of an effective union – and the independence and sensitivities of national courts are respected.' It offered little in a domestic context.

4. His last option was his preferred option: 'a supreme court severed from the legislature, established as a court in its own right, re-named and appropriately re-housed, properly equipped and resourced and

---

(2001) p 113; see Le Sueur and Cornes (2000) Current Legal Problems 53. It will be recalled that in constitutional courts overseas, it is often felt desirable to have as constitutional judges those who have a far wider political and professional expertise than ordinary judges.

[88] See LeSueur and Cornes (2000) Current Legal Problems 53 for further suggestions. The Government is not persuaded of the case for a Supreme Court: HL Debs Vol 636 col WA 3 and col WA 72; HC Debs Vol 388 col 734.

affording facilities for litigants, judges and staff as, in most countries of the world, are taken for granted.' The Judicial Committee would continue to sit for as long as demand for its services continues and a unified administration could serve both courts. One may ask, as Bingham does not, why the devolved business should not go to this new court? Why does the Judicial Committee of the Privy Council appear so suitable for these questions? Litigation on such questions has been slight in number but that may not always be the case.

Lord Bingham does not dwell on the qualities required for appointment nor the appointment process itself. The *Pinochet* episode, that was addressed briefly in Chapter 4, p 164 et seq served one useful function. The proceedings brought home the shortcomings in the secretive processes by which senior judges are appointed in the UK – basically on the approval of the Lord Chancellor who sounds out the opinions of professional elites before making his recommendation to the Crown via the Prime Minister. It also highlighted how little was known about those most senior of judges who will be increasingly asked to rule as judges on constitutional problems. Although one might not opt for the Senate style open hearings in the US where prospective appointments to the Supreme Court – the 'Supremes' – are grilled on all aspects of their professional and personal lives by senators, some serious accommodation will have to be made especially in the appointment of judges who are to deal with increasingly explosive and sensitive questions of law on devolution in the UK. A ground swell of opinion, of which Bingham's is eloquent testimony, is developing in the UK that such questions should go before a newly created Constitutional or Supreme Court which might also be an appropriate body to hear final appeals under the HRA 1998 (Chapter 9 below). This would remove the jurisdiction of the Privy Council and Judicial Committee of the House of Lords respectively. Some form of open appointments procedure could also be introduced for prospective members of this new court in the hope of uncovering any unhelpful biases or proclivities. On the other hand, it would be disastrous if we had a constitutional or supreme tribunal comprised only of the politically correct. There is a Judicial Appointments Commission which oversees the appointment of judges but it takes no part in the selection and appointment process. It is secretive.

Sensitivity to the desirability of the presence of Scottish and Northern Irish judges in any such court is obviously acknowledged. Now Welshness (language?) is being advocated. An attempt by a women's rights group to intervene in proceedings involving an all male Appellate Committee dealing with a dispute between an alleged rape victim's right not to have her past sexual history subjected to cross-examination and the defendant's right to a fair trial was unsuccessful. The Fawcett Society wished to argue that an all male Appellate Committee was not an impartial tribunal for the purposes of Article 6. Le Sueur and Cornes point out that women judges lead the German and Canadian top courts and appointments of women and ethnic minority members to the US Supreme Court has been a policy of successive Presidents.[89]

It is also common to see political agreement about the appointment of supreme judges (as in Germany and Spain) to achieve 'balanced tickets' and open political favouritism is not uncommon in the US.

Among the most important innovations sparked off by devolution is likely to be a change in our top court. There is no room for two courts here.

Regional devolution in England

The government has established regional development authorities to coordinate economic development in the regions. Regional chambers were developed in Labour's first period in office, their 'central task to provide 'a level of scrutiny of regional development authorities.'[90] Their role increased from 2000–2001 to include a government suggestion that preparation of regional planning guidance in town and country planning should be undertaken by chambers from regional planning conferences of local authorities. These proposals have come at a time when there were perceived attacks on direct public involvement in planning decisions by the government to remove obstacles to development.[91] Chambers comprising 'stakeholders in the planning process' were increasingly assuming control over regional planning policy at the expense of local authorities. RDA plans would be examined at Chambers' hearings and feed back would be given. Chambers were increasingly acting as a focal point for regional opposition to national government policies and also facilitating policy integration. In a survey reported by Tomaney,[92] in general, regional identity was felt to be far less important than being English, British or European.

---

[89]   See LeSueur and Cornes (2000) Current Legal Problems 53 for further suggestions.
[90]   J Tomaney in *The State of the Nations 2001* A Trench ed, p 115.
[91]   See N Parry (2002) European Public Law 122.
[92]   See N Parry (2002) European Public Law 122.

London achieved its own form of government under the Greater London Authority Act 1999. A directly elected mayor is the executive scrutinised by a twenty five member directly elected Assembly. It took over few powers of central government (most had been functions of Greater London Council until abolished by government legislation in 1986 and transferred to boroughs or joint bodies). The mayor's responsibilities are in transport, economic policy, emergency services and policing and there are four functional bodies for these areas appointed by the mayor who takes responsibility for their budgets. Strategies or plans have to be produced by the mayor in a wide variety of subjects. Provision is made for some new features in local government such as Question time.

Transport has been a highly public area of dispute between the mayor and central government involving the future of London Underground. Under the Greater London Authority Act 1999, full control of London Underground would only pass to its functional entity – Transport for London TfL – after a Public Private Partnership (PPP) for its management was established. The PPP negotiated between central government and private contractors was challenged in the courts by the mayor and his transport commissioner on the grounds of its impact on safety, value for money implications and its legal basis. 'The judicial process found in the UK government's favour, but the political consequences were far from clear.'[93]

The major initiative on English regional devolution came with the publication of: *Your Region: Your Choice* (Cm 5511, May 2002), in which the government set out its plans for regional government in England. It was pointed out that England now possesses some of the few regions in the EU which do not have some form of regional democratic government.[94] England does not possess its own Parliament. Its Parliament is the UK Parliament. The eight regions would be allowed to conduct local referenda – with the possibility of one being held in the North East in 2003 – to establish directly elected regional assemblies. The first may be up and running by 2004 if necessary legislation can be passed through Westminster. They will not have the powers of the Welsh Assembly, let alone the Scottish administration, but they will probably have power to issue a precept against local authorities in their respective areas and will

---

93　Tomaney p 128 and *R (Transport for London) v London Underground Ltd* [2001] EWHC Admin 637, [2001] All ER (D) 428 (Jul). On PPP/PFI projects and management, see HC 460 (2001–02).

94　HC Debs 9 May 2002.

possess powers for economic development, strategic planning, transport and housing strategy, public health, culture and tourism and skills and employment. They will not have responsibility for police or fire services. Areas traditionally under central control, such as prisons, will remain so.

Approval of a regional assembly would mean the removal of a tier of local government and county councils are the favourite to disappear. The White Paper is not clear as to where the running costs of assemblies will come from. These are estimated at £25m pa each. Other funds would be re-allocated to an assembly; in the North East it is estimated that the budget would be £350m with power of disposal of a further £500m to quangos within its authority. Figures for the North West are £730m and £1.3 billion respectively. Borrowing powers are likely to be given but with Whitehall controls and possibly forms of capping. It will be interesting to see whether the central-local government conflict over expenditure which was a feature of public life throughout the 1980s and early 1990s will re-emerge if there is a political divergence between political representation in Whitehall and the regions.

The government has already envisaged regional authorities playing an important – if undefined role – in regional planning. Quite how they will fit in with new arrangements to remove regional and national decisions from local planning inquiries and into Parliament remains to be seen – although quite what will emerge is not clear.[95] The proposals have met with a great deal of hostility from environmental groups who in the last thirty-five years or so have been able to use such inquiries as effective vehicles of public participation. Such opportunities to confront government policy will, they believe, now be removed.

Conclusion

English devolution awaits the statute book although the Queen's Speech in November 2002 announced that legislation would be introduced to provide for the holding of referendums. Rather than producing dramatic change, the devolution that has taken place has helped to give some power back to regions, to bring government closer to the people and to help bolster local identity. These are arguably good developments. But, the real battles lie ahead when the domination of Labour politics is no longer shared

---

[95]   N Parry (2002) European Public Law 122.

throughout the UK and the British regions as is currently the case. The Westminster Parliament has retained the power to legislate for the whole of the UK,[96] but the exercise of that power in relation to Scotland in breach of the understanding and conventions relating to such a power would trigger a serious political crisis. It has been seen how the German constitutional court has developed the doctrine of *Bundestreue* – federal co-operative good faith – to help resolve dilemmas between lander and federal government.[97] We do not possess the constitutional machinery to deal with such matters and there is little scope for courts in the UK to allow conventions to undermine the express will of Parliament unless they developed the doctrine of legitimate expectation in what would appear to be a bold manner. The most interesting pressure for change that has been fomented by devolution has come with the calls for a new supreme court for the UK. While devolution has been a contributing factor in this movement, it has not been the only one.

While devolution has brought government closer to the people, it has also produced a very complicated set of constitutional arrangements in the UK. There are four very different types of government in the UK, with an additional supra-national EU level and with English regionalism about to emerge. The complexity, it has been argued, does not assist citizen comprehension and compounds a national 'democratic deficit'.[98] At the level of Parliamentary practice there are some striking anomalies. The Westminster Parliament cannot be recalled by backbenchers in a recess. Only the Government may take such action. This was shown dramatically in the summer of 2002 when war against Iraq seemed a possibility. In Scotland, the Presiding Officer of the Parliament, the equivalent of the Westminster Speaker, may decide whether circumstances require a recall. The Hansard Commission has recommended a similar power for the Speaker at Westminster.

---

[96]   Scotland Act 1998, s 28(7); Northern Ireland Act 1998, s 5(6).

[97]   The *Concordat* case of 1957 (8 BverfGE 309) which concerned regional implementation of an international agreement entered by the federal government. See *A-G for Canada v A-G for Ontario* [1937] AC 326 and J Hopkins *Devolution in Context: Regional, Federal and Devolved Government in the European Union* (2002) pp 187 et seq. Note also GATT Art XXIV: 12 the 'federal clause' ensuring compliance with the agreement by regional and local authorities.

[98]   A J Ward in J Jowell and D Oliver *The Changing Constitution* (2001, 4th ed) ch 5.

Chapter 6

'... as openly as possible ...': openness and access to information

Introduction

The previous chapter dealt with the 'closeness' of government in an era of an expanding union. The purpose of this chapter is to discuss access to information and open government in the context of wider European developments. Article 1(2) TEU declares that decisions in the EU shall be taken 'as openly as possible' which although not directly effective, it is binding on Community institutions and bodies.[1] For reasons that will become apparent, openness has become an increasingly important subject for the members of the European Union. The governing institutions of the Union have increasingly come under attack for a 'democratic deficit' and a lack of 'transparency' in their operation. These wide themes raise many questions beyond the scope of this chapter. The present concern is not only access to government-held information by individuals. It also raises questions about citizen involvement in EU activity and participation in decision-making. In Chapter 7, there will be a discussion of access to information by legislative assemblies—a dimension of growing importance in the EU.

---

[1] Case T-191/99: *Petrie v Commission* [2002] 1 CMLR 519; I have benefited from discussion with I.Harden on points raised in this chapter. See: I Harden (2001) European Public Law 165 and 'The European Ombudsman's Efforts to Increase Openness in the Union' and also S Peers both in V Deckmyn ed *Increasing Transparency in the European Union* (2002) Maastricht EIPA; A Tomkins 19 Yearbook of European Law 217 'Transparency and the Emergence of a European Administrative Law.'

The EU has not opted for an access law under the title of Freedom of Information, but its laws on access have the same objectives as such laws. Such laws allow access as a presumptive legal right to documents in any form they are kept, that is paper, computerised, or whatever, subject to well established exemptions which seek to protect the right of government to govern effectively and the right to privacy of legitimate interests. In this latter respect, data protection laws allowing access to personal records both computerised and manual (paper) are now mandatory requirements for Member States following an EU Directive, and a regulation which is binding on Community institutions.[2] The Data Protection Commissioners set up in Member States under the Directive have voiced strong opposition to the demands of EU and Member State governments for Internet Service Providers and phone companies to retain data records for many years including catalogues of web sites visited, records of email recipients, lists of telephone numbers dialled and the geographical location of mobile phones at all times they are switched on.

Exemptions within Freedom of Information legislation are usually discretionary: there are frequently exclusions which are effectively mandatory – the exclusion of the papers of the President's personal advisers, for instance, in the US. A court or tribunal usually has the final word on what has to be disclosed, circumscribed though this may be in certain sensitive areas.

Open government is wider in that it embraces access to information but also includes the right to attend government meetings unless this is clearly not feasible, to participate in policy making and consultation exercises, and rule making carried out by government agencies, public authorities, or government sponsored bodies. The right to attend and participate is again subject to clearly defined and generally accepted exemptions. 'Open government' has acquired a pejorative overtone in that it has been used as a label by governments to provide *its* version of openness, not one which citizens wish for. I find this pejorative use regrettable but in the 2001 Commission paper on *European Governance*[3] the White Paper uses the expression in a manner which falls within this criticism. The Commission did not wish to see duties to consult in legal provisions.

---

[2]   Directive 95/46/EC and for the latter Regulation 45/2001/EC (18 December 2001).

[3]   COM (2001) 428 final.

'Transparency' is frequently used in relation to EU governance to refer to a broader concept than openness and access to information; it refers to the degree of accessibility of the Union and its institutions to citizens and to citizen comprehension. This is not assisted by the complexity of the institutional relationships, their modi operandi as well as the complexity of the Treaty and the legal and administrative empire that it has spawned. A major preoccupation of the Convention under Valery Giscard d'Estaing covers the simplification of the existing Treaties as well as a new constitution for Europe. These points will be addressed by the Convention (see Chapter 14). In chapter two it was noted how a working group of the Convention had recommended that the Union should possess a single legal personality thereby removing the need for a three-pillar structure. This, it was hoped, would make the identity of the Union easier to comprehend.

The arguments both in favour and against freedom of information or access laws have been well rehearsed and need no detailed repetition here beyond what is said below.[4] The case for access to government information has been overwhelmingly accepted by most EU members – a factor noted by the ECJ and CFI on many occasions, emphatically so in the *Hautala* decision (above). The same enthusiasm to embrace citizen involvement and participation through hard law provisions has not been conceded although the problem of citizen alienation has been a focal point of Commission and national government attention. But many of the arguments about killing initiative, efficiency and slowing down decision-making by allowing citizen involvement in decision-making are finding new wind. 'The Government attaches priority to openness in the EU, which brings it closer to people, enabling them to follow and participate in decision-making ... but complete openness could have the effect of driving negotiations into the corridors, which would be the opposite of what was intended.'[5] And yet a Gallup pole, in 1993, established that over 80% of the UK population had no interest in seeking information about the Community or EU.[6]

The arguments in favour are: government, including the Community institutions, exists to protect the public interest and information is used in

---

4   See P Birkinshaw *Freedom of Information: the Law, the Practice and the Ideal* (2001, 3rd ed).

5   Foreign and Commonwealth Office *A Partnership of Nations* (1996).

6   Gallup, November 1993. In the Financial Times, 29 May 2002, 44.6% of the Irish were not at all well informed on enlargement of the Community; the EU average was 36.1%. Only the UK and Portugal were less aware of the issues.

the public interest to shape policies or actions that determine how human beings are to exist. Essential questions in the collection and use of information are: how reliable is it? How is it used? What does the information itself reveal about the process of government and the identification of the public interest? Is the information well tried and tested or is it tendentious? Secondly, information is a necessity for accountability—accountability is predicated by reliable information. If we or our representatives do not know what government is doing, how meaningful is accountability? Thirdly, reliable information is a prerequisite to establish effective and efficient government. Do governments use the best information available, make the best use of resources or provide the best form of public services? Making information available helps improve government performance. Fourthly, access to government-held information is a necessary right of citizenship. Access shows a Community's trust in the people. Fifthly, information is power and its exclusive possession especially so – both in terms of policy formulation and invasions of privacy. Sixthly, secrecy is a cloak for arbitrariness, inefficiency, corruption and other vices of power. Access to information and use of information may create valuable opportunities for wealth creation and commercial development, a factor now acknowledged by the Commission.[7]

Europe, Community and European Union

In terms of open government and access to information, the question was asked whether these are appropriate topics for the EU or EC. Is the EC because of its supra-national nature in a different category to national systems? Is efficiency in this form of government achieved at a higher detriment to democracy because of the international nature of the EC and EU? Does its international existence as an organisation involving many states, and whose laws are superior to those of the Member States in the field of Community law, put it on a different plane to national states where most of the arguments concerning openness and access to documents have been concentrated? Are there diplomatic sensitivities in the routine operations of the EC and EU which prevent freedom of information laws operating? The view has been accepted that similar arguments in support of openness and access apply, a point which is increasingly perceived by

---

[7]   *Public Sector Information in the Information Society* COM (1998) 585. On eEurope see: *Towards a knowledge-based Europe* DG Press and Communications October 2000: www.europa.eu.int/comm/education/index_en.

Community officials themselves in their attempts to enhance the legitimacy of the Community in the eyes of members and citizens.

'Transparency' of operations in the Community, which is a much wider concept than access to documents, has been a key policy objective in the EC Commission and Community institutions for over a decade. In addition, the EC has been subjected to constitutional analysis and criticism as a living constitutional organism in its own right and is not simply understood in terms of it being an exclusively international organisation and a subject of concern only to governments. The ECJ opened that trail in *Van Gend en Loos* as was seen in Chapter 2. Constitutional analyses are more likely to press for the democratic and legitimate bases for the exercise of power in the interests of the public. This is where freedom of information assumes increasing relevance. First, however, we should note the problems emerging from two sets of institutions in the EU, the committees assisting the Council and the Commission and the Comitology Committees, bodies that were referred to in Chapter 2, p 42 and the EU agencies. These bodies are not executive bodies, but advisory, information gathering and expert bodies assisting the Commission in particular in its work, policy development and implementing and drafting regulations and other laws.

Transparency, agencies and comitology

The Comitology bodies comprise committees of representatives of Member States, sometimes civil servants, and various socio-economic interests to assist in the policy formulation and law making process (see Chapter 2, p 42). They have operated in secrecy and confidentiality. We also meet the array of agencies established by the Commission. They have generated a great deal of critical attention because of their uncertain constitutional provenance. A criticism levelled against such bodies is that they are created and operate without any clear framework, objectives and without appropriate mechanisms for their control and accountability. They are not subject to any judicial control. Similar criticisms are made about agencies in the UK, where although the bodies regulating utilities and services are established in statutes, they still leave maximum discretion to regulators who may wish to pursue social objectives without a clear statutory mandate in their regulation rather than in purely economic ones such as price levels. Regulators have been accused of being engaged in too 'personalised' a regime of regulation.

In the US there is an Administrative Procedure Act and unlike the German Federal Administrative Procedure Act which was examined in Chapter 3, its sights are firmly set on collective as well as individual aspects of administrative fairness. Policy for instance has to be promulgated through rule-making procedures which are highly developed exercises in participation by interested parties, even so called 'informal rule-making'. The introduction of such procedures and stringent judicial review over the committees, and presumably agencies, operating within the EU has been warned against.[8] The EU agencies are not regulatory bodies. The committees do not exercise executive powers although the recent proposals for food, aviation safety, maritime safety and rail safety agencies may be conferred with decision-making powers, certainly in the case of the aviation agency. But they doubtless influence. My own feeling is that judicial review is likely to defer to expertise in any event – as it does in the US?[9] The role of more open procedures, more access to information and a more balanced membership of committees are factors to be considered. The new regulation on access to documents should help here, as will be seen.

The EC agencies have become fashionable objects of study and criticism because they do not easily fit into the institutional framework of the EC.[10] They are not created by the Treaty but by a body created under the Treaty either the Council or Commission using powers under Article 308 EC. While possessing no executive powers they can have a persuasive impact on policy making that may lead to exercise of executive powers by others. Information gathering is the central task in policy making in non-absolutist states and places the gatherer at a crucial advantage over other actors. To what extent are they independent in their methods, tasks and findings? If given too much independence and autonomy, how are they to be made accountable? And through what devices? Legal, judicial, budgetary, legislative oversight, audit, reporting and so on. In the US, the classic answer was the creation of a strong legislative framework for the operation of agencies and a highly developed judicial review. To this was added freedom of information and the Sunshine Act enjoining open meetings and the Federal Advisory Committee Act which requires open meetings by advisory committees and balanced membership of government advisory committees. Freedom of information laws were important in helping to

---

8   Dehousse in C Joerges and E Vos eds *EU Committees: Social Regulation, Law and Politics* (1999), ch 7. See COM (2001) 428 final, note 3 above, and the Commission's views on duties to consult.

9   See Ch 3, note 151.

10   Cf G Majone (2002) ELJ 319.

uncover the Enron scandal in 2002. The absence of such a legal framework in the UK has been criticised by the industries regulated by sectoral regulators who have claimed that there is too much opportunity for personality to dominate agency programmes.

In the EC, while the solutions or balm of agencification adopted elsewhere may not be directly appropriate, there is no doubt that there are familiar problems albeit in a setting which is operating supra-nationally and which has set up and reduplicated supra-national entities in order to mediate interstate relationships. The problem is that the state level lacks any form of control and cannot claim accountability and the supra-national level may wish for its own powers and control over such entities to be obfuscated. Most of the scandal involving EC bodies has surrounded elements of the Commission – the Cresson episode for instance involving cronyism and job placement. The concern is that agencies, and comitology committees, may assist malpractice if there are not sufficient safeguards to achieve control and accountability. The Cresson episode led to an inquiry by a Committee of Independent Experts established by the European Parliament and the recommendation of an Internal Audit Service to replace DG XX of the Commission and that all its reports would be sent to the EC auditors.[11] There was also a recommendation of an analogue of a Standing Committee on Standards in Public Life – the Nolan Committee. Codes of Conduct for Commissioners and for Commissioners and Departments do exist. In a report in January 2000, Neil Kinnock, Vice President of the Commission, agreed on the establishment of an Internal Audit Service and an Audit Progress Board to follow up reports and to monitor progress and to ensure that the Internal Audit Service's work is familiarised throughout the Commission, and one might add the agencies.[12]

What do we need to see? Should there be a clear legislative mandate for EU agencies? Should there be independent management boards? Access to information will improve with the EU Regulation of 2001 (see below) But the question of a Federal Advisory Committee Act and laws providing for

---

[11]   Committee of Independent Experts, Second Report on Reform of the Commission: Analysis of Current Practice and Proposals for Tackling Mismanagement, Irregularities and Fraud (1999). DG XX performs ex ante financial controls see I Harden etc (1995) European Public Law 599.

[12]   Reforming the Commission (2000). See A Tomkins 19 1999–2000 Yearbook of European Law (2000) 217. On the anti-fraud office in the Commission, Olaf, see Ch 11, p 481.

open meetings and public participation are not on the agenda. The EU Ombudsman has jurisdiction over the agencies and we will examine his efforts in Chapter 11, particularly the sua sponte initiative on access to information which the EU Ombudsman conducted. Parliamentary oversight and budgetary control currently exist. Does there need to be judicial review – of substance or procedure? Problems vis à vis individuals are more likely to concern employees[13] as well as contractors and contracts which are likely to be governed by the *lex loci contractus*. There is a lacuna in terms of citizens and agencies and their general accountability.

In 1999, a Council Decision replaced an earlier Decision on *Procedures for the Exercise of Implementing Powers Conferred on the Commission.*[14] The recitals stated that there should be greater consistency in the choice of committee procedure, greater involvement by the European Parliament, improvement in the information given to the European Parliament, and they should be more accessible to the public. Article 7 of the decision concerns accessibility. A list must be published of all committees assisting in the process of implementation and an annual report on the operation of the committees must be published by the Commission from 2000. The references of documents sent to the European Parliament are to be made public.

Community initiatives on openness

The ten month Convention which led to the Charter of Fundamental Rights of the EU was notable for the openness and accessibility of its proceedings. A public invitation to hear 'representatives of civil society' was made[15] and applicants for 'hearings' had to supply a short presentation 'of the organisation's viewpoint.' Priority was given to bodies 'operating at a European level.' The invitation clearly had highly organised Non Governmental Organisations in mind and one may ask how representative of a wide range of interests these are? Furthermore, the fact that the secretariat of the Convention was provided by the Council has been seen as a means of carefully controlling agendas in a subterranean manner. The Giscard D'Estaing Convention on the Constitution was not given 'openness' as one of its objects of inquiry. Its plenary sessions have been conducted in the open and submissions have been made likewise. The

13   See the 'whistleblowing' cases note 18 below.
14   Decision 99/468 [1999] OJ L184/23; Annex 3 of Joerges and Vos above.
15   Press Release 29 February 2000 SN 1872/00.

Praesidium which guides the Convention meets behind closed doors. Its themes cover: subsidiarity, simplification of the treaties, the role of national parliaments and the Charter of Fundamental Rights and its future status. Eleven specialist working parties have been established. As will be seen, the Charter has incorporated a right of access to documents as a fundamental right.

In its White Paper on *European Governance*[16] the Commission identified reform of European governance as 'one of its four strategic objectives.' (p 3). This was driven by the need to adapt governance under the Treaties to suit present and future needs and also in the context of the future of Europe for the next Inter Governmental Conference (IGC) agenda. The people of the EU 'expect the Union to act as visibly as national governments' says the White Paper. In establishing openness as one of the principles which underpin good governance, the White Paper urges active communication about its actions and policies using simple and accessible language. To openness it adds participation, accountability, effectiveness and coherence. Central government must take a more inclusive role and the Commission plans to use its europa website [www.europa.eu.int] as an inter-active platform for debate. The EU institutions should continue to develop EUR-LEX as a 'single on-line point in all languages allowing people to follow through policy proposals through the decision-making process.' It did already provide a 'one-stop shop' to access information about pending and adopted Community law [www.europa.eu.int/eur-lex/en/ index.html]. Many documents are published on-line including the European Parliament's legislative observatory: [wwwdb.europarl.eu.int/dors/oeil/en/ default/htm] and the Commission's pre-lex service [www.europa.eu.int/ prelex/apcnet.cfm?CL=en].[17]

The White Paper proposes opening up the policy-making process to get more people and organisations involved in shaping and delivering EU policy. 'It promotes greater openness, accountability and responsibility for all those involved.' It has opened up a debate with all interested parties and seeks to report by the end of 2002. There are over 2,500 organisations and people who have taken part in the governance debate including

---

[16]   Note 3 above. See J Scott and D Trubeck (2000) 8 ELJ 1; C Scott (2000) 8 ELJ 56; A Cygan (2002) Mod LR 229; A Follesdal (2003) European Public Law 73.

[17]   C Mauwet ed *The Guide to EU Information Sources on the Internet* (2002, 2nd ed). A free-phone number: 00 800 67891011 provides a helpful information service.

applicant countries. A data base of civil society organisations will be published by the Commission. It placed faith in 'a less top-down approach' and 'non legislative instruments' to achieve these ends. There was going to be up-to-date online information on preparation of policy through all stages of decision-making; in seeking to achieve greater interaction with regional and local government and civil society through European and national associations at an early stage in shaping policy it would establish 'systematic dialogue' with those bodies, introduce greater flexibility into how Community law can be implemented 'in a way which takes account of regional and local conditions', it would establish minimum standards for consultation on EU policy, and finally 'establish partnership arrangements going beyond the minimum standards in selected areas committing the Commission to additional consultation in return for more guarantees of the openness and representativity (sic) of the organisations consulted.'

Along with the promotion of a greater use of different policy tools such as framework Directives and co-regulatory mechanisms, together with regulations and simplification of EU law and encouragement of national authorities to simplify implementing measures, the White Paper commits the Commission to publication of guidelines 'on collection and use of expert advice, so that it is clear what advice is given, where it is coming from, how it is used and what alternative views are available' (p 5). The statement that 'people need to understand better the political project which underpins the Union' is rather reminiscent of the student leader's declaration in the early 1970s that 'students have a right to know why they are demonstrating'!

Finally, the European Council at Seville agreed to open up initial and final co-decision debates to the public but these were only limited amendments. The House of Lords select committee on the EU has recommended that all proceedings in the legislative process should be in public with a record of proceedings like Hansard (HL 163 (2001–02)).

Access to information

The subject of access to information had been previously addressed by the Community institutions on several occasions and in various legal provisions. In the Treaty of Rome itself, Article 287 [214] EC imposes an obligation of professional secrecy on Community officials and servants even after their duties have ceased'.[18] Article 296 [223] EC allows Member States to withhold information which they consider essential to the maintenance of their security. They may take such measures as they consider necessary for the essential interests of their security which are connected with the production of or trade in arms, munitions and war materials.[19] There is an obligation to publish legal acts of the Communities under Article 254 [191] EC and to state reasons upon which such legal acts are based under Article 253 [190] EC. Questions of legal privilege and confidentiality occur in Commission investigations, especially in competition cases. Many of these provisions have been implemented by regulations including those on historical records of the Community and security classification of documents and confidentiality of statistical data. Security classifications were changed rather controversially in 2000 as we shall see below. The Council adopted a Directive imposing obligations on Member States to allow access to environmental information held by competent national authorities.[20] The Directive has now been overtaken by the Aarhauss Convention which will shortly be implemented into UK law. Directives on public procurement or public purchasing which have to be implemented within each Member State also contain provisions on publicity and openness in the advertising and contract allocation stages of contracting along with certain other details (see Chapter 12, p 550 et seq). In its jurisprudence on fair procedure and 'rights of defence' the CFI has ruled that in competition cases a complainant investigated by the Commission was entitled to the 'whole file' and access was not determined by Commission discretion.[21]

Council and Commission Decisions and the Code on Access to Information

The new Regulation on access will be discussed below, but the background to access is instructive. As part of its own move to greater openness and

---

[18] On whistleblowing in the Commission see: Case T-82/99 *Cwik v Commission* [2000] ECR-SC-II-713 and on appeal C-340/00P (13 December 2001, unreported) and A Biondi (2003) European Public Law 39. See Tomkins note 12 above on audit reforms in the Commission.

[19] Though not so as to effect adversely competition in products 'not intended for specifically military purposes.'

[20] OJEC L 158/56 (23 June 1990): Directive 90/313/EEC.

[21] Cases T-30, 31 and 32/91 *Solvay v Commission (No 2)* [1995] ECR II-1825.

conscious of accusations of a lack of transparency, in December 1993 and February 1994, the Council and Commission respectively made Decisions on public access to documents. These Decisions followed Declaration 17 on the Right of Access to Information in the Maastricht Treaty and statements issued through the European Council, in particular those held in Birmingham which issued *A Community Close to its Citizens,* and Edinburgh in 1992. A Communication on public access to the Institutions' documents from the Commission followed a survey on public access to official documents in different states and the case for wider access was accepted. In early December 1993, the Council and Commission adopted a joint code on access to documents (OJEC C1993 166/4).

Subsequently, the Council and Commission Decisions allowing public access to documents held by them set out the time limits for responses, fees, and details for reading documents. [22] The Code allows access to 'documents', not just information. The expression 'documents' covers any medium containing existing data held by the Council or Commission although in the case of the Council Decision, it stipulates that the Council is to regard its Rules of Procedure. As well as the Code and Decisions, there was also introduced after litigation involving the Council a Code of Practice concerning access to the minutes and statements in meetings of the Council as a legislator (see below on Carvel). This was introduced after a very important ruling from the Court of First Instance when it ruled that the Council had acted in contravention of the joint Code in the following circumstances.

Carvel v EU Council[23]

An English newspaper wrote to the Council in pursuance of the Decision and Code above seeking access to Council documents including preparatory reports, the attendance and voting records, and/or the minutes of specified meetings of the Council of Ministers for Justice and for Agriculture. Under Article 9 (1) of the Rules of Procedure, as a general rule minutes have to indicate in respect of each item of the agenda 'the documents submitted to the Council' which could provide a useful index. The Council originally released certain documents, which it subsequently

---

22   Council Decision 20 December 1993: OJ L31 340/43, December 1993: Commission Decision 8 February 1994, OJ L46/58 18 February 1994.

23   Case T-194/94 *Carvel v EU Council* [1995] ECR II-2765.

claimed were released as the consequence of an administrative error. It refused access to other documents because they related to matters of deliberation in the Council and were covered by the confidentiality provisions in the Decision under Article 4 (2) and the Code. They would also breach the confidentiality provisions of its own Rules of Procedure. The applicants brought an application in the CFI seeking an annulment of the Council's decision on the basis that it amounted to a blanket refusal to release information, and that the Council had not exercised its discretion and balanced all relevant considerations in making its judgment. The Danish and Dutch governments testified that no such considerations or balancing had taken place before the decision to refuse access. It was clear from the terms of the 1993 Decision that the Council *must* balance the interests of the applicants and the Council's own interests in confidentiality of proceedings before making the decision and this had not been done. The reason why confidentiality was required was that:

> the Council points out that it works through a process of negotiation and compromise, in the course of which its members freely express their national preoccupations and positions. It is essential that those positions remain confidential, particularly if members are forced to move away from them in order that agreement may be reached, sometimes to the extent of abandoning their national instructions ... compromise and negotiation [are] vital to the adoption of Community legislation.[24]

This process would be jeopardised if parties were mindful that their positions could be made public. An attempt to get the CFI to order production to it of a report by the Council's Legal Service on the widespread use of 'statements' by national representatives to gain special exemptions from EC legislation failed.[25]

The court found for the applicants in so far as the discretion had not been exercised observing that the exercise of discretion under Article 5 (1) cannot defeat rights under the Decision. The CFI declined to make any wider ruling on access rights to Council documents. Subsequently, on 2 October 1995, the Council adopted a Code of Practice on Public Access to the Minutes and Statements in the Minutes of the Council Acting as Legislator.[26] The

---

24   *Carvel* Case T-194/94 [1996] All ER (EC) 53 at 62.
25   The Economist 16 September (1995), p 51 claimed the practice was widespread.
26   See generally, V Deckmyn and I Thompson eds *Openness and Transparency in the European Union* (1998).

Code stated that statements would be used in the minutes sparingly. Council bodies will therefore endeavour, 'wherever appropriate', to incorporate contents of the projected statements in the legislative act itself or in the statement of reasons in the case of a common position under the codecision and cooperation procedures between the Council and European Parliament when making legislation. Statements have to be compatible with the text of the Act. The Council favoured public access to statements but access may nonetheless be refused, and decisions on public access are taken by simple majority. Statements may be released as an explanation of a vote where a vote is made public under the Rules of Procedure. In the case of a statement by one or more members of the Council, the Council sought the agreement of the author(s) before deciding to make it available to the public.

The role of courts and the EU Ombudsman

Access to documents was enforced under the Code through the CFI and through the Ombudsman, both of which have developed very important general principles in reviewing decisions not to disclose documents and which are still relevant. These bodies will continue their respective roles under the new Regulation on access which has replaced the Code.

In terms of the Court, the CFI has dealt with the vast bulk of challenges and has incrementally come close to accepting that a right of access to documents is a fundamental human right – a position which the ECJ balked from adopting in *Netherlands v Council*[27] although it accepted the importance of the public's right of access to documents held by public authorities and noted that Declaration 17 of the Maastricht Treaty links that right with the democratic nature of the institutions. The Court also observed that the domestic legislation of most Member States 'enshrined in a general manner' public rights of access to documents held by public authorities as a constitutional or legislative principle.' The Advocate General observed in his opinion that 'the basis for such a right [of access] should be sought in the democratic principle, which constitutes one of the cornerstones of the Community edifice, as enshrined now in the Preamble to the Maastricht Treaty and Article 6(1) [F(1)] TEU.

---

[27]   Case C-58/94 [1996] ECR I-2169, para 35.

The CFI has accepted that in accordance with Article 6(2) TEU, decisions in the EU should be taken as openly as possible and with the 'principle of the widest possible access for citizens to information.'[28] The CFI has ruled that the joint Code applied to Third and Second Pillar documents, to committees of the Commission – the Comitology committees (above) – and to the deliberative documents of the Committee on Excise Duties which acted as a committee of the Commission.[29] The CFI emphasised in its judgments that essential procedures must be followed and decisions of the Commission would be struck down if there was a failure to attend carefully to these. In *WWF* the Court stated that when claiming exemptions, which were either of a mandatory nature when they protected a third party or discretionary when they sought to protect the confidentiality of the Commission's proceedings, the Commission must specify which documents were covered by which exemption.[30] Reasons had to be given for claiming exemptions which had to be coherent, related to a specific exemption either in the mandatory or discretionary class and must not be blanket or generalised reasons. However, in that case, and subsequent case law, the Court allowed the Commission to claim a public interest exemption for its own documentation and that which had been collected in proceedings for enforcement under Article 226 [169] EC because of the sensitivity of the interests (Member State) involved (see Chapter 11, p 482).

In *Hautala*[31] the ECJ on appeal from the CFI upheld a claimant's right to a report of the Working Group on Conventional Arms Exports drawn up under the framework of the Second Pillar. The CFI had annulled a decision of the Council denying access to the document because of its harmful potential to EU/third country relationships if produced. The report prompted the adoption by the Council of a code of practice on arms exports which was published.

Ms Hautala, an MEP, put forward two specific claims for access in addition to a third claiming denial of access was a 'breach of the fundamental

---

28   I Harden 'EUO's efforts to increase openness in the Union' citing Case T-174/95 *Svenska Journalist* [1998] ECR II -2289 para 66; Case T-309/97 *Bavarian Lager Co Ltd v Commission* [1999] ECR II-3217, para 36. I am very grateful to Ian Harden for his advice on this section.

29   *British American Tobacco International (Investments) Ltd v Commission* Case T-111/00 [2001] 3 CMLR 1572.

30   *WWF UK v Commission* Case Case T-105/95 [1997] All ER (EC) 300.

31   Case C-353/99 P [2002] 1 WLR 1930.

principle of Community law that citizens of the EU must be given the widest and fullest possible access to documents of the Community institutions, and of the protection of legitimate expectations' (para 6). The ECJ noted that the CFI ruled that exceptions to a wide general principle should be 'construed and applied strictly ... in a manner which does not defeat the application of the general rule.'[32] In *Interporc*, the CFI stated that openness is essential for democracy because it gives citizens the opportunity to understand and participate in public activities, as well as to gain the information needed to engage in 'genuine and efficient monitoring of the exercise of the powers vested in the Community institutions' (para 39). In *Hautala*, the courts emphasised that any derogations must comply with the principle of proportionality. The reason for withholding documents – to protect international relations – may be achieved by removing the passages that might harm such relations. This is known as redacting documents. The relevant provision of the Council Decision had to be interpreted in the light of the principle of the right to information and proportionality. The Council under the doctrine of proportionality would be obliged to consider the burden of sifting through documents and to balance that burden against the public interest in disclosure. The Council was obliged to consider whether partial access to documents not covered by the exceptions should be granted. It had not done so, on the basis that the Decision allowed access to documents not *information* as such and its decision was therefore unlawful.

The interpretation placed on the request by the Council and the denial that the Decision covered information as well as the documents themselves and that redaction could not take place had the effect of frustrating the public right of access 'without the slightest justification' thereby substantially reducing such a right of access.[33] A refusal to grant partial access to information not covered by the exception – which was not reasoned – would be 'manifestly disproportionate for ensuring the confidentiality of the items of information covered by one of those exceptions' (para 29). The burden on the Council of examining documents could be brought into the balance in assessing the public interest, the CFI reasoned.

---

32 Paragraph 84 and Case T-105/95 *WWF UK v Commission* [1997] ECR II-313, para 56 and Case T-124/96 *Interporc v Commission* [1998] ECR II-231, para 49.

33 Paragraph 26 and see Case C-174, 189/98P *Netherlands and Van der Wal v Commission* [2000] ECR I-1, para 27 and *Kuijer v EU Council* Case T-211/00 [2002] 1 CMLR 42.

The ECJ did not consider it necessary to decide whether the CFI was wrong to allow the claimants' case to succeed on 'the principle of a right to information' because there was an error made by the Council in refusing to consider whether a partial disclosure could be made. In other words, the decision on the fundamental right aspects was deferred. How closely a court will examine a balancing exercise where that does take place and how readily they will accept a conclusion by an institution that examination would constitute a disproportionate burden and allow it to safeguard good administration, we shall have to wait and see. This will be an issue that will emerge under the new regulation. The growing importance of the right to access will suggest that it will be seen as a fundamental right – a view endorsed by the presence of such a right in the Charter of Fundamental Rights (see Chapter 9, pp 276 and 378 below). The status of the Charter is being discussed. If it is incorporated within the new constitution, access to information will be a right of fundamental sifgnifigance.

In the *Hautala* decision the ECJ made no reference to the point, the Advocate General noted how a large number of Member States had followed the Code of the Union and had developed access laws of their own. This 'convergence of national laws ... constitutes a decisive reason for recognising the existence of a fundamental right of access to information held by Community institutions.'[34] Thirteen Member States have access laws which although they differ in detail they manifest a 'common conception in most of the Member States.'[35] A principle of access exists at state level 'and that principle is such that it would engender an equivalent principle at Community level.'[36]

EU Ombudsman

The EU Ombudsman has also been in the vanguard of a movement to make the Community institutions more open. The role of the EU Ombudsman is examined more fully in Chapter 11. Details of his powers and responsibilities may be found there (www.euro-ombudsman.eu.int). Here I concentrate on his work in access to information. The EU Ombudsman deals with complaints of maladministration. Wrongful refusal of information may

---

[34] Opinion of Advocate General Léger, para 55.
[35] Opinion of Advocate General Léger, para 58. In the case of the UK, it also had a code on access rather than a legal instrument.
[36] Opinion of Advocate General Léger, para 59. See C Lyons in P Beaumont et al eds *Convergence and Divergence in European Public Law* (2002) ch 5.

amount to maladministration. Harden makes the point that although a breach of Article 1(2) TEU does not confer rights on individuals in the CFI or ECJ, it may amount to maladministration. As Harden says, the EU Ombudsman understands openness to mean:

> the process through which public bodies make decisions should be understandable and include, when appropriate, suitable opportunities for participation; the decisions themselves should be reasoned as far as possible. The information on which the decisions are based should be available to the public.[37]

We have seen the approach of the CFI in particular above. The EU Ombudsman has made his own contribution in own initiative enquiries in Article 226 [169] EC complaints concerning enforcement where the Commission itself deals with infringement actions by complainants (see Chapter 11) and in staff recruitment cases. He has insisted on giving good reasons for decisions and amounts to 'a fundamental principle of transparency in the EU in that it allows the general public to ascertain the Community institutions' exercise of their powers.'[38] Nor, he has held, is giving of reasons limited to cases where it may assist in obtaining judicial review. The courts themselves have said that a part of the reason for giving reasons is to explain the exercise of authority over an individual.[39]

The EU Ombudsman has dealt with about the same number of cases under the Joint Code and Decisions of the Council and Commission as the courts. The Decisions identify the EU Ombudsman as a source of remedy – although he cannot enforce any recommendation to the body concerned if a 'friendly solution' fails but may issue a special report for the European Parliament. He has found that insufficient reasons were often given for refusal and that requests for 'repeat documents' and 'very large documents' as exceptions to the right of access were commonly made. The Parliamentary Ombudsman in the UK has also found authorities to be evasive and dilatory in their responses to requests for information under the current Code of Practice on Access covering Crown and other bodies

---

37   I Harden 'The European Ombudsman's Efforts to Increase Openness in the Union' note 1 above.

38   Case 788/97/PD, 26 November 1998.

39   Case 1250/2000, 19 July 2001, cited by Harden – this goes further than the basis upon which reasons are given in English law: see, however *R (Williams) v Secretary of State for the Home Department* [2002] EWCA Civ 498, [2002] 4 All ER 872, on fair procedure and disclosure.

within his jurisdiction. The EU Ombudsman has reasoned that access to Third Pillar documents is allowed because they deal with the application of Community law even if they concern a third Pillar matter or actions.[40] He also criticised the application of the authorship rule – documents authored by another person/body outside the institution could not be disclosed but the request should be sent to the author – where the documents had been co-authored by the Council and other bodies. The provision was in reality an exception to the general principle of access and should therefore be narrowly construed.[41] The EU Ombudsman has also ruled that the general secretariat of the Council are not separate from the Council so a document held by them is held by the Council.[42] Too frequently, Harden alleges, complaints have revealed the somewhat obstructive stance adopted by the Commission and Council – bodies which took a central role in the drafting of the new Regulation on access.

The most wide-ranging investigation by the EU Ombudsman into disclosure practices concerned his own initiative inquiries into Community institutions and bodies and their responses in relation to requests for access to documents. Following the lead of the ECJ in the *Netherlands v Council* decision (above), the EU Ombudsman held that 'good administration' requires rules laid down in advance to justify a refusal for a request for access. The bodies investigated all adopted rules of procedure.[43] That of the European Parliament has now been replaced by the Regulation on Access and internal rules of Procedure.

One further area of interest concerns registers of documents. In one complaint, the EU Ombudsman recommended that the Council should make publicly available a list of all measures approved in the field of the then Justice and Home Affairs pillar under Title VI TEU. The Council accepted this recommendation (Case 1055/96). The second complaint concerned the Commission's failure to maintain a public register of documents held by itself. The complaint contains invaluable advice on why keeping and publicising such a register constitutes good administration. Secondly, it is an invaluable source of assistance to a requester for official documents

---

[40]   Case 1087/96 EOAR 41.
[41]   Similar interpretation by CFI in Case T-188/97 *Rothmans International BV v Commission* [1999] ECR II-2463, para 55 IH.
[42]   Case 916/2000, 16 July 2001.
[43]   The European Parliament, Court of Auditors, European Investment Bank, European Central Bank and so on.

(Case 633/97). Both this second complaint and the third complaint concerning registers have now been subsumed by the duty in the Regulation to provide a register of documents. In the latter complaint, which concerned the Council, there had been a failure to disclose a list of all documents placed before certain committees. The problem arose from the different status of preparatory documents which were held back from its public register because they contained internal deliberations and were confidential. Nor were they referred to in provisional agendas. These were distinguished from documents that were more or less 'final' and registered. The Council accepted the general principle that all papers put before the Council should be in a register which is publicly accessible. The Council was reluctant to include papers which merely substituted for 'oral interventions' such as drafting suggestions circulated by the Presidency. What should be included, and this is crucial, are:

> unofficial documents which form a basis of the Council's deliberations, or discussions in one of its preparatory bodies, or have an influence on the institution's decision-making process, or summarise the state of play of a certain dossier. The EU Ombudsman accepted that there were understandable reasons why documents substituting for oral interventions might not be disclosed but he felt it difficult to produce objective criteria to determine the importance of short-lived documents. Furthermore, the citizen might have an interest in knowing whose proposals were successful and whose were not just as voters might wish to know how their elected representative voted. Doubtless these ruminations will feature in cases before the courts and EU Ombudsman under the Regulation.[44]

The UK Ombudsman has already investigated some information complaints which have an EC dimension. He has criticised the refusal to hand over correspondence between the European Commission and a government Ministry concerning an environmental assessment impact for a motorway widening scheme. He did not press for disclosure because all the relevant information had become public (Case A 3/94). The UK Ombudsman has also upheld complaints against government bodies to establish important principles such as the right for interest groups to be informed of certain details surrounding policy development relating to the pharmaceutical industry, and this clearly has a European dimension. The

---

[44]   Special Report from EUO to European Parliament following recommendations in complaint 917/2000/GG, 30 November 2001. The EU Ombudsman made no recommendations. I am grateful to Ian Harden for information on this complaint.

UK Ombudsman has carried on his work under the Code of Practice on Access in the UK because of the delay in bringing the Freedom of Information Act 2000 into operation and there is evidence to show that he is becoming increasingly critical of unnecessary secrecy. In fact, in 2002, he issued a critical report when the Home Secretary refused to disclose documents on a citizen request and this amounted to the first time in thirty five years that a department refused to comply with the UK Ombudsman's recommendations.[45]

The new Regulation and institutional Decisions

The Code has now been replaced by a Regulation made under Article 255 EC which introduced a new Treaty provision on access to documents. The relevant provision is in Chapter 2 of Part V of the Treaty entitled 'Provisions Common to Several Institutions'. The Regulation has been influenced by criticisms of the EU Ombudsman and the case law under the Code will indicate the strict approach that the courts are likely to take in interpretation. This basically provides that any citizen of the EU, and any natural or living person residing or having its registered office in a Member State, shall have a right of access to documents of the European Parliament, Council and Commission. This right was to be subject to the principles and conditions which were to be defined under paragraphs two and three of the Article. Basically, details of the right of access were to be in a Regulation made under Article 251 EC (co-decision procedure) within two years of the entry into force of the Amsterdam Treaty. Each of the three institutions identified above had to provide specific details in Rules of Procedure relating to access to documents (see Declaration 35, Treaty of Amsterdam).

The Commission duly drafted a much criticised Regulation and after a great deal of conflict between the Council and the European Parliament, a Regulation (1049/2001EC) was agreed which came into effect from 3 December 2001.[46] The three institutions also amended their Rules of Procedure as required in Article 255 EC setting out details on access.[47]

---

[45] *Declarations Made Under the Ministerial Code of Conduct* HC 353 (2001–2002).

[46] See P Birkinshaw *Freedom of Information: the Law, the Practice and the Ideal* (2001, 3rd ed) ch 8.

[47] For the European Parliament see: (2001/2135(REG), 13 November and Bureau Decision on Public Access to European Parliament Documents, 2001 OJ C374/1; for the Council: Decision of 29 November 2001 OJ L313/40; for the Commission: 5 December 2001 OJ L345/94.

The Regulation was much improved from that which was produced by the Commission,[48] although it is of interest to note that of the three sets of internal rules of procedure, that of the EP states that documents other than legislative documents relating to the drafting of policy or strategy 'shall be made directly accessible as far as possible.' Concern was expressed that this could work against the spirit of decisions of the CFI on 'deliberative documents' (see above).

Further developments should be noted. First of all, as seen above and in Chapters 2 and 9, a Charter of Fundamental Rights of the EU has been produced which includes in Article 42 a right to access to documents which repeats the provisions of Article 255 EC, but now makes it a 'fundamental right'. Furthermore, the Charter also includes within Article 41, concerning a right to good administration, a right of access by a person to their file and a right to protection of personal data. As will be seen in Chapter 11, a code of good administration has been produced by the EU Ombudsman and approved by the European Parliament which includes 'Requests for Information' from institutions covered by the Code (Article 22), requests for public access to documents (in accordance with the 2001 Regulation) (Article 23) and data protection (Article 21). The principle in Article 22 is subject to confidentiality and written clarification where a request is complicated or extensive. It nonetheless provides a presumption in favour of openness and one should recall that from his first annual report in 1995, the EU Ombudsman has stated that a failure to provide information as requested may amount to maladministration. Article 24 requires departments to keep adequate records of their correspondence together with documents they receive and measures they take. This provision highlights one of two important changes introduced by the Regulation vis à vis the joint Code of 1993.

The first change concerns the duty to maintain public registers of documents which had to be operational by 3 June 2002. The provision of such registers is an indispensable feature of effective access regimes. The UK government for its own Freedom of Information Act 2000 refused to impose a duty to maintain registers which would contain details of all documents held by bodies covered by the legislation. Under the UK Freedom of Information Act 2000, bodies covered by the Act will produce Publication Schemes and whether these might develop into a form of

---

48   For details see P Birkinshaw *Freedom of Information: the Law, the Practice and the Ideal* (2001, 3rd ed) ch 8.

register we shall have to see. The Regulation makes the adoption of registers mandatory for the European Parliament, Council and Commission. The second major reform concerned a significant weakness in the joint Code whereby documents authored by bodies or persons outside the institution concerned were not to be disclosed without the consent of the author. This reservation has now been removed as I shall explain.

The 2001 Regulation

The controversy surrounding this measure was noted above. The EU Ombudsman took a central role in challenging the unnecessary secrecy of the draft proposal from the Commission. The views of the European Parliament prevailed. The Regulation applies directly to the Council, European Parliament and Commission. It covers the agencies established by the institutions as well as the Comitology committees by virtue of Decision 99/468 of the Council (above).

Mindful of the case law under the earlier Decisions, the preamble emphasises the virtues of openness, participation, and more accountable administration. 'Openness contributes to strengthening the principles of democracy and respect for fundamental rights as laid down in Article 6 TEU.' Its purpose is to give the 'fullest possible effect' to the right of public access to documents.[49] Wider access should be granted to documents in cases where the institutions are acting in a legislative capacity, including delegated ones, and documents 'should be made directly accessible to the greatest possible extent'. It applies to Second and Third Pillar documents although each institution should respect its security rules.

Special arrangements should be made for 'highly sensitive documents' classified as top secret, secret and confidential (Regulation Article 9). Rules on secrecy were amended in the summer recess in 2000 in very controversial circumstances. Not only may access be denied, but their existence may not be entered on the public register.[50] The consent of the 'originator' of

---

[49]　It also provides guidance on access in ECSC and EAEC.

[50]　Rules on sensitive documents within institutions are to be made public. For the Decision of the Secretary-General of the Council of 27 July 2000 on classification, see: OJ 2000/C 239/01. Cf Article 296(1)(a) EC. A draft regulation covering archive documents (over 30 years old) has been published: COM (2002) 462 final. The most recent Decisions on classification are: Council Decision 19 March

the document has to be given for the release, or recording, of the document in a register. If consent is not given, the documents are effectively excluded from access. Security clearance at appropriate levels will have to be given to the personnel who may handle them. Informing the EP about sensitive documents shall be in accordance with arrangements between the Council, the Commission and the EP. When a MS handles a request for 'sensitive documents', it shall ensure that the principles in Article 9, and Article 4 on exemptions are respected. Maintaining appropriate levels of secrecy through legal protection has become a feature of accession to the EU and many Eastern European countries have introduced secrecy laws.

All 'agencies established by the Institutions' covered by the Regulation should apply its principles, the Regulation states; the work of the EU Ombudsman should be recalled and his successful efforts to persuade institutions not named in the former Decisions and Code to produce rules on access.

As mentioned above, the Regulation applies to documents not only drawn up by the institutions but also to those received from other bodies including Member States. The institutions should be mindful of, but not be bound by, any request by a Member State not to disclose a document which it has sent unless its consent has been given first (Declaration 35). Exceptions to access may be allowed as we shall see; the decisions of the courts and EU Ombudsman and the principles on openness that they have produced should be borne in mind (above). Provisions relating to personal data protection must be respected.

Requesters for documents may apply for a further internal review of a decision where there is a refusal to give access. This is known as a 'confirmatory application'. They may then apply to the court or the Ombudsman if refusal persists. Institutions must take steps to inform the public of the new provisions and to train staff in assisting applicants and also to provide registers of documents (see Article 11).

A few controversial points were clarified in the process of finalising the rule. The original draft which seemed to establish a hierarchy of norms on access with the Community norms very much superior to national norms

2001, 2001 OJ L 101/1; Commission Decision 29 November 2001, 2001 OJ L 317/1 (both voluminous documents) and the Institutional Agreement between the EP and Council 20 November 2002 concerning access by the EP to sensitive documents: 2002 OJ C 298/1.

gave way to a 'principle of loyal cooperation' in Member State/Community relations. As Advocate General Léger expressed the point in *Hautala* (above) with a transfer of sovereignty must come a transfer of safeguards. Member States should take care not to hamper the proper application of the Regulation and should respect the security rules of institutions. The Regulation is without prejudice to existing rights of Member States, judicial authorities and investigative bodies to access. It indicates the internal rules of procedure that will have to be amended including 'Schengen documents' concerning free movement without internal frontiers within the Community.

Article 1 sets out the purpose of the Regulation which I need not repeat.

Beneficiaries include any citizen of the Union and any natural or legal person residing or having its registered office in a Member State (Article 2). It may be applied more extensively to non-residents, natural or legal. It covers documents drawn up or received in all areas of EU – and not simply EC – activity. Access is by way of written application or 'directly in electronic form or through a register'. Article 12 makes provision for legislative documents to be directly accessible; a provision which also covers policy documents. Document is defined as: 'any content whatever its medium (written on paper or stored in electronic form or as a sound, visual or audio-visual recording) concerning a matter relating to the policies, activities and decisions falling within the institution's sphere of responsibility.'

Exceptions are of two types: mandatory and discretionary. Access *shall* be refused where access *would* (not could) undermine the protection of public interest as regards: public security (post September 11 this is likely to be viewed more sympathetically), defence and military matters, international relations and the financial, monetary or economic policy of the Community or a Member State It is also mandatory where disclosure would undermine the protection of privacy and the integrity of the individual, in particular in accordance with Community Data Protection legislation. The conflict between data protection and access to documents has featured in one very prominent case where an over resort to data protection may thwart policies on access simply because a person's name – personal data – is contained in publicly held documents. A similar problem could attach to the UK Data Protection Act 1998.

Harden describes the case (Case C-713/98) where the Commission refused access to documents relating to a meeting between business competitors and the Commission because personal names were on documents – the applicant wished to discover who was at the meeting. The case ended in a special report going to the European Parliament and a Resolution of the European Parliament (11 December 2001). There are ways around such a problem – blanking out the name if it is confidential or sensitive in the circumstances although here identity was important – but the EU Ombudsman's detailed contentions stated that information supplied by an individual is not personal data requiring protection merely because it was supplied by an individual and has their name attached to it. The European Parliament supported the EU Ombudsman that the information, including the names, should be disclosed: there was no question of personal threat or danger or invasive action and no question of confidentiality had been raised. He also believed that even if the Data Protection Directive did apply, there were three relevant exceptions to its application in this case.[51] In a note published on his web site, the EU Ombudsman distinguished between a person's public activities and his private activities relating to personal and family life protected by Article 8 ECHR.[52] The purpose of the Directive was to protect the latter and such an analysis was supported he believed by the CHR.[53]

Reasons for not allowing access will have to be given, be specific (unless that compromised the information which it was sought to protect) and be proportionate. This follows from the general principles of Community law but only Article 9 on sensitive documents refers to giving reasons in a manner which does not harm the interests protected.

Article 4(2) lists grounds on which access shall be denied where it would undermine various interests. However, under this head, there is a public

---

[51]   In the UK the Data Protection Act 1998, relevant exemptions from the non-disclosure provisions would include the Data Protection Act 1998, s 35 and note Sch 2, paras 5 and 6.

[52]   *Chappell* Series A 152-A, (1989) 12 EHRR 1: www.euro-ombudsman.eu.int/letters/en/default where further details are listed.

[53]   *Amann v Switzerland* (App No 27798/95, para 65 (2000) 30 EHRR 843); and see *R v MAFF, ex p Fisher* Case C-369/98 [2000] ECR I-6751. The spectre has been raised of publicly held documents not being released because of an official's name attached to them. The only personal data would be the official's name, it is submitted. This could fall under a variety of exemptions, see note 51 above, including a legal duty to disclose under statutory provisions but not including FOIA (FOI Act 2000, s 72), or processing is necessary to comply with statutory duties. In *British and American Tobacco* note 29 above, the applicant wished to identify the members of delegations to the committee. As the delegations had now been completed, the CFI allowed access to their identities because they could not now be influenced in their advice.

interest override allowing disclosure where disclosure is in the public interest making it to that extent discretionary. These grounds are: commercial interests of a natural or legal person, including intellectual property; court proceedings and legal advice; the purpose of inspections, investigations and audit; internal documents and preparatory documents if disclosure would *seriously* undermine the institution's decision-making process. This clearly puts the burden on the institution to justify an exception where the public interest is claimed.

Deliberative documents may be refused even where a final decision is taken where disclosure would seriously undermine the institution's decision-making process unless the public interest test applies. The case law on deliberative documents should be recalled (above p 269). Third parties shall be consulted where access to a document from them is requested to see whether an exception above applies unless 'it is clear that the document shall or shall not be disclosed.' Member States may request that disclosure of documents from that Member State is not made without its consent. This is persuasive, not binding. Following *Hautala* (above p 269) documents may be redacted and what is not covered by an exception may be disclosed. Exceptions shall apply for a maximum of thirty years but privacy and commercial interests may be protected for an extended period.

Member States are no longer effectively prohibited from not disclosing documents from an institution. Article 5 provides that in such a case it shall consult with the institution to make a decision that does not jeopardise the 'attainment of the objectives of the Regulation' unless it is clear that the document shall or shall not be disclosed.

Articles 6, 7 and 8 deal with details of making applications, time limits and confirmatory applications. Article 10 concerns details on consulting or obtaining copies of documents and charges for producing and sending copies once access is granted. Up to nineteen A4 pages and direct access in electronic form or through the register is free.

We noted that the Regulation contains a duty to provide a register of documents with appropriate identifying features and numbers and the date by which this duty has to be performed. Direct access to documents by electronic means or through a register should be allowed as far as possible (Article 12). There should be proactive efforts to assist the public in gaining access; to inform the public of the measures they enjoy under the Regulation; to develop good administrative practice and for the establishment of an inter-institutional committee to examine best practice possible conflicts and to discuss future developments on access. Annual reports must contain numbers of applications refused, reasons for refusal and the number of sensitive documents not recorded in the register. The Commission is to publish a review of the 'implementation of the principles of the Regulation' recommending its possible revision.

Data protection

Regulation 45/2001/EC[54] will apply to personal data (information) held by the Community institutions. It imposes a specific code on data protection, just as the EC Directive on Data Protection applies to Member States. The EC Treaty established that Community Acts will apply to the institutions but this Regulation sets up a specific regime for the institutions and will introduce a European Data Protection Supervisor. The Supervisor will have broad powers of investigation and enforcement. Europol and Schengen are subject to a separate regime. The scope of the Regulation only covers Community law, so the Second and Third Pillars are excluded.

The pressure from Member State governments and the EU to extend the range of data information that was gathered and kept by ISPs and phone companies was noted above.

General Decisions of the ECJ

Litigation concerning access to information had been before the European Court of Justice in varying guises before the Joint Code was agreed in December 1993. At the heart of the cases was an issue concerning human rights and some of this important case law concerned the relationship between the EC Treaty and its interpretation and the ECHR. The *Zwartveld* case revealed the ECJ in its more creative mood in a case concerning access to Commission documents. An investigating magistrate in the Netherlands submitted to the Court a 'request for judicial cooperation' insofar as he wanted the Court to order the EC Commission to hand over documents from investigations it had conducted several years before.[55] The Commission refused to accede to the requests of the magistrate and to

---

54   OJ 2001 L8/1.
55   Case C-2/88 Imm *JJ Zwartveld et al* [1990] ECR I-3365. See Ch 3.

reveal the identity of EC inspectors even though the magistrate's investigation covered serious matters concerning forgeries and unlawful practices in fish markets. The Commission's objections arose from the fact that it felt the procedure governing access to the ECJ, by way of a preliminary reference from a national court on a point of European law (Article 234 [177] EC), had been bypassed and abused. The Commission further argued that the information was protected in any event by the *Protocol on the Privileges and Immunities of the European Communities*. The relevant part of the Protocol stated that the archives of the Community shall be inviolable. Contrary to Commission arguments that disclosure might jeopardise its relations with Member States the ECJ ruled Commission reports must be sent to the magistrate save where good cause be shown for non-disclosure which would await further judicial determination. The ECJ also held that Commission officials must give evidence in the Dutch proceedings. The ECJ ruled that under Article 10 [5] EC (see below) a duty of sincere cooperation flowed from relationships between the Community institutions and Member States and Article 220 [164] EC imposes a duty on the ECJ to 'ensure in the interpretation and application of the Treaty that the law was obeyed'. These provisions justified its decision.

The European Convention on Human Rights and the Council of Ministers Recommendation Rec (2002) 2

The ECJ invokes the ECHR to interpret Community law – as part of the 'general principles of law' which that Court draws on to assist in the development of Community law as was seen in Chapter 2, pp 56 et seq. Even though the Council of Europe, the body that produced the ECHR and to which the UK is a member, had provided in Article 10 ECHR that there would be freedom of speech and freedom to communicate information, the CHR has interpreted the provision in a manner which does not provide a right of access to official information. Article 8 ECHR which protects family life an privacy, has been more successfully invoked to allow access to official or publicly held documents and to provide an independent form of arbitration for disputed claims. Decisions of the ECJ showed how narrowly the Convention would be viewed by the latter Court when asked to uphold Article 10, and Article 8.[56] This was illustrated when the ECJ gave a restrictive interpretation on that provision so that it had no effect where the communication of information was independent of the economic activity

[56]   See Ch 9, note 134.

carried on by economic agents in another Member State. In the *Grogan* case,[57] the Irish government had prohibited publication of information in Ireland about abortion services available in the UK. The information had been provided by Irish student groups unconnected with the clinics providing the service. The link between the information distributed and the economic activity was too tenuous to be regarded as a restriction on the freedom to supply services under Article 49 [59] EC.

When the same matter came before the CHR in *Open Door and Dublin Well Woman v Ireland*[58], that Court established that there had been a violation of Article 10. The services were lawful in the UK and it was not unlawful under Irish law for Irish women to seek them there. The restriction created a risk to the health of women seeking abortions. Notwithstanding 'the moral implications' this limitation of information 'called for careful scrutiny ... as to their conformity with the tenets of democratic society.' This was not mere 'commercial speech or information' for which the CHR has itself relaxed protection, albeit in controversial circumstances.[59]

In its interpretation of Article 8 of the Convention which protects privacy, the ECJ has revealed a constrictive approach so that in *Hoechst*[60] the ECJ declined to extend the protection of Article 8 and its guarantee of a right to privacy to business premises. The ECJ indicated there was no CHR case law on the point but Ryssdal has indentified two relevant decisions where Article 8 was applied: to protect a home which was also used for business premises, and also in the case of a lawyer's office in connection with criminal proceedings against a third party (see Chapter 2, p 55).[61]

Nonetheless, the Council of Europe had, through its Committee of Ministers, adopted a recommendation on access to publicly held information in 1981. In February 2002 a new Recommendation on Access to Documents was agreed by the Committee of Ministers (Rec (2002) 2, 21 February (2002). The 11th Protocol (1994) Article 40 of the ECHR provided

[57]   Case 159/90 *Society for the Protection of Unborn Children v Grogan* [1991] 3 CMLR 849.

[58]   (1992) 15 EHRR 244.

[59]   *Markt Intern v Germany* (1989) 12 EHRR 161. NB *R v General Medical Council, ex p Colman* [1990] 1 All ER 489, CA.

[60]   Case 46/87, 227/88 [1989] 2 ECR 859

[61]   Judge R Ryssdal in *The Developing Role of the European Court of Justice* European Policy Forum (London, 1995) pp 9 et seq citing *Chappell* Series A 152-A (1989) 12 EHRR 1 and *Niemietz v Germany* Series A no 251-B (1992) 16 EHRR 97.

the public with a right of access to the documents of the Court of Human Rights and hearings in public.

In one area, namely obtaining written reasons for official decisions, the ECJ has shown a far more consistent and positive approach than have English courts in insisting upon reasons for administrative decisions.[62] This followed a Treaty provision stipulating that reasons for the basis of regulations, Directives and decisions had to be given,[63] although more recently the position in English courts is improving. Obtaining reasons for decisions is a vital element in administrative justice; without reasons, challenges to official decisions on the grounds of illegality, abuse of discretion or arbitrariness are virtually impossible. Obtaining reasons is in a broad respect obtaining information although it does not involve access to documents. Some of the relevant case law concerned adequate reasons for refusal to allow access to documents and was examined above (p 268 et seq). It may well be that the approach of the ECJ has been influential on developments in English case law where although the courts have ruled that there is no general duty to provide written reasons for administrative decisions, such a duty may be inferred by the courts where a decision has a serious impact on an individual's liberty, rights or privileges (see Chapter 8, p 363 et seq).[64]

The European Parliament

Its plenary sessions are open to the public and its committees are open to the public, subject to items being taken confidentially. This is an improvement on previous practice where some committees were closed to the public. It is covered by the Regulation on access as was seen above. After initial refusals to adopt its own register of interests – the British contingent of MEPs argued taking gifts was acceptable if declared – the European Parliament agreed that there should be public declarations of gifts and payments by MEPs. They must now declare their professional activities or any other paid work or office in a public register. Financial

---

[62] *Heylens* Case 222//86 [1987] ECR 4097.

[63] Article 253[190] EC; J Schwarze *European Administrative Law* (1992) pp 1400 et seq.

[64] *R v Secretary of State for the Home Department, ex p Doody* [1993] 3 All ER 92. See P Birkinshaw *Freedom of Information: the Law, the Practice and the Ideal* (2001, 3rd ed) p 424 et seq.

interests and other sources of income must be declared.[65] Lobbying interests, of which there are about 10,000 have to be registered and a code of conduct provides guidance to MEPs.

Open government

This chapter has focused on access to information rather than opening up meetings, rule making proceedings and governmental deliberations to the public – the open government side. The open government side needs significant development in the EC/EU. The position on 'Government in the Sunshine' provisions in Community institutions is still very underdeveloped – this means laws opening up meetings to public observation. There are dangers of abuse if open government duties were present. These could include domination by elitist groups, vociferous and unrepresentative minorities, and self interested groups. Would we wish to give rights to private consumer groups to act in a representative capacity? The Community, as presently structured, is not built for participatory democracy. At best, in terms of participation, it caters for specific interest groups who may be self seeking and whose view of the public interest is possibly very loaded. The Commission has stated that maintaining special information services for governments and governmental bodies and special interest groups might be assisted by keeping a Directory on all non-profit-making organisations for the purpose of 'transparency not accreditation'.[66] There is no reference to anything approaching the US Federal Advisory Committee Act allowing public access to meetings by the Commission or its Directorates with advisory or special interest groups. If the EU is to do more than survive and if it is to attain significant meaning in the lives of citizens of Europe, the most pressing task is to establish how communities and the public can become more closely involved in a participatory democracy. These questions should be top of the agenda of the Constitutional Convention under Giscard D'Estaing which will report for the 2004 Inter Governmetal Conference. It is should also be on the front burner of the Commission's programme on *European Governance*.

---

65   www.europarl.eu.int/home/default_en.

66   COM (93) 258 Fin (CB-CO-93-290-EN-C). A Users' Advisory Council for the major users of Commission information was established: SEC (94) 114 but it ceased activities in 1997 and since 1999 there has been a DG for Press and Communications.

The views just expressed are probably largely consistent with the publicly expressed views of the Commission. It is a view which has developed as the Community has grown from an organisation created by states to facilitate a common market to a system of government that is ostensibly democratic, that increasingly and directly involves citizens and whose powers are forever increasing. Its membership is due to expand significantly. The complexity of its structures, however, makes participation and access extremely difficult for all but well organised and powerful interest groups fomenting accusations of favouritism. Machinery must be provided which affords opportunities for all interest groups. In this regard, the role of national Parliaments must not be overlooked (see Chapter 7).

Conclusion

Access to information and openness and making government closer to the people has been a European theme for well over a decade. There is acknowledgment that inspiration for such developments came from the Member States. The UK and EU both adopted a Code on Access, in the EU case backed up by legal decisions and both moved towards legislation at a comparable time. As mentioned above, thirteen Member States have access legislation. The institutions of the EU have put the web to constructive use. Open meetings laws and laws opening up advisory committees may go some way to making the Community more transparent, but the sheer size of the EU – about to increase significantly – make real citizen participation virtually impossible unless in the form of highly organised and professionalised interest groups. Openness and closeness come together. The problems identified in this chapter are ones which have to be addressed by all tiers of government; they are not restricted to any one tier. It is interesting to note that there are some crucial differences, for instance, between the UK Freedom of Information Act 2000 and the Scottish version allowing the Scottish regime to be more open in relation to documents and access. The test in Scotland for holding back information is where it causes 'substantial prejudice', in the UK Freedom of Information Act 2000 it is 'prejudice'. This includes disclosures affecting relations between administrations in the UK – a provision which cuts across the confidentiality of communications between administrations in Intergovernmental Agreements. There are fewer grounds of absolute exemption in the Scottish measure and there is no Tribunal between a Commissioner and the courts in Scotland thereby subjecting disputed claims to a quicker process of resolution. In the UK measure, an exemption allows information to be withheld where it is to be published in the future. No time-scale is referred to allowing indefinite delay. In Scotland a limit of twelve weeks from the date of request is included in the exemption and has a far more limited application. What are the differences between the English and Scottish systems that deserve an apparently more liberal regime in the latter? Are citizens disadvantaged in those Member States that do not possess access regimes?

National participation in Community affairs: democracy, the UK Parliament and the EU

National parliaments and scrutiny and information

Introduction

There are those who claim that Britain is not a very democratic country: that, along with the EU, it possesses its own democratic deficit. Our governments have a notable aversion to direct democracy and, until comparatively recently, to decision-making by referenda. Referenda were held in 1975 on whether the UK should remain in the EEC, as it then was, and there were devolution referenda in 1979, both of which failed to obtain the necessary support for devolution. It was seen in Chapter 5 how further referenda took place over devolution in 1998 and how a referendum has been promised before a commitment is given to join monetary union. Local electors in England will have the opportunity engage in a referendum on the style of leadership (ie elected mayor) for their authority.

In Ireland and Denmark, referenda are compulsory before the Treaty amendments can be implemented into those countries' laws; in the case of Ireland this has to take place where an amendment affects the constitution. Both countries have rejected Treaty amendments after Maastricht in Denmark's case, and in Ireland's, Nice. A second referendum in the Autumn of 2002 approved the amendments in Ireland's case. In France a referendum was held in 1992 without any constitutional requirement to do so in order to make constitutional amendments to accommodate Maastricht. It succeeded by the narrowest of margins. Referenda are uncertain and high risk strategies even where governments are fairly secure in their expectation of the outcome.[1] Nonetheless, it has been suggested that for major revisions of the Treaty governing the EU constitution, a referendum should take place involving all the citizens of Europe entitled to vote in European Parliament elections, a recommendation which the House of Commons Select Committee on European Scrutiny found 'impracticable'.[2]

In the UK, discussion is taking place to remove one of the most famous of participatory exercises – the public planning inquiry – from those proposals which contain national or regional implications so that there will be no opportunity for interests other than official ones to question the siting of airports, nuclear waste disposal sites or major development proposals. The government intended to move such proposals in their pre-decision stage to a Parliamentary committee where the agenda will be more easily controlled although opposition from Parliament was more emphatic than the government supposed.[3]

The upper chamber of Parliament – the House of Lords – is precisely that: an assembly of hereditary peers (now much reduced in number to 92[4]), government and opposition placemen and women, and those present by virtue of spiritual title, together with the Law Lords. Elected local government has lost many of its essential powers to unelected bodies appointed by Ministers, and election to Parliament admits of no concession whatsoever to proportional representation – although concessions have been made elsewhere on proportional representation.[5] The home of the Mother of Parliaments has looked to Parliament and representative democracy for the legitimation of public authority together with the traditional and enduring presence of the Crown. Parliament's domination by the government of the day means effectively that no comparable system of democratic government in the modern world concentrates so much power

---

[1]   It was reported that there have been over 800 referenda in recorded history, a half of these in Switzerland: Lord Norton of Louth *Memorandum of Evidence:* HC 152 – xxxiii (2001–02) section 3 citing D Butler and A Ranney eds *Referendums around the World* (1994). See the Select Committee, note 2 on referenda, and the Political Parties, Elections and Referendums Act 2000.

[2]   HC 152 – xxxiii (2001–02).

[3]   HC Debs col 441 (18 July 2002).

[4]   These are likely to be abolished in reforms on membership of the upper chamber. Some combination of elected members, members nominated by an 'independent body' and nomination by political parties is the likely replacement with battle drawn over the precise ratios.

[5]   In devolved elections and MEP elections.

in the executive. Lord Hailsham, a former Conservative Lord Chancellor, summed it up in the memorable phrase 'an elective dictatorship'.[6] In British terms democracy and Parliament are synonymous and this is our weakness and our strength. Devolution provided desperately needed legitimation for the weaknesses of the Westminster model in a pluralistic Britain.

In European terms, the 'democratic deficit' was described over a decade ago by Shirley Williams as 'the gap between the powers transferred to the Community level and the control of the elected Parliament over them, a gap filled by national civil servants operating as European experts or as members of regulation and management committees – the Comitology and other committees, and to some extent by organised lobbies, mainly representing business'.[7] An unelected body, the Commission, took a central role in policy development and law preparation and even law making without any adequate accountability or scrutiny provisions in the European Parliament or the national parliaments. Williams believed that, apart from the Ministers whose responsibilities fall within areas of Community competence, most national politicians, including government backbenchers, and leading members of the opposition and back-benchers, had no role in the Community. These politicians were losing out to national civil servants who are building expertise and influence over large areas of Community business which Parliamentarians cannot begin to match. 'The losers', wrote Wolfgang Wessels,[8] 'are the parliamentarians and parties; their patterns of interaction have not developed resources and forms comparable to those of national bureaucrats and (governmental) politicians'. The end result has been a weakening of Parliament in relation to the executive not only in matters concerning European policy and its development and oversight – especially the intergovernmental pillars – but also more generally.

Williams and Wessels wrote over a decade ago, and time, procedures and problems move on. The perennial problem of democratising an international organisation remains whether its basis be federal, confederal, consociational or whatever. The assessment given by earlier writers for Parliamentary democracy and Parliament's participation in policy development within the

---

6   Lord Hailsham, (1976) *The Richard Dimbleby Lecture: Elective Dictatorship*, BBC.
7   Shirley Williams (1990) Pol Qu Vol 61 pp 299–317.
8   Wolfgang Wessels (1989) *The Community Bureaucracy at the Crossroads* College of Europe. See K Dyson (2000) *Public Administration* 897.

EU now appear rather bleak. To leave our prognosis there would be misleading, for it overlooks the considerable achievements that the Westminster Parliament has to its credit in supervising and participating in EU policy and law making and the emerging role of the Scottish Parliament and Welsh Assembly.[9] Both the Scottish Parliament and Northern Ireland Assembly have the authority and duty to implement and observe Community law. The Scottish Ministers may draft delegated legislation implementing Community law so long as it is within the Scottish Parliament's competence and compatible with Community law. The position in Northern Ireland is very similar, but Wales differs. This power remains concurrently with UK Ministers and 'Co-ordination is therefore essential to decide how UK obligations are to be observed.'[10] A concordat of understanding commits the Scottish and Westminster executives to 'full involvement in the devolved administrations in the formulation of the UK policy position', confidentiality of discussions and adherence to the UK line by the Scottish Executive.[11] The UK remains liable under Community law for any infringements of Community law. The Scottish Executive, as seen in Chapter 5, has a presence in Brussels protecting Scottish interests.

The struggle between the executive and legislature is rarely an equal one and our membership of Europe has helped tip the balance even more obviously in the executive's favour. However, commencing with Maastricht and continuing with Amsterdam's Protocol and Nice and its Declaration on the Future of the Union (No 23), there is growing evidence that UK Parliamentarians, and other national parliaments are taking a greater role in Community affairs. The Nice Declaration noted the 'wide-ranging discussions' that would take place on enlargement with all interested parties including representatives of national parliaments and 'those reflecting public opinion, namely political, economic and university circles, representatives of civil society, etc'. Continuation of such discussions would include subsidiarity, the status of the Charter of Fundamental Rights, simplification of the Treaties to enhance accessibility and 'the role of national parliaments in the European Architecture.' In addressing these issues, the need to monitor the democratic legitimacy and transparency of

---

[9]   C Carter 'Democratic Governance Beyond the Nation State: Third-Level Assemblies and Scrutiny of European Legislation' (2000) EPL 429.

[10]   N Burrows *Devolution* (2000) p 134.

[11]   N Burrows *Devolution* (2000) pp 135–141 who sees the existing set-up providing no guarantees for an independent Scottish line on Community affairs to reflect its own interests.

the EU and its institutions is recognised. Discussions may take place but the hard evidence of attitude came with the Commission's paper on *European Governance* which revealed a very managerial and top down approach to involvement of citizenry.

Since the mid 1990s, the British government has declared its intention to press for an increased role for national parliaments and to oppose further centralisation of decision-making in the Union and 'massive new powers for the European Parliament'. The House of Lords Select Committee on the European Communities heard evidence in proceedings which formed the basis of its November 1995 report on the Intergovernmental Committee, with many witnesses arguing that the relationship between national parliaments and Community institutions constituted a 'crucial problem'.[12] Part of the problem was seen as stemming from the persistence of machinery 'devised for a five member community' (sic) according to the European Parliament's Resolution of 17 May 1995.[13] That Community could within the foreseeable future become a 27 member Community. We can trace the developments since that time below.

There is no doubt that the EU is an abstract and distant figure in the eyes of many citizens, making it an easy victim of anti-European rhetoric. The adoption of ever more liberal laws on access to documents by the EU has been an attempt to sell the institutions of the Union as more open and to engage in exercises in stakeholding. We saw in the previous chapter how they created opportunities for access to documents but not for wider and concrete rights of participation in decision-making. Discussion sessions do take place at Intergovernmental Committee and pre-Intergovernmental Committees. But in *real politik*, the meetings of the Council and Commission are not open to the public and there are limits placed on what minutes can be published – identities of countries are blanked out. Some minor reforms were indicated in the previous chapter (p 275 et seq). The UK government has recommended that the Council should meet in public when legislating. In its report in 2001 on *European Governance,* the Commission offered a somewhat threadbare set of proposals for making the future of European governance more of a citizen activity (see Chapter 5, p 226 et seq). To this

12 *1996 Inter-Governmental Conference* HL 105 (1994/5). The Government has published a White Paper: *A Partnership of Nations: British Approaches to the EU IGC* Cm 3181 (1996).

13 Ref A4-0102/95: Resolution on Functioning of the TEU with a View to the 1996 IGC.

day, most UK citizens are completely unaware of the distinction between the EU and EC, for instance. Proceedings in the institutions are too often byzantine reflecting diplomatic sensitivity and a trust in elitism in management and government.

However, it would be unfair to ignore the fact that politics and politicians in particular, not just in the EU, are held in low esteem. Corporate global domination of political agendas is accused of reducing real choice in alternatives, in the EU as well as globally. In the UK a number of notorious scandals involving MPs in John Major's government and excessive reliance on press and special advisers by Tony Blair have been particularly harmful of their own reputation and that of Parliament.[14] In the case of the institutions of the EU, however, the 'democratic deficit' is a widely perceived weakness in the legitimating apparatus of the EU and the burden of this chapter is to explain how the UK Parliament has sought to review the activities of the institutions of the EU, in particular the legislative programme of the Commission and Council and the increasing role of the European Parliament, as well as other areas of EU activity. The chapter will concentrate on legislative and policy review. It will in that context concentrate on Parliament's contribution. The House of Commons European Scrutiny Committee has strongly criticised the provision of an 'ever closer union' in the Treaty and it is the Committee's belief that national parliaments constitute the 'only way' to bridge the disconnection between citizens and the EU institutions. It showed itself in very traditional Westminster spirit in recommending an end to proportional representation for MEP elections.[15]

British constitutional culture: an obstacle to effective scrutiny?

The central position and sovereignty of Parliament in a legal and political sense in the British constitutional culture must be fully appreciated and any analysis of greater participation in EU decision-making must be focused on Parliament. However, while there is no doubting that Parliament is the

---

14   See the Nolan Committee's *Standards in Public Life* Cm 2850 Vols I and II (1995); also the report of Sir Richard Scott into the *Matrix Churchill* episode: HC 115 (1995/6). See also: HC 303 (2001–02) *Government Information and Communications* Public Administration Committee

15   Above note 2.

focal point for accountability, there is also a tendency for MPs to take their position too seriously as an 'Assembly of Kings' while Parliament is effectively by-passed in many matters of government. In the ratification of the Maastricht Treaty, the government threatened to invoke Crown prerogative powers to ratify the TEU rather than obtain legislative approval through Parliament when members of its own party and the opposition threatened to block the necessary statutory approval.[16] A vote of confidence forced the acquiescence of a sufficient number of rebel Conservative MPs, but legal challenge then ensued on the grounds that EC law had been amended and implemented without the necessary legislative support. The challenge was unsuccessful but it nonetheless highlighted the frailty of Parliament's position in EU matters where a government majority is small.[17] Such dramatic problems have not attended Blair's government, but the problem of Parliament's demotion in the constitutional scheme of things persists. Its sovereignty as a constitutional institution is to that extent illusory.

While on the British side our Parliamentary culture has emphasised the central position of Parliament, the European Treaties from the beginning gave no formal role to national parliaments in the making of EC law. Nevertheless, in 1978, the Procedure Committee of the House of Commons reported:[18]

> In no sense is it possible to speak of parliamentary 'control' of EEC legislation, and the ability of the House to influence the legislative decisions of the Communities is inhibited by practical as well as legal and procedural obstacles. The practical obstacles stem from the sheer volume of EEC legislation, the complexity of the Communities' own decision-making structure, and the very limited time available for the consideration of many proposals, including some of the most important. The legal and procedural obstacles include the fact that national parliaments have no right to be consulted, and the absence of direct control by national parliaments over legislation made by the Commission on its own authority.

---

[16] This concerned a Commons Resolution: see R Rawlings (1994) Public Law 254 and 367.

[17] *R v Secretary of State, ex p Rees-Mogg* [1994] 1 All ER 457. Others saw the parliamentary harrying of government as a vindication of parliamentary procedures.

[18] HC 588-I (1977–8).

Certainly, declarations attached to the Maastricht Treaty encouraged greater involvement by national parliaments in EU affairs and invited the Conference of Parliaments of the European Parliament and national parliaments to meet as necessary as a vehicle for consultation on the main features of the European Union. Greater exchange of information should be stepped up between the European Parliament and national parliaments and governments of Member States 'will ensure ... that national parliaments receive Commission proposals for legislation in good time for information and possible examination'.[19] Yet no formal concessions were made and the impact of the Declaration was disappointing leading to calls for significant improvement.

The movement of power to Europe which began with the Single European Act 1987 makes the contribution of national parliaments all the more crucial if there is to be any vestige of domestic democratic oversight of EU law-making and policy-making. No-one is awarded marks for stating that the European legislative process is arabesque and opaque even to those who participate in the process. The European Scrutiny Committee has described the role of the Council in the legislative process as 'secret' and 'slapdash' (HC 152 – xxxiii, (2001–02) para 67). As has been frequently pointed out, an increasing role for qualified majority voting makes it more difficult for national parliaments to influence legislative decisions in the Council by exerting pressure on Ministers in national parliaments. If the Minister's vote in the Council is in the minority and he faithfully pursued the majority wish of his national parliament, there are those who are quick to assert that the representative pressure brought to bear by the national parliament was ultimately of little effect. This ignores the democratic role of the European Parliament and the enhanced role of the European Parliament in the legislative process. 'Even if the role of national parliaments is strengthened in relation to national governments' the argument runs, 'national governments are themselves limited now in their capacity to prevent undesired outcomes.'[20] Arguably, their role has diminished with the decline into desuetude of the Luxembourg accord allowing a *de facto* national veto power.[21]

---

[19]   Declarations Nos 13 and 14, TEU App 1. The Declarations are statements of intent but were not enforceable in the ECJ.

[20]   Philip Norton, 'Addressing the Democratic Deficit' (1995) *Journal of Legislative Studies* Vol 1 No 3 pp 177–193, at p 187.

[21]   A political expedient never formally sanctioned within Community law. Its status remains uncertain.

Qualified majority voting is an unavoidable consequence of an expanding EU. At Nice, about half of the EC Treaty articles requiring unanimous decision were amended to allow for majority voting – and weighting of votes will be altered post 1 January 2005 – but unanimity still applies to legislation on tax, most social protection measures, Title IV EC on visas and immigration and Titles V and VI EU. The House of Lords Committee and others have seen the possible solution in 'double majorities': of Council votes and size of population to ensure that decisions are not adopted against the wishes of the representatives of a large proportion of the citizens of the Member States but these have been taken over by the Nice revisions.[22] What matters is the quality of final outcome and its acceptability to those bound by that outcome.

Nevertheless, institutional practice and public pressure reflect a shift of power to Europe. The Commission, it has been estimated, has between 500–1,000 committees which draw interest groups to their deliberations and it has estimated that over 5,000 permanent lobbyists operate in Brussels.[23] Since 2000, the Commission has produced an annual report on 244 relevant committees and has adopted standard rules of procedure for them.[24] The problems of the exercise of delegated legislative powers by the Commission, and the committee structure of the Commission, still exist. The Commission is not subject to systematic scrutiny by the European Parliament or national parliaments.[25] Power has shifted without appropriate adjustments to the position of national parliaments. Increased consultation rights for the European Parliament in delegated legislation have not plugged the deficit and nor have they addressed the problem from the traditions and political cultures of national systems.

More widely, in the UK the feeling that too much was being conferred on the European Parliament caused Parliament to enact in 1978 that any future

---

22   Note 2 para 243.
23   Philip Norton, 'Addressing the Democratic Deficit', (1995) *Journal of Legislative Studies* Vol 1 No 3, p 191. See R H Pedler and G F Schadler *Shaping European Law and Policy* (1996); S Mazey and J Richardson *Lobbying in the European Community* (1993). See for further references Ch 2, p 42 and Ch 6, p 259 et seq.
24   COM (2001) 783 FINAL, January 2002. The Lords Committee was influential: *Third Report* HL 62 (1998–99). Estimates on the number of committees varies considerably. See Ch 2 and note 23 above.
25   V Bogdanor has suggested that individual Commissioners should be answerable to the EP for their portfolios developing a form of individual ministerial responsibility: *Evidence* European Scrutiny Committee HC 347 (2001–02).

increase in the powers of the newly elected European Parliament by Treaty agreed by the UK government would be subject to Parliamentary approval thereby giving Parliament a *locus* in Treaty making and enhancing opportunities for consequential litigation involving third parties.[26] However, for more routine supervision of the executive in Community affairs, Parliament has relied upon scrutiny committees of both Houses. In a 1989 report, the fourth report of the Procedure Committee reported:

> Whilst the House may, by changes in its own internal procedures, find ways of bringing to bear more efficiently such authority as it retains over European legislation, it cannot by such means increase that authority nor seek to claw back powers which have been ceded by Treaty. For example, the recent extension of qualified majority voting in the Council of Ministers ... has placed constraints on the House's ability to scrutinize European legislation which can only be alleviated but not removed by changes in the practice of the House.[27]

The British government opened the 1995–1996 session of Parliament with a declared intention of increasing the role of national parliaments in Community affairs: several points needed to be addressed in their role. These included provision of more detailed information *in advance* of Council meetings and greater co-operation between national parliaments and the European Parliament. The problems facing the Commons Committee on European Legislation in its scrutiny role were stated vividly in its report *The Scrutiny of European Business*. The Committee frequently had to scrutinise documents of legal or political importance without an official text and its scrutiny was often hindered by breaches by the UK government of undertakings or of Resolutions of the House of Commons.[28] These reports are particularly damning and the practices they describe do not endear the EU to the British public when the real villain is the British government. In its 2002 report, the European Scrutiny Committee highlighted recent cases of difficulty it had experienced in failing to be given legislative documents in sufficient time (paras 33 et seq).

In a report in 2002 on the Convention on the Future of the EU, the House of Lords Select Committee on the EU observed the information that was

26   European Assembly Elections Act 1978, s 6; and see *R v Secretary of State, ex p Rees-Mogg* [1994] 1 All ER 457.
27   HC 622 I (1988/89) para 10.
28   HC 51 xxvii (1995–6) especially Part VI.

being made available via the internet but also noted an absence of indexes of papers or topics considered, the absence of a search engine and no consolidated list of documents (HL 163 (2001–02)).

Scrutiny of European legislation and policy

Following the legislation allowing accession of the UK to the EEC, in 1972 both Houses of Parliament set up committees to consider how the scrutiny of proposals for Community legislation could best be carried out.

The House of Commons Committee recommended that the House should set up a select committee to scrutinise Community legislative proposals and report on them to the House. A similar recommendation was made by the Lords Committee. Both Houses set up scrutiny committees in 1974: the House of Commons Select Committee on European Legislation – originally on Community Secondary Legislation – and the House of Lords Select Committee on the European Communities. Following a White Paper presented to Parliament in November 1998[29] a European Scrutiny Committee was established to replace the original committee in the Commons and the House of Lords Committee became the Select Committee on the European Union.

The Treaty of Amsterdam contained a Protocol on 'The Role of National Parliaments in the European Union'. This is a legally binding part of the Treaty but whether it is justiciable, and at whose prompting, is a matter of difficulty.[30] Part I concerns information for national Parliaments of Member States and states that all Commission consultation documents (green and white papers and communications) shall be promptly forwarded to national parliaments of the Member States. 'Promptly' is not defined. Commission proposals for legislation (as defined by the Council under Article 207(3) [151(3)] EC) shall be made available 'in good time' so that the government of each Member State may ensure that its own national parliament receives them 'as appropriate'. The wording leaves the provision unlikely to be a

---

[29] Cm 4095 and HC 791 (1997–98) Modernisation Committee.
[30] The Protocol is a binding part of the Treaty but the Member State government would not wish to enforce it against itself. The Commission would have to bring proceedings. See C Kerse (2000) European Public Law 81.

subject of a legally enforceable duty, apart possibly from consultation.[31] Finally, a six-week period shall elapse between the period when a legislative proposal or a measure to be adopted under the Criminal and Judicial Cooperation Pillar is made available in all languages to the European Parliament and Council by the Commission and the date when it is placed on a Council agenda for the adoption of an act or of a common position. This is subject to an exception on grounds of urgency which will have to be supported by reasons stated in the act or common position. Part II of the Protocol concerns COSAC (Conference of European Affairs Committees of national parliaments and MEPs) and this will be examined below.

The position of national parliaments has been improved by the Protocol in the Treaty of Amsterdam. Provision of information to national parliaments is no longer an afterthought in a declaration. However, the duty to provide that information 'shall be made available in good time' from the Commission and handed on to national parliaments rests ultimately upon national governments – the very bodies so frequently in abuse of their duties under Standing Orders of the House or other domestic provisions. These provisions are unlikely in reality to be justiciable. The Protocol provision for a six-week moratorium does not meet the criticism made by the House of Lords Committee noted above (and see below).

The Commons Committee

The Protocol was the outcome then of frantic lobbying by interest groups and national parliaments. The outcome in the UK was a new resolution of 17 November 1998 (Standing Order 143) from the House of Commons on the 'scrutiny reserve': that 'No Minister of the Crown shall give agreement in the Council or in the European Council to any proposal for European Community legislation or for a common strategy, joint action or common position under Title V (Second Pillar) or a common position, framework decision decision or convention under Title VI (Third Pillar)' which has not completed scrutiny or which awaits a resolution of the House. The Resolution spells out what is meant by 'agreement' but the matter is not

---

[31]   See note 88 below. But who would enforce the duty: the Commission or the relevant House of Parliament and through whom?

free of ambiguity.[32] There is a saving for a proposal which is confidential, routine or trivial or is substantially the same as a proposal on which scrutiny has taken place. The Minister may also give agreement still subject to scrutiny if there are special reasons which must be explained to the Committee or House at the first opportunity after giving agreement. In 1996, the House of Lords Committee noted a practice whereby:

> the Council's practice of discussing legislation on the basis of an 'unofficial' text – usually a Presidency compromise or a Commission working paper ... this practice 'would be unthinkable in a national parliament ... the result is an opaque process where those not directly involved have no idea what is actually on the table.' This practice effectively prevents national parliaments form carrying out any scrutiny of important legislative texts.

Standing Order 143 sets out the terms of reference for the Commons European Scrutiny Committee: 'to examine EU documents and to report on the legal and political importance of each such document and on the reasons for its opinion and on any other matters of principle, policy or law which may be affected and to make recommendations for the further consideration of any such report. Previously, the Committee only examined legislative proposals. 'EU document' includes 'any proposal under the Community treaties for legislation by the Council, or by the Council acting with the European Parliament. It also includes proposals for the adoption of common positions, joint actions and positions and conventions under the Second and Third Pillars. Pratt describes how it extends to documents published for submission to the European Council or Council of Ministers or European Central Bank.[33] This includes the preliminary draft of the Community's annual budget, green and white papers and other Commission communications. It includes other documents published by one Union institution for another institution such as the reports of the Court of Auditors. It will include any other EU document deposited in the House by a Minister of the Crown. This has included the working papers of Inter Governmental Conferences.[34] Commission proposals for legislation not involving Ministers is not included and these are not published in draft. The Standing Order includes 'related matters' including institutional and

---

[32] Over, eg, 'provisional agreements': see *Twenty third Report* HL 135 (2001–02).

[33] T Pratt 'The Role of National Parliaments in Making European Law' *The Cambridge Yearbook of European Legal Studies 1998* (1999). See also E Smith ed *National Parliaments as Cornerstones of European Integration* (1996).

[34] T Pratt 'The of National Parliaments in Making European Law' *The Cambridge Yearbook of European Legal Studies 1998* (1999) p 224.

procedural changes in the EU and 'also, occasionally, Commission legislation'.[35] This, as Pratt explains, is wider than many continental regimes for scrutiny because it includes published communications which 'are often numerous and verbose'. It enables the House to view documents before the Commission makes a firm decision or 'before the Council is invited to endorse the Commission's proposals in principle.'[36]

The UK Foreign and Commonwealth Office deposits documents covered by the Standing Order in Parliament within two working days of receipt in London. Within ten days of that deposit, the lead department will be expected to provide an explanatory memorandum signed by a Minister. It is a public document constituting the Minister's evidence to Parliament. Where an explanatory memorandum accompanies a legislative proposal it should include: a description of the subject matter, details of the legal base and the legislative procedure for the provision and any Ministerial reservations or comments on them, an assessment of whether the proposed legislation accords with subsidiary and proportionality, its impact on UK law, the policy of the government towards the document, the financial implications, and the likely timetable for the deliberation of the document by the Council.

The Committee has to decide in relation to each document whether it is legally or politically important. If neither, there is no need to report on it substantively to the House or for the House of a Standing Committee (below) to give it further consideration. About half the documents are so classified. If it is of legal or political significance then the Committee has to decide whether a report is required, but no debate. The Committee may seek further clarification from the Minister before deciding whether a debate is necessary or may await the outcome of government consultations. The Committee can recommend a debate either in one of the European Standing Committees or on the floor of the house where the document is either legally or politically important and will highlight the main issues to help focus the debate. Of the approximate 1,300 reports deposited each year (when Pratt wrote it was 1,000), about half receive substantive reports and about 50 are recommended for debate. In the case of legislative proposals, a revised or amended text is depositable and which has to be accompanied by an explanatory memorandum and which triggers a new round of scrutiny. It is

---

35   Modernisation Committee at para 6, note 29 above.
36   T Pratt 'The Role of National Parliaments in Making European Law' *The Cambridge Yearbook of European Legal Studies 1998* (1999) p 225.

expected that the Minister will keep the committee abreast of major developments in negotiations and may also provide copies of Council working documents and Presidency texts. The Committee's weekly reports – it meets weekly during sittings of the House – are published on www.parliament.uk along with specific reports. A recent report of the committee is: *Role of National Parliaments in the EU* (HC 152 (2001–02). This report recommends a joint session of national MPs and MEPs to question the Commission and Commissioners on their annual policy strategy and work programme. This 'would make the opaque process by which the Commission decides what legislation to introduce much more transparent' (paras 138–140).

A few words need to be said about the Commons European Standing Committees. The Modernisation Committee recommended five such committees but three emerged, each with thirteen members. Prior to debate in the Standing Committee, Ministers may be questioned for up to one hour which can provide a regular and invaluable opportunity to obtain important information. This may be extended by 30 minutes. They meet in public for up to two and a half hours. Motions which are agreed for the approval of the House, or failure to agree a motion in Committee, are reported by the Chair to the House. Draft motions are put by the Minister and discussed. Any MP may attend but not vote. The government puts the motion to the House, or a variation, which is agreed to or rejected, without debate. The objective of this process of scrutiny, as we shall see, is to influence the approach adopted by the Minister in the Council of Ministers. MPs may raise questions on EU matters at Question Time and in debates in the House and on Departmental Select Committees.[37] The Standing Order has provided the Committee with power to request the opinion of a variety of Select Committees on an EU document within a specified time. There are two general debates in the Commons each year before the meeting of the European Council and there are debates on the European Budget, agricultural price fixing and fisheries.

It is unclear whether a government has to comply with a Parliamentary resolution on a Commission proposal. Failure to comply would be a serious breach of Ministerial responsibility and possibly perilous but whether they are binding technically has been questioned.[38] To others, putting it in these terms is misleading; it is simply a matter of practical politics.

[37] See below.
[38] See Bradley and Ewing *Constitutional and Administrative Law* (1993, 11th ed) p 151.

Until the 1990s, there was no follow up audit by the Committee of the stage after adoption of proposals to see how the outcome tied up with negotiating strategies and objectives in explanatory memorandums. Pratt described this as a 'serious weakness'.[39] He felt that government should explain major changes which occur in the final stages and should justify them. This was particularly true in the case of the final stages of the co-decision procedure when a proposal is referred to the Conciliation Committee (as occurred with the regulation on access to documents) and then emerges as an agreed text differing 'significantly' from the common position adopted in Council and on which Parliament was informed. The Modernisation Committee agreed to a 'pre and post Council scrutiny.' Pratt describes how the 'lead department' will before a Council meeting 'in good time' provide an annotated agenda of the Council and the Committee decides whether it wants a further note on agenda items or to invite officials or the Minister to give evidence to the Committee before the Council meeting. After the meeting, the Minister writes to the Chair explaining the outcome and the Committee may invite oral or written clarification of the Minister's report. This practice was to be reviewed at the end of the 1998/99 session. It was identified as a problem in the report of the Scrutiny Committee in May 2002.

The problem is the vast legislative output of the EU and the speed at which unforeseen events occur over which the Committee has no control. It does not make for easy scrutiny and accountability. Furthermore, the Council tends to secrecy and we have seen how the regulation on access may make some inroads here. The Modernisation Committee recommended that the UK Parliament should adopt the practice of the Danish and Finnish parliaments and have a national parliament office in Brussels as a forward observation post.[40]

The Lords Committee

The Lords Scrutiny Committee[41] has always had wider terms of reference than the Commons Committee in that it may consider and report on the merits of Community proposals and on policy documents that have not

---

[39]   T Pratt 'The Role of National Parliaments in Making European Law' *The Cambridge Yearbook of European Legal Studies 1998* (1999) p 228.

[40]   Placing legislative documents and materials on the web will assist.

[41]   Which can but rarely does sit with the Commons Committee.

yet been formalised as legislative proposals including matters under the Second and Third Pillars. These proposals cover papers raising matters of principle and policy. We have seen how the Commons committee's scrutiny has expanded. The Lords Committee is noted for its detailed and well informed analysis on a wide range of topics. It may share evidence with the Commons Committee and vice versa.

A good deal of the work of the Committee is conducted through six sub-committees[42] and it has power, like the Commons Committee, to appoint special advisers. After an initial sift, documents are sent to the appropriate sub-committee which in practice may take one of three courses of action: to clear the document; to write to the relevant Minister; a to carry out a detailed enquiry. Where an enquiry is undertaken, evidence can range widely – both oral and written – and may be taken elsewhere than at Westminster. EU officials frequently give evidence along with experts from other Member States. Their reports which number about 20 to 30 each year are sent to various parties[43] and the Lords Committee decides which ones merit debate on the floor of the House. Over a half of published reports are debated in the Lords and the government has undertaken to reply to all published reports. The investigations are in greater depth than the Commons Committee and can be very substantial and informative publications.

Until 1993, scrutiny of First Pillar documents was the main activity of the Committee. It subsequently scrutinised Second and Third Pillar documents and provisions for such scrutiny were formalised in 1998 and a scrutiny reserve similar to that of the House of Commons has applied to such documents.[44] We saw above how about 1,300 such documents are deposited each year. About a quarter of documents sifted by the Chair are referred to the sub-committees. The Committee publishes its correspondence with Ministers which is relevant to scrutiny. A resolution

---

[42] Economic and Financial Affairs, Trade and External Relations; Energy, Industry and Transport; Common Foreign and Security Policy; Environment, Agriculture, Public Health and Consumer Protection; Law and Institutions; Social Affairs, Education and Home Affairs.

[43] The Government, the Commission, the EP, the UK Permanent Representative, the EU Presidency in Office and the European Committees in other national parliaments.

[44] On detailed recommendations for enhancing scrutiny, see HL 25 (1997–98) *Enhancing Parliamentary Scrutiny of the Third Pillar.*

of the HL of 6 December 1999 states that Ministers will not, except in special circumstances, agree to any proposal in the Council until it has been cleared by the Committee.[45] The Committee has expressed concern about the use by the Council of 'provisional agreements'. The argument is whether such 'PAs' are in effect agreements which the government should not enter until scrutiny is cleared (HL 135 (2001–02)). A detailed report from the Committee on *Review of Scrutiny of European Legislation* (HL 15 (2002-03)) was published in December 2002.

Departmental Select Committees

The creation of Departmentally related Select Committees in 1979 with the responsibility of overseeing the administration, policy and expenditure of their departments, executive agencies and related bodies gives them a brief broad enough to cover EC developments. The Hansard Society in its publication *Making the Law*[46] reported that the Bar Council, the Institute of Directors and the CBI all supported a greater impact from the Select Committees' scrutiny of EC legislation which should operate 'at as early a stage as possible'. In what was a very fine study of the law-making processes in the UK, despite the solecism that qualified majority voting removed Parliamentary 'control' over European legislation, the Society recommended the establishment of a new Commission for the UK to examine 'the whole legislative process within the EC'.

The Select Committee on Procedure in 1989 considered the role of Departmental Select Committees and proposals before it included the creation of European Business Sub-Committees for departmentally-related Select Committees.[47] However, the Committee on Procedure reported that most Committees displayed very little inclination to devote significantly more effort to the consideration of European legislation, some doubting whether this was in itself desirable. The record more generally of oversight from such Committees has been mixed; this tepid response on European

---

[45]   Reports include the *European Arrest Warrant* HL 89 (2001-02), *The Convention on the Future of Europe* HL 163 (2001–02) and a *Second Parliamentary Chamber for Europe* HL 48 (2001–02) and many others. Reports from the Lords Committee are on: www.Parliament.uk

[46]   The Hansard Society, (1993) *Making the Law: The Report of the Hansard Commission on the Legislative Process.*

[47]   Terence Higgins MP.

affairs is not altogether surprising. The Procedure Committee was more sanguine and should be given more encouragement in its views if oversight is to be enhanced. European legislation is an area in which the House can benefit from the sort of detailed, forensic examination of policy issues which select committees are particularly well equipped to perform, the Committee believed. The record of the Committees was mixed and inconsistent on European legislation. Too often important documents escaped effective scrutiny. It has to be said that the Committees really only have themselves to blame as one can see elsewhere from their record on oversight of expenditure. Government may not always help, but the committees do not make the most of their opportunities.

If one wished to see more effective scrutiny of legislative proposals by departmental select committees, then the recommendation that scrutiny by departmentally-related select committees would be enhanced by the establishment of a European legislation sub-committee for departmental committees has some merit. At present, little time or systematic consideration is given to European matters by the committees, although the Foreign and Home Secretaries do appear before their respective committees before meetings of the European Council and its consideration of the Second and Third Pillars of the EU and evidence is taken on these matters (see HC 698 I and 974 I (2001–02)). The Foreign Affairs Committee held sessions with the representatives appointed to sit on the d'Estaing Convention on the future of Europe. A Standing Committee was also appointed by the Commons to hear from the Convention representatives. The bulk of members on the Committee are from the Foreign Affairs Committee and European Scrutiny Committee although all MPs may attend and participate, as may members of the Lords. Some committees have shown greater interest in EC business. But on the whole, an absence of focus exists. The interdepartmental responsibility of Community economic, environmental, legal and foreign affairs policy means that no one Secretary of State or department has overall responsibility. We have seen how the role of the Commons European Scrutiny Committee has been broadened and strengthened. The Standing Order of the European Scrutiny Committee allows it to ask select committees for opinions on deposited documents. It may have been more beneficial to increase the range of inquiry of the Scrutiny Committee and to have a regular system of report on European matters from that Committee specifically to the departmental select committees which the latter may pursue. The appointment of an information officer for select committees may assist.

Greater involvement with the European Parliament – and the role of national parliaments

The European Parliament is concerned primarily with the EU interests embracing those of the Member States. National parliaments are concerned with national interests as affected by Community policy and law-making and the Community impact on those interests. The performance of their Ministers and their accountability to them is their primary concern. How do the two areas – the European Parliament and national parliaments – interrelate?

Over a decade ago, the Report of the Committee of Procedure identified three possible ways of developing links between the House's scrutiny machinery and the European Parliament following the enhanced role of the European Parliament in the legislative process after the Single European Act 1987. Co-operation and co-decision procedure have enhanced the role of the European Parliament and arguably increased the need for better links. It posited formal participation by MEPs in the business of the House. This was rejected because it would require legislation. Of greater promise was the use of MEPs as witnesses and specialist advisers. The Report believed that notwithstanding practical difficulties, the idea should be pursued. The third suggestion was the development of informal contacts with MEPs – there had in fact been a resolution of the European Parliament on Relations between the national parliaments and the European Parliament[48] which called for closer liaison between the former and the latter on all aspects of the scrutiny of European legislation.

There is no doubt that greater co-operation between the MEPs and national parliaments is desirable, but establishing an acceptable *and* effective institutional nexus has been difficult. How much of this is due to 'protection of one's own patch' is difficult to say. Both groups have a good deal to learn from each other. The question has also been examined by the departmental Foreign Affairs Committee.[49]

One of the proposals was for a Conference of Parliaments[50] which became a declaration in the TEU at Maastricht. Notwithstanding that the declaration

---

[48]   Doc A2 - 348/88 - approved 16 February 1989.

[49]   *Europe After Maastricht* HC 642-I (1992–3).

[50]   See Westlake, 'The European Parliament, the National Parliaments and the 1996 IGC' (1995) Pol Qu Vol 66, pp 59–73. See also the comments of the Commons

was widely seen as a genuine attempt to create a framework for enhanced Parliamentary involvement and provision of information, only one Assizes has been held, with 173 delegates from the national parliaments and 53 members of the European Parliament. The Foreign Affairs Committee, although recognising there was a need for improved contacts between the European Parliament and national parliaments, was not persuaded that the proposed Conference of Parliaments could be more than simply a talking-shop or an audience for an annual 'state of the union' speech from the President of the Council of Ministers. The Committee saw greater merit in the development of a 'series of bilateral contacts between the European Parliament and each national parliament and the further development of national parliaments' pre-legislative role' (paras 110–11). Respective committees of the European Parliament and national parliaments should exchange papers of mutual interest and closer co-operation between political parties in the European Parliament and national parliaments should ensue – clearly influential wording given the form of the eventual Declaration in the TEU. It wanted more bilateral contacts rather than the 'unprofitable goal of a Community wide Conference of the Parliaments'.[51] It could be argued that the 'more profitable contacts' requires a will to implement such a development. A notable development has been the invitation from the European Parliament's Finance Committee to members of national parliamentary Treasury committees to sit with them when the former is questioning members of the European Central Bank. The European Scrutiny Committee agreed with the proposal that there should be regular meetings of members of the Defence, Foreign Affairs and European Affairs Committees on national parliaments to scrutinise the European Security and Defence Policy.[52] Formal sessions of the European Parliament and national parliaments to question commissioners, officials and expert witnesses should be established and given secretarial support (para 141). The European Parliament itself has stated that the EU's democratic deficit can be remedied by strengthening both the European Parliament and national parliaments and co-operation should be based on 'complementarity'.[53]

Committee: *The 1996 IGC* HC 239-I (1995–96) and the Government Reply Cm 3051.

[51] Paragraphs 110–11.

[52] HC 152-xxxiii (2001–02) para 147.

[53] *Relations Between the European Parliament and National Parliaments in European Integration* EP A5 – 0023/2002.

Strategies to remedy the EU's 'democratic deficit' need not bring the European Parliament into competition with domestic parliaments – co-operation should be the objective. No Member State had argued that national parliaments should have a role in the European legislative process itself, though this may change. In its 2002 report, the Scrutiny committee did not recommend a veto power over EC legislation by the national parliament – that would be unworkable. It did recommend a power to refer questions on subsidiarity to a 'watch-dog' figure, however, and a meeting of MPs from national parliaments to consider aspects of subsidiarity in the Commission's annual work programme (para 134). The European Parliament is far better placed and equipped, says Westlake, to bring the Commission to account. 'As far as national parliaments are concerned, institutional reform at the Member State level', he argues 'is a more productive route than constitutional revision at the European level.'[54] It may be, however, that the d'Estaing Convention and the working groups on national parliaments and subsidiarity will promote change in the role of national parliaments (below).

After the 1996 Intergovernmental Conference the Commons Scrutiny Committee's[55] view was that 'the Maastricht Declaration on the Role of National Parliaments – Declaration No 13 – has shown just how much such statements of intent are worth. Action was needed, backed where necessary by legal requirement'.[56] It regarded the statement as a 'sham'. We have seen what occurred after Amsterdam above.

The Report considered the practices utilised by national parliaments[57] to hold the executives accountable on European items. These include devices I have already discussed and meetings and contacts between national parliaments and the European Parliament and their respective members.

One such was the formal meetings between Parliamentary Committees – the Conference of European Affairs Committees (CEAC/COSAC). The Committee believed that this latter body had been most successful when focusing upon the 'technique and practice of Parliamentary control and scrutiny rather than engaging in inconclusive political debate.'[58] It may

---

54   At note 50 above.
55   24th Report of the Select Committee 17 July 1995, HC 239-I (1994–5).
56   Paragraph 60.
57   HC 152-xxxiii (2001–02) para 147.
58   Cf the view of the Foreign Affairs Committee on the Conference of Parliaments.

seem that a limitation in this approach is that it is concerned exclusively with the exchange of information rather than affecting the formal role of national parliaments. The Report does list suggestions for role changes, however, which would give an impetus for wider constitutional development. These might include:[59]

1. making national parliaments the guardians of subsidiarity (see below);
2. giving national parliaments some responsibility for budgetary matters and the fight against fraud;
3. national MPs accompanying Ministers to Council meetings;
4. more frequent Conferences of the Parliaments;
5. in each legislature, joint committees of MEPs and MPs;
6. the creation of a European Parliament Second Chamber, composed of delegations from national parliaments; one might now suggest delegations from sub-national Parliaments.

These latter two points are given further, detailed consideration in the Report. The Report raises a number of issues apropos of a second chamber of the European Parliament, addressing fairly obvious problems such as the status of its members: ie are they representatives or delegates, what would the appropriate size be and the whole issue of the 'double or dual mandate'?[60] This practice has attracted very little support because of its onerous nature if both mandates are performed properly. Various suggestions have been put forward to specify what the chamber could do and what its powers would be. The general consensus seems to be that a second chamber – overlooking for a moment that in a way this is what the Council now is – comprised of national representatives for national parliaments would to a large extent reintroduce the European Parliament of pre 1979. The idea has, however, been floated by the Prime Minister, the German Chancellor, former French Prime Minister Jospin and numerous other political elites.

Advocacy for a second chamber of the European Parliament made up of national parliamentarians acting as a link between the European Parliament

---

[59] Paragraph 124.
[60] Until direct elections in 1979, MEPs were drawn from national parliaments. After direct elections, some countries permitted a dual mandate, but such mandates are now the exception rather than the norm: Philip Norton, 'Addressing the Democratic Deficit' (1995) *Journal of Legislative Studies* Vol 1 No 3 pp 177–193, at p 187. A common procedure for elections of MEPs in Member States has not been agreed by the Council because of different Member State constitutional traditions and sensitivities.

and national parliaments has been in existence for many years enjoying highs and lows in popularity. A recent addition has been suggestions for a second chamber of members of national and regional assemblies. To some who also gave evidence to the Lords Committee on the 1996 Intergovernmental Committee, this is a 'fifth wheel on the coach'[61] and does not have sufficient support in the European Parliament. The 'dual mandate' was not seen as a possibility or sustainable and members would have to face the issue of whether they acted as delegates or representatives and of whom.

The House of Lords EU Committee revisited the question of a second chamber in its seventh report for 2001–02. Support for such a chamber had grown and an influential report had been published by the French Senate. The Committee noted the areas where review of EU policy was weak under existing arrangements: the Second Pillar (one might add the Third in spite of increased scrutiny undertaken by UK Parliamentary Committees); and subsidiarity – who is responsible and has power for what or for clarifying competencies – 'It clearly contributes to the lack of interest in the EU that there is little understanding of how it really works;'[62] and the examination of the Commission's annual work programme.[63] The Committee was unimpressed by arguments for a second chamber. So too was the European Scrutiny Committee in its report of May 2002 although it felt national parliaments should jointly question Commissioners on their annual work programmes and policy strategies (paras 136 et seq).

Part II of the Amsterdam Protocol concerns COSAC – the Conference of European Affairs Committees of national parliaments and MEPs. The Protocol states that COSAC may make any contribution it deems appropriate for the attention of the institutions of the EU in particular on draft legal texts which 'representatives of governments of Member States may decide by common accord to forward to it' because of the subject matter. It may examine any legislative proposal or initiative relating to the establishment of an area of freedom, security and justice (Community and Third Pillar) which might have a direct bearing on the rights and freedoms of individuals. It shall inform the three major institutions of its contributions

---

[61]   Lord Howe, para 226 HL Select Committee, HL 105 (1994/5).
[62]   House of Lords European Union Committee *Seventh Report* (2001–02) para 48.
[63]   See on the Work Programme: HC 152-xxx para 58 (2001–02) and HL 141 (2001–02).

on such matters and it may address those institutions on any legislative activities of the Union in particular on subsidiarity, fundamental rights and the area of freedom, security and justice. Its contributions are not binding on national parliaments and do not prejudge their position. COSAC comprises members from the European committees of national parliaments and MEPs and meets on two occasions annually.[64]

The HLs report on a second chamber (Seventh Report 2001–02) found the procedures of COSAC to be disappointing from the point of view of attending members. There was no consensus about priorities or future role; items seemed to follow the interests of the Presidency of the day; debates became a series of set speeches. The European Scrutiny Committee reinforced an erstwhile view that its real strength lay in exchanging *information* and views and it believed that COSAC should assist in sharing best practice and information. The compliance of the Council with the Protocol on the role of national parliaments should be undertaken by COSAC, the committee believed.

There is no doubt that if national parliaments were more effectively linked up so as to provide information between themselves, this could have a profound effect on holding the Council to account. Norton cites the example of a commitment by the Commission to delay a trade agreement with Romania only for the Council apparently to renege. The European Parliament asked national parliaments to examine Ministers for their account to find that contrary to the Council line five ministers told their national parliaments that they were against, but could do nothing. This clearly constituted a blocking minority and not the voice of a lone protester! 'Mutual information was not speedy and accurate enough for the national parliaments to contradict this misrepresentation.'[65] Acting in concert by speedy and established communication – and the electronic means has been there for years – may allow for far greater influence on Ministers. It depends upon will and commitment. The French and German Parliaments have agreed a joint resolution about the shape of the 2004 Intergovernmental Committee for instance. Liaisons will be made.

---

[64] See Lord Tordoff Vol 6(4) *Journal of Legislative Studies* 1.
[65] F Wijsenbeek in Lord Plumb, et al (eds) *Shaping Europe: Reflections of Three MEPs* Federal Trust 2000, p 149 cited by Norton in evidence to the Select Committee.

The implications of co-decision

The implications for the House's scrutiny process of the co-decision procedure as set out in Article 251 [189b] EC with the aim of enhancing the role of the European Parliament were considered in December 1993 by the Select Committee on European Legislation.[66] In light of the observation that the co-decision procedure, now the dominant form of law-making in the EC, contains several points at which amendments may be made to a proposal, the Committee recommended that a new procedure be followed with regard to the timetable for scrutiny and that an amendment be made to the Resolution of the House of 24 October 1990, which constrains the freedom of Ministers to agree in the Council, to bring the stages of the co-decision procedure within the scope of the Resolution.[67] We saw how the European Scrutiny Committee now attempts to deal with such problems above. The amended Standing Order attempts to address these problems.

The Commons Scrutiny Committee is still concerned about the secrecy engendered by the co-decision procedure and the considerable use of 'trialogues' of a few Council members of the Council, European Parliament and Commission meeting in private to settle amendments or agree a text. Trialogues may also be used to avoid the formal conciliation procedure where the European Parliament and Council cannot agree and which also suits in private (para 89). Such extensive secret negotiations over legislation in a democracy are 'inappropriate.'

Extending or excluding democracy?

Some commentators have seen the problem of a lack of accountability and democratic deficit emanating from an over-mighty and unelected Commission and have suggested sweeping reforms.[68] Others take up the call for reform of the Commission positively, as in the case of Sir Leon Brittan who would retain the right of legislative initiative in the Commission. The Commission should itself be subject to efficient streamlining in organisation and should concentrate on the most pressing issues. With the growth of the power of the European Parliament over the Commission and Council 'it

---

[66]   *Scrutiny after Maastricht* HC 99 (1993/4).

[67]   Paragraphs 7–9.

[68]   M Welsh Conservative MEP *The Commission and the Parliament: Partners and Rivals in the European Policy-making Process* (1994).

may be necessary in the future to find a way to consult the electorate if gridlock between the institutions does occur'.[69]

Because the role of the European Parliament has been enhanced in the legislative programme of the EU and in the budgetary process, it is seen as the body that should hold the Commission to account by investigating individual Commissioners and by having access to all relevant information. In this manner, argues Bogdanor, something resembling the British notion of individual ministerial accountability will be produced. At present, the European Parliament only has power to insist on the resignation of the whole Commission on a two thirds majority of the votes cast on a motion of censure (Article 201 EC). An amended Article 217 EC at Nice allowed the President of the Commission effectively to demand a resignation of an individual Commissioner after obtaining approval of the College – a result of the Cresson scandal that forced the Santer Commission to resign en banc. When things go seriously wrong in the Commission, as they did in the Cresson case, and where the erring Commissioner refused to resign there was little that the European Parliament or anyone else could do. Article 217 has improved matters but, in the view of the Committee of Independent Experts set up by the European Parliament after the Cresson affair, the role of internal audit in the Commission was lamentably weak. The Vice President of the Commission agreed that there should be an Internal Audit Service and an Audit Progress Board to follow up reports and to monitor progress and to ensure that the IAS's work is familiarised throughout the Commission.[70]

The suggestion has been made that the President of the Commission should be elected by MPs of national parliaments either with or without MEPs or even by the EU franchise (the difficulty in preventing nationalism always being dominant makes this unattractive). The European Parliament, Bogdanor claims, was not consulted over the replacement of Jacques Santer by Romani Prodi as President of the Commission in 1999. The President and Commissioners as a whole are subject to approval by the European

---

69   Brittan, *The Europe We Need* (1994).
70   Tompkins 19 *Yearbook of European Law* (2000) Oxford. The Experts also recommended a Standing Committee on Standards on Public Life not unlike the Nolan Committee in the UK. Codes of Conduct for Commissioners and for departments are published on the www. See case law on whistleblowing Ch 6, p 262 et seq and *Blowing the Whistle: One Man's Fight Against Fraud in the European Commission* P van Buitenen, Politicos (2000). See the discussion at Chs 6 and 11, p 261 and p 481 on Olaf.

Parliament and are appointed by the Council (qualified majority voting). Should the President be subject to a vote of confidence by the European Parliament or should the European Parliament only approve a President who shared their majority political sympathies, as in the case of a parliamentary system and the Prime Minister who is not formally approved, but who could not be Prime Minister unless supported by the political majority in the lower house?

Reforms which seek to enhance the role of the citizen and to provide greater opportunities for participation and protection of rights are seen as a firmer basis for strengthening participatory democracy. The President of the Commission is entertaining proposals to give him greater control over the Commission by establishing a Cabinet of vice presidents (Chapter 2 p 43), although this is likely to meet insurmountable barriers from the Member States. We have noted the reforms aimed at extending rights of access to documents but these do not create rights of participation and open meetings laws. The pre-Intergovernmental Committee and Intergovernmental Committee meetings have allowed representative groups to attend[71] and public submissions were made, as they have been made to the Convention under Giscard d'Estaing deliberating the future of the EU to which 30 national parliamentarians, sixteen MEPs, 15 representatives of Member State governments, two commissioners, representatives of candidate countries and several observers have been invited to sit (see HL 163 (2001–02) for details of membership). It meets in public and in composition is not unlike the Convention which produced the Charter of Fundamental Rights for the EU.

Over the years proposals have been made for Treaty revision to secure the objective of placing the 'citizen squarely at the centre of the Union's concerns'. The European Movement some years ago grouped these around six main themes:[72]

1. improving the guarantees for citizens' rights (Charter of Fundamental Rights);
2. greater accountability of the legislative process (our present concern and note the Regulation and Decisions on access involving the Council and Commission and European Parliament);
3. safeguarding citizens' rights with respect to Police and Judicial Co-operation;

---

[71] J Shaw (2001) European Public Law 195.
[72] The European Movement *Reform of the European Union* (1994).

4. the capacity for more decisive action in the Common Foreign and Security Policy;
5. the principle of subsidiarity and the role of national parliaments (and note the views of the Scrutiny committee above on a watch-dog role);
6. the need for a short clear constitution for the EU and simplification of the treaties (two of the themes of the Giscard d'Estaing Convention).

These themes have been addressed by the Charter of Fundamental Rights, the reform of the laws on access, the role of national parliaments in overseeing subsidiarity and the Protocol on Subsidiarity and Proportionality, but sharing of information by authorities with national parliaments under the Second and Third Pillars remains an unaccountable exercise of power heightened by the reverberations from 11 September 2001. Citizens remain alienated from the EU. It is geographically remote from the vast majority of citizens, there are linguistic and cultural barriers and its organisational and structural complexity are notorious. It is a true reflection of the problem of democratising international institutions. The Commons European Scrutiny Committee was correct, in spite of all the benefits that should flow from greater openness, to highlight the continuing secrecy of the Council.

The EU Convention Working Group on national parliaments

The Working Group on national parliaments under the d'Estaing Convention reported in October 2002. Its report was brief, recommending specific wording acknowledging the active involvement of national parliaments in EU activities in any future revision of the Treaty (see Chapter 14, p 600). It drew attention to the scrutiny of governments' action in the Council and monitoring of subsidiarity and proportionality. The Council should act in public when it exercises legislative functions. Clear reasons should be given for closed doors. Records of Council proceedings should be sent within ten days to the European Parliament and national parliaments. The Protocol should be re-drafted to strengthen the role of national parliaments and preliminary agreements should not be acknowledged before the end of the six-week period in the Protocol with exceptions for urgency. Scrutiny reserves should be given a clearer status within the Council's rules of procedure; there should be strict observance of rules enforcing the setting out of periods between consideration of proposals before COREPER (the Committee of Permanent Representatives) (Chapter

2, p 41) and the Council; the Commission should transmit all legislative proposals and consultative documents simultaneously to the national parliaments, the European Parliament and the Council; the same body should also submit the annual policy strategy and annual legislative and work programme simultaneously to national parliaments, the European Parliament and the Council; the Court of Auditors should transmit its annual report likewise to those same bodies. COSAC should draft a code or guidance on desirable minimum standards for effective national parliament scrutiny and related practices. A 'process-based mechanism', ie not a separate ad hoc body, should allow national parliaments to comment on subsidiarity and proportionality in EU law-making. The role of COSAC should be clarified and strengthened with the possibility of a Congress of national parliaments and the European Parliament to discuss larger political orientations and strategies and interparliamentary conferences on specific themes. A 'European week' should be organised each year in each Member State for EU wide debate.[73]

The Group on subsidiarity added that the Commission should add to its text for proposals a 'subsidiarity sheet' allowing for case by case assessment of subsidiarity by the Council and European Parliament. An 'early warning system' should be introduced to allow national parliaments an opportunity to submit an opinion on conformity of the proposals with subsidiarity. There was also support to allow those national parliaments that had expressed an opinion to 'appeal' to the ECJ against violation of the principle after adoption of legislative acts. The Group also made suggestions for regional interests (Chapter 5, p 227).

Secrecy of Council meetings and access to documents

It was noted above how the UK government has been in favour of the Council meeting in public when it acted as a legislator. The Commons Scrutiny Committee, in its 2002 report, recommended that it should be clear what line has been taken by a Member State in Council meetings. Further, open meetings should not be confined to co-decision procedures. The European Council should meet in public when making decisions influencing legislation before the Council and the public business should give a clear indication of the line taken by each Member State Artificial stages should not be created simply to draw a distinction between private and public business (paras 20–24). Documents should not have policy stances of

---

[73]   The WG report should be read with those on subsidiarity and complementary competencies: www.european-convention.eu.int.

Member States blanked out, the Committee felt. The Council should not agree 'A points' in legislation which have been agreed by COREPER (the Committee of Permanent Representatives of the Council) officials without public discussion (para 25). The Council should have to justify going into closed session. Only minor changes emerged in relation to Council meetings after the Seville European Council (see Chapter 6, p 264).

The Regulation and Decisions passed under Article 255 EC have now replaced the former Code and decisions on access and the Code of Conduct on Public Access to the Minutes and Statements in the Minutes of the Council acting as Legislator (see Chapter 6, p 266 et seq). Although these will enhance rights of access to documents, they do not open up meetings. Their impact will be viewed with great interest.

Intergovernmental Pillars of the EU

In 1993, the House of Lords Committee[74] stated that it was essential that the Intergovernmental Pillars of the EU – covering the Common Foreign and Security Policy, Defence and Justice and Home Affairs – should be supervised by national parliaments. Third Pillar documents are included in the Amsterdam Protocol which was described above, and scrutiny of that Pillar is now far more effective, argues Kerse.[75] The Lords Committee has examined, inter alia, Europol, Schengen, mutual assistance in crime investigation, the *Corpus Iuris* dealing with fraud in the Community and the European Arrest Warrant. Both Select Committees now examine Second and Third Pillar measures.

Implementation of Community legislation and Commission delegated law-making

The House of Lords Committee had some interesting points to make on the above themes, but there have been useful contributions from elsewhere. The Hansard Society [76] has recommended an extension of the remit of the Joint Committee on Statutory Instruments (delegated legislation) with

---

[74]   HL 12 (1992/3).

[75]   C Kerse (2000) European Public Law 81.

[76]   *Making the Law: the Report of the Hansard Commission on the Legislative Process* (1993). See M Andenas and A Türk (eds) *Delegated Legislation and the Role of Committees in the EC* (2000).

regard to scrutiny not of legislation to be passed by the European Commission but of Acts and statutory instruments implementing European Directives. This is seen as necessary since 'the problems of *Factortame*[77] – where UK legislation was found to be in breach of EC law and where for the first time an English court suspended the operation of an Act of Parliament by injunction, or the *EOC* case where the House of Lords declared UK legislation contrary to Community law[78] – could well re-occur, if the present scrutiny and vetting procedures are not improved and if compliance measures are not undertaken to remove potential conflicts'. Where there is a serious breach of law in implementation of EC provisions, this can establish liability on the part of the UK under EC law.[79] Authorities have stated that the UK Parliament does not possess means of ensuring 'effective scrutiny [for implementation] of European legislation'.[80] There is no special formal means of supervising domestic subordinate legislation implementing Community measures. In fact, this role has fallen to the Joint Committee on Statutory Instruments in so far as it comes within the Committee's normal terms of reference. Occasionally, this does report on improper implementation. Nonetheless, there is room for improvement to address some shortcomings.

The Hansard Society's report sees this sort of scrutiny as being essentially a question for lawyers rather than politicians and proposes that government departmental lawyers should scrutinise proposed legislation before it is promulgated even for consultation purposes. Government lawyers prepare such legislation and they will be in the front-line in seeking to avoid or minimise such liability. One might add that this point is all the more pressing given the ECJ's rulings that Directives may have an indirect effect in so far as national legislation passed either before or after a relevant Directive must be interpreted in the light of that Directive, although as seen above (Chapter 3, p 102 et seq) there are limits to this doctrine.[81] The precise scope of this doctrine has yet to be finally established but its importance in national systems, and for relevant national legislation and regulations, is

---

[77]   *R v Secretary of State for Transport, ex p Factortame Ltd.* [1990] 2 AC 85 (HL); [1991] 1 AC 603 (ECJ and HL).

[78]   *Equal Opportunities Commission v Secretary of State for Employment* [1994] 1 All ER 910, HL.

[79]   Case C-392/93 *R v HM Treasury, ex p British Telecommunications plc* [1996] ECR I-1631.

[80]   See Bradley and Ewing, *Constitutional and Administrative Law* (12th ed) p 152.

[81]   *Marleasing SA v La Comercial International de Alimentacion SA*, Case C-106/89 [1990] ECR I-4135, ECJ.

beyond question. So also is the issue of ineffective implementation of Directives which can lead to liability where there is a sufficiently serious breach of Community law in the manner in which they are implemented.[82] In other words, expert lawyers really should be examining domestic laws and implementing measures to assess their compatibility and efficacy from the EC perspective. This is appropriate for a more technical and forensic setting than those which currently operate and would be appropriate for a body such as the Joint Committee.

The House of Lords committee has not found the process of delegation of EC legislative powers to the Commission to be seriously at fault – the familiar problem of Comitology. Although it would not be practical for EC delegated legislation as a rule to be submitted to national parliaments, 'where proposals come to light which raise matters of major significance, or which have an important impact on the interests of individuals or enterprises', national parliaments should have the opportunity to express their views.[83] In this specialist area, involvement by national parliaments was only a partial solution and the Commission should make greater use of specialist advisory committees in the formulation of delegated legislation – which as was seen in Chapter 6 has produced its own problems. The European Scrutiny Committee in its 2002 report recommended that the Commission policy and legislative powers should be clearly defined as they are in the field of state aids and competition (para 82).

The position in other Member States

The position in other Member States and the role of their parliaments differs significantly. In our formal constitution, Parliament has great importance.[84] In Denmark, Ministers cannot agree to a legislative proposal until approved by the Danish Parliament although if the Council appear likely to approve a position contrary to that agreed to by the parliamentary committee, the latter must be notified and given an opportunity to agree or disagree; in

---

[82]   Case C- 392/93 *R v HM Treasury, ex p BT plc* [1996] ECR I-1631; Cases C-283, 291 and 292/94 *Denkavit International* [1996] ECR I-5063. On non-implementation: Cases C-178-9/94, 188-90/94 *Dillenkofer* [1996] ECR I-4845.

[83]   See *Government Response* to the Lords Committee report on *Comitology* HL 62 (1998–99) and HL 15 (2002-03) p 22.

[84]   See D Millar in *Westminster and Europe* eds P Giddings and G Drewry (1996) p 333 et seq.

Finland, a Grand European Committee operates; Sweden and Austria have 'robust systems' for scrutiny. Both France and Germany made no provision for scrutiny until the treaty amendments introduced at Maastricht and the implications of these changes were examined in Chapter 2. In the Netherlands, approval of Third Pillar measures have to be obtained from the States General (Parliament).

There has been an enormous disparity in standards and types of review and scrutiny. This was reported upon most recently by the European Scrutiny Committee report of 2002. It has become very much a hot item in the last decade or so, reinforced by its inclusion in the Declaration of the Future of the EU in the Final Act of the Nice conference. The greater flow of information and ideas, if put to maximum effect, could help usher in a greater degree of efficacy and consistency in approaches. It is, furthermore, in the mutual interest of national parliaments and the European Parliament to co-operate as closely as possible and in this development, regional assemblies should be put to maximum effect. The d'Estaing Convention's working groups reported on these and other matters (above p 317).

In its report on *Review of Scrutiny of European Legislation* (HL 15 (2002-03)) the House of Lords European Union Committee set out current practice in Appendix 4.

Conclusions

The role of national parliaments has been analysed both descriptively and prescriptively in the move towards greater European integration.[85] The argument has been advanced that until the mid 1980s national parliaments, in particular those of the original Member States, were for the most part content to leave European rule-making to the supranational institutions. Norton contends that, from the mid–1980s onwards, in part prompted by the earlier accession of Member States such as the UK with Parliaments jealous of their status within the national law-making process, national parliaments began to move toward (i) specialisation (ii) greater activity and (iii) the integration of MEPs in the work of national parliaments. The first two points relate to the growth of specialist parliamentary committees

---

[85]   *Insight: Newsletter of the Centre for European Union Studies*, June 1995 pp 1–16; *and* 'National Parliament's and the European Union' (1995) Journal of Legislative Studies Vol 1 No 3, p 1 and p 177.

established to scrutinise European legislation, and the third to the attempts to close the gap which had opened up between national parliaments and the European Parliament.

The analysis offered by Norton is that national parliaments have been unable (for constitutional and procedural reasons) or unwilling (for ideological and cultural reasons) to play a significant role in European law-making; an example of the constitutional obstacles being the extension of qualified majority voting in the Council of Ministers which has limited the capacity for national parliaments to affect outcomes he suggests. As an example of the ideological obstacles, he cites the view among some Member States which are keen on the principle of European integration, viz that the supranational level is the appropriate one for the formulation and enactment of European law.

This has something of a doom-laden quality about it. Scrutiny in the UK has been significantly improved as this chapter has indicated, but it could improve further. Select Committees can work superbly well. But to do the work thoroughly is time consuming, onerous and politically unrewarding, certainly for MPs. On the surface, the Committees seem to possess procedures and powers to impose an appropriate degree of accountability. They themselves bear witness to the difficulties in practice that still persist. Both domestic committees have expressed their desire to examine the Commission's annual work programme.[86] If our MPs wish to become more effective, they must show the will to place the necessary demands upon our government. Westminster MPs must also become more involved in closer co-operation with the European Parliament. Resentment has been felt about the transfer of power and sovereignty to Europe and in the past where that resentment has been felt, it was no comfort to those aggrieved that the European Parliament is the perceived beneficiary of Westminster's loss. That was seen as part of the problem. As select committees have often observed, co-operation between national parliaments and the European Parliament is essential. This is probably the only practical way that Westminster can address the problems posed by legislative changes such as qualified majority voting and whether the perceived threat to its own democratic mandate posed by that development is real or imagined.

Is there any mileage in extending further the role of the European Parliament in the legislative process? This is the arena of democratic representation

---

[86]   See p 303 above.

in Europe. For too many in the UK it is an object of obscurity or irrelevance. It must convince the citizens of Europe, the British perhaps more than many, that it maintains the best and most effective traditions of democratic control of executive action. If the Commission and Council as Legislator are to be effectively controlled then control will only be through this forum. If we do not want this to happen but we desire an expanded EU, then we must recast our notion of European democracy. The alternative is a Community of less significance.

A suggestion which addresses these points in a bold and imaginative manner came from Professor Walter van Gerven several years ago.[87] He argues that the EU's legislative body would be bicameral consisting of the Council and European Parliament. The European Parliament would consist of elected MEPs and approximately an additional third of that number delegated from national parliaments. These latter would form special committees within their own national parliaments to assist their Parliament on European proposals and the preparation of national implementing legislation. The chairpersons of such committees from all the Member States would meet regularly to coordinate preparatory work and implementing legislation with a view to facilitating harmonisation. He makes recommendations for the division of work between the Council and European Parliament.

The function of the national parliaments is to hold its own executive to account. Enough has been said about how this role should be developed in relation to EU measures. Van Gerven's suggestion would enhance their role in European affairs. On the role of the European Parliament one should recall that the ECJ has confirmed the essential role of that body in the legislative process and how procedural safeguards on consultation protecting its position cannot be ignored.[88] The European Parliament argued that, since the Council had adopted a Regulation without complying with the consultation procedure provided for in Article 43 EC which, in conjunction with Article 113 EC, forms the legal basis of the Regulation, the latter must be annulled for breach of an essential procedural requirement.[89]

---

[87] (1996) European Public Law 81 'Toward a Coherent Constitutional System within the European Union.'

[88] *European Parliament v EU Council* ECJ Case C-65/93, [1995] ECR I-643.

[89] See Heukels (1995) 32 CML Rev 1407.

Finally one needs to assess the impact there has been from the emergence of a European Ombudsman who liaises with national ombudsmen — who, in the British case, is an officer of the House of Commons and has a wealth of experience on maladministration and grievance redress in the performance of statutory duties. Also of interest will be the practice of petitioning the European Parliament which, like the provision on the Community ombudsman, was contained in the TEU. So too the placing of Questions and questioning of Commissioners. Will these features help inform the European Parliament and, via the European Parliament, national parliaments about the impact of law-making on citizens and the difficulties caused by European institutions or the implementation of EC law in Member States? These points are returned to in Chapter 11.

The above suggestions indicate a broad range of proposals for institutional reform to enhance the democratic input into EU decision-making. We are likely to see greater efforts from our own Parliament to hold Ministers to account before approval of proposals in Council and the concomitant development of procedures in the European Parliament to hold the Commission to account. In the case of the former, the movement to greater openness in the Council is welcome even though problems remain. National parliaments must be informed in sufficient time and in sufficient detail to make an effective contribution. Furthermore, the process of devolution should be an opportunity to use appropriate *fora* to discuss the impact of European law and policy initiatives on local government and regional government. The d'Estaing Convention established a working party on national parliaments which had joint sessions with the subsidiarity White Paper. The House of Lords committee saw its outcome as 'central to the democratic accountability debate of the Convention' (HL 163 (2001–02). The recommendations of this Working Group were examined above.

Chapter 8

Principles of review

Introduction

There can be no doubt that the growth of judicial review of public administration, and the beginnings of a separate system of public law, have been the most notable development of British law over the past 30 years.[1] During this period, principles of good public administration had been developed and what officialdom regarded as a *cordon sanitaire* surrounding a great deal of its decision-making has been reduced. This has been done largely by means of judge-made law (the common law), supplementing techniques such as tribunals and inquiries and ombudsmen as a means to check the exercise of official power. More recently, the basis of these developments has been assessed from a variety of perspectives. Is this development one which is inherent in the common law or is it one that is coloured and constrained by Parliamentary sovereignty?[2] The answer to this question has important implications for the developing nature of judicial review in cases of constitutional significance as identified by Laws LJ in *Thoburn's* case (see Chapter 4, p 157 et seq).

---

[1] I lean heavily on: J Jowell and P Birkinshaw 'English Report' in *Administrative Law under European Influence* (1996) ed J Schwarze, p 273. The present chapter updates that earlier chapter. Some of the classifications in this chapter (pp 336-348) follow those in de Smith et al *Judicial Review of Administrative Action* (5th ed, 1995) ch 13. On constitutional review, see J Jowell (2000) Public Law 684 for a succinct statement.

[2] See the chapters in C Forsyth ed *Judicial Review and the Constitution* (2000).

In 1978, the procedure for seeking public law had been simplified through the procedure known as the Application for Judicial Review. This has now been replaced by Part 54 of the Civil Procedure Rules 1998 following the Woolf reforms in civil justice. The Administrative Court, renamed in October 2000 to coincide with the coming into effect of the HRA 1998, now has a power to sit in Cardiff as well as elsewhere. This is not quite the regionalisation of public law that we see in France (see Chapter 3) but it is the first in-road into London hegemony in public law procedure in England and Wales. A stronger regional presence in judicial review is sorely needed in England.

In that 30-year period courts have, most notably, established that the conferment of broad discretionary powers upon officials does not preclude judicial review. Conditions of national security may lead to caution in the scope of review, a caution illustrated by the decision of the House of Lords in *Secretary of State for the Home Department, ex p Rehman* where the law lords, upholding the Court of Appeal, were unwilling to second guess the Home Secretary's judgment of what the requirements of national security entailed.[3] To have done so would have affronted basic divisions within the separation of powers. In spite of these areas of sensitivity, the courts made considerable advances holding for instance that the 'prerogative' powers of the Crown, for so long immune from effective challenge, are not *ipso facto* exempt from review. Since the mid-1980s, the courts made more coherent the 'grounds' or 'principles' of review that require all bodies exercising public functions to act within the scope of their powers (the requirement of 'legality') in a way that is fair procedurally (the requirement of 'procedural propriety') and that is not an unreasonable abuse of power (the requirement of 'rationality'). When Professor Jowell and I wrote in 1995 that 'Under the last head we are beginning to see the articulation of principles such as proportionality and equality' it was clear that such principles have for long been embedded in the common law and on rare occasion had been given judicial endorsement.[4] It is now clear that proportionality has entered our law via the Human Rights Act 1998 and

---

[3]   [2001] UKHL 47, [2002] 1 All ER 122; unlike the Special Immigration Appeals Commission which held the Home Secretary had failed to prove his case that deportation was required on grounds of national security; see the report in (2002) New LJ 1357 on the human rights review by the Commission of the Anti-terrorism, Crime and Security Act 2001; this decision was reversed by the Court of Appeal, however: see p 372 below.

[4]   And see J Jowell and A Lester in J Jowell and D Oliver eds *New Directions in Judicial Review* (1988).

also when UK courts are asked to enforce Community rights. It is also, I would suggest, a part of the common law as we shall see, although there is still some reluctance to accept this point.[5] The same is true of legitimate expectation whether procedural or substantive although as with proportionality there was resistance to an 'alien' concept which it was felt could translate courts from bodies reviewing legality to bodies that would review the merits of government and administrative decisions.[6]

Directly effective provisions of EC law creating enforceable individual rights may be invoked in domestic courts (European Communities Act 1972, s 2 (1)) and any question about the meaning or validity of an EC legal provision must be determined according to the principles of EC law (European Communities Act 1972, s 3 (1)). National law must not create barriers or obstacles to such rights or make their realisation impossible.[7] Under the judicial review procedures now contained in CPR 1998, Part 54 – 'EC law principles have to be taken into account in cases involving rights conferred by EC law'.[8]

As the case law of *Francovich, Factortame* and other cases on liability richly illustrate[9] those principles are subject to constant evolution (see Chapter 10). Senior British judges have indicated that divergence from EC law is a justification for not applying or for changing domestic law and as we saw in Chapter 4, they have not been slow to show the way. While the judicial emphasis from the ECJ has been upon the provision of effective remedies in national systems for the vindication of Community rights, the Community has given greater emphasis to the full implementation of EC

---

5   See Lord Phillips MR in *Matthews v Ministry of Defence* [2002] EWCA Civ 773, [2002] 3 All ER 513 at para 72: 'Because we have found no interference with a convention right, no issue of proportionality arises.'

6   *R (Wilkinson) v Broadmoor Hospital* [2001] EWCA Civ 1545, [2002] 1 WLR 419. Where a decision to administer medical treatment to a mental patient without his consent under the Mental Health Act 1983, s 8(3)(b) was challenged by way of judicial review, the court was entitled to reach its own view as to the merits of the medical decision and whether it infringed the patient's human rights. The patient was also entitled to require the attendance of medical witnesses for cross-examination.

7   Case C-208/90 *Emmott v Minister for Social Welfare and the A-G (Ireland)* [1991] ECR I-4269; and see Case 199/82 [1983] ECR 3595; Case 309/85 [1988] 2 CMLR 409; Case 222/84 *Johnston v Chief Constable of the RUC* [1986] ECR 1651.

8   Law Commission Paper No 126 *Administrative Law: Judicial Review and Statutory Appeals* (1993) para 2.9 and No 226, October 1994, paras 2.8–11 (1993/4 HC 669).

9   Cases C-6, C-9-90: Judgment 19 November 1991: [1991] ECR I-5357.

law within Member States. The TEU signed at Maastricht had an Annexe containing a Declaration of Implementation of EC law.[10]

We shall see in the next chapter that the movement to fundamental rights protection has gathered full pace in the UK. This movement operated both at common law, and more recently under the Convention as incorporated by the HRA 1998. From a few old cases in which fundamental statements had been made about the basic rights of individuals before the courts, a modern law was being fashioned which sought to give fuller expression to the protection of human rights. Before the ECHR was incorporated into domestic law, individuals had a right to proceed to the Commission[11] and the CHR under Article 25 ECHR. Judicial determination of these rights in the UK was thus *indirectly* influenced by the rulings of these bodies. Although they were not obliged to do so as a matter of domestic law, the courts were increasingly taking into account the text and jurisprudence of the European Convention.[12] It was also established that English courts would allow reference both to the text of the Convention and its interpretation by the European Commission and CHR in order to resolve an ambiguity in English primary or secondary legislation.[13] In such a case the courts will presume that Parliament intended to legislate in conformity with its treaty obligations under the Convention, and not in conflict with it.[14] Limits on this practice were set down in the *Brind* case, however.[15] This case established that where broad discretionary powers are conferred on an official, and the scope of the power is not ambiguous, reference to the European Convention will not be required. The Convention was not a relevant factor to consider in the exercise of a discretion within broad powers.

In dealing with domestic provisions within Community competence, English courts have to take into account the jurisprudence of the ECJ and apply its principles of review and its remedies. Here English courts are required to have regard to the case law of the CHR as a source of general principles of

10   And see Declaration 43 of the Treaty of Amsterdam.
11   Disbanded in 1998, Protocol 11 of the Council of Europe 11 May 1994.
12   See eg *R v Secretary of State for the Home Department, ex p Leech (No 2)* [1993] 4 All ER 539.
13   M Hunt *Using Human Rights Law in English Courts* (1997).
14   *R v Secretary of State for the Home Department, ex p Brind* [1991] 1 AC 696, HL, at pp 747–48, *per* Lord Bridge; pp 749–50, *per* Lord Roskill; pp 760–61, *per* Lord Ackner.
15   [1991] 1 All ER 720.

European law.[16] In such cases the courts cannot avoid the influence of general principles such as proportionality and equality. We wrote in 1995 that 'It would be surprising if a dual-stream judicial review could be sustained for long, and it is likely that the non-European stream will increasingly be infiltrated by the principles and remedies of European Law.' This chapter assesses the developments that have taken place.

Discretion and judicial review

English law had adopted a robust attitude to procedural fairness which was re-established in the early 1960s after years of neglect. In review of discretionary powers its approach was more circumspect. Judicial review permits the courts to control the abuse of discretion: the famous decision in *Wednesbury* gives expression to that protection. Even if Parliament appears to confer unlimited or unfettered discretion upon the decision-maker, the courts will insist that that discretion is lawfully exercised.[17]

It must be emphasised that judicial review is not an appeal. Review has to respect the legitimate role of administrative discretion and we hear increasingly of the 'margin of discretion' in which official discretion has to be exercised. Although the English had no developed separation of powers, as the case with the French whose laws ordained that the ordinary courts must not meddle in matters of administration, the boundaries of official competence were clearly delineated and at times rigidly enforced. The facts of a case or the merits were the preserve of the administration. The courts may require the body to act within the limits of its powers, 'but they may not substitute their views for that of the body that is better equipped to evaluate the fact situation because of its expertise and immediate contact with the parties involved in the decision.'[18] Under the HRA 1998, the courts will be faced with situations where it is alleged that a human right which is absolute has been interfered with – such as the prohibition on torture or degrading treatment under Article 3 ECHR, or, with some exceptions, the right to life under Article 2 ECHR. In such cases, courts may be left with no alternative to a merits review as we shall see in the next chapter.

---

[16]   See Ch 3, p 95 et seq: Case 222/84 *Johnston v. Chief Constable RUC* [1986] ECR 1651.

[17]   See Lord Upjohn in *Padfield v Minister of Agriculture* [1968] AC 997.

[18]   J Jowell and P Birkinshaw 'English Report' in J Schwarze (ed) *Administrative Law under European Influence* (1996), p 277.

Outside these considerations, to give an example, the courts may not interfere with the view of a planning authority that a proposal for new land development will cause unacceptable traffic congestion – that is a matter of fact, or 'fact and degree' for the planners. The court may, however, strike down a decision to refuse planning permission to anyone who does not have local connections on the ground that the issue of local connections is beyond the scope of planning as set out in the relevant statute.

The distinction between law on the one hand and fact on the other is, however, notoriously difficult. Normally, the weighing of relevant considerations is a matter for the administrative body.[19] However, where excessive or unacceptable weight has been placed upon a particular (albeit relevant) consideration, the ground of judicial review known as 'unreasonableness' or 'irrationality' allows the courts to intervene. A margin of discretion is, under this ground, allowed to the decision-maker. The courts can only intervene if the decision is 'so unreasonable that no reasonable body could so decide.'[20] However, as we shall see, underneath this doctrine the courts do in exceptional cases review the facts and merits of a case.

When doing so, however, it is often not easy to discover the precise reason for the courts' intervention. The administrative decision is simply said to be 'unreasonable' – an epithet which can do as much to obfuscate as to elucidate. From the early 1990s, courts started to adopt forms of review that were based on those that are described as general principles of European law, both the Convention and Community law, including proportionality. Although Lord Ackner stated in *Brind v Home Secretary*:[21] 'Unless and until Parliament incorporates the convention into domestic law .... there appears to me to be at present no basis upon which the proportionality doctrine applied by the European Court can be followed by the courts of this country' such a principle had taken root. The Convention has been so incorporated but long before 2000, Professor Jowell and Anthony Lester had shown how proportionality and equality were invoked by domestic courts – where for instance a punishment was too

---

19   For the limited opportunities to review a question of fact, see *Edwards v Bairstow* [1956] AC 14.

20   *Associated Provincial Picture Houses Ltd v Wednesbury Corpn* [1948] 1 KB 223. Often referred to by the name of the case as 'Wednesbury unreasonableness'.

21   [1991] 1 All ER 720 at 735j.

severe or sought to prejudice an individual without lawful authority.[22] Proportionality seemed the best way to describe these decisions albeit that the courts were not expressing the basis of review in terms of proportionality. Proportionality is one of the principles of review adopted by the ECJ. We saw in Chapter 3, p 143 et seq how they are used by the ECJ in a manner which differs in detail from the use of the principle in Member States such as Germany.

English courts are still feeling their way after the HRA 1998 implemented the Convention and decisions may not always appear consistent. But the case law reveals that the essence of the principles is present in the common law and has been developed since *Brind's* decision which only concerned the principle of proportionality.

Proportionality[23]

Proportionality as we have seen (p 143 et seq) means several things. Basically the principle seeks to protect an individual against excessive, unnecessary and ill-considered use of public power. That may be power exercised by private bodies on behalf of a public authority. As shall be seen, as well as outlawing excessive punishment or intervention into one's position, it can expose the decision-making process of administrative bodies to ensure that they give proper and full consideration to all factors. It allows a more probing form of review that investigates reasons for acting and not one which assumes the propriety of reasons given unless they are ex facie absurd. The Court of Appeal has ruled that domestic measures imposing banning orders preventing alleged soccer hooligans travelling to overseas fixtures was not a disproportionate exercise of power and

---

[22]   'Proportionality: Neither Novel nor Dangerous' in J Jowell and D Oliver eds *New Directions in Judicial Review* (1989) and per Lords Denning and Scarman LJ in *R v Barnsley Metropolitan Borough Council, ex p Hook* [1976] 1 WLR 1052 (disproportionate punishment for street trader); *R v London Borough of Brent, ex p Assegai* (1987) 157 LG Rev 891 (banning from council meeting 'out of proportion to what the applicant had done, per Woolf LJ); *R v Secretary of State for Transport, ex p Pegasus Holidays (London) Ltd and Airbro (UK) Ltd* [1989] 2 All ER 481, QBD.

[23]   E Ellis ed *The Principle of Proportionality in the Laws of Europe* (1999); P Craig *Administrative Law* (1999, 4th ed); ch 18; R Thomas *Legitimate Expectations and Proportionality in Administrative Law* (2000).

thereby a breach of Community law.[24] Where fixed penalties of £2,000 and possible detention of a vehicle were imposed on hauliers who were discovered to have 'clandestine entrants' on the vehicles, this was said to be a breach of Article 6 ECHR guaranteeing a right to a fair trial but not a breach of Community law Articles 28 [30] EC and 49 [59] EC on the basis that they were not disproportionate.[25] Where Customs officers adopted a policy of seizing the vehicles of those who evaded duty on tobacco and alcohol, because such a policy did not allow for consideration of individual circumstances, eg personal and family use and commercial use, it was therefore a disproportionate breach of the claimant's right to enjoyment of property under Protocol 1, Article 1 ECHR.[26] The language of proportionality is finding ever increasing expression.

In 1984, Lord Diplock famously suggested that proportionality might emerge as a possible fourth ground of judicial review under domestic law, following illegality, procedural impropriety and irrationality.[27] English courts initially resisted the invitation. It is part of EU law and must be applied by domestic courts when enforcing Community rights.[28] It is a part of the ECHR law. The submission that it was a discrete head of review received its first consideration in the House of Lords in the *Brind* decision in 1991. The case concerned the ban of direct broadcasting by proscribed terrorist organisations in Northern Ireland by the Home Secretary under statutory powers. Journalists claimed this was a breach of Article 10 ECHR guaranteeing freedom of speech and a right to pass on information. Two judges categorically ruled out any role for proportionality in reviewing discretionary powers on the grounds that it was anti-democratic (it upset the decisions of politicians or those endorsed by politicians) or that it

---

24 *Gough v Chief Constable of Derbyshire Constabulary* [2002] EWCA Civ 351, [2002] 2 All ER 985 – necessity for imposing an order restricting a fundamental freedom in a particular case had to be 'strictly demonstrated'. There was no breach of Article 6 ECHR in the manner in which the scheme was organised.

25 *International Transport Roth GmbH v Secretary of State for the Home Department* [2002] EWCA Civ 158, [2002] 3 WLR 344. See *R (Hoverspeed Ltd) v Customs and Excise Comrs* [2002] EWHC 1630 (Admin), [2002] All ER (D) 498.

26 *Lindsay v Customs and Excise Comrs* [2002] EWCA Civ 267, [2002] 3 All ER 118.

27 *Council for Civil Service Unions v Minister of State for the Civil Service* [1985] AC 374, HL at 410.

28 See eg *R v Minister of Agriculture, Fisheries and Food, ex p Roberts* [1991] 1 CMLR 555; *Thomas v Chief Adjudication Officer* [1991] 3 All ER 315, CA; *Stoke-on-Trent City Council v B & Q plc* [1991] 4 All ER 221.

amounted to a merits review.[29] One judge ruled that in reviewing an interference with human rights by the Home Secretary, the power must be necessary and proportionate – and he felt it was. Lord Roskill, with whom Bridge agreed, felt that it had no relevance in the present case but it should not be ruled out in future cases.[30]

In *A-G v Guardian Newspapers Ltd (No2)*[31] Lord Goff said that:

> It is established in the jurisprudence of the European Court of Human Rights that . . . interference with freedom of expression should be no more than is proportionate to the legitimate aim pursued. I have no reason to believe that English law, as applied in the courts, leads to any different conclusion.[32]

Before and after *Brind* there were cases in lower courts where proportionality had been adopted.[33] There were situations where although not expressly resorted to, the best basis for understanding a decision was an unarticulated assumption of proportionality. This was apparent in cases where there was an infringement of the Bill of Rights 'cruel and unusual punishment' provision.[34] It was also apparent in cases where punishment seemed oppressive or excessive or in some sense out of order– where someone was doing what they were lawfully entitled to do.[35] In other situations if there was evidence that there had been an improper weighing of factors that had gone into a decision – too much emphasis had been given to one factor, courts had intervened. They were classified as therefore unreasonable. Instead of justifying their decisions on finely tuned principles that weighed and balanced considerations making up a decision, there was

---

29   Lords Ackner and Lowry.
30   *R v Home Secretary, ex p Brind* [1991] 1 AC 696, per Lords Bridge, Roskill and Templeman. See also Lord Templeman, willing to apply proportionality if appropriate (which it was not) in *R v Independent Television Commission, ex p TSW Broadcasting Ltd* [1996] EMLR 291, HL.
31   [1990] 1 AC 109.
32   [1990] 1 AC 109 at 283. See also Lord Griffiths at 273.
33   See J Jowell and A Lester in J Jowell and D Oliver eds *New Directions in Judicial Review* (1988) and post *Brind: R v Secretary of State for the Home Department, ex p Hindley* [2000] 1 QB 152 and [2000] 2 All ER 385, HL – exercise of discretion not 'disproportionate'.
34   *R v Secretary of State for the Home Department, ex p Herbage* [1986] 3 All ER 209. See P Craig *Administrative Law* (1999, 4th ed) ch 18 and (2001) LQR 589.
35   *Wheeler v Leicester City Council* [1985] AC 1054.

resort to the blanket test of *Wednesbury* which did not achieve very much in advancing the cause of public law jurisprudence.[36]

The incorporation of the ECHR into domestic law under the HRA 1998 has necessarily brought with it the principle of proportionality as developed by the CHR in those Articles where rights are not absolute and have to be balanced against individual, collective or state interests. In some cases as seen above, rights are absolute resulting in different considerations – there is no justification for torture. In *de Freitas v Permanent Secretary etc*[37] Lord Clyde observed that the contours of proportionality are:

> whether (i) the legislative objective is sufficiently important to justify limiting a fundamental right; (ii) the measures designed to meet the legislative objective are rationally connected to it; and (iii) the means used to impair the right to freedom are no more than is necessary to accomplish the objective. (at p 80)

In *Alconbury* it was suggested by Lord Slynn that proportionality should now be a part of domestic law, an enthusiasm that was not openly embraced by his fellow judges.[38] It is the obiter of one judge and should not be pressed further than justified. But the signs of change are there. What are the mechanics of proportionality?

1. Balancing the weight of relevant considerations

As Professor Jowell and I wrote in our earlier paper, there have been occasions where the courts have been prepared to strike down unreasonable decisions where either *excessive or inadequate weight* has been accorded to one or other relevant consideration.

The examples include the eviction of travellers from local authority sites. It has been held that the weighing of the various considerations relevant to the exercise of the power (such as nuisance, obstruction, or danger) against the council's legal duty to provide adequate accommodation to travellers[39] is primarily a matter for the local authority.[40] However, where the local

---

36 J Jowell and A Lester QC, 'Proportionality: Neither Novel nor Dangerous', in Jowell and Oliver eds *New Directions in Judicial Review* (1988) 51, at 59–69.
37 [1999] 1 AC 69.
38 [2001] UKHL 23, [2001] 2 All ER 929.
39 Under The Caravan Sites Act 1968, s 6.
40 Eg *R v Avon County Council, ex p Rexworthy* (1988) 87 LGR 470.

authority had ignored its duty to provide adequate accommodation for travellers in its area for over ten years, the decision to evict was held void for unreasonableness.[41] The Court of Appeal has provided detailed guidance on all the considerations that have to be weighed and balanced in deciding whether to enforce planning control by injunction in a manner which is 'proportionate' bearing in mind, inter alia, rights to family life under Article 8 ECHR.[42]

As Professor Jowell and I pointed out:

> In cases involving the Home Secretary's discretion to release life prisoners who had served their 'tariff' it has been held that the weight attached by the Home Secretary to minor crimes or misdemeanours of the prisoner was excessive, rendering the decision not to release the prisoner 'perverse'.[43] Excessive weight attached to expressions of expert opinion (in the form of a medical certificate[44] counsel's opinion,[45] or even the opinion of the Chief Justice about the release of a prisoner) can similarly render a decision unreasonable,[46] as can the reliance upon an immaterial mistake in an application for legal aid as a ground of refusal.[47]

In *Venables*,[48] giving undue weight to irrelevant considerations – a survey conducted by the *Sun* on how the murderers of Jamie Bulger should be punished – was unlawful.

---

[41] *West Glamorgan County Council v Rafferty* [1987] 1 WLR 457 ('The decision ...required the weighing of the factors according to the personal judgment of the Councillors but the law does not permit complete freedom of choice assessment...' per Ralph Gibson LJ) and see *South Buckinghamshire District Council v Porter* [2001] EWCA Civ 1549, [2002] 1 All ER 425.

[42] *South Buckinghamshire District Council v Porter* [2001] EWCA Civ 1549, [2002] 1 All ER 425.

[43] See *R v Home Secretary, ex p Benson* (1988) Times, 21 November; *R v Home Secretary, ex p Cox* (1992) COD 72 (these decisions could equally be decided on the ground that the excessive weight attached to the minor crimes and misdemeanours amounted to the taking into account considerations that were irrelevant to the statutory purpose because they did not address the question of the prisoner's dangerousness).

[44] *Devon County Council v George* [1989] AC 573.

[45] *R v Lancashire County Council, ex p Hook* [1980] QB 603.

[46] *R v Home Secretary, ex p Handscomb* (1987) 86 Cr App Rep 59; *R v Home Secretary, ex p Walsh* (1991) Times, 17 December.

[47] *R v Law Society, ex p Gates & Co* (1988) Times, 31 March. J Jowell and P Birkinshaw 'English Report' in *Administrative Law under European Influence* (1996) ed J Schwarze p 284.

[48] *R v Secretary of State for the Home Department, ex p Venables* [1997] 3 All ER 97, HL.

2. Oppressive decisions

There are numerous decisions from the field of review of sentence and release of life prisoners by the Home Secretary where a delay was unreasonable because it was 'excessive beyond belief'[49] and in the case of Myra Hindley the Court of Appeal made a direct reference to 'disproportionate' exercise of power when she claimed – unsuccessfully – that the authorities had fettered their discretion in setting a tariff of life for a convicted murderer;[50] exercise of the Home Secretary's tariff making powers – the period which a prisoner will serve as punishment – were upset in *Pierson*[51] because he had retrospectively increased a tariff and acted on considerations which were not consistent with those of the judicial function.

Under the ECHR, the CHR has probably sounded the death-knell for the role of the Secretary of State in setting tariffs for prisoners when it ruled that taking into account irrelevant considerations in refusing to release a life prisoner was a breach of Article 5(1) guaranteeing freedom from arbitrary detention, and failure to comply with the advice of the Parole Board to release the prisoner was a breach of Article 5(4) ECHR.[52]

Elsewhere excessive delay of one form or another has invalidated proceedings.[53] The case law has also considered excessively low compensation to be illegal.[54] Planning law is also rich in examples where owners of property have been excessively burdened with planning conditions.[55] In cases, now somewhat dated, where courts have interfered with decisions of planning authorities for unjustifiably interfering with the

---

49   *R v Home Secretary, ex p Handscombe* (1987) 86 Cr App Rep 59.
50   Note 33 above. See: *B v Secretary of State for the Home Department (deportation: proportionality)* [2000] 2 CMLR 1086.
51   *R v Secretary of State for the Home Department, ex p Pierson* [1997] 3 All ER 577.
52   *Stafford v UK* (2002) 13 BHRC 260. See *ex p Anderson* [2002] UKHL 46, Ch 9, p 423 where the 'death-knell' was sounded by the House of Lords on the setting of tariffs by the Home Secretary for prisoners serving a life sentence.
53   *R v Merseyside Chief Constable, ex p Calvaley* [1986] QB 424; *R v Home Secretary, ex p Phansopokar* [1976] QB 606; citing the Magna Carta 1215, c 29: 'to no one will we delay right or justice'. See also *R v Preston* [1993] 4 All ER 638, HL.
54   *Hall & Co Ltd v Shoreham-by-Sea UDC* [1964] 1 WLR 240; *Williams v Giddy* [1911] AC 381.
55   *Hall & Co Ltd v Shoreham-by-Sea UDC* [1964] 1 WLR 240.

rights of private developers where the authority seemed to be off-loading its statutory responsibilities of housing onto private developers. So, a planning condition which required the developer to construct housing to local authority specifications, to impose public sector rent controls, and imposed a requirement to take tenants from the council's waiting list was declared unreasonable.[56]

The point was made that the 'courts have always employed the equivalent of the concept of proportionality, even when not explicitly recognising it.' What became increasingly evident was that the concept of proportionality was being invoked in cases involving fundamental human rights. This was before the ECHR was incorporated into domestic law.[57]

3. Decisions infringing human rights

In the field of fundamental human rights, the courts displayed their greatest sensitivity to the legitimate use of the courts in the protection of the individual and it is here that we find the most frequent reference to proportionality. In a decision in 1995, which at the time appeared strikingly radical in some quarters[58] (although the judge accepted some would see it as pusillanimous), the test of review for the protection of human rights was spelt out by Simon Brown LJ. *R v Ministry of Defence, ex p Smith*[59] was the case that concerned the homosexuals who were dismissed from the armed forces because of their sexual orientation, not because of any conduct. Several individuals who had been in the armed services brought an application for judicial review that the decision to discharge them from the armed services on the grounds of their sexual orientation was unlawful. There was no complaint of improper conduct on their part, ie sexual relationships on armed forces property. The fact that they were homosexual alone led to their discharge. Their career records were exemplary. In his judgment, Simon Brown LJ stated (at p 448a–d) that although he thought the decision of the Minister wrong because it rested too heavily on

---

[56] *R v Hillingdon London Borough Council, ex p Royco Homes Ltd* [1974] QB 720.

[57] J Jowell and P Birkinshaw 'English Report' in *Administrative Law under European Influence* (1996) ed J Schwarze, p 289.

[58] Because the court rejected that national security was involved in the case against government assertions to the contrary.

[59] [1995] 4 All ER 427. See also Lord Woolf in *R v Lord Saville of Newdigate, ex p A* [1999] 4 All ER 860 at para. 37.

prejudice, nonetheless in the absence of the incorporation of the ECHR, the court's role was one of secondary judgment, not one of primary judgment: the constitutional balance between the executive and the judiciary had not shifted. 'In exercising merely a secondary judgment, the court is bound, even though adjudicating in a human rights context, to act with some reticence.' Even though the Minister's decision was wrong it was not *Wednesbury* unreasonable. In the Court of Appeal, Bingham MR felt the issue was 'justiciable' and the more substantial the interference with human rights the more the courts would require by way of justification before it was satisfied that a decision was unreasonable. But he rejected a call for a more probing form of review because human rights were involved. This position of sententious reticence is now highly questionable in human rights cases as will be seen below.[60]

Ex p Smith approved the positions adopted by the majority in *Brind*. The ban of broadcasting considered in *Brind* was discussed above. It was held by the majority in *Brind* that in a case involving an infringement of a fundamental human right, viz upon freedom of expression under Article 10, the person exercising a broad statutory power has to show that such an infringement could only be justified by an 'important competing public interest'[61] a point repeated in *ex p Smith*.[62] What was becoming clear before the incorporation of the HRA 1998 was that where infringements of fundamental rights were concerned the courts were giving less leeway to discretion. They were showing a lower margin of discretion to the decision maker. 'The courts in these cases do not only interfere where the decision maker acted 'perversely' or 'absurdly' or took 'leave of his senses'. Instead, they ask the question 'whether a reasonable decision maker, on the material before him, could reasonably conclude that the interference was justifiable'.[63] As Jowell and Birkinshaw indicated, this test lowers the threshold of unreasonableness and is approaching the concept of proportionality. In addition, it has been held that decisions infringing some

---

[60]   Chapter 9, p 396 and *ex p Daly* p 343 below.

[61]   *Per* Lords Bridge and Roskill in *R v Secretary of State for the Home Department, ex p Brind* [1991] 1 AC 696, HL, at 749–51.

[62]   See *DPP v Jones* [1999] 2 All ER 257.

[63]   J Jowell and P Birkinshaw 'English Report' in *Administrative Law under European Influence* (1996) ed J Schwarze, p 288. This is the test laid down by the majority (Lords Bridge, Roskill and Templeman) in the *Brind* case, [1991] 1 All ER 720. See also *R v Secretary of State for the Environment, ex p NALGO* (1992) Times, 2 December.

human rights should receive the 'most anxious scrutiny' of the courts.[64] A most anxious scrutiny, but not necessarily a judicial review, as Lord Steyn was to point out in *Daly*. In other words, the courts were beginning to familiarise themselves with the approach of proportionality; but they were at that time reluctant to follow through first principles to a logical conclusion.

I have noted elsewhere in this book Lord Diplock's statement that domestic statutes should be construed, if they are reasonably capable, of bearing a meaning which is consistent with obligations originating in Community treaties (Chapter 4, p 187 et seq).[65] In *Brind*[66] the House of Lords upheld the Home Secretary's ban (above). The Law Lords were not prepared to construe the statute in question in a manner which was consistent with Article 10 ECHR guaranteeing the right to broadcast. The very fact that the power was given in such broad terms meant there was nothing the courts could do in the face of inconsistency with international norms.[67] Unlike Lord Diplock, a 'mere canon of construction' could not be used to bring 'international law into the domestic field'.[68] A very disappointing feature of the decision was that the ECHR could not be a relevant consideration and the Home Secretary was under no duty to have regard to the Convention as such a consideration.[69]

---

[64] Per Lord Bridge in *Bugdaycay v Home Secretary* [1987] AC 514 at 531, speaking of the right to life in a deportation case. Such decisions, he said would be subject to a 'more rigorous examination'. See also Lord Templeman at pp 537–8. In the context of extradition see *R v Home Secretary, ex p Osman* (1992) Independent, 10 September. See also *National and Local Government Officers' Association v Secretary of State for the Environment* (1992) Times, 2 December applying the test to the restriction on the political activities on local government officers. See also *R v Home Secretary, ex p Brind* [1991] 1 AC 696. In *Prest v Secretary of State for Wales* (1982) 81 LGR 193, Watkins LJ said that compulsory purchase decisions must be 'carefully scrutinised', and Lord Denning MR said the Secretary of State must in such cases show that the public interest 'decisively demands ' the compulsory purchase order.

[65] Per Lord Diplock in Case 12/81 *Garland v British Rail Engineering Ltd* [1983] 2 AC 751 at 771.

[66] [1991] 1 AC 696.

[67] Broadcasting Act 1990, s 10(3) (in relation to the IBA (now ITC), and cl 13 (4) of the BBC's licence and agreement both provide that the Home Secretary may require the ITC or BBC to refrain from broadcasting matters specified.

[68] Per Lord Bridge at 748. International law was held to involve not only the Convention but also the jurisprudence of the CHR. Lord Ackner felt that the application of the presumption in this case would involve the incorporation of the Convention through the 'back door' ([1991] 1 AC 696 at 761–62).

[69] Lord Templeman dissented on this point. On the facts the Home Secretary did have regard to the Convention.

The point raised and rejected in *Brind* has been the subject of several high profile cases since 1993, which have developed points of statutory construction in English courts. The most recent of these, *R v Secretary of State, ex p Daly*[70] has been the most dramatic development to date in the incorporation of proportionality. In *R v Secretary of State for the Home Department, ex p Leech (No 2)*[71] a prisoner applied for judicial review for a declaration that delegated legislation, the Prison Rules, were ultra vires the Prison Act 1952. That Act conferred wide powers on the authorities to make rules for the regulation of prisons and the control of prisoners. The Rules stated that it was permissible to stop prisoners' correspondence on the ground that correspondence was 'objectionable or of inordinate length.' The applicant contended however that the Act did not authorise the power to stop prisoners' correspondence on the ground set out in the Rules because this interfered with his right to communicate with his solicitor and thus in effect his right to unimpeded access to the courts.[72] 'The Court of Appeal upheld this contention and struck down the Rules. They held that the more fundamental a right interfered with, the more difficult it was to imply such a power. There was no 'objective need' for such a rule, and no 'self evident and pressing need for an unrestricted power to read letters between prisoners and a solicitor.'[73]

In *R v Secretary of State for the Home Department, ex p Simms*[74] two prisoners challenged decisions to prevent them being interviewed by journalists investigating the safety of their convictions. The Home Secretary argued that a blanket ban was lawful for the maintenance of good order and discipline in prison and was justified under Standing Orders made under the Prison Act 1952 and Prison Rules and the prison authorities refused to allow interviews unless the journalists signed undertakings not to publish any part of the interview. Lord Steyn referred to evidence showing the beneficial impact of journalists on righting injustice over the previous ten years. He stated that the Home Office affidavits did not show a pressing social need which might prevail over a fundamental right of access to justice. American case law, which had allowed a great degree of judicial deference to US prison authorities 'does not accord with the approach

---

[70]   [2001] UKHL 26, [2001] 3 All ER 433.

[71]   [1993] 4 All ER 539.

[72]   *Raymond v Honey* [1983] 1 AC 1.

[73]   J Jowell and P Birkinshaw 'English Report' in *Administrative Law under European Influence* (1996) ed J Schwarze, pp 288–89.

[74]   [1999] 3 All ER 400.

under English law' (p 411c). 'It is also inconsistent with the principle that the more substantial the interference with fundamental rights the more the court will require by way of justification before it can be satisfied that the interference is reasonable in a public law sense' (p 411d). In deciding whether the Standing Orders allowed interference with a basic right, Lord Steyn held that 'even in the absence of ambiguity there comes into play a presumption of general application operating as a constitutional principle .... 'the principle of legality' and this principle leaves untouched the fundamental and basic rights asserted by the prisoner in the present case.' The Standing Order could be construed in a manner which did not have to authorise an outright ban so they were not ultra vires but the policy of the Secretary of State and the decisions of the authorities as described above were unlawful in their interference. It should be observed that *Simms* was a case under common law. So was the following.

R v Secretary of State for the Home Department, ex p Daly[75] is the most important case on proportionality. It is another case concerning a prisoner. The Secretary of State had introduced a new policy of searching cells in closed prisons in England and Wales. This was done in the absence of prisoners so that correspondence between a prisoner and their lawyer could be examined without interference by a prisoner to ensure that it was bona fide correspondence. Absence was mandatory in all cases. Daly challenged the policy arguing that the Prison Act 1952 did not authorise such a blanket policy. In reversing the decision of the Court of Appeal, the House of Lords in the judgment of Lord Bingham held that such a blanket policy infringed the prisoner's rights to confidentiality of their privileged correspondence with lawyers to an extent greater than had been shown to be necessary to maintain security, order and discipline and crime prevention. Section 47 of the Act did not authorise such interference and under the Convention any infringement was also greater than necessary in a democratic society in the interests of national security, public safety and other listed items under Article 8(2) ECHR which form the proviso to Article 8(1) which guarantees the right to privacy.

Lord Steyn agreed with the above decision expressed by Bingham and but for 'one narrow but important point' had nothing to add. That point concerned proportionality. He referred to a decision of Lord Phillips in *Mahmood* (see Chapter 9, p 383) where Lord Phillips had applied the Convention to an immigration case which occurred before the Act came

---

[75] [2001] UKHL 26, [2001] 3 All ER 433.

into effect.[76] In explaining the approach to review under the Act, he said that one should apply an 'anxious scrutiny' based on *Wednesbury* as supplemented by the test of necessity in accordance with 'European jurisprudence'.

Having made reference to the oblique reference to *Wednesbury* in the dicta of the Master of the Rolls, Lord Steyn referred to the test of heightened scrutiny adopted in cases such as *ex p Smith*. There is a considerable difference between the *Wednesbury* and *ex p Smith* grounds of review and the approach of proportionality applicable in respect of review where convention rights are at stake. Referring to the contributions of academic lawyers, he says:

> The starting point is that there is an overlap between the traditional grounds of review and the approach of proportionality. Most case would be decided in the same way whichever approach is adopted. But the intensity of review is somewhat greater under the proportionality approach. ... I would mention three concrete differences [non exhaustive]. First, the doctrine of proportionality may require the reviewing court to assess the balance which the decision maker has struck, not merely whether it is within the range of rational or reasonable decisions. Secondly, the proportionality test may go further than the traditional grounds of review in as much as it might require attention to be directed to the relative weight accorded to interests and considerations. Thirdly, even the heightened scrutiny test developed in *ex p Smith* is not necessarily appropriate to the protection of human rights. (p 446)

In this last point he noted that when *Smith* went to the CHR, the reluctant refusal of the courts in England to rule the ban unlawful was not followed in that Court which believed that the domestic courts had set too high a threshold for review which 'effectively excluded any consideration by the domestic courts of the question of whether the interference with the applicants' rights answered a pressing social need or was proportionate to the national security and public order aims pursued.'

Given this difference in the tests, they may well sometimes produce different results. This does not mean that there is now a merits review. Citing Professor Jowell, Lord Steyn agrees that the 'respective role of judges and

---

[76] [2001] 1 WLR 840, CA and note *R v Kansal (No 2)* [2002] 1 All ER 257, [2001] UKHL 62, and retroactivity on criminal matters.

administrators are fundamentally distinct and will remain so.'[77] Following Laws LJ in *Mahmood* he felt that the intensity of review would depend upon the subject matter, not only as between rights but as between fundamental rights. This would be particularly relevant in cases involving Convention rights: there were in other words different degrees of intensity among Convention rights: some are absolute, some are not, a point that was made above.[78] This point was made by Sedley J in *McQuillan* (see p 382 et seq).[79] However, even in those cases where a right to life is in question, the courts in England have not been prepared to interfere with a discretionary decision which would alter the basis of allocation of funding within the health service.[80] Such a decision would have to judge between conflicting medical opinions about the chances of success for the treatment and would effectively decide how a health authority should allocate its 'limited budget.'

Just a few brief comments to conclude this section. First of all, special consideration has been given in the HRA 1998 to the balancing of rights to freedom of speech and to pass on information and the right to privacy. This will be addressed in the following chapter. That chapter will also cover decisions involving difficult security and immigration cases given heightened sensitivity because of events in New York on 11 September 2001.

4. Managerial and policy decisions

In *ex p Smith* (above) Sir T Bingham observed that the greater the policy content of a decision, and the more remote the subject matter of a decision

---

[77] J Jowell (2000) Public Law 671; see also I Leigh (2002) Public Law 265, and for a Commonwealth overview: D Dyzenhaus, M Hunt and M Taggart (2001) *Oxford University Commonwealth LJ* 5 on internationalism and constitutionalisation.

[78] Cf Laws LJ and his decision in *Thoburn v Sunderland City Council* [2002] EWHC 195 (Admin) [2002] 4 All ER 156 (above Ch 4, p 157 et seq). It will be recalled that Laws suggested a hierarchy of norms with a superior status for 'constitutional rights'. It could be argued that Lord Steyn in *Daly* gives support for that argument, certainly in terms of intensity of review where a fundamental human right is concerned.

[79] *R v Secretary of State for the Home Department, ex p McQuillan* [1995] 4 All ER 400.

[80] *R v Cambridge District Health Authority, ex p B* [1995] 2 All ER 129 at 137. This case concerned the young child who had leukaemia and treatment as advised by specialists would have involved considerable expense. The authority refused to allocate such funding. The first instance hearing ruled the decision unlawful because it had not considered the child's right to life and quashed the decision – but did not order treatment. The Court of Appeal overruled this decision.

from ordinary judicial experience, the more hesitant the court must necessarily be in holding a decision to be irrational. We have seen how the HLs has rejected the argument that in cases of human rights a more exacting form of review should not be involved. What role does proportionality have in reviewing managerial and policy decisions?

The case above of the health authority shows how reluctant courts may be even when treatment leading to saving a life is concerned. An indication of the approach to be adopted can be seen in two cases of the House of Lords where the Law Lords refused to hold unreasonable decisions of the Secretary of State for the Environment in the exercise of powers to control the expenditure of local authorities.[81]

In both cases the standard of unreasonableness was held to be 'extreme' and was formulated to include decisions 'so absurd that [the decision maker] must have taken leave of his senses.'[82] One might ask how this differs from the standard test of unreasonableness in *Wednesbury*. In *Hammersmith and Fulham*, the question concerned the power of the Secretary of State to cap the local authority's community charge if the authority's budget was set at a level which he considered 'excessive' in accordance with principles determined by him. Lord Bridge held that the setting of a norm of local government expenditure was 'essentially a matter of political opinion', and that the question whether a local authority's budget for a year is 'excessive' cannot be judged by any 'objective criterion'.[83]

These two cases do not rule out the possibility of a finding of unreasonableness in decisions that cannot be judged by any 'objective criterion',[84] but the threshold of unreasonableness (or margin of discretion) in such cases will be high. The rationale for this has a sound constitutional basis: courts are not suited to taking decisions involving policy, the allocation of resources and economic and social preference. Decisions of this kind, should, except in extreme situations, be left for determination by

---

[81]   *Nottinghamshire County Council v Secretary of State for the Environment* [1986] AC 240; *R v Secretary of State for the Environment, ex p Hammersmith and Fulham London Borough Council* [1991] 1 AC 521.

[82]   [1991] 1 AC 521 per Lord Bridge at 596.

[83]   [1991] 1 AC 521 per Lord Bridge at 596.

[84]   See J Jowell 'The Legal Control of Administrative Discretion' (1973) PL 178 at 200ff.

elected officials.'[85] A test of what approach will be adopted in a case involving managerial discretion and Community rights and the right to protest came in the *ITF* case.[86]

Animal rights protestors were mass picketing a Sussex port to prevent lorries carrying livestock reaching vessels chartered to export them. The chief constable advised the lorry owners that he would have to reduce the police presence at the port because the strain on his manpower was reducing his ability to provide efficient and effective policing as required by law in other parts of the community. He further advised that if lorries could not safely reach the vessels with the police protection, they would be turned back from the port to prevent confrontation with the protestors. The owners claimed this was unreasonable and a breach of Article 29 [34] EC which prohibits quantitative restrictions on exports, and all measures having equivalent effect between Member States. Taking an 'overall approach', Lord Slynn believed that neither the right to protest nor the right to trade lawfully was absolute. Both had to be balanced by the Chief Constable in the light of the manpower, resources and other relevant considerations. Lord Slynn did not show any enthusiasm for upsetting the Chief Constable's judgement because an improper balance had been made. Furthermore, in discussing the claim under Article 29 [34] EC, he said that: 'What is required .... where the chief constable has common law and statutory duties to perform, is to ask whether he did all that proportionately and reasonably he could be expected to do with the resources available to him.' Decisions are taken on the information available at the time and there should be no ex post facto examination of accounts to see whether a decision was justified. 'In *Brind*', he continued 'the House treated *Wednesbury* reasonableness and proportionality as being different.[87] So in some ways they are, though the distinction between the two tests in practice is in any event much less than is sometimes suggested.' On the facts of this case believed Lord Cooke, the result under either test would be the same. This may well be true in this case as the judgments show in upholding the legality of the Chief Constable's decision, but the

---

85 It should however be noted that both these cases were coloured by the fact that the House of Commons had by resolution approved the Secretary of State's decisions. While these resolutions of course fall short of statutory authority, they do constitute strong additional evidence of the 'rationality' of the decisions.

86 *R v Chief Constable of Sussex, ex p International Traders Ferry Ltd* [1999] 1 All ER 129, HL.

87 The majority view in *Brind* was that if proportionality existed, it was a component of *Wednesbury*. They are not co-extensive and proportionality was not a discrete head of review.

same result may well not occur in all cases, particularly those concerning human rights as *Daly* so graphically shows. Even assuming that the police decision could constitute 'measures' under Article 34 [29] EC they were justified on grounds of public policy which were neither disproportionate nor unreasonable.

The principle of equality

The principle of equality is another general principle of Community law. We saw the importance of this principle in French and German constitutional and administrative law in Chapters 2 and 3. As Professor Jowell has said, equality as a principle is not often explicitly articulated in English law. In some ways it is inherent however in the constitutional principle (even in an unwritten constitution) of the rule of law.[88] Its existence under the Human Rights Act was dramatically illustrated when Collins J sitting as the Chair of the Special Immigration Appeals Tribunal declared provisions of the Anti-terrorism, Crime and Security Act 2001 incompatible with the HRA 1998 insofar as they discriminated against non-British nationals detained indefinitely in high security jails – they were being treated unequally. The decision was reversed by the Court of Appeal which held that in this situation, different treatment between nationals and aliens who posed a threat to national security was unavoidable.[89]

In elaborating the Rule of Law Dicey said that 'With us every official, from the Prime Minister down to a constable or a collector of taxes, is under the same responsibility for every act done without legal justification as any other citizen.'[90] What Dicey is expressing is a concept of what has been called formal equality, by which he meant that no person is exempt from

---

[88] J Jowell in J Jowell and D Oliver eds *The Changing Constitution* (2000, 4th ed) ch 1.

[89] *A v Secretary of State for the Home Department* [2002] EWCA Civ 1502, [2002] 46 LS Gaz R 33; unavoidable because in the absence of a safe country to receive them they could not be deported and it would be unsafe, on the 'say-so' of the Minister, to allow them to go free within the jurisdiction. Articles 5 and 14 ECHR were in issue. The Convention does not prohibit discrimination itself: see Ch 9, p 376 and (2002) New LJ 1357 for the Commission. See: *Phillips v DPP* [2002] EWHC 2093 (Admin), [2002] All ER (D) 401 (Oct) 'Discrimination against mini-cabs justifiable!' and *Gurung v Ministry of Defence* [2002] EWHC 2463 (Admin), [2002] All ER (D) 409 (Nov).

[90] A V Dicey, *The Law of the Constitution* (1885) (1959, 10th ed) ed E C S Wade, p 193.

the enforcement of the law. Rich and poor, revenue official and individual taxpayer are all within equal reach of the arm of the law.

This kind of equality, although important, is limited because its primary concern is not with the content of the law but with its *enforcement* and *application* alone. The Rule of Law is satisfied as long as laws are applied or enforced equally, that is, even-handedly, free of bias and without irrational distinction. Dicey's version of the Rule of Law requires formal equality which prohibits laws from being enforced unequally, but it does not require substantive equality. It does therefore not prohibit unequal laws. It constrains, say, racially-biased *enforcement* of laws, but does not inhibit the *making* of racially-biased laws in the first place.[91] As Professor Fuller observed, such discriminatory laws may well be in breach of the 'internal morality of law' which will lead to a denial of the rule of law in the manner in which they operate.[92] They are certainly in breach of ethical considerations of substantive justice based on equal concern and respect and humane treatment which a concept of legality would have to address and meet to satisfy a test of legitimacy.

To what extent is equality in both its senses found in the common law? First, there are some ancient duties placed upon the likes of inn-keepers, common carriers and some monopoly enterprises such as ports and harbours, to accept all travellers and others who are 'in a reasonably fit condition to be received.'[93] The reach of these laws was not sufficient to prevent racial discrimination in other public places and therefore, in the 1960s, legislation outlawing discrimination first on racial grounds, and later on grounds of sex, was introduced.[94] These laws cover discrimination in employment, education, the provision of goods and services, and some other areas in relation to racial discrimination. They have been added to,

---

[91] J Jowell 'The Legal Control of Administrative Discretion' (1973) PL 178 at 200ff.

[92] L Fuller *The Morality of Law* (revised 1969).

[93] *Rothfield v North British Rly Co* 1920 SC 805; *Pidgeon v Legge* (1857) 21 JP 743. Prior to privatisation the services of some utilities were also required to be offered without discrimination. See eg *South of Scotland Electricity Board v British Oxygen Ltd* [1959] 1 WLR 587, HL. Universal service without discrimination is now the basic presumption: see Ch 12.

[94] See generally, A Lester and G Bindman, *Race and the Law* (1972); the governing statutes are now the Race Relations Act 1976 and the Sex Discrimination Act 1975. See also the Equal Pay Act 1970.

to provide a more extensive coverage of public authorities.[95] Laws attempting to correct market distortions were also introduced (see Chapter 12).

The above laws were statutory incursions and have been added to in the form of laws outlawing discrimination on grounds of disability and religion and politics, the latter in Northern Ireland although the government announced plans in October 2002 to outlaw religious discrimination in employment in England and Wales.[96] There is the strongest authority to show that treating parties unequally at common law, where no good grounds exist is an abuse of power where it reveals 'bad faith' which includes malice, fraud, personal bias or dishonesty. These factors vitiate the legality of the exercise of power.[97]

Most decisions invoking substantive inequality have been struck down under the ground of judicial review known as 'unreasonableness' or 'irrationality'. In cases of this kind, wide discretionary power has normally been conferred on the decision-maker, and the courts – through judicial review – must be careful to allow the decision-maker a sufficiently wide margin of appreciation or discretion. Courts therefore intervene under the formula set out in the 1947 case of *Wednesbury* (see above) only when the decision is 'so unreasonable that no reasonable decision-maker would so act'[98]. The example of a clearly unreasonable decision provided in the *Wednesbury* case was that of a teacher dismissed from her post on the ground of her red hair alone.

Underneath the shadow of *Wednesbury* unreasonableness, however, a principle of equality can be discerned which has often been invoked in politically contentious case law concerning unequal treatment of rate payers whom, it was felt, were victims in some degree of socialist philanthropy.[99] Aside from the easy trap of expressing the outcome of these cases in terms of political hostility by conservative judiciary, and there doubtless was some of that, there is a concern expressed about unequal

---

95   Race Relations (Amendment) Act 2000.
96   See the EC Treaty and Directives on discrimination in Ch 9, p 375 et seq.
97   See *Nagle v Fielden* [1966] 2 QB 633; *Edwards v SOGAT* [1971] Ch 354. Both decisions of Lord Denning.
98   *Associated Provincial Picture Houses Ltd v Wednesbury Corpn* [1948] 1 KB 223.
99   *Roberts v Hopwood* [1925] AC 578; *Prescott v Birmingham Corpn* [1955] Ch 210; *Bromley London Borough Council v Greater London Council* [1983] 1 AC 768.

treatment in a manner which is not justified by the statutory schemes in question. The courts struck down abuse of housing queues to give political advantage to a prospective councillor because this was unfair on others waiting for council accommodation and suggests a concern with an absence of equality.[100] Sedley J has observed that 'discretionary public power must not be exercised ... with partiality as between individuals or classes potentially affected by it'[101] and regulations have been struck down where they manifested 'unjust and unreasonable treatment' resulting in gross inequality of treatment on the basis of the wealth of immigrants.[102] Although the courts are reluctant to question decisions concerning peer review – as for instance in assessing the quality of an institution's research portfolio for a government sponsored Research Assessment Exercise which would have financial repercussions for institutions, any evidence of discrimination of sex or a racial nature 'and more may come' in decision-making – ie unequal treatment – may impose a duty to explain why decisions were arrived at. In the absence of such factors, there was no general duty to explain why decisions were reached.[103]

Judges and lawyers generally appreciate that treating all persons as formally equal and turning a blind eye to economic or social reality can cause serious injustice. Unequal treatment is, after all, the basis of class and caste distinction. The rigours of formality are tempered very often by discretionary schemes which allow justice to be done in the individual case by way of carefully reasoned exception. The law will not allow a discretion conferred to be rigidly confined – this will be to subvert the discretion which has been given; discretion means a differentiation in decision and that decisions have to be tailored to the circumstances. A great deal of administrative justice since the 1970s has concentrated upon the balance to be struck between fixed rules and discretionary schemes, between individual certainty and individual justice on the facts.[104] Setting out guidance for the exercise of such rules is a feature of good administration provided the guidance is published and that decision makers are:

> always be prepared to listen to someone with something new to say.
> Discretion may not be fettered. The decision-maker must be willing to
> depart from a rule aimed at all equally (that is, seeking formal equality), by

---

100 *R v Port Talbot Borough Council, ex p Jones* [1988] 2 All ER 207.
101 *R v MAFF, ex p Hamble* [1995] 2 All ER 714 at 722b.
102 *R v Immigration Appeal Tribunal, ex p Manshoora Begum* [1986] Imm AR 385.
103 *R v Higher Education Funding Council, ex p Institute of Dental Surgery* [1994] 1 All ER 651 at 671g–h.
104 See generally DJ Galligan *Discretionary Powers* (1986).

allowing the applicant to show that difference in treatment is justified in the particular case (that is, in order to achieve substantive equality).[105]

The issue of equality will arise on complaints under Article 8 ECHR where an individual's right to family life and privacy may not be breached. It was seen in *Smith* above, when homosexual members of the UK armed forces were dismissed on account of their sexual orientation, the Court of Appeal felt that it could not interfere with an exercise of executive discretion despite the obvious inequality involved.[106] Subsequently, the CHR ruled the ban to be an unjustified breach of Article 8 and the British executive has subsequently changed its policy.[107]

In *R v MAFF, ex p First City Trading Ltd*,[108] the High Court refused to apply the general principles of Community law in a case which did not raise a point of law under the Community competence. The principle invoked was 'equality'. Laws J drew a rigid division between cases within the Community competence and those of a purely domestic provenance. The principle of equality has become a principle of domestic law, or more correctly, it has long been a domestic principle given fuller expression under European influence. It may be on the facts that the decision in *First City* was correct. Laws certainly spelt out how the approach in his view of Community law and domestic law differed. But it is presently contended that the principle of equality may be invoked under domestic provisions as well as under Community ones. Under Community law, unequal treatment would have to be justified on grounds satisfying tests of proportionality: that it was necessary, not excessive and represented a proper balance of relevant considerations.

Under domestic law unequal treatment by a public official would have to be justified. Justification would, on a traditional approach, only be set aside if irrational. It remains to be seen whether equality has acquired a higher status as a fundamental human right deserving of protection by an 'anxious scrutiny.'

---

[105]   J Jowell and P Birkinshaw 'English Report' in *Administrative Law under European Influence* (1996) ed J Schwarze, p 281.

[106]   *R v Ministry of Defence, ex p Smith* [1996] 1 All ER 257, CA.

[107]   *Smith and Grady v UK* (1999) 29 EHRR 493; see the ECJ cases in Ch 2 notes 89 and 166. See *R v Secretary of State for Foreign and Commonwealth Affairs, ex p Manelfi* [1996] 12 CL 65 and national security considerations.

[108]   [1997] 1 CMLR 250.

Legal certainty

'Legal certainty' has an established position in the lexicon of general principles of European Law. It is a central feature of a *rechtsstaat*: a state built on law. Common lawyers may not until recently have referred to 'legal certainty' as such, but the message this doctrine seeks to embody would readily be understood within the terms of the Rule of Law.[109] Where Dicey referred to the supremacy of regular law over 'arbitrary' action he was to some extent anticipating the doctrine of legal certainty so familiar to civil systems. Dicey's rule of law required law to be certain, that is, predictable and not retrospective in its application. Courts thus presume that legislation is not intended to operate retrospectively,[110] unless there are beneficent reasons for making its operation retrospective. In *Marks and Spencer plc v Customs and Excise Comrs*[111] the ECJ ruled that removal of a right for a complainant to claim repayment of amounts of VAT paid in breach of Community law by retroactively reducing a limitation period was a breach of legal effectiveness and of a legitimate expectation, but underlying the case is a clear breach of legal certainty. Limits have been placed on the retrospective application of the HRA 1998, although this has caused difficulties (see Chapter 9). English legal tradition placed limits on the application of international norms in English courts because the norms that bind us should be at our sufferance and consent, or reflect the custom and practice of our communities. We were an exporter of norms not an importer. Today's world is ever more compacted and universalised making national autonomy ever more impossible. However, the most striking domestic judicial endorsement of legal globalisation – the *Pinochet* judgment – still set strict limits to the retrospective operation of norms derived from international conventions.[112]

---

109   See Jowell, 'The Rule of Law Today' in *The Changing Constitution* eds Jowell and Oliver (1994, 3rd ed) Oxford.

110   See *R v Secretary of State for the Home Department, ex p Mundowa* [1992] 3 All ER 606, CA presumption against retroactivity of statute did not necessarily apply merely because some of the facts with which the statute was concerned occurred before it was passed. The case involved removal of an appeal from a specified date against the Home Secretary's discretion to deport even though the immigrant was liable to be deported before the date of that right's removal came into effect. This, the Court of Appeal held, was the clear intention of Parliament provided that the decision to deport was taken after the date of the removal of the right of an appeal on the merits.

111   Case C-62/00 [2002] 3 CMLR 9.

112   Compare the *Pinochet (No 3)* judgment [1999] 2 All ER 97, HL with *Pinochet (No 1)* [1998] 4 All ER 897, HL.

One further example viz, the preparedness of the courts to rule administrative regulations or decisions void where they are uncertain in content or effect – also shows the doctrine at work. At the same time the courts will apply tests of severance, either textual or 'substantial', to legal instruments which will allow the good part to be saved if it makes sense when detached from the offending part of the instrument unless removal of the offending part destroys the meaning or original intent of what remains or leaves the instrument ultra vires.[113]

Laws and instruments having an impact upon individuals' rights should be published.[114] The protection of a legitimate expectation (which is examined below) – is based on a notion of legal certainty preventing authorities in certain circumstances from going back on their word or expectations drawn from their behaviour. This has caused a great amount of litigation where an individual claims that a representation of entitlement has been made by an official which on further analysis amounts to an ultra vires representation. The choice is inevitably stark. Either the official is estopped from going back on the representation to avoid injustice to an individual who has innocently acted on the representation to his detriment, or an official may be encouraged to act in a manner which is ultra vires with a consequential damage to the public interest. Although use of the term estoppel was employed originally to describe the relief granted[115] the term has not been resorted to in more recent years unless the specific grounds of estoppel are established; the term carries with it specific legal technicalities. As Sedley J also advised, an official cannot be estopped from performing his lawful duty. He may, however, be required by the court to fulfil a legitimate expectation and act fairly in exercising his powers.[116]

---

113   On textual and substantial severability ie ignoring the offending parts but where a textual severability is not possible, is: *DPP v Hutchinson* [1990] 2 All ER 836, HL.

114   While it is clear that legislation and regulations must be published, difficult questions do arise about the position of administrative circulars and guidance. Where these are used to determine the rights or claims of individuals they should be published and this has happened in prison administration in England. However, not all codes or guidance are published - a position with which the Court of Appeal and Divisional Court have refused to interfere: *R v Secretary of State for the Home Department, ex p Westminster Press* [1992] COD 303, DC and *R v Home Secretary, ex p Northumbria Police Authority* [1988] 1 All ER 556, CA.

115   de Smith calls it quasi estoppel *Judicial Review of Administrative Action* (1973, 3rd ed).

116   *R v MAFF, ex p Hamble* [1995] 2 All ER 714t at 725h–j. The House of Lords has held that estoppel has no place in public law; legitimate expectation was the

After a good deal of uncertainty, much of it caused by Lord Denning, the position now is that an official cannot be bound by a representation which is ultra vires whether in a procedural or substantive sense.[117] It will be recalled that this differs from the position in German administrative law (p 144 et seq above). It is, nevertheless, true to say that courts have adopted a more flexible approach to what is ultra vires or what may amount to an unlawful refusal to exercise a discretion and that the doctrine of legitimate expectation provides assistance in a manner that would not have previously been possible (see below). But the basic statement still holds, although the courts were prepared to come to the assistance of a representee acting in good faith. A series of cases has laid down that where the authorities represent that a state of affairs will exist, or that they will behave in a particular way, they are not allowed to go back on their word and place the representee at a disadvantage.[118] They will be prevented from reneging on their representation. Until the 1970s the argument would have prevailed that to hold authorities to their representation would be a means of allowing them to fetter their discretion and thereby induce ultra vires action. Not so argued Lord Denning in a path-making judgment in 1972 known as the *Liverpool Taxis* case.[119] Where the representations did not bind the authorities to the result, but merely to the method of getting to a result and where that method improved the fairness of the process, then the authorities were not inhibiting administrative discretion but improving its exercise. So too in cases conferring amnesty on illegal immigrants where it was stated that an interview would be given before a decision was taken on whether or not to deport,[120] or where promises were made to conduct specific extra statutory procedures before a decision was taken concerning the adoption of an alien infant by naturalised British relatives.[121] Giving and then denying is a denial of legal certainty.

However, limits to withdrawing representations have been imposed where it would not be unfair to allow the authorities to withdraw from a

---

public law analogy which allowed the public interest to be considered: *R v East Sussex County Council, ex p Reprotech (Pebsham) Ltd* [2002] UKHL 8, [2002] 4 All ER 58.

[117] See P Craig *Administrative Law* (1999, 4th ed) 635 et seq.

[118] *R v Liverpool Corpn, ex p Liverpool Taxi Fleet Operators' Association* [1972] 2 QB 299, CA; *A-G of Hong Kong v Ng Yuen Shiu* [1983] 2 All ER 346, PC.

[119] See previous note.

[120] *A-G of Hong Kong v Ng Yuen Shiu* [1983] 2 All ER 346, PC.

[121] *Ex p Khan* [1985] 1 All ER 40, CA.

representation. In *Matrix-Securities v IRC*[122] which concerned tax allowances, the tax-payer could not insist that the Inland Revenue be bound by a representation in the tax-payer's favour for a variety of reasons. These included the fact that the whole story had not been told to the Inland Revenue by the tax-payer (they had not 'put all their cards up on the table'); the fact that the tax-payer had gone to a less senior authority than was necessary to obtain the representation (which also seemed suspicious) and that in the circumstances the Inland Revenue were not behaving unfairly or abusing their discretion. *Matrix Securities* reflects the balancing process nicely.

A less happy balance is exemplified by the decision of the House of Lords in *Findlay v Secretary of State for the Home Department*[123] where a change in existing policy on release of prisoners disadvantaged certain prisoners who challenged the change of policy on a number of grounds. There was considerable unease expressed by some of the judges at the manner in which the policy had been changed. Nevertheless the Court of Appeal and House of Lords refused to hold the process by which the change of policy had been brought about unlawful. Each prisoner's case, the courts believed, would still be given full, fair and careful consideration by the Home Secretary and it is important that the policy-making process not be 'fettered'.[124] This said Lord Scarman, was the extent of their 'legitimate expectation'.

Legitimate expectation

English law has long prided itself on its acute sense of, and sensitivity towards, fair procedure. This subject is acknowledged among many continental lawyers as a major contribution of the common law to public law jurisprudence. *Cooper v Wandsworth Board of Works*[125] exemplified the common law's readiness to protect individuals against over enthusiastic administrative action by public authorities, although a general principle that statutory powers must be exercised in a fair manner

---

[122]   [1994] 1 All ER 769, HL; see also *Preston v IRC* [1985] 2 All ER 327, HL and *R v Board of Inland Revenue ex p MFK Underwriting Agencies Ltd* [1990] 1 All ER 91, CA.

[123]   [1984] 3 All ER 801 (CA & HL).

[124]   But see Criminal Justice Act 1991, Part II and *Doody* [1993] 3 All ER 92, HL below in text.

[125]   (1863) 14 CBNS 180.

subsequently gave way for more than a century to over conceptualistic renderings of the range of interests to be protected where the decision was of a discretionary or executive nature. While the manner in which we conduct our criminal prosecutions and trials has attracted notorious criticism, our approach to administrative justice has shown manifestations of increasing subtlety and sophistication.[126] Much of this in recent years has developed around the doctrine of legitimate expectation which was first employed in an English case in 1969.[127] The concept had been used in German law before that time and it has been extensively invoked in English litigation to expand the range of interests that must be protected by way of a hearing or opportunity to make representations before an adverse decision is taken. In this sense it is referred to as 'procedural legitimate expectation'. The courts have shown themselves increasingly prepared to fulfil the expectation before an individual is deprived of a right or an interest, or where an official has represented that a hearing of a consultation shall take place before a decision is reached, or where s/he has acted in such a way that his/her actions create a legitimate expectation of a hearing. While its acceptance in English, German and Community law, and other systems is now apparent, it will be recalled that its existence was not upheld as a feature of French domestic law (Chapter 3). A legitimate expectation to fairness itself has, however, been seen as superfluous because fairness is a legal expectation inherent in the law.[128]

A significant development came with the decision in the GCHQ litigation[129] where the legitimate expectation of civil servants working at intelligence gathering headquarters to be heard or consulted before a decision was taken to prohibit them from trade union membership was accepted by the House of Lords; only the fact that national security was involved and that advance notice of the ban by way of a hearing might jeopardise that interest saved the government. While the courts have been cautious in preventing the development of a policy because of the fettering effect this would have if a substantive legitimation were fulfilled by judicial order, there have been additions to *procedural protection* by way of legitimate expectation. In

---

[126] Flowing from the decision of the House of Lords in *Ridge v Baldwin* [1964] AC 40 reasserting the right to natural justice in administrative decision making.

[127] *Schmidt v Secretary of State for Home Affairs* [1969] 1 All ER 904 at 909B, CA.

[128] *R v Devon County Council, ex p Baker* [1995] 1 All ER 73 Simon Brown LJ.

[129] *Council for Civil Service Unions v Minister for Civil Service* [1984] 3 All ER 935, HL.

the US Tobacco case[130] this emerging doctrine was illustrated quite clearly. Encouragement to a US company to establish factories in the UK to make nicotine substitutes, including the award by the government of development grants, could not prevent the government changing its policy on the manufacture of such substances to the detriment of the manufacturer. However, there was an expectation that the party would be consulted before the relevant regulations were made and that there would be access to relevant scientific material which the government had relied upon in arriving at its decision. In *R v Secretary of State for the Home Department, ex p Ruddock*[131] the doctrine of legitimate expectation was invoked to ensure that where a policy is announced in Parliament, it will not be changed until those relying upon its continuation have been informed of a proposed change and have been afforded the opportunity to make their views known.

When it comes to legitimate expectation of a thing as opposed to a procedure the law has been slow to take the continental lead on such matters. In Germany for instance a substantive legitimate expectation may defeat a duty expressed in law. After some diametrically opposed decisions, the authorities appear to have accepted that there is such a doctrine as substantive legitimate expectation. In *R v Secretary of State for Transport, ex p Richmond-upon-Thames London Borough Council*[132] while the court rejected the right to prevent a policy developing by invocation of legitimate expectation on the specific facts of the case, Laws J believed:

> I consider that the putative distinction between procedural and substantive rights in this context has little (if any) utility; the question is always whether the discipline of fairness, imposed by the common law, ought to prevent the public authority respondent from acting as it proposes. (at 595j)

He did believe, however, that neither precedent nor principle goes further than the enforcement of procedural legitimate expectation. That belief was about to be challenged.

The most interesting case from this time is the decision of Sedley J in the *Hamble Fisheries* case.[133] It generated a lively debate. The case involved

---

[130] *R v Secretary of State for Health, ex p United States Tobacco International Inc* [1992] 1 All ER 212 (QBD).
[131] [1987] 2 All ER 518.
[132] [1994] 1 All ER 577 (QBD).
[133] *R v MAFF, ex p Hamble Offshore Fisheries Ltd* [1995] 2 All ER 714.

fishing for 'pressure stocks'[134] and the transfer of pressure-stock licences between trawlers and to larger trawlers (aggregation) which had been encouraged by two MAFF policy statements. Subsequently, MAFF announced a moratorium on the transfer and aggregation of pressure stock licences. The plaintiff was informed that he could not use his trawler which had been subject to transfers and aggregation because it had not been licensed for pressure stocks and had no record of North Sea beam trawling. The plaintiff had carried out preparatory work altering the trawler in anticipation of employing the larger trawler for such fishing. He claimed he had a legitimate expectation in law that any changes in policy would not frustrate completion of the process of licence aggregation entitling him to fish for pressure stocks in the North Sea. He also claimed that special provision should have been made to allow licensing by track record of fishermen with track records who had entered into irrevocable commitments to acquire relevant licences demonstrating a real and genuine intent to do so.

Sedley J did not see why unfairness could not colour procedural as well as substantive expectations which were not fulfilled. He also believed that the case, involving as it did the common fisheries policy, had to make reference to EC law including substantive legitimate expectation.[135] 'What matters, therefore, in the common law both of the European Community and of Britain, is whether (in Professor Schwarze's words) the applicant can demonstrate 'an expectation which is worthy of protection'[136] (728c–d). Good administration requires that a public authority should implement its promises unless that interferes with its statutory duty.[137] Policies can of course, invariably must, be changed but they must be changed in a manner which is consistent with any intra vires act or representation which has brought about a legitimate expectation that it will be performed:

> Legitimacy in this sense is not an absolute. It is a function of expectations induced by government and of policy considerations which militate against their fulfilment. The balance must be in the first instance for the policy-maker to strike; but if the outcome is challenged by judicial review, I do not consider that the court's criterion is the bare rationality of the policy-

---

[134] These are 'species of fish which are incapable of sustaining unrestricted fishing within the limits of the applicable EC quota.' P.717.

[135] Case 120/86 *Mulder* [1988] ECR 2321; Case 152/88 *Sofrimport Sarl* [1988] ECR 2931; Case C-62/00 *Marks and Spencer plc v Customs and Excise Comrs* [2002] 3 CMLR 9 etc.

[136] At 728c–d. J Schwarze European Administrative Law (1992) at 1134.

[137] Lord Fraser in *A-G of Hong Kong v Ng Yuen Shiu* [1983] 2 All ER 346, PC.

maker's conclusion. While policy is for the policy maker alone, the fairness of his or her decision not to accommodate reasonable expectations which the policy will thwart remains the court's concern (as of course does the lawfulness of the policy). To postulate this is not to place the judge in the seat of the Minister. ... it is the court's task to recognise the constitutional importance of ministerial freedom to formulate and reformulate policy; but it is equally the court's duty to protect the interests of those individuals whose expectation of different treatment has a legitimacy which in fairness outtops the policy choice which threatens to frustrate it. (p 731c–e).

This is a passage of central importance. Sedley J is saying that in the circumstances where a Minister frustrates legitimate expectations, the judicial role is not an acceptance of the appearance of rationality of the Minister's decision but whether the decision is fair and lawful, and to assess this, the fairness of upholding the expectations and the public interest requiring a change in policy must be balanced.[138] But expectation may have to yield to policy change and provided a Minister acts lawfully, fairly and rationally a Minister may change his policy to serve the public interest. While a government must treat its citizens with solicitude, it has to be able to change its policies within its discretion properly exercised. In the case of the applicant, he had not come within two classes of exempted trawler owners by the relevant date and the Minister in order to draw a line as tightly around the existing fleet as possible to protect depleted stocks was entitled to change his policy. The applicant had a hope rather than an expectation and to allow him to succeed (along with many others in his class) might have subverted fishing policy. 'The means adopted bore a fair proportion to the end in view...' (p 735j).

This was a very sophisticated judgment using EC law to develop domestic law in a manner adopted elsewhere by Sedley J.[139] If we can learn from others, all to the good. A subsequent decision of the Court of Appeal[140] concerned a case where a time limit for making full tax returns had not been enforced for years but an informal practice of making draft returns was allowed followed by final returns. This long established practice was peremptorily terminated and the strictly formal procedure enforced causing substantial loss to the tax-payer. The court's decision in effect supported

---

[138]   P Craig (1992) 108 LQR 79.
[139]   *R v Secretary of State for the Home Department, ex p McQuillan* [1995] 4 All ER 400.
[140]   *R v IRC, ex p Unilever* (1996) STC 681.

the existence of substantive legitimate expectation although the view of the court was that the behaviour of the authorities was unreasonable. In another decision, however, the Court of Appeal categorically sought to bring quietus to the doctrine in its substantive form. Sedley's approach in *Hamble* was described as 'heresy'.[141] His reasoning was summarily dismissed and his ratio should be overruled. The dismissive tone was adopted without any regard to the sophistication or depth of his analysis and without any regard to the fact that it concerned a matter on which, in Sedley's opinion, EC law had to be considered. The approach to a question of substance, as opposed to procedure, was determined by a *Wednesbury* review of reasonableness. The case itself, which involved revocation of an early home leave scheme for prisoners was probably correctly decided. But the court rejected any test built on a balancing exercise based on fairness and proportionality; it also ignored the subject matter of *ex p Baker, ex p Khan* and *ex p Ruddock* and other cases. The Court of Appeal did hold that alleged breaches of Article 8 ECHR met the 'common law test' of pressing social need and proportionality. This was before the Convention was introduced into domestic law.

Ex p Coughlan[142] concerned a woman with severe physical disabilities who was moved to a purpose built NHS facility after an assurance that she could stay there for as long as she chose. No aspect of EC law was involved but it was held in addition to what was discussed in relation to substantive legitimate expectation that there was a breach of Article 8 ECHR (before the HRA 1998 took effect). Five years later the health authority decided to close the facility having re-classified the applicant's nursing care requirements as the responsibility of the local authority and for which she would have to pay. She would have to leave the premises. This decision on nursing care was taken after a policy statement by the NHS in the way of guidance. Although the CA held that the provision of nursing care was not the sole responsibility of the NHS it did find that the relevant eligibility criteria in this case were flawed and this did affect the decision to close the facility.

Lord Woolf, who delivered the judgment of the court of which Sedley LJ was a member, stated that there were three possible 'outcomes':

---

[141]   *R v Secretary of State, ex p Hargreaves* [1997] 1 All ER 397, CA.

[142]   *R v North and East Devon Health Authority, ex p Coughlan* [2000] 3 All ER 850, CA. See Hilson (2003) European Public Law 125.

(a) The court may decide that the public authority is only required to bear in mind its previous policy or other representation, giving it the weight it thinks right, but no more, before deciding whether to change course. Here the court is confined to reviewing the decision on *Wednesbury* grounds ... This has been held to be the effect of changes of policy in cases involving the early release of prisoners (*Findlay* and *Hargreaves* above) ... (b) On the other hand the court may decide that the promise or practice induces a legitimate expectation of, for example, being consulted before a particular decision is taken. Here it is uncontentious that the court itself will require *the opportunity for consultation* to be given unless there is an overriding reason to resile from it .... in which case the court will itself judge the adequacy of the reason advanced for the change of policy, taking into account what fairness requires. (c) Where the court considers that a lawful promise or practice has induced a legitimate expectation of a *benefit which is substantive*, not simply procedural, authority now establishes that here too the court will in a proper case decide whether to frustrate the expectation is so unfair that to take a new and different course will amount to an abuse of power. Here, once the legitimacy of the expectation is established, the court will have the task of weighing the requirements of fairness against any overriding interest relied upon for the change of policy. (pp 871–872)

But in this case there had been a promise from which the authority should not resile unless there were overriding reasons of justification. In *Hargreaves,* the duty to consider each individual case in the light of existing policy had been met. The decision to move the applicant in *Coughlan* was unfair because it upset her legitimate expectation which the authority had created in representing that the facility would be her home for the rest of her life.

The representation arises either from (i) an express promise, or (ii) a pattern or practice of behaviour. Reliance on the representation does not seem to be necessary although if an individual does not know that a representation has been made, she has not been allowed to rely upon it.[143] In *R v Secretary of State for Education, ex p Begbie*[144] Sedley LJ in the Court of Appeal

---

[143]   *R v Secretary of State for the Home Department, ex p Hindley* [2000] 2 All ER 385, HL.

[144]   [2000] 1 WLR 1115. See also: *R (Association of British Civilian Internees, Far East Region) v Secretary of State for Defence* [2002] EWHC 2119 (Admin), [2002] All ER (D) 271 (Oct), a case also relevant for the principle of equality which was unsuccessfully pleaded to challenge as discriminatory non-payment of ex gratia compensation to internees of wartime Japanese internment camps who were non qualifying British subjects.

stated that a general representation made by government may create a legitimate expectation even though there is no specific reliance of the applicant. It was sufficient that government had made known its intention. An enforceable expectation had not been made out on the facts. Revocation of a representation must be clear and unambiguous for it not longer to be 'fulfillable' by the representee.

Rights to defence

Rights to defence covers the range of practices which in English law amount to fair procedure or natural justice. As we saw in Chapter 3, p 94 the influence of English principles in this area has been considerable in Community law. It includes rights to hearings conducted fairly, legal representation, knowledge of charges of complaints against one, an absence of bias – in general, fairness in action. Crucial to success in many claims against both public and private bodies is the possession of information and evidence to establish one's case; and the right to keep legal advice privileged. In private actions, English law is generous in allowing 'discovery' or disclosure as it is now known, and inspection of the relevant documents in the possession of other parties to litigation. Judicial review allows less scope. In the case of public bodies, there are frequent resorts to what is known as 'public interest immunity' ie, the authority is allowed by a court to hold back documents in the public interest because of some apprehended injury to national security, public order or international affairs or public service. The claims are on a class basis – all documents in a class require the immunity – or a more specific contents basis. Following the *Matrix Churchill* episode in the 1990s, the government undertook never to invoke a class basis of PII again. The Freedom of Information Act 2000 does however, contain numerous class exemptions and exclusions from the Act. These matters are dealt with elsewhere.[145]

Giving of reasons

A right to adequate reasons for decisions falls under rights to defence in Community and continental systems. One of the developments with the

---

[145] P Birkinshaw *Freedom of Information: the Law, the Practice and the Ideal* (2001, 3rd ed).

greatest possible potential in domestic administrative law has been the movement towards a duty to give reasons for adverse administrative decisions. The Tribunal and Inquiries Act 1992, following earlier legislation, places tribunals and Ministers as specified under a duty to give reasons for their decisions, in the latter case following public inquiries. The Freedom of Information Act 2000 imposes a duty on bodies covered by that Act (about 100,000 and rising!) to have regard to the public interest in the publication of reasons for decisions made by the authority (s 19(3)(b)). This appears somewhat periphrastic![146] In the absence of a duty under legislation there is no general duty under common law. The courts have preferred to treat the matter as one of fairness and one which will be assessed on the requirements of the particular facts and circumstances. If there were a failure to give reasons where they would appear to be necessary to explain a course of action, the House of Lords appeared to be on the verge thirty five years ago of establishing a duty to give reasoned decisions.[147]

This dicta has not been followed although a presumption in favour of reasoned decisions may be expected in particular circumstances though the domestic courts are still wary of imposing general duties, unlike the requirement of the Administrative Procedure Act (USA) 1946 where reasons for administrative decisions have to be given.[148]

Duties to provide reasons in EC law derive from various quarters including Article 253 [190] EC Treaty where there is a duty to provide reasons for legislative instruments adopted by the European Parliament and Council, as well as by the Council and Commission. Decisions of the ECJ have established a general duty to give reasons as a general principle of law.[149] This means administrative decisions must have an adequate statement of reasons on which they are based although a dialogue does not have to be

---

[146] P Birkinshaw *Freedom of Information: the Law, the Practice and the Ideal* (2001, 3rd ed) ch 6.

[147] *Padfield v Minister of Agriculture, Fisheries and Food* [1968] AC 997. For an emphatic example of the duty, though probably overstated in terms of the law, see: *R v Lambeth London Borough Council, ex p Walters* (1993) 26 HLR 170 (QBD).

[148] P Birkinshaw *Freedom of Information: the Law, the Practice and the Ideal* (2001, 3rd ed) ch 9.

[149] Eg Case 222/86 *UNECTEF v Heylens* [1987] ECR 4097; Case 7/61 *Commission v Italy* [1961] ECR 317 Case C-166/95 P *Commission v Daffix* [1997] ECR I-983; and Case C-269/90 *Technische Universität München* [1991] ECR I-5469 (Ch 3, p 146 et seq).

entered over the reasons.[150] Without this, the Community courts will be obstructed in their review powers. The influence of French and German administrative law have been influential in this development.[151]

Nevertheless the progress of the common law is not glacial. Recent decisions of senior courts have emphasised that a body operating as a tribunal with a duty to decide the rights of an individual – and one includes the private law rights of employment as well as the public law rights – and a duty to act judicially, must give reasons for its decisions 'to enable the parties to know the issues to which it addressed its mind and that it acted lawfully'.[152] In the absence of reasons there is no way of establishing whether justice has been done or has been seen to be done. Nothing, not even national security, dictated against the giving of 'short' reasons. In the context of particular statutory powers, the court may infer adverse reasons for a decision where no reason has been given:

> The only significance of the absence of reasons is that if all other known facts and circumstances appear to point overwhelmingly in favour of a different decision, the decision-maker who has given no reasons cannot complain if the court draws the inference that he had no rational reason for his decision.[153]

A striking development took place in *Doody v Secretary of State for the Home Department.*[154] *Doody* is an emphatic vindication of the duty to give reasons for adverse decisions where necessary as a distinct feature of administrative justice involving an individual. The Home Secretary was appealing against a decision of the Court of Appeal that prisoners mandatorily sentenced to life imprisonment for murder were entitled to be told by the Home Secretary what period or periods had been recommended by the judiciary as necessary for the purposes of retribution and deterrence and that prisoners should be given an opportunity to make representations to him before the Home Secretary determined what that period – 'the penal

---

[150] Cf *Sytraval and Brink's France v Commission* Case T-95/94 [1995] ECR II-2651.

[151] In France a loi requiring the giving of reasons for decisions was passed in July 1979.

[152] *R v Civil Service Appeal Board, ex p Cunningham* [1991] 4 All ER 310 at 320, CA per Lord Donaldson MR.

[153] Lord Keith in *Lonrho plc v Secretary of State for Trade and Industry* [1989] 2 All ER 609 at 620, HL.

[154] [1993] 3 All ER 92.

element' – should be. The House of Lords held that the prisoner was entitled to an opportunity to receive information and to make representations and further, and here the Law Lords overruled the Court of Appeal, that the prisoner was entitled to receive reasons for the Home Secretary departing from the period recommended by the judiciary which the prisoner should serve for the purposes of retribution and deterrence. Lord Mustill, giving the judgment of the court, held that there was no general duty to give reasons for administrative decisions. However, in appropriate circumstances, such a duty may be implied. Much turned on the peculiar nature of mandatory life imprisonment in England; nonetheless, 'the modern climate of administrative law' dictated that the prisoner should be informed of the reasons for the disparity. It was true that the decision of the Home Secretary on the penal element is susceptible to review in the courts. But the following indicates the philosophical thrust of Lord Mustill's reasoning:

> To mount an effective attack on the decision, given no more material than the facts of the offence and the length of the penal element, the prisoner has virtually no means of ascertaining whether this is an instance where the decision-making process has gone astray. I think it important that there should be an effective means of detecting the kind of error which would entitle the court to intervene, and in practice I regard it as necessary for this purpose that the reasoning of the Home Secretary should be disclosed'. (at p 111)[155]

The general move towards greater openness was set back somewhat in the decision of the High Court in *R v Higher Education Funding Council, ex p Institute of Dental Surgery*[156] which was referred to above. A dental school wished to be given reasons for its research rating which would be crucial in determining its grant entitlement from the government. The general 'openness' in the approach of the statutory Funding Council and the 'oracular' nature of its decision made the 'allocation of grades inapt for the giving of reasons notwithstanding the undoubted importance of the outcome to the institutions concerned'.[157] Fairness did not require that questions of 'academic judgment' alone required reasons for decisions although the court accepted that in matters of academic judgment reasons

---

[155] Indeed, compare this with the decision of the ECHR in *Wynne v UK* (1994) 19 EHRR 333.
[156] [1994] 1 All ER 651 (QBD).
[157] Sedley J at p 669h.

must be capable of being formulated or articulated. Somewhat teasingly, the judge believed there was no agreed criteria by which the panel would judge the point on the scale to which each institution was to be allocated in spite of the need for uniformity and consistency in approach. The court accepted that there was nothing on the surface of the decision to suggest that the decision was so aberrant that reasons were called for and the court would be reluctant to excavate too deeply below the surface of the decision:

> But it is necessary for public decision-making bodies to appreciate that there are already some circumstances (eg where unlawful race or sex discrimination is alleged), and more may well come, in which their legal position may well depend on their ability to account intelligibly for their decisions by explaining not simply how but why they have reached them. This much, we think, bears a practical relationship to the movement of the law towards open or 'transparent' decision-making to which Lord Mustill refers in *Doody's* case. (At p 671GH)

Interim relief

Interim relief falls under a variety of possible principles of law: these include legal effectiveness and legal certainty. It is not in itself a principle of law, but its absence or presence has the most important consequences for the maintenance of the rule of law. It is also an area which has been spectacularly influenced by Community law.[158] The decision of the ECJ in *Factortame*[159] ranks as one of the most important decisions affecting the UK government not only in its relations with the Community and its law but also in terms of the effects it had on general principles of administrative law within the English jurisdiction.

The factual background is sufficiently well known and needs no rehearsing (Chapters 2, 4 and 10, pp 87, 195 and 454). The limits placed on the registration of non-UK fishing vessels under the terms of the UK Merchant Shipping Act 1988 and regulations thereunder were challenged by Spanish nationals whom the Secretary of State had refused to register under the terms of British law. Their challenge was based on the fact that the non-registration was in breach of Community law, in particular the Common Fisheries policy and various doctrines accepted by EC law viz, principles

---

[158] Interim declarartions may now be awarded under the CPR 1998, r 25.1(b).
[159] *R v Secretary of State for Transport, ex p Factortame Ltd* [1990] ECR I-2433.

of proportionality, legitimate expectation, acquired rights, non-retroactivity, non-discrimination and equal treatment and respect for fundamental rights recognised by EC law. The House of Lords ruled that English courts had no power to issue orders, by way of injunctions or any other means, which could disapply an Act of Parliament. To do so would be repugnant to the doctrine of the legislative supremacy of Parliament. The thrust of the development of Community law since the Treaty of Rome and the clear implications of the rulings of the ECJ seemed to be overlooked as did the terms of the European Communities Act 1972, s 2(1). More specifically, the House of Lords ruled that injunctions would not issue against the Crown and its servants. They were barred by the Crown Proceedings Act 1947. This conclusion reversed decisions of lower courts which had held that on the Crown Office side, ie judicial review, injunctions were available against the Crown and, it must be said, was decided without a full review of all the existing authorities.[160]

Subsequently the ECJ ruled in effect that a national court must set aside a national law which of itself prevented the court granting interim relief in a case before it and where the refusal would impair the full effectiveness of the subsequent judgment to be given on the substantive issue of the rights claimed under Community law. The judgment was nicely phrased to address a particular point which often arises in interim proceedings: as relief by injunction to maintain a status quo or to prohibit the operation of an activity (or a law) is discretionary, one of the considerations the court will take on board will be the extent to which damages will be an appropriate remedy in the event of the successful pursuit of the action/application by the claimant. Where damages by themselves are not entirely appropriate then this might weigh heavily in favour of an injunction to prevent irreparable damage to the claimant.

In the subsequent or No 2 hearing, the House of Lords were then left with little option but to rule that where either the enforcement of the law or resistance to the operation of a law was sought, the court would usually have to apply interim measures to avoid what would otherwise be irremediable damage. Where a public authority was seeking to enforce the law, the balance of convenience would have to be assessed in particular with regard to the importance of upholding the law of the land in the public

---

160 *Factortame Ltd v Secretary of State for Transport* [1989] 2 All ER 692, HL. See eg, *R v Secretary of State for the Home Department, ex p Herbage* [1986] 3 All ER 209.

interest with due regard to stability and the duty to enforce the law in the public interest. To restrain an 'apparently authentic law' of the domestic system should only be exceptionally taken where a challenge to its validity was prima facie so firmly based as to justify such action. On this basis, the applicants had a strong case to present to the ECJ that the evidence presented by the Secretary of State against their claim was not sufficient to outweigh the 'obvious and immediate' damage which would continue to be caused to them if they were to be granted no interim relief and the balance of convenience was in their favour. An interim injunction was therefore issued.[161]

The relief, by injunction it should be noted, had now been awarded against the Crown with the approval of the House of Lords. Subsequently, the question was to arise whether an injunction would apply against the Crown in a case not involving any EC element – in effect, could it be argued that the ruling in *Factortame* only applied to cases where there was an EC element but that it had no relevance to cases involving only domestic law. The case where this was tested was *M v Home Office*.[162]

The facts are long and complicated but essentially they involve the removal from the jurisdiction by executive action of an alien seeking asylum in breach of an undertaking given to a High Court judge in an application for leave to move for judicial review not to do so. The undertaking was given on behalf of the Secretary of State. The Secretary of State further failed to keep the judge informed of a continuing situation and failed to protect the position of the alien at various crucial stages. In doubting dicta of the House of Lords in the first *Factortame* case, the Law Lords ruled unanimously that under the Supreme Court Act 1981, s 31, the court could issue coercive orders against Ministers of the Crown in their official capacity and under Ord 53, r 3(10) Rules of the Supreme Court, interim injunctions could be issued against Ministers. In addition, where a Minister acted in disregard of a court order, the Minister and the department could have a contempt of

---

[161] *Factortame Ltd v Secretary of State for Transport (No 2)* [1991] 1 All ER at 106, HL; see further *R v HM Treasury, ex p BT plc* [1994] 1 CMLR 621, CA; and *R v Secretary of State for National Heritage, ex p Continental TVBV* [1993] 2 CMLR 333 (QBD) and [1993] 3 CMLR 387 (CA) – pornographic broadcasting by satellite from Denmark proscribed by order. 177 reference and no injunction issued. And see: Case C-143/88, 92/89 *Zuckerfabrik etc* [1991] ECR I-415 and case law, Ch 4, p 207 et seq on interim measures against domestic provisions implementing allegedly unlawful Community measures.

[162] [1993] 3 All ER 537, HL.

court finding entered against them. Although these were neither personal nor punitive against the department or the Minister in his official capacity, a finding of contempt would demonstrate that there had been an interference with the administration of justice and costs could be entered against the respondent. It would then be for Parliament to determine the consequences of the court ruling. Interestingly, the Law Lords ruled that an injunction could be awarded even before leave to apply for judicial review had been given.

This judgment is an essential contribution to the maintenance of the rule of law in Britain and there is no doubt that the decision in *Factortame (No 2)* was a crucial development along the road to interim relief in public law proceedings. To allow interim relief where Community law was involved but not where a question of domestic law only was raised was seen to be inconsistent and unsatisfactory: 'It would be most regrettable if an approach which is inconsistent with that which exists in Community law should be allowed to persist if this is not strictly necessary' believed Lord Woolf (at p 564h). Lord Templeman saw the decision to grant an injunction as a vindication of the rule of law itself.[163]

Conclusion

This chapter has described the revolution in English administrative law that has taken place under European influence. That revolution has seen the application of principles derived from Community and other European legal systems applied in a domestic context and not only to cases involving Community competence. Judicial review in England has grown in maturity and sophistication, and I question to what extent that would have occurred without that European influence. I do not believe there was an inevitability that our judicial review would have developed as it has left to its own devices. Perhaps the most dramatic development in this area concerns the arrival of a degree of judicial review appropriate to scrutinise with sufficient forensic precision decisions allegedly interfering with fundamental human rights. It is to that subject generally and the HRA 1998 that the focus will now shift.

---

[163] 'My Lords, the argument that there is no power to enforce the law by injunction or contempt proceedings against a Minister of the Crown in his official capacity would, if upheld, establish the proposition that the executive obey the law as a matter of grace and not as a matter of necessity, a proposition which would reverse the result of the civil war [AD 1642–1649].' Lord Templeman at 541.

Chapter 9

Citizenship and protection of human rights

This chapter is concerned with human rights and the revolution that has taken place in the protection of human rights in the UK in the last ten years. The concept of human rights is one which today is associated with membership of the human race; it embraces those rights which are fundamental features of human co-existence, dignity and self-respect. To deny those rights to anyone is to deny that person's full existence as a human being regardless of position, status, wealth, power or hierarchy. Historically, such rights were associated with liberal democratic states building upon the traditions of natural law and flowed from citizenship. Perhaps the most famous critique of this position is that of the young Marx in *On the Jewish Question* where he asserted that the protection of human rights and democratic society could, in a capitalist society, only be given in circumstances of economic dependency.[1] The 'freedom' that suppressed Jews in Germany craved for would only see them free within a materially inegalitarian society. They would still face a life of economic enslavement.

This critique has long lost its appeal. But the link with citizenship is still important. When the Americans captured and took allegedly Taliban and Al-Qaeda fighters to Camp X-Ray (or Delta) at its Guantanamo base in Cuba early in 2002, it was in order to avoid any protection such captives might be given under national systems based on their nationality (in some cases UK) and to avoid any protection such individuals may have been awarded under the US constitution if on US territory. They were denied, probably

---

[1]   K Marx *Early Writings* Penguin Books (1975). For more recent scepticism: T Campbell et al eds *Sceptical Essays in Human Rights* (2001).

wrongfully, the status of prisoners of war by the US authorities in order to avoid any embarrassing inquiries and protection under international law. This is not to say that the US authorities intended to abuse the prisoners in any inhumane way; they simply wished to be free from any legal restraint in their ability to extract information from them. But being free from constraint in the exercise of power is a path to tyranny and oppression. The captured individuals were denied any rights of citizenship or international protection. When the relatives of a UK national incarcerated in Camp X-Ray asked the English Court of Appeal to force action on the part of the Foreign Secretary, Lord Phillips said the action of the US authorities was 'legally objectionable' but beyond the jurisdiction of the Foreign Secretary.[2] This approach stands in stark contrast to the decision of the Special Immigration Appeals Commission (SIAC) when in July 2002 it ruled that it was contrary to the discrimination provisions in the ECHR to detain aliens in high security jails under legislation which did not apply to UK citizens. The ECHR applies to all persons within a jurisdiction of a member of the Council of Europe. Nonetheless, the world is still divided into citizens and aliens, a point emphasised by the Court of Appeal in reversing the SIAC's decision in holding that different treatment was unavoidable.[3]

Citizenship has been invoked to attempt to give desperately needed legitimacy to the EU. Weiler and others have shown how the attempt to address the legitimacy crisis at the heart of the Union has repeated the notion of national citizenship and a national demos, or people. A demos may take several forms, as Weiler has suggested, and need not be a replica of a national version of citizenship. He has suggested a 'supranational civic citizenship' to override nationalistic connotations.[4] The TEU speaks of an ever closer union among the *peoples* of Europe, not the people. The Union 'places the individual at the heart of its activities, by establishing the citizenship of the Union and by creating an area of freedom, security and justice.'[5] The movement from a European Economic Community to a European Community and then to a European Union at Maastricht was symbolised by the introduction of European citizenship in the Maastricht Treaty, but as Craig and de Burca point out, although this established the first 'formal constitutionalization of European citizenship' in fact 'the idea

---

[2]   *R (Abassi) v Secretary of State* (2002) Times, 8 November. It was an arbitrary detention in a 'legal black hole.'

[3]   *A v Secretary of State for the Home Department* [2002] EWCA Civ 1502, [2002] 46 LS Gaz R 33: (2002) New LJ 1633.

[4]   J H H Weiler *The Constitution of Europe* (1999) ch 10.

[5]   Preamble, *Charter of Fundamental Rights of the European Union.*

of European citizenship and the rhetoric of a 'People's Europe' had been in circulation for a long time.'[6] Most recently, the Giscard d'Estaing preliminary draft constitution has brought forth 'dual citizenship' where individuals may choose either national or EU citizenship – the implications are not spelt out.

Citizenship is used in many senses and is not a coherent but a protean concept. There may be social citizenship implying notions of solidarity and collectivity and mutual support; it can refer to economic and market citizenship which is more individualistic; to cultural citizenship; national citizenship which has predominated as a matter of legal definition – or subnational and transnational citizenship; it may refer to post-national, global and political citizenship. It is not clear where EU citizenship is aiming for.

The Treaty established Citizenship of the Union stating that Union citizenship is the entitlement of every person holding the nationality of a Member State (Article 17 EC). Such citizens enjoy the rights of the Treaty and are subject to duties imposed under the Treaty. It is made clear that citizenship of the Union shall complement and not replace national citizenship. Article 18 EC confers the right on every citizen of the Union to move and reside freely within the territory of the Member States, subject to the limitations and conditions laid down in this Treaty and by measures adopted to give it effect. Under Nice revisions, the Council may adopt provisions if necessary to give effect to this objective where the powers are not provided by the Treaty.[7] Furthermore, the ECJ has in several cases emphasised the fact that discrete rights may flow from citizenship.[8] European citizenship is a long term and uncertain process, but a process nonetheless.[9] Further amendments are likely to emerge from the d'Estaing Convention.

It appears that Article 18 EC gives no right of free movement for citizens beyond those in the Treaty and secondary legislation. It has no effect on

---

6   P Craig and G de Burca *EU Law: Text, Cases and Materials* (2002, 3rd ed) p 755. See N Barber (2002) 27 EL Rev 241.

7   The requirement for unanimity has been removed. Social security and other matters cannot be affected under Article 18(2).

8   Especially *Grzelczyk* Case C-184/99 [2001] ECR I-6193. See A Biondi (2003) European Public Law 39 at 45.

9   J Shaw (1997) European Public Law 413.

internal rules restricting freedom of movement of citizens *within* a Member State.[10]

Citizenship of a Member State remains the sole decision of a Member State subject to any relevant treaty provisions. Union citizenship is in addition to and not a replacement for Member State citizenship. Additional rights include power to stand in municipal and European Parliament elections as an elected representative for another Member State of which an individual is not a citizen (derogable), the right to the protection of any Member State's diplomatic services in a third country where there own Member State is not represented; and the right to write to any Community institution in one's own language and to receive a reply in that language. Some rights are conferred on both EU citizens and any persons resident in a Member State: these include the right to petition the European Parliament, the right to apply to the Ombudsman for him to investigate a complaint, and the right to apply to the Council and Commission and European Parliament for access to documents under Article 255 EC and its implementing Regulation (see p 275 et seq above).

The Commission reports on the citizenship provisions in Articles 17-21 EC every three years and the Council, acting unanimously, may adopt provisions strengthening or adding to these provisions (which may require constitutional amendment at Member State level). The point has been made that these new citizenship rights do not add up to a significant pile of beans: they are very limited in what they give, they do little to counter the feeling of small people in a big abstract Community although as we have seen (Chapter 6), the provisions on access to information seek to address this problem, and they emphasise the distinction between citizens and third country nationals witnessed ever more vividly by the masses seeking entry to the Union along its Eastern borders and across and under the Channel. The legitimacy of the Union was a matter at the forefront of the agenda that led to Amsterdam and Nice. Eastward and outward expansion is likely to increase problems of 'legitimacy' still further as greater inclusion leads to a feeling of lesser exclusivity on the part of existing citizens.

---

10   *R v Secretary of State, ex p Adams* [1995] All ER (EC) 177; UK had not signed Protocol 4 of ECHR giving a right to move freely *within* the territory of a Member State: Commission App Nos 28979/95 and 30343/96 *Adams and Benn v UK* (1997) 23 EHRR CD 160. This position on constraints *within* the Member State was made clear in Case C-299/95 *Kremzow v Austria* [1997] ECR I-2629 and also in *Land Nordrhein-Westfalen v Uecker and Jacquet v LN-W* Cases C-64/96 and 65/96 [1997] 3 CMLR 963.

Rights flow from citizenship, but human rights are due to individuals irrespective of citizenship: the universality of human rights derives from the 'moral principle of each person's personal and equal autonomy' which according to the 1998 Bangalore principles 'transcends national political systems and is in the keeping of the judiciary.'[11] It must be added that such autonomy should not be blind to differences in economic and social standing; such differences can lead to oppression as pronounced as that exercised by tyrants.

Discrimination[12]

One of the most important of human rights in contemporary society is the right not to be unjustly discriminated against. The rights of free movement within the Community carried with them implicit rights not to be discriminated against on grounds of nationality in order to protect the economic Community and a common market. Article 12 contains a specific provision prohibiting discrimination on grounds of nationality. The Treaty also contained in its original version a prohibition on discrimination in relation to pay in so far as Member States were to ensure equal pay for equal work and subsequently work of equal value between men and women. The reasons for this may have been economic rather than socio-political.[13]

The addition of Article 13 EC at Amsterdam, which has accompanying directives,[14] extends the power of the Council under stated procedures to

---

11   Lord Lester (1999) EHRL Rev 273.

12   M Bell *Anti Discrimination Law and the European Union* (2002); *The Ombudsmen Against Discrimination* (2002) Office for Official Publications of the EC.

13   See in relation to France, P Craig and G de Burca *EU Law: Text, Cases and Materials* (2002, 3rd ed) p 846 but it was recognised by the ECJ as a social and economic right and as a 'foundation of the Community': Case 43/75 *Defrenne v Sabena* [1976] 2 CMLR 98. See *Deutsche Telekom v Schröeder* Case C-50/96 [2000] ECR I-743, para 57 for a powerful statement that economic goals are subservient to social goals which gave expression to the Charter of Fundamental Rights of the EU.

14   One directive concerned 'implementing the principle of equal treatment between persons irrespective of racial or ethnic origin' – the race Directive – the other was concerned with 'establishing a general framework for equal treatment in employment and occupation' – the Framework Directive: 2000/78/EC, 27 November 2000. There was also a proposal 'establishing a Community action programme to combat discrimination (2001–2006) and a 'Communication from the Commission on certain Community Measures to combat discrimination.'

take 'appropriate action to combat discrimination based on sex, racial or ethnic origin, religion or belief, disability, age or sexual orientation.' The Charter of the Fundamental Rights of the European Union (p 388 et seq below) declares that everyone is equal before the law (Article 20) and in Article 21 adds to those prohibited areas of discrimination listed in Article 13 EC: 'colour, social origin, genetic features, language, political or any other opinion, membership of a national minority, property or birth.' The present non-legal status of the Charter will be discussed further below.

The Council of Europe did not, however, make protection from discrimination one of the articles of the ECHR, unlike the International Covenant on Civil and Political Rights. The Convention provided in Article 14 that rights were to be enjoyed without discrimination so that protection of one's right to privacy did not depend upon whether one was black or white, Catholic or Protestant. In the field of discrimination there has been a new addition from the Council of Europe in Protocol 12 to the ECHR which provides a free-standing guarantee of the fundamental human right to equal treatment without arbitrary or unfair treatment.[15]

These will add to the British contribution to anti-discrimination measures contained in legislation from 1975 and 1976 on sex discrimination and race relations respectively. To these were added measures outlawing disability discrimination and provisions in Northern Ireland on religious and political discrimination and a Race Relations (Amendment) Act 2000 which seeks to apply indirect and direct discrimination provisions to activities of public authorities not covered by earlier legislation. Under this Act, all public bodies[16] have to publish racial equality plans by 2003. Plans were announced to make religious discrimination unlawful at work in England and Wales in October 2002. A variety of Commissions has been established under these acts to investigate and give assistance in cases of discrimination.

See House of Lords Select Committee on the European Union *Ninth Report* (1999–2000) and *Fourth Report* (2000–01).

[15] See A Lester (2000) Public Law 562. On the Article 14 right to enjoy ECHR rights free from discrimination in an English case, see *Wandsworth London Borough Council v Michalak* [2002] EWCA Civ 271, [2002] 4 All ER 1136, CA.

[16] 43,000 named but 100,000 or so are covered by the Freedom of Information Act 2000.

Human rights before the Human Rights Act 1998

The reluctance of English law historically to recognise human rights is well known.[17] We did not possess a statement of rights in bold type which proudly proclaimed the existence of the right but which then may be qualified by countervailing rights and duties. We started with a range of legal duties and powers in others to interfere with our actions and what was left were our liberties – residual and contingent.[18] English law's great strength was seen in the presence of independent judicial procedures and their real protection as opposed to idealised rights on paper. Nowhere was this better expressed than in habeas corpus and the power of a court to demand that a detained person be brought before it so that detention could be justified on grounds established in law – a procedure which famously ended slavery in England.[19] In fact this hallowed procedure had become somewhat threadbare by the 1980s and superficial justifications for detention seemed to meet with judicial approval.[20] Nonetheless, the aura that the remedy attracted was given renewed vigour in discussions concerning the European Arrest Warrant and the prospect of British nationals languishing forever in hostile gaols overseas. Incorporation of habeas corpus would at least ensure that British safeguard which had passed into folklore along with an Englishman's home and his castle.

There is no doubt that the re-emergence of administrative law principles in the 1960s was a contributory factor to a growing sense of inadequacy in our legal apparatus to protect human rights where these were not given specific protection in statute or common law. The contributions of Lord Denning and Lord Reid in particular in the 1960s and 1970s were pivotal in helping to place public law on a more coherent basis and *Conway v Rimmer*[21] was one case which displayed, perhaps for the first time, an unwillingness to accept the *ipse dixit* of the executive. In this case the House of Lords established that a court could look behind an official certificate claiming a Crown privilege not to disclose documents required by a claimant in litigation. The court could make its own judgment. It was

---

[17] C Palley *The United Kingdom and Human Rights* (1990).

[18] See *Duncan v Jones* [1936] 1 KB 218 and *DPP v Jones* [1999] 2 All ER 257 where the traditional approach was not followed in the House of Lords: H Fenwick and G Phillipson (2000) Public Law 627.

[19] Though not the empire! *Sommersett's Case* (1772) State Tr 1. Cf the US Supreme Court in *The Antelope* 23 US (10 Wheat) 64.

[20] Sir Simon Brown (2000) Public Law 31.

[21] [1968] AC 910.

a case of true constitutional significance. *Conway v Rimmer* was followed by *Anisminic*[22] which sent shock waves through an older generation of government lawyers when the House of Lords decided that courts were the final arbiters of legality.

We were to wait another twenty years to see significant developments in protection of substantive rights. What these cases did was to ensure that the courts would have the final say on questions of law and legal interpretation and would attempt to allow applicants for justice to be informed, when necessary, of information which might assist their case: the case law made no contribution to enhancement of human rights. This was despite the fact that the UK government had signed up to the ECHR in 1950 and after ratification in March 1951[23] it came into effect as a part of the UK's international obligations in 1953. It was an agreement binding in international law and on accepted principles of English legal doctrine, it had no binding force in English law. The government believed in its White Paper *Rights Brought Home: the Human Rights Bill* (Cm 3782), that the traditional British approach to the Convention had not sufficiently emphasised its importance.

In his admirable work on *Using Human Rights Law in English Courts*[24] Murray Hunt writes how in the 1970s, English courts were generally content to interpret statutes in a manner which conformed with the ECHR and, after some initial reluctance, to develop the common law in accordance with the principles of the Convention. This was at the time of Sir Leslie Scarman's powerful work *English Law: The New Dimension* (1974) which highlighted the potential of the ECHR to invigorate the protection of human rights in the UK, both in its own right and as a part of Community Law. The Convention, and its case law, was a part of the *acquis communautaire* and therefore a part of the body of law that the UK government had agreed to accept as binding in the Treaty of Brussels. Such a direct impact of the CHR would however have been resisted. It remained persuasive. Indeed, their hostility was not infrequently displayed towards the Convention by

---

22   [1969] 2 AC 147.
23   UK first state to ratify but this did not originally cover Art 25 ECHR on individual petition which the UK ratified in 1966. France did not ratify the ECHR until 1974 and Art 25 in 1981.
24   (1997).

domestic judges both English and Scottish.[25] Other approaches to the Convention were not hostile, but failed to give full weight to the contribution of the Convention to English law.

In retrospect, a water-shed occurred in the House of Lords judgments in two cases in particular in the early 1980s. Both cases occurred in subject areas where administrative justice and the concept of human rights had been sadly deficient. In the first of these, *Raymond v Honey*[26] a prisoner wished to make an application to the court to commit the prison governor for contempt and this was stopped by the governor. Until the late 1970s the courts had refused to supervise prison administration even to the extent of refusing to review decisions of boards of visitors who heard disciplinary cases against prisoners when there were allegations of unfair procedure. This changed in 1979 when the Court of Appeal overturned a ruling of the Divisional Court and held that proceedings of boards of visitors were susceptible to control by judicial review.[27] Prisons were no longer a complete 'no go' area although large areas of prison administration remained beyond effective challenge. The words of Lord Wilberforce in *Raymond* that 'a prisoner retained all those rights ... that were not taken away by necessary implication ...' predicated a more rights conscious approach in English law, although it was qualified – here a right to access to justice which is a basic human right.[28] It also foreshadowed a particular approach to judicial construction of legislation that would not allow interference with basic rights unless the power of interference that was claimed was spelt out precisely in the legislation.

In the second case, *Bugdaycay v Secretary of State* Lord Bridge put forward a test of judicial review which anticipated the more exacting standards of review that we are now accustomed to when human rights are in question. There were degrees of scrutiny and the more invasive action was vis à vis individual liberty, the more carefully the court would appraise the means and method of the exercise of power. In *Bugdaycay,* an applicant for refugee

---

25   Indeed, in *Kaur v Lord Advocate* 1981 SLT 322, and *Moore v Secretary of State for Scotland* 1985 SLT 38, it was stated that the ECHR cannot be used as an aid to the interpretation of a UK statute. Lord Ross in *Kaur* observed on the practice of 'distinguished judges in England' ...'I find such a concept extremely difficult to comprehend' at 329. The English approach was approved in *T, Petitioner* 1997 SLT 724, 734.

26   [1983] 1 AC 1.

27   *R v Hull Prison Board of Visitors, ex p St Germain* [1979] QB 425.

28   Letters to the prisoner's lawyer were lawfully stopped under prison regulations.

status feared that he would be deported to a country that might subsequently send him to a country where he risked persecution. Although the decision on asylum was within the discretion of the Secretary of State:

> The most fundamental of all human rights is the individual's right to life and, when an administrative decision under challenge is said to be one which may put the applicant's life at risk, the basis of the decision must surely call for the most anxious scrutiny. [29]

While these cases had been decided in an atmosphere that was more concerned with the promotion of human dignity, there were other cases that were more indicative of the limits the courts were prepared to place on their use as facilitators of human rights' protection. Moreover, a fairly restrictive line was being adopted in relation to freedom of the press and freedom of speech in spite of spirited dissenting judgments from Lord Scarman in several cases. But it was one particular episode of litigation which brought home the poverty of judicial protection of human rights. It was both nadir and zenith. The case was *A-G v Guardian Newspapers*. The case concerned the notorious episode surrounding the government's attempts to ban reporting by newspapers of the contents of the book: *Spycatcher*. The courts initially gave the government every assistance in their attempts to impose prior restraint orders prohibiting publication – even of events which were widely known and reported elsewhere. There was a true *cri de coeur* from Lord Bridge in his dissenting judgment in the House of Lords when the vista and enormity of unbridled executive power were paraded before his eyes.[30]

When the case came before Scott J the following year for judgment on the final as opposed to interim injunctions the respect for the Convention and its influence were unmistakable.[31]

In the government appeal to the House of Lords, Lord Goff observed that he could see no inconsistency between domestic law and Article 10 ECHR on freedom of speech:

> This is scarcely surprising, since we may pride ourselves on the fact that freedom of speech has existed in this country perhaps as long as, if not longer than, it has existed in any other country in the world. The only

---

29   [1987] 1 All ER 940, HL at 952b–c, per Lord Bridge.
30   [1987] 3 All ER 316, 346–47.
31   See Scott J [1988] 3 All ER 545 at 570, 580–82.

difference is that, whereas art 10 ... proceeds to state a fundamental right and then to qualify it, we ... (where everybody is free to do anything, subject only to the provisions of the law) proceed rather on an assumption of freedom of speech and turn to our law to establish the established exceptions to it.[32]

What followed was the unfolding of the common law of human rights. The ECHR and the common law had been placed on an even pedestal in terms of their capability of protecting human rights. The common law was now to take precedence. The litigation involving the *Derbyshire County Council v Times Newspapers Ltd* before the House of Lords made this dramatically clear.[33] In this case the law lords held that a public such as a local authority or government department could not sue for defamation. It was a serious inhibition on freedom of speech. The case was decided on the basis of common law principles.

Some English judges have decided cases in recent years by using the language of fundamental human right never heard before in our judicial discourse. Where a prisoner was effectively denied access to the courts because he was incapable of making a legal aid contribution the statutory order imposing a compulsory contribution was declared ultra vires because it interfered with 'a citizen's right of access to the courts'.[34] This approach is emanating from the common law and cases have covered freedom of the press[35] and allocation of scarce resources where a right to life is involved in medical treatment.[36] In the latter case the decision of Mr Justice Laws concerning a refusal to treat a young child with a life threatening condition because the child's right to life had not been considered by the authority was reversed with almost indecent haste by the Court of Appeal fearing budgetary crisis in hospital management.[37] Allocation of interventionist medical resources, 'even where life is at stake, is ordinarily not justiciable.'[38]

---

[32]   *A-G v Guardian Newspapers Ltd (No 2)* [1988] 3 All ER 545 at 660. But this makes such rights subject to the will of the legislature and competing claims such as defamation which is often used by the powerful to restrict free expression, revealing sources of publication for similar purposes and so on.

[33]   [1993] AC 534.

[34]   *R v Lord Chancellor, ex p Witham* [1997] 2 All ER 779 (QBDC) and Laws J expression 'a common law of human rights'.

[35]   See *Derbyshire County Council v Times Newspapers* [1993] AC 534.

[36]   *Ex p D* (1995) Independent, 14 March.

[37]   [1995] 2 All ER 129 (see p 345 et seq above). See *R v Secretary of State for Social Services, ex p Hinks* (1980) 1 BMLR 93.

[38]   Stephen Sedley *Freedom, Law and Justice* (1999) p 53.

Ten years ago, Lord Browne Wilkinson felt secure in stating that:

> It is now inconceivable that any court in this country would hold that, apart from statutory provision, individual freedoms of a private person are any less extensive than the basic human rights protected by the ECHR... the [English] judges have asserted that the Convention confers no greater rights than those protected by the common law.[39]

More recently, English courts have asserted that the common law's protection of fundamental human rights is not only coextensive with the ECHR, but also recognises a hierarchy of rights ie, some *are* more important than others and enjoy a pre-eminent status. The most eloquent expression of this view comes from Sir Stephen Sedley in his judgment in *McQuillan*:

> Once it is accepted that the standards articulated in the Convention are standards which both march with those of the common law and inform the jurisprudence of the European Union, it becomes unreal and potentially unjust to continue to develop English public law without reference to them. Accordingly, and without in any way departing from the *ratio decidendi* of *Brind*, the legal standards by which the decisions of public bodies are supervised can and should differentiate between those rights which are recognised as fundamental and those which, though known to the law, do not enjoy such a pre-eminent status. Once this point is reached the standard of justification of infringements of rights and freedoms by executive action must vary in proportion to the significance of the right which is in issue.[40]

Sedley's dicta have been adopted subsequently, as we saw in Chapter 8 to provide a distinction between review of discretion where a fundamental right is involved and those cases where such a right is not involved. Even within human rights there are distinctions between those that are absolute such as the prohibition on torture or inhuman and degrading treatment or non-retroactivity of criminal charges and penalties and those that allow a proviso to their exercise.

The self confidence of judicial development of human rights has continued in cases such as *ex p Daly* and *ex p Simms* (see p 342 et seq above) where the courts have refused to interpret legislation in a manner which overrides

---

[39]   (1992) Public Law 405 – while acknowledging the influence of the ECHR through its use by the ECJ.

[40]   [1995] 4 All ER 400 at 422h–j.

fundamental human rights simply by implication.[41] In *R (Mahmood) v Secretary of State*, the Court of Appeal stated that the HRA 1998 would not operate retrospectively but the common law nonetheless would insist on compliance with Article 8 ECHR in a case concerning a deportation order issued by the Secretary of State. Protection under common law had to be consistent with that under the Convention, felt Lord Phillips MR.[42] The deportation was allowed to proceed.

Would, then, the protection of human rights have occurred even if the UK had not been a party to the ECHR, had not joined the Community and this membership had not led ultimately to the enactment of the HRA 1998? The answer must be a profound 'No'. In the eyes of our governors, the UK's moral superiority was vindicated at the end of the Second World War. It would have seemed strange not to have signed up to an international treaty on human rights that the UK had taken a lead role in drafting and promoting. The underlying assumption was that such a Convention would have little relevance to the UK and its government. It was never envisaged that the UK would become one of the most frequent of defendants in the dock at Strasbourg. Ignorance, possibly contempt for matters European were likely to have been as deep-rooted in 1945 as they were twenty and more years later when the Community membership was being negotiated, a feature we noticed in Chapter 4. The call for a United States of Europe by Winston Churchill in 1946 at Zurich concentrated essentially on a union of France and Germany under the UN and overseen by the allies. He did not see the UK as an active participant in such a union. 'We are with Europe, but not of it. We are linked but not compromised. We are interested and associated, but not absorbed.'[43]

In the UK, the common law promotion of human rights had been the preserve of some senior judges in the higher courts. The HRA 1998 makes human rights a central feature of the business of all judges. Besides, it has a Parliamentary and executive dimension as we shall see. The common law patriation of human rights would most likely not have occurred unless the UK had been a party to the Convention and had been subject to its constant

---

41   See *R (Morgan Grenfell) v Special Comr Income Tax* [2002] UKHL 21, [2002] 3 All ER 1, HL and protection of legal professional privilege.

42   [2001] 1 WLR 840. Laws J was more traditional in his approach stating that the courts could not stand in the shoes of the Minister. See I Leigh (2002) Public Law 265.

43   M Wolff *The Collected Essays of Sir Winston Churchill* Vol 2 (1976) p 184.

pressure for change and reform in our law and administrative practice. As I have mentioned in Chapters 2 and 3, the UK's membership of the European Community also helped produce a mindset that was receptive to change in fundamental legal concepts and in approaches to fundamental legal rights.

We saw in an earlier chapter how the ECJ had advised in *Opinion 2/94* that the EU lacked the competence to accede to the Convention and how the human rights tradition of the ECJ had been criticised for displaying a lack of full commitment to human rights. The Convention was inspired by and based upon the 1948 Universal Declaration of Human Rights adopted by the UN General Assembly on 12 December 1948. In spite of deficiencies in human rights protection, 'the two instruments enabled the work of building a European community to proceed without a separate human rights foundation.[44] The EU adopted a Charter of Fundamental Rights at Nice in 2000[45] as we saw in Chapter 2, p 63 et seq although at British insistence this was not made a part of the Treaty which would become a binding part of Community law. The European Convention commenced its work on the consideration of the EU's constitutional future in early 2002 and one of its important themes for the UK was the role of the Charter of Fundamental Rights and whether the EU should accede to the ECHR. The UK has denied that the Charter has legal effect within the UK although other Member States disagree (see p 63 et seq). It is time to turn to the incorporation of the ECHR.

The European Convention on Human Rights[46]

The Convention [Cmd 8969 1950] provides in Article 1 that the High Contracting Authorities shall secure to everyone within their jurisdiction the rights and freedoms in Articles 2 to 18 of the Convention. These rights are ostensibly rights mainly *not* to be interfered with in various ways. In Berlin's famous terminology they are mostly negative rights and not positive rights; rights not to interfered with or to be left alone as opposed to rights to be able to do things. To be allowed to do something implies a

---

44   P Alston *The EU and Human Rights* (1999) OUP p 3.

45   (2000) OJ 364/01.

46   For detailed and up to date accounts of the Convention and its case law, see: M Janis, R Kay and A Bradley *European Human Rights Law* (2000, 3rd ed); C Ovey and R White *European Convention on Human Rights* (2002); R Blackburn and J Polkiewicz eds. *Fundamental Rights in Europe* (2001)

right to a means of doing something which places financial or resource burdens on others, rights which carry collectivist undertones. Campaigners, for instance, advocate realisation of social rights such as employment, welfare, a decent life and a healthy environment, open government, a world free of tyranny and famine. These are not in the ECHR but forms of them are contained in the EU Charter. The UK has not incorporated the UN Covenant on Economic, Social and Cultural Rights or the Council of Europe's Social Charter (1996).

Although some of the rights may be couched in negative terms they are on closer inspection positive. Article 1 requires High Contracting Parties 'to secure to everyone within their jurisdiction the Convention rights.' We saw in Community law how press diversity could be an aspect of freedom of speech under Article 10 (p 61 et seq above). Furthermore, the interpretation of Convention Rights by the CHR and now disbanded Commission – and the Court's interpretation prevails – has been used in a manner which has made rights positive in areas such as privacy and family life and their interpretation to provide a right of access to information (see p 413 et seq). The right to life in Article 2 has been interpreted to include a right for relatives to have an independent investigation into the circumstances of the death. The rights in the Convention are conventional individual and individualist rights which are easily accommodated within mainstream liberal and conservative philosophy.

The 'Convention' incorporated into UK law by HRA 1998, s 1(2) and (3) and Schedule 1 does not include the whole of the Convention and is subject to any reservations or derogations set out in the Act.[47] The Schedule does include Articles 2 to 18 (excepting Article 13 which is concerned with an effective remedy for breaches of the Convention within participating states and Article 15) and the First Protocol and the Sixth Protocol. What, in brief, does it protect?

Article 2 protects the right to life: 'Everyone's right to life shall be protected by law. No-one shall be deprived of their life intentionally save where death is duly imposed after a criminal conviction in a court of law for which death is the penalty provided by law. Article 2(2) contains various provisos and

---

[47] *Brogan v UK* (1988) 11 EHRR 117 and Art 5(3) – this derogation has itself gone although a new derogation was included in the Anti-terrorism, Crime and Security Act 2001, s 23 covering Art 5(1): SI 2001/3644 and 4032; see *A v Secretary of State for the Home Department* note 3 above. For derogation under the ECHR, see Art 15.

this – apart from Article 3[48] – is a common feature of the Convention rights. The provisos add qualifications or balance the rights against other rights: individual or collective.

Article 3 prohibits torture or 'inhuman or degrading treatment or punishment.' It is stated in absolute terms.

Article 4 states that no-one shall be held in slavery or servitude and no-one shall be required to perform forced or compulsory labour. There are various savings in relation to what constitutes forced or compulsory labour.

Article 5 guarantees the right to liberty and security of person. Article 1(a)–(f) sets out circumstances where liberty and security may be curtailed after lawful conviction, arrest and detention in a variety of ways.

Article 6 guarantees a right to a fair and public trial 'in the determination of his civil rights and obligations or of any criminal charge against him'. The hearing should take place within a 'reasonable time' and should be before an 'independent and impartial tribunal.' A public hearing is subject to certain qualifications. The term 'civil rights' has fomented a considerable degree of litigation.[49] It has been held not to cover an investigatory procedure as opposed to an adjudicatory one[50] nor certain administrative procedures.

Article 7 provides that there shall be no finding of criminal guilt unless the behaviour constituted a criminal offence under national or international law when it was committed; criminal punishment shall not be retrospective. Only such penalties may apply as existed at the time of the offence. There is a proviso covering acts which at the time of commission were 'criminal according to the general principles of law recognised by civilised nations.'

Article 8 states that 'Everyone has the right to respect for his private and family life, his home and his correspondence. There shall be no interference by a public authority with this right except such as in accordance with the law and is necessary in a democratic society in the interests of national security, public safety or the economic well-being of the country, for the prevention of disorder or crime, for the protection of health or morals, or for the protection of the rights and freedoms of others'.

---

[48] Articles 6, 7 and 12 all have limited qualifications.
[49] A Bradley (1995) European Public Law 347.
[50] *Fayed v UK* (1994) 18 EHRR 393: Article 13 was actually in question.

Article 9 states that everyone has the right to freedom of thought, conscience and religion. It is subject to provisos.

Article 10 proclaims that everyone has the right to freedom of expression including the freedom to hold opinions, to receive and impart information and ideas without interference by public authorities and regardless of frontiers. Certain forms of licensing are permitted. These freedoms, since they carry duties and responsibilities, may be subject to restrictions and penalties prescribed by law and are necessary in a democratic society in the interests of national security, to prevent disorder or crime, to protect health, morals, or the rights and freedoms of others. Lawful restrictions may be imposed to protect such rights.

Article 11 provides the right of lawful assembly and association including the right to join a trade union.[51] It is subject to provisos similar to those in Article 10.

Article 12 provides for a right to marry according to the national laws governing the exercise of this right.[52]

Article 14 prohibits discrimination of the enjoyment of Convention rights on a series of grounds now contained in the EU Charter (see p 376 above).

Article 16 allows political restrictions to be placed on aliens.

Article 17 seeks to prevent rights from being abused and Article 18 places limitations on the use of restrictions of rights.

The First Protocol as implemented provides for the protection of property; a right to education; a right to free elections[53]; and the Sixth Protocol abolishes the death penalty with savings for time of war or imminent threat of war, ie treason.

---

[51] *Wilson v UK* CHR [2002] IRLR 568, ECtHR.
[52] *Goodwin v UK* [2002] IRLR 664: failure to allow a post operative male to female transsexual to marry a male was a breach of Article 12. See *A v Chief Constable of West Yorkshire* [2003] 1 All ER 255.
[53] See *Matthews v UK* (1999) Times, 3 March, ECtHR and a ruling on a breach of this protocol involving a provision adopted by the EU (Ch 3, p 59). On a rejection of a convicted prisoner's right to vote, see *R (Martinez) v Secretary of State for the Home Department* [2001] EWHC Admin 239.

This is the Convention as incorporated into domestic law by HRA 1998, Sch 1.

The Charter of Fundamental Rights of the EU

We saw in Chapter 2 that the ECJ had given an opinion that the EU as presently constituted was not empowered to accede to the ECHR, although the Treaty on EU makes specific reference to the Convention and it is a part of the *acquis communautaire*. The protection of human and fundamental rights within the Community judicial system has not been a resounding success as we saw. Following a convention comprising representatives as described in Chapter 7, p 316, a Charter of Fundamental Rights of the European Union was solemnly proclaimed at the Nice European Council in December 2000 after approval from the Council, European Parliament and Commission.[54] The Official text (European Communities 2001 accessed through <http://europa.eu.int>) is accompanied by explanatory text which is not meant to have any 'legal value'. The failure to place the Charter within the EC Treaty deprives it of legal value although it might be suggested that by implication the Articles themselves do have legal value. The Charter is 'addressed to' the Institutions of the Community (see Article 7 EC) and to Member States only when the latter are implementing Community law although the extent of the derogation is not clear (see Chapter 2, p 63 et seq). It has already been used by the ECJ and CFI as a source of further inspiration in its case law although it is not directly binding. The extent to which it may evidence an influence on our domestic law, both within and outside Community competence will have to be seen. Its provisions must be examined.

The Charter is broader than the Convention, considerably so, although all the major provisions of the Convention are repeated and in some cases extended. The Charter claims to build upon the constitutional traditions and international obligations common to the Member States, the TEU itself – particularly in relation to equality, non-discrimination – Community treaties, social charters adopted by the Community and Council of Europe – see in particular Chapter IV on 'Solidarity' which gives economic and

---

[54]   Proceedings were in public, all preparatory drafts were on the internet. The EU Ombudsman, representatives of the Economic and Social Committee and Committee of the Regions as well as representatives of civil society and of applicant countries were heard.

employment rights including workers' rights 'at appropriate levels' (as laid down by Community law) to information and consultation 'in good time' (Charter, Article 27) – and finally the case law of the ECJ and CHR.

Chapter I covers 'Dignity' including the right to integrity of the person aimed at repeating the principles in the Council of Europe's Convention on Human Rights and Biomedicine.[55] It prohibits reproductive cloning but not 'other forms of cloning.' Chapter II provides protection for 'Freedoms' including the protection of personal data (Article 8) as well as privacy and family life (Article 7) and freedom of the arts and sciences (Article 13) and freedom to choose an occupation and right to engage in work (Article 16) and to conduct a business (17) and asylum (Article 18). Chapter III protects equality and non-discrimination: 'everyone is equal before the law' (Article 20) and builds heavily on EC Articles 2, 3(2), 12, 13, 141(3), 151(1) and Article 6 TEU and case law, and also includes rights of the child (Article 24) from the NY Convention on the Rights of the Child and the rights of elderly and disabled (Articles 25 and 26). Chapter IV concerns solidarity as we saw above and covers employment rights – both individual and collective – social rights such as social security (Article 34) – and a right to preventative health care and medical treatment (Article 35) and access to services of general economic interest ie utilities (Article 36) and environmental protection (Article 37) and consumer protection (Article 38). Chapter V embraces the rights of citizenship and as well as rights to vote and to stand as a candidate, there are rights which we have seen elsewhere such as 'the right to good administration' (Article 41), the right of access to documents (Article 42 and see Chapter 5), the right to make a reference to the EU Ombudsman (Article 43), and to petition the European Parliament (44) and to freedom of movement (45). Chapter VI covers the right to justice including an effective remedy and to a fair trial and legal aid where necessary to ensure effective access to justice (47) and rights in criminal proceedings (Articles 48, 49, 50).

The rights in the Charter may only be limited where necessary and where such limitations are proportionate and genuinely meet objective needs of general interest recognised by the Union or the need to protect the rights and freedoms of others. The phrasing is similar to that employed by the CHR (see p 396 et seq) and also comes from the ECJ.[56] The rights in the Convention as interpreted by the CHR and repeated by the Charter set the

---

[55] ETS 164 and 168.
[56] Case C-292/97 *Karlson* [2000] ECR I-2737, para 45.

threshold of standard to be applied and may be extended by 'Union law'. The very breadth of the Charter, and the very considerable power it would give to the ECJ and CFI, make it at first sight an unlikely candidate for incorporation into UK laws. The working group under the EU Convention has strongly supported incorporation of the Charter into the EU constitution (CONV 354/02 WG II 16, Chapter 14, p 600). The group also favoured a power to be included in a revised Treaty to allow accession by the EU to the ECHR.

The Human Rights Act 1998 and 'incorporation' of the European Convention on Human Rights

Until the HRA 1998, the Convention was and is binding in international law; it was not binding in domestic law. The Convention's major use until the HRA 1998 was in its use as an aid in the interpretation of statutory provisions which were unclear and it was used to assist the interpretation of, and help develop, the common law. Where the common law provided no rights eg to be free from telephone tapping, it was ruled, questionably, that the Convention could be of no assistance.[57] One of the drafters of the Convention was Lord Kilmuir a future Conservative Lord Chancellor and the UK was the first state to ratify the Convention.[58] Although the common law was seen as deficient in protecting human rights because of its proprietory basis and bias we have seen the impact of more recent judicial statements showing a fairly widespread belief that human rights protection under the common law is consonant with the protection offered by the Convention. The rights in the Convention, it was proudly proclaimed, echo back to those contained in the Magna Carta.[59]

Unsuccessful attempts to introduce a Bill of Rights had been made in the House of Lords on several occasions, most recently in 1995 by Lord Lester QC. Lester's Bill would have entrenched the Bill rather in the fashion of the European Communities Act 1972 (see Chapter 4, p 181) although it was toned down in Committee. In the Lords debate on Lester's Bill, three senior

---

57   *Malone v Metropolitan Police Comr* [1979] Ch 344. On human rights articles in *Public Law*, see Le Sueur (2002) Public Law 395.

58   For the history of events behind the Convention see: Lord Lester of Herne Hill (1984) Public Law 46; and Marston, below.

59   Sir Edward Gardiner QC, HC Debs col 1224 (6 February 1987) and see eg Lord Goff in *Spycatcher* [1988] 3 All ER 545. On the British contribution to the Convention, see G Marston (1993) ICLQ 796.

judges: Lord Taylor, Lord Brown Wilkinson and Lord Donaldson stated they did not seek powers to strike down Acts of Parliament.[60] This self denying ordinance was in contradistinction to Lords Woolf and Sir John Laws who in extra-judicial publications had expressed the opinion that Acts of Parliament might under certain conditions lay themselves open for such an assault (see Chapter 14 p 621 et seq). These views were criticised without mentioning names when Lord Irvine the Lord Chancellor referred to 'extra judicial statements of judges' asserting such a power in judges.[61]

As part of the New Labour Government's plan to introduce major constitutional change within the UK, a White Paper was produced stating the Government's intention to incorporate the European Convention into English, Scottish and Northern Irish law.[62] Contemporaneously, a bill to incorporate the Convention – the Human Rights Bill (now the HRA 1998) was published. This latter practice was unusual but it falls in line with the government's promise to publish Bills of significance well in advance of their presentation to Parliament to allow for public comment. The Freedom of Information Bill was also published in draft consultation form and was subject to pre-legislative scrutiny by committees in the Commons and Lords. There was initial discussion on whether the Bill 'incorporated' the Convention or simply provided 'a body of interpretative principles' which would give 'better effect' to the Convention. However, in the Second Reading of the Bill, the Home Secretary used the expression 'incorporate' as did the Lord Chancellor subsequently and that is now the commonly used term. What the HRA 1998 does not strictly do is to make the Convention *itself* a part of English or UK law because the Convention includes the CHR and certain articles and provisions which are not scheduled – to make it such a part of domestic law would have been to give sovereign power to the Convention and as we shall see, this is expressly not the case. In so far as parts of the Convention are scheduled in the HRA 1998, they *are* a part of UK law and are binding subject to the terms of the Act. What the HRA 1998 does is to make it unlawful for public authorities to act in contravention of Convention rights which are

---

[60] HL Debs Vol 560, cols 1143 et seq (25 January 1995).

[61] HL Debs Vol 572, col 1255 (5 June 1996).

[62] *Rights Brought Home: The Human Rights Bill* Cm 3782 (HMSO, 1997). See Lord Irvine (1998) Public Law 221 and M Hunt (1998) Public Law 423. On the balancing of rights and duties by the courts post-ECHR incorporation see Sir J Laws (1998) Public Law 254. The question of a Bill of Rights for Northern Ireland remains on the table; Harvey (2001) EHRRev 48.

scheduled in the Act (s 6) and it attempts to ensure that in interpreting domestic statutes and regulations, judges shall ensure as far as it is possible to do so that they are read and given effect in a way which is compatible with Convention rights (s 3).

Interestingly the government did not believe that the European Communities Act 1972 was an appropriate model for incorporation of the ECHR because 'it is a requirement of membership of the EU that Member States give priority to directly effective EC law in their own legal systems' (para 2.12):

> To make provision in the Bill for the courts to set aside Acts of Parliament would confer on the judiciary a general power over the decisions of Parliament which under our present constitutional arrangements they do not possess, and would be likely on occasions to draw the judiciary into serious conflict with Parliament. There is no evidence to suggest that they desire this power, nor that the public wish them to have it. Certainly, this Government has no mandate for any such change.[63]

In presenting the case for incorporation the government outlined the problems about the ECHR – its delay, their 'foreign' quality, ie they are enforced by non-British institutions, 'and there will be another distinct benefit. British judges will be enabled to make a distinctively British contribution to the development of the human rights of Europe' (para 1.14). Convention law would be highly influential, but not supreme. The relative weakness of the ECHR in certain respects in protecting fundamental rights, and the limits of its contribution to UK law have been identified.[64]

Domestic judges were quick to see the opportunities for interchange and exchange of views with the Strasbourg CHR a development that will formally

---

[63] Paragraph 2.13. The White Paper looked at the Canadian Charter of Rights and Freedoms 1982 which allows courts to strike down legislation unless the statute effectively disallows this; the New Zealand Bill of Rights 1990 which requires past and future legislation to be interpreted consistently with its provisions unless this is not possible; and Hong Kong where a distinction is made between legislation passed before and after the Bill of Rights Ordinance (1991).

[64] See D Fottrell who makes unfavourable comparison with the International Covenant on Civil and Political Rights: (2002) PL 485 and Lord Steyn ibid p 473.

be assisted by co-option of British judges onto the CHR as occasional judges.[65] Their example may be drawn upon and followed by other judges:

> I do myself think that one of the greatest advantages of having incorporated the Convention is that it makes it possible to have a dialogue with the Court in Strasbourg. Of course, we do have a lot to learn from them but I venture to suggest they have a great deal to learn from us, not least in areas which are unfamiliar to most Continental jurists, ... [jury trial cited] ... They [CHR] are now, for better or worse, getting our views on these questions and one would hope that they would treat those with the same serious respect with which we treat their judgments, when though of course we have a duty ultimately to take account of their jurisprudence, whereas they have no duty to take account of ours.[66]

The Convention would be interpreted in the context of domestic law. While a domestic jurisprudence more finely nuanced to domestic conditions would develop, domestic jurisprudence would make its own contribution. The 'English court is not a Strasbourg surrogate' said Laws LJ.[67] The duty on domestic courts, he continued 'is to develop, by the common law's incremental method, a coherent and principled domestic law on human rights.' As other judges saw the position, it was a continuation of a process already embarked upon in English law. It is 'artificial' said Lord Phillips MR:

> [T]o consider English domestic law and the European Convention separately. The Human Rights Act 1998 has made that Convention part of the constitution of the UK, but the Convention sets out values which our laws have reflected over centuries. The need, so far as possible, to interpret and give effect to statutory provisions in a manner which is compatible

---

65   See for instance Sir J Laws in *McGonnell v UK* (2000) 30 EHRR 289 on confusion of judicial and political roles in Royal Court of Guernsey and Art 6. Laws wrote a separate judgment concurring and emphasising each Art 6 case had to be decided on its merits; note also Arden LJ and her judgment *Z v UK* on negligence in performance of a statutory duty (see Ch 10, p 470 et seq).

66   Lord Bingham Joint Committee Human R Oral Ev 26 March 2001, Q 130. See also the views of Lord Hope in Ch 1, p 20 above. On judicial interaction at international level: C.McCrudden (2000) 20 Oxford Journal of Legal Studies 499 'A Common Law of Human Rights: Transnational Conversations on Constitutional Rights.'

67   *R (Prolife Alliance) v BBC* [2002] EWCA Civ 297, [2002] 2 All ER 756, para 33.

with Convention rights is now a mandatory discipline, but it is not a novel approach.[68]

In the absence of a power to outlaw statutes, judges were given a power under HRA 1998, s 4 to award a declaration of incompatibility where a statute leaves no option but to contravene a Convention right. Nine such declarations appear to have been issued as I write,[69] although some have been successfully appealed to the Court of Appeal and House of Lords. The declaration does not invalidate a statute itself; a declaration has no impact on the operation or enforcement of the provision and it is not binding on the parties to the proceedings (s 4(6)(a) and (b)). Special provisions exist to give notice to the Crown where a court is considering making a declaration of incompatibility (s 5).

The crucial sections on interpretation of the HRA 1998 and Convention rights are s 2, 3 and to some extent s 8(4). Basically, s 2 states that a court or tribunal must take into account any judgment, decision etc of the CHR, any opinion or decision of the Commission (which no longer exists) or decision of the Council of Ministers of the Council of Europe (now removed). Rules will provide for the manner in which such judgments or decisions are to be taken into account in evidence. It should be noticed that the court or tribunal *must* take these items into account. This is a mandatory instruction followed by a *power* as to how the court considers the judgment. Judgments must not be ignored; but they are not binding on UK judges. There is room for 'dialogue' said Lord Hoffman:[70]

> The Bill would of course permit United Kingdom courts to depart from existing Strasbourg decisions and upon occasion it might well be appropriate to do so.... For example, it would permit UK courts to depart from Strasbourg decisions where there has been no precise ruling on the matter and a commission opinion which does so has not taken into account subsequent Strasbourg case law.[71]

The CHR as well as the Commission, treated the Convention as a flexible document which was not susceptible to binding precedent although one

---

[68]   *Saadi* [2001] EWCA Civ 1512, [2001] 4 All ER 961, para 68. See also Laws J in *R (Prolife Alliance) v BBC* [2002] EWCA Civ 297, [2002] 2 All ER 756.

[69]   Including the Collins J decision in the SIAC note 3 above which was successfully appealed and *R v Secretary of State for the Home Department, ex p Anderson* [2002] UKHL 46, [2002] 4 All ER 1089.

[70]   *R v Lyons* [2002] UKHL 44, [2002] 4 All ER 1028, para 46.

[71]   Lord Chancellor HL Deb Vol 513 col 514.

could rightly expect, in Dworkin's famous phrase 'articulate consistency' in its interpretation. The CHR does not approach its task on the basis of original intent – what was the intention of the original framers of a measure in drafting the measure. It treats the Convention as a 'living instrument' which 'must be interpreted in the light of present-day conditions.'[72] Interpretation may change over time in the light of changed circumstances. In *Saadi* Lord Phillips MR said:

> The Convention was a living instrument and when interpreting it and considering the Strasbourg jurisprudence, it was necessary to bear in mind that its effect might change in step with changes in the standards applied in member states.[73]

It is a reciprocal process.

As with all treaties, it must be interpreted 'in good faith in accordance with the ordinary meaning to be given to the terms of the treaty in their context and in the light of its object and purpose.'[74] The object and purpose of the Convention – protection of human rights – means that the CHR will not usually interpret provisions narrowly where the object and purpose would be undermined and interpretation will be in a manner to ensure that 'safeguards are practical and effective.'[75] 'This is not to say ... that the Court of Human Rights aims to corral State action within unreasonable bounds, since restrictions on rights will often be justified. But in delimiting the rights themselves, the Court of Human Rights prefers to take a broad approach in order to secure that the Convention is effective. The legitimacy of each restriction on those rights is then separately considered, on its own merits.'[76] The CHR frequently uses phrases which are 'independent of their meaning' under domestic law say the authors and 'does not necessarily follow the phraseology' used in domestic law.[77]

Where it is established that a Convention right has been infringed by a restriction, the CHR asks itself four questions to establish whether such a

---

[72]   *Loizidou v Turkey* (1995) 20 EHRR 99, para 71.
[73]   [2001] EWCA Civ 1512, [2001] 4 All ER 961, para 36.
[74]   Vienna Convention on the Law of Treaties, Art 31.
[75]   *Loizidou v Turkey* (1995) 20 EHRR 99.
[76]   P Duffy and P Stanley *Current Law Statutes* 1998, ch 42, pp 42–4; J Jowell (2000) Public Law 671.
[77]   P Duffy and P Stanley *Current Law Statutes* 1998, ch 42. See also S Grosz, J Beatson and P Duffy *Human Rights: The 1998 Act and the European Convention* (2000).

restriction/infringement is legitimate, unless the right is an absolute one such as the right not to be tortured. In cases under the HRA 1998, domestic courts must establish whether a breach has actually occurred before proceeding further to interpret any purported authorisation or intent in legislation.[78] These four questions or tests are:

1. Is the restriction/infringement lawful which means prescribed by *law*? Informal administrative guidance is not sufficient.

2. Is there a legitimate purpose or objective; very rarely is such a purpose not legitimate, eg national security, but the following two tests help establish whether such a purpose justifies the restriction;

3. Is the restriction necessary in a democratic society? This introduces the doctrine of proportionality in making the assessment or in balancing the interests of the state on one hand – the collective welfare – and those of the individual on the other. Does the restriction/ infringement amount to an overreaction or unjustifiable interference or is the method of interference necessary? Can less invasive measures achieve the legitimate objective?[79] Under Article 10, the court will ask whether the restriction fulfils a 'pressing social need'. As I indicate below, the CHR will apply a 'margin of appreciation' to the exercise by the state of its powers. I will examine *R v Shayler* below where this question is analysed by the House of Lords.

4. Is the restriction discriminatory? If it does appear to discriminate on any of the wide grounds in Article 14, is there any 'reasonable and objective justification' for the discrimination. If not, the measure may well be in breach of Article 14.[80]

It may be that UK judges might simply disagree with a decision of the CHR or Commission. It was envisaged, rightly so, that the occasion when this might happen would be rare. There would be a tendency to talk around an unhelpful decision. It has been held that where an interpretation of a Convention right by an English court differs from that of the CHR, the interpretation of the former is binding on English courts.[81] Counsel must adopt a responsible attitude in using the HRA 1998.[82] They should avoid the temptation to 'try it on' by making excessive or exaggerated use of the new jurisprudence.

---

[78]   Lord Lester of Herne Hill QC (1998) EHRLRev 665.
[79]   *Handyside v UK* (1976) 1 EHRR 737, para 49.
[80]   *Belgian Linguistics Case (No 2)* (1968) 1 EHRR 252, para 10.
[81]   *R v Central Criminal Court, ex p Bright* [2001] 2 All ER 244.
[82]   *Daniels v Walker* [2000] 1 WLR 1382.

As well as seeking to give UK judges opportunities to develop ECHR principles in a domestic setting there are other reasons why the giving to CHR decisions a 'binding' quality would be questionable. This is apart from any argument based on sovereignty and the UK government clearly did not wish to make the convention and its case law sovereign. The CHR, as we have seen, does not apply a rigid form of precedent but treats the Convention as a 'living document' subject to development. Furthermore, the CHR has adopted the 'margin of appreciation' in its approach to questions of application of the Convention to national practices. By this means, the CHR regards itself as subsidiary to national protection of human rights and has to pay full respect to national interpretations on eg 'obscenity' but this does not give to national systems a *carte blanche* – there are boundaries beyond which national systems must not transgress. While UK courts will not adopt an approach based upon a margin of appreciation, they will nonetheless display deference to executive discretion – a deference which will vary according to subject matter and which will be less pronounced where human rights are in issue as we shall see below. In the case of some rights, there is no margin of discretion at all. It will not adopt the *Wednesbury* test of whether a decision appears reasonable on the surface by a bare demonstration of rationality (see Chapter 8, p 331). As Laws LJ has made clear, the margin of appreciation is a test of international law by which the CHR accepts that there may be a range 'of different views and approaches relating to the matter in hand.' It cannot dominate the approach of the domestic court to the margin of discretion because the domestic court is a part of the 'culture and practice' in which it is operating.[83] It is also quite clear that UK courts will apply proportionality to the exercise of official power both as a consequence of the Convention rights and the jurisprudence of the CHR.

The HRA 1998 reverses the decision in *Brind* which was examined in Chapter 8 so that the Convention will apply to the exercise of power exercised by officials which interferes with a Convention right. Where a balance has to be struck between an individual right and pressing social or collective needs, it will be asked whether that exercise was proportionate which includes an assessment of all relevant facts, that the exercise was necessary – not convenient but necessary, and lastly in accordance with the law. In *ex p Smith*, Simon Brown LJ believed that the effect of incorporation would be to make 'the primary judgment (subject only to a

---

[83]   *R (Prolife Alliance) v BBC* [2002] EWCA Civ 297, [2002] 2 All ER 756, para 33.

limited "margin of appreciation") one for the courts'; a result he described as a 'shift' in the 'constitutional balance'. Duffy and Stanley believe that shift has now taken place.[84]

In debates, the Lord Chancellor stated that in 99% of cases that arise there will be no need for declarations of incompatibility.[85] The reason for this was explained by the Home Secretary when he said the in almost all cases the courts will be able to interpret the legislation compatibly with the Convention.[86] How should statutes be interpreted under the HRA 1998?

Interpreting statutes

Section 3 bears the legend 'Interpretation of legislation'. It states that:

> So far as it is possible to do so, primary legislation and secondary legislation must be read and given effect in a way which is compatible with Convention rights.

Legislation will be interpreted so as to be compatible with the Convention 'so far as possible' unless, quite obviously, it is clearly impossible to do so. This rule of construction will apply to past and future legislation: it is to that extent, prospective and retrospective. But the Act only takes effect in relation to actions or decisions of public authorities occurring after 2 October 2000.[87] The HRA 1998 only comes into play where a court is satisfied that a breach of a convention right has actually taken place (above). We have already seen the views of the Lord Chancellor [88] and the Home Secretary.[89]

---

84 *Current Law Statutes* (1998) ch 42. Cf Lord Steyn in *ex p Daly* on Simon Brown's test of review (p 344).

85 HL Debs 585 col 840.

86 HC Debs Vol 306 col 778.

87 *R v Kansal (No 2)* [2001] UKHL 62, [2002] 1 All ER 257 upheld (by majority) but criticised the decision in *R v Lambert* [2001] UKHL 37, [2001] 3 All ER 577 which decided that the HRA 1998 could not apply to *appeals* being heard *after* the HRA came into effect. Although *Lambert* was erroneous, 'it would be wrong to depart from so recent a decision.' See: Beyleveld et al (2002) *Legal Studies* 185 for criticism in not applying the 1966 Practice Direction.

88 HL Debs Vol 585 col 840.

89 HC Debs Vol 306 col 778.

The government did not wish to give overriding power to the judiciary because of the importance which it attached to Parliamentary sovereignty. It is nonetheless a binding obligation upon judges so to interpret legislation in a manner consistent with Convention rights *where that is possible*. Lord Slynn has opined that courts should, in the absence of some special circumstances, follow Convention case law although this approach may not be universally held (see, however, Lord Hoffman below in *Alconbury*). Where there are two possible interpretations, judges must opt for that interpretation which upholds the ECHR. The words 'So far as it is possible to do so' mean that where the statute is absolutely clear in its intent, and that intent is contrary to the Convention, there is likely to be little that a court can do but apply the statute. The courts cannot override the clear will of Parliament when expressed patently in a statute. In undertaking their task, judges must acknowledge that the techniques of the legislature and the judiciary are different. The obligation must be performed with regard to its limitations.[90] But matters of interpretation are rarely that simple. In Chapter 4, p 186 et seq we saw a line of cases dealing with interpretation of domestic measures in a manner which conformed with the wording of EC directives and Treaty provisions and, with a couple of exceptions, how English courts had made every possible effort to achieve consistency.[91] Although the HRA does not impose the same duty of interpretation as the European Communities Act 1972, where possible, the imperative to achieve consistency is clear. While creative and constructive imagination might be required, anything approaching re-legislating by judges or radically altering the effect of the legislation may pass over to the impermissible.[92] The interpretative obligation certainly 'goes far beyond the rule which enabled the courts to take the convention into account in resolving any ambiguity in a legislative provision' before the HRA 1998 was effective.[93]

Lord Steyn has, however gone further than fellow Law Lords or the Lord Chief Justice. In *R v A (No 2)*[94] he interpreted the Youth Justice and Criminal

---

[90]   *R v Lambert* [2001] UKHL 37, [2001] 3 All ER 577, para 79.

[91]   The *Litster* line of cases: ch 4 p 189 et seq.

[92]   *Poplar Housing etc* [2001] EWCA Civ 595, [2001] 4 All ER 604; see *Re S (Minors)* [2002] UKHL 10, [2002] 2 WLR 720, para 41.

[93]   Lord Steyn in *R v A* at para 44; *Rights Brought Home: the HR Bill* Cm 3782 (1997) para 2.7. In *R v Lyons* [2002] UKHL 44, [2002] 4 All ER 1028 Lord Hoffman believed that interpretation of the Convention, in a case which did not involve the HRA 1998, was not within the Law Lords' jurisdiction: para 41.

[94]   [2001] UKHL 25, [2001] 3 All ER 1.

Evidence Act 1999, s 41(3)(c), which sought to give protection to a rape complainant from being cross-examined on her sexual history, to provide nevertheless an accused with the opportunity 'to put forward a full and complete defence by advancing truly probative material.' (see paras 44 and 45). The defendant's right to a fair trial under Article 6 necessitated such an interpretation although the interpretation 'linguistically may appear strained'. He believed that the HRA 1998, s 3 requires the court to subordinate the niceties of the language of s 41(3)(c)[95] to broader considerations of relevance judged by logical and commonsense criteria of time and circumstance (ie broader than the language allowed). 'Logically relevant sexual experiences between the complainant and the accused' should be admitted and this was a necessary implication in allowing the accused a fair trial under Article 6. A trial judge will have to decide whether the evidence (and questioning) should be admissible to ensure a fair trial having taken all due regard to protect the complainant from indignity and humiliating questions (sic). 'A declaration of incompatibility is a measure of last resort. It must be avoided unless it is plainly impossible to do so.'[96]

Lord Steyn has commented extra-judicially that:

> Traditionally the search has been for the one true meaning of a statute. Now the search will be for a possible meaning that would prevent the need for a declaration of incompatibility. The questions will be (1) What meanings are the words capable of yielding? (2) And, critically, can the words be made to yield a sense consistent with Convention rights? In practical effect there will be a rebuttable presumption in favour of an interpretation consistent with Convention rights.[97]

This is a positive duty of interpretation and as such goes far beyond existing practice where norms of international law may be invoked to interpret a domestic measure which was ambiguous. It has been argued, as was seen in Chapter 4, that this limited presumption was in fact giving

---

95   Section 41(3)(c) concerned 'consent' of the victim and dealt with sexual behaviour of the victim that was 'so similar' and which took place as a part of the event for which the accused was charged or to any other sexual behaviour of the victim which took place '*at or about the same time*' as the event for which the accused was charged and the similarity between that behaviour and the event in question cannot reasonably be explained as a coincidence. The behaviour in *A* was separated by three weeks.

96   Lord Steyn *R v A* at para 44.

97   Lord Steyn [1998] EHRLR 153 at 155.

way to a more robust application of international norms to interpret domestic measures (p 163 et seq above). Be that as it may, the scope and power of the new norms of interpretation are beyond question.

The HRA 1998 provides that a Minister would have to make a written statement in Parliament before the Second Reading that a Bill is compatible with the Convention; if he cannot he has to state that it nonetheless is the government's wish to proceed with the Bill (s 19). Parliament would have the opportunity to clarify the Bill. If the government is of the view that the Bill is not compatible and Parliament legislates on that basis that is likely to be conclusive where words in breach of a Convention right only allow one interpretation. Guidance on compliance with the HRA 1998 obligations will be revised to assist departments and drafters of Bills and regulations of the Convention's requirements. No minister would have overall responsibility for promoting human rights.[98] The HRA makes provision for derogations and reservations from the Convention and its Protocols.

The role of the Joint (Lords and Commons) Human Rights Committee, established in January 2001, will be of considerable importance here in assisting Parliamentary scrutiny.[99] Statements by ministers tend to be bare assertions. The Committee may summon witnesses and take evidence and its terms of reference include: consideration of human rights matters in the UK excluding individual cases; proposals for remedial orders (below) including those made under the fast track procedure and whether in respect of such orders, the attention of the House needs to be drawn to them because of matters such as defective drafting or that further elucidation is required.[100] Compatibility with Convention rights is not specifically within the terms of reference but in July 2001, the Committee re-affirmed its resolve to examine legislation brought before Parliament under its power to examine 'matter's relating to human rights in the UK.'[101] The Committee 'takes on board relevant ECHR jurisprudence, other human rights obligations and a range of academic literature in the human rights field' forming 'valuable

---

[98]   Cm 3782 para 3.5. No Ministry of Justice although the Lord Chancellor is reported to be keen on such a Ministry: see Lewis and Birkinshaw *When Citizens Complain: Reforming Justice and Administration* (1993). The Lord Chancellor's Department is the sponsoring department for the Act.

[99]   D Feldman (2002) Public Law 323.

[100] Cf the terms of reference of the Joint Select Committee on Statutory Instruments.

[101] See D Bonner and C Graham (2002) European Public Law 177.

research sources.'[102] Its two reports on the Anti-terrorism, Crime and Security Bill were particularly directed and critical on many points. The White Paper spoke of a Human Rights Commission – so common in Canada[103] – as a future possibility, not a commitment. It has not come to pass. A Human Rights Commission has been established in Northern Ireland[104] and there is continuing discussion about introducing a Northern Ireland Bill of Rights, with the possibility of a Northern Ireland version of a constitutional court.

Since the Act was brought into effect in October 2000, although statements of compatibility have been made since late 1998, there has been one bill on which a statement of compatibility was not made. This was the Communications Bill 2002 and resulted from a judgment of the CHR concerning banning of political advertising (see HC 191 and HL 24 (2002-03) p 8 et seq). As noted elsewhere, in the Anti-terrorism, Crime and Security Bill, cl 23, the government derogated from Article 5(1) when it sought powers to detain non nationals 'under remand conditions' who were suspected of being international terrorists. For bills enacted before the HRA 1998 came into effect, any potential inconsistency is likely to be open to interpretation in a manner which maintains a construction which complies with the ECHR. Where a subordinate instrument contravenes a Convention right, it will be invalid and open to quashing unless the primary legislative power under which it was made 'prevents the removal of the incompatibility' (s 3(2)(c) and see s 6(2)(b)) ie, the primary power necessarily involves an infringement by secondary instruments.

What is a 'public authority'?

Section 6(1) of the Act makes it unlawful for public authorities to act in a way which is incompatible with the Convention rights. Section 6(2), however, provides that basically, where primary legislation leaves no alternative to action which breaches convention rights, section 6(1) does not apply. Along with ss 3(2)(b) and (c) and 4(4)(b) and (6)(a), section 6(2)

---

102 D Bonner and C Graham (2002) European Public Law 184.

103 The government examined approaches adopted in Canada, New Zealand and Hong Kong all of which countries took different approaches from strong judicial control to Parliamentary control.

104 *Re Northern Ireland's Human Rights Commission's Application for Judicial Review* (2002) Times, 25 June (HL) the Law Lords held that the NIHRC has capacity to make submissions on human rights law to the Northern Ireland courts.

seeks to leave unaffected the validity of any offending legislation. Section 7 stipulates that nothing in the Act creates a criminal offence.

'Public authorities' will be understood broadly to include all agents of central and local government, statutory and prerogative bodies and police, as well as courts and tribunals themselves – where for instance the latter fail to protect human rights in a case before them. The question of what is a public body has been an important issue in judicial review since the decision of the Court of Appeal in the *Datafin* case in the 1980s although the case law was not consistent.[105] The jurisprudence of the CHR would also have to be referred to as this has identified bodies whose actions may incur responsibility on the state.

The expression also includes 'private persons' when exercising public powers: 'any person certain of whose functions are functions of a public nature' but not where the function is private in nature. It will include hybrid bodies and quangos when exercising public functions. Disparities will arise where a private body performs a function which is also performed by a public body if that function is considered private. *All* acts of public authorities proper are covered by section 6. It does not include either House of Parliament – except for the House of Lords in its judicial capacity. Guidance on 'functions of a public nature has come from the courts.[106]

In *R (Heather) v Leonard Cheshire Foundation* the Court of Appeal held that a voluntary sector home for disabled residents whose placements were funded by a local authority could exercise their rights under the Convention against the local authority but not against the home which was not exercising public functions.[107] The authority was exercising statutory powers under the National Assistance Act 1948 and remained liable to the residents under Article 8. It had not contracted out its functions. Lord Woolf advised that authorities might wish to bear in mind in the future that when they arrange for private bodies to supply such a service, claimants may require the contract between the authority and the private undertaking to include a clause providing for convention rights to be

---

[105]   *R v Panel on Take-overs and Mergers, ex p Datafin* [1987] 1 All ER 564, CA. See also *R v Disciplinary Committee of the Jockey Club, ex p Aga Khan* [1993] 2 All ER 853 and *R v Cobham Hall School, ex p S* [1998] ELR 389 and *R v British Council, ex p Oxford Study Centre* [2001] EWHC Admin 207, [2001] ELR 803.

[106]   *Poplar Housing etc* [2001] EWCA Civ 595, [2001] 4 All ER 604.

[107]   [2002] EWCA Civ 366, [2002] 2 All ER 936, CA.

maintained by the undertaking. The court reasoned that like a private school, which was not exercising public functions, the home could not be said to be exercising public functions simply because those functions could be exercised by a public authority and were paid for by a public authority. If this were the case there would be a distinction between those who were privately funded and those who were publicly funded: 'there was no material distinction between the nature of the services the foundation had provided for residents funded by a local authority and those provided to residents funded privately.' Funding was 'relevant' but not 'determinative'. The undertaking was not itself exercising statutory powers in exercising its functions.

Ironically, the court believed it was proper to bring proceedings for judicial review under the CPR, Part 54 and it was not an abuse of process. Part 54 deals with public law procedure and it might appear to cause some confusion if a divergence is appearing between those bodies that are judicially reviewable and those functions which are not public but reviewable by Part 54, even if the review consists in holding that the HRA 1998 does not apply to the functions. It may not be doctrinally pure, but at least it resolves the issue in one court. Where 'a bona fide contention was being advanced, although incorrect, that the foundation was performing a public function, that was an appropriate issue to be brought to the court by way of a judicial review.' Lord Woolf has been anxious to prevent technicalities prejudicing the award of relief under the new reforms, and there is an understandable reluctance to foist duties owed by the state in its broadest sense onto private bodies to introduce a direct horizontal effect. Nonetheless, the public/private divide raises difficulties which our courts have yet to resolve.

In *R (A) v Partnerships in Care Ltd*,[108] duties in the case of a private hospital were cast directly on the hospital after a health authority arranged for their discharge by the hospital and in addition patients were admitted under compulsion under the Mental Health Act 1983, s 3; the patients' care and treatment aimed at returning them to the 'community' was a 'matter of public concern and interest' and the managers of the hospital were performing as a 'functional public authority'.[109] In *Poplar Housing* the Court of Appeal said that a generous definition of public authority and public

---

[108] [2002] EWHC 529 (Admin), [2002] 1 WLR 2610.
[109] In the case of private prisons disciplinary functions have always been Crown responsibilities since prisons were privatised.

function should be given a 'generous interpretation' for the HRA 1998, s 6.[110] However, the fact that a body performs a function which otherwise would be performed as a duty by a public authority does not make that necessarily a public function. Hybrid bodies may perform both public and private functions under s 6(3). An act may remain private if performed by a hybrid body even though a public authority is under a duty to provide that the act is done.[111] The state may not be able to absolve itself from its duty, but that does not mean a private contractor is performing a public duty. 'What can make an act, which would otherwise be private, public, is a feature or a combination of features which impose a public character or stamp on the Act.'[112] Particular features may include statutory authority for what is done; the extent of control by a public authority, how closely the acts of a private body are enmeshed with those of a public body, the closeness of relationship between the public and private body (regulation by itself is not enough) joint membership of the bodies and whether the private body was created by the public body to fulfil its tasks and whether a relationship between a public authority and [as here] a tenant was assumed by the private body. The body under challenge was a registered social landlord (a housing association which in *R v Servite Houses, ex p Goldsmith* [2001] LGR 55, was held not to be a body susceptible to judicial review) and the public authority was the former landlord of the sitting tenant who was now claiming a breach of Article 8 by the registered social landlord in its service of a notice to quit on her. While the problem is very much a question of fact and degree, the position here is that the local authority and the registered social landlord were so closely assimilated that the registered social landlord was performing a public function in housing the tenant and then seeking possession.

There had, however, in *Poplar* been no breach of Article 8.[113] The degree of assimilation explained in *Poplar* was not present in the *Leonard Cheshire* case. The extent to which some difficulties, but far from all, may be resolved through an indirect horizontal effect can be explored below.

---

110   *Poplar Housing and Regeneration CA Ltd v Donoghue* [2001] EWCA Civ 595, [2001] 4 All ER 604.

111   *Costello-Roberts v UK* (1993) 19 EHRR 112; cf Case C-188/89 *Foster v British Gas plc* [1990] 3 All ER 897.

112   *Poplar etc* para 65. See *RSPCA v A-G* [2001] 3 All ER 530 and *Marcic v Thames Water Utilities Ltd* [2002] EWCA Civ 65, [2002] 2 All ER 55.

113   See para 75 of *Poplar* on the extent of the duty of interpretation in the HRA 1998, s 3.

Some procedural points

Section 7 will allow individuals and 'organisations' to raise a human rights argument in any proceedings brought against them – whatever level of court – or in proceedings which they bring against a public authority by direct challenge. The government preferred the rights to be invoked as they arose 'rather than confining their consideration to some kind of constitutional court'. If an individual wishes to bring a breach of the Convention directly to the courts, s/he will be able to do so; it creates a discrete right of action. There is, however, a time limit of 'one year' from the date on which the act complained against took place – the date of enactment etc in case of legislation – which is extendible on generous grounds but which is subject to any rule imposing a 'stricter time limit'. In judicial review the period to bring review is three months (subject again to any shorter period specified in rules).

Where Convention points are raised on judicial review applications, locus standi will have to be established. The test of standing to bring proceedings in all cases is whether the person seeking relief is a 'victim' – this is more confined than the traditional test of locus standi in judicial review where Part 54 requires a claimant for relief to establish a 'sufficient interest' in the matter and the courts have shown that they are more relaxed about allowing public interest groups to bring proceedings under judicial review.[114] The Convention[115] allows the CHR to receive applications from 'any person, Non Governmental Organisation or group of individuals.' This has included companies, although the breach must be of a kind that is capable of injuring a company.[116] The Convention jurisprudence has not established that there is an *actio popularis*. While it has sometimes been

---

[114] *R v Secretary of State for Foreign Affairs, ex p World Development Organisation* [1995] 1 All ER 611; *R v Inspectorate of Pollution, ex p Greenpeace (No 2)* [1994] 4 All ER 329; *R v Secretary of State for Foreign etc Affairs, ex p Rees-Mogg* [1994] 1 All ER 457. On time limits for seeking judicial review, see: *R (Burkett) v Hammersmith and Fulham London Borough Council* [2002] UKHL 23 [2002] 1 WLR 1593.

[115] Article 34 though previously Art 25 in so far as the Commission received applications and on which most of the case law developed; Art 34 is now mandatory.

[116] See R Clayton and H Tomlinson *The Law of Human Rights* (2000) OUP and supp paragraphs 22.21 et seq. See *R v Broadcasting Standards Commission, ex p BBC (Liberty intervening)* [2000] 3 All ER 989, CA for a domestic approach.

liberal[117] it has also been restrictive.[118] It will be recalled that s 11 safeguards existing human rights including those in common law (including judicial review with its potentially more liberal rules on standing, and under EU law) as well as a right to resort to Strasbourg if no success is obtained in domestic courts.) It should also be recalled that under Part 54, the court may allow *amicus* briefs to be heard on judicial review applications (CPR, r 54.17).

Courts or tribunals will be able to award whatever remedies lie within their normal powers and as they consider just and appropriate (s 8) where they find unlawful conduct: crucially here in the case of the courts this includes damages and awards of injunctions, but as seen above breaches of the Convention will not be criminal offences (unless otherwise a crime eg torture is an assault and grievous bodily harm). Section 8(3) places a limit on awards of damages in that they must be 'necessary' to afford just satisfaction having taken into account all the circumstances of the case.[119] Awards of damages on Convention grounds will take account of principles developed by the CHR in awarding compensation so that domestic awards will be 'equivalent'.[120] It is interesting that the government has allowed a human rights issue to be raised under a collateral challenge to be made by way of a defence as well as direct challenges.[121] A collateral challenge is a challenge to the legality of a measure on which a prosecution or a contract is based but where the illegality is raised as a defence and not as a direct challenge to the measure itself.

[117] As in the *Open Door* decision where the CHR allowed the Art 10 complaint to proceed and left open the question of an Art 8 application; the Commission HR had not allowed the Art 8 application to proceed when made by the clinic: (1992) 15 EHRR 244.

[118] *Leigh v UK* (1984) 38 DR 74. A journalist was not a victim of a rule punishing for contempt disclosure of documents obtained in discovery in litigation: *Hilton v UK* (1988) 57 DR 108.

[119] See s 9(3) on limits against courts.

[120] Section 8(4); see D Fairgrieve (2001) Public Law 695 for a discussion of the possibilities of how principles will develop. NB the case law on damages, and these have not been automatic on finding of a breach, is under pre-Protocol Art 50 not Art 41 as referred to in the HRA.

[121] In *R v Wicks* [1997] 2 All ER 801, HL Lord Hoffman did not believe that it was possible 'to construct a general theory of the ultra vires doctrine which applies to every statutory power, whatever the terms of the policy of the statute' at 815j. Basically, collateral challenge may be raised in the lower courts on procedural or substantive grounds but the statutory framework in question may make such challenges inappropriate. See also: *Boddington v British Transport Police* [1998] 2 All ER 203, HL.

It was seen above how the government have not attempted to allow courts to set aside Acts of Parliament where there is a breach of the Convention by a legislative provision but higher courts will be able to make a 'formal declaration' that a provision is incompatible with Convention rights under s 4.

The HRA 1998 allows for a 'fast track' procedure under s 10 'for compelling reasons' to amend legislation by Order approved by positive resolution of both Houses where a declaration of incompatibility has been issued by the court or where a decision of the CHR after the section in the HRA 1998 came into effect against the UK renders a provision of a statute incompatible with the Convention. By this means, the government may amend statute by delegated legislation and although there are precedents for this[122] it attracted vociferous criticism as an abuse of executive power. Approval of a draft order may be waived where there is a case of emergency in which case the Houses will be notified along with other procedural safeguards (see Schedule 2). By this means Parliamentary sovereignty is maintained; judges may declare incompatibility, the executive may (but are not compelled) take remedial action and Parliament will approve the order. In the case of orders made under the urgency provisions Parliament has to approve the order within 120 days of it being made – otherwise orders shall cease to have effect.

Acts of the Scottish Assembly are subject to the HRA 1998 and must comply with the Convention both when enacted and in Bill form (see Chapter 5, p 231). Disputes will be referred to the Judicial Committee of the Privy Council. It was noted how the Convention rights came into effect in Scotland and Northern Ireland under the provisions of the devolution legislation and so took effect before 2 October 2000. In the case of the Northern Ireland and Wales devolution statutes, there is a saving provision to protect NI Ministers and devolved administrations when they exercise powers which by virtue of provisions in a Westminster statute(s) mean that they have no choice but to breach a convention right (HRA 1998, s 6(2), GoWA, s 107(4)(a) and NIA s 71(3)(a) and (4)(a)). Such a provision is not repeated in the Scotland Act and s 57(3) of that Act only allows a saving power in relation to several functions of the Lord Advocate.

---

[122] The so-called 'Henry VIII clause' and under Deregulation and Contracting Out Act 1994 as amended. See, eg, *R (H) v Mental Health Review* [2001] EWCA Civ 415, [2002] QB 1 and SI 2001/3712. Amendment may be made by legislation: see Nationality etc Act 2002, s 125 and Sch 8.

Judges and the constitutional order

The HRA 1998 has invigorated the human rights debate in the UK. In *R v DPP, ex p Kebeline*[123] Lord Hope expressed the view that although:

> The Human Rights Act is not yet in force, the vigorous public debate which accompanied its passage has already had a profound influence on thinking about issues of human rights. It is now plain that the incorporation of the ECHR into our domestic law will subject the entire legal system to a fundamental process of review and, where necessary, reform by the judiciary. (p 838h)

But incorporation has had its detractors fearful that the judiciary's new weaponry will promote them in the political arena where they will be encouraged to make policy decisions on controversial subjects which are inherently political, which should be accepted as such, and which are best resolved through that process.[124] So much is envisaged in Lord Hope's statement above although the reference to 'entire legal system' would include law-making in Parliament. A judicial training programme under the HRA 1998 was established under Sir Stephen Sedley and Sir Robin Auld. This was attacked by John Griffiths as 'highly suspect, subversive of the judicial process and likely to interfere with the course of justice' (*The Guardian* 9 April 1999). In reality, Parliament has been criticised for becoming very much a tool of the executive and an ineffective opposition is not able to subject government to appropriate criticism in the elected chamber. In the case of the Anti-terrorism, Crime and Security Act 2001, change was forced by an unelected Lords and there is no guarantee that that chamber will continue its critical role and even if it did, the Parliament Acts would allow an Executive to get its way if prepared to delay. The 'political process' means to all intents 'the executive process' and that is to make it a judge in its own cause on those very matters which concern fundamental rights, the realisation of which are bothersome to its agenda.

---

[123] [1999] 4 All ER 801 breach of Art 6 alleged in Prevention of Terrorism (TPs) Act 1989 which reversed onus of proof but before the HRA 1998 came into effect; the HRA 1998 was not operative.

[124] See J Griffith's criticism of Sir S Sedley's book *Freedom, Law and Justice* (1999) in (2001) LQR 42 (Sedley's Reply ibid 68) and see Griffith (2000) Mod LR 159 and criticism of Sir John Laws. Both Lord Irvine and Lord Woolf have spoken of the relationship between the judiciary and politics under the HRA: www.lcd.gov.uk/speeches/2002/lc011102.htm and www.britac.ac.uk/pubs/src/tob02/index.html.

I make some points below about how the judiciary are using Convention articles in a distinctly domestic fashion.

One further point which might call for comment is the fact that while the Convention rights may be applied by courts and tribunals, there is no mention of the public sector ombudsman within s 2 – this requires courts or tribunals deciding an issue under the Convention to have regard to the jurisprudence of the Convention institutions and decisions of the Council of Ministers. Clearly such ombudsmen will be public bodies covered by the Act under s 6 but they are not referred to as bodies applying judgments and decisions of Convention institutions. This may well be a sorry omission because in several jurisdictions the contribution of ombudsmen to the protection of human rights is acknowledged (see Chapter 12). The Bill concentrates on 'unlawful' action by public authorities and the remit of UK ombudsmen covers maladministration not illegality although the boundary between the two is sometimes impossible to draw. Also our major ombudsmen are circumscribed in that they should not investigate where there is a legal remedy and it is not reasonable for the complainant to pursue a judicial remedy[125]

Special cases and flash-points

Before the HRA 1998 was enacted and still to the present day, stories have been rife concerning the impact incorporation would have on restricting reporting activities of the Press because of a new right to privacy which would be imposed by an over eager judiciary – especially to help the Royal family. The rights could be invoked against the courts where the latter would be acting unlawfully in not upholding Convention rights introduced under the HRA 1998. There have been conflicting statements from the Lord Chancellor about the impact of Article 8 ECHR on the British model of press self-regulation under a code administered by the Press Complaints Commission. However, as is obvious to anyone with a knowledge of the Convention, article 8 rights have to be balanced against other rights including those of free speech under article 10. There is no reason why the balancing should inevitably be lop-sided and unfavourable to one side or the other in a disproportionate manner. Nonetheless, extra safeguards were introduced into the Bill (the HRA, s 12) to protect 'genuine investigative journalism' and these seek to make prior restraint of publication more

---

[125]   *R v Comr for Local Administration, ex p Croydon London Borough Council* [1989] 1 All ER 1033.

difficult than previously.[126] Additional safeguards were also provided for religious groups who were fearful of restrictions on freedom of conscience under Article 9 ECHR by invocation of Article 8. Section 13 asks a court to have 'particular regard' to rights under Article 9 if they are called into question by eg, homosexuals who wished to go through a marriage ceremony in a church whose teaching did not recognise such a marriage.

One immediate flash point in addition to privacy protection concerns the discrepancy between English provisions which compel the answering of questions which may well be self incriminating, usually in the investigation of financial offences and a decision of the Court of Human Rights which has ruled that the UK statutes allowing such compulsion are in breach of the Article 6(1) ECHR.[127] In the light of the existing statutory provisions and their clear expression and authorisation, the domestic courts remained powerless.[128] The Court of Appeal[129] has ruled that the whole scheme of the HRA 1998 preserved Parliamentary sovereignty and the Court could not quash convictions subsequently found by the CHR to breach the Convention. This decision was upheld by the Law Lords.[129a]

How has the Human Rights Act 1998 been used?

In his work on *A Bill of Rights for Britain* Ronald Dworkin argued that a benefit of incorporation of the Convention into a Bill of Rights would be that it would allow domestic judges to make their contribution to a jurisprudence of human rights. We have seen how this is already taking place and how the HRA 1998 allows for co-opted judges from the UK to sit

---

126 The section is not restricted to prior restraint.

127 *Saunders v UK* (1997) 23 EHRR 313. The offending provision was the Companies Act 1985, s 434 – now modified by the Youth Justice etc Act 1999, s 59 and Sch 3. The CHR did not award compensation in *Saunders*. See the CHR in *Allan v UK* (2002) Times 12 November concerning Articles 6 and 8 and use of covert recordings of telephone conversation.

128 *R v Morrissey* (1997) Times, 1 May; *Secretary of State for Trade and Industry v McCormick* [1998] 2 BCLC 18. And note *R v Chief Constable RUC, ex p Begley* [1997] 4 All ER 833, HL: there was no common law right of access to a lawyer during police interviews; there was a clear intention of Parliament that a person arrested under the Prevention of Terrorism (Temporary Provisions) Act 1989, s 14 (1) was not to have such access. The court accepted that Art 6 ECHR did not assist.

129 *R v Saunders etc* [2001] EWCA Crim 2860, [2002] 2 Cr App Rep 210.

129a *R v Lyons* [2002] UKHL 44, [2002] 4 All ER 1028.

on the CHR. Lord Hoffman has entered a note of caution that: 'The 1998 Act was no doubt intended to strengthen the rule of law but not to inaugurate the rule of lawyers.'[130] The impact of the Act in some high profile cases has been dramatic but the actual statistics on the use of the HRA 1998 in case law has not been so. The Lord Chancellors' Department has reported on litigation involving human rights in a statistical update the most recent being published in November 2001. Le Sueur and Cornes state that public law litigation is not a 'significant part' of the Law Lords' case load; those cases tend to be more sensational perhaps as in the *Shayler* trial and judgment (below).

Of 1,971 cases in the Court of Appeal (Criminal Division) in the period April – June 2001, 123 included a human rights point (6.2%) compared with 277 of 2,491 cases (11.1%) in the first quarter after implementation and 161 (8.6%) of 1,872 in the second quarter. 'In general human rights issues continue to be raised as additional points to existing cases and could have been lodged even if the Act had not been in force.'[131] In the Court of Appeal (Civil Division) from 2 October 2000–June 2001, 123 human rights cases had been determined, and 95 were outstanding. No further details are provided. In the Administrative Court, of 1,078 cases received between April–June 2001 (1,264 between January-March 2001), 261 (24%) raised human rights issues compared with 21% in the previous quarter. 'It is apparent that the vast majority of those cases could have been lodged irrespective of implementation of the Act.'[131a] In the QBD, there were 8 cases citing the HRA (2 April–2 July 2001); in the same period 18 cases in the Chancery division; and in the first half of 2001 only one case in the Family Division. From 2 October 2000 until the end of June 2001, 214 cases had raised a human rights point in the Crown Court – less than 0.5% of cases. In county courts between April and June 2001, less than 0.01% of cases raised a human rights point. In magistrates' courts, cases raising human rights points constituted 'a small fraction of the overall caseload.' A majority (85%) of these were in criminal cases: Article 6 was raised in two thirds of those cases, Article 5 in 15%, 11% Article 8 and two cases raised Article 14. Article 6 was raised in 40% of cases on the non-criminal side in which a human rights point was taken. Magistrates acknowledged when giving reasons that in cases where a human rights issue had been raised they were 'a factor in the decision in 87% of criminal cases and 57%

---

[130] *R (Alconbury) v Secretary of State* [2001] UKHL 23, [2001] 2 All ER 929, para 129.

[131] HRA 1998: *Impact on Court Workloads*. LCD, 5 December 2001.

[131a] HRA 1998: *Impact on Court Workloads*. LCD, 5 December 2001, p 2.

of family cases. In 45% of criminal cases and 23% of family cases where the issue was raised they were the 'sole determining factor.'[131b] In immigration appeals, human rights were mentioned as a secondary factor in 4,547 cases until August 2001 (32% of cases), but only as a primary factor in 75 cases in the same period. The HRA has not 'affected the Immigration Appellate Authority's ability to deliver its business. Between April and June 2001, 52 legal aid certificates were issued by LSC regional offices for cases that raised significant points of human rights law. 37 of those were judicial review certificates – the total number of judicial review certificates in that period was 1416 an increase driven by immigration work. The 'impact of the Act on legal aid expenditure is likely to be limited.'[131c]

Case law

It is not my intention to trot through an exhaustive list of case law. Reference points for details on the case law involving the HRA 1998 can easily be found elsewhere.[132] The impact of the Convention has been felt particularly in the area of freedom of speech and privacy; in Article 6 in relation to a right of access to justice and a fair trial; in Article 5 and detention[133] There has also been some interesting use of Article 2 on the right to life.

Article 10 and openness: the Commission has been prepared to accept a right of access to information to be informed about environmentally dangerous activities. The CHR has not accepted that Article 10 confers a right to information – it confers a right to have information passed on in a freedom of speech sense. The CHR has however ruled that a right to privacy and family life under Article 8 may allow the court to infer a right of access to information to protect the Article 8 right.[134] The CHR has also ruled that a right to life under Article 2 includes the right to have a suspicious death

---

[131b] HRA 1998: *Impact on Court Workloads.* LCD, 5 December 2001, p 3.

[131c] HRA 1998: *Impact on Court Workloads.* LCD, 5 December 2001, p 3.

[132] See eg EHRL Rev which has regular surveys of case law under the HRA 1998: see ibid (2001) 181 E Salgad and C O'Brien and (2002) at 432 J Arkinstall and C O'Brien.

[133] In the Anti-terrorism, Crime and Security Act 2001, s 23 the government derogated from Art 5(1) (SI 2001/3644).

[134] Or to have an independent determination: *Gaskin v UK* (1989) 12 EHRR 36; Cf decisions in *Guerra v Italy* (1998) 26 EHRR 357 and *McGinley and Egan v UK* (1998) 27 EHRR 1; *Kerojarvi v Finland* (2001) 32 EHRR 8 and Art 6 compared with *McGinley* point and *MG v UK* [2002] 3 FCR 289.

investigated by an efficient and effective process of investigation to uncover relevant information about the death; this commonly applies where there has been a death in custody or at the hands of police or armed services.[135] The Court of Appeal, reversing the High Court, has held that such an inquiry did not have to be in public and did not have to guarantee the right for relatives to participate. 'Pragmatic flexibility' should determine the procedural requirements which would differ with circumstances (see Chapter 13, p 575).[136]

In *Ex p Wagstaff* the High Court ruled that the Secretary of State had acted unlawfully in holding an inquiry in private into the murder of the victims of Dr Harold Shipman and Article 10 had been breached. The Secretary of State felt that a private inquiry under the National Health Service Act 1977, s 2(b) was appropriate would be quicker and would reveal more information.[137] Advice from Lord Chancellor's Department in 1991 on the form of inquiry after a disaster causing death was not published until 2000.[138] The Minister also felt that privacy of relatives justified a private inquiry; they had not been consulted on this (although they had been invited to attend). *Wagstaff* represented a novel and unexpected use of Article 10.

However, the Administrative Court held[139] that the government decision to hold the foot and mouth inquiry in private was not a breach of Article 10. The government wanted a forward looking inquiry to advise on future action in the light of any similar event and wished to avoid the expense and delay of the inquiry conducted by Lord Phillips into the BSE and new variant CJD epidemics (at about £30,000,000). Simon Brown LJ examined why some inquiries had been held in public noting the views of various judges as to why they should be held in public as well as those of Professor Sir Ian Kennedy after the *Learning From Bristol Inquiry* into the use of deceased person's body parts without permission. At Bristol, cross

---

[135]   *McCann v UK* (1995) 21 EHRR 97; *Hugh Jordan v UK* (2001) 11 BHRC 1: *McShane v UK* (2002) Times, 3 June, ECtHR; *Edwards v UK* (2002) Times, 1 April.

[136]   *R (Amin) v Secretary of State for the Home Department* [2002] EWCA Civ 390, [2002] 4 All ER 336.

[137]   *R v Secretary of State for Health, ex p Wagstaff* [2001] 1 WLR 292. Not under s 1 and under the Tribunals of Inquiry (Evidence) Act 1921; cf the Allitt inquiry was in private: *Compton v Secretary of State for Health* (9 July 1993, unreported) and in *Taylor v UK* there was an alleged breach of Art 2 after this litigation – Commission rejected application.

[138]   Cm 4558 (2000) *Thames Safety Inquiry.*

[139]   *R v (Persey) v Secretary of State for the Environment, Food and Rural Affairs* [2002] EWHC 371, [2002] 3 WLR 704.

examination was permissible but not resorted to; the inquiry nonetheless took over three years to submit its final report. The reasons identified for holding an inquiry in public were: for accountability, to get to the truth, to assuage anxiety, to act as a 'communal catharsis' to purge the sense of horror and degradation felt in the community after shocking events. Simon Brown felt that there was no legal presumption to openness in all inquiries – each inquiry turned on its merits. Sometimes there is benefit in holding a public inquiry but taking evidence in closed session. 'Inquiries in short come in all shapes and sizes' and it would be wrong to assume a single fit for purposes, felt Simon Brown LJ. Sometimes openness may appear a necessity, but where competing judgments came into play, 'and the judgment as to where the balance falls may be thought pre-eminently a political one.' (para 42) In *Wagstaff* there were many reasons why the inquiry should be public not least because the Secretary of State had wrongly identified the wishes of relatives, the terms of reference were very broad and although there was no finding of a legitimate expectation nonetheless there 'many people received the clear impression that the inquiry would sit in public.' (para 44) This inquiry was clearly distinguishable from *Wagstaff* – there was a narrower set of terms of reference than in *Wagstaff* and a much more complicated set of factors to consider that were not within the court's own field of expertise.

Simon Brown LJ categorically rejected the argument that an Article 10 right was involved. Basically, his view was that the court in *Wagstaff* wrongly interpreted Article 10 to give what it cannot provide: a positive right to information as opposed to its true conferral of a right to freedom of speech and a right not to have the supply of information stopped for no good reason. It is wrong for the state to prevent the provision of information by one person to another; it does not create a duty on the state to supply information itself. 'Article 10 prohibits interference with freedom of expression: it does not require its facilitation.'[140] The judgment about the benefits of a closed inquiry over an open one is basically a judgment for government not the courts and could have been justified by Article 10(2), even if Article 10 had any relevance. Article 6 ECHR makes provision for hearings in public but only courts are mentioned. In *R (Howard) v Secretary of State for Health* the decision in *Wagstaff* was criticised and the court

---

[140] Paragraph 53; see para 57 and *Decision on Application by Cable News Network (unreported 25 October 2001; and Petition No.2 of BBC* [2000] HRLR 423 – Art 10 does not confer right on TV companies to film events which were in any event being broadcast by other means; the inquiry has an inherent right to control its own proceedings.

confirmed the approach taken in *Persey* above. *Wagstaff* laid down no general rule of law on open inquiries. It was a decision for the Secretary of State.[141] Findings and recommendations are usually published.

Article 10 and free speech: The case law shows the clear imprint of the impact of Article 10 in cases dealing with confidentiality, copyright[142] and defamation although the courts have been vigilant to invoke common law standards of freedom of expression to curb unnecessary restraint. A defence of political privilege has not as yet been accepted without reservation – that comment about politicians or those in the public limelight is protected by a qualified privilege even where inaccurate provided that the inaccuracy if not intentional or reckless. In *Reynolds v Times Newspapers Ltd* the House of Lords formulated a series of tests to be answered by journalists and publishers before publishing material in order to gain the protection of a qualified privilege.[143] In *Loutchansky v Times Newspapers Ltd (No 2)*[144] the Court of Appeal added to the *Reynolds* decision in holding that in establishing whether a qualified privilege attached to a publication (here suggesting the claimant was a Russian crime boss and involved in money laundering and smuggling of nuclear weapons) the question to be posed was not whether it was in the public interest to publish an untruth, but whether it was in the public interest to publish the article, true or false. Qualified privilege tolerated factual inaccuracy for two reasons: not to deter the publication sued upon and to encourage the future publication of truthful information. However, each individual publication of defamatory material in English law gives rise to a right of action which had not been displaced by the American 'single publication rule' ie that limitation runs from the original publication and not the last of repeat publications and this rule of English law does contravene Article 10 ECHR. The position of archive material would 'normally' be protected whether in hard copy or on the internet by placing an appropriate warning against treating it as the truth.

A particularly interesting decision came in *McCartan Turkington Breen v Times Newspapers Ltd* where the Law Lords were responsive to a plea for a wide definition of a public meeting in order to give a qualified privilege to

---

[141]   [2002] EWHC 371, [2002] 3 WLR 704. *Howard* involved an inquiry under the National Health Service Act 1977, s 2 as in *Wagstaff.*
[142]   *Ashdown v Telegraph Group Ltd* [2001] EWCA Civ 1142, [2001] 4 All ER 666, CA below
[143]   [1999] 4 All ER 609, HL.
[144]   [2001] EWCA Civ 1805, [2002] 1 All ER 652.

statements made (and not made) at a press conference on private premises.[145] There was judicial criticism of counsel's over reliance upon the HRA when ordinary canons of construction and reliance on common law freedom of expression would suffice to reach a just conclusion which held the meeting to be public and one protected by the privilege. Nonetheless, said Lord Steyn 'Even before the coming into force of the Human Rights Act 1998, the principle of freedom of expression attained the status of a constitutional right with attendant high normative force ... Now freedom of expression is buttressed by the Human Rights Act 1998. The convention fulfils the function of a Bill of Rights in our legal system. There is general agreement that the Act is a constitutional measure...' (p 928)

The final case can be dealt with briefly which does not signify its non-importance. The facts of the *Shayler* case are notorious. Shayler was a former member of the security service who was charged with breaches of the Official Secrets Act 1989, ss 1(1) and 4(1) for disclosing 'classified and top secret' documents to journalists. He had signed two Official Secrets Act declarations and a further contractual undertaking not to disclose information without authority. He was eventually tried and on a preparatory hearing the judge decided that he had no defence to the disclosures – which he alleged were of wrongdoing in the security service – under Article 10 ECHR.[146] His contention was the disclosures were made to alert the public to serious wrongdoing in the security service. They were made in the public interest. If section 1(1) did not allow such a defence it breached his rights under Article 10. It should be interpreted to comply with his convention rights or a declaration of incompatibility should be made, he contended. The statute's relevant sections contained no public interest defence, Lord Bingham ruled, a reading that was clear in consulting the White Paper leading to the Official Secrets Act 1989.

Having emphasised the importance of freedom of speech and provision of information for democratic government, Lord Bingham said:

> Despite the high value placed by the common law on freedom of expression, it was not until the incorporation of the ECHR into our law that this fundamental right was underpinned by statute.[147] On article 10(2) and tests to be applied in restricting freedom of speech 'necessary' has

145 [2000] 4 All ER 913.

146 *R v Shayler* [2002] 2 All ER 477, HL. The CA felt that a defence of necessity may be applicable but not on the facts of the case [2001] EWCA Crim 1977, [2001] 1 WLR 2206.

147 See *Vogt v Germany* (1995) 21 EHRR 205 and Art 10 ECHR.

been strongly interpreted: it is not synonymous with 'indispensable', neither has it the flexibility of such expressions as 'admissible' 'ordinary', 'useful', 'reasonable' or 'desirable': *Handyside v UK* (1976) 1 EHRR 737, 754. One must consider whether the interference complained of corresponded to a pressing social need, whether it was proportionate to the legitimate aim pursued and whether the reasons given by the national authority to justify it are relevant and sufficient under article 10(2): *The Sunday Times v UK* (1979) 2 EHRR 245, 277–278, para 62. (Para 23)

The thrust of the decisions of the CHR has been 'whether, in all the circumstances, the interference with the individual's convention right prescribed by national law is greater than is required to meet the legitimate object which the state seeks to achieve.' (para 26) A variety of internal safety valves existed by which complaint could be made or the former officer could seek permission to publish his complaints/information via ultimately the Cabinet Secretary. Bingham hoped that requests for authorisation to disclose would be granted where no adequate justification existed for denying it and that authorisation would be refused only where such justification existed. (para 31) A refusal would be challengeable on a judicial review. This in line with Lord Steyn's analysis in *Daly* (Chapter 8, p 344 et seq) and constitutes a far more searching scrutiny where fundamental rights are at issue. Where the appellant required legal assistance there may be restrictions on what can be disclosed to that lawyer but 'I cannot envisage circumstances in which it would be proper for the service to refuse its authorisation for any disclosure at all to a qualified lawyer from whom the former member wished to seek advice.' A court might wish to follow the suggestion of appointing special counsel (vetted) to represent the applicant's interests.[148] A complete denial of evidence would be a breach of Article 6(1) ECHR.

A sweeping blanket ban would fall foul of the rights guaranteed in Article 10(1) and would not survive the rigorous and particular test required under Article 10(2). 'The crux of this case is whether the safeguards built into the Official Secrets Act 1989 are sufficient to ensure that unlawfulness and irregularity can be reported to those with the power and duty to take effective action, that the power to withhold information is not abused and that proper disclosures are not stifled. In my opinion, the procedures discussed above, properly applied, provide sufficient and effective

---

[148]   *Rehman v Secretary of State for the Home Department* [2000] 3 All ER 778 paras 31-32 Lord Woolf (CA): ie the procedures before the SIAC: evidence would not be specific to avoid the harm that it was intended to prevent.

safeguards' and included the necessity for the consent of the Attorney General before a prosecution could be commenced. (para 36) The relevant provisions of the Official Secrets Act are compatible with Article 10. This was the unanimous decision.[149]

Lord Hope felt the problems raised by the case had not been really been faced up to by the legislature. The Official Secrets Act is 'vulnerable' because it 'lacks the necessary degree of sensitivity.' But Shayler had chosen not to use the safety valves.[150] The HRA 1998 allowed the raising and articulation of arguments over matters which just three years ago would not have been raised. Conversely, the last time such a high profile prosecution took place under the former Official Secrets Act of 1911, the jury acquitted the defendant under measures which were far broader and more draconian, but under which the jurors effectively had the final say on where the public interest lay.[151]

Article 8 and the right to privacy:[152] In several cases the courts have almost developed a law of privacy from Article 8, the most celebrated being *Douglas v Hello! Ltd* where Sedley LJ's dicta constitute the most powerful statement of the impact of the Article on the development of the common law.[153] However, both that case and *Venables v News Group* are explicable

---

[149] Lord Scott had reservations about Lord Hutton's comments that disclosure of any information may undermine the service in paras 99-100; submissions from press and TV of disclosures and reports were not addressed in the judgment.

[150] Cf ECJ approval for EC staff regs requiring clearance before publishing material is consistent with Art 10 – Stanley Reynolds *Connolly v Commission* Case C-274/99 P [2001] ECR I-1611. See his use of Feldman at para 76. See para 79 for the test to be adopted in a judicial review of a decision refusing authorisation to publish.

[151] *R v Ponting* [1985] Crim LR 18. The proceedings in *Shayler* involved a preparatory hearing under the Criminal Procedure and Investigations Act 1996 to make rulings on questions of law relating to the case (criminal prosecution). These concerned the questions of a public interest defence and compatibility of the OSA, ss 1 and 4 with Art 10 ECHR.

[152] Article 8 also protects family life: see *Clarke v Secretary of State for Transport* [2002] EWCA Civ 819 and Romany gypsies. Scottish courts have held that Article 8 does not engage a right to fox-hunting! *Adams v Lord Advocate* Court of Session (OH) (8 August 2002, unreported). See in the CHR *Taylor-Sabori v UK* (2002) Times, 31 October and surveillance of pager messages via private telecommunications system. On retention of finger-print and DNA samples, *R (S) v Chief Constable of South Yorkshire Police* [2002] EWCA Civ 1275, [2003] 1 All ER 148

[153] [2001] 2 All ER 289, CA.

on grounds of common law confidentiality. *Venables*[154] concerned the intended publication of information about the two murderers of James Bulger which would have been a breach not only of their rights under Article 8, but also Articles 2 and 3. Indeed in awarding an injunction, despite protests of a breach of the press rights under Article 10, the judge was more moved by the force of Articles 2 and 3 rather than 8 and protection of these rights by injunction preventing the press releasing details of their whereabouts and new identities. This was justified under Article 10(2) to protect their rights to confidence to prevent physical injury to them.

In *A v B* Lord Woolf laid down guidance on what is a central feature of the HRA 1998's attempt to protect freedom of the press.[155] This is under the HRA 1998, s 12. The press anxieties that s 12 was intended to assuage were examined above (p 412). It was feared that privacy rights would gain an unjustifiable advantage which would be used by powerful individuals, politicians and otherwise, to hide information which in the public interest should be made public. The public interest would suffer. In *A v B* a newspaper intended to publish allegations of sexual relationships between a Premier league soccer player and two casual partners; the information had come from the partners. Section 12(3) basically provides that before awarding an interim injunction which might affect the Convention right of freedom of expression, no such relief is to be granted to restrain publication before trial 'unless the court is satisfied that the applicant is likely to establish (at trial) that publication should not be allowed.' The court in such interim proceedings must have particular regard to the importance of any Convention right to freedom of expression and where journalistic, literary or artistic material may be in involved or is claimed to be involved the extent of its actual or pending public availability or of the public interest in publishing the material.[156]

In overturning the judge at first instance who had awarded an interim injunction, the Lord Chancellor's Department gave detailed guidance on the future treatment of s 12. His judgment is a remarkable fillip to freedom of speech and publication which takes on board the full thrust of Article 10(1) in a manner which many felt did not properly protect the legitimate sexual secrets of individuals. A clear distinction was drawn between protection of confidences in marriage, or more stable partnerships, and

154 [2001] 1 All ER 908.
155 [2002] EWCA Civ 337 [2002] 2 All ER 545.
156 Section 12(4) which also applies to full hearings.

those of a casual or fleeting nature.[157] Furthermore, the two parties who had intercourse with the claimant wished to divulge their story, for profit, and this touched upon their Article 10 rights; the soccer player was a role model for young boys and a feeling of hypocrisy tainted his behaviour and there was a public interest in the public knowing about his sexploits off the field to help expose hypocrisy. Under Guideline (xii), Lord Woolf said 'Any interference with the press had to be justified irrespective of whether a particular publication was in the public interest' or as some said it was merely interesting to the public. 'The fact that under s 12(4) the court is required to have particular regard to whether it would be in the public interest for the material to be published does not mean that the court is justified in interfering with the freedom of the press where there is no identifiable special public interest in any particular material being published.' Regardless of its quality, the court should not interfere with its publication. Guidance was also given on future judicial use of the direction in s 12 to have regard to any privacy code in weighing the balance. 'Once it is accepted that the freedom of the press should prevail, then the form of reporting in the press is not a matter for the courts but for the Press Complaints Commission and the customers of the newspaper.'[158] (para 48)

This case was followed by *Campbell v Mirror Newspapers plc* in which after Woolf's decision, Morland J ruled that the famous super model Naomi Campbell was entitled to have protected her confidential information relating to her attendance at Narcotics Anonymous for therapy.[159] This, it was held, was confidential information – in the form of personal details and photographs – and there was no public interest in its being published although it is not a prior restraint case because the claimant was not seeking to prevent publication – publication had already taken place and she was seeking damages after the event. The Court of Appeal reversed this decision and dealt with the case as one concerning a breach of confidence while acknowledging that courts were identifying 'the principles by which the law of confidentiality must accommodate the Article 8 and Article 10 rights.' Although the Court accepted that even celebrities are entitled to private space, the claimant's denial that she was a drug addict justified the publication of the story of her addiction and the disclosure of her

[157] See *Theakston v MGN Ltd* [2002] EWHC 137 (QB), [2002] EMLR 398.
[158] Generally, many old precedents now only of historic interest – plea for brevity and cites with approval Morritt VC in *Imutran Ltd v Uncaged Campaigns Ltd* [2001] 2 All ER 385 on *American Cyanamid* which appears contrary to the intention of s 12!
[159] [2002] EWHC 499 (QB), [2002] EMLR 30.

attendance at Narcotics Anonymous was not sufficiently sensitive to attract a right to protection under principles of confidentiality. Although the case was not concerned with the HRA 1998, s 12(3), the Court of Appeal ruled that the Data Protection Act 1998 protection for journalism, literary and artistic use was not confined as a defence to prior restraint, ie as is the case with s 12(3). The exemption applied where a breach of processing sensitive personal data (eg a publication) has occurred and includes the period *after* the publication.[160]

What emerges from Lord Woolf's judgment in *A v B* and from the *Campbell* decision is that contra Sedley LJ, the courts are not developing a common law of privacy; they are basing their judgments upon the established law of confidentiality as *influenced* by the HRA 1998, Articles 8 and 10 and the HRA 1998, s 12. It may, however, be only a question of time before a set of facts emerge which are not protected by confidentiality and which a law of privacy alone can protect.[161] All sets of facts will have to be weighed very carefully from the point of view of Article 10 and Article 8 or other rights. In spite of the very strong judgment in *A v B*, Article 10 is not an automatic 'trump card'.

Article 6: cases coming to the Privy Council and CHR have raised questions about the independence and impartiality of a tribunal determining the civil rights of applicants and rights to a fair trial.[162] The sensitivity of this for the position of the Lord Chancellor and the Law Lords was also seen in Chapter 5. Article 6 was raised in the very important decision of the CHR in *Osmond* and other cases which I examine in the next chapter where the manner in which the question of negligence was dealt with in English case law was brought into question by that court and which led to a sustained exchange of views between the Law Lords and the CHR.[163] In *Rehman* the

---

160   [2002] EWCA Civ 1373, [2002] 42 LS Gaz R 38.
161   *Douglas v Hello!* came close to this because of factual uncertainties but injunctions were not awarded.
162   See Ch 5, p 248 et seq and *McGonnell v UK etc*. See also *Runa Begum v Tower Hamlets London Borough Council* [2002] 2 All ER 668, CA: whether County Court and reviewing officer complied with Art 6 in a homeless case application; homeless application 'civil rights' for Art 6. See also: *R (Beeson) v Dorset County Council* [2001] EWHC Admin 986, [2001] All ER (D) 448 (Nov) and *R (Adlard) v Secretary of State for the Environment etc* [2002] EWCA Civ 735, [2002] 1 WLR 2515 and *R (Bono) v Harlow District Council* [2002] EWHC 423 (Admin), [2002] 1 WLR 2475.
163   See *Matthews v Ministry of Defence* [2002] EWCA Civ 773, [2002] 3 All ER 513, CA and not allowing a service man to sue for negligently inflicted injury when in the armed services.

House of Lords had the opportunity to revisit criticism made in earlier case law on the manner in which decisions involving national security had been dealt with (see below). One dramatic decision of the CHR has ruled that prison governors hearing cases against prisoners had acted in breach of Article 6 in not allowing legal representation where the disciplinary would have amounted to a criminal charge outside prison. Nine hundred prisoners faced early release as a consequence of serving longer periods in gaol after breaches of the Convention in the disciplinary hearings.[164] The decision raised the distinct possibility of removing disciplinary functions from governors. The Law Lords have also ruled that the setting of a tariff for a convicted murderer by the Home Secretary was a breach of Article 6, a decision anticipated by developments in Scotland and Northern Ireland.[165]

The decision in *Alconbury* came as an enormous relief to the executive.[166] The Divisional Court ruled that the exercise by the Secretary of State of appellate powers under planning and related legislation whereby the Secretary of State called in a planning application to be determined by himself rather than by an inspector – or in other instances where he 'recovered' appeals for his own determination from an inspector or made orders – were in breach of Article 6(1). In such cases, the Secretary of State wished to apply a question of policy, or to formulate a policy in respect of such issue of general public importance which he considered rendered it inappropriate for the decision to be made by an inspector. Of 500,000 planning applications each year, 130 are called in and of about 13,000 appeals, about 100 are recovered. As Tuckey LJ said, 'the vast majority of appeals are decided by inspectors' (p 946, para 61). The Secretary of State accepted that he was not an independent and impartial tribunal for the purposes of Article 6, he was nevertheless subject to control by the High Court and this ensured compliance with Article 6. Under the Town and Country Planning Act 1990, s 288, the applicant for planning permission may apply to the High Court to have a decision of the Secretary of State

---

164 *Ezeh and Connors v UK* (2002) 12 BHRC 589 App Nos 39665/98 and 40086/98, ECtHR.

165 *R v Secretary of State for the Home Department, ex p Anderson* [2002] UKHL 46, [2002] 4 All ER 1089. A declaration of incompatibility was also issued in relation to the Home Secretary's powers under the Crime (Sentences) Act 1997, s 29. On Art 5 and prisoners, see *Stafford v UK* (2002) 13 BHRC 260, ECtHR. In *R v Lichniak* [2002] UKHL 47, [2002] 4 All ER 1122, the Law Lords ruled that a mandatory life sentence for murder under Murder (Abolition of Death Penalty) Act 1965, s 1(1) did not breach Articles 3 or 5 ECHR.

166 [2001] UKHL 23, [2001] 2 All ER 929.

quashed on grounds that it was not empowered to be made or that any relevant requirements were not complied with. Where the statutory application to quash was not available, the applicant would have to rely upon judicial review. The existence of judicial review brought the procedure within the requirements of Article 6(1), he believed. The Divisional Court ruled that the procedure adopted by the Secretary of State did breach Article 6 and as this was authorised by the legislation and statutory instruments, a declaration of incompatibility was issued by the court.[167] The role of the reviewing court did not provide a 'full jurisdiction' to deal with appeals on questions of fact and the merits but was confined to a review of legality with limited powers to find errors of law where a fact, for instance, was not supported by evidence.[168] The scheme itself did not comply with Article 6, the Divisional court held (see paras 85 and 86; the challenge under purely domestic law failed.)

A 'leap-frog' appeal was allowed to the Appellate Committee, in this case the judgment of which would have 'far-reaching consequences' for the government. The appeal was allowed. Much was made of Commission and CHR case law that had upheld UK practice in relation to planning decisions whereby a two stage procedure involving an administrative body subject to review in the court did comply with Article 6.[169] A power to re-hear on the merits or policy was not required. A power to quash where there was 'misunderstanding or ignorance of an established and relevant fact' was well established.[170] In para 51 Lord Slynn points out that review in Community law under Article 230 EC is similar to review in domestic law. There is of course proportionality in Community law (see Chapter 8) and a margin of appreciation in making economic assessments. In considering proportionality, Lord Slynn said:

---

[167] That court distinguished *Bryan v UK* (1995) 21 EHRR 342 and relied on a Scottish case: *County Properties Ltd v Scottish Ministers* 2000 SLT 965; in *Bryan,* inspector made final decision not Minister; Lord Hutton found 'some weight' in this submission but not of sufficient force to distinguish the instant case from *Bryan's* case, para 188.

[168] See *Stramek v Austria* (1984) 7 EHRR 351; *Findlay v UK* (1997) 24 EHRR 221 – court martial; *Belios v Switzerland* (1988) 10 EHRR 466; *Bushell v Secretary of State* [1980] 2 All ER 608 cf Slynn, para 47.

[169] *Chapman v UK* (2001) 10 BHRC 48); *Varey v UK* App No 26662/95 (27 October 1999 Commission). The CHR has ruled that judicial review is and is not an effective remedy under Article 13: *Vilvarajah v UK* (1991) 14 EHRR 248 and *Kingsley v UK* (2000) 33 EHRR 13.

[170] *Secretary of State for Education and Science v Tameside Metropolitan Borough Council* [1976] 3 All ER 665 at 675 etc.

> I consider that even without reference to the 1998 Act the time has come
> to recognise that this principle is part of English administrative law, not
> only when judges are dealing with community acts but also when they are
> dealing with acts subject to domestic law.

He invited the other Law Lords to rule on that question of principle at this
stage of the procedure. Even if proportionality were not a part of domestic
law, the power of review was sufficient to comply with Article 6. Lord Nolan
agreed with Slynn but did not think powers of review had to be extended
(they have been under the HRA 1998). Lord Clyde felt similarly on this
point to Nolan (para 169). Hoffman did not feel the issue of 'the limits of
judicial review' needed to be addressed.

Lord Hoffman also allowed the appeal but his concern was directed more
to the type of issue in question in *Alconbury* – a decision purely on the
public interest or a policy decision which is best made by a body which is
democratically accountable. It is a decision which has to be rendered
politically accountable and not one which requires a power to come to an
opposite decision on the merits of a policy. Its legality including its fairness
could be challenged. Were Article 6 (and the HRA 1998, s 2(1)) to require
a merits review, this Hoffman would have great difficulty accepting: 'The
House is not bound by decisions of the CHR and if I thought the Divisional
Court was right to hold that they compelled a conclusion fundamentally at
odds with the distribution of powers under the British Constitution, I would
have considerable doubt as to whether they should be followed.' No such
dramatic safety valve was required: the Divisional Court had misunderstood
the jurisprudence of the CHR! [171]

According to Lord Clyde 'Planning matters are essentially matters of policy
and expediency, not law.' (para 159) They are primarily matters for the
executive to resolve, not the courts.

---

[171] Lord Hoffman considered 'administrative' cases discussing whether a breach of
Article 6 could take place (is it a civil right etc) and if so, has a breach actually
taken place. Hoffman's preference would be to say that the 'administrative stage'
ie before the Secretary of State, did not fall within Art 6 and one concentrates
purely on the adequacy of the judicial review, or the act does fall within Art 6 but
the administrator's partiality can be cured by 'an adequate and impartial judicial
review' para 135; Lord Hutton felt that the CHR had departed from the
Commission ruling in *Kaplan v UK* (1980) 4 EHRR 64 and had ruled that ministerial
decisions were within Article 6(1) but were covered by the existence of judicial
review.

Lord Hutton argued that: 'the Strasbourg jurisprudence recognises that where an administrative decision to be taken in the public interest constitutes a determination of a civil right within the meaning of Article 6(1), a review of the decision by a court is sufficient to comply with Article 6(1) notwithstanding that the review does not extend to the merits of the decision.

An area where the UK had encountered particular difficulty in relation to administrative procedures had concerned those where the Secretary of State has decided to deport an alien in exercise of his powers to act for the public good on the grounds of political, diplomatic or national security grounds. This has been tested in the courts on several occasions and the response to criticism from the CHR for the approach taken by English courts can be seen below under national security.

Article 5 (detention): Another case to cause momentary anxiety for the executive was the decision of the High Court in *Saadi*.[172] The claimants for review were four Iraqi Kurds who claimed asylum on arrival in the UK. Claims for asylum, both generally and from Iraqi Kurds, had been 'escalating' (para 3 of the judgment for figures). They were detained in a reception centre established to deal with the problem of large numbers of asylum seekers under powers in the Immigration Act 1971 (para 16(1) of Sch 2). The aim was to make decisions on asylum within about seven days. The claimants, none of whom had been detained for more than ten days, challenged their detention and at first instance it was held that detention under the 1971 Act was authorised. However, it was in breach of Article 5(1) and their right to liberty since it was not justified by the exception to that article in Article 5(1)(f) namely the lawful arrest or detention of a person to prevent his effecting an unauthorised entry into the country or of a person against whom action was being taken with a view to deportation.[173] This decision in particular was the cause of the Home Secretary, David Blunket's attack on lawyers and their use of the HRA 1998 to undermine public interest.

Collins J appreciated the inconvenience of his decision noting that justice and convenience were often not on speaking terms.[174] Lord Phillips on

---

[172]   *R (Saadi) v Secretary of State for the Home Department* [2001] EWCA Civ 1512, [2001] 4 All ER 961.

[173]   Decision of Collins J, 7 September 2001.

[174]   Repeating a point made by Lord Atkin in *General Medical Council v Spackman* [1943] AC 627.

appeal observed that if Collins J were correct, 'a cornerstone of the government's current procedure for processing applications for asylum is removed.' What Lord Phillips MR did was to interpret the Article 5 right in the light of domestic law – it is artificial to treat the rights under the Convention and domestic rights separately, he argued. Policies restraining the powers to detain aliens who come to 'our shores' 'do not result from any conscious application of Article 5 of the Convention. They result from recognition, that it is part of our heritage, of the fundamental importance of liberty.' The Secretary of State had determined that detention of about a week is not unreasonable and a short detention can be justified where this will enable speedy determination of his or her application for leave to enter. 'In restricting detention to such circumstances he may well have gone beyond what the CHR would require. We are content that he should have done so.' (para 67) The Master of the Rolls found that 'no disproportionality is demonstrated in this case' – detention had not gone on for too long (para 66, Court of Appeal). But it might be considered 'objectionable' if such persons were detained for 'any significant length of time' in the absence of good reasons such as a risk of absconding or misbehaving. Not only was detention justified within the statutory framework, it was lawful within the Convention. Its legitimacy [detention] should receive 'strict scrutiny.' The Law Lords rejected the appeal.[175]

This case stands in complete contrast to the position adopted under Community law in interpreting directives as we saw in Chapter 4, p 186 et seq. As the White Paper insisted, Community law was legally binding upon domestic courts whereas Convention law will be subject to local interpretation. *Saadi* shows how powerful that local influence can be.

How enriched and different has our law been and become because of this European influence? One area has shown signs of activity: national security.

National security

I have written elsewhere of the almost complete zone of immunity the courts have given to claims of national security in the past.[176] It was a famous judgment of the ECJ which first invoked fundamental rights from Article 6

---

[175] [2002] UKHL 41 – detention justified 'for a short period in acceptable physical conditions as being reasonably necessary.'

[176] *Freedom of Information: the Law, the Practice and the Ideal* (2001, 3rd ed).

ECHR to rule that a certificate stating that an act discriminating against the claimant issued by the Secretary of State was issued on the grounds inter alia of national security denied the claimant her fundamental right of access to justice. The impact of the certificate was to terminate her claim to compensation for sexual discrimination against the Chief Constable of the Royal Ulster Constabulary.[177] Other cases have also challenged as breaches of ECHR provisions UK government practices based on national security grounds which had sought to prevent applicants in Northern Ireland seeking compensation for denial of Article 6 rights.[178] Widespread change to legislation has had to be made to ensure rights against discrimination may be investigated in spite of national security considerations.[179]

Elsewhere the power of the Secretary of State to issue a certificate under the Data Protection Act 1998, s 7(1) exempting the Security Service from responding to a request by a person (an MP) who requested the Service to disclose whether they processed personal data on him, and if so, what they were, has been successfully challenged. The response had been given in 'non committal terms' – the service neither confirmed nor denied the existence of such data – and this was challenged before the Data Protection Tribunal under the Data Protection Act 1998, s 28(4). This involved powers under Data Protection Act 1998, s 28(5) in which the Tribunal may determine whether the Secretary of State has 'reasonable grounds' for issuing the certificate. Such a reply could be made where reasons of national security made this 'necessary'. It was accepted that where the service lawfully determines that a positive response would be harmful to national security, a non-committal policy (neither confirmed nor denied) would be permissible. But it was not permissible to adopt a blanket policy which relieved the service from the obligation to consider whether or not national security would be harmed by a 'positive response to the particular request.' There were no reasonable grounds to permit the service to respond in such wide terms by issuing the certificate, it was contended. The appellant also contended that the present case is a case where a positive response could have been given to his request. But the Tribunal did not consider it necessary to consider the individual circumstances of his request but

177 Case 222/84 *Johnston v Chief Constable RUC* [1986] 3 All ER 135.
178 *Tinnelly and McElduff* (1998) 27 EHRR 249: *Devenney v UK* (Application No 24265/94) (2002) Times, 11 April.
179 Employment Relations Act 1999, Sch 8; Race Relations Act 2000, ss 7 and 8 (only one national security certificate under RRA 1976) and Northern Ireland Act 1998, ss 90–92 and Sch 11.

restricted its inquiry to the issue of informing a requester whether or not his personal data are being requested. Did the Minister have reasonable grounds for issuing the certificate in such terms? The tribunal concluded the Minister did not have reasonable grounds for issuing the certificate 'which this unnecessarily wide effect'. The certificate concentrated on 'circumstances in which data were acquired or held by the service rather than the consequences for national security if data were released or their existence acknowledged at the time of the request.' The certificate was therefore quashed.

The Tribunal applies the principles of judicial review as applied by the courts. These principles have now been reinforced by the HRA 1998, especially in this area Article 8, and by doctrines of proportionality which apply to the construction of the Data Protection Act 1998. As the decision of the Tribunal shows these (and this is the case law discussed in this chapter and Chapter 7) clearly have given added weight in the protection of that right.[180]

In *Chahal v UK*, the CHR found a breach of Article 13 and rights to an effective national remedy. This article was not incorporated within the HRA 1998. Chahal, who was subject to deportation on grounds of national security, was not allowed to challenge evidence against him and judicial review did not allow a sufficiently anxious form of review of the decision made by an informal body of 'three wise persons'.[181] To circumscribe further effective challenge before the CHR, the government introduced a special procedure under the Special Immigration Appeals Commission Act 1997 establishing the Special Immigration Appeals Commission (SI 1998/1881). Rehman was a Pakistani national who was subject to an order of deportation because his presence here was not conducive to the public good on grounds of national security certified by the Home Secretary. He was accused of being involved with, and fund-raising for, Islamic terrorist groups. The Secretary of State was empowered to make two statements to the Special Immigration Appeals Commission: an open one and a closed statement. Rehman could see the former but not the latter although following a procedure adopted in Canada, a security vetted advocate can be appointed to present the case for the appellant while the latter may be excluded. The open statement stated that the security services 'assessed' that he directly

---

[180] *Norman Baker v Secretary of State for the Home Department* Decision of Information Tribunal, 1 October 2001.
[181] (1996) 23 EHRR 413.

supported terrorist activities in the Indian sub-continent although those involved were unlikely to carry out acts of violence in this country. He was also 'partly responsible' for an increase in the number of Muslims who have undergone forms of military training and indoctrination into extremist beliefs and 'some basic weapons training'. His activities in the UK were intended to further the cause of terrorist organisation abroad. The appeal was heard in open and closed sessions hearing 'open' and 'restricted and closed' information.

The Commission decided that 'on a high civil balance of probabilities' the charge against the appellant had not been made out. They had not been satisfied that the continuing presence in the UK of the appellant was a danger to national security. The question of national security was a question of law that it had jurisdiction to decide – one could say it was jurisdictional and was not a matter exclusively for the Home Secretary. It was not satisfied with the Home Secretary's definition of terrorism which the Commission believed was activity 'targeted against the state, its system of government or its people.' Finally the various grounds on which a deportation could be ordered on grounds of public good in the interests of national security, or of international relations between the UK and any other country or for other reasons of a political nature, were disjunctive not cumulative.

An appeal against the Commission's decision to the Court of Appeal was successful. Basically, it held that the wrong standard of proof had been applied by the Commission and it had given too narrow a definition of 'terrorism' which it had equated with defence of the realm.[182] It had made mistakes of law. In the House of Lords, Lord Slynn accepted that the Commission was given a power to review the discretion of the Secretary of State where it 'should have been exercised differently' or where any decision was not in accordance with the law or any applicable rules. This was necessary to comply with the judgment against the UK in *Chahal v UK* (above). Although the review of discretion infers a power of merits review whether the discretion should have been exercised differently 'will normally depend on whether on the facts found the steps taken by the Secretary of State were disproportionate to the need to protect national security.' There must be some possibility of danger to the security or well being of the nation, said Slynn. The Secretary of State cannot simply give any reason.

---

[182] *Secretary of State v Rehman* [2001] UKHL 47, [2002] 1 All ER 122; [2000] 3 All ER 778, CA. See *Council of Civil Service Unions v Minister for the Civil Service* [1985] AC 374; Security Service Act 1989, s 1(2).

There must be some probative material. 'There must be material on which proportionately and reasonably he can conclude that there is a real possibility of activities harmful to national security but he does not have to be satisfied ... that all the material before him is proved and his conclusion is justified, to a 'high degree of civil probability.' (para 22) But all Law Lords felt that the definition of terrorism adopted by the Commission was too narrow. It does not have to be targeted; the threat may be global and unspecific, indirect and consequential. 'The cumulative effect may establish that the individual is to be treated as a danger' said Lord Woolf in the Court of Appeal and 'the executive is the best judge of the need for international cooperation to combat international terrorism and counter terrorist strategies' (Lord Steyn). In making this judgment, a security service officer may be as concerned with the presence of an alien who not only in fact has endangered national security but who is a *danger* to national security – a future risk. There was complete agreement that the grounds of deportation in the Immigration Act 1971, s 15(3) were not disjunctive; the Secretary of State did not have to hang his colours to only one mast; they could be read together and as such reinforced the 'global' approach adopted by the appeal court.

Although it might easily be seen as a judicial apologia for non-involvement in this area of supreme executive sensitivity, the approach is an improvement on previous case law. It should be recalled that the hearing was in May 2001. Judgment was on 11 October 2001. In between in September 2001 were the horrific events in New York. Lord Steyn had made up his mind after hearing argument in May. Lord Hoffman wrote his judgment before the events of 11 September.

For the latter, the position came down to the inappropriateness of the Commission – a judicial organ – meddling in high matters of state. While national security was a question of law, 'in the interests of national security' was a question of policy which courts were ill equipped to address. The judicial controls were establishing that a factual basis exists, but the evaluation is for the executive. This is subject to the proviso that an opinion must be of a kind that no reasonable Minister could reasonably have held. Last of all, if an Article 3 right (torture) is in issue, 'the European jurisprudence makes it clear that whether deportation is in the interests of the national security is irrelevant to rights under Article 3.' (para 54) On the burden of proof, Lord Hoffman felt that its application was not really appropriate where we are discussing not past facts but future risks. It is not a criminal trial. The Commission has to be advised about its limitations in the appellate process – it is not 'the primary finder of fact' – that is the

Secretary of State with all his 'advisers'. In evaluating a risk, a 'considerable' margin will have to be given to the person evaluating the risk. Really its role is a *Wednesbury* review in a secondary and not a primary sense.[183]

Fundamental human rights – What remains?

The potential for the Act implementing the ECHR to be truly revolutionary in our legal and political consciousness should not be understated. It is a constitutional change which has had the most dramatic impact on the way judges and lawyers think – and not simply in the obvious areas of public law and criminal law and procedure. Perhaps surprisingly, the Lord Chancellor's Department has reported that about a dozen issues raised on human rights case law could be described as 'new' (www.lcd.gov.uk). But the HRA's model of human rights is built on traditional liberal individualistic lines. Its makes no concessions to the third generation of human rights such as a healthy environment, transparency and openness and access to information about the way we are governed in a global economy, and rights to sustenance.[184] The attempts to use Article 10 and 8 to make inroads into closed decision-making were seen above. In imposing duties on courts and tribunals to use the jurisprudence of the Convention institutions, the legislation could introduce an 'indirect horizontal effectiveness' insofar as judges will have to interpret duties in private relationships with reference to the Convention and Act. The Convention jurisprudence has imposed liability on the state where its failure to remedy an abuse by a private individual led to a breach of Article 8 by the state.[185] It is agreed that the Act does not *bind* private parties exercising *private* powers or 'functions' and has no direct horizontal effect. But statutory, and specifically, common law provisions will have to be interpreted in the light of duties binding on courts under the Convention which have not hitherto existed: the duty to recognise and enforce human rights and a duty not to allow them to be overborne by other rights in individual

---

[183] See *ex p Smith* Ch 8, pp 339 et seq.

[184] See *Marcic v Thames Water Utilities Ltd* [2002] EWCA Civ 65, [2002] 2 All ER 55 where a successful claim was made for common law nuisance and a breach of Article 8.

[185] *X and Y v Netherlands* (1985) 8 EHRR 235. There is a horizontal application of human rights under the Basic Law in Germany: B Markesinis (1999) LQR 47 and *Always on the Same Path* (2001) ch 8. In Irish law, basic constitutional rights are horizontally effective: *Meskell v Córas Eireann* [1973] IR 121 at 132–33 and *Lovett v Logan* [1995] ILRM 12.

relationships. *Douglas* and *Campbell* both illustrate this impact as between private parties. In *Ashdown v Telegraph Group Ltd*, the Court of Appeal was not persuaded that a breach of copyright by a newspaper which had published the contents of the diaries of a former politician without permission was justified by Article 10. Although on the facts, Article 10 could not be successfully invoked by the newspaper, its potential invocation against a private individual was beyond dispute.[186] The question of such effect spawned a great deal of academic comment as the Bill was enacted and before it came into effect. There was a wide range of diverging opinion.[187] There can be no doubt that the HRA 1998 will influence legal relationships between individuals. In the *Leonard Cheshire* case discussed above (p 403) Lord Woolf spoke of guarantees of the HRA 1998 protection being written into the contract between the authority and service provider. Lord Woolf suggested a resident, as well as the authority, could enforce the contract against the provider. Would the authority have to draft a clause specifying that the contract was enforceable at the suit of a resident?[188] The problem of 'horizontality' will not go away. The HRA 1998 could help subject private power relationships to constitutional norms of good behaviour.

---

[186] [2001] EWCA Civ 1142, [2001] 4 All ER 666; Morritt J's judgment can be criticised for not giving sufficient weight to the HRA 1998 argument although correct in conclusion.

[187] H W R Wade (2000) LQR 217 who was firmly of the view that some provisions of the incorporated Convention were directly effective between individuals; Sir R.Buxton opposed this view (2000) LQR 48; M Hunt who believed that indirect horizontal effect would be produced – powerfully argued although some of the examples did not work (1998) Public Law 423; I Leigh (1999) ICLQ 57. See Mummery LJ in *JA Pye Ltd (Oxford) v Graham* [2001] EWCA Civ 117, [2001] Ch 804: not necessary to discuss in the case the effect of the HRA 1998, s 6(1) on private law issues arising between one citizen and another. I am grateful to Mike Varney for this reference.

[188] See Contracts (Rights of Third Parties) Act 1999. I am grateful to Gordon Anthony for raising this point with me.

Chapter 10

Principles of liability[1]

The area of liability is one of the most contentious of litigated subjects in the recent jurisprudence of public law, both domestically and in the EU. The interrelationship of the exercise of statutory powers and negligence liability has been described by Lord Brown-Wilkinson as a 'nightmare world.'[2] If I may take Community law first, the decisions of the ECJ which established a liability for breaches of Community law by Member States, even though no such liability was established in the Treaties, have rightly been regarded as one of the most significant contributions by that court to the jurisprudence of Community Law – and it is a jurisprudence which was inspired by a specific EC Treaty provision enjoining the ECJ to seek inspiration from the laws of Member States – the second paragraph of Article 288 [215] EC. Walter van Gerven has, however, expressed the view that further inspiration from Article 288 is required on questions related to 'causation' and other matters left to national courts.[3] Questions of liability have also produced one of the most engaged dialogues between the CHR and the English courts as shall be explained.

The basic problem, if that is not too dramatic an expression for the English position, has been the reluctance of English law to establish liability for the wrongs of public authorities. By liability I refer to a liability in damages for culpable wrong whether brought about by negligence, some other

---

[1]   I am grateful to Martina Kunnecke for helpful comments on this chapter.

[2]   M Andenas and D Fairgrieve in M Andenas ed *English Public Law and the Common Law of Europe* (1998) at p 286.

[3]   W van Gerven in J Beatson and T Tridimas eds *New Directions in European Public Law* (1998) pp 38 et seq.

private action such as nuisance, a breach of statutory duty under one of literally hundreds of statutes or for misfeasance of public office which I shall refer to below.[4] The following chapter does not offer a treatise on liability. We are well served by domestic[5] and European accounts of the law.[6] What the chapter seeks to achieve is an explanation of the relationship between domestic and European principles of liability and to ask whether domestic law can be adapted in line with European approaches, and whether there is anything to be gained from such adaptation.

There are numerous reasonably routine cases where public authorities have been found liable for tortious wrongdoing and have had to pay for damages in domestic law. The difficulty arises in those areas where such wrongdoing, usually negligence, is wrapped up within the exercise of statutory powers or duties. To impose liability may inhibit the exercise of discretion and judgement in a manner that hinders effective public service and protection of the public – the latter being the reason why a statute was passed in the first place. People providing public services may simply act with a fear of litigation uppermost in their mind and not the public interest. The courts have also been reluctant to interpret statutes in a manner which creates rights owed to individuals under private law but I do not develop this point.

Historically, the reluctance to allow government bodies to be sued in England was evidenced by the doctrine, still surviving in many states, of sovereign immunity.[7] In England, the Crown could not be sued in its own courts. This doctrine of immunity, which did not extend to non-Crown public bodies,[8] was finally brought to an end with the Crown Proceedings Act

---

4   See Lord Browne-Wilkinson in *X v Bedfordshire County Council* [1995] 3 All ER 353, HL for the categorisation of actions against public authorities. There can be no action for 'careless' performance of a statutory duty in the absence of a common law duty of care situation. Such a duty may arise as a result of the statute or as a consequence of the manner of its performance.

5   See P Craig *Administrative Law* (1999, 4th ed) ch 26.

6   Craig *Administrative Law* (1999, 4th ed); T Heukels and A McDonnell eds *The Action for Damages in Community Law* (1997); B Markesinis, J-B Auby et al *Tortious Liability of Statutory Bodies: A Comparative and Economic Study of Five English Cases* (1999); P Craig (1997) LQR 67; D Fairgrieve, M Andenas and J Bell *Tort Liability of Public Authorities Comparative Perspective* (2002); M Wathelet and S van Raepenbusch (1997) 33 CDE 13. From a previous generation: H Street *Governmental Liability: A Comparative Study* (1953).

7   J Bell and A Bradley *Governmental Liability: A Comparative Study* (1991).

8   *Mersey Docks and Harbour Board v Gibbs* (1866) LR 1 HL 93; *Geddis v Proprietors of Bann Resevoir* (1878) 3 App Cas 430.

1947 which allowed the Crown to be sued in those circumstances where an individual in his or her private capacity could be sued. English law had always held an individual acting under Crown authority liable for his wrongs in his *personal* as opposed to *official* capacity.[9] The 1947 Act now allowed official recourse to the Consolidated Fund for payment of damages for tortious injuries committed by a Crown servant in the course of their employment. The Crown and the servant are made jointly and severally liable. 'Crown' here means a governmental institutional capacity and not the monarch personally.

Unlike French law, English law does not allow an action for damages for ultra vires action which does not involve some form of tortious activity.[10] As it is expressed, there is no tortious liability *per se* for ultra vires activity or for a breach of a public law duty. 'The breach of a public law right by itself gives rise to no claim for damages. A claim for damages must be based on a private law cause of action.'[11] Community law will allow a remedy in damages where there is a sufficiently serious breach of Community law which contains an obligation owed to an individual by a Member State without the need to establish any additional factors such as negligence or deliberate abuse.[12] In France, although liability does arise from illegal acts or failures to act, damage has to be established which flows directly from the illegal action or decision.[13]

Sedley LJ has remarked on the absence from English law of a right to damages for abuse of power falling below misfeasance of public office which is very difficult to prove. Misfeasance of public office concerns the exercise in bad faith of public power that causes injury to the claimant. The tort is constituted by a deliberate use of public power to injure an individual (targeted malice) or knowingly or recklessly acting outside one's legal powers and causing injury to the individual of which the official was aware

9   *Entick v Carrington* (1765) 19 State Tr 1029; *Raleigh v Goschen* [1898] 1 Ch 73.

10 *R v Knowsley Metropolitan Borough Council, ex p Maguire* (1992) 90 LGR 653; W Reid (1993) *Public Law* 221.

11 Lord Browne-Wilkinson in *X v Bedfordshire County Council* [1995] 3 All ER 353, HL at 363h.

12 Case C-5/94 *R v MAFF, ex p Hedley Lomas* [1996] ECR I-2553: the breach of Art 29 [34] EC – quantitative restrictions on exports – was sufficiently serious a breach to justify liability.

13 The damage has to be caused by the illegality: see D Fairgrieve, M Andenas and J Bell *Tort Liability of Public Authorities Comparative Perspective* (2002) p 297 and N Brown and J Bell *French Administrative Law* ch 8.

or to which s/he was recklessly indifferent.[14] In speaking of an absence of a right to damages where misfeasance is not present, Sedley LJ said:

> [Their absence] does not necessarily mean that the door is closed to them in principle but the policy implications of such a step are immense, and it may well be that – despite the presence for some years of the rules of a power to award damages on an application for judicial review – a legal entitlement to them cannot now come into being without legislation.[15]

It was seen in Chapter 3, p 123 et seq how liability for public bodies in France is catered for by *droit administratif*, unless areas are removed to the civil law by statute. One such area that has been so removed is motor vehicle accidents. It is worth re-emphasising a few more points concerning public liability in France. Where English law tends to rely upon various forms of subjective or objective degrees of fault in the absence of a statutory right owed to an individual, French law has dispensed with the concept in a variety of areas. It must be said, however, that damages in French public law are not as generous as in common law although there is less reluctance to compensate for pure economic loss than in England.[16]

Where an area carries a special risk, as in new forms of medical treatment, no negligence may have to be established in France because the victim should not bear the 'risk' of such new treatment.[17] The theory of risk is in fact a highly developed basis of liability in French public law and covers areas such as dangerous activities where it would be unfair to place the risk of such activity on an individual victim.[18] In fact, where a victim suffers from public action without any question of fault or illegality, that person may be entitled to compensation where harm is done to advance the public good. The basis of liability may be found in Article 13 of the Declaration of

---

[14] For misfeasance, see *Three Rivers District Council v Bank of England (No 3)* [2000] 3 All ER 1, HL and M Andenas and D Fairgrieve (2002) ICLQ 757 for a study of this case and related cases in a comparative perspective.

[15] *F&I Services Ltd v Customs and Excise Comrs* [2001] EWCA Civ 762, [2001] All ER (D) 280, para 73 commenting on M Fordham and G White (2001) JR 44.

[16] See W van Gerven *National, Supranational and International Tort Law* (1998); B Markesinis in 2001 *Current Legal Problems* 591 ed M Freeman.

[17] CAA Lyon, 21 December 1990, Gomez; CE, 3 November 1997, Hopital Joseph-Imbert D'Arles; N Brown and J Bell *French Administrative Law* p 184.

[18] N Brown and J Bell *French Administrative Law* pp 193 et seq.

the Rights of Man 'equality before public burdens'.[19] In German law, the analogous principle is known as *Sonderöpfer*. Similarly, in France where legislation has the effect of damaging an individual's interests, compensation may be payable but only where, inter alia, the victim can show special damage.[20]

Where fault has to be established, a distinction is also drawn in France, as we saw in Chapter 3, p 123 et seq between *faute simple* and *faute lourde*.[21] The distinction is between simple or ordinary degrees of fault and very serious fault. The latter has been associated with very difficult and demanding exercises of judgment and the case law, where fault is required, had moved more towards a *faute simple* basis of liability although *faute lourde* was recently required in a case concerning banking regulation.[22]

The wind of change

Two major developments have occurred which impacted on the English law of liability. First of all, as part of its developing jurisprudence, the ECJ has used the pressure point of liability to ensure the *effet utile* of EC law; that is, it has sought to encash real rights for those who are injured by the actions of Member States that breach EC law and where the earlier doctrines of sovereignty of EC law and direct effect (Chapter 2, pp 46 and 97 et seq) may not be sufficient to provide adequate relief for one reason or another. A failure to receive compensation for damage or loss may be one such reason. A 'victim' may complain to the Commission under enforcement proceedings and the Commission is empowered to take action under Article 226 EC which may involve the award of fines if breaches are established on the part of a Member State by the ECJ under Article 228 EC (see Chapter 11, pp 481 and Chapter 3, p 109). But this does not compensate the victim. Therefore, from the early 1990s, the Court fashioned a liability in basically

---

[19] R Errera [1986] *Current Legal Problems* 157, at 171–2; N Brown and J Bell *French Administrative Law* p 184. In England, compensation schemes administered on a discretionary basis may be created.

[20] CE 14 January 1938, La Fleurette.

[21] Andenas and Fairgrieve (2002) ICLQ 757 above. And also between faute de service and faute personnelle as we saw in Ch 3, pp 123 et seq.

[22] Cf the Conseil d'Etat in Kechichian AJDA 2002, 136 and Ch 3, p 123. The liability of the regulator was set at 10% of the loss because the main cause of injury was the activities of the fraudulent bank.

tort/delict where there was a culpable breach of Community law.[23] This was in contradistinction to its earlier approach that remedies for breaches of directly effective rights in EC law were primarily a matter for domestic courts. A remedy of restitution had been fashioned by the ECJ where money had been wrongly paid in breach of EC law[24] or as a defence where wrongly demanded. But elsewhere the ECJ had been silent as to remedy. In *Bourgoin*, the English Court of Appeal determined, by a majority, that breaches of directly effective rights were remediable by public law judicial review;[25] no rights in private law were created and therefore no damages could be claimed in the absence of a breach of a private law obligation.[26] The dissenting judge, Oliver LJ, pointed out that there is a paradox in a right being owed to an individual where there is no individual remedy enforceable by that individual. A right to have the law enforced is a right owed to everyone: but a failure to receive reparation for damage caused to an individual is to possess no right.

Secondly, the CHR has found breaches of Articles of the ECHR, particularly but not exclusively Article 6 ECHR guaranteeing fair, independent and timely trials in the determination of an individual's civil rights and obligations. The circumstances in which such findings occurred were those in which a contracting state, in that Court's opinion, had failed to provide an opportunity for judicial redress of a grievance. Access to the courts and judicial determination of the dispute and any rights in issue had been denied or prevented. It was prevented by the application of precedent in preliminary proceedings known as applications to strike out the case where public authorities sought to have actions 'struck out' before trial because they disclosed no cause of action – there was no case in law to answer. The view of the English courts has been that such denial had not taken place (see below p 464 et seq).

There is in fact a third aspect of this discussion which concerns the award of damages under the HRA 1998 for breaches of the ECHR and where UK

---

23 The juridical nature of the tort is subject to some controversy: see M Hoskins in J Beatson and T Tridimas *New Directions in European Public Law* (1998) ch 7 and below.

24 Case 222/82 *Apple and Pear Development Council v Lewis* [1983] ECR 4083.

25 [1985] 3 All ER 585, CA; there is a notable dissent by Oliver LJ.

26 In *Garden Cottage Foods v Milk Marketing Board* [1983] 2 All ER 770, HL the majority believed that a breach of Art 82 [86] EC would be compensable in damages which were an adequate remedy thereby refusing an interim injunction.

judges may award damages in accordance with HRA 1998, s 8 for such breaches. I deal with this point towards the conclusion of this chapter.[27]

Why the fuss?

Before I look at EC law and decisions of the CHR, I must examine more closely the issue that causes so much difficulty. In discussing liability of public authorities, we are not talking about simple negligence committed by public authorities. If a NHS doctor amputates the wrong leg, a school teacher while running between classes accidentally injures a child by knocking her over in the playground, or a police car runs over a pedestrian in circumstances amounting to negligence, there is liability. There are problems of proof, litigation anxiety, the role of insurance companies and all the other difficulties associated with accident litigation. In some areas, Parliament may have excluded liability as in the case of those in the armed services who were injured as a consequence of the negligence of other members of those services (Crown Proceedings Act 1947, s 10). The Crown Proceedings (Armed Forces) Act 1987 sought to amend the law to allow service men injured after the 1987 Act was enacted to bring proceedings. In *Matthews v Ministry of Defence* the Court of Appeal ruled that immunity prior to that date was not a breach of the HRA 1998.[28] In other areas it is common to impose a liability under statute for regulators only where they acted with malice; in other words negligence is excluded. There would also be difficulties claiming for pure economic loss under negligence.[29] The case of the boxer Michael Watson who was seriously injured in a fight with Chris Ewebank and whose condition was aggravated by the absence of adequate medical facilities at the arena led to a successful action in negligence against the British Boxing Board of Control (a non-statutory

---

27   D Fairgrieve (2001) Public Law 695.

28   [2002] EWCA Civ 773, [2002] 3 All ER 513.

29   Eg the Financial Services and Markets Act 2000, s 102; there is a saving for acts which are unlawful under the HRA 1998, s 6(1): see Ch 9, p 402. On the reluctance of the courts to impose a duty of care on regulators to investors, see: *Yuen Kun Yen v A-G of Hong Kong* [1988] AC 175; *Davis v Radcliffe* [1990] 2 All ER 536, both in the Privy Council. The role of the Parliamentary Ombudsman where maladministration is alleged, as in the Barlow Clowes investment scandal should not be overlooked: for the report HC 76 (1989–90) and P Birkinshaw *Grievances, Remedies and the State* (1994, 2nd ed) ch 5. See also: *Reeman v Department of Transport* [1997] 2 Lloyd's Rep 648 on health and safety regulation.

self regulatory body) a ruling which the latter claimed would bankrupt it. The case is instructive as to why liability may be excluded or limited in the case of statutory bodies.[30]

The 'problem' occurs in cases where there is a question of judgment, discretion and choice involved in the exercise of a statutory power and the use of what are frequently scarce resources which depend upon the outcome of the exercise of judgment or discretion. The old case of *East Suffolk Rivers Catchment Board v Kent* illustrates the problem.[31] In this case a catchment board which had powers to take action after sea flooding was accused of being so dilatory that the plaintiff owner of flooded land claimed damages against the Board for the period beyond which their land was flooded as a consequence of the Board's alleged incompetence. 14 days was a reasonable period – 164 days was the actual time it took to clear the land. In finding for the Board, the judges felt that the real cause of the flooding was the original act of nature and not the incompetence of the Board. The Board had a power to act; they therefore had a power not to act. If punished for acting incompetently, their decision next time might be to do nothing. The courts at that time would not have established a liability for doing nothing in such circumstances – there was no positive duty to act, although it may have introduced questions of enforcement of duties owed to the public through a mandamus or mandatory order as it is now called. The case has been seen as an early example, though not the first by any means, of the junction point between public law and control of powers and their exercise, and the question of common law liability.

If there is a power to act; there is unavoidably a power not to act. If a finding of negligence attaches to acting, the public authority's response may well be not to exercise the power on a following occasion. If a power involves fine tuning judgement on a question of balancing risks and benefits in the introduction of a social policy, or allocating scarce resources, courts inevitably believe that they are ill-equipped to make such decisions by deciding whether objectively the authorities should have come to a particular conclusion. It effectively involves second guessing a judgment on its merits whereas judicial review involves a question of illegality and process, not merits. The developments in judicial review to fathom decision-making more deeply which were addressed in Chapter 8 may make such

---

30   Not because of insolvency but because of the sheer expense (anticipated) of successful actions. See *Watson v British Boxing Board of Control* [2001] QB 1134, CA.

31   [1941] AC 74. M Bowman and S Bailey (1984) Public Law 277.

distinctions less compelling but courts are notably reluctant to review discretion in areas concerning financial management and economic policy (Chapter 8, p 345 et seq).

The approach of English courts in cases where it is alleged that there has been negligence in the exercise of a statutory power has been dogged by a great deal of confusion which did much to add to the complexity of the subject. The basic approach until 1995 was that where a discretion was conferred, a party injured by the negligent exercise or non-exercise of that discretion had to prove first of all that the exercise was ultra vires and secondly that the exercise was a negligent breach of a duty of care owed to the victim in tort. The authority had to be in some way outside their lawful discretion before liability could attach because otherwise they would be held liable in tort where they otherwise acted lawfully.[32] The two stage process was not unlike the early position in EC law where before one could sue for damages for injury caused by an unlawful measure, a claimant first had to have an application for a judicial review of the measure in question upheld under what was Article 173 EC.[33] This position in Community law has long since changed.

In cases where there is a failure to exercise a power, where the authority fail to do anything as a consequence of their discretion, the requirement that such failure amounts to an unlawful exercise of discretion as a preliminary to a breach of duty of care to a victim becomes more apparent. If the authority decides quite legitimately not to exercise a power, then its decision is lawful and it can face no liability. It is only where it abuses its discretion or chooses not to exercise it at all that it is acting unlawfully. In these circumstances, its decision may be open to attack on the ground that it is an abuse of a discretion and a breach of duty of care. In *Anns v London Borough of Merton*, damage was caused to buildings as a result, it was alleged, of inadequate inspection of foundations by building inspectors. The authority argued that as they possessed a statutory power to inspect they had a power not to inspect which they could exercise with impunity. Basically, Lord Wilberforce believed that the power was one which must be exercised reasonably so if they exercised their discretion unreasonably in the *Wednesbury* sense, they were outside the realm of their legitimate authority. Once outside their legitimate area of authority,

---

[32] Lord Diplock in *Home Office v Dorset Yacht Co Ltd* [1970] AC 1004, Cf Lord Reid in the same case. Lord Wilberforce in *Anns v London Borough of Merton* [1978] AC 728. See P Craig (1978) LQR 428.

[33] *Plaumann and Co v Commission* Case 25/62 [1963] ECR 95.

they may become liable in negligence for those whose injuries were caused by the negligence. The problems of causation in any subsequent trials would have been considerable.[34]

Where a discretion is exercised to do something, the courts have felt a reluctance to become involved with an exercise of a policy decision to do X rather than Y because this will involve them second guessing on judgments which are either politically based (how do you allocate resources between education or health care), very sensitive, or simply not susceptible to the judicial process. In the case of elected bodies, such decisions should be contested and accountable through the electoral process.

A way of approaching this problem was to say that discretion contained a policy element and an operational element. One was a thinking, one was a doing. If in the exercise of a power I negligently build faulty flood defence barriers and a neighbour's property is damaged as a consequence, I am liable. If however, I, together with other officials, make a policy decision to build in some parts rather than others, then this is in the policy area and the courts would either be inclined not to subject the decision to scrutiny or, which has the same effect, to decide that for reasons of policy it is not appropriate to hold authorities liable for the exercise of such a power. I overlook difficulties arising from nuisance.

A judicial reluctance to intervene and impose liability in cases involving sensitive judgement was evidenced in *X v Bedfordshire County Council*. Lord Browne-Wilkinson gave the leading judgment with which, basically, all the other Law Lords agreed.[35] There, the decisions of a local authority acting through a psychiatrist employed by it and social services' personnel were not to be subjected to a duty of care in common law where they decided to remove a child from its mother on what, it transpired, were mistaken grounds. In a joined appeal, an authority took no steps for almost five years to place children on a Child Protection Register despite reports of sexual abuse and failed to take the children, who were subject to appalling living conditions, into care. It would not, on the *Caparo* principles be 'fair, just or reasonable' to impose a duty of care.[36] The imposition of a duty of care would seriously inhibit the ability of the various officials to perform their

---

[34]   [1978] AC 728. This aspect of Anns was not overruled in subsequent litigation.
[35]   [1995] 3 All ER 353, HL; the case also concerned appeals dealing with provision of special education needs.
[36]   *Caparo Industries plc v Dickman* [1990] 2 AC 605.

statutory functions; they would forever be looking over their shoulders and performing their duties with unwarranted apprehension.

The policy operational/divide had not met with a warm reception in Browne-Wilkinson's judgment in *X v Bedfordshire County Council* nor in other judgments in case law before the House of Lords.[37] The difficulty, said Browne-Wilkinson, is to establish whether a decision is a policy decision because the courts cannot enter upon 'an assessment of such policy matters.'[38] Like divisions in all difficult areas, they are rarely clean cut in all but the most straightforward of cases. If policy descends too far into the operational level, there could be too wide an immunity for negligence. If the operational sphere drifts too far into the policy area, the courts may be making too great an inroad into government prerogative and their decisions could have serious repercussions for the public purse. It is, said Lord Wilberforce 'a distinction of degree'[39] and is not a touchstone of liability 'but is rather expressive of the need to exclude altogether those cases in which the decision under attack is of such a kind that a question whether it has been made negligently is unsuitable for judicial resolution...'[40] In *Phelps* (see below), Lord Slynn believed that the policy/operational division may serve a useful purpose – 'there is some validity in the distinction' provided it is not overmilked.[41]

In *X and Y v Bedfordshire County Council*, Lord Browne-Wilkinson offered the following analysis of where the law stood in relation to liability for abuses of discretion and common law liability in negligence in the realm of policy:

> From these authorities I understand the applicable principles to be as follows. Where Parliament has conferred a statutory discretion on a public authority, it is for that authority, not for the courts, to exercise the discretion: nothing which the authority does within the ambit of the

---

[37] See Lord Hoffman in *Stovin v Wise* [1996] 3 All ER 801, HL; see Lord Nicholls in *Stovin* at 814 'But the boundary [between the two] is elusive, because the distinction is artificial and an area of blanket immunity seems undesirable and unnecessary. It is undesirable in principle that in respect of certain types of decisions the possibility of a concurrent common law duty should be absolutely barred whatever the circumstances. An excluded zone is also unnecessary because no statutory power is inherently immune from judicial review.'

[38] *X v Bedfordshire County Council* [1995] 3 All ER 353 at 370.

[39] [1977] 2 All ER 492 at 500.

[40] Lord Keith in *Rowling v Takaro Properties Ltd* [1988] 1 All ER 163 at 172.

[41] *Phelps v Hillingdon London Borough Council* [2000] 4 All ER 504, HL.

discretion can be actionable at common law. If the decision complained of falls outside the statutory discretion, it *can* [emphasis original] (but not necessarily will) give rise to common law liability. However, if the factors relevant to the exercise of the discretion include matters of policy, the court cannot adjudicate on such matters and therefore cannot reach the conclusion that the decision was outside the ambit of the statutory discretion. Therefore a common law duty of care in relation to the taking of decisions involving policy matters cannot exist. (at 371b-c)

But could such questions of policy involve breaches of the HRA 1998? For example a policy of open prisons for dangerous prisoners and Articles 2, 3 and 8 (Chapter 9, p 385 et seq)?[42]

In *Barrett v Enfield London Borough Council*, Lord Slynn with whom two judges agreed, seemed to repeat the orthodox approach starting with Lord Reid's and Lord Diplock's speeches in *Dorset Yacht*.[43] *Barrett* concerned an allegation of negligence by social workers in the manner in which they had taken decisions under statutory duties and powers in relation to a child (now an adult) who had been taken into care and whose treatment in care and while with foster parents, it was alleged, had caused him serious psychiatric damage. Following *X*, the defendant authorities sought to have the decision struck out as disclosing no cause of action. The decision was allowed to proceed because the Law Lords were not satisfied that the claims might not be successful and *X* was distinguished. In *X*, the decision involved teams of specialists making decisions leading to a child not being placed in care. In *Barrett* the decisions in question were not so complex in terms of numbers involved and *led* to a child being placed in care where the alleged negligence took place in the exercise of powers in relation to his upbringing:

Where a statute *empowers* an authority to take action within its discretion, then if it remains within its powers, the authority will not normally be liable under the statute, unless the statute so provides, or at common law. This, however, is subject to the proviso that if it purports to exercise its discretion to use, or it uses, its power in a wholly unreasonable way, it may be regarded as having gone outside its discretion so that it is not properly exercising its power, when liability in damages at common law may arise. It can no longer rely on the statutory power or discretion as a defence because it has gone outside the power. (Lord Slynn at 209–10)

[42]   See for the HRA 1998, Art 8 ECHR and nuisance claims *Marcic v Thames Water Utilities Ltd* [2001] 3 All ER 698 and *No 2* [2001] 4 All ER 326.

[43]   [1999] 3 All ER 193, HL. See P Craig and D Fairgrieve (1999) Public Law 626.

Lord Slynn did qualify what Lords Reid and Diplock, and also presumably Wilberforce said, however about the need to show that a discretionary decision was ultra vires or unlawful *before* one could argue negligence. 'I share Lord Browne-Wilkinson's reluctance to introduce the concepts of administrative law into the law of negligence'. He did not think that Lords Reid and Wilberforce were saying that an action in negligence could never be brought where an act has been done pursuant to the exercise of the discretion:

> A claim of negligence in the taking of a decision to exercise a statutory discretion is likely to be barred, unless it is wholly unreasonable so as not to be a real exercise of the discretion, or [it is likely to be barred] if it involves the making of a policy decision involving the balancing of different public interests; acts done pursuant to the lawful exercise of the discretion can, however, in my view be subject to a duty of care, even if some element of discretion is involved. Thus accepting that a decision to take a child into care pursuant to a statutory power is not justiciable, it does not in my view follow that, having taken a child into care, an authority cannot be liable for what it or its employees do in relation to the child without it being shown that they have acted in excess of power. It may amount to an excess of power, but that is not in my opinion the test to be adopted: the test is whether the conditions in *Caparo Industries plc v Dickman* [above] have been satisfied. (at 211 f–h)

In exercising a power, the authority through its servants may simply act negligently and cause injury. The *Caparo* test, to remind readers, asks is it 'fair, just and reasonable' to impose a duty of care and a liability in common law?

In *Phelps v Hillingdon London Borough Council*, decided after *Barrett*, Lord Slynn said an issue was non justiciable where there were competing public interests to be balanced, or where [a decision] 'has been dictated by considerations on which Parliament could not have intended that the courts would substitute their views for the views of Ministers or officials that the courts will hold that the issue is non justiciable on the ground that the decision was made in the exercise of a statutory discretion.'[44]

Lord Hutton, with whom Lords Nolan and Steyn also agreed, was even more emphatic in scrapping the two stage test from the earlier case law

---

[44]   [2000] 4 All ER 504 at 517c–d.

where *decisions* under a discretion (and in this case relating to an individual) were taken negligently:

> I consider that where a plaintiff claims damages for personal injuries which he alleges have been caused by decisions negligently taken in the exercise of a statutory discretion, and provided that the decisions do not involve issues of policy which the courts are ill-equipped to adjudicate upon, it is preferable for the courts to decide the validity of the plaintiff's claim by applying directly the common law concept of negligence than by applying as a preliminary test the public law concept of *Wednesbury* unreasonableness. (at 225f–g)

Any decision on a policy upon which the court *is* able to adjudicate and which concerns a decision to do or not do something, usually by a group, team or committee, may attract liability in negligence if it is unreasonable or irrational in the *Wednesbury* sense.[45] That seems to be in Slynn's analysis and possibly in Hutton's: 'the decisions do not involve issues of policy which the courts are ill-equipped to adjudicate upon'. In other words, are there issues of policy on which courts can adjudicate?

In cases involving *non*-exercise of a statutory power, it will be seen below that the courts have ruled that the decision not to exercise a power must be ultra vires and even then, there is a great reluctance to impose liability save in exceptional circumstances.[46]

Liability in Community law

The cases in domestic law are ostensibly far removed from those we are about to examine. In domestic law, the difficulty has been concerned with cases where a liability for damage should be imposed in the exercise or non-exercise of statutory powers. In the Community cases, the question concerns the liability of a Member State for failing to follow and apply Community law where an individual allegedly suffers injury as a

---

[45]   Not all ultra vires behaviour in public law may amount to negligence. Negligent decision-making, or negligent failure to take a decision *may* be *Wednesbury* unreasonable where a person or body have acted in such a way that no reasonable body etc could have made such a decision – where they have taken leave of their senses, defied logic etc. Misinterpreting rules or acting procedurally incorrectly *may be virtually impossible* to classify as negligence.

[46]   *Stovin v Wise* [1996] 3 All ER 801 p 462 below.

consequence. The ECJ has given a broad interpretation to what bodies are 'state bodies' for purposes of establishing Member State liability and it includes bodies irrespective of their public law status although they were governed by public law.[47]

Although the ECJ had decided that there must be a judicial remedy in a national court for breaches of directly effective EC law[48] it was the 1990 decision in *Francovich* which set the present law on its dramatic development.[49] The point was made in *Francovich* that 'it is a principle of Community law that the Member States are obliged to make good loss and damage to individuals by breaches of Community law for which they can be held responsible.' The principle was 'inherent in the system of the Treaty.'

In that case employees brought domestic actions against the Italian government for a failure to implement a Community Directive dealing with insolvency of employers and consequential payment of wages to employees. The employees had been deprived of their wages because of the failure by the Italian government to implement the Directive. On a reference to the ECJ, the court based its judgment establishing liability on two grounds: ensuring the effectiveness of Community law, and a breach of Article 10 [5] EC requiring Member States to take all appropriate measures to ensure fulfilment of Treaty obligations or Community tasks. The conditions to establish liability were that the rights in question in the Directive must be capable of conferring rights on individuals; secondly, the content of those rights must be capable of being identified from the provisions in the Directive;[50] and thirdly, there must be a direct causal link between the breach of the State's obligation and the harm suffered by the injured parties. The provision of an effective remedy for a breach of Community law was a matter of *Community* law enforced through national courts. On their part, national courts must make good loss or damage on the basis of national rules on liability; furthermore, there were parameters

---

[47]   Case C-302/97 *Kolne v Austria* [1999] ECR I-3099; Case C-424/97 *Haim v KVN* [2000] ECR I-5123. On liability for *individuals* for breaches of Treaty provisions, see Van Gerven in Case C-128/92 *Banks v British Coal* [1994] ECR I-1209 and Case C-453/99 *Courage Ltd v Crehan* [2001] ECR I-6297 on Art 81 [85] EC.

[48]   Case 222/86 *UNCTEF v Heylens* [1987] ECR 4097; Case 222/84 *Johnston v RUC* [1986] 3 All ER 135.

[49]   Case C-6 and C-9/90 [1991] ECR I-5357.

[50]   See *Three Rivers District Council v Bank of England (No 3)* [2000] 3 All ER 1, HL for a situation where the Law Lords held that a Directive did not create duties and rights for individuals.

within which a national court had to operate so that remedies had to be no less favourable than those operating under national law (equivalence) and a national remedy must not make it impossible or excessively difficult to obtain a remedy (effectiveness).

As observers have claimed, what *Francovich* represents is a movement by the ECJ from a model of law based on 'rights' illustrated by the courts' judgments on supremacy and, in particular, direct effect which were examined in Chapters 2 and 3, to a system that is to be built on remedies. In both cases, the ECJ felt the developments were necessary in order to ensure the efficacy of Community law through the creation and realisation of individual rights. In *Francovich*, the court was faced with a 'right' that was not directly effective; it was not clear on whom the duty under the Directive fell: the employer or the State. It was clear that the state was in breach of its duty under Community law and for that it faced liability.

It has become clearer that while the basic provisions on liability and a right to compensation for breach of Community law were established by the court, the conditions under which national courts regulate the bringing of actions in terms of both procedure and substance are under the control of national courts and national law, although this is not a matter solely for national courts, as seen below. Questions of 'substance' would refer to such items as causation, quantum (amount of damages) and awards of interest; the former to limitation periods or other time factors, burden of proof and who may bring an action (eg a relative etc – though quaere whether these in reality amount to matters of substance).

There were two further crucial safeguards to which passing reference was made above. The domestic court had to treat the claim under EC law in a manner no less favourable (comparable/equivalent) to similar claims under domestic law. In *Bourgoin* for instance, if the English court had given damages to a purely domestic claim involving breach of a directly effective right in a statute (a European expression) to an individual (as Oliver LJ dissenting suggested above) then a remedy only in public law, which is what the court believed it could award if anything, would be less favourable. Furthermore, the secondary factors concerning substance and procedure could not be employed in a manner by a domestic court which would undermine or render ineffective the EC remedy (make it impossible in practice to enjoy the right to compensation). If an English court were to insist on a level of fault in excess of that required by European Law in order to establish liability this could render the EC remedy ineffective. If for instance the EC remedy was based on negligence but the English court insisted on a finding of intent or recklessness, that would have such an effect.

These two points are part of a more general background right: that in enforcing or not enforcing Community rights, there must be no discriminatory practice. *Francovich* was one of the most heavily criticised decisions to date of the ECJ. The reliance upon the principle of effectiveness and Article 10 providing for a duty of cooperation in particular was felt to be illustrative of a court that was abusing judicial office and was redolent of those debates about the US Supreme Court and its decisions on equal protection and civil rights in the 1950s and 1960s – the court was not enforcing the law but was engineering fundamental social change in a manner that was not justified by the legal provisions.[51]

Francovich was however to be the spring-board for further litigation involving Member State liability for breaches of Community law, a development which owed much to the inspiration of the approach to liability adopted in Member States and by the ECJ's resort to Article 220 [164] EC which simply states that in its interpretation and application of Community law the Court shall ensure that 'the law is observed'. The ECJ has commented that Article 220 has allowed it to take inspiration from the courts of Member States.[52] Tridimas quoting R Posner says Article 220 [164] EC does no less 'than to grant the Court jurisdiction to create "constitutional doctrine by the common law method".'[53] The resort to Article 220 allows a reference to the laws of Member States to act as an inspiration for the development of public liability and is given specific support for this by virtue of the second paragraph of Article 288 [215] EC. This Article concerns the basis of liability for Community institutions in non-contractual cases. It stipulates:

> In the case of non-contractual liability, the Community shall, in accordance with the principles common to the laws of the Member States, make good any damage caused by its institutions or by its servants in the performance of their duties.

51 Sir Patrick Neill *The European Court of Justice: A Case Study in Judicial Activism* (1995).
52 *Brasserie* and *Factortame* Joined Cases C-46/93 and C-48/93 [1996] ECR I-1029.
53 T Tridimas *The General Principles of EC Law* (2000) p 11.

The Treaty said nothing about Member State liability therefore it is for the Court, the ECJ has said, in pursuance of Article 220 [164] EC ... 'to rule on such a question in accordance with generally accepted methods of interpretation, in particular by reference to the fundamental principles of the Community legal system and, where necessary, general principles common to the legal systems of Member States.'[54] Article 288(2) [215(2)] EC directs the ECJ to the principles of law common to the Member States to establish liability for Community institutions and 'reflects the obligation on public authorities to make good damage caused in the performance of their duties.'[55]

Francovich involved a failure to implement a Directive within the time-scale. It was a clear and flagrant breach of duty. The provisions in the Directive were of a kind that conferred rights which belonged to individuals – those made redundant – although they were not as explained directly effective. What would be the situation if a Member State breached provisions of Community law in a variety of other different ways? In this respect, it makes no difference which branch of government of the Member State is in breach of Community law; a breach by the legislature can be just as damaging as a breach by the courts or by the executive. But there may be differences in the type of legal instruments through which a breach occurs. Where a discretion is involved in implementing Community norms through legislation, the approach of the Community courts may differ from the case where an administrative decision by national authorities is taken in breach of a Community norm, or a national court from which there is no appeal refuses to follow a decision of the ECJ and to refer a question to that Court. Under the European Communities Act 1972, domestic courts when applying Community law are supposed to adopt what Community courts state the point of Community law to be. In the latter two cases, the degree of discretion involved is unlikely to be as great as where a legislative choice is to be made. And it may be that a particular form of legal instrument has been used to prevent challenge in domestic courts; this would certainly be the case in the UK where an Act of Parliament was the offending item. It could not, subject to Community law itself, be challenged in domestic courts. Indeed, even where delegated domestic legislation is approved by Parliament, a court may rule on their vires with the parent statute but cannot

---

54   *Brasserie and Factortame* para 27. See W van Gerven in J Beatson and T Tridimas eds *New Directions in European Public Law* (1998); J Steiner (1998) EPL 69.

55   W van Gerven in J Beatson and T Tridimas eds *New Directions in European Public Law* (1998) para 29.

impose liability for the ultra vires nature of the measure in the absence of a Community aspect. The answer to these questions became apparent in litigation involving the UK and Germany in particular.

Community law was given a relatively free rein to develop the law of tortious liability concerning Community institutions. Article 288(2) EC provides, as we have seen, that the ECJ may draw on the *the principles common to the laws of the Member States,* and make good any damage caused by its institutions or by its servants in the performance of their duties.[56] This liability, with modifications, was influenced very considerably by French law. However, where there was a question of choice involved in the application of economic policy, then a ruling that a regulation was null and void (which was originally required before being allowed to sue for damages) would not be sufficient to establish liability where a victim alleged damage as a consequence of the application of such a regulation. There would have to be a finding that there has been 'a sufficiently serious breach of a superior rule of law for the protection of the individual.' This was a doctrine which the ECJ formulated in the famous *Schöppenstendt* case,[57] a case concerning agricultural markets. Public authorities (PAs) can only 'exceptionally and in special circumstances incur liability for legislative measures which are the choices of economic policy' and 'the Community does not therefore incur liability unless the institution concerned has manifestly and gravely disregarded the limits on the exercise of its powers.'[58] It is now clear that where a decision, as opposed to a legislative measure, involves an appropriate measure of discretion then the *Schöppenstendt* test applies.[59]

In *Mulder v EC Council* the Advocate General Walter van Gerven wrote that the expression 'manifestly and gravely disregarded the limits on the exercise of its powers' qualifies the words a 'sufficiently serious breach'.[60] In the case of legislative measures (and decisions) carried out pursuant to a broad discretion, he continued, 'the public authority is allowed a certain margin of error.' 'Only where the PA's error is inexcusable, that is to say where it could reasonably not have committed it, have powers been

---

56 Article 288 EC. On immunity for servants, and liability for the institutions, see Art 12 of the Protocol on the Privileges and Immunities of the Communities.
57 Case 5/71 *Zuckerfabrik Schoppenstendt* [1971] ECR 975.
58 Case 83, 94/76, 4, 15, 40/77 *Bayerische* [1978] ECR 1209 at 1224.
59 Case C-352/98 *Bergaderm SA v Commission* [2000] ECR I-5291.
60 Case C-104/89, 37/90 [1992] ECR I-3061.

manifestly and gravely disregarded and there therefore has been a sufficiently serious breach (of a superior rule of law for the protection of individuals) (para 15). He alluded to the factors that the ECJ had previously adverted to determine whether 'a manifest and grave disregard of discretion' and therefore 'sufficiently serious breach' had been made out. This case concerned the Common Agricultural Policy of the Community and its implementation, ie difficult economic judgments were involved:

> i) the particular importance of the principle infringed by the regulation (in those cases the principle of equality) and hence the (objective) seriousness of the breach; ii) the fact that the disregard of that principle affected a [limited] and clearly defined group of commercial operators or economic agents.... iv) the fact that the principle in question was infringed without sufficient justification.

This combination of factors persuaded the ECJ to find the Community liable for the wrongful and total exclusion of producers from the milk production market.

Brasserie and Factortame III is the leading case on post *Francovich* liability. The importance of *Factortame* lies in the fact that it is establishing a liability for Member State breaches of EC law, regardless of whether the legal provisions being breached are directly effective, as in *Factortame,* or not. In *Francovich*, it will be recalled that the Directive in question was not directly effective. In other words, in *Factortame*, there were alternative remedies that a plaintiff could pursue in national courts, a point raised in proceedings by the governments of several Member States as a reason to deny liability where there was a breach. These pleas were not accepted by the ECJ.

It has been seen how in previous stages of the *Factortame* litigation there had been an allegation of breaches of Treaty provisions by the UK government by virtue of the Merchant Shipping Act 1988 insofar as the non-registration of Spanish owned shipping vessels under regulations made under the Act led to allegations of breaches of the Treaty (see below). In earlier proceedings, the House of Lords had little alternative but to issue an interim injunction disapplying the Merchant Shipping Act 1988 because the enforcement of the Act clashed with, indeed prevented the realisation of, prima facie rights of the applicants under Community law.[61] The Spanish

[61]   See p 367 et seq above.

ship owners now wanted compensation for the wrongful prohibition of their engagement in business.

In *Factortame III*, which was reported together with *Brasserie du Pêcheur* where Germany was the defendant, the claimants sought to establish the basis on which damages could be awarded against the UK government for a breach of Community law.[62] The specific breaches included: Article 43 [52] EC when their application to register a vessel as a British fishing vessel under the Merchant Shipping Act 1988, which sought to prevent all vessels from registration unless they had a substantial British connection, was refused on the grounds of failing to satisfy British nationality requirements. These were set out in the Act. In *Brasserie*, there was an allegation of a breach of Article 28 [30] EC by Germany when it prevented imports of French beer which did not conform with German beer purity laws.

In *Factortame III*[63] the ECJ in its judgment establishing the terms for liability for breaches of Community law, said:

> The conditions for [state liability of breaches of Community law] cannot, in the absence of particular justification, differ from those governing the liability of the Community in like circumstances [under art 288(2)]. The protection of the rights which individuals derive from Community law cannot vary depending on whether a national authority or a Community authority is responsible for the damage. (at 363)[64]

In particular, the principle of state liability for loss and damage caused to individuals as a result of breaches of Community law for which the state could be held responsible, which was inherent in the system of the Treaty, applied to any case in which a Member State breached Community law whatever the organ of the state. In the case of breach by a national legislature, where it was acting in a field in which it possessed a wide discretion to make legislative choices, the conditions of individual entitlement were: the rule of law breached was intended to confer rights on individuals; the breach was sufficiently serious showing a manifest and grave disregard of the limits of discretion; and there was a direct causal

---

[62]   Cases C-46/93 and C-48/93 [1996] ECR I-1029.

[63]   [1996] All ER (EC) 301.

[64]   Tridimas has criticised the comparison of liability for Member State's acts with liability for legislative acts of the Community as 'not necessarily accurate.' T Tridimas *The General Principles of EC Law* (2000) p 333. See E Deards (1997) European Public Law 117.

link between the breach and the damage sustained. In the area of wide discretion to make legislative choices a finding that a breach was sufficiently serious could not be contingent upon a concept of fault beyond that identified above. It could not, for instance, be dependent upon a misfeasance of public office which requires intention, malice or recklessness. Reparation for the loss or damage caused by a breach of Community law has to be commensurate with the loss sustained and a national court must determine the criteria for determining the amount. These criteria must be formulated on the basis of comparability and effectiveness and non-discrimination as was outlined above.

The system of rules which the ECJ has evolved to establish liability for legislative measures takes into account 'the complexity of the situations to be regulated, difficulties in the application or interpretation of the texts, ie legislative documents, and ... the margin of discretion available to the author of the act in question.' At para 56 of the *Factortame III* judgment, the ECJ spell out the factors to consider to establish whether there is a manifest and grave breach of Community law in order to establish liability:

> The factors which the competent [national] court may take into consideration include the clarity and precision of the rule breached, the measure of discretion left by that rule to the national or Community authorities, whether the infringement and the damage caused was intentional or involuntary, whether any error of law was excusable or inexcusable, the fact that the position taken by a Community institution may have contributed towards the omission, and the adoption or retention of national measures or practices contrary to Community law.

It only needs to be said that in *Bergaderm* the ECJ ruled that the test to be applied to obtain damages from the Community was that applied to assess whether a Member State was liable for breaches of Community law: the conduct alleged against the Community must involve 'a sufficiently serious breach of a rule of law intended to confer rights on individuals.'[65] Where a Community institution has limited discretion an absence of ordinary care and diligence would suffice. Where a wide discretion is involved, a higher standard would be required amounting to a manifest and grave disregard of one's discretion.[66]

---

[65]   *P Bergaderm and Goupil* Case C-352/98 P [2000] ECR I-5291.
[66]   *Comafrica and Dole Fresh Fruit Europe v Commission* Case T-225/99 [2001] ECR II-1975.

Back to the House of Lords

When *Factortame* came back to the House of Lords after this ruling under Article 234 [177] EC by the ECJ, the Law Lords ruled that the breaches of Community law were 'sufficiently serious' even though it involved a discretion relating to legislative choices. The nationality requirements were in breach of 'clear and fundamental' articles of the Treaty prohibiting discrimination (old Articles 7 and 52).[67] Although the provisions in the Act were 'pushed through' to make them effective, they were not however, intentionally or recklessly unlawful. Lord Slynn observed that the government had acted for what were accepted as legitimate, if unlawful, reasons. The Commission had advised the UK government that this was the case – although this was not conclusive in itself but it is of importance – leading, as English courts in interim proceedings had accepted, to 'serious and immediate' damage.[68] Further, legal advice should have caused the government to perceive the weakness of its case. The evidence indicated that the government intended to press ahead with its policy – reinforced by the fact that it was enshrined in legislation and was thereby not susceptible to attack in domestic courts. The qualifications based on domicile fell for the same reason and with some circumspection, so did those on residence. Liability was established. A claim of exemplary damages having failed in the Divisional Court was not pursued further.[69]

Lord Clyde spelt out some considerations that might help determine whether a breach of Community law was sufficiently serious including matters referred to by the ECJ in its judgment as well as the breach of a superior rule of law such as legitimate expectation in *Mulder II* (above), the presence or absence of settled case law, ambiguity and lack of clarity, the state of mind of the infringer and persistence with measures which are

---

[67]   [1999] 4 All ER 906, HL.

[68]   The Divisional Court awarded an interim injunction but this was successfully appealed to the Court of Appeal; the House of Lords awarded an injunction after the decision of the ECJ in Case C-213/89 *Factortame I* [1991] 1 All ER 70; and decisions of the ECJ *R v MAFF, ex p Agegate* Case C-3/87 [1989] ECR 4459 and *R v MAFF, ex p Jaderow* Case C-216/87 [1989] ECR 4509; *Factortame II* [1991] 3 All ER 769 and *EC Commission v UK* Case 246/89R [1989] ECR 3125.

[69]   Because the action was classified as a breach of statutory duty. Given the House of Lords judgment on exemplary damages in *Kuddus v Chief Constable of Leicestershire Constabulary* [2001] UKHL 29, [2001] 3 All ER 193 it may be this restrictive approach will be abandoned.

known to infringe Community law, and the existence of a defined and possibly limited group of claimants.[70]

Subsequent case law from the ECJ has established that 'manifest and grave disregard of its powers' under Community law by a Member State is constituted by a failure to implement a Directive by the required date; such a failure to implement in itself constitutes a sufficiently serious breach.[71] In the case of administrative decisions where no legislative discretion is present (although there may well be administrative discretion) a straightforward breach of Treaty provisions may well of itself be sufficiently serious as a breach to incur liability. In *Hedley Lomas v UK*, a breach of Article 29 [34] EC prohibiting quantitative restrictions on exports – in this case of live sheep to Spain allegedly slaughtered in Spain in breach of a Directive seeking to prevent unnecessary suffering on the part of animals – was a sufficiently serious breach in itself because of the flagrant breach of basic provisions of the Treaty. No application of legislative discretion was present. This was notwithstanding arguments from the UK government that there were public interest grounds for preventing the export.[72] In the *BT, ex p HM Treasury* case the UK was found not to be liable where it had failed properly to implement a Directive on purchasing contracts in the telecommunications sector.[73] The Directive was not clearly worded and was 'reasonably capable of bearing the interpretation given to it' by the UK government in good faith. No guidance was available in case law and the Commission had raised no objections when the regulations implementing the Directive were notified to it. Any breach was insufficiently serious and did not give rise to any duty of reparation.

The breach of an important principle of law would qualify as a 'manifest and grave' disregard of duty. But what precisely is that? Lord Slynn for instance spoke of 'fundamental norms' of the Treaty as if there were different levels of norms within the Treaty itself. Clearly, the phrase covers provisions dealing with the four basic freedoms, discrimination and Article

---

70 He did not think, however, that one necessarily disregarded the view of the Commission 'at one's peril'.
71 Cases C-178, 179, 189 and 190/94 *Dillenkofer v Germany* [1996] ECR I-4845, ECJ.
72 Case C-5/94 *R v MAFF, ex p Hedley Lomas (Ireland) Ltd* [1996] ECR I-2553, ECJ.
73 Case C-392/93 *R v HM Treasury, ex p BT plc* [1996] ECR I-1631, ECJ; also Case T-20/99 *Denkavit* [2000] ECR II-3011 and Case C-319/96 *Brinkman* [1998] ECR I-5255 to similar effect.

249 [189] EC on implementation. What others can be covered? It would appear to cover breaches of the fundamental principles such as legitimate expectation, proportionality and equality and a breach of fundamental rights. Failure to give reasons for a decision has not attracted such protection.[74] The ECJ has also ruled that the duty to give reasons for legislation under Article 253 [190] EC does not cover a national legislature implementing Community measures.[75]

If we step back to view the prospect, what we see is the creation of a principle of liability by the ECJ to provide an effective remedy for breaches of EC law with the detail of implementation provided by domestic courts. This reverses the original position where the establishment of the basic principles for an effective remedy was a matter for the domestic courts.

National courts

The decision of the House of Lords on the question of liability for breaches of Community law established, as we saw, that the breaches in question were sufficiently serious. Just how important the role of the national court is in this process can be seen when the case joined with *Factortame*, *Brasserie du Pêcheur*, was remitted to the German courts for them to make the assessment on the existence and/or nature of the breach. In *Brasserie*, the ECJ was asked to rule on general principles of liability in a case from Germany concerning the prohibition of beer imports into Germany from France because of the German purity law on beer. The German law stipulated that the description 'beer' could only apply to products satisfying German laws on purity. The ECJ's general ruling on liability has been discussed above but it should be noted that in Article 226 [169] EC proceedings, the ECJ had ruled that the prohibition on marketing beers from other Member States which did not conform with the purity law contravened Article 28 [30] EC – the prohibition on quantitative restrictions on imports. In the proceedings before the ECJ, while the question of liability seemed clear in relation to the prohibition of the word 'beer' to products produced as beer lawfully in their own state by virtue of a series of judgments including the

---

[74] Case 106/81*Kind v EEC* [1982] ECR 2885; Case T-390/94 *Aloys Schroder etc v Commission* [1997] ECR II-501, paras 54 et seq.

[75] Case C-70/95 *Sodemare v Regione Lombardia* [1997] ECR I-3395. The obligation would cover administrative decisions of national authorities in a Community competence.

famous *Cassis de Dijon*,[76] a different gloss may have been placed on a prohibition on use of 'additives' because the prohibition of these was not clear until the decision on Article 226 [169] EC proceedings in 1987.[77]

When the case was remitted to the German courts for decision on liability, the domestic courts established there was no liability in somewhat questionable circumstances. The additives law did not amount to 'a sufficiently serious' breach of Community law. The prohibition on the use of the word 'beer' was linked to contents and this concerned the question of additives, and any breach in a law on additives was not sufficiently serious. Any such breach in prohibiting the word 'beer' had no direct causal connection with the damage suffered through the 'designation breach'.[78] It seems remarkable that no causal connection could be established between the designation prohibition and the loss suffered. And in the case of *ex p Gallagher* although the ECJ ruled that there had been a breach of Community provisions in the manner in which the claimant, an Irish national, had been issued an expulsion order to deport him to Ireland from the UK, the Court of Appeal ruled that the deportation would have taken place anyway despite the breach so that any breach was not a causal factor in any injury.[79] If it is felt that national courts are evading their duties to establish liability where it ought to be established, or to provide an effective and equivalent remedy, this may well lead to further action for breaches of Community law or to enforcement by the Commission.[80]

In determining how the breach should be classified for the purposes of providing a remedy, a matter for the national court the ECJ believed (para 58), the Divisional Court in *Factortame (No 5)* felt it was a breach of statutory duty.[81] The Court of Appeal was not so sure and the Law Lords

---

[76]   Case 120/78 [1979] ECR 649. Such a ban must satisfy the test of proportionality.

[77]   [1987] ECR 1227. See the Advocate General in *Brasserie* at para 116.

[78]   The German decision is: *Brasserie du Pêcheur SA v Germany* [1997] 1 CMLR 971. On questions of the effectiveness and equivalence of national remedies, see: Case C-94 and 95/95 *Bonifaci and Berto v INPS* [1998] 1 CMLR 257; Case C-261/95 *Palmisani v INPS* [1997] 3 CMLR 1356 and C-373/95 *Maso and Gazzetta v INPS* [1997] ECR I-4051.

[79]   *R v Secretary of State for the Home Department, ex p Gallagher* [1996] 2 CMLR 951 following [1996] 1 CMLR 557.

[80]   See M Andenas and D Fairgrieve in M Andenas ed *English Public Law and the Common Law of Europe* (1998), for more illustrations establishing the 'sufficient seriousness test' in English courts.

[81]   [1998] EuLR 456. See Lord Diplock in *Garden Cottage* [1984] AC 130, HL. Is the action not like a breach of statutory duty owed to an individual? The governing measure after all is the European Communities Act 1972. One of the problems

remained silent on this point, only noting that such a classification fell to the national court. It has been argued that the action for Member State liability is not an action for breach of a statutory duty because the Community approach differs from the English law in a variety of ways in terms of causation, mitigation and defences available.[82] A new tort of 'state liability for breaches of Community law' has been called for.

The influence on domestic law

The question posed by this development in liability in European law is: to what extent will it influence the law on liability in a domestic setting? Where the basic conditions of liability are established in EC law, any exercise of power in breach of those principles and which satisfy the necessary criteria, will establish liability. Exceptions have not as yet been forthcoming. In English law, on the other hand, the court will ask to what extent is it fair, just and reasonable to impose a duty of care in a particular situation? In some circumstances the answer has been an unequivocal, or almost unequivocal, negative one so that the police, financial regulators, social workers taking decisions not to take children into care are not placed under such a duty of care. Many factors may militate against the establishment of a duty of care including disruption of effective public service, resource implications or other aspects of public policy. Only if the question is it fair, just and reasonable is answered in the positive will the English court proceed to examine the application of legal principles to the specific facts of the case to establish negligence, foreseeability, causation and so on. On the specific facts of *Factortame* or *Brasserie du Pêcheur*, there would be no likely prospect of liability where the facts raised a purely domestic question of law because there would be no liability for legislative acts. And this would be true not only for primary legislation but also for secondary legislation. It is hard to imagine how secondary legislation approved by Parliament could satisfy the criteria for liability in any area outside the HRA 1998. But how useful a test could the manifest and grave disregard of its powers and a sufficiently serious breach of law be in a domestic setting in order to establish liability?

---

with defining the action as a breach of statutory duty was the fact that the Divisional Court believed that exemplary damages could not be awarded for such a claim. See *Kuddus* [2001] UKHL 29, [2001] 3 All ER 193. See *Factortame (No 7)* [2001] 1 CMLR 1191.

82 Hoskins in J Beatson and T Tridimas eds *New Directions in European Public Law* (1998) ch 7.

We have seen elsewhere how tensions brought about by disparities between domestic and Community law have been raised as reasons for modelling our laws directly on Community law (Chapter 8, p 368 et seq). This point was certainly in the mind of Lord Woolf in *M v Home Office*. Is there a case for modelling our law of liability for wrongdoing by public bodies in areas of statutory and common law overlap on the Community model?[83] In the Court of Appeal in *Factortame (No 5)* it was stated that the inquiry into sufficient seriousness in relation to legislative discretion is taken on a 'basket or global approach, involving weighing the relevant considerations' as we saw above.[84] This arguably is not unlike the approach taken by English courts to assess whether it is 'fair, just and reasonable' to impose a duty of care and it has been suggested that the Community approach can be the basis of an examination to ask whether an exercise of discretion is such that it amounts to culpable negligence because an act, or crucially non-act, was outside the authority's discretion.[85] In *Barrett,* Lord Hutton said 'in each case the court's resolution of the question whether the decision or decisions taken by the defendant in exercise of the statutory discretion are unsuitable for judicial determination will require ... a careful analysis and weighing of the relevant circumstances.' (at 225g–h) English law has been reluctant to provide relief by way of damages in liability cases involving statutory duties and powers because of the impact upon the public purse if actions succeed and the possible inhibiting effect such claims may bring in the exercise of powers or judgement by administrators. Recent years have been notable for the efforts by the courts to prevent statutes being construed so as to give remedies to injured parties where there is an allegation of a breach of a duty in a statute eg *X v Beds CC*, *Phelps* and *Barrett* all provide examples of this reluctance.[86] Where a statutory power is involved rather than a duty, the fact that a power was chosen by Parliament has been seen as reinforcing the belief that Parliament did not intend to create a right of action.[87] In *Stovin v Wise*, Lord Hoffman believed that for a liability to arise for a decision which resulted in a non-

---

[83]   See P Craig in J Beatson and T Tridimas eds *New Directions in European Public Law* (1998) ch 6 and the same author in M Andenas (ed) *English Public Law and the Common Law of Europe* (1998) ch 8.

[84]   Lord Woolf in the Court of Appeal.

[85]   M Andenas and D Fairgrieve in M Andenas (ed) *English Public Law and the Common Law of Europe* (1998).

[86]   And note that the existence of statutory complaints procedures or remedies may help to negate the existence of a common law duty of care: Lord Hutton in *Barrett* at 228h et seq.

[87]   Lord Hoffman in *Stovin v Wise* [1996] 3 All ER 801, HL.

exercise of a power, the decision to do nothing would have to be irrational and there would have to be 'exceptional grounds' for holding that the policy of the statute intended individuals to be compensated for loss if the power were not exercised. Such exceptional circumstances might fall under examples of 'general reliance' – where the public expected that a power to protect them generally because of its importance or complexity would be exercised and the authority knew that there would be a general reliance on that power being exercised. Hoffman thought these circumstances were extremely limited but a statutory 'may' could potentially become a common law 'must'. A power could become a duty.

There has also been a reluctance to establish liability in negligence where it is alleged that a power has been exercised negligently. There is also a reluctance to become involved in the policy dimension of decisions because courts are not equipped to make decisions on allocation or balancing of expenditure and distribution of risks;[88] such a reluctance may not be so keenly felt where action is unlawful and a remedy in public law without damages is felt to be more appropriate. There is a shift in emphasis occurring. We have seen how *Barrett* provided a more claimant-friendly approach in cases of social welfare and how *Barrett* distinguished *X v Beds*. In *Phelps* the House of Lords ruled that actions could be maintained against educational psychologists and London Education Authorities for breaches of common law duties of care and could go to trial for determination on the facts. As was clear in *Barrett*, where negligence is alleged in the exercise of a discretion which is justiciable, the statutory wording and context will have to be examined in each case to establish whether there has been negligence.

We shall have to see whether the advent of liability for breaches of Community law will cause English courts to review the position of liability of public authorities. *Barrett and Phelps* may indicate a change in emphasis in that the insistence on a dual test based on abuse of public authority and the imposition of a duty of care is no longer required to establish liability. The question is: is this a situation covered by a duty of care and is there unreasonable behaviour on which a liability should be established? In some cases, as indicated by Lord Hoffman, it may not be possible not to ask questions about vires before establishing liability. But even in cases of a failure to exercise a power, can an attempted resolution not be found by

---

[88]   Lord Keith in *Rowling v Takaro Properties Ltd* [1988] AC 473 at 501.

asking: is this manifestly disregarding the proper exercise of power and does it constitute a sufficiently serious breach of law? It seems somewhat high-handed to dismiss such a proposal without more because of the different manner in which the Community courts operate.[89]

The Court of Human Rights

The second sphere of European influence on questions of liability has been the CHR. In particular that Court has been critical of the approach taken by the House of Lords and the method it adopts to establish whether a duty of care should be imposed in a particular relationship. The first judgment, *Osman v UK*[90] concerned a refusal of English courts to allow a plaintiff to sue the police where the police had failed to prevent the claimant – a youth of 16 years – being attacked (and his father and his deputy head-teacher's son murdered) by a teacher of the youth who had developed an obsessive attraction for the boy. The police had been warned on numerous occasions of the obsessive nature of the teacher's actions. The action was struck out because following the decision in *Hill v Chief Constable of West Yorkshire Police*[91] in which it was held that the police were immune from civil action arising from their investigation of crime,[92] it disclosed no reasonable cause of action. This 'water-tight immunity' said the CHR was a disproportionate restriction of the applicant's right of access to a court and constituted a breach of Article 6(1) ECHR guaranteeing a hearing for the determination of one's civil rights and obligations by an independent and impartial tribunal established by law.

The CHR ruled that the acceptance of the immunity, without an opportunity to allow enquiry into whether there were public interest exceptions which

---

89   J Allison in J Beatson and T Tridimas eds *New Directions in European Public Law* (1998) ch 12. On Allison's other concerns, see Andemas and Fairgrieve in J Beatson and T Tridimas eds *New Directions in European Public Law* (1998) ch 14. Allison argues that a public private divide is required for such a development. There is no such divide in Community law and this divide is precisely present in the case law from *Dorset Yacht* onwards in England. See M Hoskins in J Beatson and T Tridimas eds *New Directions in European Public Law* (1998) ch 7 on categorisation of Community liability.

90   (1998) 29 EHRR 245.

91   [1989] AC 53; *Osman v Ferguson* [1993] 4 All ER 344.

92   Cf the case of the negligent disclosure of an informer's identity where a duty of care was held to exist and which had been breached.

allowed the case to be heard on its merits, amounted to an unjustifiable restriction on an applicant's right to have a determination on the merits of his or her case.

The interesting point about this case is that it reflects the approach of a civil jurisdiction's to a judicial decision on the merits. In a civil system, there will be in existence a general codified rule determining liability. Each case will contain its own specific details to which the court will apply the general rule. In civil case law, the court is not the oracle of the law as is the case in a common law jurisdiction where the court develops precedent which is binding in subsequent cases. When establishing a new duty of care situation in common law a 'court should proceed incrementally and by analogy with decided categories'. The outcome (decision) then establishes binding precedent. A judicial decision does not create a binding precedent in a civil system which subsequent courts must follow, as in the situation in *Osman* before the Court of Appeal where that court had to follow the ratio decidendi of the House of Lords. The law in a civil system is contained in the code. In reality, there is more opportunity to establish something like precedent in a civil system than this brief description allows and there is ample opportunity to circumvent unhelpful precedent in the common law process by distinguishing precedent.[93] There is no doubt that the approach of the unanimous CHR on Article 6 caused extreme difficulty for English judges as articulated by Lord Browne-Wilkinson in *Barrett*.[94] The case, it will be recalled, concerned allegations of serious psychological damage suffered by the plaintiff as a consequence of negligence in the way powers relating to his placement in care by a public authority had been exercised – the authority had negligently failed to safeguard his welfare.

The Law Lord felt that the CHR in *Osman* did not understand the manner in which negligence operated in English courts. His view basically was that the CHR has assumed that the claimant Osman had a right in English law which the claimant was prevented from vindicating in judicial proceedings by virtue of the exclusionary rule set out in *Hill's* case (above). The claimant, according to the CHR, must be given an opportunity to argue

---

[93]   Cf Karl Llewellyn and 64 techniques for distinguishing precedents in *The Common Law Tradition*; see W Twining *Karl Llewellyn and the Realist Movement* (1985) pp 237–39.

[94]   [1999] 3 All ER 193, HL. See Lord Hoffman (1999) MLR 159. The CHR was not unanimous in its decision on other Articles where breaches were alleged.

his case *on the merits*: this was his right under Article 6(1). Because the English court had not balanced whether the public interest in an efficient police force was, or was not, proportionate to the damage suffered by the plaintiff, there had been a breach of Article 6. According to the CHR, the 'applicability of such exclusionary rule has to be decided afresh in each individual case' said the Law Lord (at 199a–b). The English court had denied Osman the opportunity to have any evidence relating to the proportionality of the application of the exclusionary rule in his case.

In order to establish a liability in negligence, the threefold test pronounced in *Caparo Industries plc v Dickman* has to be satisfied.[95] This seeks to establish not only whether it is a kind of damage that is foreseeable and that there is a sufficient proximity of relationship between the claimant and defendant. It also has to be satisfied that it is 'fair, just and reasonable' to impose liability as was discussed above. In a lengthy passage, Lord Browne-Wilkinson set out the approach that judges should take to the question of whether a duty of care should be imposed:

> In a wide range of cases public policy has led to the decision that the imposition of liability would not be fair, just and reasonable in the circumstances...In all these cases and many others the view has been taken that the proper performance of the defendant's primary functions for the benefit of society as a whole will be inhibited if they are required to look over their shoulder to avoid liability in negligence. In English law the decision as to whether it is fair, just and reasonable to impose a liability in negligence on a particular class of case of would-be defendants depends on weighing in the balance the total detriment to the public interest in all cases from holding such class liable in negligence as against the total loss to all would-be plaintiffs if they are not to have a cause of action in respect of the loss they have individually suffered. In English law, questions of public policy and the question whether it is fair and reasonable to impose liability in negligence are decided as questions of law ... [and] ... that decision will apply to all future cases of the same kind. The decision does not depend on weighing the balance between the extent of the damage to the plaintiff and the damage to the public in each particular case. (at 199e–j)

So although the CHR had, in his estimation, misunderstood the modus operandi of negligence law in England, Lord Browne-Wilkinson was uncertain what the outcome would be if the House of Lords upheld the

[95]   [1990] 1 All ER 568.

order of the Court of Appeal striking out the action – what would happen were the case to go subsequently to the CHR. To recall, an application to strike out occurs when a party to litigation argues that there are no reasonable grounds for bringing or defending a claim (CPR 1998, r 3.4). Given the impact of *Osman*, and the fact that Article 6 'would soon be a part of English law' by virtue of the HRA 1998 'it is difficult to say that it is a clear and obvious case for striking out.' The order to strike out the action was therefore overruled. 'In the meantime one can only hope that the law applicable under Article 6 is further interpreted' the Law Lord said somewhat wishfully (at 200b–c).

The view of the other Law Lords was that *Barrett* was distinguishable from *X* because it concerned a case of negligence after a child was taken into care as opposed to an allegation of negligence in *failing* to take a child into care. But Lord Browne-Wilkinson's brief judgment had clearly fastened on what appeared to be considerable doctrinal differences.

But it is pertinent to point out that *Barrett* and *Phelps*[96] were determined very much in the shadow of *Osman*. *Phelps*, it will be recalled, was the decision where it was held that employees of an educational authority viz, educational psychologists and teachers, could owe a common law duty of care to pupils in exercising their statutory duties and powers, and their employing authorities could be vicariously liable. The onus was clearly on the defendant authority to establish: i) whether there was any overriding reason in principle why that person ought not to owe a duty of care and ii) why, if that duty was breached, the authority as employer or principal ought not to be vicariously liable.' In *Phelps*, Lord Clyde said:

> The test of fairness [is it fair, just and reasonable] has the advantage of flexibility, enabling the court to define the boundaries of claims for negligence in the light of new situations and the recognition that incremental growth may require to be controlled, albeit at the risk of some uncertainty at least in the prediction of the directions in which the law may develop. But this test may also have regard to the particular facts and circumstances of a particular case. Broader considerations may not alone be determinative. Thus in *Osman v UK* [the CHR] required account to be taken of such matters as the gravity of the negligence in question, the assumption of responsibility by the police for the safety of the eventual victim, and the seriousness of the harm sustained. Even where sound policy

[96]   [2000] 4 All ER 504, HL.

reasons can be put forward for excluding a claim it is not thereby necessarily
to be excluded. (534h et seq)

The case law, then, reveals a growing reluctance to strike out and a desire
to allow cases to proceed to trial. This follows Browne-Wilkinson's
comments in *Barrett* about deciding novel and difficult areas without full
reference to all the facts. The point is repeated in *Phelps.* In *S v
Gloucestershire County Council* the Court of Appeal,[97] following *Barrett*,
ruled that social work cases did not fail as a class. It was a case where
children were taken into care and where they alleged sexual abuse while
being fostered out and that they had suffered damage as a result of the
authority's negligence. The Court held that when deciding what was and
was not justiciable, and in determining what was just, fair and reasonable,
the judicial role might require a more extensive investigation than was
possible on pleadings (the paper documents) alone; it might be necessary
to conduct a 'detailed investigation' of the facts. Furthermore, if a strike-
out application would fail under CPR 1998, r 3.4[98] – the statement discloses
no reasonable grounds for bringing or defending the claim – an application
for summary judgment under r 24.2[99] would not succeed unless the court
was satisfied that it had all substantial facts relevant to the allegations of
negligence which were reasonably capable of being before it, those facts
were not disputed or there was no real prospect of disputing them and
there was no real prospect of oral evidence affecting the court's assessment
of the facts. In other words, a court has to be sure it has all relevant facts,
and what may be relevant facts, before it. A proper consideration of these
factors would ensure compliance with Article 6 ECHR. As Lord Bingham
summed up the position in an extra judicial capacity: 'Appellate courts are
usually and rightly restive if asked to decide questions of law without
reference to detailed findings of fact.'[100]

Are English courts beginning to concentrate more on the breach than the
duty as Craig and Fairgrieve suggest[101] and as the CHR (and one may add
ECJ) practices? Is there in any words a greater emphasis placed on
examining the detailed allegations of negligence rather than on striking

---

97   [2000] 3 All ER 346; see also *W v Essex County Council* [2000] 2 All ER 237,
     HL.
98   Formerly Ord 18, r 19, RSC: 'plain and obvious cases'.
99   This states that summary judgment may be given by a court where the claimant
     has no real prospect of succeeding on the claim and there is no other reason why
     the case or issue should be disposed at trial.
100 Lord Bingham 'A New Supreme Court for the UK', Constitution Unit, May 2002.
101 P Craig and D Fairgrieve (1999) Public Law 626.

out on broad policy considerations? And to continue, is this not what the ECJ concentrated upon in cases alleging breaches of Community law (above)?

In spite of all these developments, judges are at pains to emphasise, as is clear in *Barrett* and *Phelps*, that establishing liability for breaches of statutory powers are unlikely to be successful with any degree of frequency. Even in a duty of care situation, there are many factors that will help to negate negligence including the complexity of judgement involved in making a sensitive decision and the number of actors involved from different statutory agencies.

If influence is coming from Europe, the direction of the influence is not all one way. The appeals that were the subject of *W* (which were heard together with *X v Bedfordshire County Council* in the House of Lords) were subsequently brought to the Commission of Human Rights and subsequently the CHR. *TP and KM v United Kingdom*[102] concerned the decision to take a child into care because of suspected sexual abuse by the mother's partner, as it happened on unjustifiable grounds. The upholding of the application to strike out the claim by the Law Lords in this case was not a breach of Article 6 ECHR, the CHR held. This was because the action in *TP and KM* was against the authority for vicarious liability; but the duty in that case was owed by the social worker and doctor involved in the case to the authority, not to the claimant. The authority was not being sued for a direct liability so there was no application of the 'fair, just and reasonable' test which ruled out liability on an exclusionary basis as in *Osman*. There was, the CHR ruled, no legal basis for the claim.[103] Lord Browne-Wilkinson's judgment in *Barrett* was cited at length in the CHR judgments. There was, the CHR believed, no reason to hold that the striking out procedure *per se* offended Article 6.[104]

---

[102] App 28945/95, [2001] 2 FCR 289. See further: *DP v UK* [2002] 3 FCR 385 and *E v UK* [2002] 3 FCR 700 and Art 13 ECHR.

[103] There was a breach of Art 8 in so far as the mother had not been allowed to view a video of the child giving evidence in which she could have seen immediately that there was a case of mistaken identity and this did not allow her to participate in a decision affecting her daughter and their interests: see *McMichael v UK* 24 February 1995 Series A no 307-B, (1995) 20 EHRR 205. Because no procedures were available to contest this decision on access, there was also a breach of Art 13. Damages were assessed at £10,000 each for the mother and child 'on an equitable basis' but 'without further justification' Carnwarth (2001) PL 475 at 478.

[104] Commission by majority found a breach of Art 6.

An even clearer indication of the influence of the English approach being taken on board by the CHR came in *Z v United Kingdom*.[105] This case concerned another of the cases involved in *X* in which children suffered horrendous and prolonged parental ill-treatment and where it was alleged that the authority had been in breach of statutory and common law duties. It will be recalled that the Law Lords upheld the striking out of the case for disclosing no cause of action.[106] The applicants claimed a breach of Article 6 in that their claims were struck out. There was also a claim for a breach of Article 3 in relation to 'inhuman or degrading treatment' over a four and a half year period and a claim for a breach of Article 8.[107] In making the Article 6 claim, the applicants relied on *Osman* and the finding 'that domestic courts should be able to distinguish between degrees of negligence or harm and give consideration to the justice of a particular case' (para 83) The UK government argued that Article 6 guaranteed a right of access to an independent tribunal only where an individual's rights were in question. It does not bear on the question of whether a specific substantive right to compensation actually exists. Alternatively, the dispute had been subject to a fair and public hearing involving three levels of domestic courts and, as the CHR stated, the claimant was supported by legal aid. It had received a full hearing of the relevant issues. The restriction on access to a court was in pursuit of a legitimate aim and proportionate to preserve the efficiency 'of a vital sector of public service.' (para 86) The domestic courts had weighed up the policy factors involved and 'a very substantial margin of appreciation would therefore be appropriate in any international adjudication.'

The CHR found for the UK government on the Article 6 point. Basically, the arguments on a striking out application assume that the alleged facts are true and whether, that being assumed, they disclose a cause of action. Although the decision to strike out did close the case, the English court established there was no arguable case in law for the existence of a duty in the relationship between the children and a social services authority. This did not operate as an exclusionary rule or immunity which prevented access to the courts. There was a careful balancing of policy factors by the House of Lords, the CHR believed. In a paragraph which seems to give very broad

---

[105] App No 29392/95, [2001] 2 FCR 246.
[106] Awards for criminal injuries were made by the Criminal Injuries Compensation Board.
[107] The claim under Art 3 was successful; the CHR felt there was no need to discuss the claim under Art 8.

support for the UK government's case, the CHR stated that Article 6 does not guarantee the *content* of any substantive right. 'It is not enough to bring Article 6(1) into play that the non-existence of a cause of action under domestic law may be described as having the same effect as an immunity, in the sense of not allowing the applicant to sue for a given category of harm.' (para 98) The Court also noted the domestic case law which followed *X* and how that had refined the questions of law involved, one might add to the applicants' favour. The Commission which had found for the claimants in *Z* had applied the ruling in *Osman* before that case's understanding of the English law of negligence had been developed by *Barrett* and other case law. The CHR was satisfied that the law of negligence includes the fair, just and reasonable test and that the Law Lords decision on this point does not operate as an exclusion. 'In the present case, the Court is led to the conclusion that the inability of the applicants to sue the local authority flowed not from an immunity but from the applicable principles governing the substantive right of action in domestic law. There was no restriction on access to a court...' and no breach of Article 6. (para 100). The decision of the CHR on this point was 12–5.

The applicants' civil rights were involved but there had been a fair hearing. In paragraph 89, the CHR refers to the fact that although the applicants' rights were involved, that same finding could not be said to arise in future cases where the principle in *X is* applied by English courts. Might the CHR be tempted to follow *Osman* in such cases and argue that there has been an exclusionary rule in effect if the particular circumstances of the case were not examined? Such arguments are countered by the fact that a finding of a breach of Article 3 was established in *Z*. This related to the failure by the authority to relieve the children from the dreadful depradations that they were suffering at the hands of their parents. Authorities will now have to calculate this obligation under the HRA 1998 in assessing how they respond. There was also a finding of a breach of Article 13 ECHR because of the absence of an effective remedy within domestic law. The ombudsman, Criminal Injuries Compensation Board and domestic complaints' procedures were not sufficient alone or cumulatively to satisfy the requirements of Article 13 (see Chapter 11). Damages were awarded to the four applicants of £40,000, £132,000, £112,000 and £36,000 respectively.

English courts have moved a great deal to accommodate the judgment in *Osman*. Lord Browne-Wilkinson bemoaned the absence of understanding in the CHR of English law of negligence and spent the remainder of his judgment explaining how the approach in domestic courts did comply with Article 6. It is of interest to note that an English judge, Dame Elizabeth Arden, sat as an ad hoc judge in *Z* and in a separate concurring judgment stated that in *X* the decision was 'fully and carefully reasoned' by the Law Lords. It 'could not be regarded as the product of arbitrariness and it applied to closely defined circumstances.' Appearances of ad hoc judges is becoming more common and under the HRA 1998, s 18 allows for the secondment of British judges to the CHR without having to resign their domestic office. It will encourage judicial confluence.

The Chairman of the Law Commission, Sir Robert Carnwarth has been critical of the decisions in *Z* and *TP*. His criticism is directed to the finding of a breach of Article 8 in the latter case. This concerned the failure by the authority to provide to the mother the video of the interview of her child with the social worker which would have revealed that a case of mistaken identity had been made and that the abuser was not the mother's partner. He believed the failure was an error of judgement in a 'difficult and sensitive area' which was not culpable. The CHR finds it difficult to draw a distinction between a failure to fulfil a positive obligation and mere failures of judgement, he believed. There is a discrepancy between English law and the CHR's tendency to award damages for procedural lapses. In *Z*, he anticipated a future problem arising from the finding of a breach of Article 3 in the case and the award of damages and the line of English case law that established that there would be no liability for breaches of statutory duties in the area in question, social services, or for negligence. A vista is opening up for claims under the HRA 1998 for breaches of Article 3. Even if this is correct, this is not likely to change the 'state of lamentable obscurity and confusion' in which public liability in English law finds itself.[108]

Damages under the Human Rights Act 1998

The HRA 1998, s 8(1) allows a court to 'grant such relief or remedy, or make such order, within its powers as it considers just and appropriate.'

---

[108] Carnwarth quoting McKinnon LJ *Kent v East Suffolk Catchment Board* [1940] 1 KB 319, 332. See *Kingsley v UK* (app No 35605/97) (2002) Times, 4 June: ECtHR did not think it appropriate to award monetary compensation for loss of procedural opportunities or for distress, loss of damage allegedly flowing from the outcome of domestic proceedings.

Damages may only be awarded by a court with power to award such. The power is circumscribed by a requirement to take into account all the circumstances of the case and that 'the court is satisfied that the award is necessary to afford just satisfaction to the person in whose favour it is made.' (s 8(3)) There has been discussion of the precise nature of this remedy – is it a breach of statutory duty as the Law Commission has suggested (and this would be my preference), a new tort or something else? There will be questions about the degree of fault required, if any, for a damages award and how the remedy will fit in with the usual parsimony of English judges in finding liability on public authorities; the manner in which they have dealt with questions of policy has been an exemplar of this. Fairgrieve highlights some differences in approaches between the CHR and English courts on eg, questions of strict causation and a 'loss of opportunity' approach favoured by the CHR and anticipates possible developments in relaxation of approaches by English courts to questions of pecuniary loss.[109] It will doubtless be a long and interesting development.

Finally, it will be recalled that the CHR in *Z* did not find the existence of alternative forms of relief sufficient to satisfy the requirements of Article 13 – the right to an effective remedy. As I argue in Chapter 11, internal complaints procedures and ombudsmen are essential features of good and responsive administration. Ombudsmen must not breach the ECHR as incorporated into domestic law and although independent they are not tribunals. There is evidence that the courts are taking them more seriously in the UK than hitherto. Had they been bound to apply the Convention rights in their investigations in accordance with HRA 1998, s 2, as are courts and tribunals, they would be in a much stronger position perhaps to assuage some of the concerns of the CHR.[110]

---

[109] Fairgrieve (2001) PL 695; J Wright *Tort Law and Human Rights* (2001). French administrative courts have been more relaxed than English courts in allowing claims for pure economic loss: Andenas and Fairgrieve (2002) ICLQ 757, 777. On damages for 'maladministration' and a breach of Article 8 under the HRA for failure to provide suitably adapted accommodation for a disabled tenant, see *R (Bernard) v Enfield London Borough Council* [2002] EWHC 2282, [2002] All ER (D) 383 (Oct).

[110] So too would a commitment by Government and public authorities to accept their recommendations.

Placing limits on national remedies

It has been seen elsewhere how the ECJ has ruled that remedies within Member States for breaches of Community law are primarily a matter for domestic courts subject to the principle of equivalence – the principles must apply in the same way to domestic and Community law and that remedies must not be applied in a manner which effectively deprives an injured party of a remedy. The decision in *Marshall (No 2)*[111] – which was concerned with a ceiling placed by national law on awards of compensation for discrimination contrary to Community law and a refusal to pay interest on sums awarded – has illustrated dramatically that where obligations are imposed on Member States and where these confer rights on individuals, adequate compensation for damage caused by a breach of those rights must be provided. National provisions which imposed an upper limit on the amount of compensation payable or which excluded an essential component of compensation for the purpose of restoring the right – equality of treatment under Directive 76/207/EEC – were not consistent with the proper implementation of Article 6 of that Directive. Article 6 was also directly effective even though it gave discretion to the State to choose between different solutions to achieve the objectives of the Directive. Being directly effective, it could, therefore, be relied upon by an individual to avoid the application of a national provision which did not conform to Article 6. Where the content of Community rights can be determined sufficiently precisely on the basis of the provisions of a Directive alone, then the fact that the Member State has a choice among several possible means of achieving the objectives of a Directive does not of itself exclude the possibility of individual enforcement.

The full impact of the decision in *Marshall (No 2)*, has, however, been diluted by subsequent decisions where it was held that social security payments that were wrongfully withheld did not attract interest payments as in *Marshall (No 2)* because the award in *Marshall* was compensatory for discrimination whereas payment of arrears of social security wrongfully withheld did not constitute reparation for injury sustained. This was the case even though the claim had been denied on discriminatory grounds.[111A] Allowance was made for the fact that the state cannot be prejudiced in organising its finances! More recent case law has seen the ECJ advise that interest may be awarded where an unlawful demand for taxation has been

---

[111]   Case C-271/91 *Marshall v Southampton and South West Hampshire Area Health Authority (No 2)* [1993] ECR I-4367.

[111A]   Case C-66/95 *R v Secretary of State, ex p Sutton* [1997] ECR I-2163.

made.[112] Nor is the state prohibited from placing a cap on awards of compensation in all cases so that a maximum compensatory award of three months salary might be justifiable where a person wrongfully refused employment on grounds of discrimination was in any event less well qualified than the successful candidate and would not have been offered the job notwithstanding the discrimination.[113]

Limitation periods

Another striking decision affecting practice and procedure was the decision in *Emmot*.[114] The ECJ decided that prescription or limitation periods cannot begin to run vis à vis rights based upon a directly effective Directive until the Directive has been fully implemented into national law. It was accepted that an individual cannot know about his or her rights under a Directive until it has been implemented into national law. This decision owes much to the doctrine of legal certainty.

Like *Marshall (No 2)* the principle established in *Emmott* has been qualified by subsequent decisions of the ECJ. In *Steerhorst-Neerings*[115] a national rule restricting the retroactive effect of a claim for benefit relating to a Directive that had been incorrectly transposed into national law was not a breach of Community law but a matter of 'sound administration' and financial balance as payments made in a year must be met from contributions in that year. The ECJ subsequently ruled that even if these considerations were not present restricting retroactive awards of wrongfully withheld social security payments was not inconsistent with Community law.[116]

Restitution

Until recently, the received wisdom was that claims in restitution for payments made following ultra vires demands by authorities, typically for

---

112 Case C-410/98 *Metallgesellschaft and Hoechst v IRC* [2001] ECR I-1727.
113 *Draehmpaehl v Urania Immobilienservice* Case C-180/95 [1997] ECR I-2195.
114 Case C-208/90 *Emmott v Minister for Social Welfare and the A-G (Ireland)* [1991] ECR I-4169.
115 Case C-338/91 [1993] ECR I-5475.
116 Case C-410/92 *Johnson v Chief Adjudication Officer (No 2)* [1994] ECR I-5483. See also Case C-66/95 *R v Secretary of State for Social Security, ex p Sutton* [1997] ECR I-2163.

tax, or for repayment of advances or expenditure under ultra vires contracts were not recoverable.[117] Specific statutory provisions might allow for the repayment of money unlawfully demanded. Where no such provision is made, the common law ruled that payment under a mistake of law by the tax-payer would not be recoverable. This doctrine was applied strictly causing manifest injustice because the real cause of the payment was not a mistake by the tax-payer but the unlawful demand of the authorities. The House of Lords in a judgment in 1992 declined to follow earlier precedents and have held that in such circumstances the tax-payer is allowed to recover. The judgments were influenced by developments in various common law jurisdictions and, critically for present purposes, by the decision in *Amministrazione delle Finanze dello Stato v SpA San Giorgio.*[118]

This case established that a person who pays charges levied by a Member State contrary to Community law is entitled to repayment of the charge, such right being regarded as a consequence of, and an adjunct to, rights conferred on individuals by the Community provisions prohibiting the relevant charges. Reliance upon EC law was particularly apparent in the judgment of Lord Goff who made the following point:

> I only comment that, at a time when Community law is becoming increasingly important, it would be strange if the right of the citizen to recover overpaid charges were to be more restricted under domestic law than it is under Community law.[119]

The same judge also believed that the principle applied to demands not based upon an ultra vires factor but intra vires mistake (a distinction that is becoming less important in English law), but in the circumstances this was purely obiter. In terms of ultra vires contracts made by public authorities, the view was that they were not subject to restitutionary claims by innocent contracting parties, especially in the absence of a failure of consideration. This view has now come under question and indeed following notorious litigation in England which ruled that contracts

---

117 *W Whiteley Ltd v R* (1909) 101 LT 741; *Twyford v Manchester Corpn* [1946] 1 All ER 621.

118 Case 199/82 [1983] ECR 3595.

119 *Woolwich Equitable Building Society v IRC (No 2)* [1992] 3 All ER 737 at 764, HL. On more recent comments along this and related themes, see: Lord Bingham 'A New Common Law for Europe' in B Markesinis ed *The Coming Together of the Common Law and the Civil Law* (2000). See *Fairchild v Glenhaven Funeral Services Ltd* [2002] UKHL 22, para 32 [2002] 3 All ER 305 cited in Andenas and Fairgrieve (2002) ICLQ 757.

involving 'rate swaps' transactions for interest rates between banks and local authorities were ultra vires subsequent decisions allowed restitution, albeit in circumstances which have attracted much criticism.[120]

Conclusion

On the question of liability for tortious wrongdoing, the test invoked by the ECJ to establish liability in cases where a discretion is exercised, viz whether there is a sufficiently serious breach of law whereby a Member State manifestly and gravely disregards the limits of its discretion may help to address some of the difficulties English courts have encountered in this area. Should the expression include abuses of discretion in the *Wednesbury* sense – 'they must have taken leave of their senses' – and disproportionate exercise of power? Or is the way forward to concentrate on a breach of a duty of care. It is axiomatic in English law that if a power is given, it should not be exercised negligently. However, where questions of policy choice are involved, especially but not exclusively in relation to collective resource allocation, no test is likely to overcome judicial reluctance to intervene in decision-making.

English judges are also likely to remain reluctant to impose a duty of care where this will be seen to hinder the performance of services owed to the public and which requires difficult questions of judgement and discretion.[121] However, some inroads into this reluctance have been made already as has been seen in this chapter. Andenas and Fairgrieve argue that the decision by the Law Lords to allow the claim of misfeasance in public office by investors in the failed BCCI bank to proceed against the Bank of England, the regulator, shows a preparedness to 'liberalise' the law on liability. The burden facing claimants is nonetheless substantial.[122]

---

[120] *Hazell v Hammersmith and Fulham London Borough Council* [1991] 1 All ER 545; the follow-up litigation was: *Westdeutsche Landesbank Girozentrale v Islington London Borough Council* [1996] 2 All ER 961, HL and *Kleinwort Benson Ltd v Lincoln City Council* [1998] 4 All ER 513, HL where German and other authorities were extensively referred to. See *Restitution* Law Commission Cm 2731 (1994) and Local Government (Contracts) Act 1997.

[121] See eg, *K v Secretary of State for the Home Department* [2002] EWCA Civ 775, [2002] All ER (D) 509 (May).

[122] *Three Rivers District Council v Bank of England (No 3)* [2001] UKHL 16, [2001] 2 All ER 513. Above note 14.

Finally, any question of liability for ultra vires activity or inactivity *per se*, ie outside the sufficiently serious test and without accompanying tortious action, is a matter for Parliament. Were such a liability to be introduced, very difficult questions of causation and damages would arise. The award of damages under the HRA 1998 will also be watched with interest to see what influence the jurisprudence of the CHR will have. An unjustified and disproportionate interference with a human right is likely to attract damages.

Questions of liability and attendant issues are quintessentially lawyers' 'stuff'. Questions of money are the meat and gravy of legal practice. Yet in this area of traditional concern, we have seen the most striking of dialogues and developments between our domestic system and European systems influencing the way in which our law progresses. As pointed out, the development is not all one way. The result should not be exaggerated; but the influence should not be denied.

Chapter 11

The EU Ombudsman, complaints and internal complaints and grievance procedures

Ombudsmen and internal complaints procedures – the background

In this chapter we examine the role of the EU Ombudsman and his office and the operation of internal grievance mechanisms. The EU Ombudsman was established under the Maastricht Treaty in 1992. He is appointed through election by the Parliament, his 'seat' is the European Parliament and he must be an EU citizen. He enjoys the same 'rank' as a judge of the ECJ. The Courts of the EU do of course provide a system of remedies for citizens for breaches of Community law but only where the object of attack is a Community institution; the more usual manner in which litigation involving an individual ends up before the court is on a preliminary reference from a national court under Article 234 [177] EC. Since the Treaty of Nice, the CFI has become a court of general jurisdiction for all actions for annulment and illegal failure to act and it may be called upon to give preliminary rulings in areas laid down in its statute. Individuals, as we saw in Chapter 2, faced considerable barriers in overcoming access rights to the courts under Article 230 EC, a difficulty which the decision of the ECJ in *Union de Pequenos Agricultores*[1] is likely to maintain. The EU Ombudsman is meant to provide accessible and flexible, as well as cost free, means of redress for individuals.

---

[1] Case C-50/00 P [2002] 3 CMLR 1 which did not follow the Opinion of the Advocate General and the decision of the CFI in *Jégo-Quéré et Cie SA* Case T-177/01, [2002] All ER (EC) 932. See Chapter 3, p 106 et seq for discussion. See also Case C-253/00 *A Muñoz Y CIA SA v Fraumar Ltd* [2002] 3 CMLR 734 and Case T-598/97 *British Shoe Corpn Footwear Supplies v Council* [2002] All ER (EC) 385.

The provision of an ombudsman accompanied the power of the European Parliament under Article 193 [138c] EC to establish a temporary Committee of Inquiry to investigate alleged contraventions or maladministration in the implementation of Community law. A request must come from a quarter of its members and was famously invoked to investigate the Cresson affair.[2] It also accompanied a new right of 'any citizen of the Union' along with any natural or legal person to petition the Parliament on a matter falling within the EC's 'fields of activity' and which affects them or it directly.[3] There is an agreement between the European Parliament and the EU Ombudsman concerning the 'mutual transfer of complaints and petitions in appropriate cases.'[4] In 2001, two petitioners were transferred from the European Parliament to the EU Ombudsman and nine from the EU Ombudsman to the European Parliament. The EU Ombudsman cannot deal with complaints about the Committee of Petitions because this is regarded as a 'political matter'.[5] The European Parliament may send these petitions to the Commission which may deal with them as a complaint under Article 226 [169] EC.

The chapter begins by looking briefly at an area which has attracted a great deal of attention from the EU Ombudsman, namely the procedures adopted by the Commission to deal with alleged infractions by Member States of Community law. Many of these Article 226 EC procedures are initiated after complaints are made by individuals, companies or persons, about Member State activity. The primary purpose of the procedure from the Commission's point of view is that of ensuring compliance with Community law by Member States. Those who make complaint, as the Commission point out, are often left frustrated that their complaint is not satisfactorily concluded

---

[2]   See Ch 6, p 261 et seq.

[3]   Under Arts 21 and 39 TEU, the European Parliament may ask questions about the Second and Third Pillar areas, make recommendations, be informed and consulted about those matters and hold an annual debate

[4]   The agreement is outlined in the 1995 EU Ombudsman *Annual Report.* See generally: www.euro-ombudsman.eu.int.

[5]   Under Art 197 [140] EC, members of the Commission may attend all meetings of the Parliament and shall be heard at their request on behalf of the Commission. The Commission shall reply orally or in writing to questions put to it by the European Parliament or by its members. Details are governed by internal regulations of the European Parliament (Arts 40–42 of the regulations) governing oral questions for a Parliamentary commission, political groups or at least 29 deputies; a question time for individual MEPs; written questions which have no limit for number and which are published along with answers in the Official Journal series C.

to their satisfaction.[6] While the ECJ gives a wide berth to the Commission under Article 226 EC procedures (below), it should be noted that the case law provenance of individual enforcement for breaches of EC law in *Francovich* and *Factortame* were both decided after the Commission had brought Article 226 EC proceedings to the Court, and in the former case after interim measures were awarded in the Commission's favour, and in the latter final judgment was given in the Commission's favour. Article 226 EC, which was addressed briefly in Chapter 3, p109 et seq is one of several compliance and enforcement mechanisms in the Treaty.[7]

Following the Cresson affair, the anti-fraud office in the Commission (Olaf) was established. It may act, inter alia, on complaints from 'whistleblowers' (europa.eu.int/comm/anti_fraud/index_en.html).[8] The Court of Auditors may also conduct investigations arising from complaints, but it is not a complaints remedial body (www.eca.eu.int).

Article 226 EC complaints

A brief examination of the role of Article 226 EC will be made. Complaints received by the Commission are largely about national regimes and breaches of, or failures to comply with, EC law. It also receives complaints about its own activities in addition to complaints under Article 226 EC.[9] Under Article 211 EC first indent, the Commission is under a duty to 'ensure that the provisions of this Treaty and the measures taken by institutions pursuant thereto are applied.' Article 226 EC provides the principal means of enforcement of this duty and it says that if the Commission considers that a Member State has failed to fulfil an obligation under the Treaty, it shall deliver a reasoned opinion on the matter after giving the State concerned the opportunity to submit its observations.[10] Non-compliance with this

---

6   See *18th Annual Report*, COM (2001) 309.

7   See eg Art 237 [225] EC for enforcement powers of the Board of the European Investment Bank and the Council of the European Central Bank.

8   Commission Decision 99/352 establishing Olaf and Council Regulation 99/1073 concerning investigations. See *Rothley v European Parliament* Case T-17/00 [2002] 2 CMLR 737 and Case T-17/00 [2002] 2 CMLR 766 and a challenge by an MEP to rules of the EP amending its rules and requiring MEPs to cooperate with Olaf.

9   See Art 211 EC first indent; Declaration 19 Maastricht Treaty; the Commission produces an annual report on its activities under Art 226 EC.

10   See F Snyder (1993) Mod LR 19; R Mastroianni (1995) European Public Law 535; R Rawlings (2000) 6 ELJ 4 on the variety of functions of the Art 226 EC procedure: part diplomatic, part law enforcer, part complaint resolver.

opinion within a prescribed period may cause the Commission to bring the matter to the ECJ – the judicial stage which may lead to an order from the ECJ. In 2000, the Commission issued 460 reasoned opinions and referred 172 cases to the ECJ under Article 226 EC. These figures are similar to other recent annual statistics on the procedure.

This is preceded by the administrative stage which is split into two phases: the informal which may lead to closure of the file or to a decision to investigate the complaint. The latter decision leads to the formal phase which may subsequently lead to a reasoned opinion (above). Its sources of information come from complaints as well as its own enquiries. A standard complaints form has been produced.[11] The EU Ombudsman in *The Citizen, the Administration and European Law*[12] noted how the citizen who complained was somewhat alienated from the procedure despite the procedure being an important means of making states comply with EC law. The sense of alienation was enhanced where no directly effective rights were concerned. The procedure and practice of the Commission were highly criticised. The Commission have argued that technically, the complainant is not a party to proceedings and has no locus standi to claim documents or to receive a copy of the reasoned opinion which under the procedure the Commission must serve on the Member State in order for the Member State to be informed of the case against it. The CFI has not been prepared to assist complainants to obtain documents concerned with the letter of formal notice to the Member State, process of investigation, or of drafts or final copies of reasoned opinions. This confidentiality applies even after the 'matter has been brought before the Court of Justice'.[13] The procedure is built around negotiation, as Snyder graphically illustrated some years ago[14] in which political and diplomatic elements feature prominently.[15] The procedure is a graphic illustration of the dilemma facing the Community of little people in big societies in which supra-national and national sensitivity and disagreement have to be resolved by politico-diplomatic processes in which the individual has little place.

---

11   [2002] OJ C 244/5: http://europa.eu.int/comm/secretariat-general/sgb/lexcomm/ form_en.htm.
12   FIDE XVIII Congress, 1998 *Rapport General* (1999) pp 314 et seq at 323; see Barnard in the report on UK in the same volume.
13   Case T- 191/99 *Petrie v Commission* [2002] 1 CMLR 519, 11 December 2001; see also Case T-309/97 *Bavarian Lager Co v Commission* [1999] ECR II-3217 and Case T-105/95 *WWF UK v Commission* [1997] ECR II-313. See COM (2002) 725 final, 11/12/02.
14   F Snyder (1993) Mod LR 19.
15   P Craig (1992) 12 OJLS 456.

The point was made emphatically by the EU Ombudsman that an individual who complains to the Commission is doing so as a citizen *qua* citizen, not simply as an informer.[16] Too often, the administrative stage has not convinced complainants that the procedure under Article 226 EC represents 'a legitimate method of enforcing Community law' because of the high premium placed on negotiation and persuasion to achieve compliance and to avoid a judicial reference.[17] The suspicion of political interference is present. Complaints in national reports in the 1998 *Fide* publication also highlight inconsistency, over reliance on secrecy as well as discrimination eg, non-use of the complainant's language. The EU Ombudsman has himself received complaints about the procedure under Article 226 EC and perceived shortcomings in the way it has been conducted. These have contained allegations of delay and a lack of reasons for findings as well as the above shortcomings.[18] It was not satisfactory simply to say that the manner in which a complaint was dealt with was a matter of discretion for the Commission. The EU Ombudsman reported that even though there are limits to what a court can do to enforce compliance with Article 226 EC – judicial review of decisions under the procedure is not available – and the ECJ cannot enforce the Commission to refer a complaint to the court, the powers the Commission adopted to deal with a complaint were not limitless and were bounded by fundamental rights and general principles of law. Where the Commission decides not to bring an infringement before the ECJ, it should give reasons the EU Ombudsman believed. The *real politik* is that this could cause embarrassment where there had been political involvement by a Member State. But how can this be reconciled 'with a citizenship of the Union which is based on the Rule of Law.'[19]

The EU Ombudsman did initiate an own initiative investigation into Article 226 EC pre-litigation procedures in 1997.[20] The Commission promised to improve procedural fairness although further complaints were made about what were seen as procedural lapses by the Commission and the Commission was found to be at fault.[21] In his report for 2001 (p 165), the EU Ombudsman observed that the Commission was, in October 2001, 'in

---

16   P Craig (1992) 12 OJLS 456, p 324.
17   P Craig (1992) 12 OJLS 456, p 324.
18   *Annual Report 1996* EU Ombudsman (1997) pp 66, 75.
19   J Soderman *FIDE Report* (1999), p 20.
20   See EU Ombudsman *Annual Report 1997* (1998): 303/97/PD.
21   See EU Ombudsman *Annual Report 2001* (2002): Complaint 995/98/OV failure to state reasons for the closure of a complaint file; 1267/99/ME failure to register complaint; 493/2000/ME failure to provide adequate reasons; 1194/2000/JMA failure to follow its own procedures.

the process of drafting' its procedural code for Article 226 EC pre-litigation proceedings but that in fact there seemed to be no progress in drafting rules in its role as 'Guardian of the Treaty'! Below, I discuss the *Code of Good Administrative Procedure* produced by the EU Ombudsman and which the Commission has accepted and which will also apply to Article 226 EC procedures and complaints. In October 2002, the Commission published a communication to the EP and EU Ombudsmen in its 'relations' with Article 226 complainants (COM (2002) 141 final – OJ C 244/5).

A further development may see closer links between the EU Ombudsman and national ombudsmen who may receive complaints about alleged breaches of Community law in their Member State by their own authorities. I pick up on this point below.

The EU Ombudsman and complaints[22]

Under Article 195 [138e] EC, the EU Ombudsman is empowered to receive complaints from any citizen of the EU or any natural or legal person residing or having a registered office in a Member State and which concerns maladministration in the activities of Community institutions or bodies. There is no requirement for locus standi or 'interest'. Article 41 TEU extends jurisdiction to Third Pillar subjects, but no similar provision covers the Second Pillar. In his 1998 Annual Report, the EU Ombudsman defined maladministration as occurring when 'a public body fails to act in accordance with a rule or principle which is binding upon it.' In his 1995 Annual Report, the EU Ombudsman gave various illustrations of maladministration but the European Parliament pressed for a definition. This definition has been approved by the European Parliament and the Commission. Examples given in the EU Ombudsman's Guidance on complaining include: administrative irregularities and omissions, abuse of power, negligence, illegal procedures, unfairness, malfunction or incompetence, discrimination, avoidable delay, lack of, or refusal to supply information. While this list is not as long as the UK Parliamentary Ombudsman's, it openly refers to legal concepts such as negligence.

---

[22]   See J Soderman (1997) European Public Law 351 and I Harden 'When Europeans Complain: The Role of the European Ombudsman' 3 (2000) Cambridge Yearbook of European Legal Studies 199 (2002); and K Heede (1997) European Public Law 587.

Complaints about the judicial work of ECJ or CFI are not admissible. The remit includes complaints from Community staff on personnel matters and in this respect the EU Ombudsman differs from the UK ombudsmen who cannot investigate personnel complaints. He may also investigate complaints relating to contractual tendering, unlike the UK ombudsmen. Unlike the UK ombudsmen he can conduct an own initiative investigation and he does not have to wait for a complaint. In this respect he is like many other ombudsmen. The most important of these has been his investigation into the practice and policy of disclosure of documents to the public adopted by every institution in the Community (Chapter 6, p 271 et seq). Complainants may approach the EU Ombudsman directly or via an MEP. In the case of the UK Ombudsman, a complaint may only be made via an MP but it may be that this will change when plans for combining the public sector ombudsmen into a single office – a sort of 'one-stop-shop' – come to fruition.[23]

The EU Ombudsman cannot investigate complaints where the alleged facts are or have been the subject of legal proceedings. Public sector ombudsmen in the UK are warned off investigating complaints where there is a legal remedy unless in all the circumstances of the case it is it is reasonable to do so. The courts have been quite strict in their interpretation of this provision although they have shown some tolerance where an ombudsman complaint would uncover evidence that would not be obtained on a judicial review and which was essential for successful complaint.[24] The EU Ombudsman has faced opposition from the Commission who have argued that a legal matter should go to the Courts and not be subject to an ombudsman investigation. The EU Ombudsman has resisted such opposition pointing out that such a limitation is not in the Treaty and the UK ombudsman is one of the few to have such a limitation spelt out in statute. The EU Ombudsman has taken up a reference from the Irish ombudsman which concerned interpretation of an EC legal rule which the latter felt was being interpreted over restrictively by the Commission. The EU Ombudsman insisted that he could investigate whether an institution has acted 'lawfully' in accordance with the agreed definition of maladministration.[25] He expressed surprise that the Commission was still

---

[23] Only France has an MP filter and Sri Lanka. On creating a single public sector office in the UK, see: HC 612 (1999–2000).

[24] *R v Local Comr for Administration etc, ex p Liverpool City Council* [2001] 1 All ER 462, CA.

[25] *Annual Report 1999* (2000) pp 17 et seq.

pressing this point although the Commission undertook to review the position. Subsequently the EU Ombudsman was able to report that the Commission had accepted his interpretation.[26]

Article 195(1) [138e] EC provides that where he establishes an instance of maladministration after an investigation, he must refer the matter to the institution concerned. That body has three months to inform the EU Ombudsman of its views. The EU Ombudsman has to forward a report to the European Parliament and to the institution. The person who makes the complaint has to be informed of the outcome.

The EU Ombudsman submits an annual report on the outcome of his inquiries to the European Parliament which is published. The EU Ombudsman is appointed after each election to the European Parliament and his tenure endures for the duration of that Parliament. He may be re-appointed. Like a Commissioner, he may be dismissed from office by the ECJ if the European Parliament (in the case of a Commissioner it is the Council or Commission) believes he no longer fulfils the conditions required for the performance of his duties or if he is guilty of serious misconduct.' He will be completely independent in the performance of his duties taking and seeking instructions from no-one. He has to provide a 'solemn undertaking' before the ECJ on his independence.

Powers and procedures of the EU Ombudsman

The powers of the ombudsman are set out in a statute adopted by the European Parliament on 9 March 1994.[27] Community institutions and bodies are 'obliged to supply to the EU Ombudsman, at his request, with any information which he requests from them unless there are duly substantiated grounds of secrecy.' This information must not be divulged by the EU Ombudsman. Member State authorities are also obliged to provide the EU Ombudsman with all necessary information save where such information is covered by laws or regulations on secrecy, or by provisions preventing it being communicated. Where information is requested from a Community institution which has come from a Member

---

26   *Annual Report 2000* (2001) pp 202 et seq.
27   OJ L113, 4.5.1994, p 15. Under Art 14, the EUO has adopted implementing measures.

State, and which is classified as secret by law or regulation,[28] that Member State has to consent to disclosure. Other documents originating in a Member State may be given after the Commission has informed the Ms The EU Ombudsman must not divulge the content of such reports. Complainants may also request confidentiality.

Officials and servants of Community institutions must testify at the request of the EU Ombudsman; 'they shall speak on behalf of and in accordance with instructions from their administrations and shall continue to be bound by their duty of professional secrecy.'[29] This provision has caused the EU Ombudsman concern and is open to abuse and he has described it as 'unnecessary and inappropriate.' He has called for them to be removed and for the EU Ombudsman to have full access to the files and documents and for officials to be under a clear duty to give 'full and truthful testimony' to the EU Ombudsman.[30] Member States authorities are obliged to provide the EU Ombudsman with information that may help to clarify instances of maladministration by Community institutions or bodies as requested via the Permanent Representatives of the Member States to the EC. There is a saving for information which by law or regulation is secret or where provisions prevent it being communicated. In the latter case, the Member State *may* allow the EU Ombudsman to have the information providing he undertakes not to divulge it. Presumably, this means to the complainant or anyone outside his office. Where such assistance is not forthcoming, he shall inform the European Parliament which can make 'appropriate representations'. Complaints of inaccurate information or not providing information comprise the largest single category of complaint to the EU Ombudsman. Although information collected must be treated in confidence, the EU Ombudsman is obliged to disclose facts to the competent authorities

---

28 UK classifications are non-legal measures.

29 EU Ombudsman Statute Art 3(2); for an EU Ombudsman suggested revision see *Annual Report 1999* (2000) pp 22–23 and this will be reported on in his Annual Report for 2001 (July 2002) – a redraft by the European Parliament which removed this qualification was awaiting comment by the Commission and which would have to be approved by the Council on a qualified majority voting *Annual Report 2001* (2002) p 24; and on use of the power see pp 23–24. There is no provision, as in the case of UK ombudsmen to take evidence on oath. The Commission has refused to allow a Commissioner to testify: Harden 'When Europeans Complain: The Role of the European Ombudsman' 3 (2000) Cambridge Yearbook of European Legal Studies 199 at 217.

30 *EU Ombudsman Annual Report 1998* (1999) p 13 and *Annual Report 1999* (2000) p 12; on his instructions to his own staff see: *Annual Report 2000* (2001) para 2.7.2 'Inspection of documents'.

which he considers might relate to criminal law. The preamble states that provision should be made for co-operation with ombudsmen and similar bodies in Member States. The EU Ombudsman addressed this very topic at the 1998 FIDE conference and I will return to it below.

A complaint must be made within two years of the date on which the facts on which it is based came to the attention of the person lodging the complaint and there has to be 'appropriate administrative approaches to the institutions and bodies concerned.' This means that the body complained against must be given an opportunity to address the issue and find a solution before a complaint is made to the EU Ombudsman. Article 2(8) of the EUO statute specifies in particular that complaints about working relationships, ie employment disputes, must follow procedures laid down in staff regulations. The EU Ombudsman must inform a complainant as soon as possible of the action he has taken on it. The EU Ombudsman is under a duty 'as far as possible' to seek a 'friendly solution' with the body complained against to eliminate the maladministration and to satisfy the complainant. He assumes the role of conciliator when appropriate. On a finding of maladministration, he has to inform the body complained against and may make draft recommendations. The body has to send a detailed opinion to the EU Ombudsman within three months. If the opinion is unsatisfactory, it may be followed by a report by the EU Ombudsman to the European Parliament and the body complained against which may contain recommendations. The complainant is informed of the outcome, any opinion expressed by the body complained against and any recommendations made by the EU Ombudsman. There is no reference to any power to recommend payment of compensation.

The EU Ombudsman's mandate covers the EU institutions and bodies.[31] It does not cover national bodies even when implementing Community provisions – unlike the original Spanish proposal that the EU Ombudsman should cover Community rights of individuals at all levels including Community, national, regional and municipal level. The EU Ombudsman has not supported such a mandate and has expressed the view that subsidiarity demands that national bodies attend to such matters. The EU Ombudsman does receive queries from national ombudsmen about

---

[31]   For a hybrid body within his jurisdiction: the European University Institute, see complaint 659/2000/GG: *Annual Report 2000* (2001), para.3.1.4. See Harden 'When Europeans Complain: The Role of the European Ombudsman' 3 (2000) Cambridge Yearbook of European Legal Studies 199 at 227-28.

Community law and replies either directly or refers the request to an appropriate authority.[32] The EU Ombudsman has, however, encouraged a system whereby national ombudsmen assist him in enforcing Community law in each Member State. A website and a Summit (consisting of several internet forums) have existed since September 2000 to exchange information and views on Community law matters between the EU Ombudsman and national ombudsmen, and it is hoped regional and even municipal offices (http://www.euro-ombudsman.eu.int).

The proportion of complaints outside the mandate is about 70% – many of these relate to national institutions and a very large number concern free movement of persons. Having national ombudsmen assist in free movement provisions would be particularly appropriate now that visas, asylum and foreigners' rights are a part of the Community legal framework[33] and are effected through national authorities. The UK did not sign up to the provisions that were brought into the Community pillar by the Amsterdam Treaty but for those countries that did agree, the EU Ombudsman has pressed the case for assistance in enforcing Community law. In his 1998 Annual Report he believed that the citizen's rights to seek enforcement of Community rights via national courts and ombudsmen should be specifically referred to in the Treaty. This would cause insuperable difficulties for the UK ombudsmen whose remit is designed to ward them off complaints where there is a legal remedy. Furthermore, although the UK public sector ombudsmen are public authorities and cannot therefore act in contravention of the ECHR, the HRA 1998 did not impose a duty on ombudsmen, unlike courts and tribunals, to 'take into account' the jurisprudence of the CHR etc when determining a question which has arisen in connection with a Convention right.[34] It is not clear therefore to what extent the UK ombudsmen informally invoke the standards of the ECHR in determining complaints, some of which would be very relevant to their work. It is clear that human rights jurisprudence is taken into consideration by other ombudsmen but their ability to engage in legal interpretation is far more evident than the case with UK public sector ombudsmen.[35] It is this ability to engage in legal matters that the EU Ombudsman is building

---

[32] *Annual Report 2000* (2001), para 3.7. The UK Ombudsman is the only national ombudsman who cannot have a complaint transferred to her office by the EU Ombudsman.

[33] *Annual Report 2000* p 11 ME 00014 EN.

[34] HRA 1998, s 2(1) and Ch 9, p 364 et seq.

[35] This is not the case with several private sector ombudsmen in the UK.

upon in establishing a network for decentralised application of Community law. All 'public authorities must be subject to the Rule of Law. It can never be good administration to fail to act in accordance with the law.'[36] Ombudsmen should receive advice on Community law to enable them to assist courts in overseeing the application of Community law, the EU Ombudsman believed. Such a network would assist the courts and the Commission, not obstruct them.

In 1998, twelve Member States had national ombudsmen and some of these had ombudsmen at regional and municipal levels; Germany and Luxembourg have Parliamentary committees to deal with petitions which fulfil certain ombudsmen functions. Italy has regional ombudsmen. National ombudsmen do not exist in those countries.

UK public sector ombudsmen may recommend an award of compensation for maladministration causing injustice which, if paid, is done so on an ex gratia basis. Such sums can be considerable and the *Financial Times* (25 May 2002) reported that the Parliamentary Ombudsman had recommended an award of £4.7 million to a business which had been the victim of errors by the Office of Fair Trading. The Barlow Clowes episode in the late 1980s which involved maladministration by the DTI in the supervision of a rogue trader led to awards of £150m.[37]

There is no provision in the Treaty or the EU Ombudsman Statute for a Community institution or body to award compensation for maladministration. Where the conditions for contractual or non contractual liability under art 288 EC are met, the award of compensation may be possible. A friendly solution may include a recommendation for monetary compensation providing some limited flexibility.[38] Article 41 of the Charter of Fundamental Rights of the EU includes the right to have the 'Community make good any damage caused by its institutions or by its servants in the performance of their duties, in accordance with the general principles common to the laws of the Member States.' In complaint/inv 1230/2000, the Commission referred to the payment as 'ex gratia'.

---

[36]   J Soderman *FIDE Report* (1999), p 19.

[37]   See Ch 10, note 22.

[38]   See I Harden 'When Europeans Complain: The Role of the European Ombudsman' 3 (2000) Cambridge Yearbook of European Legal Studies 199 and cases 1109/96 and 390/99.

Own initiative investigations have included: access to documents; a code of practice on good administrative behaviour; opposition from the Commission where a complaint had arguably a legal remedy although it had not been lodged with the courts (CFI, ECJ) and secrecy in appointments in the Commission. An own inititative investigation in 1999 led to recommendations on access to Interpol's documents by requesters and Interpol agreed to be bound by Council Decision 93/731. This has now been replaced by a Regulation and a Council Decision as we have seen (see Chapter 6). The subject of a code on good administrative procedure has now seen significant development.

Facts and figures on complaints

By far and away the greatest object of complaint to the EU Ombudsman in admissible complaints investigated is the Commission – the 'Guardian of the Treaties'. In 2000, the Commission involved 83% of such inquiries.[39] The European Parliament is 7%; the Council 2% and others 8% including the ECJ on a permissible complaint relating to personnel.

The largest single subject of such complaints was denial of access to information but legal errors constituted 6% and 'negligence' 7% and failure to fulfil obligations at 2%.

Complaints to the EU Ombudsman in 2001 numbered 1,874. There were 4 own initiative inestigations.

Code on good administrative practice

We saw how the EU's Charter of Fundamental Rights was adopted at Nice in December 2000 (Chapter 9, p 388 et seq). Interestingly the Charter includes as fundamental rights of citizenship the right to good administration and the right to complain to the EU Ombudsman against maladministration. The Code spells out in greater detail what the Charter's right to good administration in Article 41 CFR should mean in practice. The EU Ombudsman had campaigned to have a code of good administrative practice accepted by Community institutions for some years before it was

---

[39] *Annual Report 2000* (2001) p 224. In 2001, the figures were 77%, 7% and 2% respectively: *Annual Report 2001* (2002) p 271.

formally adopted. Even although the Charter of Fundamental Rights was solemnly proclaimed by the three institutions at Nice, they have not 'shown themselves to be serious about applying it in practice.'[40] He published a report on his own initiative inquiry into the existence and the public accessibility of a Code of good administrative behaviour.[41] The report drew inspiration from the legal administrative codes in existence in Member States including: Portugal, Italy, Spain, Denmark, Finland, Sweden, Austria, Germany, Greece, Belgium, the Netherlands and what was then a French draft text of 1998–99. The report drew further inspiration from those states which possessed no law of administrative procedure but which had eg an Ombudsman's guide to Standards of Best Practice for Public Servants, the UK Citizen's Charter (now a part of the Better Government initiative[42]) and the Belgian Charter for the Users of Public Services as well as Organisation for Economic Cooperation and Development (OECD) publications *Improving Ethical Conduct in the Public Service* (1998) and *The Administration and You* (1996). Because the take up by EC institutions had been somewhat lethargic, the EU Ombudsman recommended a form of 'European Administrative law' which could take the form of a Regulation using the procedure under Article 192(2) EC. The legal base would be Article 308 EC. No Regulation has been forthcoming (see Chapter 14) but in September 2001, the European Parliament adopted the Code and also adopted in the same resolution a proposal for a Regulation containing the Code. The EU Ombudsman is also called upon in the resolution to apply the code when examining whether maladministration is present 'so as to give effect to the citizen's right to good administration in Article 41 of the Charter.'[43]

The Code applies to the institutions of the Community and their officials. The Code emphasises the importance of acting according to law. Interestingly, the UK Parliamentary Ombudsman has advised that mindless observance of legal technicality can constitute maladministration. Decisions affecting the rights or interests of individuals shall have a basis in law and that their content must comply with the law [Article 4]. Decisions must be made on the basis of equality and without any unjustified discrimination based on 'nationality, sex, race, colour, ethnic or social

---

[40] *Annual Report 2001* (2002) p 11.

[41] April 2000: OI/1/98/OV.

[42] See *Making a difference in public services* (11/02) HM Treasury: www.hm_treasury.gov.uk/pspp.

[43] EU Ombudsman European Code of Good Administrative Behaviour.

origin, genetic features, language, religion or belief, political or any other opinion, membership of a national minority, property, birth, disability, age, or sexual orientation. [Article 5] Proportionality in behaviour has to be respected including a duty to 'respect a fair balance between the interests of private persons and the general public interest.' [Article 6] Powers should not be abused or used for improper purposes [Article 7]. Officials must be impartial and independent avoiding all political, personal, family and national interests or pressures. [Article 8] Proper weight should be given to all relevant factors and irrelevant factors should not be considered. [Article 9] Officials should act with consistency, respecting legitimate expectations and should only depart from normal administrative practices where there are legitimate grounds in an individual case which have to be recorded in writing. [Article 10] Officials shall act 'impartially, fairly and reasonably.' [Article 11] Officials should display courtesy and be as helpful as possible at all times. Questions should be answered completely and accurately as possible. Errors must be corrected and apologised for remedying it in the most expedient manner and the member of the public should be advised of any rights of appeal. [Article 12] Correspondence must be replied to in the language of the original communication. [Article 13] Every letter or complaint shall be acknowledged within two weeks unless a 'substantive reply' can be sent within that period. The official replying shall provide the name and telephone number of the official dealing with the matter and service to which he or she belongs. No acknowledgment need be sent where correspondence is vexatious or repetitive. [Article 14] Correspondence wrongly directed to a service shall be re-directed to the correct service and the complainant will be notified of the matters under Article 14 [Article 15]. The content of Article 16 can be dealt with below for reasons that will become apparent.

Prompt responses should be adhered at all times and for all communications. A two-month time limit is set which may be extended because of complicated features in which case the complainant has to be advised as soon as possible and a decision should be notified to the complainant/author in the 'shortest time'. [Article 17] Decisions which may possibly adversely affect the interests or rights of an individual should state the grounds on which it is based indicating clearly the relevant facts and its legal basis. Decisions shall avoid 'brief or vague grounds or which do not contain individual reasoning.' Where a large number of similar cases occur, and it is not possible to communicate in detail the grounds, any citizen who subsequently requests an individual reasoning shall be provided with such. [Article 18] Appeal rights, including complaints to the EU Ombudsman, should be communicated together with essential information. [Article 19] Decisions affecting the rights or interests of individual persons should be communicated as soon as the decision has been taken. [Article 20] Personal data should be protected according to Regulation 45/2001/EC (European Parliament and Council) (OJ L8/1, 12/1/2001) [Article 21].

Where there is a request for information, this shall be provided to a requester by the responsible official and s/he shall give advice on how to initiate a request taking care that the information communicated is 'clear and understandable.' If oral requests cannot be responded to because of their complexity or 'comprehensive' nature, the official shall advise the requester to formulate the request in writing. If the information is confidential, art 18 has to be followed. Misdirected requesters shall be advised on the proper destination of their request including the 'Institution responsible for providing information to the public.'. [Article 22] A request for access to documents shall be dealt with according to rules laid down by the Institution and in accordance with Regulation EC No 1049/2001 (OJ L145/43, 31/5/2001 see Chapter 6). Requests may be made orally but a requester may be required to formulate it in writing. [Article 23] Adequate records must be kept of all incoming and outgoing (ie not internal) correspondence, documents they receive and measures taken [Article 24] Institutions must take effective measures to inform the public of rights under the Code including where possible making the text electronically available on its website. The Commission shall publish and distribute it as a brochure on behalf of 'all institutions.' [Article 25] Failure to comply with the above provisions may be the subject of a complaint to the EU Ombudsman [Article 26]. Each institution shall review its implementation of the Code after two years of operation informing the EU Ombudsman of the results of the review. [Article 27]

Article 16 of the Code

I reserved until last Article 16 which deals with 'rights to be heard and to make statements.' This states that where the rights or interests of individuals are involved then at every stage, the rights of defence are respected. 'Rights of defence' is a rather legalistic phrase involving the right to be advised on procedure, to have access to information on file relating to a dispute, to be given a hearing and to meet any adverse allegations or presumptions with one's own comments. It means being fully informed of the case against one and being allowed to comment upon and challenge that case in a hearing. It is of course close to our own fair procedure/natural justice and like fair procedure, there are accompanying issues concerning legal representation, precise content and timing of the right and so on.[44]

The Article goes on to explain that every member of the public shall have the right, in cases where a decision affecting their rights or interests is to be taken, to submit written comments and when needed, to present oral observations before the decision is taken. Rights of defence is perhaps an unfortunate phrase suggesting heavy-handed formality. Before the Code was drafted, the EU Ombudsman office engaged in examination of informal processes to resolve complaints/grievances before more formal avenues are attempted. The difficulty is that the English love of informality is not repeated on the continent and it is probably better to look upon Article 16 as an attempt at internal and fair resolution by way of a complaints procedure difficult though this may be in continental eyes. It was noted above how under staff regulations Article 90(2) there is a procedure involving complaints to be made by staff against 'appointing authorities' ie employers within the EC institutions and which comprises an internal procedure. In Chapter 6 there was a reference to the internal procedures within the institutions to deal with review of decisions to refuse access to documents under the Regulation on access to documents. The confirmatory application procedure for access to documents is conceptually very close to an internal complaints procedure. Internal review procedures have to be in place to deal with internal reviews under the UK Freedom of Information Act 2000.

As we have stated, a Resolution of the European Parliament has called upon the Commission to submit a proposal for a Regulation containing the *Code*. 'Incorporating the Code in a Regulation would emphasise to both citizens and officials the binding nature of the rules and principles it contains.' [p 5 Code]

In September 2000, the Commission adopted a code of good administrative behaviour which contains many of the features of the EU Ombudsman code. It specifies that complaints may be made to the Secretariat General of the Commission or to the EU Ombudsman.[45] It only applies to officials

---

44   J Schwarze *European Administrative Law* (1992) p 1243.
45   OJ L267 20.10.2000. and www.europa.eu.int/comm/secretariat_general/code/ index_en.

of the Commission. Other EU bodies and officials have adopted the EU Ombudsman Code.

Internal complaints/grievance procedures

Reference was made to internal procedures not only in the *Code of Good Administrative Behaviour*: the subject was given some recognition in the Charter of Fundamental Rights which states that a right to good administration under Article 41 includes 'the right of every person to be heard, before any individual measure which would affect him or her adversely is taken.'

The movement towards widespread provision of internal complaints/ grievance procedures in public bodies for citizens, through which citizens may make complaint about aspects of such bodies' services and administration, has its origins in the mid-1970s. More latterly such procedures have emerged in privatised industries and organisations under contract with public bodies to provide publicly financed services. In the UK, there were serious shortcomings in the established methods for dealing with complaints and grievances against public authorities. In 1987, the OECD noted that 'equal access by all citizens to the public administration and to the established complaints system – a basic right in the constitutional principles of OECD Member countries – is not always, nor necessarily, ensured by the structures of representative democracy.'[46] The report indicated that there may be a need to create procedures between public bodies and existing external agencies such as ombudsmen and courts to provide effective means of redress for in-house administration (p 120).

Part of the response of governments in their attempts to deal with the complexity of public service delivery has involved arrangements whereby public services are provided through private bodies by contractual arrangements or 'contracting out', and now in many countries by privatisation, sometimes as a means of balancing budgets. Delivery of public services through private bodies has not removed the need for effective internal complaints procedures – it has enhanced that need. The European Union Ombudsman (EU Ombudsman) remarked in case 630/96 that the Commission remains responsible for the quality of administration of work carried out by an 'intermediary organisation'. It is therefore assumed

---

[46]   OECD *Administration as Service: The Public as Client* (Paris, 1987).

that the provision of effective internal complaints procedures for the public will cover the contracted out as well as in-house administration.[47]

In *The Administration and You* (1997), the Council of Europe spoke of the right of everyone to make representations to an administrative authority which has a corresponding responsibility to accept and deal with representations properly. Furthermore, in Recommendation R (86) 12, the Council urged conciliation procedures – an earlier Recommendation R (81) 7 had noted the use of *conciliateurs* in France – and alternative dispute resolution procedures to relieve the excessive workload on the courts and enhance access to justice.[48] Access to justice, it is presently maintained, is enhanced by the existence of effective, objective and open complaints procedures.

Many commentators previously noted how unresponsive public bodies were to citizens or recipients of such bodies' services when there was a perceived shortcoming or failure in service. There were glaring deficiencies that helped alienate public bodies and public service providers from public sentiment and support.

It has to be said that many public bodies still have a good deal to do in order to provide effective and fair complaints procedures in the UK, in spite of the enormous consciousness raising in recent years on this subject. One must never rest complacent. The Citizen's Charter Unit in the Cabinet Office conducted a survey in May 1997 which showed that public satisfaction with the way public bodies dealt with complaints remains low. But the whole approach has changed enormously. In Ireland, for instance, the Ombudsman has written that: 'In the past public bodies may have considered complaints as irritants interfering with their normal work and/ or as criticisms of their decisions against which they had to defend themselves'.[49] Now, a more constructive approach was called for.

The really significant advance came with the 1991 Citizen's Charter movement led by the then Prime Minister John Major – although its philosophical provenance came from a Cabinet Office publication in 1988.[50]

---

[47]   *Annual Report 1997* (1998) pp 231–32.
[48]   Alternative dispute resolution is now encouraged under the CPR 1998 in England and Wales and the EU has published a Green Paper on alternative dispute resolution in civil and commercial law (April 2002): see (2002) New LJ 1670.
[49]   *Settling Complaints* (1998) Office of the Ombudsman, Dublin.
[50]   *Service to the Public*, HMSO (1988).

The Citizen's Charter promoted a corpus of principles of public service in a ten year programme to 'improve public service'. In 1996, the government reported that the programme had set in motion a 'fundamental change in culture in our public services.'[51]

The principles were: explicit standards; openness; information; choice; non-discrimination; accessibility; and finally when things went wrong, there should be an opportunity for effective redress and feed-back to public service providers of vital information:

> At the very least, the citizen is entitled to a good explanation, or an apology ... There should be a well publicised and readily available complaints procedure ... lessons must be learned so that mistakes are not repeated. Nobody wants to see money diverted from service improvement into large-scale compensation for indifferent services ... the Government intends to introduce new forms of redress... to stimulate rather than distract from efficiency.

In Ireland, the Irish Ombudsman has written as follows:

> While there is greater emphasis nowadays on improving the quality of service, the standards are set by the public bodies themselves and they also devise the systems and procedures for achieving these standards. The effectiveness of these procedures and the relevance of the standards set can, however, be judged or assessed properly only by reference to the very people – the public – for whom the service is provided. A good internal complaints system will provide essential feedback from the public and will benefit the body ... (Settling Complaints, (1998))

It is quite clear from a perusal of the literature that this subject has relevance to the European Community/Union, in spite of the differences between the normal range of welfare and other responsibilities assumed by the nation state when compared with Community institutions.

Relevance for the Community

The EU Ombudsman has noted that the Community institutions do not provide typical welfare state services like education, social security or housing. Also Community spending programmes in fields such as

---

[51]   *The Citizen's Charter – Five Years On* Cm 3370.

agriculture and social policy 'normally involve national bodies as the administrative authorities in direct contact with individual citizens' – a point encouraging constructive national/regional relationships as was seen in Chapter 5.[52] In the UK these bodies will be expected to have complaints procedures! However, increasingly the Commission and agencies are engaging directly with the EU citizens and residents; many complaints concern contractual matters where courts may be a daunting experience for ordinary citizens.

While there are set procedures for disputes in specific areas, as well as internal Commission guidance for dealing with complaints about breaches of Community Law by national authorities, little is known about how Community institutions deal with complaints from the public about their own officials or their own activities. The EU Ombudsman has opened many windows and pressed for a code as we have seen. The Ombudsman also pointed out the existence of a draft *Code of Conduct for European Commission Officials in their relations with the public* which one might add could contain details of any complaints procedures along with details of services and practices. Alleged breaches of the code could be dealt with via an internal complaints procedure for the public. In the work of the Irish Ombudsman, it was felt such a procedure would:

1. provide a means through which the public could tell the body how well it is doing in its efforts to provide an improved level of service
2. serve as a quick and efficient means to resolve difficulties
3. avoid extra time and cost involved in additional appeals
4. promote good relations and communications
5. encourage a positive attitude towards the administrative system
6. indicate where problems exist in the provision of services
7. highlight shortcomings
8. help avoid unfavourable publicity

Complaints, grievances et al?

What is a complaint? Is it the same as a grievance? In simple terms a complaint is a statement in written or oral form that something has gone wrong regardless in fact of whether anything has gone wrong. It is the complainant's perception that is important though that does not mean that anyone who complains will get what they want. It is also distinguished

[52]   FIDE Vol III (1998) p 318.

from a simple request for information or clarification. A grievance is an unresolved complaint or one that is not resolved to the satisfaction of the complainant. We shall see that in a UK context, this distinction has largely been maintained in the provision of internal procedures for complaint and further review of that attempted resolution where this was unsuccessful.

What are complaints for or about? First of all to respond to an expression of dissatisfaction or unhappiness, well-founded or not. They are a means to ensure that published standards of performance, and this is an increasingly common duty, are met. They compensate individuals when things have gone wrong. They help ensure that service will be improved.

Complaints also operate at different levels. There can be a complaint about service delivery; inaccurate assessment; rudeness; late performance; discrimination and so on. There can be complaints which have a systemic impact where large numbers of individuals will be similarly affected by a mistake with enormous consequences for public expenditure. There can be complaints about policy so that for instance, policies on education, or housing, or competition are wrong and damaging. As we shall see, some attention has been given in government literature to complaints about policy but most procedures are directed to the first kind of complaint although nothing can effectively prevent the second form of complaint arising. Treasuries may impose limitations on what can be done or legislative or constitutional constraints may impose inhibitions. The Citizen's Charter emphasised consultation of users in the planning and implementation of programmes of service, ie in the formulation of policy and this has been given greater emphasis in the New Labour government's *Better Government* initiative from its first term of office. Information about complaints procedures in UK public authorities and also about written consultation exercises are available on the internet.[53]

A fourth type of complaint is not so much a different form of complaint but it is one where there are important consequences for policy. The complaints reveal something to be seriously wrong with an adopted policy. Here the information gathered from the complaint has been used to change policy or practice.

---

[53] www.servicefirst.gov.uk/index/comp_ps.htm and www.cabinet-office.gov.uk/
servic.../2000/consult/code/Consultationcode.htm.

Many complaints arise from poor communication or/and inadequate information and publicity. Very often the quality of service or what is provided is not clearly set out so recent years have seen increasing attempts to set out service and performance criteria, sometimes in the form of a 'contract' between authorities and citizens. This can be discussed under the advantages, as well as possible disadvantages, of internal procedures.

Advantages of internal complaints procedures

A UK Cabinet Office Complaints Task Force published advice in 1993 for public sector bodies on essential aspects of good complaints systems. Much of this work has been developed in subsequent publications which are examined below. In stating that much depended upon ethos and positive culture, the Task Force advised on what to avoid and what could be achieved. The basic thrust is that complaints and treatment of complaints must be taken seriously.

Alongside this advice which has now been built upon by central government, the Commission for Local Administration produced guidance on good practice for authorities within the local ombudsmen's jurisdiction. One of these was entitled *Devising a Complaints System*. The main reasons for having an internal complaints system, and which are reasons with a very wide potential, are:

1. individuals are now more aware of their right to voice critical comments and suggestions for improvement;
2. increasing emphasis is being given by public bodies to providing services of the highest affordable standard;
3. greater emphasis is being given to the importance of promoting and developing customer care;
4. as an integral part of customer care policy and quality assurance programmes a complaints system can show that an authority cares about their constituents;
5. complaints systems need not be defensive but can be positive ways of improving customer satisfaction and enhancing services;
6. well publicised complaints procedures are part of government and opposition philosophy on the rights of citizens
7. An effective complaints procedure will help to resolve the dissatisfaction of citizens about the service they should have, or believe they should have received. To be effective it will provide: a

straightforward means for customers or their representatives to make a complaint – it will be accessible and conspicuous, simple to use; a procedure for investigating a complaint objectively which will be as speedy as possible working according to pre-determined time limits though these may, with explanation, have to be waived; keep the complainant informed about progress and eventual outcome; provide redress where required; ensure that action is taken to avoid recurrence; feedback necessary information to officials, managers and politicians to ensure relevant information is taken into account when decisions are taken on resource allocation, benefit conferral, prioritisation, quality assurance and forward planning.

Specific benefits for officials and consumers arising from complaints procedures include the following.

Management/Officials

Effective internal complaints procedures help increase the responsiveness of service providers:

> Responsiveness in general is increased if an organisational capacity is created which is responsible for analysing complaints... and has the authority to propose changes in the performance of administrative tasks. (OECD, 1987, p 54)

However, administrative reform should not be driven by information gleaned from complaints alone. Complaints are the 'tip of the iceberg of dissatisfaction' (p 97). While complaints procedures are *a part* of responsiveness, greater responsiveness will hopefully reduce grievance.

Effective procedures help ensure that standards of service are met by providing essential information to management. Allowing officials and citizens to participate in their design will help prevent alienation and defensiveness.

Complaints procedures which are effective offer adequate redress when things go wrong. At the EC level, this will help to reduce resentment and enhance the popularity of bodies which may not be as popular in Europe as they could be.

They help to improve service. The public will respond positively if services are improved and administration will become more responsive if effective complaints procedures are in place.

They will help officials in their work by giving them a greater understanding of the impact of their work.

Effective grievance procedures available for all complaints and not just 'serious' ones will help identify the vexatious and unmeritorious complainant. The absence of such open procedures encourages the pushy and those without merit to gain advantages by secret deals. As was once so well expressed: the 'noisy wheel' gets the grease syndrome.

It helps bring officials closer to those they serve.

Complainants

They help to promote a perception among complainants of justice and equity in their treatment. Procedures will have to aim for objectivity. A sense of fairness will not be present where procedures are felt to be partial.

They are part of the process, along with reasoned decisions, of increasing openness and transparency. They are important in themselves but they help achieve larger purposes.

They reduce resentment. Often what people want is a good explanation not compensation. They help reduce the feelings of helplessness and alienation felt by many who are aggrieved by official decisions. They help citizens feel closer to administration to feel they 'belong'. They can help the Community to be more wanted by its community.

In helping to achieve responsiveness and a greater sense of belonging, it does not mean that a response always has to be 'Yes, you can have what you want'. Although members of the public have inalienable rights, they also have obligations. Effective complaints procedures are part of a process whereby government

> engages the public's active participation in and understanding of administration and of its democratic context ...

Effective complaints procedures can be an additional means of heightening citizens' sense of their own and governmental responsibilities (OECD 1987, p 124).

Complaints procedures and other forms of review in Member States

In the UK and in other EC Member States where a decision is challenged, higher internal review of a decision by a more senior official is fairly common. The Council of Europe has highlighted the existence and importance of internal formal appeals.[54] Although the UK government likes to take credit for the fact that the Citizen's Charter and its successor programmes have been influential on a world-wide basis, different countries have adopted Charters for different reasons and use them for different purposes. The evidence seems to suggest that while internal processes for complaints handling are not unknown, the preoccupation that the British have shown is not widespread, although under Ireland's *Delivering Better Government* programme, there is increasing evidence of internal complaints procedures.

France[55]

The existence of consultative bodies to help complainants is common; a striking example is CADA the Commission which deals with complaints about access to documents and which makes recommendations in relation to access to documents. CADA is under a legal duty to give an *avis* to complainants and the administration in a dispute on access. In about 80% of cases, the *avis* (opinion) of the CADA is accepted. Similarly in tax disputes, there is a legal duty to resort to an administrative commission which comprises fonctionnaires and laymen before going to courts. It operates on an informal basis without lawyers and again in the region of 80% of tax complaints are resolved satisfactorily by this process. In many areas of domestic regulation, eg sporting bodies such as football leagues,

---

54   The Administration and You (1997) p 43.
55   On alternative dispute resolution in France, see N Brown and J Bell *French Administrative Law* (1998, 5th ed) pp 29–30, 302–303; special advisory committees exist to attempt informal resolution of contractual disputes between public bodies and contractors: see Ch 3, note 98.

clubs must go to an administrative body to deal with their complaint and this again is a legal requirement. Where people are dissatisfied by an administrative decision they can write to the Minister or Director of service asking for the decision to be rescinded. This will clearly set in motion an internal review but refusal to amend a decision will then lead to the usual channels of challenge – mediateur and tribunaux administratifs/Conseil d'Etat. Indeed, a decree of 1983 put this opportunity to put a case to a civil servant on a formal legal basis (Décret 83–10250). Citizens can ask for internal reviews by the same authorities or by higher authorities although the service will be sensitive to the fact that these processes cannot be used as unjustifiable delaying processes. Harden has described how departmental delegates of the French Ombudsman attempt to resolve disputes informally and locally.[56]

There has been a good deal of discussion to set up mediating/complaints bodies to reduce the numbers of cases coming to courts but there has been government opposition to this because of cost factors, manpower etc. However, it is agreed that such bodies should be trusted, competent, impartial, speedy and responsive. Municipalities will have their own practices and will depend upon local factors.

It was felt that complaints procedures were desirable because they could avoid unnecessary and complicated litigation. Secondly, since the starting point between the citizen and the state was an unequal one, some remedy should be provided to assist the complainant. Administration will not provide such a procedure of their own accord – this was largely true in the UK – and the administration has the time, resources, expertise and so on whereas the complainant does not.

Germany

An informal remedy which is available throughout public law (and for which there appears to be untypically no statutory basis) is the so-called *Aufsichtsbeschwerde* or supervision complaint. This derives its name from the fact that the next higher authority will deal with the matter. There is no time limit and no particular form to be observed, no *locus standi* requirements and the process has no suspensive effect – but then, the only right which a person resorting to this remedy has is to obtain an answer.

[56] Note 22 above.

If the complaint is not directed against the content of administrative action, but rather the way in which it has been conducted by a particular officer or agent, this is called *Dienstaufsichtsbeschwerde* or service supervision complaint, which will take the matter to the next higher authority who is in charge of supervising this particular person. Textbooks seem to attach little importance to this remedy.[57] This remedy should not be confused with the formal remedy of *Widerspruch* (objection) against administrative decisions (*Verwaltungsakt*). This is governed by *Verwaltungsgerichtsordnung* (Administrative Court Code), ss 68 et seq. Before being allowed to apply for judicial review, a person who is affected by an administrative decision must generally first lodge this formal objection within a month from the time of the decision. This objection will take the case to the next higher administrative authority, which has the power to alter the initial decision of the authority.

There are hardly any ombudsmen as such, but both the Federal and Lander Parliaments possess Petitioner Committees of elected representatives who investigate complaints concerning public authorities. These committees are very active. Under Article 17 Basic Law and Lander equivalents, everyone has the right individually or jointly with others to address written requests or complaints to the appropriate authority or parliament. This allows complaints to be made to the administrative authorities on *general* matters. At Federal level, complaints are regulated by the *Gemeinsamen Geschäftsordnung der Ministerien (GGO 1)*.

Practices elsewhere

In the 1998 FIDE report, national reports identified internal procedures where there were opportunities for an internal review and for representations to be made to a higher grade official, either formally or informally: see eg the reports of France, Belgium, Spain, Finland, Sweden, Portugal etc. In Sweden, an internal review is authorised under the Swedish Administrative Procedure Act which can amend an administrative decision. This opportunity may only be used where the 'amendment can take place quickly and simply and does not adversely affect any person'[58] (FIDE p 304). In Holland, an internal administrative 'objection' must be made in many cases before an appeal is allowed to the courts. This objection can be made by

---

57   Hartmut Maurer *Allgemeines Verwaltungsrecht* (1997, 11th ed) p 532.
58   FIDE Vol III (1998), p 304.

representative groups such as environmental groups, action groups and residents' associations and in some cases is recognised specifically in law, eg for the Consumer Association or the Animal Protection Society. The review is an extensive review taking into account all new circumstances and facts.[59] There are limits on amending a decision when an individual may be adversely affected.

In Ireland, there are both internal review and complaints procedures in operation in some bodies. The complaints procedures are non-statutory. In some instances they are integrated, ie in a Complaints and Appeals Service. Many public bodies are developing internal complaints procedures

In the UK an internal review or appeal may operate informally – as under the 1994 *Code of Practice on Open Government* – or they increasingly operate under a statutory scheme. When freedom of information laws come into operation, the UK government has proposed an internal review of an adverse decision that will be covered by statutory provisions, although the detail will be contained in a code of guidance. 'Confirmatory decisions' are allowed in the access to documents regimes in the Council and Commission and other Community bodies as noted above. These might bear some similarity to complaints procedures insofar as someone is dissatisfied with a decision and another person is looking at it afresh.

There are, however, several differences in kind. An internal appeal is often concerned with the correctness of an individual decision according to some pre-existing legal or administrative criteria or rules. It might be concerned with the merits of a decision – was discretion exercised to reach the right decision in this case? The thrust of the review is the correctness of the original decision according to some established criteria. The grounds of appeal may be more or less widely defined but do not include all issues covered by maladministration.

A complaints procedure is concerned not simply with correctness, but failures of service, behaviour, wrong application of the rules, harsh consequences of a rigid application of certain criteria, setting the wrong standards, inadequate explanations and responsiveness. In short the much wider territory of maladministration rather than legality or technical correctness per se. However, illegality and incorrectness are maladministration and being 'legal' does not mean that maladministration

[59]   FIDE Vol III (1998), p 279.

is not present in a decision (see below). A complaints procedure may not involve looking again at the merits of a decision, but in some cases it might. A complaints system can deal with all claims and any exclusions should be explicitly justified according to published criteria.

Internal appeal is precisely that: an *internal* process. It is concerned primarily with the internal accuracy of official decision-making. The process of decision-making remains internal and discreet. It is more bureaucratic and legalistic in its tendencies. Internal appeal might concentrate on procedural regularity which although necessary is not sufficient to ensure responsiveness.[60] Complaints processes are external insofar as full explanations will be given to foster openness; increasingly citizens and staff are invited to participate in the design of the procedures; regular contact with the complainant throughout the complaint process is maintained and they are often invited to meetings.

There is no doubt that if two separate processes of internal appeal and complaints hearing are present, there is scope for confusion in spite of their qualitative differences. Indeed, where internal appeal exists in bodies in the UK for instance, they will be expected to provide complaints procedures under the initiatives discussed above. This might be an argument for suggesting that review should be brought within the ambit of complaints procedures and share, where possible, in the external features of such procedures although their task will be specific: was the initial decision correct according to some pre-existing criteria? It may even be that this is occurring.

Some of the differences in the objectives of these two sets of procedures were spelt out in the 1987 OECD study. In bureaucracy, rules are used to decide cases:

> Equality of treatment is a rule about cases not people ... Responsiveness requires that the administration treat the client as an entity not as a 'case' or 'fragment' relating to a particular set of rules vested in a particular part of the administration.

However,

> Responsiveness might lead to rulelessness [sic] and consequent lack of control' (p 30). 'Administrative controls protect important values in the

[60]   OECD *Administration as Service: The Public as Client* (Paris, 1987) p 120.

democratic system. But they may reinforce rigid and inward looking administration. Controls may need to be adjusted to enable the administration to act responsively; but change must be carefully designed to protect the efficacity (sic) of control' (p 118).

Internal complaints procedures, ombudsmen, tribunals and courts

How do complaints procedures relate to the other bodies identified above? It is a common feature that if internal processes exist, the ombudsman will expect them to be resorted to unless there is a compelling reason why not. In some case there are administrative measures to investigate complaints: Article 226 is such an example (above). They may not be individual oriented. In the case of the Statute on the European Union Ombudsman, Article 2.4, for instance: 'A complaint ... must be preceded by the appropriate administrative approaches to the institution and bodies concerned.' This provision clearly implies that if a suitable internal complaints procedure exists, it should be used before a complaint is taken to the Ombudsman. The complaints procedures will, as already stated, cover basically the same ground as ombudsmen – maladministration – and UK and Irish ombudsmen supply copious guidance for authorities within their jurisdiction on what good and bad practice are. Ombudsmen are increasingly the last or very often third stage in a complaints process after the internal procedures are finalised.

One point that has arisen in the UK, and this arose from the very early days of the Citizen's Charter, concerns the overlap between such procedures and established Ombudsmen. Indeed, Ombudsmen felt threatened by their existence for a variety of reasons: they might be a deliberate attempt to undermine ombudsmen by taking work away from them and giving the work not to *independent* persons but to bodies that were inherently a part of the body that was complained against. They could confuse the public into believing that they were the ombudsmen and deprive the real ombudsmen of the benefit of their service.[61] In tune with the appeal to the market driven philosophy of the then (and present) government in the UK, it was suggested that Ombudsmen should enter the market of dispute resolution mechanisms and compete with other bodies

---

[61]   *Implications etc.* HC 158 (1991/92).

for the custom of citizens. This did not come to fruition and Ombudsmen very clearly are hierarchically superior to internal mechanisms.

However, the British and Irish Ombudsmen Association did seek to control the use of the name 'Ombudsmen' and established criteria which had to be satisfied before the appellation could be used and refused to admit to the Association anyone who did not satisfy the criteria of independence. The Parliamentary Ombudsman also advised that the expression 'ombudsman' should not be used by internal bodies. This has not been respected in some cases. Furthermore, ombudsmen have stated that not possessing an internal procedure *may* indicate evidence of maladministration.

In relation to courts, an important development has been the use of the existence of internal procedures to reduce opportunities for legal remedies. Where they exist, English courts will expect parties seeking judicial review to use them *before* they can come to court. Limitation periods would run from the date of the final decision of a complaints body (cf the position in Finland where resort to an internal review for a 'correction' does not 'suspend' the operation of limitation periods to apply to the courts although there is no time limit in which an application for administrative review may be made and such an application may be made even though an appeal to the courts has been launched).[62] Their existence may also prevent the existence of statutory rights recognisable by the courts.

Generally, internal complaints procedures are more likely to be seen by judges as a sensible and welcome attempt by public authorities to settle disputes before the necessity of resorting to expensive and over-worked courts or the ombudsman. If complaints procedures are driven by an ideology or are invested with too much power then this may well attract an exacting standard of review in the courts.

A check-list for the design and operation of a complaints procedure

The checklist to follow in setting up a complaints system is: set out service standards; inform the user about complaints systems; remove barriers to complaining; explain the stages of the procedures; meet any special needs;

---

[62]   FIDE Vol III 1998, p 201.

provide support and assistance to those who need it; obtain the views of those who use the procedures.

It is remarkable how often internal complaints procedures involve three distinct stages. Documentation often speaks of complaint resolution by service staff. If that fails, there should be reference to a point within the section/department/directorate involved. A third stage might involve an independent person outside the section and might take the form of a review panel or an ombudsman. This has become a very typical set-up in the UK in health, police, utility and other complaints and is similar to recommendations from the Irish Ombudsman.

UK government thinking on complaints procedures – and the Irish model provides many similar features – is contained in the Cabinet Office's *How to deal with complaints* and has been updated by guidance issued on the internet (see above).[63] This built on the recommendations of the Complaints Task Force in the Cabinet Office. In particular, it emphasises the desirability of internal complaints procedures, a further review procedure where the first stage is not successful and which should be separate 'from line management' and then advising complainants of where to go should they remain dissatisfied viz, ombudsmen or other statutory procedures. Additional items included publishing information at least once a year on:
1. the number and type of complaints;
2. how quickly they were dealt with;
3. users' satisfaction;
4. actions taken as a result.

Further points included putting details of complaints procedures on the internet (see above). Freephone numbers should be used. It emphasises necessary precautions to avoid discrimination against complainants: make clear they will not suffer any adverse consequences, allow access to necessary documents and personnel but allow complaints to be made confidentially where this is required – although confidentiality should not be used to prevent important information for service improvement being disclosed – monitoring services provided to those who have complained and allowing complaints to be made to others who are not dealing directly with complainants and carrying out surveys of those who have made a complaint. The Irish model usefully advises that different languages should be provided for.

[63] June 1998, *Service First – the New Charter Programme* Cabinet Office.

The second stage 'review arrangements' which it urges upon public authorities concerns complaints about maladministration and failures to meet service aims and targets. It does not cover formal appeals about decisions based on statutory requirements or complaints about policy (p 3). However, for internal complaints staff should be trained to deal with complaints about policy even if 'they cannot change things' (p 37).

There is certainly a greater emphasis on all staff knowing about effective complaint redress mechanisms. The government's Freedom of Information Act 2000 and accompanying guidance includes a *duty* on all public services to publish their complaints procedures for dealing with freedom of information complaints where a request for a reconsideration is made by an applicant whose request for information is denied. Details of general complaint procedures should be items which authorities under the Act should publish in their Publication Schemes which are introduced under Freedom of Information Act 2000 and which start to take effect from November 2002 for central government, and will be phased in over the following nineteen months for other public authorities. The Freedom of Information Act 2000 embraced not only an enormous range of public bodies but included privatised utilities, bodies in the private sector carrying out statutory tasks and bodies under contract with public authorities to provide public services.

Examples of complaints processes in existence cover adequate arrangements for monitoring complaints, staff and public participation in their design, familiarising all staff with their existence and giving proper publicity to them. The principles for good procedures should be written in clear simple language and in *all relevant languages* and cover complaints about operations and policy and should be subject to regular review. They should spell out clearly when a complaint should go to the next stage. These stages are: on the spot reply (informal); referral, investigation and reply; internal review; external review. It might be advisable to use an easily identifiable colour for complaints forms to ensure they are not misplaced. Complaints should be dealt with as expeditiously as possible according to set time limits.

Replies should: aim to answer all the points of concern appropriately; be factually correct; avoid jargon; be signed by the officer responsible; contain a contact number; inform the person what to do next if still not satisfied. A willingness to meet with complainants is important and is certainly identified as good practice.

The guidance offers advice on remedies, including compensation. This question has been a vexed issue in the UK. A report into the Parliamentary Commissioner for Administration investigated the total confusion of practice and procedures for making compensatory payments.[64] The situation verged on anarchy. In central government, the position is discretionary governed by Treasury Guidance known as *'Dear Accounting Officer'* Letters. The guidance was revised in 1996. The available guidance states that staff should provide information which will allow complainants to identify whether a service is below par. Suitable remedies should be offered and should ensure that staff are aware of the options; try to give remedies that complainants wish for though within reason and obvious constraints; survey complainants to see whether they received the remedy they wanted. Remedies might include:

1. an apology;
2. an explanation;
3. an assurance that the same thing will not happen again;
4. specifying what action will put things right;
5. financial compensation. 'This should always be an option, even though it may only be relevant in a few cases. Make sure that your users know how to get financial compensation. Front line staff should have the authority to make small payments.'[65] In local government, where there are greater legal restrictions on making compensatory payments because of the statutory basis of local government administration, the Commission for Local Administration has produced detailed guidance on remedies and financial compensation.

Chief Officers in all public administration, or in bodies under public private partnership arrangements, should be held personally responsible for effective complaints handling. And this would be reflected in job descriptions and performance appraisals, including decisions on performance related pay. It would, as the Select Committee said, be a contractual undertaking by senior officers. In turn managers should recognise and reward staff who handle complaints well. Some authorities have made handling complaints a part of formal appraisal of staff:

> For staff who deal direct with the public, the assessment of their ability to handle customers well is a major determinant of their appraisal... the appraisal itself reaffirms the authority's commitment to customer care

[64] *Maladministration and Remedies* (HC 112, 1994/95).
[65] *Service First – the New Charter Programme* p 39.

and provides these staff with the opportunity to say what they feel is going well or badly and what help they need to do the job better. (p 43).

Complaints procedures should be separated from disciplinary procedures. Greater publicity, provision of information, consultation with representatives of user groups and staff and delegation for complaints handling to 'the lowest possible level' will help reduce the cost of administering such schemes and any consequential demand for more resources. Recording complaints should be done in a consistent and detailed fashion. It should be simple, practical and not onerous and should be useful for monitoring complaints. There are details on the minima that should be recorded and these include: name, address and telephone number of complainant; date of receipt; details of the complaint, putting it into a category depending upon the subject; remedy requested; immediate action to be taken.

Needless to say there are many questions that will have to be addressed before an adequate complaints process can be established. As well as training, building up commitment and resource and personnel issues, the following will need specific attention:
1.   Define a complaint and what is not included. Who can complain?
2.   Details of how to complain should be spelt out: all addresses including email, phone and fax numbers should be provided.
3.   Set out the stages of any procedure, details on recording of complaints, any form that they should be in – informal at first but thereafter in writing? Who takes action?
4.   Political involvement and how to respond.
5.   Time limits.
6.   How to deal with special cases: eg very senior officials as subjects of complaint, or financial impropriety.
7.   How should anonymous complaints be responded to?
8.   What remedies are available? Provide advice on other remedies and next steps.
9.   Establish a senior officer to coordinate and manage complaints arrangements to ensure consistency, promote efficiency and facilitate monitoring. Do not call this person an Ombudsman.
10.   How will the complaints procedures tie in with any existing procedures required by law or currently in operation, eg disciplinary procedures?
11.   How can procedures be best publicised and most widely disseminated? And, for instance, what is the best use of the internet for publicising internal complaints procedures?

Conclusion

Such practices exist widely in public bodies in the UK. In this field the UK has been a brand leader. There is scope for internal and informal processes to deal with grievances in an 'on the spot' fashion. The point has been made that internal complaints procedures established under Freedom of Information Act 2000 might cause unnecessary delay and deter people from going to ombudsmen. If such procedures operate according to fixed time scales there is no reason why they should cause delay. Ombudsmen themselves take a considerable period to investigate and report and then agree a settlement with the body concerned. If justice can be done by avoiding that route, so much for the good. Complaints procedures should operate as a facilitator of justice, not a barrier. They are an important part of the justice debate which concentrates inevitably on courts and often only grudgingly looks to other devices – domestically or in Europe.

Chapter 12

Competition, regulation and the market[1]

This chapter looks at several related themes. These themes centre around the market and regulation, competition and liberalisation and the impact Community norms are having on national regimes. First of all, competition law seeks various objectives. One of these is to prevent a market imbalance that may operate against the interests of the consumer and the public interest. This may occur where prices or service provision are seriously distorted because of the dominance of one provider, manufacturer or retailer in a market. Secondly in some markets, the service is deemed so essential that special provisions are considered necessary to ensure the universal delivery of the service. These services comprise utilities and essential services. The provision of essential services is, in some traditions, seen as the primary *raison d'etat*. In others, the failure to provide essential services will have serious political repercussions but the state's responsibility is to ensure that the market ie, private sector suppliers, provides the service under regimes that seek to meet the public interest. These involve varying degrees of regulation which basically means directing, ordering, exhorting or encouraging particular forms of behaviour in terms of charging policies, standards of service, interconnection between providers at different levels in the market eg the telecom or energy network, and disconnections from eg energy or water supply, the latter of which are prohibited under the Water Industry Act 1999, Sch 1. Community competition law is concerned with the impact of agreements and practices which affect competition within the Community and market integration.

[1]   I am grateful to Mike Varney for his helpful comments on a variety of points in this chapter.

Whether the state provides a service to the public directly, or whether it regulates a service provided by private sector companies is a matter of tradition and political preference. The state cannot afford, whatever the arrangement, to ignore such industries. Even where a service is provided by a private concern, there is very often a considerable degree of state subsidy. This is true of rail transport in the UK even before the administration of Railtrack plc in 2002 and its replacement by a non-profit making Network Rail. Furthermore, decisions affecting some services, such as energy, can only be made at governmental level: a clear case being whether to renew or de-commission nuclear power stations.[2] The state/private sector dichotomy, it is argued, no longer aptly describes the reality of economic interests today. A new sector has emerged, the public-service sector in which ideas about citizenship are of striking importance and which produces a 'distinct and distinctive' body of law for such services known as public service law which Freedland sees as closely related to public law and labour law.[3]

The Commission has received a great deal of criticism for its stances adopted in regulation and enforcement of competition and it is frequently subject to legal challenge. Criticism is not uncommon in regulatory regimes and is certainly true of UK and US regulatory bodies. Economic philosophy on competition policy has been particularly influential, driven by the free-market ideology of the Chicago school on the one hand and the more interventionist Harvard school on the other. Regulatory regimes influenced by such schools of thought impact on powerful interests. There is a great degree of complexity associated with regulation in the EU and it is attracting increasing interest far beyond the field of competition.

First of all there are many bodies assisting the Commission in other fields of regulation: here we encounter the notorious comitology bodies comprising committees of representatives of Member States, sometimes civil servants, and various socio-economic interests to assist in the policy formulation and law making process. We referred to these in Chapters 2

---

[2] Complete public ownership of nuclear power came to an end with the privatisation of British Energy although when BE's share price collapsed in 2002, the government was forced to assist BE by granting extensive loan facilities.

[3] M Freedland 'Law, Public Services and Citizenship – New Domains, New Regimes?' in M Freedland and S Sciarra *Public Services and Citizenship in European Law* (1998) OUP, ch 1; see also W MacLauchlan 'Public Service Law and the New Public Management' in M Taggart *The Province of Administrative Law* (1997) Hart, ch 6.

and 6 (pp 42, 259). They have tended to operate in secrecy. We also meet the array of regulatory bodies established by the Commission – many of them in areas having nothing to do with competition. They have generated a great deal of critical attention because of their uncertain constitutional provenance. Some agencies, such as Europol and the European Food Agency are likely to have an increasing impact on EU citizens. Only two agencies, claims Majone, have executive powers.[4] The Commission does have executive powers and its role in competition enforcement and market regulation is pivotal.

Before examining competition law and its trend towards convergence, mention should be made of one market where special provision has been made in order to achieve more open competition and transparency: public purchasing or public procurement. I examine this in the final section of this chapter. What the chapter does is look at the interrelationship between competition law, various regulatory problems and the extent to which markets in essential services, as well as public markets, may be rendered more open and transparent. As we shall see, not all are convinced that greater transparency is a virtue in itself and maintaining effective and efficient markets may be better achieved by other stimuli.

Competition law

One of the clearest examples of EC influence on domestic law has been in the field of competition law. Accompanied by an enormous amount of economic theorising, the purpose of competition law is basically to prevent abuse of economic power in the market place in a manner which prevents disadvantage to consumers and ultimately the general welfare. There is wide disagreement between economic theorists, and between lawyers, and between economic theorists and lawyers about the advantages and disadvantages of monopoly, predatory pricing and so on, whether markets should be left alone or regulated in some fashion, and if so, how?[5]

The provisions of the UK Competition Act 1998 dealing with abuse of dominant position and restraint of trade are largely modelled on the EC Treaty Articles 81 and 82 [85 and 86] EC (see below). The Competition Act

---

4   G Majone (2002) ELJ 319.
5   R Bork *The Antitrust Paradox: A Policy at War with Itself* (1978); G Amato *Antitrust and the Bounds of Power* (1997).

1998 recast our competition law although provisions on mergers and some other matters are dealt with in other legislation and are currently under consideration in the Enterprise Bill.[6] Competition policy has been a dominant feature of Community law and policy since the inception of the EEC. The Preamble to the EC Treaty refers to 'fair competition', Article 2 EC refers to a high degree of competitiveness as a purpose of the Community and Article 3 EC includes as an activity of the Community a 'system ensuring that competition in the internal market is not distorted'. Some areas of economic activity such as steel and coal, nuclear energy, military equipment, agriculture and transport are outside the competition rules of the EC and have their own regimes under the Treaty of Rome as amended, such as Part Three Title II on agriculture, or other treaties such as the ESC Treaty and Euratom. In the case of military products, any Member State may under Article 296(1)(b) [223(1)(b)] EC 'take such measures as it considers necessary for the protection of essential interests of its security which are connected with the production of or trade in arms, munitions and war material; such measures shall not adversely affect the conditions of competition in the common market regarding products which are not intended for specifically military purposes.' The list of products which was first drawn up in 1958 is not published. This area is excluded from the Directives on procurement which I examine below. Regulated industries or those in areas of special economic importance merit special attention to which I shall return.

Competition law has been seen as a means of ensuring an integrated common market within what is still called a Common Market although more often referred to now as a single market. It may be that more recently the concentration on integration has not retained its central preoccupation as the emphasis shifts to decentralisation of competition enforcement via

6   Mergers are dealt with under Fair Trading Act 1973 as amended; there is an EC regulation on mergers (amended by Council Regulation 1310/97/EC and which came into force on 1 March 1998) which is highly controversial because it may affect two or more non-EC companies who wish to merge: see *Gencor v Commission* Case T-102/96 [1999] ECR II-753 and the GE/Honeywell episode Case COMP/M.2220 Commission Decision (3/7/01). The CFI has made some very controversial rulings affecting the Regulation concerning *Airtours/ Firstchoice* Case T-342/99 [2002] All ER (EC) 783, *Schneider/Legrand* Cases T-310/01 and T-77/02 and *Tetra Laval/Sidel* Cases T-5/02 and T-80/02, [2002] 5 CMLR 1182, 1271 where the CFI ruled that the Commission had not justified the case for vetoing mergers. A Green Paper was published at the end of 2001 on mergers and the Commission has proposed a special competition court to deal with competition cases. It has felt that the CFI has ruled on the 'merits' of its decisions and not their legality.

national agencies and authorities and a draft regulation on decentralisation of decision-making has been produced.[7] Guidelines will be introduced by the Commission to attempt to ensure consistency in practice between the Member States' competition authorities and the European Competition Network will address this question. Competition law, albeit adjusting relationships between individual actors or undertakings, is in effect a form of public law whereby the state intervenes in the market place to readjust an imbalance or create a balance that the operation of the market has necessitated. A market is a network of buyers and sellers of goods or services and competition is the process by which a share in the market is increased. A Commission *Notice on the Definition of the Relevant Market for the Purposes of Community Competition Law*[7a] defines precisely that – the relevant market. This borrows some features of US Anti Trust law which was devised from 1890 and which itself adopted features of common law on restraint of trade.[8] Although the notice is not legally binding, the UK Office of Fair Trading has said it will adhere to its principles and Whish describes how it is also influential in New Zealand and Australia.[9] Percentages of market share are important for a variety of thresholds triggering possible action under EC and UK competition law.[10] As well as Articles 81 and 82 which will be examined briefly in a moment, EC competition law is contained in Articles 83–89 [87–94] EC. Articles 87–89 EC deal specifically with government assistance or 'state aids' to undertakings which distorts or threatens to distort competition. Under provisions on state aids, for instance, the Public Private Partnership involving the London Underground had to be approved under Community law.[11] The provisions on competition exist alongside the provisions on the four basic freedoms of the Treaty of Rome: free movement of goods, persons, capital and freedom to provide services.

In enforcing and overseeing competition law, the Commission – Director General (DG) Competition (formerly DG IV) – acts as a regulatory authority

---

[7]   This should take effect from 1 May 2004. To the original competition provisions there have been added many social, egalitarian and environmental objectives inter alia as well as the purpose of economic and monetary union.

[7a] OJ C372/5 1997.

[8]   Which feature from *Dyer's* case in 1414. See P Craig (1991) Public Law 538.

[9]   Whish *Competition Law* (2001, 4th ed) p 23.

[10] See Whish *Competition Law* (2001, 4th ed) pp 41–3 for examples of these percentages.

[11] The loan and aid facilities to British Energy (note 2 above) by the UK government was attacked for breaching state aids provisions.

and much of its regulation is achieved by various soft law devices such as informal settlements or 'comfort letters' which ask businesses whether they would be happy to deal with the matter informally so that the Commission can close its file and not go to formal decision. Very often, businesses will have to accommodate behaviour of practices to achieve such an informal settlement. Soft law techniques are also employed in other areas such as state aids. DG IV has always had to rely upon domestic authorities to enforce that law while also viewing this area as a leading exponent of European wide policy because of its perceived – by the Commission – importance in integrating markets making the Community a truly common market.

Competition law and regulation are seen as necessary where it is no longer possible to rely upon free markets and self interest, enlightened or otherwise, to produce what the public interest requires or necessitates. This might range for instance from the best deal for consumers in terms of price, service or standards and could cover manufactured goods, services such as those provided by lawyers or accountants, or utilities, or it might involve regulation for purposes of safety, environmental pollution, waste disposal and so on.

Competition and the Commission

The Commission has played a central role in the development of the detail of competition law and policy. Originally, EC competition law was shaped by German inspiration and competition law because Germany was the European state with the first developed laws on competition. German influence has continued with developments at the national level influencing Community law. That law has now been adopted throughout Member States as we shall see specifically in the case of the UK below. Maher says that Article 82 [86] EC was very much a product of 'German ordoliberal thought, requiring dominant firms to act as if they were subject to competition, such that a failure by a company to meet its special responsibility would be construed as an abuse of its dominant position.'[12] Competition law is a stunning example of European Public law now that many regimes have based their national laws on Articles 81 and 82.

[12] I Maher in P Craig and G de Burca eds *The Evolution of EU Law* (1999) p 602. She made the point that as she wrote, all heads of DG IV had been German, p 602.

First of all, what do the provisions of Articles 81 and 82 [85 and 86] EC seek to achieve? Article 81 prohibits 'all agreements between undertakings, decisions by associations of undertakings and concerted practices which may affect trade between Member States and which have as their object or effect the prevention, restriction or distortion of competition within the common market.' Some agreements are emphasised as falling within the provision.[13] Prohibited agreements or decisions are void. As mentioned above, Article 81(3) EC allows for exemptions. Article 82 EC prohibits as incompatible with the common market insofar as it may affect trade between Member States 'any abuse by one or more undertakings of a dominant position within the common market or in a substantial part of it.' Particular examples of abuse are emphasised.[14] In both cases, there is the provision that it may affect trade between Member States. Where trade is clearly not so affected, it is not a matter for Community law. These articles are directly effective not only on state bodies and emanations of the state but also on private undertakings.[15] In the judgment in *Courage Ltd v B Crehan*, the ECJ ruled that damages may be awarded against an individual who is injured as a result of a breach of Article 81(1) and even though that claimant is a party to an agreement.[16] There is in addition an EC Merger Regulation which was referred to above.

[13] In particular those which (a) directly or indirectly fix purchase or selling prices or any other trading conditions; (b) limit or control production, markets, technical development or investment; (c) share markets or sources of supply; (d) apply dissimilar conditions to other trading partners placing them at competitive disadvantage; and (e) impose supplementary agreements having no connection with main agreement

[14] In particular: imposing either directly or indirectly unfair purchase or selling prices, limiting production, markets or technical development to the prejudice of consumers, applying dissimilar conditions to equivalent transactions placing other trading partners at a competitive disadvantage, imposing supplementary obligations as in note 13.

[15] See *Garden Cottage Foods Ltd v Milk Marketing Board* [1983] 2 All ER 770, HL – an assumption that breach of Art 82 EC may lead to imposition of damages on an individual. See Whish *Competition Law* (2001, 4th ed) pp 361–62 on third party enforcement under the Competition Act 1998.

[16] Case C-453/99 [2001] ECR I-6297. See W van Gerven's Opinion as Advocate General in Case C-128/92 *HJ Banks and Co Ltd v British Coal Corpn* [1994] ECR I-12091209 and Case C-390/98 [2001] ECR I-6117. A P Komninos (2002) 39 CML Rev 447 on the *Courage* decision. Article 81(3) EC is not directly effective, but the decentralisation process will transfer enforcement to national authorities. For the draft regulation on decentralisation see: doc 500PC0582.

However, central to the regime is Regulation 17/62/EEC made under Article 83 EC.[17] Under this regulation, which is to be replaced by a new regulation, agreements which may contravene Article 81 EC have to be notified to the Commission so that they may obtain negative clearance (that is the agreement is not caught by the Article) or exemption. 'Behaviour' under Article 82 EC may also receive negative clearance. The Commission has power to fine undertakings in breach of Articles 81 or 82 EC up to 10% of their world-wide turnover. These are drastic powers introduced very much, Maher believes, under German influence. Fines may be reviewed in the Court (the CFI) which can vary, reduce or cancel the fine. Maher describes how the ECJ and now the CFI have been very insistent on fair procedures being adopted by the Commission in its investigations given that its multiplicity of roles may lead to abuse.[18] This attention coupled with under resourcing has caused the decision-making process to be convoluted and slow leading to only a small number of formal decisions each year. Maher says this has led to a concentration on short, informal pre-notification procedures leading to informal resolutions in which analysis and policy are not made explicit. Reference has already been made to Comfort letters. The Commission, based on information in its possession, does not make a formal decision but states that it intends to take no further action, perhaps on the ground that Article 81(1) or 82 EC do not apply, or that the grounds of exemption in Article 81(3) EC apply. Comfort letters are not binding on national courts and could in theory, although not in practice, lead to confusion if a national court was asked not to recognise such a letter.

The Commission is the investigator, prosecutor and decision-maker in competition matters as well as being a rule maker under powers conferred by the Council – a recent illustration being Regulation 2790/99/EC on vertical block exemptions. 'Block exemptions' involves exempting agreements on a generic basis from the operation of Article 81 so that they do not need to be notified to the Commission. Decisions of DG Competition have to be adopted by the College of Commissioners. There are about 420 staff in the DG with an additional 25 or so from national competition authorities. Maher, in her study of the relationship between EC competition law and intellectual property rights – where there is no specific Community law on the latter and where competition law has been used to fill lacuna left by the absence of Community law and the existence only of national laws

---

[17]   A new Regulation was planned for 2002 COM (2000) 582 coming into effect on 1 May 2004.
[18]   Note 12 above.

– describes the DG as closed and 'unresponsive' to developments.[19] A lack of transparency characterises its decision-making. The Legal Service of the Commission has to be consulted on every legally binding decision[20] although in all but contentious issues the decision is effectively made by the Commission. There has been a preponderance of lawyers and a concentration on legal methods in the Commission unlike, Maher claims, the US where economists have dominated and where the consumer interest has been more apparent. It is not clear that economics has been that supportive of the consumer interest in the States, certainly in shaping regulatory policy. Many outcomes in the Community are in fact negotiated by members of the Commission just as they are in the UK by the Office of Fair Trading, part of whose brief covers competition law and policy.

Since 1992, Maher believes, there has been an increased emphasis on decentralisation so that national competition authorities are increasingly relied upon to enforce Community law leading to the alignment of Community and national laws and qualifying the early preoccupation of market integration through a directed competition policy. She refers to this as arguably, the fourth phase of the development of competition law. In fact Gerber has described how three prior stages of competition policy saw the investment of great powers in the Commission, its consolidation and then concentration by the Commission on state activity in markets covering public procurement, state aids and state monopolies.[21] As stated above, a draft regulation on decentralisation has been published.[22]

Although the ECJ and now the CFI have adopted an exacting approach towards the Commission in the fairness of its procedures in competition investigations, a more lenient approach to the Commission has been taken by the courts in relation to the right to silence and the use of self incriminating material obtained from those investigated in competition enforcement than that taken by the CHR in relation to the right to silence in criminal investigations. The latter has ruled that such practices are a

---

[19]   I Maher in P Craig and G de Burca eds *The Evolution of EU Law* (1999), p 600.
[20]   Citing L Laudati in G Majone ed *Regulating Europe* (1996).
[21]   D J Gerber 'Constitutionalising the Economy: German Neo-Liberalism, Competition Law and the "New" Europe' (1994) 42 Am J Comp Law 25 at 73 cited in Maher. See Gerber *Law and Competition in Twentieth Century Europe: Protecting Prometheus* (1998).
[22]   Note 16 doc 500 PC 0582.

breach of Article 6 ECHR.[23] The ECJ has not interpreted Article 6 in such a manner to give a comparable right not to give evidence against oneself in Commission investigations.[24] The ECJ may well have been sympathetic to the fact that the Commission were seeking to enforce a central policy in integrating the Community and that fundamental rights had to be seen in that light (see Chapters 2 and 9 pp 55 and 388).

The Commission also feels under pressure to resort to block exemptions which were addressed above whereby agreements which satisfy criteria set out in the regulations do not have to be notified but enjoy automatic exemption. As well as block exemptions which were introduced by a Regulation made by the Commission acting alone under powers conferred by the Council, there are also individual exemptions granted by the Commission. However, it is expected that notifying agreements for individual exemption will be terminated with effect from 1 January 2003 (subsequently 1 May 2004) and competition authorities in Member States will be allowed to give exemptions. There have also been important developments affecting Article 81(3) EC and vertical agreements (agreements at different levels in the market eg manufacturer and supplier) and also in relation to treatment of horizontal co-operation agreements (agreements at the same level in the market eg, retailer and retailer).

Many EC and also other non-member European countries, especially in the middle and east of Europe, have based their competition laws on EC law including in some cases the EC Merger Regulation. In the case of the latter countries, such a development has been imposed through trade agreements with the EU leaving little alternative to other parties.[25] There has been an impetus towards establishing a Euro-Mediterranean Economic Area from Algeria to Turkey which will lead to Euro-Mediterranean (Association) Agreements, some of the provisions of which will be based on EC law. Among Member States, UK law provides an interesting example of this phenomenon of alignment.

23   *Funke v France* (1993) 16 EHRR 297.
24   Case 374/87 *Orkem v Commission* [1989] ECR 3283 – see K Lenaerts and J Vanhamme (1997) 34 CML Rev 531. On Community/national cooperation in investigations, see Case C-94/00 *Roquette Frères* (22 October 2002, unreported).
25   Van den Bossche [1997] ECLR 24.

The UK Competition Act 1998

Dissatisfaction with the UK legislation on restrictive trade practices and anti-competitive practices had existed in the UK for many years. Common law provisions on restraint of trade agreements and monopolies go back centuries as we saw above. The law on restrictive trade practices was form based and concentrated on the particular form an agreement took; it was not effects based looking at an agreement and the effects that it had on competition. The law was very complicated and often caught harmless agreements while doing nothing to prevent abuses; it was not effective in controlling cartels and sanctions were weak; the powers of the Director General of Fair Trading (DGFT) to obtain information on cartels were puny; the law was not very effective in dealing with unilateral behaviour of firms with significant market power; last of all, it was very different from EC law even though firms very often had to comply with domestic and EC law.

Reform had been debated for over twenty years and even after it was recommended that such change should take its framework from the EU and the then Articles 85 and 86 EC, it took a further ten years to produce such changes to the law.[26] The provisions of the Competition Act 1998, or most of them, were to come into effect on 1 March 2000. The Act repeals the Restrictive Trade Practices Act, Resale Prices Act and the provisions on anti-competitive practices in the Competition Act 1980. The provisions in the Fair Trading Act 1973 dealing with investigations into monopolies and mergers is retained although this has been subject to proposals for change in 1999 and October 2000. The regime in the UK (sic) prior to the 1998 Act was a particularly idiosyncratic British hotch-potch.

The Competition Act 1998 aims to sweep away cartels – agreements restricting or distorting competition. The most important provisions in the Act are in Part I. The first chapter of Part I introduces prohibitions based on Article 81 EC, and chapter two prohibitions are based on Article 82 EC. The Act gives very significant powers of investigation and enforcement to the DGFT and sector regulators with whom he has concurrent powers eg the Director General of Telecommunications, the gas and electricity regulator, water and so on. A completely new Competition Commission is

---

[26]   Government papers in 1988 (Cm 331), 1989 (Cm 727) and 1992 (Cm 2100). See Green and Robertson eds *The Europeanisation of UK Competition Law* (1998).

established and its tasks include hearing appeals against decisions of the DG and regulators.

Part II is concerned with investigations by the DGFT into Articles 81 and 82 EC. It gives to a High Court judge power to issue a warrant authorising the DGFT to enter and search premises in connection with a European Commission investigation where the Commission request this. Part III amends the monopoly provisions of the Fair Trading Act 1973 especially in relation to information gathering. Part IV makes a variety of other amendments.

A large number of guidelines have been published by the DGFT and also by the regulators in compliance with duties on the former, and powers for the latter. These have been published conjunctively.[27] A large number of regulations have been published as well as DTI consultation documents.

The Chapter I prohibition is contained in s 2 and agreements excluded from the terms of s 2 are in s 3 which has to be seen along with s 50 which excludes further agreements.[28] This in simple parlance means that s 2 is based directly on Article 81 but only for agreements etc which are implemented within the UK and not those falling under the provisions of the common market. Section 2(1) is as follows:

> agreements between undertakings, decisions between undertakings, decisions by associations of undertakings or concerted practices which –
> (a) may affect trade within the UK, and
> (b) have as their object or effect the prevention, restriction or distortion of competition within the United Kingdom are prohibited *unless they are exempt in accordance with the provisions of this part.*

The italicised words import the effect of Article 81(3) EC which relates to agreements or category of agreements, decisions or category of decisions or concerted practices or category of concerted practices which basically have beneficent market effects, but in different wording. The section continues to repeat the specific examples of agreements, decisions or practices which are prohibited. Any prohibited agreement etc, is void by virtue of s 2(4). The reason for the repetition of the EC provisions was to

---

27   www.oft.gov.uk.
28   SI 2000/310. Section 50 covers vertical and land agreements.

avoid inconsistency and conflict: 'our objectives ... are best served by ensuring that the domestic prohibition is interpreted in such a way as to avoid inconsistency with the way Articles 81 and 82 EC themselves are interpreted by the European Court.'[29]

Excluded agreements include mergers and concentrations – because they are caught by other provisions, or those caught by other enactments, or professional rules[30] but the Secretary of State has considerable powers to exclude additional agreements. Sections 4–11 deal with exemptions which cover individual exemptions, in spite of their proposed removal from EC law, and block exemptions as well as 'parallel exemptions' ie those that would be exempted under EC law but for technical reasons do not require an exemption under EC law – they do not affect trade between Member States. Sections 12–16 deal with notifications of agreements, practices etc to the DGFT. Parties do not have to notify agreements but they do have to ensure that the agreement does not breach any Chapter I or II prohibitions.

It was noted above that while s 2 is very similar to Article 81 EC, it is not absolutely identical. It refers only to trade within the UK and not between Member States while Article 81 EC is concerned with the Community dimension. Any agreement which covers both forms of trade will be subject to both regimes and could potentially be subject to fines under both. Where this is the case there are provisions seeking to avoid double jeopardy[31] and the DGFT has issued guidance on which is the appropriate office to conduct an investigation and undertakings may have to notify the authorities under both provisions.[32]

It is clear that many questions will be raised that will call into question interpretations dependent upon Community law. Does, for instance, 'severability' apply to contracts void under s 2(4)? In EC law, Article 81 EC has been interpreted to allow severability of offending agreements allowing non-offending parts to survive.[33]

---

29   White Paper August 1997, cited by S Corry and B Rodger *Current Law Statutes* (1998) ch 41, pp 41–20.

30   See Sch 4. Such rules must be designated by the Secretary of State.

31   The Commission has drafted various Co-operation Notices

32   See *Is Notification Necessary?* at www.oft.gov.uk.

33   Case 56/65 *Société Technique Minière v Maschinenbau Ulm GmbH* [1966] ECR 235.

With only very slight modifications, the Competition Act 1998, s 18 draws on Article 82 EC for its inspiration in prohibiting an abuse of a dominant position. It has to be established that the undertaking(s) has a dominant position in a market; a market is analysed from three perspectives: product market, geographical market and temporal market.[34] There has to be an 'abuse' of the dominant position by the undertaking(s). Section 18(2) spells out kinds of behaviour that may amount to abuse by a dominant undertaking. Like Article 82 EC, this is not an exhaustive list. There is no provision, as in s 2, for exemptions for abusive conduct which may produce benefits. The DGFT has followed the thinking which operates at the Community level so if it can be established that there is an 'objective justification' for the behaviour it may not be regarded as an abuse even though it restricts competition in some way. Finally, Article 82 EC refers to conduct in a 'substantial part' of the Community. Section 18 omits the qualifying 'substantial' and simply refers to a dominant position within the UK. It can refer to a market in any part of the UK including localised markets.[35]

Conduct may be excluded from s 18 if within s 19. Persons (which includes undertakings) may notify conduct for the consideration of the DGFT or for the DGFT's guidance or decision.

The interrelation of EC and domestic law on competition

Whish has pointed out that the possibility of conflict between EC and domestic law on competition may arise for several reasons in spite of the massive influence of EC law and in addition to the fact that the underlying objectives are different. There are still differences in their respective treatment of mergers and complex monopolies as well as areas under common influence such as vertical agreements. Authorities may generally reach different conclusions. Article 10 EC, as has been seen on numerous occasions in this book, provides for cooperation and this works both ways and is reciprocal. Regulation 10 of 17/62/EEC and the EC Merger Regulation provide for co-operation between national and Community authorities in the enforcement of Articles 81 and 82 EC and in the control of mergers

---

[34]   Case 27/76 *United Brands v Commission* [1978] ECR 207.
[35]   See *South Yorkshire Transport v Monopolies and Mergers Commission* [1993] 1 All ER 289, HL.

respectively. According to the jurisprudence of the ECJ,[36] EC law takes precedence if it is stricter in exemptions but what if national law takes a stricter approach in either individual or block exemptions?[37] A draft Regulation recommending replacement of Regulation 17/62/EEC states that where EC law applies it will take effect to the exclusion of domestic law. National authorities are likely, however, to end up with more devolved power (above).

Section 60 of the Competition Act 1998 seeks to ensure that questions arising under the relevant part of the Act in relation to competition within the UK law will be dealt with in a manner which is consistent with 'the treatment of corresponding questions arising in Community law in relation to competition within the Community.' The section seeks to ensure this only so far as is possible 'having regard to any relevant differences between the provisions concerned'.

The duty is not absolute compliance but consistency and compliance with Community law unless the domestic court is driven to an alternative conclusion. There are substantive and procedural differences between the two regimes. In the case of the former, EC law aims to ensure the fulfilment of Community policy which includes removal of barriers in trade between Member States; this objective does not apply to trade within a Member State as was spelt out in the Act in ss 2 and 18. Whish also emphasises that the objective of EC law is market integration whereas in UK law it is elimination of agreements and practices prejudicial to competition.

In the case of the latter there is an appeal to the Competition Commission from decisions of the DGFT and regulators whereas in EC law the CFI may only provide judicial review. Methods for calculating fines are different.

Section 60(2) and (3) provide that at any time that a court (including the Competition Commission, DGFT and sectoral regulators)[38] determines a question arising under this part of the Act, it must act to ensure there is no inconsistency between application of principles and decisions of the court and principles laid down in the Treaty, by the ECJ (including the CFI but not Advocates General). Those bodies must also 'have regard to any

---

[36] Case 14/68 *Walt Wilhelm* [1969] ECR 1.
[37] See Whish *Competition Law* (2001, 4th ed) pp 323–29. NB effect of s 60 below in text.
[38] Section 60(4) and (5).

relevant decision or statement of the Commission.' This is so far as compatible with provisions under that part of the Act dealing with competition and regardless of any other requirement so to do.

Furthermore, the government spokesperson in the House of Lords accepted that s 60 includes the general principles of Community law which we looked at in Chapter 3. To recall, these include proportionality, equality, legitimate expectation and equality, rights of defence and so on.[39] Principles laid down in the Treaty would include sovereignty and direct effect but this would be in relation to a domestic issue, not a Community one and so the European Communities Act 19872, s 2(1) would not be the governing provision here – prohibitions in Chapters 1 and 2 would not be entrenched as against future legislation.

Under EC law, actions by third parties injured by a breach of Articles 81 and 82 EC are allowed. The Act is silent on the rights of third parties in the event of breaches of prohibitions. In the House of Lords, Lord Haskell stated that private actions would be possible by analogy with Articles 81 and 82 EC and s 60: 'There is no need to make an explicit provision in the Bill to achieve that result. Third party rights of action under the domestic regime are to be the same as those under Articles [81 and 82 EC].'[40] The UK Enterprise Bill (enacted 2002) provides for private actions in damages to be brought in the Competition Commission Appeal Tribunal.

Inquiries and investigations

The DGFT and sectoral regulators are given wide powers to conduct inquiries and investigations into cartels and abuses of dominant position. These are contained in ss 25–29 of the Competition Act 1998.[41] The provisions improve the position of the DGFT vis à vis the earlier regimes

---

[39]   Cf *Society of Lloyd's v Clementson* [1995] CLC 117; *Gibbs Mew plc v Gemmell* [1999] ECC 97; *Connaught Restaurants Ltd v Indoor Leisure Ltd* [1994] 4 All ER 834.

[40]   HL Debs Vol 583 cols 955–966. The earlier decision of the ECJ that parties to agreements cannot bring actions however under Art 81: *Chemidus Wavin Ltd* [1978] 3 CMLR 514 must now be seen in the light of the *Courage* decision above note 16.

[41]   See OFT: *Powers of Investigation* and *Under Investigation* at: www.oft.gov.uk/ html/comp-act/technical_guidelines/index.

but they will now operate within the context of the HRA 1998. The powers include written requests for information, entry without or with a warrant (the latter are more extensive). The DGFT has followed Commission practice when exercising powers under Regulation 17/62/EEC and will allow a lawyer to be called if none is present 'in-house' (an employee) where 'it is reasonable in the circumstances'. Under the Act it appears there is a wider definition of what is protected by legal professional privilege in investigations.[42] In EC law, communications with 'in-house' lawyers is not privileged and nor are communications with lawyers who are not qualified in a Member State. Combined investigations are therefore likely to pose considerable problems added to by the fact that where material is privileged, in an EC case the matter is referred to the CFI. In a domestic investigation, it might be subject to a judicial review but is more likely to be a matter arising in any appeal to the Competition Commission. Whish believes joint investigations are unlikely. A further point of difference concerns self incrimination. The standards incorporated by the HRA 1998 include the ECHR's decision in *Funke v France* which commentators agree gives more protection than the ECJ's decision in *Orkem v Commission* as was noted above.[43]

Agreements may be notified to the DGFT either for guidance or for a formal decision. A summary of decisions is kept in a register and published by the Office of Fair Trading in a *Weekly Gazette*. Guidance is not made public. The DGFT may issue directions of an interim or final nature where there are breaches of Chapter I or II prohibitions. These may be enforced through the courts. In setting penalties, the DGFT (and any domestic appeals tribunal or court) must take account of fines issued by the Commission, or by EC courts 'or by a court or other body in another Member State'. This presents two problems: first of all in setting fines up to 10% of turnover, a

---

[42] See the Competition Act 1998, s 30.

[43] [1993] 1 CMLR 897 and Case 374/87 [1989] ECR 3283 respectively and see above. See also *Mannesmannröhren-Werke AG v Commission* Case T–112/98 [2001] ECR II–729 continuing this trend. *Saunders v UK* (1996) 2 BHRC 358 also established a stricter test than the common law for self-incrimination and the English courts have refused to make the operation of the HRA 1998 retrospective to nullify the earlier convictions: *R v Saunders etc* [2002] EWCA Crim 2860, [2002] 2 Cr App Rep 210. Article 46 ECHR did not confer rights on parties in domestic law which could override the clear intention of Parliament: cf the unfairness resulting from non-disclosure of evidence under common law principles explained in *Rowe and Davis v UK* (2000) 30 EHRR 1 and see *R v Davis, Johnson and Rowe* [2001] 1 Cr App Rep 115.

different basis is used to establish turnover under the Competition Act 1998 and EC provisions. Secondly, the effects of agreements or conduct for instance may be different in different Member States.

Interesting questions may also be present in whether references may be made to the ECJ on a point arising solely under the Act but where EC law is relevant. Earlier case law of the ECJ suggested limitations where EC case law was not binding but was a matter to which regard should be had.[44] Section 60 of the Competition Act 1998 (above) establishes as we have seen a qualified duty to maintain consistency with Community case law. More recent case law of the EC courts suggests that where a ruling on Community law is necessary in order to give a proper construction to purely domestic rules a ruling may be given.[45] The ECJ stated that a reference may be allowed where a point of domestic law corresponds with Articles 81 or 82 EC: 'A request from a national court may be rejected only if it is quite obvious that the interpretation of Community law bears no relation to the actual facts of the case or to the subject matter of the main action'[46] (para 17).

A final point to make is that the Enterprise Act 2002 will give huge powers of investigation into markets under Part 4 which may be launched in the public interest under chapter 2 of the Act.

The emergence of Agencies

Before we examine competition law and services of general economic interest and then regulation of European markets in utilities there needs to be an examination of agencies in the EC. The Commission in the shape of DGIV has championed a market integration approach into its work as the supervisory body for EC competition law. It is not a regulatory authority in a pure sense but it engages in many tasks undertaken by regulatory authorities: it acts in an executive capacity, it legislates, it investigates and makes judgments – its decisions have the full effect of a court's judgment until set aside by a court.

---

[44]   Case C-346/93 *Kleinwort Benson Ltd v Glasgow City Council* [1995] ECR I-615.

[45]   Case C-130/95 *Bernd Giloy* [1997] ECR I–4291; Case C-28/95 *Leur Bloem* [1997] ECR I-4161.

[46]   Case C-7/97 *Bronner* [1998] ECR I-7791 para 17: see Whish *Competition Law* (2001, 4th ed) p 360.

To assist the Commission in many of its responsibilities concerning eg, the environment, health and safety at work, medicinal products, racism and xenophobia and harmonisation of the internal market, various agencies have been created. Their role is largely advisory and information gathering. They may work in conjunction with national networks to facilitate the task of information collection and dissemination. While the agency concept is a familiar one in many countries, EU members and non-EU members, and none more so than the famous regulatory agencies of the US they may take many forms. For instance, executive agencies in the UK are very often part of public service provision and not regulatory bodies as such. The domestic Food Standards Agency, the Environmental Agency and the Civil Aviation Authority share some characteristics but far from all of the US style regulatory agencies. These agencies in the US formulate policy, they adjudicate claims and they legislate for the areas that they regulate.[47] The EU agencies are not analogues of US or UK agencies. Many Member States are developing agencies to engage in regulatory activities. It was seen in Chapter 3 (p 134) how in France the Conseil d'Etat had been somewhat hostile to such bodies.

As we have seen, a notable example of regulatory agencies in UK law has involved the regulation of utilities by the sectoral regulators. Originally, it was envisaged that regulators would be a short-term creation and that once markets in public service industries were subject to competition there would be no more need for regulators. Their role has however, been enhanced. In the Utilities Act 2000, gas and electricity were combined in the Gas and Electricity Markets Authority. The original Utilities Bill had contained provisions affecting telecommunications and water but these were dropped as the Bill progressed through Parliament. A new regime for telecoms is contained in the Communications Bill and in new Directives. Licensing as such in telecoms will disappear.

What is of interest is that the regulators of utilities in the UK have wide powers to regulate in the public interest and to enforce, concurrently with the DGFT, Chapters I and II prohibitions under the Competition Act 1998 in relation to the respective industries. The regulators may either use the Act or enforce licence conditions (the industries require licences to operate) where appropriate. The Act, a concurrency regulation and Guidelines exist

---

[47] For a straightforward account, see: P L Strauss *An Introduction to Administrative Justice in the United States* (1989).

to ensure smooth blending of these powers[48] and there is also a Concurrency Working Party which is chaired by a member of the Office of Fair Trading and which includes members from all the regulators. This seeks to deal with information sharing and also to decide upon who should have jurisdiction in a particular case. Meetings are confidential and minutes are not published. This may change when the Freedom of Information Act 2000 is operative. A disagreement that cannot be resolved by application of the Guideline will be sent to the Secretary of State.

In fact, before these additions of the Competition Act 1998, regulated industries claimed that the regulators had too much power. Their original brief to regulate the price formula, oversee licence revisions and apply competition to the privatised industries has in some cases been overtaken by social considerations concerning eg universal coverage, establishing service standards with general quality indicators and rights to compensation for individuals, and preventing disconnections involving impoverished families. After privatisation, such disconnections initially increased in the energy, water and telephone utilities. However, such interventions have been described as 'pragmatic' and 'varying from industry to industry' and undemocratic.[49] The Labour government elected in 1997 saw universal service on fair terms as a central feature of a 'fairer society'.[50] By 2002, it saw reform of social service provision as a means of achieving greater social justice. The Utilities Act 2000 provides new duties on regulators concerning the interests of low income consumers and the chronically sick and the regulator will 'have a duty to heed guidance issued by the minister on social and environmental matters.'[51] Section 9 contains a new overriding duty on the regulator to protect the interests of consumers by promoting competition. This covers prices and conditions of supply, continuity and availability and quality of supply. In the Green Paper preceding the Act, it stated that due weight has to be given to interests of consumers 'long-term, medium-term, immediate or short-term.' Furthermore, some of the agencies have operated in a remarkably open manner when discussing eg, licence revisions or pricing formulas not always, perhaps, to the liking of the industries.

---

[48] T Prosser in B Rodger and A MacCulloch eds *The UK Competition Act: A New Era for UK Competition Law* (2000) p 225.

[49] Prosser (2001) Law & Contemporary Problems, 63, 72.

[50] DTI *A Fair Deal for Consumers: The Response to Consultation* (1998).

[51] Prosser (2001) Law & Contemporary Problems, 73.

The UK agencies operate in areas where provision is made under EC law for the application of competition law which I will investigate in a moment. But that application is qualified. They also operate in markets which are subject – some activities eg telecommunications, more than others – to efforts to liberalise markets in Europe making them more open and allowing for the possibility of more market penetration and competition by non-national concerns.[52] But public utilities whether publicly or privately owned, like public employment, are subject to some of the strongest of national controls. In the case of public employment the control is allowed in the Treaty.[53] In the case of services of general economic importance, the treaty is agnostic as to ownership.[54] To what extent could or/and should markets in publicly dominated sectors or utilities be opened up?

An interesting development is unfolding. On the continent, services of general interest are heavily influenced in several countries by the French concept of 'public service'. This was introduced in Chapter 3. Under the French constitution, specifically the Preamble of 1946, it stipulates that national public services or de facto monopolies are to become public property. This has not been rigidly interpreted by the Conseil Constitutionnel.[55] This entails the performance of an activity in the general interest, under a public or private provider with equality of treatment, adaptation to changing needs and security of supply.[56] The service will be defined in law and will invariably involve a monopoly to ensure effective provision. Limits will be placed on the right to strike for employees in such services. Transparency and some degree of participation of consumers in

---

52   See Directives 2002/19/EC and 2002/22/EC which effectively remove the requirement for licensing. On the rail regulator and decisions to enforce access agreements on Railtrack, see *Re Railtrack plc* [2002] EWCA Civ 955, [2002] 4 All ER 435; on access disputes in telecoms: *Mercury Ltd v DGT* [1996] 1 WLR 48 and also on the DGT: *R v Director General of Telecommunications, ex p Cellnet* (1998) Times, 7 December.

53   Article 39(4) EC which provides that the provisions in Art 39 (freedom of movement and abolition of prejudice etc) do not apply to public employment.

54   Article 295 EC which provides that the Treaty shall in no way prejudice the rules in Member States governing the system of property ownership.

55   Concessions to private companies are common especially in water supply. In the privatisation decision of the Conseil Constitutionnel the draft loi authorising privatisation in the mid-1980s was held to be constitutional although this was subject to important qualifications regarding how assets were to be evaluated and priced on the sale: see C Graham and T Prosser *Privatizing Public Enterprises* (1991) 97 et seq.

56   Prosser (2001) Law & Contemporary Problems, 76, citing Debene and Raymundie 52:3 AJDA 183, 186 (1996).

the regulation of services have become common. The French model has been seen as a bastion of national champions enshrined in a special legal regime – most details of which are contained in detailed legislation and regulations which confer special privileges. In its 1994 annual report, the Conseil d'Etat (see Chapter 3) spoke of the threat to *service public* and its ethics by the laissez faire approach of the Treaty. The English model with its concentration on privatisation, liberalisation and competition is also seen as a threat to the concept of *service public* with its end objective of social solidarity entailing forms of redistribution. How has European initiative been influenced by and how is it influencing these national traits? In a 1996 Communication, the Commission identified the concept of a European universal service as follows:

> The basic concept of universal service is to ensure the provision of high-quality service to all at prices everyone can afford. Universal service is defined in terms of principles: equality, universality, continuity and adaptability; and in terms of sound practices: openness in management, price-setting and funding and scrutiny by bodies independent of those operating the services. These criteria are not always all met at national level, but where they have been introduced using the concept of European universal service, there have been positive effects for the development of general interests services.[57]

Regulated markets

These markets are often referred to as utilities and invariably enjoy a special position and relationship within a state structure.[58] There has been an inevitable tendency for the state to own the industry in question, nationalisation, or to regulate a utility serving the public by a public body which seeks to ensure standards of service and price controls. The period in the UK since the early 1980s has been characterised by an era of privatisation in which publicly owned industries or businesses are sold to the public in the form of shares. The state often held on to the 'Golden share' allowing it to retain crucial powers in the management of the company. The ECJ in June 2002 ruled that retention of golden shares in

---

57   *Services of General Interest in Europe* [1996] OJ C 281/03, para 28. The latest papers on services of general interest are: COM (2001) 580 and 598 and see p 545 below. See C Scott (2000) European Law Journal 310.

58   Defence and pharmaceutical production possess their own regulation, policy formulation and complaints procedures.

privatised companies by France and Portugal contravened the free movement of capital provisions of the Treaty because of a lack of precision and wide discretionary powers in the manner in which the controls over share transfers and company take-overs were exercised. In the case of Belgium, however, the state control was of a limited temporal nature and a right of appeal for shareholders had been established, and the state interest in seeking to guarantee supplies of gas in cases of real emergency was a legitimate need. These provisions made the holding of the golden share compatible with fundamental provisions of Community law.[59]

Because invariably a monopoly is unleashed onto the market by such a process of privatisation, it may be expected that special regimes will have to be established in order to avoid the abuse of a monopoly. Competition authorities are not usually equipped to deal with such a position in which there simply is no, or no effective competition, by design.[60] For this reason, regulatory authorities were established by Parliament in the UK to regulate the activities of such industries especially by price controls and standards of service. Public enterprise – which goes further than utilities – has been an area where the sovereignty of the state has been witnessed in a traditional sense, indeed some see it as a consummation of state sovereignty. The question is: to what extent will EC norms interfere with traditional notions of sovereignty as expressed either in public ownership or state created monopolies?

Articles 81 and 82 EC, and accompanying articles, and the provisions on state aids apply to public enterprises and undertakings granted special or exclusive rights by the state by virtue of Article 86(1) EC.[61] They are not excluded from competition provisions. Article 86(2), however, states that in the case of services of general economic interest, they are subject to rules on competition but 'insofar as the application of such rules does not obstruct the performance, in law or in fact, of the particular tasks assigned to them.' It continues that development of trade must not be affected to such an extent as would be contrary to the interests of the Community.

---

59   Cases C-483/99, 367/98 and 503/99 *Commission v France, Portugal and Belgium* [2002] 2 CMLR 1213, 1249, 1265, ECJ.

60   When BT was privatised there were two competitors: Mercury and Kingston Upon Hull's network. By 2000, there were about 150 companies offering fixed-line services.

61   Along with state aids this reduces the incentive for nationally or publicly owned enterprises because they cannot be subject to a different regime.

The ECJ has vacillated somewhat, as will be seen, in its application of this provision and the manner in which it has protected market interests and in the manner in which it has protected the interests of social solidarity. It has been argued, and it has also been questioned, that the new Article 16 EC introduced at Amsterdam into the general principles of the Community, advances the presumption in favour of the *service public* ethic.[62] It is hardly surprising that such an argument is made because Article 16 EC was drafted by France.[63]

Article 16 EC seeks to highlight the importance of public service provision. It refers to 'the place occupied by services of general economic interest in the shared values of the EU as well as their role in promoting social and territorial cohesion.' It continues by stating that the Community and Member States 'shall take care that such services operate on the basis of principles and conditions which enable them to fulfil their missions.' This is to be achieved within their respective powers and within the scope of application of this Treaty and without prejudice to various Articles (73, 86 and 87 EC).

Ross sees in this formulation the possibility that the values represented by services of general interest 'can be read as representing at least a minimum overlapping Union consensus or, going further, might even sustain the beginnings of a concept of universal personhood. Such claims risk sounding emptily grandiose, and they admittedly contain no particular path for concretising rights, but they do testify to a solidarity which may be a necessary precondition to challenge market-ruled local systems of welfare supply.'[64] It might become a focus for discussion of the 'key attributes' of modern European society and European citizenship.

Furthermore, the Charter of Fundamental Rights of the EU contains the following provision which to borrow Ross's phrase may indicate that it is a declaration of social objectives rather than a limited derogation from the free market and competition. It says:

> The Union recognises and respects access to services of general economic interest as provided for in national laws and practices, in accordance with

---

62   M Ross (2000) European Law Review 22. Hancher in P Craig and G de Burca eds *The Evolution of EU Law* (1999) is not so convinced.

63   See, A Lyon-Caen and V Champeil-Desplats eds *Services publics et droits fondamenteux dans la construction européenne* (2001) Paris.

64   M Ross (2000) European Law Review 22.

the Treaty establishing the EC, in order to promote the social and territorial cohesion in the Union.

'General economic interest' has never been defined by the court but the concept of certain goods or services which if left to the operation of the markets would not be guaranteed – or at least not on a basis of universal provision – seems close to the mark.[65] The EC Treaty, as seen above, is agnostic as to whether there is public or private ownership of public goods or services.

Article 86 EC recognises that states may confer exclusive or special rights on certain firms but not so as to conflict with other Treaty provisions.[66] Article 86(2) EC states that such undertakings (and those having the character of revenue producing monopoly) are subject to competition rules in so far as the application of such rules does not obstruct the performance, in law or in fact, of the particular tasks assigned to them. The development of trade must not be affected to such an extent as would be contrary to the interests of the Community. The Commission must ensure the application of these provisions and may issue 'appropriate Directives or decisions to Member States' (Article 86(3) EC). This power has been used to seek to ensure transparency in the use of funds for state aids.[67]

In earlier case law, the ECJ placed primary emphasis on detriment to the market when analysing whether the application of competition rules 'obstructed performance'.[68] Service of general interest is not mentioned in Article 86 EC as a value to be given special status. Nonetheless, the ECJ has since adopted a looser test which is arguably more sympathetic to the environment in which the public service operates.[69] In assessing whether breaches of Articles 81 and 82 EC are justifiable, the concession in Article 86(2) EC made it 'necessary to take into consideration the economic conditions in which the undertaking operates, in particular the costs which it has to bear, and the legislation, particularly concerning the environment,

---

[65]   W van Gerven, Opinion Cases C-48/90 and C-66/90.
[66]   C-157/94, *Commission v Netherlands* [1997] ECR I-5699: Member State must not oblige or encourage organisations to behave in a way that would be a breach by the Member State of obligations binding on it.
[67]   Hancher in P Craig and G de Burca eds *The Evolution of EU Law* (1999) p 727.
[68]   *France v Commission* Case C-208/88 [1991] ECR I-1223.
[69]   *Corbeau* Case C-320/91 [1993] ECR I-2533.

to which it is subject.'[70] Such approaches are likely to be enhanced by the new Article 16 EC and Article 36 in the Charter of Fundamental Rights of the EU.[71] The Court has ruled that for the exemption in Article 86(2) EC to apply, it does not have to be established that the application of competition rules will prevent the commercial survival of the undertaking. It is sufficient that application would obstruct the performance of the special obligations incumbent upon the undertaking, eg universal service. This is to balance the interest of the state in using such undertakings for instruments of economic policy and the Community's interests in achieving a competitive and integrated market. This attitude in the ECJ which saw it balancing competing interests rather than simply basing deliberation upon economic detriment was manifested in several cases in the late 1990s.[72] The balancing would be subject to familiar tests of necessity and proportionality.[73]

Hancher has described case law on Article 82 EC as 'opaque' and 'erratic'. Edwards and Hoskins have suggested that the case law reveals a view of the provision which establishes limited sovereignty in Member States and limited competition at the Community level. Limited sovereignty means that a state cannot create exclusive rights with impunity under Community law as some are illegal. There was no distinction between the existence and exercise of exclusive rights.[74] Limited competition means that states may grant exclusive or special rights if these are *necessary* in the public interest or to allow them to perform services in the general economic interest.

In order to establish whether a legal monopoly should be allowed, it must perform commercial or market activities. If not, Articles 81, 82 and 86 EC do not apply. The Court has also been sensitive about being drawn into over committing itself in areas such as gas and electricity supply where there has been little in the way of harmonisation legislation and guidance on application of competition rules and there is little in the way of competition

---

[70]   *Almelo* Case C-393/92 [1994] ECR I-1477 at para 49 cited in Ross (2000) European Law Review 22.

[71]   Ross (2000) European Law Review 22.

[72]   *Commission v Netherlands* Case C-157/94 [1997] ECR I-5699; *Commission v Italy* Case C-158/94 [1997] ECR I-5789; and Case C-160/94 *Commission v Spain* [1997] ECR I-5851. See, however, *Chemische Afvalstoffen Dusseldorp* Case C-203/96 [1998] ECR I-4075.

[73]   Not unlike, argues Ross (2000) European Law Review 25, the 'disapplication of normal rules in favour of higher interests recognised in Community law ... a cornerstone in balancing Community and national regulation of markets.'

[74]   Case C-202/88 *France v Commission* [1991] ECR I-1223.

in the EC in these areas. Hancher notes that several barriers exist to prevent judicial intervention in such areas not the least being state discretion to organise public services and that in infringement proceedings, 'it is for the Commission and not the Member State to come up with alternative forms of providing collective goods which are less restrictive than a reservation of monopoly rights to particular undertakings.'[75] By removing monopoly and enhancing liberalisation, the Court may have to ensure that any diminution of a Member State's provision of essential services is replaced by a Community capacity or a capacity elsewhere in the Community which complies with competition law and policy. This is not realistic in many areas so national or regional provision will continue.

Hancher makes the point that a combination of Articles 81, 82 and 86 EC may in fact produce a Commission which acts more like a Community regulator of public or exclusive rights service. It has gone beyond the Court which has been ready to strike a balance and give protection to exclusive rights truly serving a public interest in the provision of core economic activities as opposed to those which did not serve such core activities. The Commission's approach, argues Hancher, may produce a regulator as interested in the structure of the market and the state's failure to ensure that that structure will become a competitive one.[76] 'They can also arise because, at least, in the Commission's view, the relevant national sectoral regulators do not operate effectively to deal with a structural situation.'[77] Market liberalisation in telecommunications emerged from the dual influence of competition measures and harmonisation measures. These were accompanied by decisions of the Commission affecting national regulation and to these were added a large array of provisions which sought to shape the way national decisions were made on, for instance, agreements allowing access to networks by competitors. This may not always produce decisions that the Commission wish for for a variety of reasons, eg the national authority is not as independent as the Commission would wish, or its exercise of powers is coloured in a subtle way. They have been accompanied by reminders from the Commission that national regulatory decisions may be set aside. This has led to calls for a super regulatory authority to oversee national regulation more effectively. As Hancher expresses the point: in

---

[75] Hancher in P Craig and G de Burca eds *The Evolution of EU Law* (1999) p 733
[76] Hancher in P Craig and G de Burca eds *The Evolution of EU Law* (1999) p 738.
[77] Hancher in P Craig and G de Burca eds *The Evolution of EU Law* (1999) p 738. The performance of these differs.

the field of telecommunications, national governments have surrendered their power to manage certain areas of the economy by adopting secondary legislation of the Community:[78]

> Whereas ten years ago, the provision of telecommunications services was not only closely regulated and controlled at national level, but was also the primary preserve of national, publicly owned monopolies, as at 1998 this sector must be wholly exposed to market forces. In this context, state regulation will be permitted primarily as a way of ensuring that market forces are actually able to work in practice, as well as to correct certain market externalities. Member States have lost the power to organise their national markets along monopolistic lines or to preserve the provision of certain services to certain firms. Market integration has become the priority. Externalities are defined in Community and not national terms.[79]

Hancher accounts for the emergence of the national regulatory authority as a consequence of these developments. As such these bodies are outposts of the Commission effectively enforcing Community norms as 'decentralised Community regulatory bodies'[80] and where the concept of a Community collective service or good has become a Community concept contained in the Directive and no longer a national one. It could be argued that this reflects French influence at the Community level where norms of public service law have entered Community discourse. But such factors have also been increasingly influential in the UK where regulators have been under increasing legislative pressure and de facto initiative to advance social values.

Several points need to be made. First of all, in 2002 telecommunications is the only area where such a striking development has been made and this is because of judicial decisions and secondary legislation.[81] A universal

---

[78]   Hunt (1997) EPL 93 has described how in the development of Community telecommunications policy there is 'a complete lack of openness in that process'. The Director General of Telecommunications – the industry regulator – in the UK has no *locus* because the national representative is the Department of Trade and Industry. However, ECTRA has been a 'key group in recent policy development' and is constituted by an ad hoc high level committee of national regulators. There are many other areas of secretive Community/MS policy development. To whom does one make an application for access under the Code, and how will decisions be challenged if made by a Member State?.

[79]   Hancher in P Craig and G de Burca eds *The Evolution of EU Law* (1999) p 722. See also E Szyszczak *20 Yearbook of European Law* 35.

[80]   Hancher in P Craig and G de Burca eds *The Evolution of EU Law* (1999) p 723.

[81]   Eg, 88/301/EEC; 90/388/EEC; 96/16/EC.

service provision is contained in one of these Directives – although it covers thirty pages. The energy market had been resistant to European liberalisation and concentrated on standard unification, environmental protection and the Directives allowed wide-ranging derogations.[82] There was agreement at the Barcelona summit in 2002 that the energy sector would be opened up for industrial but not domestic consumers. It has to be said that those developments relating to the industrial sector went further than many anticipated. The Commission is also committed to a framework Directive on services of general interest by the end of 2002 and a new package of telecoms Directives have been agreed for implementation by 2003. Domestic regulations implementing the Postal Services Directive have set out a universal service at a uniform tariff throughout the UK – the first time such provisions were set out in law.[83] In the case of post, water and transport these are not regarded as 'normal market commodities' although there has been considerable penetration in the UK market by non-UK companies. Some Member State markets remain impenetrable to integration in areas of services of general interest – others may have regulatory regimes that allow for greater degrees of market penetration.[84] In broadcasting, cable and satellite are more amenable to regulation at the EU level and the terrestrial level has been subject to regulation in terms of free movement of goods. Digital broadcasting and cable and satellite delivery mechanisms are more susceptible to market operations. They nonetheless carry considerable problems in relation to regulation and competition. With the convergence between telecoms and broadcasting which is recognised in the new Directives, there will also be a convergence of regulation in the delivery of telecoms and broadcasting. The Directives provide that there will be no licensing of cable as a delivery mechanism but the delivery of a broadcasting service may be regulated.[85]

Secondly, the UK regulatory apparatus which separated service provision from regulation had been devised and had met with considerable success – too much the industries might say! – before there was any significant EC influence. In fact, the British model was influential in Europe and even France, after initial reluctance and opposition from the Conseil d'Etat has

---

[82]   [1997] OJ L27/20 – electricity; [1998] OJ L204/1 – gas. See F Botchway (2001) 26 ELR 3.

[83]   Postal Services Act 2000. In July 2002, there were calls for additional fees for delivery to domestic addresses and small businesses before 9.00am!

[84]   The *Financial Times* reported on an EU power market by 2007, 26 November 2002.

[85]   Directive 2002/20/EC, para 20 Preamble.

adopted the agency model;[86] so too has Italy whereas Germany is still discussing the need for a specialist agency. Had there not been a two way process of influence here?

The implementation and impact of the EC procurement Directives

The language of contract has achieved overriding significance in the process of UK government and public service. The term is used in many senses to cover not only purchasing in a traditional sense, but use of contract as a means of achieving governmental goals, policy delivery and service provision. In litigation involving the Motor Insurers' Bureau in the UK, Lord Cooke referred to a type of contract used by government 'as instruments of policy and administration'.[87] And yet 'government contracts' as a subject has assumed the role of a Cinderella or poor step-child both in the law curriculum, even for public law courses, and in legal consciousness in Britain until comparatively recently. For an area of activity which sees government departments and agencies alone spending £13 billion pa on civil procurement[88] this may appear surprising. And this figure does not include expenditure on defence procurement, by local authorities, police authorities, health bodies and quasi government. At the EC level, the Cecchini report famously reported how in 1986 central and local government expenditure on construction and supplies contracts amounted to 15% of Community GDP, a figure now standing at over 10%.[89] Services alone, it has been estimated, account for 25% of public procurement.[90]

---

[86]   'The Conseil d'Etat is not too keen on these new kinds of exotic bodies whose multiplication it considers to be a reflexion of the decline of the state's authority' N Lenoir in B Markesinis ed *The British Contribution to the Europe of the Twenty-first Century: The British Academy Lectures* (2002) ch 17 citing Annual Report Conseil d'Etat 2001, *Etudes et Documents du Conseil d'Etat* (Paris, La Documentation Francais, 2001).

[87]   *White v White and Motor Insurers' Bureau* [2001] 2 CMLR 1, para 35.

[88]   *Modernising Procurement* HC 808 (1998/99), p 1. This figure did not include defence expenditure nor employment contracts. The 1995 *Government Procurement Progress Report to the Prime Minister* HM Treasury 1994/5 estimated that £60 billion was spent pa on central government contracting.

[89]   S Arrowsmith (2002) European Law Review 3.

[90]   De Graaf (1992) 1 Public Procurement Law Review 317. The Commission Green Paper *Public Procurement in the EU: Exploring the Way Forward* (1996) estimated that each year 720 billion ECUs were spent by European – ie, Member State – contracting authorities.

In legal terms the existence of government contracts was simply non-problematic: it was subsumed under the rubric of contract law and it would therefore be assumed that the general principles applying to contracts of public authorities would be the same as those applying to commercial or other contracts and would be governed by principles of private law. After all, would this not follow inevitably from Dicey's view of the Rule of Law as it applied to the UK – that the same regular and supreme law applied to all and all were equal under the law. Various academic authors had provided accounts of how under the veneer of Dicey's explanation/apologia of the British constitution there was a subterranean world of government procurement which bore no relation to the law of contract as written in contract texts.[91] But, although a description of subterranean practices was undoubtedly useful and well informed, it could not act as a substitute for a jurisprudence of public contracts which had to a considerable extent emerged in parts of the continent and in the US, for instance. In France, the existence and sophistication of *contrats administratifs* is well known.[92]

Without doubt, the single most important legal development affecting public contracts has been the EC Directives on public procurement and I shall address these in a moment.[93] I have outlined the fact that there has been an absence of legal culture in the development of our public law of contract. Recent years have highlighted developing trends towards judicial involvement by way of judicial review and restitution which will doubtless generate litigation.[94] There have also been statutory interventions,

---

91   See J Mitchell *The Contracts of Public Authorities: a Comparative Study* (1954); C Turpin *Government Procurement and Contracts* (1989) and the earlier and excellent *Government Contracts* (1972); I Harden *The Contracting State* (1992); Arrowsmith *Government Procurement and Judicial Review* (1988); and her *Government Contracts and Public Law* (1990) 106 Law QR 227 and (1995) 111 Law QR 235; and A C Davies *Accountability: A Public Law Analysis of Government by Contract* (2001); H Collins *Regulating Contract* (1999). There is a very useful bibliography in J M Fernández Martín *The EC Public Procurement Rules* (1996).

92   Brown and Bell *French Administrative Law* (1993, 4th ed) ch 8. On the US, see J W Whelan *Cases and Materials on Federal Government Contracts* (1985).

93   Eg, Council Directives 93/37/EC, 93/36/EC, 92/50/EC, 89/665/EC, 92/13/EC and 97/52/EC.

94   *R v Independent Television Commission, ex p TSW Broadcasting Ltd* [1996] EMLR 291 set out clearly the limited approach the courts would take on commercial matters where they were asked to review the exercise of a discretion in relation to commercial broadcasting. See also: *R v Independent Television Commission, ex p Virgin Television Ltd* [1996] EMLR 318; *R v Director of Passenger Rail Franchising, ex p Save our Railways* (1995) Times, 18 December;

especially in local government covering contractual terms, ultra vires contracts and 'best value' in-service delivery.[95] In addition to this case law, and the Directives which I discuss below, there is increasing evidence that the courts may be ready to address public contracts in a manner that does not simply assume that a contract entered into by a public authority may in all circumstances be equated with an ordinary private law contract between two private parties. Initially, the case of *R v Lord Chancellor, ex p Hibbit*[96] provided little in the way of optimism that a view different from that obtaining in English law would prevail. In that case, a decision by the Lord Chancellor's Department to award a contract for court shorthand reporting to a new firm and not the applicant company which had held the contract since 1907 was not subject to judicial review. This was in spite of a clear denial by the public authority of legitimate expectation and unfair treatment of the unsuccessful contractor by the respondent department. The contract was a private law matter lacking any appropriate 'statutory underpinning' or other 'sufficient public law element'.

Conversely, the point has often been made in England: why should public authorities not be bound by private law jurisdiction when exercising licensing powers in relation to markets, transport facilities, taxis etc? The answer is that in those latter areas the authority is exercising power in a regulatory and supervisory manner which necessarily involves an assessment of the public interest. Furthermore, in the case of local authorities, there is a statutory framework for the exercise of such licensing powers which carries with it a strong indication that the exercise of power is controllable by judicial review – the public law remedy. So much was perhaps conceded by the judge in *Hibbit* who felt that if the court were confronted by a monopoly situation in which a public authority had power to determine the right of a person to earn a living the court might be more willing to exercise its public law jurisdiction.[97]

R v National Lottery Commission, ex p Camelot Group plc [2001] EMLR 43. On striking off from a list of tenderers, see: *R v Bristol City Council, ex p D L Barrett*, Jackson J (6 July 2000, unreported).

[95]   The Local Government Act 1988, Part II, the Local Government (Contracts) Act 1997 and the Local Government Act 1999.

[96]   (1993) Times, 12 March. See also: *R v Hammersmith and Fulham LBC, ex p Beddowes* [1987] QB 1050.

[97]   D Oliver (1993) Public Law 214 and her reference to *Nagle v Fielden* [1966] 2 QB 633; and *R v Wear Valley District Council, ex p Binks* [1985] 2 All ER 699. See also *R v Barnsley Metropolitan Borough Council, ex p Hook* [1976] 3 All ER 452; and *R v Basildon District Council, ex p Brown* [1981] 79 LGR 655.

Other case law has acted on this 'public law presence'. In *R v Lewisham London Borough Council, ex p Shell UK Ltd*[98] the applicant for public law relief was part of a multi-national group of companies with subsidiaries trading in apartheid South Africa although it did not so trade itself. There was a considerable black population living in the area of the respondent local authority and the authority decided to boycott the goods of the company provided alternative goods were available at a reasonable price elsewhere. This it claimed was done in pursuance of statutory duties under the Race Relations Act 1976 to promote good race relations. It was held that although the authority may boycott the goods, and also seek to persuade other authorities to do likewise to help achieve good race relations, it had here used its statutory powers for an ulterior purpose to compel the company to sever all links with South Africa. Trade with South Africa was lawful and their actions were extraneous, impermissible and unlawful. An authority cannot use its powers to punish someone for doing something that was lawful. This was precontractual use of statutory powers. The interesting question would have been: what would have happened had the authority terminated contracts for the same reason? Would the court have similarly held that the ulterior use of the powers rendered a termination unlawful, or would they have relied upon breach of contract if there were a breach?[99] If there had been no breach, then what?

R v Legal Aid Board, ex p Donn & Co[100] is a more striking progression. Legal Aid Boards allocate publicly funded contracts for various legal functions including legal representation in litigation. Firms of solicitors tender for the contracts. The applicants for judicial review had tendered for a contract to represent victims of 'Gulf War Syndrome' in actions against the Ministry of Defence and which arose from the Iraqi invasion of Kuwait. Because of procedural flaws in the tendering process, including the loss of tender documents by the Board and an improper mode of decision-making, the decision not to allocate to the applicants was judicially reviewed because the court held the decision was justiciable in public law. The court treated the decision-making process and its consequences as

---

[98] [1988] 1 All ER 938.

[99] See *R v Ealing London Borough Council, ex p Times Newspapers* (1986) 85 LGR 316. Stopping the purchase of newspapers by public libraries was unlawful to support former employees of the newspaper were in an industrial dispute with the owners: s 7 Public Libraries and Museums Act 1964. See *Wheeler v Leicester City Council* [1985] 2 All ER 1106 where suspension of a contractual licence was successfully attacked because the authority had invoked impermissible grounds.

[100] [1996] 3 All ER 1.

an 'indivisible whole' – ie both the selection of solicitors by the Board and the work that they were selected to perform – and irrespective of whether there might be a remedy in private law[101] the public dimensions of the decision made it reviewable in public law. The procedural errors of the committee had to be corrected. On behalf of the respondents it was argued that simply because the work in question was publicly important did not make it a public law issue.[102] The court in *Donn* did not accept the analogy of cases in which a contract of employment had been in question and which the courts consistently treat as a private law governed matter.[103] There was a public interest in the proper allocation of public money to protect the important rights of individuals in which the Board was the exclusive and final arbiter of selection. There was also a public interest in the representation of the alleged victims of negligence by the Ministry of Defence. Although the presence or absence of a 'statutory underpinning' had been important in some cases to establish whether a function was public or private, as in *Hibbit*, the absence of such a quality was not fatal because it may be recognised by the common law.[104] Ognall J stated that there was '"a vital public interest" in the procedurally regular and fair conduct of the selection process which, at common law, brings the process within the aegis of public law.'[105] When the National Lotteries Commissioner in the Autumn of 2000 decided to continue discussions with one bidder for the renewal of the licence to operate the lottery and ceased discussions with the existing operator, the decision was judicially reviewed in public law for amounting to a breach of fair procedure.[106]

The Directives on Procurement are however, the closest we come to a code on public procurement confined as they are to the pre-contractual stages of public procurement. They have no relevance to disputes between contracting parties. In the UK standard practice for awarding contracts

---

[101]   *Sed quaere?* Is it because an alternative remedy may not have been *appropriate* - which really begs the question.

[102]   See *ex p Hibbit* above. A statutory or prerogative position of employment may be protected by public law process in appropriate circumstances especially to provide procedural protection.

[103]   Note the position of staff cases in EC law and the position of public sector employees in France: see *McClaren v Home Office* [1990] ICR 824; *R v Lord Chancellor's Department, ex p Nangle* [1992] 1 All ER 897.

[104]   *R v Independent Television Commission, ex p TSW Broadcasting Ltd* [1996] EMLR 291, HL; per Steyn LJ in the Court of Appeal: (1991) Times, December 30.

[105]   *Donn* above at p 11.

[106]   *R v National Lottery Commission, ex p Camelot Group plc* [2001] EMLR 3.

was via closed tender or negotiated procedures. This was largely unknown territory to all but governmental insiders and some contractors on selected lists. Numerous abuses where markets were rigged by contractors' 'rings' necessitated, it was felt, closed practices. But those very practices themselves led to allegations of abuse and fraud by officials.[107]

The Treaty of Rome as amended contains provisions which have an impact upon procurement : on the free movement of goods (Articles 23–31 [9, 10, 30–37] EC); establishment and the free provision of services (Articles 43–55 [52–60] EC)—but only Article 183(4) [132(4) EC] concerning Member States and overseas countries and territories specifically refers to procurement and Article 296(1) [223(1)] EC has a direct impact on defence sector procurement (see above). A commentator believes that this omission by the Treaty makers related not only to the fact that public contracts concerned sensitive matters on a privileged instrument for intervening in the economy 'and pursuing a wide range of social, political, and economic objectives'[108] but also because the Treaty merely provided the framework for future legislation concerning the Common Market and furthermore because in the early years non-tariff barriers to trade did not over concern the Member States.

The Directives, as is well known, seek to apply constraints to public procurement in works and supplies contracts and were subsequently applied to contracts for services and contracts made by publicly or privately owned utilities. They are accompanied by a remedies Directive and there is a specific remedies Directive for utilities.[109]

The Directives establish qualitative selection criteria and award criteria for contracting. The former determine the professional, economic, financial and technical suitability of interested bodies to tender or to be invited to do so. Once through this hurdle, tenders are assessed through two awarding criteria according to which the award must be decided: the lowest price or

---

[107] For the position before the reforms in Directives and the SIs, see P. Birkinshaw (1990) FIDE Report, *L'Application dans les Etats Membres des Directives sur les Marchés Publics* FIDE 14th Congrès, Madrid (1990) Rapport Britannique P Birkinshaw.

[108] See Fernandez Martin op. cit. note 91 above p 5.

[109] Directive 92/13/EC. The other directives are: EC Council Directives 93/97, 93/36, 92/50, 89/665 and 97/52. There is also an Unfair Terms in Consumer Contracts Directive (Directive 93/13/EC) which is implemented by SI 1994/3159 and it applies to consumer contracts for services provided by public as well as private bodies.

the most 'economically advantageous tender' on the basis of relevant factors depending upon the contract eg price, delivery date, after-sales service, technical assistance. Where public authorities, which is given a broad contextual definition, and utilities covered by the Utilities Directive award contracts and where contracts are above certain thresholds of value, the Directives seek to increase the transparency of the award of public contracts. This they do by making recourse to the open or restricted procedures through competition the norm and imposing a duty to justify resort to non-competitive negotiated procedures which may only be utilised in specific circumstances and subject to certain conditions. The duties on contractors to provide information about awards both before and after the award and also both to the Commission as supervisory authority and contractors in the bidding process were significantly increased in the revised Directives. This is arguably the most important improvement in the amendments. Unsuccessful bidders, or those not selected to bid, have to be given reasons for rejection if requested and there are important duties requiring pre-contract information which means that contracting authorities have to publish in the *Official Journal of the EC* (OJEC) indicative notices making public the total of procurement which they envisage awarding during the following year. Post-award information also has to be published in the OJEC indicating results of an award and this applies to all three types of award and must indicate the criteria applied in the award and the price. Reports also have to be produced by contracting authorities on each contracting award procedure with details about the awards and this must be produced to the Commission if requested. In the most recent consolidated version of the Directives, the opportunity to use procurement by contracting authorities for instrumental purposes has been abandoned.

Before the significant developments relating to the procurement Directives which began in the early 1990s, they had been implemented by Treasury guidance and departmental circulars — a questionable means of implementing EC legal measures. These Directives have now been implemented into UK law by statutory instrument, ie delegated legislation, although not without problems in the case of the Utilities Directive which caused litigation which led to a leading decision on the consequences under Community law of failing to implement a Directive properly, albeit under a genuine and honest mistake.[110] Many of the provisions are directly effective but their transposition into domestic law reinforces the position

---

[110] *R v HM Treasury, ex p British Telecommunications plc* [1996] All ER (EC) 411; Case C–392/93, ECJ.

of domestic courts as enforcement mechanisms and the regulations will have to be interpreted to give effect to the objectives of the Directives in the light of ECJ case law.

If we take the Public Services Contracts Regulations,[111] the regulations commence with an interpretation clause which defines a service contract as a contract in writing for consideration (whatever the nature of the consideration) under which a contracting authority engages a person to provide services but this does not include a contract of employment or other contract of service; public works contracts; public supply contracts; utility contracts as covered by the Part of Sch 1 of the Utility Regulations in which the utility is specified; or a contract under which a contracting authority engages a person to provide services to the public within its responsibility and under which the consideration given by the contracting authority consists of or includes the right to exploit the provision of the services. The regulation describes how services are split into services contracts under Part A (which are subject to the full range of obligations) and Part B (subject to a less extensive regime) (and see Sch 1) and reg 3 defines contracting authorities. This was interesting in itself because it constituted one of the first attempts to map out in a legal instrument the 'state' in a UK context. Regulation 6 contains general exclusions; thresholds are contained in regulation 7. Part II concerns technical specifications and Part III deals with procedures leading to the Award. Part IV concerns Selection of Services Providers including criteria for rejection of services providers, information as to economic and financial standing as well as ability and technical capacity. Part V covers the Award of a Public Services Contract including criteria, contract award notices, information about contract award procedures including the giving of reasons to unsuccessful services providers and on specified occasions the name of the successful party (if evaluated under reg 21). A detailed record also has to be kept of specified facts and circumstances under reg 10(2) where there is a resort to the negotiated procedure. This record must be reported to the Treasury if requested for onward transmission to the Commission. Part VI deals with a miscellany including design contests, subsidised public services contracts, employment obligations, statistical and other reports, responsibility for obtaining reports, publication of notices, sub-contractors and under reg 30: 'A contracting authority shall comply with such requirements as to confidentiality of information provided to it by a services provider as the services provider may reasonably request.'

[111] SI 1993/3228.

However, in our present discussion it is the remedies provisions which provides the most interesting example of the development of public contracts. This is contained in reg 32 'Applications to the Court'. The UK government opted for a remedy before the ordinary courts and not before a specialised tribunal or arbitration body where the duties under statutory instruments implementing the EC Directives were breached. The means of challenge is by a statutory procedure – which the courts appeared initially to treat as a judicial review – with a limitation period of three months; this is the same period as for judicial review but much shorter than the usual period of six years for breaches of contract. The Court of Appeal has ruled that where an action was brought 15 months after the date of the acts which were alleged to be a breach of the Directive and Regulations on public service contracts (Article 30 and 3(2) Council Directive 92/50/EEC and/or reg 8 of the 1993 Regulations) it was correctly struck out by the judge at first instance for being out of time.[112]

Interestingly a challenge was made to the brevity of the limitation period which allegedly constituted a breach of Community obligations. The limitation period could not be less favourable than that relating to similar domestic claims (principle of equivalence) and could not be so framed as to make it virtually impossible or excessively difficult to obtain reparation (principle of effectiveness). In applying the principle of equivalence, the domestic court had to look not merely for a domestic action that was similar to the claim asserting Community rights but one which was in 'juristic structure' very close to the Community claim. In the absence of such a comparator the domestic system was at liberty to set whatever limitation period seemed best. There was no such comparator in the domestic system either for an action of breach of statutory duty, by way of judicial review or under the Local Government Act 1988, ss 17 or 19 (which provided for regulation of the terms to be included in local authority contracts). The three month limitation period was therefore not open to attack. There is a very strong ground for arguing that the closest case is a breach of statutory duty where the limitation period is 6 years for a comparable claim. This is reinforced by reg 32(7) which speaks of the award of injunctions under the Crown Proceedings Act 1947 and which refers to private law actions; in other words, the private law context is reinforced. Furthermore, the Court of Appeal held, the regulations did not contravene the principle of effectiveness.

[112] *Matra Communications SA v Home Office* [1999] 3 All ER 562, CA.

The regulation states that the obligation to comply is a 'duty owed to services providers.' A breach of such a duty shall not be a criminal offence but is *actionable* by any services provider who, in consequence, suffers, or risks suffering, loss or damage. '*Actionable*' is clearly the language of rights under private law and not judicial review.

In *R v London Borough of Tower Hamlets, ex p Luck*[112a] there is an interesting illustration of the interrelationship between judicial review and remedies under the statutory instrument. Judicial review can only apply to those areas where the regulations have no reference; review, if available, is supplementary to the regulations.[113] The various sets of regulations state that the powers of the court under the regulations are 'without prejudice to any other powers of the Court' including judicial review. In the Court of Appeal, the view seems to be that remedies under the regulation are predominant, and where a remedy is available under reg 32 of the service regulations, this is the route that must be followed. There is no scope therefore to upset a contract that has been awarded by seeking a judicial review under judicial review procedure. The only situation where a judicial review might apply is where there was no remedy under the regulations for an abuse or illegality. This was not the position in *Luck* as the tenderer wanted a remedy in addition to the entitlement in damages.

An interesting point in relation to the conclusion of the contract was raised in *Ealing Community Transport v Ealing London Borough Council*.[114] This concerned the provision of 'special needs' transport services under a restricted procedure. The claimant, ECT, had unsuccessfully tendered for the contract and instituted proceedings alleging a breach of reg 32. The authority had sent a letter of acceptance to the successful tenderer and argued that the contract was thereby 'entered into' and the only available remedy was in damages. The claimant argued that further necessary formalities had to be complied with before the contract was concluded. The Court of Appeal agreed with the authority that the contract was concluded by its letter; it left open the possibility of attack in judicial review on the grounds of collusion or bad faith. The contract award had been announced in a public meeting by the authority three weeks before the letter of acceptance and there would have to be appropriate procedures to review the award of a contract *before* the contract was entered into.[115]

[112a] [1999] COD 294.
[113] See (1999) 3 PPLR CS 72.
[114] (30 July 1999, unreported), CA.
[115] See the decision of the ECJ in *Alcatel Austria AG* Case C-81/98 [1999] ECR I-7671.

The statutory instruments allow a remedy by way of injunction against the Crown before the House of Lords decision in *Re M*[116] allowed this remedy against an officer of the Crown acting in his official capacity on the public law side of proceedings. Decisions or actions in breach of the statutory instrument may be set aside and all procedures leading to awards of contracts may be suspended and damages awarded for the breach unless the contract has been entered into in which case damages are the only remedy.

Proceedings may not be brought unless the services provider wishing to bring proceedings has informed the contracting authority of the breach or apprehended breach of duty towards the former under reg 32(1) and of their intention to bring legal proceedings for the breach. The giving of a notice does not, however, prevent the contract otherwise being concluded by the authority with another contractor. This duty of notice has been interpreted as requiring a strict adherence by the Court of Appeal. The same case also insisted on a strict adherence to the publication of award criteria when the authority intends to make an award on the basis of 'the most economically advantageous' offer.[117]

The Utilities statutory instrument, reg 32(8) seems to allow wider claims made by contract providers to damages and other relief although there is a clear limitation to damages once the contract is entered into in reg 32(6). The same statutory instrument is also of interest in that the Utilities statutory instrument (following the Utilities Remedies Directive) has a conciliation procedure which an unsuccessful contractor may invoke by requesting the Minister (sic) to forward that request 'as soon as possible to the Commission'. Regulations have also allowed utilities to have recourse to 'attestation' which is a certificate from an independent body stating that the utility's procurement procedures comply with EC requirements thereby avoiding various formalities.[118]

---

[116] [1993] 3 All ER 537 – although the *Factortame* Case C–213/89 [1991] 1 All ER 70 preceded the implementing SIs. *Re M* is very important because it involved the award of a mandatory order against the Crown where *no question* of EC law was involved unlike *Factortame*.

[117] *R v Portsmouth City Council, ex p Coles and Colwick* (1996) 81 BLR 1, CA.

[118] Directive 92/13/EC, art 4 and SI 2001/2418.

In works contracts local authorities must state in the invitations to tender the criteria on which such awards will be made.[119] However, in awarding such contracts to its own labour force and not accepting the lowest offer, the authority was not entering into a contract made with 'pecuniary consideration' because it could not contract with its own department.[120] *R v Secretary of State for the Environment, ex p Harrow London Borough Council* (1996) 29 HLR 1 concerned a judicial review of a Secretary of State's decision relating to contracts to manage publicly owned housing. Harrow LBC—a local authority—wanted to transfer housing management contracts to UK Housing Associations who could later accept transfer of ownership of the properties under English law. Harrow argued that in this case the 'most economically advantageous tender' included that which best fulfilled the long term objectives of the authority—the transfer of housing management—under art 36 (1)(2) Council Directive 92/50. The Secretary of State had rightly refused approval on the grounds that the restrictions were unlawful under Directive 92/50.

On other matters the case law has been low key and less than sensational.[121] In the early 1990s, there was a feeling that a sea change in public law litigation would be brought about by virtue of the implementation of the Directives. The change in practice brought about by legal requirements has been enormous – and before the regulations were introduced the Directives were implemented by administrative circular and Treasury guidance. Compared with case law developments relating to public contracts outlined elsewhere in this chapter,[122] the litigation has been minimal and concerned with procedural points.

The effectiveness of the Directives in realising their objective of introducing more open competition within the area of public procurement has been

---

[119] Regulation 20(3), 71/305 EC as amended.

[120] *R v Portsmouth City Council, ex p Coles and Colwick* (1996) 81 BLR 1, unreported, CA – note these were applications for judicial review

[121] See eg, *R v Brent London Borough Council, ex p O'Malley* (1997) 30 HLR 328, CA where the work in question did not fall within the Works Directive and the regulations; *Resource Management Services v Westminster City Council* [1999] 2 CMLR 849 which concerned a breach of the services Directives; and *Keymed (Medical and Independent Equipment) Ltd v Forest Healthcare Trust* [1998] ELR 71 where the limitation period under the public services regulation was extended. See also the *Harmon* decision discussed by S Arrowsmith (2000) PPLR 120.

[122] See notes 94-104 above.

questioned. One argument is that they seek to achieve too much.[123] One commentator has argued that the emphasis on transparency may not be the best way of achieving greater liberalisation within public purchasing markets and there should be greater emphasis upon self audit or removal of companies from regulation where they have a good track record of compliance.[124] Greater reliance upon national authorities to enforce the law may produce that bias towards national systems which Cecchini observed almost twenty years ago.[125] One question which the procurement rules have to address more fully is the growing resort to contract through the Public Private Partnerships which has become a preferred means of the present UK government delivering essential service provision such as hospitals, schools, roads, transport systems and local authority services. In many cases, these are effectively the only way that new facilities may be built. The preferred method for allocating such contracts is through a negotiated procedure – ie the most confidential procedure. Guidance has been issued by the Commission on PPPs and proposals to amend the Directive only cover such negotiated procedures.[126] But as has been pointed out elsewhere, we have not developed a notion of contract to address the wide public interest involved in such mechanisms being employed to provide for collective welfare.[127]

---

[123]　JM Fernandez-Martin *The EC Procurement Rules* (1996).

[124]　S Arrowsmith (2002) ELR 3.

[125]　See p 546 above.

[126]　S Arrowsmith (2002) ELR 3, p 12. See *R (Kathro) v Rhondda Cynon Taff County Borough Council* [2001] EWHC Admin 527, [2002] Env LR 15 and an unsuccessful challenge by third parties to the award of a PPP contract by negotiated procedure.

[127]　See M Freedland 'Public Law and Private Finance: Placing the Private Finance Initiative in a Public Law Frame' in C McCrudden ed *Regulation and Deregulation* (1999). Also R Thomas 'Private Finance Initiative: Government by Contract' (1997) European Public Law 519.

Part three

Some questions and future issues

Chapter 13

Does European public law exist?[1]

This penultimate chapter is concerned with European public law and whether it exists today and if it does, what form and ambit it possesses. Although it might be thought more appropriate to have placed this chapter at a very early stage in the book, my own feeling was that discussion of what has preceded can now more usefully be placed in the European public law matrix.

Forms of European public law have existed since Roman law and continued through the Holy Roman Empire and the Canon Law of the Church. In the nineteenth century, Napoleon's wish to see a European system and a European law to buttress that system and to which he made such significant contribution in his code of civil law also displayed tendencies towards a European legal system. His resort to the Conseil d'Etat which became the inspiration for modern French public law – *droit administratif* – and which had a lasting influence on much of Europe and national systems of public law as well as on EC/EU law, accelerated that trend. No doubt the significant alterations to German administrative law under Nazism may well have been imposed throughout Europe had Nazism succeeded. Whatever its present format, the European public law I have in mind does not possess the totalitarian mould of some of these past practices. As we know, British lawyers and English lawyers in particular and politicians, have been very sensitive about European influences. There has been a long history of sensitivity. *Praemunire* – arguing for the content of Canon law on matters

---

[1] This chapter was given originally as a paper at the Institute for European Studies, Queen's University, Belfast: Queen's Paper on Europeanisation No 9/2001.

of state and church in England – has in the past been regarded as treasonable and due punishment exacted. Discussions about a European Arrest Warrant have given recent expression to that sensitivity. I shall set out what I mean by the term European public law below.

The scope of public law

A few points about public law should be recalled. Public law denotes that system of law that deals with our public affairs. It denotes the public sphere, defines its extent, the relationship between different tiers in the public sphere and between those tiers and individuals, corporate or personal, citizen or alien. Public law is primarily concerned with the exercise or non-exercise of public power, sometimes by private actors, and its fairness, rationality, legality and proportionality.

All law reflects the history and culture of the society in which it evolved or in which it was created. Historical factors certainly set limits to the transposition of legal norms from one legal system to another but such factors should not be used to deny the possibility of mutual influence between systems.[2] Public law tends to be more dependent upon historical and cultural factors, and particularly political practice and culture than private law.[3] Revolutionary political practice and colonisation may have spread their influence and helped to shape structures of public law in many states. However, today, aspects of public law may lend themselves more readily to mutual influence because of a sharing or pooling of public power, and because invariably strict limits are set by domestic courts on enforcing various public laws of foreign states. Until there is such a pooling, public law systems tend to be 'cocooned'.

'Public law' also takes very different forms in other comparable European systems where it is applied and enforced through special courts and where its separation from private law is not as ambivalent and uncertain as in English and Northern Irish law. Clearly, this is to a significant extent the result of the existence of a separation of powers doctrine in many European countries, once again under French influence.[4] A substantial case for the resistance of the English system to a French style or form of public law has

---

2   See G Anthony (2000) 14 Yearbook of European Studies 83 for a very helpful review and analysis. See his *United Kingdom and European Law: The Dynamics of Legal Integration* (2002).

3   J Schwarze *European Administrative Law* (1992) ch 1.

4   N Brown and J Bell *French Administrative Law* (1998, 5th ed).

been made out recently and is based upon the absence of state traditions and a separation of powers in Britain and Northern Ireland.[5] The absence in the UK of a French-style public law is not in doubt: the assertion that there is an absence of a system of public law is highly contentious and indeed we, and I refer to all UK jurisdictions, are well on the way to a developed system of public law. EPL has been central to that process. I believe there is something far more fundamental brewing than simply the introduction of new procedures for judicial review and an 'Administrative Court' of the High Court from October 2000 in London and Cardiff and with powers to sit elsewhere.

What do we mean by European public law?

We have various competing contenders.
1.   The law of the EU – it is without doubt a form of European public law based on a system of administrative and increasingly constitutional law including its own Charter of Human Rights (not a legally enforceable part of the Treaty of Rome because of amongst others, the UK's objections but the d'Estaing Convention is likely to recommend that it becomes a part of the new constitution for the European Union). The Community law of judicial review was based on French practice and so were some essential procedures including the purely declaratory form of judgment – they cannot be judicially enforced.[6] EU law is concerned with relations between institutions of the EU, Member States and EU institutions, citizens and citizens of non-Member States and EU institutions and regulatory law. This latter is increasingly dominant: competition law which affects non-Member States; environmental law; data protection law the EU provisions on which have so upset the US, broadcasting Directives and so on.
2.   A 'common law of Europe' – 'what a terrible thing' is a common reaction although it forms the content of an increasing number of legal scholars' research agendas in both public and private law. It is terrible if seen as some monolith imposed from above without regard to national sensitivities within each Member State and beyond – 'beyond' includes the growing list of prospective new members, members of the Council of Europe and so on. What its adherents aspire to is a

---

5   J Allison *A Continental Distinction in the Common Law* (1999 pb).
6   French administrative courts now invoke the doctrine of 'astreinte' as a means of enforcing judgments (see Ch 3). These basically are fines. Fines were introduced for failures to abide by judgments of the ECJ by Member States under Art 228 EC. These do not cover the institutions of the Community (Ch 3, p 109 et seq).

body of laws increasingly drawing on common influences and inspirations. I have to accept that the boundaries of such a common law are limitless; there are global vistas to a common law of human rights as there are global limitations based on political and religious ideologies.

3.   The ECHR. Its scope is as wide as membership of the Council of Europe. This quite rightly has some claim to the epithet European public law. Its success has created a back-lash among English lawyers in particular where there is a resentment about the fact that a Treaty drafted by, inter alios, English lawyers to attempt to prevent a repetition of atrocities of the second world war has been used more against the UK than any other signatory state.[7] The English judges have been quick to assert a patriation over the incorporation of the Convention into UK laws by the HRA 1998 – and even before that incorporation, case law had been illustrative of the reliance of the common law upon its own traditions for the protection of human rights – often with an American and Commonwealth contribution.[8] It has been observed that the margin of appreciation doctrine does not apply in the application of the HRA 1998 by domestic courts although discretion will be appropriately respected.[9] This means that in interpreting the domestic provisions under the HRA 1998, special account will not have to be given to local standards and traditions. In an Irish context, this is dramatically illustrated by abortion and the constitution of the Republic of Ireland.[10] However, Laws LJ has stated that the ECHR will be interpreted with a local gloss by domestic courts. Such a practice is perhaps anticipated in the formulation of the HRA 1998 which instructs domestic courts that they must take into account, not slavishly adhere

---

7   M Hunt *Using Human Rights Law in English Courts* (1997).

8   In particular *Derbyshire County Council v Times Newpapers Ltd* [1993] 1 All ER 1011, HL; *Reynolds v Times Newpapers Ltd* [1999] 4 All ER 609, HL.

9   Domestic courts will respect executive discretion in sensitive areas where the Convention applies and where a balance has to be struck between individual rights and collective welfare and where the rights are not expressed in absolute terms: see *R v DPP, ex p Kebilene* [1999] 4 All ER 801, HL per Lord Hope at 843–44. An exacting scrutiny will be exercised where interference with human rights is invasive and serious: see *R v Secretary of State for the Home Department, ex p Daly* [2001] UKHL 26, [2001] 3 All ER 433; *Alconbury etc* [2001] UKHL 23, [2001] 2 All ER 929. For a Northern Ireland gloss, see: *In the Matter of an Application by 'A' for Judicial Review* NIHC, 20 June 2001. See also P Craig (2001) Law Quarterly Review 589.

10   *Open Door Counselling v Ireland etc* (1992) 15 EHRR 244 at para 63. See also W van Gerven as Advocate General in Case C-159/90 *SPUC v Grogan* [1991] 3 CMLR 849.

to, the jurisprudence of the Convention when determining a question relating to a Convention right.[11] Lord Philips MR has observed how the ECHR is a living instrument 'and when interpreting it and considering the Strasbourg jurisprudence, it is necessary to bear in mind that its effect may change in step with changes in the standards applied by Member States.'[12]

4. The impact of EU law and the ECHR on the laws of Member States, and the impact in turn, of the law of Member States on EU law, in particular, as well as on each other. This is what I have in mind when speaking of European public law. There is a variety of processes through which this may take place. EU law may be applied directly in domestic courts when a question of EU law is involved.[13] It 'supplants' domestic law. It can also be applied indirectly when it is used to interpret domestic provisions. A reference on a preliminary ruling sends back the interpretation of a point of EU law referred to the ECJ by the national courts for the latter courts to apply.[14] In some cases, there has been too much scope for 'local texture'. In other cases, the ECJ has been directorial, eg the Sunday shopping saga in the UK where that Court had to give a ruling on the proportionality of the Sunday trading laws under the Shops Act 1950.[15] A domestic court may apply EU law directly when it decides a question of EU law and a reference is not necessary.[16] The last situation concerns those areas where there is a spill-over from EU (or ECHR or other European influence) so that that law, or those laws, influence a question of purely domestic law. Craig distinguishes this from a more general influence such as that which is generated by the development of general

---

[11] Under the HRA 1998, s 2(1): see Ch 9. See Laws LJ in: *R (on the application of M) v Metropolitan Police Comr* [2001] NLJR 1213. In *R v Central Criminal Court, ex p Bright* [2001] 2 All ER 244, it was held that English courts must follow the interpretation of the Court of Appeal and House of Lords on the judgments of the ECHR (Ch 9 p 396).

[12] *R (on the application of SB Saadi) v Secretary of State for the Home Department* [2001] EWCA Civ 1512, [2001] 4 All ER 961, CA. The Law Lords rejected the appeal: [2002] UKHL 41, [2002] 4 All ER 785.

[13] *R v MAFF, ex p First City Trading* [1997] 1 CMLR 250 and the limits of this approach. For a greater willingness to acknowledge European and not simply EC influence, see Sedley J in *R v MAFF, ex p Hamble* [1995] 2 All ER 714.

[14] Under Art 234 EC (Ch 2, p 43 et seq).

[15] *Stoke-on-Trent City Council v B & Q* Case C-169/91 [1993] 1 All ER 481, ECJ and only after great confusion; see R Rawlings (1993) 20 Journal of Law and Society 309.

[16] NB the limits seen by Laws J in *R v MAFF, ex p First City Trading* [1997] 1 CMLR 250.

principles of eg judicial review (see below).[17] The former refers to a felt compulsion to develop domestic provisions so that there is no inconsistency between an area of domestic and EC law.[18] There is clearly a close association between the developments identified under this heading and that contained in 2. above under a 'common law of Europe'.

The next steps

The focus of this last heading allows us to ask – is there something novel arising; something which is not already a self contained system of law but something which has made our law significantly different? It may relate to areas of law or to principles of law of widespread applicability. We cannot say that European public law has a separate existence in its own jurisdictional confines applied in its own courts. It is much more amorphous than that and its progress more like osmosis. But in an English context, the European influence has been staggering and what is happening is that our principles of common law and our process of judicial reasoning are changing, and have changed, dramatically. This latter point was made many years ago by Lord Denning when he demonstrated how English law was to be interpreted in the light of EC provisions so that overriding effect was to be given to those provisions.[19] It has continued in a multi-dimensional manner since then and has included not only the impact of Directives on domestic provisions[20] but also the range of materials that are referred to when domestic courts interpret EC provisions to achieve 'convergent

---

[17]   P Craig *Administrative Law* (1999, 4th ed) pp 318–19.

[18]   See eg: *M v Home Office* [1993] 3 All ER 537, HL and Case C-213/89 *Factortame Ltd v Secretary of State (No 2)* [1991] 1 All ER 70 and the question of interim relief against an officer of the Crown by way of injunction; see also *Woolwich Equitable Building Society v IRC (No 2)* [1992] 3 All ER 737 at 764. An interesting variation on this theme concerns cases of 'reverse discrimination' where a case containing, perhaps completely fortuitously, an EC element is decided differently to a case raising almost identical but purely domestic aspects, leaving a real sense of injustice over differential treatment: see Case C-370/90 *R v IAT and Singh, ex p Secretary of State for the Home Department* [1992] ECR I-4265 and N Nic Shuibhne in P Beaumont et al eds *Convergence and Divergence in European Public Law* (2002) ch 10.

[19]   Case 129/79 *McCarthys v Smith* [1979] 3 All ER 325: the Treaty of Rome is not just an 'aid to the construction of statutes' 'it is an overriding force'.

[20]   *Litster v Forth Dry Dock and Engineering Co Ltd* [1989] 1 All ER 1134 (Ch 4, p 190 et seq).

construction'.[21] This process is not always smooth as a judgment of Lord Hoffman illustrates where he refused to interpret a domestic provision in a manner which gave full effect to EC requirements in the Equal Treatment Directive because such an interpretation would impose obligations on individuals horizontally.[22]

The next step involves identifying whether similar developments are taking place in the legal systems of other Member States. This includes discovering whether principles of law are entering into domestic systems via the EU and ECHR. They are more likely to enter via these systems which have themselves absorbed principles of domestic law such as proportionality, legitimate expectation and which subsequently develop such principles than they are to enter through the direct influence of other national systems. This latter would face enormous barriers eg, national public law reflecting different historical, political and cultural traditions tied up in doctrinal differences and procedural eccentricities and aberrations.

My point is that a community sharing law and a legal system is going to be far more readily influenced by such law in its own outlook and substance than would individual legal systems where, for instance, there are significant differences about the status of constitutions and the role of a constitutional court.Think of the difference between the German and French and our own traditions here (see Chapter 2), the role of academic lawyers and political theorists in shaping the doctrine of what is the state and what does it stand for or signify.[23]

The civil traditions on the continent have seen the systematising of law and doctrine and the establishment of the 'rights' of individuals in an abstract formulation. In the common law tradition there has been a resistance to intellectualising the issue: pragmatic incrementalism and a concentration on procedures which seek to get power wielders to justify their action rather than making grand declarations of civil right are the legacies of that tradition. Just over a year ago, I took part in a Council of Europe mission in Trieste which sought to provide guidance on good practice in controlling executive

---

21   *Three Rivers District Council v Bank Of England (No 2)* [1996] 2 All ER 363; and *Pickstone v Freemans plc* [1988] 2 All ER 803, HL. See Sedley LJ in *R v Durham County Council, ex p Huddleston* [2000] 1 WLR 1484.

22   *R v Secretary of State for Employment, ex p Seymour-Smith* [1997] 2 All ER 273, HL at 279 and cf the *Marleasing* line of cases on consistent interpretation and the limits of that doctrine (Ch 4, p 191 et seq).

23   K Dyson *The State Tradition in Western Europe* (1980).

power by Parliamentary, judicial and ombudsman techniques to Balkan and south-eastern European countries. They all seemed to possess very advanced systems or had a subtle appreciation of advanced systems of public law, built I would guess on French (and possibly other European experience.) To them the common law systems seemed eccentric and antediluvian.

The eccentricity covers various points:
1. In that part of public law known as administrative law, for instance, the focus in England and Northern Ireland on control of inferior jurisdictions and procedural control. This makes it the most confined 'system' of administrative law in the advanced world, though to leave the appraisal at that point would be misleading (below).
2. In France, the development of public law was as much about articulating the concept of public service as it was about accountability of power. Administrative efficiency and solidarity were uppermost in the design of *droit administratif.*
3. In Germany, post-second world war, a concentration on substantive rights and control of subjective discretion via principles of review that would cause unqualified reaction from the executive in the UK as an unjustified interference with the merits of public decision-making. Individual security and protection were paramount and such factors required a full substantive review.
4. The procedural differences between these forms of public law are enormous.

Post-1972, and indeed after some considerable delay, proportionality has entered our discourse in English and Northern Irish law; German law is becoming more relaxed about procedural matters although it has experienced difficulties in relation to the overriding importance of EC procedural requirements.[24] There has been a heightened awareness of human rights in both France and the UK. In Germany, the source of human rights would be the constitution rather than the ECHR which is an ordinary law in Germany. In France and the UK, the ECHR has been highly influential but both have relied upon internal resources, in the English case on a fairly dramatic resort to principles of common law. This has prompted predictable responses from unsurprising sources.[25] I cannot speak with authority on

[24] *Land Rheinland-Pfalz* Case C–24/95 [1997] ECR I-1591.
[25] Griffith (2001) LQR 42 and Sedley (2001) LQR 68 in reply. This concerned Sedley's Hamlyn Lectures: *Freedom, Law and Justice* (1999).

France but in England, I have no doubt that that catalysing influence of Europe is responsible for this change. Change of this nature would have to be mediated via an international order and mediation; whereas change of specific legal provisions may be influenced by comparative approaches.[26]

I think these points, and especially in relation to the UK are well illustrated by several powerful illustrations:

1. The HRA 1998 and patriation of human rights. The scheme of the Act preserves Parliamentary sovereignty but allows judicial review of devolved legislation in Scottish and Northern Irish courts. What is left for the common law? The answer is found in the HRA 1998, s 11 which safeguards a person's existing human rights – 'any right or freedom conferred on him by or under any law having effect in any part of the UK' – including common law. The implications for this and for the courts' development of a human rights jurisprudence are profound.

2. The legal community's perception that it is a part of a wider legal order. Not only that it is a part of a wider legal community, but that a preparedness has arisen to absorb principles of international law as principles of domestic law or as principles to help shape domestic law. The striking feature here is the *Pinochet* judgment, especially *No 1.* where Lord Steyn in particular interpreted norms of national law as affected by norms of international law in so far as they affected former heads of state and acts of torture.[27] Even in the retraction of the *Pinochet (No 3)* decision after the first proceedings and their decision were ruled void, a former Head of State could still be liable for acts against humanity committed *after* the relevant Convention was ratified and for acts which were a crime in the UK at the time they were committed.[28] The latter judgment still represents an about turn which has been notable for twenty-five years or so and goes far more widely than use of treaties or international law to interpret the common law. Until comparatively recently, this in fact amounted to little more than

---

[26] See *Kleinwort Benson Ltd v Lincoln City Council* [1998] 4 All ER 513, HL and Lord Goff's reliance on continental and commonwealth precedents to decide an issue of unjust enrichment.

[27] *R v Bow Street Metropolitan Stipendiary Magistrate ,ex p Pinochet Ugarte* [1998] 4 All ER 897, HL. For reservations, see Slynn at 913d and 915c–e. G Robertson *Crimes Against Humanity* (2002, 2nd ed).

[28] *R v Bow Street Metropolitan Stipendiary Magistrate ,ex p Pinochet Ugarte* [1999] 2 All ER 97, HL.

the common law filling holes left in international space. It did not involve a re-assessment of domestic law under international standards.[29]

We need to develop this latter point. English law and lawyers, and I would guess Irish, for centuries took delight in their isolation and isolationism. 'English law becomes more insular, and English lawyers become more and more utterly ignorant of any law but their own' after the reign of Edward I said Maitland and long before the final rejection of Roman law and Rome. Dualism – the realms of international and domestic law inhabit different spheres – helped maintain that legal isolation and helped also to frame (or accompany and complement) doctrines of sovereignty and Parliamentary supremacy which still notionally hold sway in the UK. This was wrapped up in the notion of the political constitution and not a legal constitution which some lawyers and most politicians see as the ultimate and inescapable condition of life.[30]

Sovereignty, a balanced constitution, and the all embracing use of the Crown for every feature of government helped produce that belief in:

A constitution so blessed that it seemed to be,
Not one but all mankind's epitome. (Apologies to Dryden)

I have to admit that I have attended lectures by eminent French lawyers on Europe's contribution to French public law only for the theme to transmute into France's impact on European law! I will now concentrate on some of the changes that have helped make European public law a topic worthy of examination in England – and one could add Northern Ireland. I have to leave to others the impact of European public law on their own jurisdictions.

European public law and change

1. A change in our jurisprudence

The master theory of recognition of legal validity has been Professor Hart's Rule of Recognition.[31] A legal system must have a master rule which allows

---

29 The starting point in the modern era is Lord Diplock's judgment in Case 12/81 *Garland v British Rail Engineering Ltd* [1982] 2 All ER 402 although that case was confined to statutory interpretation.

30 J A G Griffith 'The Political Constitution' (1979) Mod LR 1.

31 H L A Hart *The Concept of Law* (1961).

officials to identify what is legally valid. The attack on this theory by amongst others, Ronald Dworkin, has been a focal point of jurisprudential discussion for the last thirty years.[32] In Chapter 10 of his acclaimed work, Professor Hart addresses the question of international law – there is an open acknowledgment that there is no rule of recognition in international law and so the analysis of the previous nine chapters, of what is essentially a municipal legal system, has limited relevance for that sphere. This argues Hart is not fatal to the existence of an international legal order. The absence of a rule of recognition in this legal order is not fatal because arrangements are far more truly pluralistic and multi-faceted at the international level. One may question whether the absence of a rule of recognition at the municipal level, as Hart describes it, *is* fatal to the existence of law at that level. Many have criticised the view of sovereignty implicated by Hart's theory of law arguing that we have moved into a world where sovereignty is no longer a central feature of a domestic system, let alone in international relations.[33] Is it more accurate to suggest that our Rule of Recognition has changed, or more accurately perhaps its non-existence is becoming more apparent not only in the international sphere but also in the domestic sphere? Both Lord Woolf and Sir John Laws have questioned whether Parliamentary sovereignty exists in its pristine form and the former has asked whether it would be unassailable if put to particular uses – like for instance, limiting the scope of judicial review.[34] Lord Woolf has repeatedly urged caution against an overreaction by British Ministers to events in New York in September 2001. What is clear is that whether it is accurate to describe a master rule in such terms, it has to accommodate at the domestic level a much wider range of internationally inspired influences than Hart ever perceived. It must accommodate a developing form of 'standard openness' in relation to such influences. This 'standard openness' or 'openness of standards' allows outside influences to be more widely and more pervasively felt.

2. A change in our legal reasoning

We have known since the early 1980s that a more purposive form of reasoning would be incorporated in legal reasoning where interpretation

---

[32] R Dworkin *Taking Rights Seriously* (1977) and *Law's Empire* (1986).

[33] N McCormick (1993) Mod LR 1 and *Questioning Sovereignty* (1999) OUP. See P Allott *Eunomia: A New Order for a New World* (1990).

[34] Lord Woolf (1995) Public Law 57 and Sir J Laws (1995) Public Law 72 and (1996) Public Law 622.

of legal measures incorporating EC provisions was concerned. We have noted prior domestic provisions and sex equality and Lord Hoffman's reaction above. This has developed. In the case of *R v Durham City Council, ex p Huddleston*[35] the Court of Appeal went to (what some may describe as) extraordinary lengths to apply indirectly as between individuals a Directive that had not been implemented. The applicant (claimant) argued they were being penalised by horizontally directly effective provisions – the very thing Lord Hoffman in *Seymour-Smith* claimed could not be achieved. Sedley LJ believed that the unimplemented Directive in question was directly effective upon the public authority and thereby imposed duties that a public authority had to follow in the exercise of its power. Any consequences on individuals were purely coincidental and not directly effected.[36] The decision, reversing a lower judgment, would have been unthinkable only a few years ago and displays a far more sophisticated grasp of the interplay between EC and domestic law. In the *Dan TV* case there was a reading of a Directive concerning transmission of, as it happened, football matches involving national teams in a manner which protected the rights of Danish nationals to view the match according to criteria drawn up by Danish authorities, even though the decision in this case was made by the UK Independent Television Commission. This outcome did best justice to a sort of equality of viewing right rather than market determined rights – the latter of which the Court of Appeal had followed in its interpretation of the Directive.[37]

3. Principles of judicial review

This is perhaps the most dramatic development but possibly not the most significant. To the standard heads of review adumbrated by Lord Diplock one can now add proportionality and *ex p Daly* and *Alconbury* and particularly the judgments of Lords Steyn and Slynn respectively;[38] and

---

[35] [2000] 1 WLR 1484.

[36] And see *R v Human Embryology and Fertilisation Authority, ex p Blood* [1997] 2 All ER 687, CA.

[37] *R v Independent Television Commission, ex p TV Danmark 1 Ltd* [2001] UKHL 42, [2001] 1 WLR 1604.

[38] *R v Secretary of State for the Home Department, ex p Daly* [2001] UKHL 26, [2001] 3 All ER 433; *Alconbury etc* [2001] UKHL 23, [2001] 2 All ER 929. See the judgment of Laws LJ in *Gough v Chief Constable of the Derbyshire Constabulary* [2001] EWHC Admin 554, [2001] 4 All ER 289 at paras 62–81 and the Court of Appeal [2002] 2 All ER 985.

substantive legitimate expectation and the judgment of the Court of Appeal in *R v North and East Devon Health Authority, ex p Coughlan.*[39] These cases, and others, show a far more subtle and supple approach to judicial review which subjects a decision to a more probing review in the interests of justice, leaving the merits to those with political responsibility or those who are responsible to politicians.

4. Human rights and a growing maturity and sophistication in judicial review[40]

The growing intensity of review commensurate with the importance of the subject matter is now a widely practised and accepted feature of judicial review – to such an extent that it is now claimed constitutional review is taking place in the UK.[41] In the *Daly* decision, Lord Steyn pointed out in his important judgment that the more exacting scrutiny of decisions affecting human rights under the *Wednesbury* formulation may still not give sufficient protection to human rights.[42] Such heightened reviews will be subject of course to critical political comment concerning the overstepping of the boundaries between the judiciary and the executive and which in civil jurisdictions will be seen as an abuse of the separation of powers. I am not sure that what the British courts have done is any more dramatic than what has happened in France or Germany; there, the doctrine of separation of powers has not interfered with striking developments in judicial protection of the individual.

5. English courts on openness

I think that there have been striking developments in relation to advancing openness and the role of the courts. The story begins in *Conway v*

---

39   [2000] 3 All ER 850, CA. See *R v Secretary of State for Education etc, ex p Begbie* [2000] 1 WLR 1115, CA.

40   See the celebrated dicta of Sedley J in *R v Secretary of State for the Home Department, ex p McQuillan* [1995] 4 All ER 400 at 422 h–j.

41   Cases cited in *R v Secretary of State for the Home Department, ex p Daly* [2001] UKHL 26, [2001] 3 All ER 433 and see Chs 4 and 8 above.

42   He specifically cited the case of *R v Ministry of Defence, ex p Smith* [1996] 1 All ER 257 where the Court of Appeal refused to rule the MoD policy proscribing homosexuals in the armed forces and the CHR decision in *Lustig-Prean v UK* (1999) 29 EHRR 548 which found against the UK government.

Rimmer[43] and the famous decision on government immunity (or Crown privilege as it was called) from disclosure orders in litigation but a major development came with *Johnston v Chief Constable of the RUC*.[44] My own belief is that this accompanies the enhanced protection of human rights which has been evident for some time. It is not a direct response to European influence although *Johnston* concerned Community law; there has generally not been much of an influence on such matters in Community law (see Chapter 2). If we look at the Convention, this concentrates on freedom of speech and communication of information which have been influential,[45] but the ECJ has let some valuable opportunities slip by in dealing with litigation concerning rights of access to documents.[46] French law has been important because of a presumption of giving reasons; a feature which was late of development in the UK.[47] The question which arises is whether access to information and openness are human rights and whether they will be seen as such by UK courts, and if so, what limits they will place on such a right? While much of the inspiration may be enriched by a human rights culture – and to repeat I have doubts whether this would have occurred without a European influence – there is also a considerable international common law influence. The domestic catalogue is striking: see *Turkington*[48] and an extension of the concept of public meetings; *Reynolds*[49] and freedom of speech; English cases on public inquiries into Harold Shipman's murders and coroners' inquests;[50] and the influence of Convention case law and even the recent *R v Shayler* and the acceptance of 'necessity' by the Court of Appeal as a possible defence to an unauthorised disclosure under the Official Secrets Act 1989, s 1.[51] Convention case law includes the ground-breaking decision in the CHR

---

43   [1968] AC 910.

44   Case 222/84 [1986] 3 All ER 135, ECJ. Certificates signed by the Secretary of State barring further judicial proceedings on the grounds of national security amounted to a denial of the right to judicial protection of the plaintiff's rights to equal treatment under EC law; see also *Tinnelly and McElduff v UK* (1998) 27 EHRR 249.

45   *A-G v Guardian Newpapers (No 2)* [1988] 3 All ER 545.

46   Most notably in *Netherlands v Council* (see Ch 6, p 268 et seq). The CFI has brought forward some interesting advances. See P Birkinshaw *Freedom of Information* (2001, 3rd ed) and I Harden (2001) EPL 165 and Ch 6.

47   Now contained in the Freedom of Information Act 2000 in a circuitous fashion.

48   *McCartan Turkington Breen v Times Newspapers* [2000] 4 All ER 913, HL.

49   *Reynolds v Times Newspapers* [1999] 4 All ER 609, HL.

50   *R v Secretary of State for Health, ex p Wagstaff* [2001] 1 WLR 292. See however, Ch 9, p 414 et seq where the courts have subsequently qualified such an approach.

51   Court of Appeal Criminal Division [2001] 1 WLR 2206. This 'vexed and difficult' point was not taken up in the House of Lords (Ch 9, p 417 et seq).

concerning the inquiry into deaths arising from the struggle against terrorism and the right to life under Article 2 ECHR (the right to life entailed a right to proper investigation into the death).[52] The Court of Appeal has emphasised the 'pragmatic' nature of the CHR's decisions in these cases and reversed the High Court which held that such inquiries must be in public and must allow the relatives a right to participate in the inquiry. Any inquiry and any investigation were 'adjectival' to the substantive right in Article 2 and procedures were not fixed in rigid rules but were subject to 'pragmatic flexibility' in interpretation depending upon the particular facts. Democratic accountability, said Lord Woolf, did not necessarily require a public inquiry.[53]

Are the courts outdoing themselves – just as in cases of competition between different levels of legislature in a federal or devolved system? It is interesting to note how the UK Parliament and the Scottish Parliament produced Freedom of Information Acts which differed considerably in their contents leading to speculation of conflict emerging between disparities caused by a more liberal access regime north of the border. Like a pluralism of legislatures, a pluralism of courts means a pluralism of ideas.

6. The area of government liability

This might appear somewhat recondite an area, even more so than the previous areas and one particularly for the lawyers. It has been a subject that has attracted more critical attention from lawyers than any other in the discussion of European public law (Chapter 10).[54] The last twenty years have seen attempts to limit the scope of governmental liability by making it difficult to succeed in actions against public authorities in the UK. In

---

[52] *Jordan v UK* (2001) Times, 18 May, unreported.
[53] *R (Amin) v Secretary of State for the Home Department* [2002] EWCA Civ 390, [2002] 4 All ER 336, CA. Lord Woolf emphasised that the parents of the murdered man were invited to participate in an internal inquiry but declined, the Prison Department admitted serious fault on their part, there was an internal inquiry by the Prison Department, a police investigation, an investigation by the Commission for Racial Equality, and a conviction for murder leaving no doubt where the responsibility lay. No further information to establish civil liability was required. However, L Blom Cooper points out that the mental health of the murderer was not a subject of investigation, nor the subject of male prisoners and mental health generally: (2002) Public Law 391.
[54] J Beatson and T Tridimas *New Directions in European Public Law* (1998); M Andenas *English Public Law and the Common Law of Europe* (1998).

France, illegality is a ground of liability, although the measure of damages is very constrained and damage has to be proved. In England, illegality *per se* is not actionable. There has to be an additional breach of duty owed in private law to an individual. What was notable in England was that after some ground rules on liability were established in the 1970s in a case concerning the failure to exercise discretionary powers,[55] the courts displayed a growing reluctance to allow actions to succeed against public authorities on the grounds that there were other remedies available which often provided far less in the form of compensation, if any at all;[56] other cases decided it was wrong as a matter of policy for actions in negligence to succeed against various parties: the police in the exercise of powers of criminal investigation;[57] social workers in their powers to take children into care;[58] and generally a reluctance to establish liability where what was asserted was the breach of a power rather than a breach of a duty.[59] Then there arose a series of cases from the ECJ where liability for damages was established where first of all a Member State failed to implement a Directive within time and the Directive was not directly effective.[60]

There followed the equally momentous decision in *Factortame (No 3)* where the ECJ ruled that a 'sufficiently serious' breach of Community Law by a Member State which caused damage to an individual and where the provision in question conferred rights on individuals was actionable for damages at the suit of that individual.[61] The EU was opening the way to liability where the English courts, and I assume Northern Irish courts, were restricting opportunities.

In the decision in *Osman v UK*, the CHR held that the UK was in breach of Article 6 ECHR when the English courts struck out an action for disclosing no cause of action when a police authority was sued for negligence in the manner in which police officers had exercised their powers of investigation.[62] Such an action interfered with public policy because if

---

55   *Anns v Merton London Borough Council* [1978] AC 728.
56   Where a remedy is provided in the statute the courts invariably interpret this to exclude liability under common law for breach of statutory duty.
57   *Hill v Chief Constable of West Yorkshire* [1988] 2 All ER 238.
58   *X v Bedfordshire County Council* [1995] 3 All ER 353, HL.
59   *Stovin v Wise* [1996] 3 All ER 801.
60   Case C-6, 9/90 *Francovich* [1991] ECR I–5357.
61   Case C-48/93 [1996] ECR I-1029, ECJ.
62   *Osman v UK* [1998] 29 EHRR 245 and *Z v UK* [2001] 2 FCR 246. See also *TP and KM v UK* [2001] 2 FCR 289.

successful, it would have an inhibiting and potentially deleterious effect on police discretion. This approach, the CHR ruled, interfered with a right to a fair trial under Article 6. The reaction from the House of Lords in subsequent litigation was that the claimant had not been denied a fair trial: the action was not allowed to proceed because it was not 'fair, just and reasonable' to an authority to allow it to be sued for its police investigation or social services' responsibilities and for difficult questions of judgment it had to make. Liability would inhibit the proper exercise of its duties and powers.[63] The question of *liability* in law *had* been given a full and proper hearing. This judgment of Lord Browne-Wilkinson had an impact on the CHR and is one of the clearest cases I know where such an influence has been given to the CHR by an English court.[64] The end result of the mutual interrelationship has been a liberalising of opportunity for relief by way of claims for negligence (see Chapter 10).[65]

One further point of interest in relation to liability for damages involves the power of a court under the HRA 1998 to award damages for breaches of Convention rights and in the exercise of which power, and any amount, they must have regard to the decisions of the CHR.

7. The question of interim relief and injunctions

Our substantive law, it has often been remarked, is to be found in the interstices of procedure. This is amply demonstrated by the litigation in *Factortame* which was addressed above (see Chapter 8) and where one of the questions involved the availability of an interim injunction against an officer of the Crown – previous authority was overwhelmingly, though not absolutely, against this form of relief being issued against an officer of the Crown. After initial reluctance, the Law Lords ruled that such relief had to be given if necessary to comply with Community law. As Lord Bridge

---

[63] *Barrett v London Borough of Enfield* [1999] 3 All ER 193, HL.

[64] *Z v UK* above. See Lord Phillips in *R (on the application of SB Saadi) v Secretary of State for the Home Department* [2001] EWCA 1512, [2001] 4 All ER 961, CA.

[65] In *TP and KM v UK* [2001] 2 FCR 289, the ECtHR ruled that there was a breach of Art 8 ECHR even though on the facts a breach of Art 6 had not been established. In *Z*, a breach of Art 3 was established by the CHR although a breach of Art 6 was not. Where there was a breach of Art 3 which remained unremedied, there could be a further breach of Art 13. The latter has not been incorporated; Art 3 prohibiting torture and degrading treatment has been: see R Carnwarth (2001) Public Law 475.

explained, when the penny finally dropped, so much was implicated by the European Community Act 1972 and the jurisprudence of the ECJ.[66] The well-known 'spill-over' of the holding of the case to a purely domestic situation is well known, but nevertheless striking.[67]

It would take a matter of procedure to fire antagonism between British judges in our higher courts – although behind procedure there is inevitably an issue of susbstance. The point of law involved the question of which law should govern the award of interim measures against a Secretary of State who had issued regulations made under an allegedly unlawful EC Directive. The application of EC law was more favourable to the government case than domestic law. The matter was eventually ruled moot as the Americans say and so no reference to the ECJ was necessary, but it highlights in a very dramatic way the importance of the question of which law governs in a matter on which the Community has an interest.[68]

8. Increasing harmonisation or approximation in essential areas

Competition, data protection, environmental protection and access to environmental information, procedures for public procurement and so on have all been subject to detailed implementation to increase harmonisation or approximisation of domestic provisions. Media regulation is a very sensitive question given language and cultural differences. What may be required is more of an approximisation and not a uniform application and standardisation. The impact of the European Monetary Union (EMU) on constitutional fundamentals hardly needs any appraisal save to note that much of our budgetary materials are drawn up to be consistent with the EMU requirements. The impact of the EMU on our domestic budgetary programmes is already being keenly felt and the insulation of monetary policy from overt political pressure was one of the first steps taken by the incoming government in 1997 (see Chaper 14).

Bringing all these cases together, I will attempt to assess where we are in terms of the existence of European public law. It is not a distinct body of law applied in a distinct body of courts or jurisdiction. It is a body of

---

66 Case C-213/89 *Factortame (No 2)* [1991] 1 All ER 70 at 107–08 per Lord Bridge.
67 *M v Home Office* [1993] 3 All ER 537, HL. G Anthony (1998) European Public Law 253.
68 *R v Secretary of State for Health, ex p Imperial Tobacco Co Ltd* [2000] 1 All ER 572, CA; on appeal [2001] 1 All ER 850, HL.

evolving principles, shaped by a variety of jurisdictions and their mutual intercourse. It embraces many systems of law and is applied in many legal systems. It is, if you like, becoming a sort of axiology although I would be wary of any scientific association. I do not think values are scientifically deductible concepts. In one form, European public law represents a body of legal, ethical and moral precepts shaped in the matrix of Western legal thought. European public law is the application of legal principles to legal problems within Member States and within the EU and ECHR. It is part of that fabric which lawyers and judges must draw on but which is not present in any single code or set of codes. But the application of these precepts cannot be ignored; to do so is to fail to understand underlying and central developments in English, British and Northern Irish law and Irish law and other systems as well. To ignore it is not to know the basis on which law is contemporaneously applied and developed. It is quite simply to be a bad lawyer or to possess an inadequate basis on which to identify law. In some areas, the shape is more definite: the areas that are subject to approximation illustrated in the paragraph above are examples. European public law also, I believe, largely accounts for the period which has seen the richest development in our public law, ie post-1980. The great developments from the 1960s rightly celebrated by Lord Diplock in the famous *GCHQ* case[69] were in fact nothing more than the development of domestic principles of judicial review long ago known but for so long disregarded. European public law represents something qualitatively and quantitatively different from anything we or others have experienced before.

When I say 'quantitatively' I am referring to the size and momentum of the development but not something which is easily counted. It represents the outcome of a pooling of legal traditions and thought which because of their own richness and depth makes this a constantly developing process. Its elasticity is very much at home in a common law framework. The next stage will see demands for a codification of principles of European public law [70] and perhaps for a European constitution – our respective constitutions have certainly experienced profound and irreversible

---

[69]   *Minister for the Civil Service v Council of Civil Service Unions* [1984] 3 All ER 935, HL.

[70]   See the contributions by Schwarze, Chiti, Jowell and Birkinshaw etc in J Schwarze *Administrative Law under European Influence* (1996). Chiti has argued that there are dangers in that the Charter of Fundamental Rights agreed at Nice may have a restrictive influence on the development of a human rights jurisprudence by national courts and by the ECJ.

development since the birth of the Community (see Chapter 14).[71] I have no hesitation in harnessing in ill-placed enthusiasm which such calls could all too easily become but there may be a place for a limited codification. It might stiffen the sinews, summon up the blood and sharpen the mind if there proved to be a judicial retreat from protection of individual liberties which some have witnessed in recent decisions of the House of Lords and Court of Appeal.[72] A limited expression of principles would not allow a process of ossification to thwart the development I have spoken of. The common law needs to be open; but it also needs encouragement from time to time.

In short, because European public law is not easily cut, dried and displayed, that does not mean it so vague as to be practically meaningless. 'But I would regard these [arguments] as tainted by the perennial fallacy that because something cannot be cut and dried or nicely weighed or measured therefore it does not exist' said Lord Reid in a seminal decision on fair procedure in the 1960s.[73] I would apply the same note of caution against those who argue that European public law does not exist.

The problems

I do happen to think that this is all very exciting. But it is not all a one-way ticket to paradise. Not all legal traditions welcome flexibility in legal development. And certainly most non-lawyers do not. If we are not fixated on a rigid separation of powers, we, in particular our politicians, certainly expect a division of labour in matters of government. European public law will be seen as an attempt to subvert time honoured divisions to make the judge a legislator and administrator; to make the law and to decide on the merits of decisions. It may well become associated with incursions into executive decision-making. Different traditions have different approaches to these problems.

---

[71] J Schwarze ed *The Birth of a European Constitutional Order* (2000).

[72] See *Secretary of State v Rehman* [2001] UKHL 47, [2002] 1 All ER 122 and *R (on the application of SB Saadi) v Secretary of State for the Home Department* [2001] EWCA Civ 1512, [2001] 4 All ER 961, CA; affd [2002] UKHL 41, [2002] 4 All ER 785.

[73] *Ridge v Baldwin* [1964] AC 40.

Particular problems include:

1. A growing centrality of law and legal process in matters of government. The complaint of being administered by judges and the delay, expense and uncertainty of increasing juridification. Conversely, we may be over heavily judged by administrators where there is a sudden shift when national security requires an adjustment or where for instance it is felt that a court has gone too far – and it is interesting how the role of the ECJ has been restricted post-Amsterdam and Nice;[74]
2. A concentration on courts and subjection of administrative processes to over legalisation and strict compliance with Article 6 ECHR may freeze up attempts to create processes of informal justice which seek to minimise reliance on formal systems of justice. These latter tend to be expensive and remote from ordinary citizens. In other words we should use tribunals, ombudsmen and internal processes and not ignore them (Chapter 11). European traditions on internal review are highly bureaucratic and legalistic and subject to specialised administrative courts: *justice retenue* and *justice déléguée*.

My final point concerns the use of law as a surrogate political system; many traditions in Europe – and in the EC and the ECHR – are not as open in terms of allowing access to courts by interest groups as English law. English law – common law generally as witness American and Indian models in particular – is more relaxed on the question of locus standi and English law has a long tradition in terms of the use of courts to achieve collective or political objectives. One purchases wholesale. An interesting EU example came with the *WWF* litigation on access to documents where a pressure group in the form of a trust was allowed to bring complaint to the CFI about an alleged breach of the Commission Decision on access.[75] *WWF* had applied under the Decision and had been refused. Decisions on standing under Article 230 [173] EC have been strictly applied in the case of regulations and decisions addressed to others, a tradition which continues (see Chapters 3, p 106 and 11, p 479).

---

[74] There seemed no role for the ECJ when decisions were taken to suspend membership of the Union or Community for breaches of the ECHR by Member States. Post-Nice, there is a role for the Court to ensure that the procedure is followed correctly.

[75] Case T–105/95 *WWF v Commission* [1997] ECR II-313.

Conclusion

The developments I have spoken of are dramatic and long-lasting. They have changed the way in which British lawyers are operating and thinking – and not just those at the cutting edge of public law development. Although I have concentrated on Europe, I have no doubt that mutual influence and cross-fertilisation are part of a global development and it is a part of a redefinition of the Rule of Law. This is a rule of law that is not fixed in Dicey's privatisation of the constitution – our private rights are the source of the constitution – but one which attempts to address more fully the exercise of power on behalf of, or at the sufferance of, the public interest under appropriate conditions of fairness, rationality and openness. In the terms in which I have discussed it, I have no doubt that European public law exists.

Chapter 14

Future considerations

In this concluding chapter, I will take the opportunity to speculate on future developments and their impact on our European public law. The focus will be on that impact within a British context, although I will wish to make some observations about wider ranging factors. We in the UK are still part of a Commonwealth of nations, most of which have inherited features of the common law but those nations have been highly influential, some more than others, in giving ideas on the common law's development to the English. Discussion of Australian, New Zealand, Canadian and Indian case law is common in English judgments.[1] Recently in South Africa, freedom of information laws have been adopted which go far further than UK laws in imposing duties on private sector bodies to disclose information to the public.[2] The 1996 constitution of South Africa includes incorporation of the widest ranging economic, social and political rights. It stands in complete contrast to the UK which has steadfastly refused to incorporate into domestic law provisions of the Social Charter of the Council of Europe and the UN Covenant on Economic, Social and Cultural Rights. These influences may have a greater impact on our domestic law and our domestic law may, under European influence, have more influence in these other jurisdictions. There are clear links between English and US common law, and the federal administrative law of the latter was influential in our law in

---

1   *Derbyshire County Council v Times Newspapers Ltd* [1993] 1 All ER 1011, HL; *Reynolds v Times Newspapers Ltd* [1999] 4 All ER 609, HL. See: D Dyzenhaus, M Hunt and M Taggart 'The Principles of Legality in Administrative Law: Internationalism and Constitutionalism' (2001) Oxford University Commonwealth LJ 5.

2   I Currie and J Klaaren *The Promotion of Access to Information Act Commentary* (2002).

the 1960s and 1970s – it may be so again and the influence of regulatory law is still being felt. The influence of English legal thought may be more pronounced in the US academy than in US courtrooms or agencies. The English experience is a part of the 'Western' heritage being an amalgam of Christian tradition and doctrine, Roman law and the enlightenment although along with the US, the Roman law influence was not significant as a systemic force in England. In spite of the developments catalogued in this book, that absence still sets us apart from our European neighbours and together with our linguistic affiliation, makes our affinity with the US stronger than that of any European partner.

The themes this chapter will concentrate upon will be: economic and monetary union; the establishment of a European written constitution and the impact of such a development upon domestic constitutional arrangements; the case for codifying European administrative law; and finally, some comments on the theme touched upon above, the impact of European public law beyond Europe. I will conclude with an appraisal of future directions.

Every chapter in this book has raised questions about the development of our constitutional and administrative law in a European context. This is not the place to repeat the discussion of such matters as qualified majority voting, subsidiarity, openness and transparency, the role of national Parliaments in scrutinising EU laws and policies, the protection of human rights and the emerging agenda of judicial review and liability of public bodies as influenced by European legal concepts. These and other themes inform the contents of this book. It is the place, however, to make some wider comments about future developments and their implications.

Economic and Monetary Union (EMU)[3]

Perhaps no other issue has been cast in terms of its capacity to win or lose national elections as the EMU. The EMU was introduced in three stages, the first in 1990, the second introducing the transitional European Monetary Institute in 1994 and the last stage on 1 January 1999. The basic idea behind the EMU is the maintenance of price stability and economic

---

[3]   P Beaumont and N Walker eds *The Legal Framework of the Single European Currency* (1999); F Snyder in P Craig and G de Burca eds *The Evolution of EU Law* (1999) ch 12.

growth. Through these objectives, it is hoped that greater cohesion will be introduced in economic and monetary policy and in economic performance among Member States. National governments will cede their ultimate control over national monetary policy and this will be the responsibility of an independent European Central Bank (replacing the European Monetary Institute) together with a European System of Central Banks.[4] This centralising policy was introduced, paradoxically some believe, in the same Treaty that introduced subsidiarity. Economic integration will rely upon existing institutions. The European Central Bank has power to make regulations and take decisions and may enforce obligations under these by fines and periodic penalty payments, subject to conditions. It is subject to judicial review within the provisions of Article 234 EC. It may also issue opinions and give recommendations. Monetary policy will be developed according to criteria set out in the Maastricht Treaty (Article 105 EC), the statute of the European Central Bank and the Stability and Growth pact agreed by the European Council,[5] and individual convergence pacts and stability programmes agreed between the Commission and individual Member States.

The third, and crucial, stage of monetary union will involve an irrevocable fixing of exchange rates for Member States currencies and the adoption of a single currency for participating members at those rates together with full responsibility by the ECB and ESCB for monetary policy and intervention by the latter in third country currencies. A single currency – the Euro – was introduced for those countries that are members of Monetary Union on 1 January 2002 and smooth transition was effected within two months. Members of the EMU must also guarantee the independence of their national central banks. Broad guidelines on economic policy within the EMU will be agreed by qualified majority voting in the Economic and Finance Council (ECOFIN) consisting of the finance ministers of Member States. Some decisions will already have been agreed and discussed informally by the Euro-X committee of Euro area finance ministers.[6] In the

---

[4]   The ECB and ESCB will be independent of all other bodies: Article 108 EC and Article 7 ECB Statute. They shall not take instructions from Member States, Community institutions or any other body. The ESCB is composed of the ECB and the national central banks of Member States whether participating in the single currency or not. See C Ziliodi and M Selmayr *The Law of the European Central Bank* (2001); C Goodhart 37 *Government and Opposition* (2000) p 190. See F Amtenbrink *The Democratic Accountability of Central Banks* (1999).

[5]   Providing guidance on interpretation of legal provisions.

[6]   See R Ware *EMU: the constitutional implications* Research Paper 98/78 House of Commons Library.

ECB, each participating Member State will be represented on the Governing Council by the governor of its national central bank. The President of the Council of Ministers and a member of the Commission may participate in meetings of the Council, but may not vote. Decisions will be by straightforward majority. An executive board comprises a President, a Vice President and four other members. Executive board members are members of the Governing Council. The European System of Central Banks (note 4) is to support an open market economy and free competition 'favouring an efficient allocation of resources.' The European System of Central Banks is governed by the Governing Council and Executive Board of the ECB.

An Excessive Deficit Procedure concerning Member State debts and budgets is contained in Article 104 [104c] EC along with Protocol No 5 EC and an accompanying Regulation. Deficits and debts have to be kept within ratios set out in the Protocol on Excessive Deficit Procedure in the Treaty. This involves regular supply of information from Member States to the Commission. Further provisions concern opinions, recommendations, action and reports by the Commission and an Economic and Financial Committee, established under Article 114 EC, and Council including action by the latter where its recommendations are not complied with. In this latter case, failure to comply with a Council decision could result in the imposition of fines on the Member State.[7] There is no bail-out provision for a Member State that cannot meet its debts (Article 103 EC) but Article 100 EC does allow for financial assistance where there are severe difficulties caused by 'natural disasters or exceptional occurrences.' For participating states, Article 100 EC replaces Article 119 EC. The latter addresses the possibility of mutual assistance where a Member State faces difficulties over its balance of payments because, eg of an overall disequilibrium in its balance of payments.

There are twelve countries in the EMU.[8] The UK has opted out of monetary union having previously in September 1992 pulled out of the Exchange Rate Mechanism of the European Monetary System because of the then crisis of the collapse in value of Sterling.

To meet the convergence criteria to join the EMU, states must establish a 'high degree of price stability' by satisfying tests on currency stability.

7   I Harden in P Beaumont and N Walker eds *The Legal Framework of the Single European Currency* (1999) ch 4.
8   Those not participating are: the UK, Sweden and Denmark. Greece's participation was delayed.

They must also show the sustainability of their government's financial position by ratios of debt and deficit to GDP and other indicators. Once a member, the EMU places limitations on the freedom of national governments to formulate monetary policy with immediate impacts on fiscal and economic policy. It does not impose uniform taxation. There is no direct control over the size of the public sector in Member States and the latter may set its own fiscal policy subject to the discipline of monetary union. Budget deficits must be no more than 3% of GDP; there are controls over government debt; and there are controls over interest rates which are set by the European Central Bank. Direct borrowing from the central bank or the European Central Bank by a Member State is prohibited, as is privileged access to financial institutions. The European Central Bank alone has the right to authorise issue of bank notes.

The model of the EMU was based upon the German monetary model with its central independent bank[9] and indeed the BVerfG had decided in two judgments that the EMU was consistent with German constitutional traditions of democracy.[10] In the latter judgment, it had accepted that the notoriously flexible application of the convergence criteria was lawful.[11] These criteria are suffused with discretionary aspects and such discretion is reinforced by the individual convergence pacts. The range of factors to be considered by a community of expert technocrats is not, simply, a matter which is easily susceptible to judicial challenge. Although the ECJ has jurisdiction over the European Central Bank, any decisions on meeting convergence criteria, which are extremely flexible, are likely to be given an extremely wide berth by that court.[12]

The fact that price stability was an objective of the German political order and the Community order brought fears within some Member States that a policy of hard money and a strict financial discipline might carry with it disastrous consequences for weaker economies with a real threat of

[9] Independence is not actually guaranteed in the constitution. Decisions of the *Bundesbank* can be suspended for two weeks by the government. See Goodhart above.

[10] See Ch 2, note 126

[11] Flexibility is shown by the fact that Germany, Belgium and Italy did not appear to meet the convergence criteria. France in 2002 faced budget cuts to maintain the criteria. One possible remedy was further privatisation in France of electricity, Air France and France Telecom. France chose to ignore budgetary constraints! This flexibility will help the UK and any request to be admitted.

[12] P Craig in P Beaumont and N Walker eds *The Legal Framework of the Single European Currency* (1999).

catastrophic political upheaval. Such a scenario would be unlikely to be of pressing concern to financial technocrats who bear no *political representative* responsibility for their actions. They would be desensitised to the political consequences of their actions: rising unemployment, increasing poverty and hardship. In September 2002, for instance, it was reported that Italy and France in particular were seeking a 'more flexible interpretation' of the stability pact because they were both in danger of breaching the 3% GDP limits in their budgets – in the case of France it was reported that the government had rejected the budget limitations imposed by the stability pact. The Germans and Portuguese were also very close to that limit whereas the Finns wanted to ensure the pact was not interpreted too loosely.[13]

In terms of monetary union, the threat to Britain has been expressed as one affecting the sovereignty of Parliament and national sovereignty. A similar problem was perceived in France where the constitution was amended to allow for membership of the EMU.[14] In the case of the UK, the disappearance of Sterling and the withdrawal of Bank notes with the Sovereign's image upon them have been played for all they are worth in the popular press.[15] In terms of the sovereignty of Parliament, Parliament has had little if any say in monetary matters and its role has always been restricted to voting through or rejecting the budget and auditing expenditure. The real threat will be to executive supremacy vis à vis Parliament in these matters. Historically, the executive has had complete control – subject to international market forces and then international constraints connected with borrowing via the International Monetary Fund – over monetary policy. That freedom consisted in the ability to inflate the economy and devalue the price of money to enable British exports to compete more effectively in world markets and ease economic constraints at home which would help to induce a 'feel-good factor' especially before elections. Increasing public debt to invest in public services could be a very popular ploy with the electorate, for instance, where that electorate is reluctant to pay higher taxes. The implications for price stability and inflation are obvious.

[13]   *Financial Times* 4 September 2002. Germany has been formally warned by the Commission for its budget deficit.

[14]   The Conseil Constitutionnel ruled that: 'a State will be deprived of its own competencies in an area in which the fundamental conditions for the exercise of national sovereignty are at issue'. Cited by J-P Duprat (1995) Public Law 133 at 136.

[15]   The Queen's head on coins will be allowed.

Exercising legal controls over monetary policy will be world upsetting in British constitutional terms and will clearly diminish the opportunity that our governments possess to manipulate monetary policy to suit political purposes. On the other hand there are those who see enormous problems if the levers which are tied in so tightly to political sensitivity and which thereby provide the opportunity to respond to a genuine need and to react to public difficulty are removed. An independent central bank with responsibility to Parliament would be a novel development, but one which an influential Commons Select Committee recommended some years ago.[16] On coming to office in 1997, one of the first acts of the new government was to announce legislation to give the Bank greater independence, but not an independence that would qualify for Stage Three of the EMU (below).

The operation of the Rule of Law in England and Britain was traditionally seen as an individualistic concern: the protection of the individual rights of equals. This was highlighted in Chapter 4. So far as collective processes of government were concerned, its currency was less persuasive. In executive processes where wide discretion was best left unconfined, it might have been difficult to discern the existence of the supremacy of regular law. One such area clearly involved monetary policy.

In the European System of Central Banks the Maastricht Treaty provided a schema of central banking and conduct of monetary policy 'which is alien to traditional British ways of thinking about these subjects'.[17] Indeed, the concept of an independent European Central Bank which is created by Treaty and which operates under law 'is not best calculated to appeal to British politicians schooled in a tradition of purely political responsibility for a monetary policy in whose conduct the central bank is the intimate, but ultimate subordinate, partner in the Treasury.'[18] Establishing the independence of the national central bank from interference from the government of the member state will be revolutionary in a British context. Traditionally the Bank of England has operated informally under political instruction with a back up power for the Treasury in its governing statute to issue directions to the Bank after consulting the Governor.[19] This formal power of control has never been exercised. The German model is present

---

[16] HC 98 (1993–94): the former Treasury and Civil Service Committee.
[17] Daintith, T (1995) Public Law 118.
[18] Daintith, T (1995) Public Law 118.
[19] Bank of England Act 1946, s 4.

in the independence of the European Central Bank and also in the federal organisation of the ESCB.

Reforms have been introduced in the UK in that the quarterly report on inflation is published as are the minutes of the meeting of the Monetary Policy Committee established under the Bank of England Act 1998, initially after a six-week interval (s 15), subsequently reduced informally to two. Reforms have also been suggested from various parties[20] which would introduce a precise legislative basis through statute and regulations for the Bank of England 'to achieve and maintain stability in the general level of prices'. This would be without reference to general economic policy. The government would have power temporarily to set aside the monetary targets with the approval of Parliament. Nonetheless, as Daintith says, the operation of the monetary policy has been high on discretion and low on transparency.

The British historically opted for weaker forms of democratic accountability for monetary policy through the Minister to Parliament and not for any formal-legal framework of accountability to the courts or even to Parliament although under the terms of the European Communities (Amendment) Act 1993, s 3 a duty on the Governor to report to Parliament which is subject to approval will arise on our entry into Stage Three of monetary union. The provisions on monetary union in Maastricht and subsequent treaties would represent a fundamental shift in our constitutional development to a more formal legal mode of delivering monetary policy and achieving accountability.[21] The problem faced by other Member States' constitutional arrangements concerns the question of whether they would be unable to control the realisation of the stability requirements and their fulfilment without thereby violating the principle of democratic government if 'expedient' decisions were taken out of government's hands. How strong, for instance, was the democratic control over the convergence criteria for the third stage? As seen in Chapter 2, constitutional challenges were overcome. The British resolution was the opt out from stage three of monetary union until, that is, Parliament gives its approval. The Chancellor of the Exchequer originally announced that it was unlikely that the UK

---

20 Centre for Economic Policy Research *Independent and Accountable: A New Mandate for the Bank of England* (1993) and the Treasury and Civil Service Committee of the Commons *The Role of the Bank of England* HC 98 (1993/4); and that committee's *Accountability of the Bank of England* HC 282 (1997/8).

21 Daintith, note 17 above.

would enter monetary union until effectively 2002, although in October 1998, he indicated the government's willingness to proceed to stage three after a referendum. 2004 is now the earliest feasible date for entry and as I write, that is swiftly receding especially as an election would be looming. Lord Neill, when chair of the Committee on Public Standards, reported that the government should face restrictions on its expenditure of public funds to advance the case for joining monetary union which it might otherwise wish to advance and that it should furthermore adopt a neutral stance before a referendum. The case for and against should be evenly funded.[22] Two-thirds of the British public, it is estimated, are against joining the EMU.

The Chancellor announced that five criteria would have to be satisfied before a clear and unambiguous case can be made for joining the EMU. 'The determining factor underpinning any government decision on membership of the single currency is the national economic interest and whether the economic case for joining is clear and unambiguous. If it is, there is no constitutional bar to joining.'[23] The tests involve sustainable convergence between Britain and the economies of a single currency; whether there is sufficient flexibility to cope with economic change; the effect on investment; the impact on the UK's financial services industry; and whether membership is good for employment. In September 2002, some additional studies to establish criteria for price convergence were reported including the impact of the Euro on price rises, the housing market in the UK and Europe, the flexibility of the UK labour market, impact on business and financial markets, the experience of a single currency in the US, the impact of 'economic shocks', impact on trade and the robustness of the impact of the eurozone's framework for stability and growth.[24]

One of the very first things that the incoming government did in May 1997 was to announce that the Bank of England was to be independent in setting monetary targets, although it was also subsequently announced that it was to lose its powers to regulate banks to the Financial Services Authority (rules governing when prudential supervision becomes a matter of financial stability, for which the Bank is responsible, were set out in a Memorandum of Understanding between the Bank and the Financial Services Authority).

[22] *The Funding of Political Parties in the United Kingdom* Cm 4057 Vol I (1998), p 169: Political Parties, Elections and Referendums Act 2000.

[23] *The Government's policy on Economic and Monetary Union* available on the Treasury website: www.hm_treasury.gov.uk

[24] *Financial Times* 7 September 2002.

The Bank of England Act 1998 placed these announcements on a legislative basis. While the Act does give independence to the Bank, by removing the Treasury's power of direction in monetary policy under the 1946 Banking Act, it gives formal legal objectives to the Bank to maintain price stability and subject to that, to support the economic policy of Her Majesty's Government, including its objectives for growth and employment.[25] A Monetary Policy Committee is created with half its membership appointed by the Chancellor of the Exchequer but with the casting vote in the Governor or his Deputy. A duty is placed on the Committee to publish whether it has decided to take any action to meet its objectives and what the action was, but this does not include intervention in financial markets. If such latter intervention is decided upon, the Committee shall decide whether immediate publication would be likely to impede the intervention's purpose. The duty on the Committee to publish its minutes after these meetings was explained above.

The Bank has very wide powers to demand information from banks and financial bodies. It is under a duty to publish reports on monetary policy decisions and inflation and its approach to meeting statutory objectives.

Interestingly, the Treasury retains reserve powers to issue instructions on monetary policy to the Governor where satisfied that directions are necessary in the public interest and in 'extreme economic circumstances' (s 19). Otherwise the Bank will set interest rates independently. Such an order by the Treasury has to be positively approved by Parliament by statutory instrument.

Were the UK to enter the EMU, up to one-third of this legislation would have to be repealed. The Governor of the Bank of England could not be a delegate of the Monetary Policy Committee of the Bank of England but he would have to vote on the European Central Bank in his own right and the European Central Bank would be responsible for the inflation target not Her Majesty's Treasury. The Monetary Policy Committee would only be an advisory body, not an executive one. The Treasury would have to give up its right to override the Bank in exceptional circumstances. The influence of the EMU is already being felt within the UK. As early as 1998, the Treasury's Economic and Financial Strategy made explicit reference to compliance with the convergence criteria set out in Maastricht and the

[25]   In New Zealand monetary targets are set by contractual agreement between the central Bank and the Government: see note 20.

Community's Stability and Growth Pact. The Maastricht Criteria are used 'as a useful means for the enhancement of domestic control over the spending aggregates forming one side of the equation through which the key Maastricht figure of general government financial deficit is calculated.'[26]

The Bank of England Act 1998 represents a considerable restriction on the traditional British way of leaving monetary policy to virtually unbridled political forces. Although considerable legal changes will still be required for monetary union, there is no doubt that the Act is a step in the direction of such union. It will mean a considerable development in the pooling of monetary policy and sovereignty under the European Central Bank which will be subject to judicial review. Given the complexity of the decisions and judgments involved in the EMU, successful review is unlikely except in the rarest of circumstances. And judicial review can only provide legal accountability. Accountability may be political, financial, operational, managerial as well as legal. The European Central Bank has to provide an annual report on its activities to ECOFIN and the European Parliament, as well as to the Commission and the European Council. The President will also have to present this report to the first two bodies which may decide to hold a general debate. The President shall be invited to participate in Council meetings when it discusses the European System of Central Banks and the President and members of the Executive Board may by invitation or their own request be heard by European Parliament committees. Pressure has been applied through national parliaments to engage in joint sessions between themselves and the European Parliament to examine the President.

The change to the British constitutional controls to monetary policy introduced by the EMU will be obvious – although they have been anticipated by developments in place now for over four years. These involve independence, a greater role for law and an overriding emphasis given to expert and technocratic financial communities. The EMU is a considerable development in the pooling of sovereignty, a pooling which both the EC and now EU represent and which is the major reason for the detestation to which the EMU is subjected by the right in British politics. A single currency throughout the whole Union will provide the greatest impetus to the creation of a federal European entity and will raise questions about the nature of a European constitution.

[26]   T Daintith and A Page *The Executive in the Constitution* (1999) p 147.

A constitution for Europe?[27]

Do we need a new constitution or can we say that Europe now has its constitution: the Treaty as amended and the ECHR? The Amsterdam Treaty makes reference to the European Charter on Social Rights which is not a part of UK domestic law. For international bodies, treaties are the traditional constituent documents. Constitutions apply to the state in conventional constitutional discourse, national or regional although it is open to any club, society or group to frame its *raison d'etre* or objectives in a 'constitution'. The Convention on the Future of Europe was mandated by the European summit at Laeken in December 2001 to investigate the areas identified by the Intergovernmental Committee at Nice as central to the future of Europe and to make recommendations. The identified areas in the Final Act of the Nice conference were: subsidiarity; the question of the status of the Charter of Fundamental Rights of the EU; simplification of the Treaties; and the role of national parliaments (and regional) in the 'European architecture.' These points have been examined within this book. There is evidence of a new political urgency in the question of a constitution for Europe. The UK Foreign Secretary in August 2002 advocated the need for a written constitution for the EU and recommended this as the main aim of the Convention under Valéry Giscard d'Estaing.[28] This sign-posted a change in UK government policy.

Only two years prior to this the UK Prime Minister had urged a statement of guiding principles to provide political but not legal guidance. Such a constitution, he recommended, would set out in a simple set of principles, expressed in 'plain language', what the EU is for. It would 'reassure the public that national government will remain the primary source of political legitimacy.' A written constitution would be a legally binding document enforceable by the ECJ. The creation of such a constitution would help legitimise the institutions of the EU and flows from strategic calculations. While the impetus for a federal Europe has waned, and was never supported by the present British government, a written constitution would enshrine the basis for intergovernmental co-operation and not federalism. The overriding emphasis would be against increasing centralism, although some areas such as crime control and investigation, immigration and

---

27   A Euro Barometer poll in December 2001 showed 58% of Britons favoured an
      EU constitution: *The Guardian* 22 February 2002.
28   *Financial Times* 28 August 2002. www.european-convention.eu.int for the
      convention and www.europa.eu.int/futurum/index_en.htm.

environmental regulation would require more effective central coordination and direction.

The Convention has been examined in various parts of this book. It established working groups to investigate specific areas: subsidiarity; the Charter of Human Rights and incorporation of that and/or the ECHR into the Treaty; legal personality for the EU; the role of national parliaments within the Union architecture; complementary competencies of the Union in relation to Member State; economic governance. In July 2002, four further groups were established to investigate: internal security and justice; simplification of legislative procedure; external relations and representation of the EU abroad; and finally, defence and security. An eleventh group on social Europe was added. The outcome of this vast inquiry will not be binding and the government assured Parliament in the UK that the report would be discussed in national parliaments before governments moved forward. No specific reference was made by the House of Lords Select Committee report on the Convention to regional assemblies (HL 163 (2001-02). Evidence to the committee said that at the Convention plenary hearings which are in public, the MEPs were the most coherent group; national parliamentarians the least coherent from the 105 full members although the Convention altogether comprises 207 members.

While these discussions involve the widest ranging review of the constitutional basis of the Union, there are also sub-texts developing about the future of the Council and Commission in particular. The most comprehensive contributions to the Convention had come from the Commission and Member States. In COM (2002) 257 final, the Commission President set out his list of objectives and developed these at Seville in June 2002. He wanted a reformed Commission involving an inner Cabinet with delegated powers to one of nine vice presidents which would clearly undermine the collegiate basis of the Commission. This would be reduced in size from a possible 27 members after ratification of the Nice treaty. A constitutional treaty would, the Commission argued, be in two parts: first of all a section dealing with constitutional principles and the Charter of Fundamental Rights; a second part would set out practical procedures and 'more flexible voting rules'. The Commission wants stronger economic co-ordination instruments and wishes to give greater emphasis to the EU as a global player in which it would take a lead role. Qualified majority voting would apply in foreign affairs (Common Foreign and Security Policy: CFSP). The Presidents of the Council and Commission should be one role elected by the European Parliament for five years.

The larger Member States are not in favour of these initiatives; smaller Member States are more warmly disposed. The UK, France and Spain have supported an elected President of the Council, serving possibly for five years. This would strengthen the position of the Council internationally. The Convention chair, Giscard d'Estaing was concerned that an apparent split into two camps meant that not only 'the Convention will be blocked, but also Europe will be blocked.'

But whose vision of Europe would prevail? A constitution is an empty bottle into which any content may be poured. Even a constitution of simple principles to guide future development and enlargement could differ enormously in its basic direction. Walter van Gerven argued some years ago that the recent development of the Community has witnessed less concentration on distinctness and sovereignty, more on co-operation between systems of law and increasing constitutional coherence.[29] If this is true, any constitutional settlement would have to be in the broadest and most flexible of terms. Agreement is unlikely on any thing other. The Amsterdam Treaty is pragmatic, less visionary than that of Maastricht and the Nice Intergovernmental Committee saw constitutional matters excluded until the subjects identified in the Nice Declaration on the Future of the EU were identified (Chapter 2 p 63 et seq above).

Visions of a new Europe and a new constitution for Europe often either wish to give full vent to European federalism or wish to see the Member States more clearly defined as Masters of the Treaties and limits placed on the competence of the Community institutions. The UK vision appears to go between the two of these approaches, but what detail would it come up with on, for instance, subsidiarity? What would be the precise role of the ECJ and of national parliaments in a *simple* document? What specificity would be given to human rights protection? Would, in other words, the constitution simply be a 'link' back to the Treaties? And what would be the connection between a simple constitution as a statement of principle and simplified Treaties? Furthermore, if a simple constitution for the EU were introduced, what impact would this have on the UK where there is no written constitution, simple or otherwise, but a vast array of constitutional statutes and conventions, practices and understandings? There is in the UK a vast corpus of constitutional law, much of it untouched by judicial decision although devolution and human rights litigation will force through changes on these constitutional matters. Senior judges have recognised a

---

[29]   Walter van Gerven (1996) European Public Law 81.

hierarchy of statutes in the UK which is a product of the common law and which allows European supremacy to be recognised within a matrix of Parliamentary sovereignty, but one may add, a sovereignty which itself may be assuming a changing identity. Would such a development for the EU necessitate a written constitution for the UK? If so, what would it contain? Would it be the occasion to qualify doctrines such as Parliamentary sovereignty – and if so, why? Would there be any realistic chance of such a qualification given the Blair government's and the Conservative Party's predilection for a pristine version of Parliamentary sovereignty?

Suggestions for a constitution for Europe have been made before. The European Constitution Group, a free market and right of centre group, drafted a constitution[30] which emphasised the free market and commercial freedoms, made clear that powers were delegated from Member States to the EU subject to limits defined in the constitution and which could be 'repatriated', which protected fundamental freedoms, which provided a Chamber of Parliamentarians from Member States, and a Union Chamber and made provision for the powers of the European Council, the Council of Ministers and the Commission. A new Court of Review would be able to hear an *actio popularis* challenging the vires of the decisions or actions or laws of officers or institutions of the Union and would hear references from the ECJ, the International Court of Justice or 'any national court or tribunal' for the interpretation of the Union constitution or law, or the law and constitutions of Member States (sic).

The Union's powers would be limited so as to give primacy to subsidiarity and local action and subsidiarity would be a fully justiciable principle. The subject matter of legislative powers of the EU would be clearly defined. Member States could secede from the Union and any laws discriminating against a Member State which did secede would be unconstitutional.

What further alternatives could we identify? One which clearly identifies ultimate and complete sovereignty with the Community? Such a prospect is rapidly receding. A power to accede to the ECHR and/or to incorporate the Charter of Fundamental rights as a legally binding part of the EU? Such a prospect may be advancing. What of greater involvement of national parliaments in the European legislative process and even a second chamber of MPs from Member States? What of greater participatory and access

---

[30] *A Proposal for a European Constitution* European Constitutional Group (1997).

rights for citizens of the Union to EU affairs? How would these objectives be put into effect so as not to subvert the Union and impede efficient governance? The question of national parliaments was examined in Chapters 4 and 7. But one point that was not examined concerned the role of national parliaments in setting the Community budget – that list of expenditure and income over an annual period. It has not attracted much legal attention, but it is of vital constitutional importance. This is especially so, should the EMU prompt greater redistributive tendencies within the Union to support weaker economies.

Domestically, there is pressure for a greater role for Parliament in Community budgetary affairs. The House of Lords Select Committee on the European Communities has observed that the process of setting the Community budget makes a mockery of scrutiny arrangements.[31] There is also a great deal of support in other Member States for a fuller role for national parliaments in the EC budget proposals and national contributions. UK contributions are not subject to voting or supply arrangements but are paid direct out of the Consolidated Fund (European Communities Act 1972, s 2(3)). The Treasury must pay providing it is satisfied that the demand to pay is lawful. There is no annual appropriation procedure in the legal sense. UK contributions are taken into account in the annual national budget and Parliament is informed in that context. Changes to the Own Resources Decision (the EC revenue ceiling) require legislation in Westminster (eg the European Communities (Finance) Act 2001). Both scrutiny Committees are informed by the Treasury of EC budgetary developments but time for analysis is woefully short. A mass of paper has to be scrutinised within six weeks by very hard pressed committees. There are audits conducted. But Westminster's authority to investigate Community expenditure is limited to Community expenditure which passes through government departments in the UK. Furthermore, the UK's contributions to the EC budget are not hypothecated to any particular expenditure, whether within or apropos of our net contribution outside the UK public sector. It is not therefore possible to perform a Value For Money audit of the contributions themselves.

No-one can realistically expect a complete harmonisation of constitutional practices, a complete integration of such practices into one constitution.

---

[31]   14th Report Select Committee on European Communities (1995–6); *Westminster and Europe: Proposals for Change* G Leicester, EPF, 1997; HL 36 (1998–99).

Any attempt would be futile. But there appears to be scope to achieve a coordination of fundamental objectives. Incorporation of the Charter of Fundamental Rights into the basic constitution – which the UK government opposes – is a workable objective for the future.[32] But who can doubt that such incorporation could cause serious difficulty if the interpretation given to its provisions by the ECJ is not as extensive as that given to similar rights by national courts or by the CHR? Furthermore, when this coordination is in the process of realisation or achievement, there will be a corresponding weakening of strong versions of national sovereignty. The point was put with uncanny prescience by de Smith over thirty years ago:

> If however, the Community develops characteristics of a political federation, and if the incongruity of the orthodox position of Parliamentary Sovereignty becomes increasingly apparent in a context of expanding EC law, then a climate of opinion will doubtless develop in which heterodoxy will thrive and prevail. The legal concept of Parliamentary Sovereignty may then drift away into the shadowy background from which it emerged.[33]

But no-one should underestimate the power of forces opposing such developments.

A final point to make is that while the EU has internationalised our constitutional affairs in a more juridical and possibly egalitarian manner than was the case with the Commonwealth, we have to be careful that a fortress Europe does not become the end of our ambition in a turbulent, divided and very unequal world order. An Antipodean lawyer's hopes of seeing an international common law of human rights emerge from growing trends in internationalism is a hope worth cherishing.[34]

---

[32] See Chs 2 and 9, pp 63 and 388 above and note: Case C-173/99 *Broadcasting, Entertainment, Cinematographic and Theatre Union* and the Opinion of Advocate General Tizzano [2001] 1 WLR 2313. See P Oliver FIDE 2002, Ch 2, note 1.

[33] S A de Smith (1971) Mod LR 597 at 614.

[34] Lord Cooke 'The Dream of an International Common Law' in *Courts of Final Jurisdiction: The Mason Court in Australia* C Saunders ed (Sydney 1996); D Dyzenhaus, M Hunt and M Taggart 'The Principles of Legality in Administrative Law: Internationalism and Constitutionalism' (2001) Oxford University Commonwealth LJ 5; C McCrudden (2000) OJLS 499 on a common law of human rights.

The preliminary draft constitution of the Convention

In October 2002, the preliminary first draft of a constitution for Europe was published by the d'Estaing Convention. Much of it was outline in form and is likely to be changed significantly before any, or any final, agreement. National opposition was expressed to possible titles for the union, including the 'United States of Europe'. Whatever the new entity's name, provision is made for it to possess 'legal personality'. The subject working group believed that this would apply to the EC and EU as a single entity (and also Euratom). By implication, this would see the end of the three pillar structure and help simplification (see pp 68 and 257 above).

Part One covers constitutional structure in which diversity is recognised, national identities retained, policies at the European level closely co-ordinated and in which certain 'common competencies' will be administered on a 'federal basis'. Under Title II of Part One, dual citizenship – 'national and European' – is envisaged whereby citizens 'will be free to use either as he or she chooses.' The possibility of incorporating the Charter of Fundamental Rights is raised: either a reference to the Charter, a statement that the Charter is an integral part of the Constitution but with its articles contained in another part of the Treaty or an annexed protocol, or full incorporation. Presumably this mode would reflect the degree of *bindingness* of the Charter but it is far from clear how. The working group on the Charter recommended that it should be a legally binding component of the constitution. There was also strong support for a power in a revised Treaty allowing accession by the European Union to the European Convention on Human Rights (chapter 2, p 62 et seq).

Title III covers EU competence and states that any competence not conferred on the Union remains with Member States while also explicitly establishing the primacy of Union law in the exercise of competencies conferred on the Union. The categories of Union competence will be listed pin-pointing those that belong exclusively to the Union and those that are shared. In promoting subsidiarity and proportionality in law making, the role of national parliaments will be addressed. Title IV states that the Union will have a single institutional structure in which the institutions are enjoined to provide and promote 'open, effective and unostentatious administration.' The European Council will be defined along with its composition and tasks. The composition and duties of the Council and Commission would be listed and there would be Presidents of the European Council, the Council and the Commission. The European Parliament may be empowered to introduce a motion of censure on the Commission and what the consequences of such a motion may be. The possibility of a Congress of the Peoples of Europe is included although details would still have to be discussed. The different instruments available to the institutions to exercise their competencies are to be listed.

Title VI deals with the democratic life of the EU in which citizens are equal vis à vis the institutions and in which the principle of participatory democracy will be spelt out. Procedures for European Parliament elections will be uniform in Member States and the legislative debates in the Council and European Parliament will be public – it is far from clear what this will cover. Title VII concerns finances and Title VIII concerns the EU in the world. These are in bare outline form. A procedure for voluntary withdrawal from the Union might be included.

Part Two deals with EU policies and their implementation covering the internal market, the EMU, policies in specific areas, internal security, areas where supporting action may be taken by the Union, external action including commercial policy and CFSP. Part Three will deal with general and final provisions.

There is much yet to discuss and finalise, let alone agree upon.

If something along these lines comes to pass, and it will set the constitutional template for Europe for the next fifty years or so if it does, what impact would this have on the pressure for a written constitution for the UK? Noreen Burrows wrote that in a country 'whose constitutional mantra is that there is no written constitution, the deference to the written word in the devolution process is astonishing.'[35] This is a reference to the legislation, secondary legislation, codes and concordats encapsulating the devolution process. Masterman and Mitchell observe that this may not be evidence of a constitution in the making so much as a significant increase to the 'set of laws, rules and practices that create the basic institutions of the state and its component and related parts.'[36] I am not sure that this is 'astonishing'. Who would wish to make fundamental commitment unless evidenced in the written word? This can be done through law or other codes; it does not necessarily require a written constitution. If we possessed a written constitution, would this increase the support for a

---

[35]   Burrows *Devolution* (2000) p 2.

[36]   Masterman and Mitchell in A Trench ed *The State of the Nations 2001* (2001) p 195 quoting HLs Select Committee on the Constitution, HL 11 (2001-02), para 50.

constitutional court as opposed to a supreme court, the latter as we saw in Chapter 5 was the preference of Lord Bingham (p 247 above)? I think we would have to ask what improvement would a written constitution make to existing arrangements – or do we wish to change such arrangements? The chief target here would doubtless be Parliamentary sovereignty so that the devolution settlement and protection of human rights could be constitutionally entrenched. The position of the Crown – both personal and political – would also have to be addressed. Is it time for change? There is no point in fixin' something that ain't bust unless one wants to change what the 'thing' is and does.

Should national or European administrative law be codified?

The subject of codification of administrative law in England and Wales and one might add Northern Ireland – Scotland is based upon different traditions but there is no reason why the same basic principles need not apply – has caused a rigid division of opinion amongst practitioners and academics in the UK.[37] On the one hand it is felt that codification will ossify that spur of judicial ingenuity which drives the common law and the development of its principles; as indeed, some argue, would a written constitution and a judicially enforceable Bill of Rights. On the other hand there are those who argue that the complexity of the modern state demands an Administrative Procedure Act, and that the judicial record on these matters is subject to serious fluctuations in the standards on, eg fairness and openness that courts demand in governmental and administrative decision-making. The Americans in a common law system perceived this necessity in 1946 when Congress enacted the Administrative Procedure Act and the Australians have also seen the need for a 'new administrative law' putting onto a legislative basis the operation of the Administrative Review Council, the Administrative Appeals Tribunal and the ambit of judicial review under statutory as opposed to inherent common law power although the latter still exists in Australia. Many Member States now have Administrative Procedure Acts or codes on administrative procedure, although their content and detail differs significantly.[38]

---

[37]   Sir Harry Woolf in *Protection of the Public* (1990) p 122 favoured *non-statutory* principles of good administration.

[38]   Portugal, Spain, Italy, Denmark, Finland, Sweden, Greece, Holland and Luxembourg. Germany as we saw in Chapter 3 has an Administrative Procedure Act. France is notable, but explicable, by its absence.

There is a great deal of legislation relating to administrative law in the UK and in England and Wales: the Tribunal and Inquiries Act 1992 which followed earlier statutes and rules made thereunder cover inquiries and tribunals scheduled in the Act and these are increasingly sophisticated. Section 31 of the Supreme Court 1981 sets out the procedure for judicial review along with the CPR 1998, Part 54. The Parliamentary Commissioner Act 1967 as amended deals with the Parliamentary ombudsman. Other statutes deal with ombudsmen for local government, the health service and other regimes. These public sector ombudsmen are likely to be established in a 'one-stop' ombudsman commission.[39] A Freedom of Information Act was enacted in 2000, to come into effect as regards individual access in 2005. Regulations, codes and civil service guidelines deal with appointments and good practice and so on, but much of this is 'hit or miss'. The basic guidance on the conduct and exercise of administrative power comes from judicial decisions and increasingly from the reports and guidance of ombudsmen, Select Committees in Parliament and the Committee on Standards in Public Life. These are making greater and more systematic efforts to collect together 'good practice' guidance from their investigations for use by officials.[40]

Whole areas, however, are left out of the picture especially the independent regulatory agencies whose advent in the US in fact precipitated the development of administrative law in the US. So too, the movement to public private partnerships in the UK and government by contract, events occurring both in the UK and elsewhere, have created a new climate for the exercise of public power and fairness for those affected by the exercise of such power. In the UK there is a growing crisis concerning their lack of coherence, their perceived lack of fairness and the uncontrolled nature of their discretionary powers. The public/private interface in Britain long ago spawned a beast known as Quangos – quasi-autonomous non-governmental organisations – which in constitutional terms are hybrids and often private in form carrying out public tasks. Their only effective form of control is *ex post facto* investigation by the National Audit Office or Audit Commission, although there may sometimes be the possibility of judicial review. The Human Rights Act and the Freedom of Information Act may touch private bodies performing public functions. In Chapter 6 and elsewhere, the role of comitology committees and agencies in the

---

[39] HC 612 *Review of Public Sector Ombudsmen in England* (1999–2000).
[40] See the *Powers, Work and Jurisdiction of the Ombudsmen* Select Committee on the Parliamentary Commissioner for Administration, HC 33 Vol I (1993/4).

Community was identified together with the problems such bodies introduced in terms of transparency and accountability.

I do see a benefit from a statute covering domestic law which would create a body to oversee the totality of administrative justice in the modern state and not just the easy parts: those parts in other words which statute increasingly fails to reach. Our law on judicial review procedures has been reformulated.[41] A wide-ranging review has taken place on tribunals.[42] Informal processes, which abound in England and Wales, remain informal and largely unregulated.[43] A decade ago, Professor Lewis and I called for a Ministry of Justice to replace the confused role of several government departments in overseeing aspects of the justice system.[44] While more and more tasks have been located within the Lord Chancellor's Department, there is an irony in the fact that that department is headed by a figure whose multiplicity of roles is a clear contravention of the letter and spirit of the ECHR.

There should be a clearer duty to set out in legal terms the powers of bodies carrying out public tasks and a general principle that all bodies performing such tasks operate fairly and openly. The advent of public/private partnerships, both in the UK and Europe, and indeed the wider world context as illustrated dramatically in the earth summit in Johannesburg in 2002 where so many responsibilities were falling to combinations of public and private bodies in some form of union with 'civil society', reinforces the necessity. As part of the US Administrative Procedure Act there is a Freedom of Information Act and in Australia freedom of information forms part of the new administrative law. Appointments to bodies exercising power on behalf of the state – public or private in form – and terms thereof should be spelt out and should be a matter of public record. Advisory committees should be embraced by legal requirements of openness and rights of public admission as currently exists in the US. Contracts and terms involving some form of public expenditure or oversight must be published as should monitoring appraisals of the performance of such contracts. Where a party is expected to act in a judicial capacity there should be a duty to appoint

---

[41]   CPR 1998, Part 54 following the Bowman Report *Review of the Crown Office List* LCD (2000).

[42]   Sir A Leggatt *Review of Tribunals* (2001).

[43]   P Birkinshaw in M Partington ed *The Leggatt Review of Tribunals: Academic Seminar Papers* (2001).

[44]   N Lewis and P Birkinshaw *When Citizens Complain: Reforming Justice and Administration* (1993).

an independent and disinterested party although decisions on policy in areas such as planning and finance might require judicial oversight as opposed to judicial decision.[45] The duties to provide compensation, including we would argue for unlawful administrative action, should be spelt out. With enhanced rights to information would come rights to be consulted and to participate in decision-making in those public and hybrid bodies through whose embrace the public interest is developed.[46] Our constitutionalising should not ignore those trans-national companies who manage our affairs: in Johannesburg (above) companies did not want to be under constraints to disclose information to governments in third world countries because of 'damage' to their commercial position.

Many of these principles would derive to a considerable extent from the increasingly sophisticated decisions of the courts in England developing the common law, and indeed from decisions of ombudsmen. However, in the case of judicial review itself we should have to consider very carefully whether there was a disadvantage in seeking to codify the powers and grounds of judicial review. A detailed code on judicial review could stifle development and it might be in the interests of government and Parliament to achieve this very objective by enacting a feeble safeguard as the basic threshold. One would not wish to kill the inspiration of the common law at its creative best. Conversely, areas have been identified that would benefit from codification.

As observed above, many Member States now possess an Administrative Procedure Act. Should there be such a provision for EC institutions? If so, should there be a provision covering Member States, assuming that any problems with competence on the subject matter of harmonisation of administrative justice are not insurmountable. Should there be a Directive setting out the requirements of good administrative practice? Or should it be left to a Recommendation or soft law form of exhortation?[47] If in a Directive, these would apply when domestic bodies were refusing, denying, conferring or enforcing Community rights. The Charter of Fundamental Rights it will be recalled applies when Member States are applying or derogating from Community law, although the Charter does not as yet

---

[45] *R (Alconbury)* v *Secretary of State* [2001] UKHL 23, [2001] 2 All ER 929.

[46] Council of Europe Recommendation Rec (2001) 19: *The Participation of Citizens in Local Public Life;* Consultation and Communications (1997) OECD.

[47] C Harlow (1996) European Law Journal 3; J Schwarze *Administrative Law under European Influence* (1996); Lord Millett (2002) Public Law 309.

impose a legal duty (p 63 et seq). The EC has shown an increasing interest in the realisation of rights via effective remedies and procedures in *specific* areas; once again procurement is a good example and competition another. Has the time also arrived for a statement to embrace Community institutions themselves?

On balance, I am in favour of a legal code of good administrative practice provided the principles are stated in a broad and flexible manner – they will have to apply to very different legal regimes. The common themes would embrace: judicial independence; administrative integrity and independence; rights to compensation for unlawful public action; fairness in procedure; decisions based on relevant, probative and substantial evidence; due care and diligence in collecting evidence and material; proportionality and principles of review; deprecation of arbitrariness; non-retroactivity; reasons for decisions and action; transparency and openness and access to meetings and documents covering public, hybrid and private bodies engaged in decision-making affecting the public welfare. 'Commercial in Confidence' must not be an obstacle to the full operation of the rule of law.

I would also suggest that an Administrative Review Body should be established to review administrative justice in the EC and in its ever increasing Member States. Both America and Australia had and, in the latter case, still have very successful bodies fulfilling these tasks: the Administrative Conference of the US and the Administrative Review Council.[48] It goes without saying that such a body is also needed for our domestic law to map out the ever changing contours of justice and administration and to assess what the impact of Community law will be on the relationship between the two. A need for such a body at EU level may now be identified and close co-operation, but not hierarchical domination, between the Union and national bodies should be prescribed.

The EU Ombudsman has produced a code on good administrative procedure which was examined in detail in Chapter 7. The code has been adopted by a variety of EU bodies and the Commission has adopted its own code. These concentrate on individual rights, but omit participatory

---

[48] The American body ACUS was killed off in the attack on public bodies in the 1990s as an easy victim of anti-federal sentiment. Its work on advising all branches of government on administrative justice was widely regarded as enlightened and very successful and it did more to protect citizens from power's all embracing grasp than those agencies and bodies that survived the cull of Newt Gingrich's contract with America – the downsizing of the state.

rights. The code is a 'soft law' measure and the evasion of the Charter of Fundamental Rights by Community institutions, as observed by the EU Ombudsman (Chapter 2, p 65) should be recalled. The code could provide inspiration (p 491). Furthermore, the Convention group examining complementary competencies or 'supporting measures' as it preferred, supported the adoption of a power in the Treaty to adopt rules on good administration for EU institutions. The Treaty should also contain, it suggested, a clause underlining the common interest in the efficiency of national implementation of EU legislation. The EU should adopt supporting powers to facilitate exchange of information and personnel and to support training and development programmes.

National limits to common European standards

The question poses immediate problems for British lawyers because of the absence of a written constitution; 'and what do the English or the British mean by a constitution?' is a problem frequently asked of our students and posed by those not familiar with the British system, and sometimes by those who are! However, three particular problems of a constitutional order or nature which will hinder the movement towards common European standards of administrative law may be identified. These are:

Parliamentary sovereignty, and nothing in the Treaty of Rome or the Treaty on European Union has obliterated that doctrine as the linchpin of the British State, at least from the perspective of British judges and nothing that was said above has altered that basic fact, difficult though its realisation may be as long as we remain a member of the Community (see Chapter 4).

The absence of a separate public law system in England, Wales and Northern Ireland and to an extent Scotland is the second feature. At one level public law permeates everything in the UK: land use and ownership, employment, education, financial regulation and so on. Its breadth is really quite staggering but so too is its lack of order. It will also be apposite to say a few words about the use of prerogative powers in contemporary British government. The implication of Parliamentary sovereignty is that there are many politicians and civil servants, and as importantly lawyers, who would argue that the lead on something as important as standards on administrative justice should come from Parliament; and Parliament, has been notably reluctant to legislate a general code in this field, content to lay down specific and unrelated provisions.

No distinct public law system. The boundaries between public law and private law are not distinct. Public bodies exercising public powers may affect one's private interests in which case one's claim may be best pursued in private law procedure by way of a claim or an originating summons – a view reinforced by a decision in 1992 of the House of Lords which seemed to be adopting a more pragmatic approach as to which procedure was relevant where a private law issue was present in a public law matter and subsequently endorsed by the reformulation of judicial review procedure under the CPR 1998, Part 54.[49] This decision seems to be introducing a degree of flexibility where previously the House of Lords had sought to minimise uncertainty for public bodies by holding that such bodies should be challenged exclusively by public law process save in some special circumstances.[50] To complicate matters further, rights which are of a private law nature in common law eg contract and tort/delict must be brought by private law procedure even where a public body is allegedly in breach of those rights[51] whereas private law bodies exercising *de facto* public powers may be challenged by way of public law judicial review. The end result was a good deal of uncertainty as to whether a claim should be pursued in private law or public law process. The positive side is that courts often do strive to achieve justice rather than formalistically apply the law – a *justizstaat* rather than a *rechtsstaat* and in many instances a remedy will be found. This is not a Kadi system of justice as Max Weber believed and all Member States no doubt have their own quirks. However, there are significant differences on some matters viz, limitation periods, locus standi and access to documents or disclosure by the parties to litigation and cross examination. We would have to give thought to guidance on standards for public and private wielders of power affecting significant portions of the population eg banks, building societies and insurance companies. In a way something along these lines is happening already with the Directive on Unfair Contract Terms which provides rights of class actions against private bodies. The CPR 1998, Part 54 do seek to remove some of the anachronisms that plagued the public private division and the courts have declared the virtues of flexibility that the new rules contain.[52] It has even been suggested that the new rules of procedure prompt the thought that

---

[49]   *Roy v Kensington Family Practitioner Committee* [1992] 1 AC 624.

[50]   *O'Reilly v Mackman* [1983] 2 AC 237; and see *Wandsworth London Borough Council v Winder* [1985] AC 461; *Davy v Spelthorne Borough Council* [1984] AC 262.

[51]   *R v East Berkshire Health Authority, ex p Walsh* [1985] QB 152, CA.

[52]   *Clark v University of Lincolnshire and Humberside* [2000] 3 All ER 752, CA.

the public/private division in judicial relief can be cast aside.[53] The courts in England have certainly applied the *Wednesbury* test designed to control abuse of public power to review the exercise of discretion in contractual relationships.[54]

Prerogative powers: a few words are apposite. Governmental action in the UK is still suffused by a large shaft of prerogative powers – that residue of arbitrary power residing in the Crown and invariably, but not exclusively, exercised by its Ministers. All systems of administrative law confront areas of non-justiciability or non-reviewability. An enormous advance was made in 1984 in the GCHQ litigation when it was held that the prerogative was reviewable in those areas where individuals stood to be affected by its *exercise*[55] and where review was appropriate. Given the subject matter of prerogative powers eg declaration of war, then on many occasions when it is exercised its operation will remain outside review, although Parliament may refuse to vote supply, however unlikely that may be. In *R v Secretary of State for the Home Department, ex p Bentley*[56] the exercise, or non exercise of the Royal Pardon – a prerogative power – was successfully reviewed in the High Court and in other cases where an individual's rights are involved the prerogative has been susceptible of judicial review.

National space: more generally, there is an evident movement towards the establishment of what Snyder a decade ago called 'domestic political space'. This means that Member States must take, and must wish to take, more of the initiative in enforcing and developing appropriate rules of law and procedures to advance Community objectives and broad legal principles, or even to go their own way in pursuit of certain key objectives. This is evidenced by the increased resort to subsidiarity, the resort to 'opting out' of Treaty provisions, an excessive adherence to the letter rather than the spirit of EC law thereby frustrating its effective application.[57] Even the wide resort to Article 10 [5] EC which has been addressed elsewhere in this book amounts to an admission that a task is beyond the Community institutions and it cannot act alone. However, there is a positive side in

---

[53] D Oliver (2002) Public Law 91 and *Common Values: The Public Private Divide* (1999).

[54] *Equitable Life v Hyman* [2000] 2 All ER 331, 338–9 and [2000] 3 All ER 961, 972; *Paragon Finance Ltd plc v Nash* [2001] EWCA Civ 1466, [2002] 2 All ER 248.

[55] *Council of Civil Service Unions v Minister for the Civil Service* [1985] AC 374, HL.

[56] [1993] 4 All ER 442, QBD.

[57] F Snyder (1993) Mod LR 19.

that the Community cannot do everything and nor would anyone sensibly wish for that even if, inconceivably, Member States were prepared to budget for such a responsibility. The secret of all successful constitutional arrangements is to establish where the constitutional tasks and the administrative functions are best effected and how. This is creative and constructive and not simply negative.[58]

European public law beyond Europe

I spoke earlier of the heritage that shaped the Western world: the forces of Christianity, the enlightenment and Roman law. What is the practical legacy of these influences? The legacy can be seen in those traditions and principles which are central to Western societies: a belief in the pre-eminence of the rule of law over arbitrary and tyrannical action; a belief in fair procedure; a growing awareness of openness and transparency in decision making affecting the public; increased importance of human rights protection and a widening perspective on the rights to be protected by such provisions to embrace environmental and social and economic rights as well as rights to be informed and to information on how power is exercised.

In so far as Member States have influenced legal regimes by a process of colonisation, the legal systems in such countries may be influenced by developments that arise from the mutual influence of domestic and European legal orders. They may well show us the way forward; witness the constitution building in South Africa and the sophistication of the concepts of administrative justice and freedom of information that were developed there.[59] These are among the most advanced in the world. Witness public interest litigation in India.[60] But as I write, there are increasing signs of hostility by Europeans to the world beyond Europe; indeed beyond the Member States and racism has found powerful support among governments as well as civilians.

---

[58]   See the Convention WG on 'Complementary Competencies' CONV 375/02 WGV 14 p 222 above and Temple Lang, J *What Powers Should the European Community Have?* Institute of European Public Law, University of Hull (1993).

[59]   H Corder and T Maluwa eds *Administrative Justice in Southern Africa* (1997).

[60]   U Baxi *The Future of Human Rights* (2002); and ed *Law and Poverty* (1988).

Fortress Europe and global jurisprudence

Globalisation is a much heralded process involving the domination of world economies by multi-national and often American dominated companies operating on capitalist and exploitative competitive lines. The communications revolution and the ease with which capital may be moved and invested throughout the world have removed much of the significance of national boundaries from the point of view of such companies. But movement of people does not benefit from similar freedom. The world is a closed and hostile place for the economic underclasses. Free movement within the Community is not matched by free movement into the Community. Immigration and nationality laws are the preserve of nation states and their operation, together with laws regulating asylum seekers, seek to establish ever more restrictive regimes to keep foreigners – inevitably third or poor world individuals – out.

Jurisprudence has also been globalised.[61] Law and legal regimes are increasingly internationalised. This book has been an examination of such a process in Europe. Economic power will bring dominant forms of law and legal expression usually based on free market philosophy, freedom of contract and choice of law clauses favourable to mighty companies. Alston has noted (p 64 above) how secretive are details concerned with human rights instruments in development cooperation and trade agreements between the EU Commission and developing countries. The overall picture is 'unsatisfactory'.[62] Access to country strategy papers and to national indicative programmes is 'highly restricted'[62a] 'despite their importance in ensuring that human rights are taken adequately into account in policy-making.' Access to complaints channels about such matters are inadequate, he feels, because the European Parliament lacks information, the Court of Auditors does not deal with individualised matters and the ECJ's remit is confined. He has called for a Human Rights Commissioner and a Directorate General in the Commission to address such subjects together with a European Human Rights Monitoring Agency possibly developing the Vienna Monitoring Centre on Racism and Xenophobia.[62B]

---

[61]   See Ch 1, note 12.
[62]   P Alston et al (eds) *The EU and Human Rights* (1999) p 38.
[62a] P Alston et al (eds) *The EU and Human Rights* (1999) p 38.
[62b] P Alston et al (eds) *The EU and Human Rights* (1999) p 38. And see de Witte in Alston.

Fortress America and resistance to Europe

The events of 11 September 2001, while projecting America into the role of global defender against terrorism, also reinforced her citizens' sense of isolation from the world. The US's refusal to abide by environmental constraints agreed at Kyoto are well known, as is her opposition to the International Criminal Court's jurisdiction over her citizens.[63] Less well known is the opposition to the EU Directive on Data Protection because of the hostility of US companies to alien standards going beyond anything the US has produced for controls on personal data when used by private companies.[64] Human rights has also been a contested area, especially over the widespread use of the death penalty in America and the problem this causes extradition arrangements between members of the Council of Europe and the US. US commercial protectionism in steel and other products has caused serious rifts to develop in EU/US relationships. We should not be over negative nor forget the influence of US law and thought on human rights development, the freedom of information and government in the Sunshine developments, nor the field of Alternative Dispute Resolution, and the United States' entrenchment of freedom of speech protection. It reveals at once amazing sophistication and xenophobic defensiveness. The undermining of freedom of information legislation in the US since the beginning of 2002, laws which for more than a generation were held out as an exemplar to the rest of the world, is a worrying development. No-one can deny the awful trauma of 11 September and the threat posed to innocent lives everywhere. No-one can deny the threat posed to security. But the strength of Western civilisation and democracy is built on tolerance and understanding, wisdom and compromise. They have grown through the acquisition of knowledge. There is a quality of opportunism about the movement back to a secret state but a development that has global implications. Abusers of power, any abusers and any power, flourish in darkness and ignorance.

---

[63]   A summons was issued in France against Henry Kissinger to give evidence about the disappearance of French nationals in Chile and the events surrounding General Pinochet are notorious: see Ch 4, p 165 and below. Russia, China and India had not signed the ICC treaty as of July 2002. European nations were largely in favour. See G Robertson *Crimes Against Humanity* (2002, 2nd ed). And Cm 5590 on the International Criminal Court and the ICC Act 2001.

[64]   A Charlesworth 'Clash of the data Titans....' (2000) European Public Law 253.

Eastward democracy

We face a dramatic eastward expansion of the EU with several candidate states lined up for membership now Nice is ratified by all present Member States. Human rights protection is a central feature in accession agreements but what of *acquis communautaire* and *acquis de l'Union* comprising traditions in eastern states and their inclusion in such acquis? Such traditions may say more about collective social values and social solidarity than those existing in current Member States. Is there not room for their place in the acquis?

European public law and international legal order

The EU is the most developed international arrangement for the pooling of sovereign powers and the most sophisticated in producing its own system of law. But it is not alone. There is the Inter American Human Rights System which was originally modelled on the ECHR and which possesses an Inter American Commission on Human Rights as well as a court.[65] Its reach covers the Western hemisphere. In terms of trade agreements which provide dispute settlement machinery, the World Trade Organisation which has responsibility for the GATT and its protocols resort to independent panels to make judicial decisions.[66] China is a recent member. Specific rule-bound trade agreements cover US/NAFTA for North America. Asia has seen ASEAN and South America MERCOSUR. The result has been an internationalisation of legal norms, operating at various levels of efficacy and detail so that the division into monist and dualist states will increasingly lose much of its significance. The decision in the *Pinochet* judgments, even the final version which was necessitated after the procedural errors of the first judgment[67] revealed a domestic court far more inclined to accommodate international norms than had previously been the case in England. Ancient doctrine informed us that norms of customary international law were a part of the common law.[68] But English law

---

[65] S Davidson *The Inter-American Human Rights System* (1997).
[66] The general Council of the WTO is responsible for establishing and administering the GATT dispute settlement machinery: S Davidson (1997) The Canterbury Law Journal 437 at 462 et seq J Weiler ed *The EU, the WTO and the NAFTA* (2000). See N Douglas Lewis *Law and Governance* (2001) ch 10 on protection of environmental, social and health aspects under a new world order.
[67] Chapter 4 p 165.
[68] Blackstone *Commentaries* Vol IV, p 55.

witnessed a rigid division between the different layers of legal spheres. We are still a considerable way from realising a new international legal order but a more flexible approach to the relationship between domestic and international spheres is clearly under way. Why should British courts not accept that international norms protecting human rights are a part of the domestic order even though they have not been implemented by the legislature?

The operation of substantive constitutional law

Our membership of the Community has coincided with, or enhanced, the use of law as a political resource increasing opportunities for the analysis of political issues in juristic terms. Our membership in the Community has seen an increase in the phenomenon of 'juridification' – the resort to litigation to resolve institutional conflict. Whether this is cause or effect is unclear. Various commentators described law as the key instrument of European integration.[69] This phenomenon of juridification was evident in the passage of the Maastricht Bill amending the Treaties through Parliament which was later challenged in the courts. It is clear that many opportunities have been opened up to challenge decisions through the courts that would otherwise fail at the first step.[70] This is particularly important in the UK where there is no written constitution or entrenched Bill of Rights and no tradition of constitutional adjudication – at least not since the seventeenth century.

As the House of Lords Select Committee has stated on the question of human rights and citizenship:

> The law and practice of all the component parts of the EU is based on respect and protection of fundamental rights. The Treaty on EU makes this more explicit in requiring the Union to respect fundamental rights as guaranteed by the ECHR and by the constitutional traditions of Member States ... The ECJ have in their judgments applied an increasingly wide range of general principles of human rights, derived both from the European Convention and on national constitutional principles. They have sought

---

[69]   See J Weiler *The Constitution of Europe* (1999). But on continuing constitutional discourse at the political level in relation to the IGC see B de Witte *Convergence and Divergence in European Public Law* eds P Beaumont et al (2002) ch 3.

[70]   *Factortame* and *Johnston* (Ch 4, pp 194 and 427 et seq).

to apply the case law of the European Commission and Court of Human Rights.[71]

In Chapter 4 it was seen how the Directives on equal treatment and protection have been used by courts to make rulings on incompatibility and to interpret offending domestic measures in a manner which is consistent with EC norms (p 184 et seq). Britain has gone further than many Member states in requiring a detailed legal framework to address racist discrimination and in Northern Ireland discrimination arising from political or religious factors; matters on which Community law until recently was silent (see Chapter 9).[72] The operation of Article 13 EC introduced at Amsterdam and its accompanying Directives which extend the definition of discrimination will be viewed with great interest.

Integration of economic activity at the European level requires policies aimed at achieving greater degrees of harmonisation, or approximisation as it is now preferred, in fiscal policy, employment rights, health and safety, consumer protection and environment to name a few. While in some fields there have been notable developments, others have simply been subjected to an opt out. In the former case the environment is possibly a striking example: Environmental Impact Statements, water and air quality and access to environmental information have either come from or have been highly influenced by Community provisions and those deriving from international agreements such as Aarhus.[73] There are signs of increasing 'juridification' in the environmental field under the prompting of Community provisions.[74]

The courts have made significant contributions towards greater openness and fairness in the operation of public bodies both under the HRA 1998 and under common law doctrine (see Chapter 9). An enhanced sensitivity

---

[71]   HL 105 (1994/5) para 283. But not where a question of Community law did not arise: see *Grogan* Case C-159/90 [1991] ECR 4685 and *Kremzow v Republik Österreich* Case C-299/95 [1997] ECR I-2629.

[72]   Race Relations Act 1976, Fair Employment (Northern Ireland) Act 1989 both as amended and Disability Discrimination Act 1995 and Disability Rights Commission Act 1999. M Bell *Anti Discrimination Law and the European Union* (2002).

[73]   See *Human Rights and the Environment* M. Déjeant-Pons et al Council of Europe (2002).

[74]   See eg the '*Greenpeace*' litigation in [1994] 4 All ER 329 and 352 and *R v Durham County Council, ex p Huddleston* [2000] 1 WLR 1484.

to the constitutional implications of freedom of speech and other rights has been apparent and have encouraged constitutional debate by the judiciary.

It is also clear that our membership of the Community has, as I indicated above, increased the tendency to use litigation to resolve institutional constitutional conflict.[75] *Factortame* and *Rees-Mogg*[76] are clear examples of constitutional litigation that would not have been possible under purely domestic provisions. English law may be, according to Hobbes, 'the public conscience' but our judges have not been the grand interpreters of the pattern of politics. Theirs has traditionally been a limited role in matters affecting the constitution.

The process of European juridification has proved to be complex for English courts in certain areas and the results have sometimes been chaotic. In the Sunday Shopping saga, the compatibility of UK legislation prohibiting Sunday trading was challenged as a contravention of Article 28 [30] EC. After the ECJ left it to English courts to apply a test of proportionality to the application of the English law and decided that a restriction of Sunday trading was acceptable providing it was not out of proportion with the beneficial effects of such trade, differing results were achieved in courts up and down the land on the application to identical facts of the ruling laid down by the ECJ.[77] On a further reference from the House of Lords to the ECJ, the latter decided on the evidence that the Shops Act 1950 was proportionate with the aims of Article 28 [30] EC.[78]

The whole saga brought out some sensitivities of British judges towards a role that required them, as some of them saw it, to act as legislators and policy formulators in a relatively unbridled fashion. They showed themselves to be ill at ease with Community legal principles. Hear for instance, Hoffman J in *Stoke-on-Trent City Council v B & Q plc* on the Sunday trading saga:

[75]   M Capelletti, M Seccombe and J Weiler eds *Integration through Law: Europe and the American Federal Experience* (1987); and see J Weiler 'The Transformation of Europe' (1991) Yale LJ 2403 and *The Constitution of Europe* (1999) and R Rawlings (1994) Public Law 254 and 367.

[76]   *Factortame (No 2)* [1991] 1 All ER 70, HL; *R v Secretary of State for Foreign and Commonwealth Affairs, ex p Rees-Mogg* [1994] 1 All ER 457; and see Case 222/84 *Johnston* [1986] 3 All ER 135 and Case 150/85 *Drake v Chief Adjudication Officer* [1986] 3 CMLR 43; and the Sunday Trading case law: see notes 78 and 79 below.

[77]   R Rawlings (1993) *Journal of Law. and Society* 309.

[78]   *Stoke-on-Trent City Council v B & Q* Case C-169/91 [1993] 1 All ER 481, ECJ.

Who is to decide whether shops should be allowed to open on Sundays? Is it to be Parliament or this court? ...

The Member states of the Community differ widely in their histories, customs and social and cultural values. It was certainly not the object of the Community to introduce uniformity in all these matters. The purpose of the Treaty was to bring about a European Common Market but not to interfere with national law and customs which did not constitute obstacles to the establishment of such a market. But there are many provisions in the Treaty expressed in language capable of being given a wider or narrower interpretation. According to the way they are interpreted, they may have more or less of an impact on questions of social policy which in member states are strongly felt to be matters for national decision. It is the function of the Court of Justice of the European Communities in Luxembourg to interpret the Treaty and for the national court to apply it. In its interpretation of the Treaty the European Court has tried to tread a careful line which admits both boldness in advancing the objects of the Treaty and sensitivity to the domestic interests of member states. In applying the Treaty as interpreted by the Court, the national court has to be aware of another division of powers: not between European and national jurisdiction, but between legislature and judiciary. The fact that the European Court has said that a particular question is one for decision by the national court does not endow that court with quasi legislative powers. It must confine itself within the area of judicial intervention required by the Treaty and not trespass on questions which are for democratic decision in Parliament.[79]

Administrative law has been described as constitutional law in action and the subject of procedural rights – 'fair play in action' – is the British way of describing natural justice. For almost 40 years the courts have developed and extended the range of decision-making that is covered by duties to give hearings, to allow legal representation, to extend consultation and to insist that reasons are given for adverse decisions. The courts have

---

[79] [1991] 4 All ER 221 at 223g and 224b–e. His reticence to become involved in policy questions led him to ask whether the Sunday Trading laws represented a compromise between competing interests which a 'reasonable legislature' could adopt. It was not the domestic court's role to ask whether the competing interests had been properly balanced according to tests of proportionality. For criticism of this statement, see Walter van Gerven as Advocate General in *Stoke-on-Trent City Council v B & Q plc* [1993] 1 All ER 481 at 512.

opened up the administrative process in a manner which is staggering compared with the situation less than two decades ago. Some of this might be explicable in terms of the influence of the Community and ECHR and of course the influence of the latter on the former.[80] Even a decade ago, the European impact on our public law was given prominence in the Law Commission's report on *Administrative Law: Judicial Review and Statutory Appeals,*[81] particularly the consultation paper published in 1993. This is particularly true in the case of the Council of Europe's and latterly the EU's provisions on Data Protection, the latter of which have been compared to a law on privacy protection. It is not and our law is notoriously weak in protecting personal privacy as several eminent judges have noted although here as elsewhere the HRA 1998 will exert its influence (see p 419 et seq).

It remains the case that the absence of an entrenched Bill of Rights and the supremacy of Parliament means that Parliament can legislate out of existence any judicial decisions which protect citizens' rights in a manner which causes inconvenience.[82] This political fact has meant that an increasing resort was made to the ECHR by British lawyers. The UK had more cases before the European Commission and CHR than any other western European country. This fact explains why government in the UK wished to patriate the Convention and to leave its interpretation to domestic judges under European influence. These points were examined in Chapter 9. The government, with control of Parliament, still exercises the whip-hand on human rights but the HRA 1998 has, to repeat, been a force for the good and will make avoidance of human rights protection more difficult in the future.

We do, however, see the influence of doctrines of European systems and the doctrine of the ECJ influencing domestic legal thought. This is true in cases where 'legal certainty', 'equality', 'legitimate expectation'[83] and 'proportionality' have been influential on English judges in making judgments.[84] In *ex p Hamble,* for instance, Sedley J gave a judgment on

---

[80]   European Policy Forum *The Developing Role of the European Court of Justice* August 1995.

[81]   HC 669 (1993–4).

[82]   *Burmah Oil v Lord Advocate* [1965] AC 75 or decisions may be circumvented by passing statutory regulations.

[83]   *R v MAFF, ex p Hamble* [1995] 2 All ER 714 etc. See Ch 8.

[84]   Even where the courts have applied proportionality to assess the balancing of competing claims, the English courts have basically ruled that a reasonable allocation of resources satisfied a proportionality test: *R v Chief Constable of*

legitimate expectation, both procedural and, more crucially, substantive which was remarkable for its grasp by an English judge of European judicial and academic literature. Such expertise is becoming more apparent in other judges. The prospect has for some time been realised of a twin track approach where in deciding cases involving EC law the principles of EC law are invoked without qualification, as they ought. It is only a matter of time before this approach affects purely domestic case law. Such a case has already been seen in dramatic circumstances in *Re M*.[85]

In that case it was seen how an applicant for asylum was deported from the UK contrary to a court order. The Secretary of State was held to be liable in contempt proceedings and was susceptible to an interim injunction from the court despite the fact that it was formerly considered impossible to award an injunction against servants of the Crown acting in their official capacity. A Department could also be subject to contempt proceedings. A constraining feature of the decision of Lord Woolf was that in *Factortame* an injunction had been issued against such a servant to prevent breaches of Community law authorised by an Act of Parliament – described by Bingham LJ in the Court of Appeal hearing of the case as a 'constitutional enormity' – enjoining the Secretary of State to act contrary to the express will of Parliament when that expression's lawfulness or otherwise had yet to be established. To allow a 'twin track' process – one for domestic law and one for Community law was undesirable, thought Lord Woolf:

> It would be most regrettable if an approach which is inconsistent with that which exists in Community law should be allowed to persist if this is not strictly necessary.[86]

In terms of individual security and economic security, the cases involving Spanish ship-owners attempting to avail themselves of UK fishing quotas which they were wrongly denied have been noted. There are also dramatic cases concerning Irish nationals which were addressed in Chapter 9, pp 374, 382.[87] A point made earlier is re-emphasised. Some English judges

---

 Sussex, ex p International Trader's Ferry Ltd [1997] 2 All ER 65, CA and [1999] 1 All ER 129, HL; and see Hoffman J in *Stoke-on-Trent City Council v B & Q plc* Case C-169/91 [1993] 1 All ER 481 at 512.

[85] *Re M* [1993] 3 All ER 537, HL. This case has not been followed in Scotland: see T Mullen and T Prosser 'An Introduction to Scottish Public Law' (1995) European Public Law 46. See *Gairy v A-G Grenada* [2001] UKPC 30, [2002] 1 AC 167.

[86] At p 564h.

[87] *Adams* [1995] All ER (EC) 177 (DC); *McQuillan* [1995] 4 All ER 400.

have decided cases in recent years by using the language of fundamental right unheard in our judicial discourse for over three hundred years. Where a prisoner was effectively denied access to the courts because he was incapable of making a legal aid contribution the statutory order imposing a compulsory contribution was declared ultra vires because it interfered with 'a citizen's right of access to the courts'.[88] This approach is emanating from the common law and cases have covered freedom of the press and allocation of scarce resources where a right to life is involved in medical treatment. In the latter case the decision of Laws J was reversed with almost indecent haste by the Court of Appeal fearing budgetary crisis in hospital management (see Chapter 8, p 345).[89] Lord Browne-Wilkinson has stated that:

It is now inconceivable that any court in this country would hold that, apart from statutory provision, individual freedoms of a private person are any less extensive than the basic human rights protected by the ECHR... the [English] judges have asserted that the Convention confers no greater rights than those protected by the common law.[90]

In the famous *Spycatcher* case, Lord Goff observed that he could see no inconsistency between domestic law and the ECHR art 10 on freedom of speech. His words were quoted above (p 380).[91] This is a little partial because the Convention may provide greater protection than the common law. But there can be no denying that the threshold of consciousness for human rights protection has been raised substantially.

There are those who would see such a comparison as exaggeration. Nevertheless, the feeling is widely present that all cannot be quite the same again. This spirit of adventure has been influenced by our presence in the EC and by the Convention. The source of reference is increasingly cited as common law: the underlying impetus has come from European influence. In a case concerning asylum seekers, regulations which denied income benefit entitlement to those seeking asylum other than on arrival or who

[88] *R v Lord Chancellor, ex p Witham* [1997] 2 All ER 779, QBD and Laws J expression 'a common law of human rights'.
[89] [1995] 2 All ER 129. See also *R v Ministry of Defence, ex p Smith* [1996] 1 All ER 257, CA.
[90] (1992) Public Law 405 – while acknowledging the influence of the ECHR through its use by the ECJ.
[91] *A-G v Guardian Newspapers Ltd (No 2)* [1988] 3 All ER 545 at 660. But this makes such rights subject to the will of the legislature and competing claims which are often used by the powerful to restrict free expression, revealing sources of publication for similar purposes and so on.

awaited appeal having made unsuccessful claims for asylum, were ultra vires the 1993 governing legislation in that they drastically interfered with the right to asylum and, more interestingly, they undermined human rights to such an extent that the common law could not tolerate it:

> As for there being no obligation for maintaining poor foreigners ... the law of humanity, which is anterior to all positive laws, obliges us to afford them relief, to save them from starving.[92]

In an article in 1995, Lord Woolf wrote of the judicial response were Parliament to abolish judicial review by legislation. This would constitute an attempt to 'undermine in a fundamental way the rule of law on which our unwritten constitution depends' a role which 'predates our present form of Parliamentary democracy and the Bill of Rights'. This is what he had to say:

> However, if Parliament did the unthinkable, then I would say that the courts would also be required to act in a manner which would be without precedent. Some judges might choose to do so by saying that it was an unrebuttable presumption that Parliament could never intend such a result. I myself would consider there were advantages in making it clear that ultimately there are even limits on the supremacy of Parliament which it is the courts' inalienable responsibility to identify and uphold. They are limits of the most modest dimensions which I believe any democrat would accept. They are no more than are necessary to enable the rule of law to be preserved.[93]

The growing constitutional sensitivity of our courts is very much directed to individual human rights. It is also evident in the interpretation by the Privy Council (a special committee of Law Lords and other judges) of written constitutions of former colonies concerning the constitutionality of the death penalty[94]

---

92   Simon Brown LJ in *R v Secretary of State for Social Security, ex p Joint Council for the Welfare of Immigrants* [1996] 4 All ER 385, CA citing Lord Ellenborough CJ (1803) 4 East 103. This case was subsequently reversed by legislation but a further judicial ruling held that a duty to assist asylum seekers existed under the National Assistance Act 1948: *R v Hammersmith London Borough Council, ex p M* (1996) Times, 10 October. It is a continuing and ever-more repressive saga under the Nationality, Immigration and Asylum Act 2002.

93   Lord Woolf (1995) Public Law 57 at 69 interestingly entitled '*Droit Administratif*: English Style'.

94   See eg, *Reyes (Patrick) v R* [2002] UKPC 11, [2002] 2 AC 235, *R v Hughes (Peter)* [2002] UKPC 12, [2002] 2 AC 259, *Fox (Bernhill) v R* [2002] UKPC 13, [2002] 2 AC 284. See D O'Brien (2002) PL 678.

Sir John Laws has gone even further and has suggested that there is a form of natural law above Parliamentary legislation.[95] His judgment in *Thoburn* setting out the arena for constitutional adjudication should be juxtaposed (p 157 et seq). Nonetheless, old traditions die hard. The incorporation of the ECHR and the introduction of freedom of information legislation seem set to be controlled ultimately through Parliament, in deference, the government has argued, to Parliamentary supremacy.[96] This reminds us that even Dicey appreciated the dangers in maintaining the Rule of Law with the doctrine and practice of Parliamentary sovereignty.

Some, however, view the growing constitutional confidence of the judiciary with alarm because of the dangers in upsetting the delicate equilibrium in a balanced and unwritten constitution.[97] The suggestion of Sir Richard Scott that the duty of Ministers to be accountable and to provide information to Parliament should be a judicially enforced one may be one such illustration.[98] There are also those whose reaction has been one of rabid hostility, a view commonly held by members of previous Conservative governments and editors of the popular press. There is nothing new in political hostility to 'interfering judges' who are bending the rules to suit their own needs or advance their own political creeds. In the past the point has often been made by left of centre politicians resentful of 'class warriors' undermining social reformist legislation. An expanding judicial role will upset politicians who feel their patch invaded. The important point is whether an expanding role is based upon principle and supported by authority or whether it is derived from some form of expedience. I do not feel there is any significant evidence to suggest the latter. There is a good deal to support the former. There is a good deal to support the view that the influence of Europe on our legal thought is born of 'articulate consistency' and not judicial fashion or expansionism.

---

95   Sir J Laws 'Law and Democracy' (1995) Public Law 72. See Sir S Sedley 'Human Rights: a Twenty-First Century Agenda (1995) Public Law 386. Sir John Laws has also emphasised that duties as well as rights flow from justice: 'The Limitation of Human Rights' (1998) Public Law 254.

96   See also *R v Parliamentary Comr for Standards, ex p Al Fayed* [1998] 1 All ER 93, CA and unwillingness of the courts to review a report of an officer of Parliament.

97   See Lord Irvine of Lairg QC (1996) Public Law 59 and Lord Bingham CJ giving the inaugural lecture of the Judicial Studies Board reported in Times, 6 November 1996.

98   Sir R Scott 'Ministerial Accountability' (1996) Public Law 410 at 426. Under the Freedom of Information Act 2000, the government has power to override the Information Commissioner's decision.

Conclusion

The absorption of ideas nurtured in other national systems and articulated in Community law has been a staggering development. Europe is impacting upon our substantive law, our legal techniques and our legal culture in ever more dramatic ways. In a way, this is not surprising because the doctrine of Parliamentary sovereignty has forced lawyers to be more inquisitive of other systems of law, more resourceful and acquisitive in what they utilise to interpret legislation and to advance the principles of the common law. The development of the principles of public law, which have emerged from the common law, will help the latter to address and review the myriad forms of contemporary executive power. We are not alone in seeking inspiration from Treaty provisions or Community law. It was widely argued that the doctrine of subsidiarity contained in the Treaty of Maastricht and reinforced in Amsterdam may be invoked to support arguments for stronger regional and even local government vis à vis central government in the UK (Chapter 5). 'Subsidiarity' was inserted as part of an Article in that Treaty (Article 5 [3b] EC) at British and German insistence to keep powers within Member States and to address the Community/ Member State relationship. More generally, the feeling is present that we face a situation which is pregnant with possibility and that the European influence has coincided with a period in which our domestic public law has been in its most creative phase.[99] We no longer have a fixation with questions of *vires* and jurisdiction as did previous generations of English administrative lawyers.[100] Increased pressure to make decision-makers justify the exercise of their powers is a feature shared by many Commonwealth courts and clearly owes a great deal to international human rights' norms and their influence within domestic regimes.[101] Our new public law will owe much to European influence although doctrines developed elsewhere such as legal certainty, legitimate expectation and proportionality may take a different shape in English soil. But take root they have.

[99] See eg *R v Home Secretary, ex p Fire Brigades Union* [1995] 2 All ER 244, HL: the Secretary of State was acting unlawfully in introducing a scheme outlined in legislation by prerogative powers.

[100] Although naturally *vires* still has an essential role to play: see *R v Secretary of State for Foreign Affairs, ex p World Development Movement Ltd* [1995] 1 All ER 611, QBD where the Government was ruled to have acted outwith the powers of the Overseas Development and Cooperation Act 1980, s 1 in awarding £234m from the Overseas Aid Budget to pay for the Pergau Dam project in Malaysia.

[101] D Dyzenhaus, M Hunt and M Taggart 'The Principles of Legality in Administrative Law: Internationalism and Constitutionalism' (2001) Oxford University Commonwealth LJ 5; C McCrudden (2000) 20 OJLS 499.

Index